THE CAMBRIDGE HISTORY OF
AMERICAN WOMEN'S LITERATURE

The field of American women's writing is one characterized by innovation: scholars are discovering new authors and works, as well as new ways of historicizing this literature, rethinking contexts, categories, and juxtapositions. Now, after three decades of scholarly investigation and innovation, the rich complexity and diversity of American literature written by women can be seen with a new coherence and subtlety. Dedicated to this expanding heterogeneity, *The Cambridge History of American Women's Literature* develops and challenges historical, cultural, theoretical, even polemical methods, all of which will advance the future study of American women writers – from Native Americans to postmodern communities, from individual careers to communities of writers and readers. This volume immerses readers in a new dialogue about the range and depth of women's literature in the United States and allows them to trace the ever-evolving shape of the field.

DALE M. BAUER is Professor of English at the University of Illinois, Urbana-Champaign.

THE CAMBRIDGE
HISTORY OF
AMERICAN WOMEN'S LITERATURE

*

Edited by

DALE M. BAUER

CAMBRIDGE
UNIVERSITY PRESS

CAMBRIDGE UNIVERSITY PRESS

Cambridge, New York, Melbourne, Madrid, Cape Town,
Singapore, São Paulo, Delhi, Mexico City

Cambridge University Press
The Edinburgh Building, Cambridge CB2 8RU, UK

Published in the United States of America by Cambridge University Press, New York

www.cambridge.org
Information on this title: www.cambridge.org/9781107001374

© Cambridge University Press 2012

First published 2012

Printed in the United Kingdom at the University Press, Cambridge

A catalogue record for this publication is available from the British Library

Library of Congress Cataloguing in Publication data
The Cambridge history of American women's literature / edited by Dale M. Bauer.
pages   cm
Includes bibliographical references and index.
ISBN 978-1-107-00137-4
I. American literature – Women authors – History and criticism.   2. Women and literature – United
States – History.   I. Bauer, Dale M., 1956–
PS147.C37   2012
810.9′9287 – dc23   2012004206

ISBN 978-1-107-00137-4 Hardback

Contents

Contents

Contents

Contents

Illustrations

Acknowledgments

My thanks go to many friends for their guidance. My greatest thanks go to the thirty-two contributors, whose work has been amazing.

As always, to Gordon Hutner, my partner, for all of his advice. And to our sons, Jake and Dan, my thanks for their energy.

I am grateful to the University of Illinois for a sabbatical, during which I edited and wrote the Introduction to the *History*.

To Ray Ryan, who has been the best guide in making this *History* a pleasure to imagine and to produce. A sincere thanks to Nathalie Horner at Cambridge for her dedication to the details, and to Maartje Scheltens, for her expert guidance during production.

My thanks to Jo Breeze and especially Ann Lewis for their intense and productive, lively work.

Notes on contributors

Jennifer Ashton is the author of *From Modernism to Postmodernism: American Poetry and Theory in the Twentieth Century* (Cambridge University Press, 2005). She has also published scholarly articles in *ELH, Modernism/Modernity, Modern Philology, American Literary History* and *Interval(le)s*, and she is one of the founding editors of the online forum *nonsite.org*. She teaches at the University of Illinois at Chicago.

Jennifer J. Baker is Associate Professor of English at New York University, where she specializes in eighteenth- and nineteenth-century American literature and intellectual history. She is the author of *Securing the Commonwealth: Debt, Speculation, and Writing in the Making of Early America* (2005).

Dale M. Bauer is Professor of English at the University of Illinois, Urbana-Champaign. Author of three books on feminist theory, American women writers, and sex expression, she has also edited (with Phil Gould) *The Cambridge Companion to Nineteenth-Century American Women Writers*. She is currently working on the career of E. D. E. N. Southworth.

Susan David Bernstein, Professor of English, and Gender and Women's Studies, at the University of Wisconsin-Madison, is the author of *Confessional Subjects: Revelations of Gender and Power in Victorian Literature and Culture* (1997) and the editor of two novels by Amy Levy, *The Romance of a Shop* and *Reuben Sachs* (2006), as well as the co-editor with Elsie B. Michie of *Victorian Vulgarity: Taste in Verbal and Visual Culture* (2009). Forthcoming is her article, "Transatlantic Magnetism: Eliot's 'The Lifted Veil' and Alcott's Sensation Stories" in *Transatlantic Sensations*. She is completing her next book, *Roomscape: Women Readers in the British Museum from George Eliot to Virginia Woolf*.

Patricia Bizzell is the Reverend John E. Brooks, S.J. Professor of Humanities at the College of the Holy Cross. She regularly teaches courses in women's studies and in the theory and practice of rhetoric. Among her publications is *The Rhetorical Tradition*, co-authored with Bruce Herzberg, which won the NCTE Outstanding Book Award in 1992. She was given the Conference on College Composition and Communication Exemplar Award in 2008. In addition to nineteenth-century American women's activist rhetoric, she is interested in global Englishes, and taught at Sogang University in Seoul in the summer and fall 2011 terms.

LESLIE BOW is Professor of English and Asian American Studies at the University of Wisconsin, Madison. She is the author of '*Partly Colored': Asian Americans and Racial Anomaly in the Segregated South* (2010) and *Betrayal and Other Acts of Subversion: Feminism, Sexual Politics, Asian American Women's Literature* (2001). Her work has appeared in the *Utne Reader*, the *Michigan Quarterly Review*, the *Southern Review* as well as in numerous other academic journals and anthologies. She recently edited a scholarly reissue of Fiona Cheong's novel, *The Scent of the Gods* (2010), and is editing the four-volume *Asian American Feminisms*. Currently working on a book entitled *Racist Love*, Leslie is also a contributor to *Progressive* magazine and the Progressive Media Project through which her op-ed columns appear in newspapers across the United States.

JODI A. BYRD is a citizen of the Chickasaw Nation of Oklahoma and an Assistant Professor of American Indian Studies and English at the University of Illinois, Urbana-Champaign. She has had articles appear in *American Indian Quarterly, Cultural Studies Review*, and *Interventions*. She is also the author of *The Transit of Empire: Indigenous Critiques of Colonialism* (2011).

MARY CHAPMAN is an Associate Professor of English at the University of British Columbia and the co-editor of *Treacherous Texts: US Suffrage Literature 1846–1946* (2011) and *Sentimental Men: Masculinity and the Politics of Affect in American Culture* (1999). Her essays on suffrage literature have appeared in *American Literary History, American Quarterly, Canadian Review of American Studies*, and *US Popular Print Culture 1860–1920* (2011). She is currently completing a book project titled *Making Noise, Making News: US Suffrage Print Culture and Modernism*.

RYNETTA DAVIS is an Assistant Professor of English at the University of Kentucky where she teaches nineteenth- and early twentieth-century African American literature. She is currently completing a book project titled *Racial Love: The Nineteenth-Century Black Romance Narrative*.

ANDY DOOLEN is Associate Professor of English at the University of Kentucky. He is author of *Fugitive Empire: Locating Early American Imperialism* (2005) and journal articles on American literature, slavery, African American writing, and republican theory. He is currently finishing a book on the culture of US expansionism from 1803 to 1830.

JOHN ERNEST, the Eberly Family Distinguished Professor of American Literature at West Virginia University, is the author or editor of ten books, including *Liberation Historiography: African American Writers and the Challenge of History, 1794–1861* (2004), *Chaotic Justice: Rethinking African American Literary History* (2009), and *A Nation Within a Nation: Organizing African American Communities before the Civil War* (2011).

STEPHANIE FOOTE is at the University of Illinois, Urbana-Champaign. She has written numerous essays on US regionalism, nineteenth-century US literature and culture, and queer culture.

NANCY GLAZENER is an Associate Professor at the University of Pittsburgh. She is the author of *Reading for Realism: The History of a US Literary Institution, 1850–1910*, published in the New Americanists Series at Duke University Press in 1997. Her recent scholarship includes articles about print culture, ethics, modern personhood, and literary history. She is at work on two book projects: *Literature in the Making: A History of US Literary Culture in the Long Nineteenth Century* and *Ethics at the Edge of Liberalism: The Arts of Moral Personhood in US Fiction*.

SUSAN M. GRIFFIN is Professor and Chair of English at the University of Louisville. She is the editor of the *Henry James Review*. Her most recent book, co-edited with Alan Nadel, is *The Men Who Knew Too Much: Henry James and Alfred Hitchcock*.

SANDRA M. GUSTAFSON'S most recent book, *Imagining Deliberative Democracy in the Early American Republic*, was published by the University of Chicago Press in 2011. She is the editor of *Early American Literature* and a member of the English faculty at the University of Notre Dame.

MELISSA J. HOMESTEAD is Susan J. Rosowski Associate Professor of English and Program Faculty in Women's and Gender Studies at the University of Nebraska-Lincoln. She is the author of *American Women Authors and Literary Property, 1822–1869* (Cambridge University Press, 2005) and many essays on American women writers, such as Susanna Rowson, Augusta Jane Evans, Sarah Orne Jewett, and Willa Cather. She is also co-editor of a Broadview edition of Catharine Sedgwick's New York novel of manners *Clarence; or, A Tale of Our Own Times*.

GORDON HUTNER is the author and editor of several books and articles on American literary studies, including Hawthorne, immigrant autobiography, Jewish American fiction, and the tradition of cultural critique. His most recent book is *What America Read: Taste, Class, and the Novel, 1920–1960*. He is the founding editor of *American Literary History*.

JEAN M. LUTES is Associate Professor of English at Villanova University, where she teaches modern American fiction. She is the author of *Front Page Girls: Women Journalists in American Literature and Culture, 1880–1930* (2006) and she has published articles on American women's writing in *Legacy*, *American Literary History*, *American Quarterly*, *Arizona Quarterly*, and *Signs*. Her current book project is tentatively titled "Crying Out Loud: Emotion, Mass Culture, and Women's Narratives in Early Twentieth-Century America."

JOHN MARSH is Assistant Professor of English at Pennsylvania State University. In addition to numerous articles and reviews, he is the editor of *You Work Tomorrow: An Anthology of American Labor Poetry, 1929–1941* and the author of two forthcoming books, *Hog Butchers, Beggars, and Busboys: Poverty, Labor, and the Making of Modern American Poetry* and *Class Dismissed: Why We Can't Teach or Learn Our Way Out of Inequality*.

HEIDI SLETTEDAHL MACPHERSON is Pro Vice-Chancellor of Research and Innovation at De Montfort University, England. She has written widely on American, Canadian, and

British women's literature. Her most recent books are *Courting Failure: Women and the Law in 20th Century Literature* (2007), *Transatlantic Women's Literature* (2008), and *The Cambridge Introduction to Margaret Atwood* (2010).

BRENDA MURPHY is Board of Trustees Distinguished Professor of English at the University of Connecticut. She has published fifteen books and a wide range of articles that reflect her interest in placing American drama, theater, and performance in the broader context of American literature and culture. Among her books are the *Cambridge Companion to American Women Playwrights* (1999), *The Provincetown Players and the Culture of Modernity* (2005), *American Realism and American Drama, 1880–1940* (1987), *Congressional Theatre: Dramatizing McCarthyism on Stage, Film, and Television* (1999), and *Tennessee Williams and Elia Kazan: A Collaboration in the Theatre* (1992).

KIMBERLY O'NEILL is Assistant Professor at Quinnipiac University. Her current research focuses on US cultural production during periods of hemispheric political conflict. She examines writers who engaged the 1910 Mexican Revolution, 1959 Cuban Revolution, and the 1970s–80s Central American Crisis to argue that both Anglo and Latina/o journalists and literary intellectuals contested US interventionism.

ELIZABETH RENKER is Professor of English at The Ohio State University and is the author of *The Origins of American Literature Studies: An Institutional History* (Cambridge University Press, 2007); *Strike Through the Mask: Herman Melville and the Scene of Writing* (1996); and the introduction to the Signet classic edition of *Moby-Dick* (1998). She has also published an array of articles on nineteenth-century poetics; on the history of the curriculum, with a focus on the subject area called "English"; on American literary realism; on pedagogy; and on the authors Herman Melville and Sarah Piatt. She is the recipient of three distinguished teaching awards.

SUSAN M. RYAN, Associate Professor of English at the University of Louisville, is the author of *The Grammar of Good Intentions: Race and the Antebellum Culture of Benevolence* (2003). Her current book project is titled *The Moral Economies of American Authorship*.

CHERENE SHERRARD-JOHNSON is Professor of English at the University of Wisconsin-Madison where she teaches nineteenth- and twentieth-century American and African American literature, cultural studies, and feminist theory. She is the author of *Portraits of the New Negro Woman: Visual and Literary Culture in the Harlem Renaissance* (2007) and a forthcoming biography of Harlem Renaissance writer Dorothy West.

CAROL J. SINGLEY is Professor of English and director of graduate studies at Rutgers University-Camden, where she teaches American literature, childhood studies, and children's literature. She is the author of *Adopting America: Childhood, Kinship, and National Identity in Literature* (2011) and *Edith Wharton: Matters of Mind and Spirit* (Cambridge University Press, 1995). She is also the editor or co-editor of six volumes, including three on Wharton and *The American Child: A Cultural Studies Reader* (2003). Her current work explores literary and cultural constructions of childhood, especially in relation to kinship and adoption.

STEPHANIE SMITH is a Professor of English at the University of Florida. Examining the intersections of science, literature, politics, race, and gender, her essays appear in such journals as *differences, Criticism, Genders, American Literature,* and *American Literary History.* She is the author of *Conceived By Liberty* (1995) and *Household Words* (2006), as well as three novels. She has held fiction residencies at Dorland, Norcroft and Hedgebrook. Currently she is at work on a book about publishing and American letters, *The Muse and the Marketplace,* and has just signed a three-novel contract with Thames River Press (London).

JENNIFER TRAVIS teaches in the English department at St. John's University in New York. She is the author of *Wounded Hearts: Masculinity, Law, and Literature in American Culture* and the co-editor of *Boys Don't Cry? Rethinking Masculinity and Emotion in the US.* She is completing a new manuscript titled *A Call to Harms: Injury and Identity in the US.*

JONATHAN VINCENT is Visiting Assistant Professor at the University of Louisville. He recently finished a study on the relationship between war memory in literature and the development of the American state, "Dangerous Subjects: US War Narrative, Modern Identity, and the Making of the National Security State, 1877–1964."

KIRSTIN R. WILCOX teaches in the Department of English at the University of Illinois, Urbana-Champaign. Her work in progress centers on poetic exchanges among women writers in periodicals of the early republic. She also writes about transatlantic transmission of women's poetry in the long eighteenth century and literature pedagogy.

SUSAN S. WILLIAMS is Professor of English and Vice Provost for Academic Policy and Faculty Resources at Ohio State University. She is the author of *Confounding Images: Photography and Portraiture in Antebellum American Fiction* (1997) and of *Reclaiming Authorship: Literary Women in America, 1850–1900* (2006) and also edited the Bedford College Edition of *The Scarlet Letter.* Her current work focuses on the abolitionist publisher James Redpath and his relationship to American literary culture.

HANA WIRTH-NESHER is Professor of English and American Studies at Tel Aviv University where she is also the Samuel L. and Perry Haber Chair on the Study of the Jewish Experience in the United States and the Director of the Goldreich Family Institute for Yiddish Language, Literature, and Culture. She is the author of *City Codes: Reading the Modern Urban Novel* (Cambridge University Press, 2008) and *Call It English: The Languages of Jewish American Literature,* the editor of *What is Jewish Literature?,* and the co-editor of the *Cambridge Companion to Jewish American Literature.* Her numerous essays include studies of Virginia Woolf, Henry James, Philip Roth, Isaac Bashevis Singer, James Joyce, Saul Bellow, and Amos Oz. She is currently writing a book about the role of Hebrew in Jewish American literature.

LYNDA ZWINGER is Associate Professor of English at the University of Arizona and Affiliate Faculty in Women's Studies. She specializes in theory of the novel, the American novel, popular film, and psychoanalytic and feminist/women's theory and criticism.

Introduction

DALE M. BAUER

Why create a new *Cambridge History of American Women's Literature*? Why is this the time to analyze the breadth and range of scholarship that the last thirty years have inaugurated in American women's literature and to discuss what we have left to do? Because now is the time to move beyond 1980s paradigms and 1990s elaborations to include a wider vision of this literary history. Since 1980, mode after new mode of interpretation has been added to change how American women's writing might be studied, whether through new historicism or affect theory, including models of modern woundedness and "the female complaint." Much important recovery work has already been done, giving us many authors to read and analyze, but much more remains: too few writers have been explored in their entirety (like Lydia Maria Child or Catharine Sedgwick). More important, as Susan Williams argues, thinking of women's writing as a non-oppositional strategy has helped us to begin to study women's writing, not in resistance to the male canon, but as a new field altogether. We are still discovering ways of historicizing and recombining this literature, rethinking contexts, categories, and juxtapositions. And perhaps most exciting these days is the reading of women transatlantically, hemispherically, or through "deep time," giving us transnational, global, and comparative ideas about women's writing.

The impetus for this book is to assess the major renovation of US women's literature in the past thirty years. This volume will also deal with the critical trends of reading women's writing, especially the rise of feminist theories that created new rubrics and new methodologies, and will recognize the larger geographical links that shaped women's visions. This *History* further outlines American canon formation – especially in terms of racial and ethnic identity, sexual and gendered perspectives, as well as hemispheric and transnational writing.

Much prior scholarship on American women's writing has examined its relationship to the male canon, so much so that anthologies typically repeat the same groupings of female talent, from Bradstreet to Dickinson to Wharton and Cather. By contrast, new anthologies, like *The Aunt Lute Anthology of US Women Writers* (2004), have expanded recovery work. The editors of the *Aunt Lute*, Lisa Maria Hogeland and Mary Klages, call for a "complicated, contradictory, and multiple" volume. Yet at a moment when studies in American literary history are ever expanding to more specific histories and geographies, such complications are hard to teach as a whole (*Aunt Lute*, xxxi). Including such figures as Tituba, Jarena Lee, Lydia Sigourney, and Frances Osgood, among many others, *Aunt Lute* is the kind of anthology we need to introduce previously unknown women authors. To that end, this *History* vivifies the study of women's writing within US culture and makes anthologies like *Aunt Lute* even more valuable and accessible.

A mere chronology of women's writing will not do enough to meet the scholarly needs of subsequent generations. Nor can a new history just include the major women writers. It should not be content to locate the most fruitful theoretical or cultural or historical ways of unveiling these texts, although doing so has marked many of the contributors' careers. Instead, a new literary history can discern how changes in the practice might also shape American women's writing as a field. This *History* provides a much broader array of texts, approaches, theories, and debates about what is significant in US women's writing and demonstrates new rhetorics for reading these works.

One of the narrative continuities among chapters in this volume is the sustained focus on political and social history, as well as on the cultural studies of women's writing and its various audiences. The authors in this volume describe – and illustrate – how women wrote for a "civil society" (Kelley, *Learning to Stand and Speak*), a literary culture, a set of educational and social practices that created a community of authors and readers.

This new sense of reading and dialogue animates this volume. Religious topics, for example, were once among the most prominent scholarly subjects; we need now to draw on studying religion in early American women writers to discover ways of appreciating and reimagining the spiritual concerns of such modern women writers as Dorothy Day and Kathleen Norris. And not just the early Norris whose conservative novel *Mother* helped to establish "Mother's Day," but the writer who later gave us profound ways to think about time and space in her poetry and essays.

These essays also give us ways to read authors such as Margaretta Bleecker Faugères and Jane Johnston Schoolcraft, prolific writers who ought to be known more than they are today. Moreover, this *History* shows us how to go beyond the association of an author with one text. At the same time, one of the challenges in writing this *History* has been assessing, say, Charlotte Perkins Gilman, whose 1892 story, "The Yellow Wall-Paper," was once considered a feminist triumph. In the last ten years, however, critics have complicated this triumph by acknowledging Gilman's casual racism and quite conventional support for eugenics. Reading one Gilman story – like "The Yellow Wall-Paper" – does not give readers a true sense of how Gilman's career broadly developed, from the horror story about Silas Weir Mitchell's rest cure, to her groundbreaking *Women and Economics* (1898), to the utopian vision of *Herland* in 1915, to her autobiography where she celebrates will power over every other personal and professional value. One famous story cannot, however, offset the burden of Gilman's vitriolic hatred of Asians and African Americans, minorities that she attacks in "Parasitism and Civilised Vice" (1931). Both Susan Griffin and Stephanie Smith show how recognizing Gilman's complex commitments and engagements repays new scholarly attentions.

This *History* is unconventional insofar as the essays' contributors have gauged the needs of today's literary studies and extend the literary thematizations of such issues as women's pain and suffering, resistance, and styles that result in our past concern with sympathy, sentiment, or sensation. Instead, as some recent critics have done, they have moved to more material bases for study and can imagine, say, Emily Dickinson's disease as epilepsy, or her anger as a result of violence, rather than continuing to focus on her agoraphobia, or her affection for Susan Huntington Gilbert Dickinson. Many contributions to this book are author-centered, yet the contributors offer a much more nuanced and wider range of the different audiences for which these women wrote. This *History* charts the newly emerging subjects in the field, even as it also traces how that canon has changed over time, while elaborating on how women writers shaped the literary, social, or cultural values of their day.

Here the *Cambridge History of American Women's Literature* offers a set of larger connections that researchers and students all need if we are to make sense of the changing modes of women's writing – from religion, to education, to popular influence, to rhetorical power. New recoveries of women writers have been published and need the new contexts provided by these contributors who have focused on such comprehensive changes to American literary studies. Following certain recovered works was one major task, such as the Schomburg Library of Nineteenth-Century Black Women's Writing or the Rutgers Series of American Women's Writing, or the Legacies of Nineteenth-Century American Women Writers Series from the University of Nebraska, which has published Julia Ward Howe's *The Hermaphrodite* (1846; 2004) and Elizabeth Stoddard's *Two Men* (1888; 2008). Consider the popular achievement of someone like Fannie Hurst and the interest she held for the masses of readers who took her seriously. Why, some contributors ask, have some authors proved less than influential over time, though their contemporaneous prominence was major? What sort of values do women writers in their historical arena advocate? A prominent modern writer like Mary Austin, for instance, changed her career when she gave up writing about the West for a new focus in the 1910s as a proto-radical feminist writing about a "woman of genius" (1912) and later – in *No. 26 Jayne Street* (1920) – about World War I politics. In Austin's case, such commitments, including a foray into ecological criticism, may change within a single woman's career, let alone within a single historical period.

One compelling imperative for this *History* is the study of a single career, one whose length and variety has been insufficiently appreciated. E. D. E. N. Southworth was probably the most popularly read writer in the nineteenth century, with fifty novels (first serialized in reading magazines) to her credit. Yet few today know even the broad outlines of this amazing career in its entirety. Why, as a community of scholars, are we satisfied to establish the success of the serial and the novel *The Hidden Hand* (1859; 1888), and then ignore the rest of her writings? From the 1840s to the 1890s, this prolific novelist engaged an encyclopedic array of topics: the death penalty, abolition, insanity, religious diversity, none of which is approachable via her best-known but by no means most representative novel. (Southworth wrote, for instance, about a Jewish woman converting to Christianity in *Self-Raised* [1876], as well as a woman marrying a Jewish man in *Miriam, the Avenger* [1856].) Critics in this volume focus on such singular writing careers whose specific contours continue to engage readers, while other authors emerge as case studies that reorient how we might read a general direction of women's writing.

Here are some other challenges that this *History* confronts:

- How long does it take for new recoveries of women writers to find their place in the literary canon? Do new Histories of American women's writing need to appear in order to illuminate a changing audience?
- Are revision and resistance the two major models allowed to critics who want to include women into the canon? Some of the best critics use these modes, and some try to redefine what women's writing is, what Susan Friedman now calls "writing for women."
- Have we finally recovered enough forgotten voices, or should we still pursue the hundreds of writers to recover? Consider that, in her most

recent study, Nina Baym has now assembled over 500 women authors devoted to writing about the American West.

- What does it mean to develop new terms in order to revise the history of a literary movement like naturalism, as Jennifer Fleissner has done in *Women, Compulsion, Modernity* (2008), from the perspective of female writers who saw themselves compulsively "stuck" in a particular model of culture? Or to revise American realism according to emotions and the experiences of the body, as Jane Thrailkill has done in *Affecting Fictions* (2007)?

- What happens after the debate about private and public spheres explodes, as it did after *No More Separate Spheres!*, the collection based on an *American Literature* 1998 special issue? Under what circumstances does a separate category of "women's writing" seem to bring us back to this divide?

- Do we need even more specific subdivisions of Histories, ever-narrower groups of women, like Plains, Hmong, Afro- or Anglo-Caribbean women writers? Or another study like Hillary Chute's on women and graphic writing? Do we need another *History* with geographical categories like "Appalachian culture," which includes Muriel Rukeyser, Harriette Arnow, and Denise Giardina?

Elaine Showalter's *A Jury of her Peers* (2009) argues that women's literary cultures have often "disappeared" in our culture. She asks, for one example, why did Susan Glaspell, the early twentieth-century feminist writer, "disappear from literary history" (xi). What are our critical responsibilities to once-popular writers? The great achievement of Showalter's book is its power of memory insofar as she recovers these writers for literary historians and scholars. It is not enough that women's writing scholars remember Susan Glaspell. All Americanists should, as Showalter argues. For instance, and perhaps rightly, Showalter argues that Harriet Beecher Stowe is the most important American women writer: "Her achievements and her wide influence make her the most important figure in the history of American women's writing" (109). Yet on what grounds? What, in our history since 1852, could have stimulated as important a novel as *Uncle Tom's Cabin*? The antebellum era created the context for her writing – and a serious context above all – yet Toni Morrison's novels, by the same token, have also exerted incredible influence in the twentieth century, comparable to Stowe's in the nineteenth. For Showalter, it is a matter of the individual reader's values: "I said, OK, this is my view, these are my judgments; here they are, you can argue with them" ("Back Talk," 29). Her crucial personal stakes on issues of literary history is laid out throughout her volume.

Yet the days when a single scholar could decidedly do justice to creating a unified vision of the whole of American women's literature seem past. As engaging as Showalter's judgments are, her monumental book does not aim to elaborate historical or cultural contexts in order to deliver a message about what women's writing meant to accomplish. What if an author does not find the right context – someone like Gertrude Atherton, who mostly imagined her own literary world? Or perhaps we still have not figured out the context itself, as for her *Patience Sparhawk* (1897), a novel about the death penalty, or for *Black Oxen* (1923), about a now-forgotten therapy for women's aging.

The same might be true of *A New Literary History of America* (2009), edited by Greil Marcus and Werner Sollors, where the contributors are more aware of specific readings than they are of the larger context of women's writing. That volume offers coverage that means to be distinctive for a twenty-first-century audience, based on "meetings of the minds" about American literary history. The roster of women writers that results from this conversation is quite familiar to scholars of the last thirty years: Bradstreet, Wheatley, Rowlandson, Fuller, Stowe, Cummins, Dickinson, Alcott, Ida Wells, Queen Lili'uokalani, Wharton, Mamie Smith, Dorothy Parker, Zora Neale Hurston, Margaret Mitchell, Elizabeth Bishop, Maya Angelou, Toni Morrison, Alice Walker, Adrienne Rich, Gayl Jones, Harriet Wilson, Hong Kingston. Their volume details where scholars of women's writing are in American Studies and where we need to go to keep American Women's writing both new and important in opening canons of US culture.

For Marcus and Sollors, the history of American women's writing is still subsumed into an established canon. Yet as literary modes change, so do most of the women writers addressed. While someone like Emma Dunham Kelley Hawkins – who wrote *Four Girls at Cottage City* (1891) and *Megda* (1895) – was once considered a black woman writer, later critics have learned the truth about her Caucasian identity. As these critics, like Cherene Sherrard-Johnson, have shown, the frontispiece for *Megda* might merely be deceiving, or perhaps Hawkins was passing in order to publish her evangelical novels. Often, our judgments depend on how much of a single author's career we have read or, in other cases, how much we know about the history of how women wrote, "from the individual to the divine, from the momentary to the eternal," as John Ernest explains how nineteenth-century African American women wrote to transcend contingent historical events, aiming, as they did, for a Christian eternity.

Methods

This *History* depends on a variety of ways to read women's writing both historically and theoretically. Some contributors work on particular periods (Gustafson, Baker, Doolen, Chapman, Lutes, March, Hutner, Macpherson), but others choose single authors as exemplary cases of what happens to women in their literary cultures (Ryan, Homestead, Davis). And still others offer persuasive narratives about the way literary canons have been formed. One contributor has imagined the invention of the entirety of a literary culture (Glazener), while another focuses on the figures of reading communities of women by books written by women about women (Griffin). In this way, this *History* has a broadly cultural dynamic at its base, which pursues not only what is written, but also what is read or heard, what is debated, and what consequences women's writings have created.

Neither genre nor form, nor period nor era limits these various essays. Most important, contributors have been asked to present a current view of their areas of study and to offer a vision for what is to come. Some essays focus on the official and unofficial dates of significance for women's writing: 1774 and the Edenton Tea Party; 1848 and the Seneca Falls convention; the 1890s and writing in the Indian territories; the 1920s and women's national voting rights; the 1960s and '70s and the emergence of Women's Studies courses in universities and colleges. Unofficial dates are crucial, too: 1907, the unofficial date for the start of the suffrage movement; 1910, perhaps the birth of the modern. While these dates may be merely occasional or absolutely fixed, they represent many critical junctures that women used to figure their defeats and triumphs.

Some of the following essays introduce women authors who have been barely read, like Susan Blow and the Concord School (Glazener), the 1845 play *Fashion* (Murphy), or Maria Gowen Brooks (Renker), while others introduce better-known authors in terms of one or another of their unstudied texts, such as Child, Sedgwick, and Wright. Some contributors introduce the kind of literary and cultural criticism that has created new ways of reading, especially as Jean Lutes does in writing about "psychic interiority" and the middlebrow novel. The discussions here are not only new in their emphasis on what has been done already, but, even more crucially, what is left to make of women's writing. In so doing, there is not one particular method – either historical, cultural, formalist, reader-response, thematic, or psychoanalytic – dominating these essays or the polyvalence of women's writing.

The *Cambridge History of American Women's Literature* explores how women's writings have defined specific communities or opposed major trends and movements in American culture. For the salient feature of American women's writing has been its position at the forefront of a changing American scene, as well as its creating of individual forms for the inner life of those political and social worlds. Central to this *History* is an account of the reception of women's literatures, from the historical novels of the early 1800s to the domestic realism and sentimentalism of the mid-nineteenth century, to the naturalism and modernism of early twentieth-century modes, and finally to the pluralism – of multicultural literature to postfeminism of contemporary writing.

It is not just the new content or the ever-widening force of women's writing that preoccupies the scholars gathered here. Particularly useful is the force of our contributors' calls for new methodologies: for instance, Kirstin Wilcox's desire to see studies of the many more women authors based in colonial literature who wrote for manuscript, but not print culture; Susan Ryan's insistence that our methodologies have to change, perhaps through the Wright American fiction index (a collection that attempts to include every novel written between 1851 and 1875, which gives us insight into long-forgotten works). What does it mean to read metropolitan and rural print sources for reviews and commentary on women authors? As so many of the authors here contend, the close-reading model will not do enough to launch an argument about the "cultural work" – in Jane Tompkins's famous phrase – of women's writing or even the anthropological turn such writing may take. A "distant" reading – from the outlook of a whole career, like Sedgwick's – might be more what we need for the future of American literary studies.

One of the key contributions of this *History* is its focus, too, on common terms for each period – from "Revolutionary rhetoric" (Baker) to "parlor rhetoric" (Bizzell) to "postfeminism" (Macpherson); "moral authority" (Ryan); "racializing the novel of manners" (Sherrard-Johnson) to "female woundedness" (Travis); "eighteenth-century colonialism" (Doolen), to "sentimental identification" and "transatlantic sympathies" (Bernstein), to "regional literature / material place" (Foote) to "psychic interiority" (Lutes), and what Stephanie Smith elsewhere calls the "household words" that inform the lives of women "on the edge of tomorrow." All these terms transform the rhetorics of each field: from "poetess poetry" to "geographic sentimentalism" to "moral authority" to "domestic realism" to "labor drama" and "cosmopolitan writing," and finally to an incredible array of women's war writing (Vincent). And there are new questions that unfold, dealing with assimilating in America and Jewish history (Wirth-Nesher) or which writers might belong in a new category such as "Asian American chick-lit" (Bow), or who will next address the "Latin American diasporas" (O'Neill). And scholars now need to figure what editors of journals and magazines, such as Charlotte Porter and Helen A. Clarke's 1889 *Poet-Lore*, did for female authors (Glazener).

Some essays offer finely tuned case studies of individual authors or suggest how, for example, African American writings/memoirs have to be read significantly through their "improvisational performance" (Ernest) or through "historical trauma studies" (Travis). Others crystallize individual careers by suggesting how these women were read (Griffin) and how their books changed in the process. Reviews are crucial, as are changes in career, as Child's abolitionism and children's fiction reveal. As Homestead suggests, there is no single "Sedgwick voice" but, rather, a series of voices in her prodigious career. It may be that we need to create many more woman-authored studies – with extended careers like Sedgwick's, Southworth's, Ferber's, or Joyce Carol Oates's.

Such arguments like Bizzell's for a present feminist rhetoric are key to claims about where we are going with the study of American women's writing. Many essays warn against the presentism of so much criticism – especially reading moral authority from a twenty-first-century perspective – but other contributors want that rhetorical edge. In producing such calls as Bizzell's and asking such polemical questions as Ashton does in her essay about modern and contemporary poetry and the rise of neoliberal capitalism, this *History* is not definitive but has a design of its own – one that crystallizes why we are devoted to covering work that new methods and new texts will realize. We may need to recover a "silent language" of an alternative mode of history (Ernest) or the "voiceless speech" of an entire campaign (Chapman) or even discover newer terminology to analyze the "decolonial action" of Indian/Native American writers (Byrd).

In fact, I hope the readers of this *History* will recognize how very different these essays are and have to be. One of the great pleasures of this volume is to be found in the difference in the essays: from literary history – like Singley's and O'Neill's – to Ashton's sharp theoretical claims about why we do the work we do and its values and repercussions, and to Zwinger's approach to the complex questions about sexuality. There are so many subjects, more kinds of women writers, more ways of reading – from autobiographers and biographers, to women editors in publishing, to lesbian work, to many exemplary single careers – that I trust readers will see the ongoing need for focusing on women's writing in the USA.

Works cited

Baym, Nina. *Women Writers of the American West, 1833–1927*. Urbana: University of Illinois Press, 2011.

Berlant, Lauren. *The Female Complaint*. Durham, NC: Duke University Press, 2009.

Chute, Hillary L. *Graphic Women: Life Narrative and Contemporary Comics*. New York: Columbia University Press, 2010.

Fleissner, Jennifer. *Women, Compulsion, Modernity*. Chicago: University of Chicago Press, 2008.

Green, Chris. *The Social Life of Poetry: Appalachia, Race, and Radical Modernism*. New York: Palgrave Macmillan, 2009.

Hogeland, Lisa Maria and Mary Klages *et al. The Aunt Lute Anthology of US Women Writers*. San Francisco: Aunt Lute Books, 2004.

Kelley, Mary. *Learning to Stand and Speak: Women, Education, and Public Life in America's Republic*. Chapel Hill: University of North Carolina Press, 2006.

Marcus, Greil and Werner Sollors, eds. *A New Literary History of America*. Cambridge, MA: Belknap Press, 2009.

Showalter, Elaine. *A Jury of her Peers*. New York: Knopf, 2009.

"Back Talk" with Christine Smallwood. *The Nation*. March 30, 2009, 29.

Thrailkill, Jane. *Affecting Fictions*. Cambridge, MA: Harvard University Press, 2007.

Williams, Susan S. *Reclaiming Authorship: Literary Women in America, 1850–1900*. Philadelphia: University of Pennsylvania Press, 2006.

1

The stories we tell

American Indian women's writing and the persistence of tradition

JODI A. BYRD

American Indian women's writing presents a quandary when one attempts to provide an historical overview. Within the larger nationalistic framing of an "American canon," the whos, whats, and wheres of American Indian women's writing are often informed by colonialist ethnographies, national borders, and anthropological categorizations when they are not lumped into a single ethnicity or generic "Indian" racialization to parallel other ethnic literatures. And then there is the question of when to start. Does it include those pre- and post-contact oral traditions about women's roles in creation stories, in the bringing of corn to the people, or perhaps the Cherokee story of the seven menstruating women who stopped Stone Man? Even if those stories were not necessarily created or even told by women? If one prefers to prioritize "early American" writing, does one start with captivity narratives, and the white colonial serial pathologies and desires that produced Mary Rowlandson and the mass-murdering Hannah Dustan? Does one include Mary Jemison and Eunice Williams and their accounts of becoming Indian? Which borders does one use to identify American Indian women's writing? Does it include Canada, Mexico, or Peru? Which US borders at which historical moment? And what of treaties and the borders produced and maintained by indigenous nations? Is writing produced in Indian Territory in the 1890s, before Oklahoma became a state in 1907, necessarily US literature? And then there is the problem of language.

As all these questions might suggest, American Indian women's writing offers distinct challenges to the spatial, temporal, regional, national, and racial categorizations that have often functioned *de rigueur* to define American women's writing at the site of canon building. Writing by American Indian women has often been framed as something of an enigma, or at least a genre-bending conundrum of expectation and identity that is often tolerated and occasionally noted along with American Indian writing in general, but it is not usually valued by dominant literary histories charting the development of something that might be delineated as "American" literature. And even that project, of writing American Indian literature, by men or women, into "America" ends up replicating the paternalistic and colonialist agendas of eradicating indigenous nations and their inherent sovereignty by adding it to the mosaic of US national literature.[1] Or in the case of someone like Mary Austin, author of *The Land of Little Rain*, American Indians are the source material onto whom a newly formed American literature might be grafted.[2] "The significance of Amerind literature," she writes in her essay, "Non-English Writings: Aboriginal" for *The Cambridge History of American Literature: Later National Literature Part III* (1921), is not

> [to] the social life of the people which interests us. That life is rapidly passing away and must presently be known to us only by tradition and history. The permanent worth of song and epic, folk-tale and drama, aside from its intrinsic literary quality, is its revelation of the power of the American landscape to influence form, and the expressiveness of democratic living in native measures... The earlier, then, we leave off thinking of our own aboriginal literary sources as the product of an alien and conquered people, and begin to think of them as the inevitable outgrowth of the American environment, the more readily shall we come into full use of it... (633–4)

Indians are a sign of the past, though we have no history; we represent the natural world, though we have no art to do so. We are traditional and cultural artifacts within a museum of American progress, the key to a deeper connected relationship to land for Americans more broadly, though Indians in and of ourselves can have no land or presence or future on that land.

By any definitional stretch, then, American Indian women's writing does not exist within such paradigms because American Indians cannot produce a vibrant presence that disrupts the colonialist trajectory that relegates us to the already dead and gone. Or at least that was what I was told as a graduate student when I set out to delineate American Indian literature as my historical area for my comprehensive exams. What I soon realized is that American Indians are often defined by what we are not. Not a canon, not "good literature," not authentic, not alive, not present, and certainly not colonized. We exist somewhere in the interstices, and as a very minor chord to the larger movement of American literature. To acknowledge American Indian presences prior to 1492 disrupts foundationally the affective narratives of immigrant arrival that have served to cohere an "American" literature. Our very nativeness and indigeneity stand in the breach of colonialist desire to refill such nativity with settler colonial histories, dramas, and identities.[3] At the same time, to focus on post-contact literary contributions by American Indian women writers serves to cement the idea that indigenous peoples were only dreamed up by Europeans to the extent that we exist with no antecedents or foremothers. So how then might one account for or provide a literary history of American Indian women's writing that does not capitulate to anthropological, salvage narratives on the one hand that document cultural distinctions at the moment of their passing, or the assimilationist narratives of recovery and inclusion that depend upon a recursive grafting of American literary traditions onto American Indian traditions that then serve as the justification for the eradication of indigenous nations external to the United States?

At some level, then, the contexts, issues, and concerns surrounding American Indian women's writing cannot be separated from issues of settler colonialism, and whether one looks at Cherokee Beloved Woman Nancy Ward (c.1738–c.1824), Ojibwe poet Jane Johnston Schoolcraft (1800–42), Paiute writer and activist Sarah Winnemucca (1844–91), Muscogee Creek author S. Alice Callahan (1868–94), Mohawk author E. Pauline Johnson (1861–1913), Yankton Dakota writer Zitkala-Ša (1876–1938), Laguna Pueblo author Leslie Marmon Silko (1948–), Muscogee Creek poet Joy Harjo (1951–), or Ojibwe novelist Louise Erdrich (1954–), there are central themes that do emerge across the eighteenth, nineteenth, twentieth, and twenty-first centuries of American Indian women's writings. At heart, American Indian women's writing is fundamentally political at the same time that it is inherently literary. It is embodied as lived experience at the same time that it draws upon cultural traditions that have existed since time immemorial. It is multivocal, multilingual, transcultural, intertextual, spatial, and temporal. But above all, American Indian women's writing is responsible to and for community, sovereignty, and land. And oh yes, it is intimately connected to history and the reimagining of decolonial futures for indigenous peoples.

Oral traditions and tribal histories

In order to contextualize the importance of community, sovereignty, and land to American Indian women's writing, it is necessary to provide a few preliminary salvos for those unfamiliar with American Indian Studies. There are currently more than 565 federally recognized American Indian nations and Alaska Native villages in the lands that now constitute the United States.

Each of those 565+ federally recognized nations and communities has its own languages and cultural traditions, and its own treaties and their own diplomatic, government-to-government relationships with the United States. Some of those nations remain on their traditional homelands while others have been removed and relocated hundreds of miles from the territories that defined them prior to European arrival. Oklahoma, created out of the fragmentation of Indian Territory into land allotments, has over thirty-eight federally recognized tribes and nations – from most of the indigenous cultural and geographic regions of what is now the United States. At some level, the only thing giving coherence to "American Indian" as a categorical delineation is the force of ongoing US colonialism, and most American Indians define themselves through their tribal or national affiliations. Each tribe and nation has its own citizenship requirements, and each functions as self-governing and self-determining. Prior to the creation of the United States, there were hundreds more communities, cultures, and languages. The Americas were far from uninscribed earth at the time of contact, and were richly peopled by communities with intricate governmental, social, and cultural structures that maintained and cultivated relationships with the land. Those structures continue still today.

Often when scholars attempt to provide a linear trajectory of American Indian literary productions to mirror the larger progression of the rise of an American national literature, they tend to fall upon a series of tropes. The first is to evoke, as the "authentic" expression of early American literary aesthetics, the traditional oral stories and songs that have been recorded and translated into English by anthropologists and ethnologists such as James Mooney, John R. Swanton, Henry Rowe Schoolcraft, Alice Fletcher, and others. For instance, the seventh edition of the *Norton Anthology of American Literature* (2007) begins with American Indian creation stories and trickster stories as well as including chants and songs to represent the diversity of indigenous cultural aesthetics that pre-date print culture, and Karen L. Kilcup's *Native American Women's Writing: An Anthology c.1800–1924* opens with traditional narratives and songs that include the Iroquois creation story of the Woman Who Fell From the Sky as recorded by Harriet Maxwell Converse (1908) and James Mooney's version of Nun'yunu'wi, the Stone Man, published in 1900. The importance of oral tradition to the study of American Indian literature has been well discussed by scholars such as Paula Gunn Allen (Laguna Pueblo), Greg Sarris (Coast Miwok/Pomo), Vine Deloria, Jr. (Standing Rock Sioux), and Kimberly Blaeser (Anishinaabe) to name just a few. According to Wilma Mankiller, former Principal Chief of the Cherokee Nation of Oklahoma, "An entire body of knowledge can be dismissed because it was not written, while material written by obviously biased men is readily accepted as reality" (*Mankiller*, 20).

By looking at the materiality of indigenous textualities that exist outside the paradigm of written text, the world of indigenous literary production opens into a larger field of interdisciplinary contexts. Certainly stories and songs stand as evidence of what Robert Warrior (Osage) has delineated as "intellectual trade routes," the intricate networks of indigenous knowledge that traverse space and time to provide cultural continuities that resist those histories that continually write indigenous peoples out of existence (*The People and the Word*, 182). As Stephanie Fitzgerald (Cree) and Hilary E. Wyss remind us, "While Native people may not have traditionally utilized alphabetic literacy, rock painting, pictographs, painted and carved baskets and boxes, wampum belts, birchbark scrolls, and other forms of material culture constitute 'texts' that can and should be read within a Native context" ("Land and Literacy," 275).

According to Lakota scholar Craig Howe, tribal histories structure time and narrative through modes that differ radically from the linear, sequential narratives arising from written traditions. Indigenous histories depend upon relationships to "specific landscapes, waterscapes, and skyscapes" and are "event-centered: here something happened and a particular person or being was present" ("Keep Your Thoughts Above the Trees," 162). "Event-centered histories that aspire to achieve an indigenous tribal perspective," Howe continues, "must be composed of at least four dimensions – spatial, social, spiritual, and experiential – that conceptually define tribalism from its origins in the American Indian Old World to its resurgence in the New World of today" (164). The spatial refers to the interconnection between land and people, the relationship to ancestors and the immediacy of space to tribal cultures. The social dimension emphasizes the national and community specificities of indigenous peoples, those components that make one Chickasaw rather than Lakota and tie one to an intricate web of kinship genealogies that extend through land and time. The tribal social dimension focuses on community rather than the individual identities, a self-in-relation rather than a self-made self. The spiritual dimension, according to Howe, embodies the "moral and ethical standards by which tribal members conduct their interactions not only with the land but also with each other and with outsiders" (166). Finally, the experiential component that Howe identifies as necessary for tribal histories and, by extension, tribal aesthetics resides in the embodied and lived elements of the spatial, social, and spiritual components of tribal histories and depends upon the multisensory elements of communal activities and ceremonies (166–7).

The use of oral traditions within certain American literary histories to designate early American Indian textual productions does not always or necessarily reflect Craig Howe's discussion of tribal histories arising from specific landscapes, waterscapes, and skyscapes, and can run the risk of what Robert Dale Parker has diagnosed as a form of modernist nostalgia, especially when deployed as a means to map American literature onto and into indigenous lands and traditions. "That nostalgia," Parker writes, "helps open the door to the naïve identification of orality with Indianness in a world of print literacy that condescends to orality, even as condescension is the tacit accomplice of romanticizing exaltation" (*Invention*, 4). And certainly, both condescension and romanticization have accompanied many of the literary histories of American Indian writings and have participated in the construction of the two enduring stereotypes about American Indians within US cultural archives: hostile and noble savages with their gendered princess and squaw counterparts.

The noble savage, according to Paula Gunn Allen, "is seen as the appealing but doomed victim of the inevitable evolution of humanity from primitive to postindustrial social orders" (*The Sacred Hoop*, 4). As a romanticized figure, the noble savage is often represented as environmental orator or as a tragic leader depressed by the sheer inevitability of white dominance and is often romanticized as the only true "authentic" Indian voice. The princess, the female version of the noble savage, shares a similar fate; she is forever caught between her people and the white man she loves, a virginal, lovelorn figure who sacrifices her own happiness in order to help the white man she loves overcome the savagery of her own people. Think Disney's Pocahontas. On the flipside of the noble savage are the hostile savages who "capture white ladies and torture them, obstruct the westward movement of peaceable white settlers, and engage in bloodthirsty uprisings in which they glory in the massacre of innocent colonists and pioneers" (5). These barely literate, howling savages are the original terrorist threat, the horde that lurks in wait for the oncoming stagecoach, and their mate is the Indian squaw, a beast of burden who drudges, toils, and bears litters of papooses. She is the sexually promiscuous, degraded Indian woman who is abused by Indian and white men alike. These persistent stereotypes inform sports mascots, science fiction epics, and cowboy diplomacies, and are the root justifications for colonization and genocide. The passing of the noble savage is regrettable, tragic, and predetermined; the hostile savage is too dangerous to live and is, in fact, to blame for every violence the colonist inflicts upon the whole race of people.

American Indian women's writing emerges out of the nexus of tribal histories and the violences of settler colonialism and responds to, resists, and disrupts the rote stories US culture continues to produce to justify the ongoing displacements and removals of American Indian peoples and nations from their lands and from historical remembrance. Drawing upon spatial, social, spiritual, and experiential modes of literary aesthetics, stories by and about American Indian women demonstrate the power women have in traditional communities and the intellectual trade routes that oral tradition provides. Some non-Native literary critics have expressed concerns that "Many readers of early Native American women writers may need to suspend ordinary reading practices that value 'consistency' and 'unity'" (Kilcup, *Native American Women's Writing*, 6). What one finds in the writings by American Indian women across time is a sophisticated intertextual, multidirectional consciousness that engages tribal histories, the genocidal logics of an assimilative colonialist invasion, and the continuance of stories to inform resistance and resurgence. From Jane Johnston Schoolcraft and Zitkala-Ša to Leslie Marmon Silko and Joy Harjo, American Indian women have relied upon oral traditions and their narrative structures and aesthetics to produce texts consistent with tribal paradigms whether or not those forms are recognized or valued by outside readers. As Silko has explained, "We are all part of the old stories. Whether we know the stories or not, the stories know about us. From time immemorial, the old stories encompass all events, past and future" ("An Expression of Profound Gratitude," 205).

Captivity narratives

Typically, when anthologies of American literature attempt to provide a linear progression of women's writing in the United States, what usually follows the obligatory inclusion of oral tradition to signal indigenous "pre-historical" and "pre-literate" roots are the Indian captivity narratives from eighteenth- and nineteenth-century New England particularly. As a genre, captivity narratives are distinctively American and have influenced textualities as wide ranging as slave narratives to Herman Melville's *Typee* to the twenty-first-century wars in Iraq and Afghanistan. According to Kathryn Zabelle Derounian-Stodola, "'the captivity narrative' encompasses any story with a captor (usually from a minority group) and a captive (usually from a majority group)" ("Introduction," xi). Though the idea that Indians were minorities in their own nations is both ahistorical and ethnocentrist as it assumes always and already that American Indians constitute minorities in our own lands, captivity narratives predominated the cultural imagination of the late eighteenth-century American colonies at that moment when the population numbers shifted to such a degree that the colonialists outnumbered citizens of indigenous nations. Still, Derounian-Stodola draws some useful taxonomies. "Almost invariably," she writes, "the Indian captivity narrative concerns the capture of an individual or several family members rather than larger groupings, and its plot is most commonly resolved with the captive's escape, ransom, transculturation, or death" (xi). These narratives, especially those that center on white women and children, were wildly popular and over 500 were published in the eighteenth and nineteenth centuries. They emphasize the violence Indians supposedly posed to the frontier settlements, and offer discourses on redemption and divine providence to intervene and recommit the captive to the glory of a Christian and Protestant god. Often, too, as is the case with the captivities of Hannah Dustan (1657–1736), Eunice Williams (1696–1785), French Nancy (1730–1820s?), and Mary Jemison (1743–1833), to name a few, the narratives are filtered through white settler men: John E. Seaver, Cotton Mather, John Williams, and Horatio Bardwell Cushman.

For some scholars, Indian captivity narratives raise the question of who constitutes an "Indian" subject position within written and spoken texts, especially those narratives of women like Jemison, Williams, and French Nancy who chose unredemption and lived their lives out as Seneca, Kahnawake Mohawk, and Chickasaw women respectively rather than return to their lives in the British and French colonies. For Karen Kilcup, one of the primary concerns of American Indian women's writing is the question of identity, a question that is not resolvable through blood quantum, community recognition, class, or education but is located at the interstices of assimilation, acculturation, intermarriage, and privilege (*Native American Women's Writing*, 2–3). Given the multifocal transubjectivities that emerge within the field about what constitutes an American Indian text, it may be useful not only to pluralize American Indian literature into literatures as Kilcup suggests, but to be mindful of the colonialist and racist assumptions that continue to circulate around American Indians and the texts they produce. Indian captivity narratives mythologized certain ideas about Indianness, helped solidify colonialist attitudes towards Indian savagery and depravity, played to emerging US nationalistic masculinities that sought to protect white womanhood from racial threat, and appealed to fantasies about becoming native in a land that was still new and uncertain to settlers. The genre has furthermore engrained a certain expectation of subjectivity, of who is able to be "captive" and the emphasis on white women's narratives often denies, forgets, or blatantly ignores the experiences so many indigenous men and women had as they were stolen from their communities and families and forced to attend boarding schools. A final caveat about captivity narratives: a text that has Indians in it does not an indigenous text make.

Certainly Mary Jemison, Eunice Williams, and other captives often chose to remain with their adoptive families, and through the course of time assimilated into their new nation's kinship structures, genealogies, and social worlds. While one could and perhaps should consider how Jemison and Williams draw from the cultural codes and tribal histories that deploy social, spatial, spiritual, and experiential dimensions that help shape indigenous aesthetics, there are also colonial and racial implications that emerge from continuing to place whiteness, even if it is disaffected or transculturated, at the center of representational politics in constructing literary histories. Kahnawake Mohawk scholar Audra Simpson argues that captivity narratives about women like Mary Jemison and Eunice Williams perform an alchemy of race and citizenship that has continued repercussions for white and Indian women captured today in the service of settler colonialism. "This alchemy," she writes, "was one that became legal, and we may understand as a move from white into red, a social and political moment in North American history wherein such political and legal recognitions were possible" ("From White into Red," 252). Read in this way, Eunice Williams's transformation from settler into Kahnawake Mohawk is, Simpson argues, "a shadow logic to that of *claiming* and *owning* land," particularly in the context of the Canadian 1876 Indian law that legally determined who was an Indian and disenfranchised and removed Mohawk women who married white men and conferred Indian status on white women who married Mohawk men (253). "A feminist analysis that squares itself with questions of indigeneity," Simpson continues, "will ask how Eunice Williams's captivity narrative contributes to the expropriation of land and to the reformulation of Indigenous gender and governmental systems" (255).

White women's Indian captivity narratives, though they may in some cases exist liminally between white and Indian narrative traditions, have lasting implications for how white settlers have legally and imaginatively conceptualized race and citizenship, belonging and nation, gender and desire, at the same time that they have wittingly or unwittingly reinscribed anti-Indian racial logics that demonize indigenous peoples or target them for literal and cultural annihilation. And for this reason, within the larger body of American Indian women's writing, captivity narratives have become one of those literatures of empire against which American Indian writers such as Zitkala-Ša, Louise Erdrich, and Leslie Marmon Silko write back. Following in the vein of postcolonial texts such as Jean Rhys's *Wide Sargasso Sea* or Aimé Césaire's *A Tempest* that reframe the canonical texts of the British empire, Louise Erdrich's poem "Captivity," assumes Mary Rowlandson's voice to disrupt her Calvinistic repudiation of the Wampanoag society and people in her 1682 captivity narrative, *The Sovereignty and Goodness of God*. Erdrich's poem, originally published in 1984 in her poetry collection *Jacklight*, interweaves sentences from Rowlandson's text into the verse of the poem to fill in the silences of the original narrative and woman's captivation. Erdrich's Rowlandson is haunted by her captivity and the unfilled desire for the Wampanoag man with whom she traveled and lived briefly. After she returns to her white husband and finds herself alienated from a land that had begun to open for her during her captivity, her Calvinist surety and supremacy begin to fracture: "Rescued, I see no truth in things" ("Captivity," 11). Zitkala-Ša's *American Indian Stories* (1921) and Leslie Marmon Silko's *Gardens in the Dunes* (1999) detail the other side of captivity through the experiences of Indian girls coerced by missionaries and the US government to attend boarding school.[4]

Nineteenth and early twentieth centuries

Though the archive of early nineteenth-century American Indian women's writings continues to expand as more and more texts are recovered, the larger movements of key texts may start with the Cherokee women's petitions against Removal presented to the Cherokee National Council in 1817, 1818, and 1821 (1831?) and include Cherokee Catharine Brown's conversion narrative published originally by Rufus Anderson in 1824. But for poetry and fiction, the timeline starts with Ojibwe Jane Johnston Schoolcraft (Bamewawagezhikaquay) who began writing poems and traditional stories in 1815. Born in Sault Ste. Marie, Schoolcraft grew up in the Great Lakes region as part of a mixed-blood family – her mother was Ojibwe and her father Irish. According to Robert Dale Parker, Schoolcraft wrote approximately fifty poems in English and Ojibwe. In addition, she transcribed and translated traditional oral stories and songs into both English and Ojibwe (Schoolcraft, *The Sound the Stars Make*, 1–2). Her work negotiated a changing world that saw shifts "not only from Ojibwe and French-Canadian cultural dominance to the dominance of the encroaching United States, but also from British rule to US federal rule, with the accompanying changes in language and religions as well as shifts in the sense of centering cultural identity from Ojibwe and French to English and from Montreal to Washington and New York City" (5–6).

In 1823, she married cultural anthropologist Henry Rowe Schoolcraft, and she had a deep influence on his ethnographic work in the Great Lakes Region.

Jane Johnston Schoolcraft's profoundly significant work was often overshadowed by her husband, and her importance as one of the earliest American Indian women authors producing literature in English and Ojibwe was underplayed. According to A. LaVonne Brown Ruoff, Henry represented Schoolcraft in his own work "as an emblem of assimilation and as a liaison between Indians and non-Indians more than as a writer and intellectual" ("Early Native American Women Authors," 83). What one finds in her writings, however, is a complex and sometimes conflicting engagement with the cultural and national influences that shaped her world. While many of her poems demonstrate a writer influenced by the Romantic poetic conventions of the time, she also produced poems in English and Ojibwe that evoke land, space, and cultural continuance that demonstrate not so much the emblematic assimilation her husband emphasized but rather a complex Ojibwe subjectivity that was able to draw upon the full influences that shaped her world. Poems such as "To the Pine Tree" and "The Contrast," according to Parker, "engage the personal and the familial with what we might call a nationalist commitment to place and people that can resonate powerfully for the later history of Indian literary and political self-consciousness and sovereignty" (*Invention*, 50). Her poem "On leaving my children John and Jane at School, in the Atlantic states, and preparing to return to the interior" was written in Ojibwe, and in a new translation by Dennis Jones, Heidi Stark, and James Vukelich, engages with Ojibwe ontological connections between being and land when Schoolcraft writes, "To my home I shall return / That is the way that I am, my being / My land" (Schoolcraft, *The Sound the Stars Make*, 142–3). Her writings draw upon the social, spatial, spiritual, and experiential elements of tribal history and challenge any essentialist or dismissive readings of her work.

Paiute author, activist, and orator Sarah Winnemucca's *Life Among the Piutes: Their Wrongs and Claims* (1883) was one of the first autobiographies written by an American Indian woman. Born some time around 1844 in the lands that are now known as Nevada, Winnemucca was part of a prominent family of leaders within the Paiute Nation. As a liaison with and translator for the military as the United States waged campaigns against Native peoples in the Great Basin region, Winnemucca remains a controversial figure. In 1879, Winnemucca (Thocmetony, Shell Flower) went on the lecture circuit in an attempt to draw attention to the struggles of her people in the face of corrupt US Indian agents and continued encroachments by white settlers in pursuit of land. Often positioning herself and allowing herself to be promoted as an Indian Princess, Winnemucca negotiated the often fraught sexist and racist assumptions about American Indian women through what some have argued was a form of cultural mediation. As an activist, she supported the Dawes General Allotment Act (1887) and advocated for native lands to be apportioned in severalty to citizens of indigenous nations in the hope that it might help stave off the violence of, and protect American Indians from, white settlers. Her autobiography draws upon Paiute oral traditions and tribal histories and at the same time bears witness to the racialized and gendered violences of colonialism.

S. Alice Callahan (Muscogee Creek) was the first American Indian woman to publish a novel, and her book, *Wynema: A Child of the Forest*, has spawned controversy ever since. Callahan was born in Sulphur Springs, Texas, to a white mother and a mixed-blood father who was a prominent figure within Creek national politics. The Muscogee Creek's traditional homelands are in what are now Georgia, Alabama, Florida, and South Carolina, and they were removed in the 1830s along with the Cherokee, Choctaw, Chickasaw, and Seminoles to Indian Territory. *Wynema*, published in 1891, was profoundly influenced by the December 29, 1890, massacre at Wounded Knee, and the novel criticizes the United States government for its barbarity and violence towards Indians, and its hypocrisy in denominating Indian peoples uncivilized. It was also written and published at the height of the debates concerning the 1887 Dawes General Allotment Act, and the novel contains a Socratic dialogue on whether to allot the Creek nation. The plot focuses on the friendship of a white southern Methodist woman, Genevieve Weir, who has taken a teaching job in Indian Territory, and her full-blood Muscogee student, Wynema Harjo. The book opens with a dedication "To the Indian tribes of North America who have felt the wrongs and oppression of their pale-faced brothers" and sets out to "open the eyes and hearts of the world to our afflictions and thus speedily issue into existence an era of good feeling and just dealing toward us and our more oppressed brothers" (*Wynema*, front matter). Muscogee Creek scholar Craig Womack critiques the novel for being "a remarkably 'un-Creek' work, which is not the same thing as saying that she is not a Creek writer. She is a bad Creek writer who has written a marginally Creek novel, at least from one Creek reader's perspective, and I would say her novel squelches any Creek voices, or any other Native perspectives" (*Red on Red*, 120).

Callahan's text is, admittedly, written in conversation with other sentimental novels of the period and as a result shares commonalities with Okanogan Mourning Dove's *Cogewea* (1927). Susan Bernardin argues that Callahan, like Zitkala-Ša, Mourning Dove, and other *fin-de-siècle* Native women writers, "mobilized an array of conventional narrative forms as a means of rewriting the terms of nationalism, reform, and federal policy" at the intersections of "Euroamerican women's reform culture, Native women, and national Indian policies" ("On the Meeting Grounds of Sentiment," 210). Womack is correct to a certain extent that the main characters in *Wynema* are the white Genevieve and her suitor Gerald Keithly, but rather than suggest that the novel fails to present a Creek perspective, it might also make sense to read the novel as a reflection upon whiteness and the power white women and men have within colonial regimes, a perspective that might well be a Creek woman's. The fractured alliances and hostilities between whites and Creeks in Indian Territory, the tensions between stereotypes and misrepresentations of Creek life that the white characters both engage in and critique in the text, and the white characters' ventriloquization of anti-Allotment arguments in counter to Wynema's initial support of the proposed policy are multiply inflected and raise interesting questions about critiques of whiteness within indigenous studies. In her essay "A Strong Race Opinion: On the Indian Girl in Modern Fiction" published originally in 1892, Mohawk poet E. Pauline Johnson objects to the double-standard of characterization that meets the Indian girl when she appears in American texts. While the American woman is "vari-coloured as to personality and action," Johnson writes, "Not so the Indian girl in modern fiction, the author permits her character no such spontaneity, she must not be of womankind at large, neither must she have an originality, a singularity that is not definitely 'Indian.' I quote 'Indian' as there seems to be an impression amongst authors that such a thing as tribal distinction does not exist among the North American aborigines" (*Collected Poems and Selected Prose*, 178). Though Callahan's *Wynema* deploys certain stereotypes and generalities about Creek culture, she at least passes Johnson's Indian version of the Bechdel test:

> Let us not only hear, but read something of the North American Indian "besting" some one at least once in a decade, and above all things let the Indian girl of fiction develop from the "doglike," "fawnlike," "deer-footed," "fire-eyed," "crouching," "submissive" book heroine into something of the quiet, sweet womanly woman she is, if wild, or the everyday, natural, laughing girl she is, if cultivated and educated; let her be natural, even if the author is not competent to give her tribal characteristics.[5] (183)

Johnson's 1892 essay still resonates with and indeed anticipates twenty-first-century calls for native literary nationalisms.[6]

Red power and postcolonial tales

The year 1968 saw the publication of Kiowa author N. Scott Momaday's Pulitzer Prize-winning novel *House Made of Dawn* and marked a turning point within American Indian literary production as the Red Power movement of the 1960s and '70s revitalized indigenous struggles and drew attention to issues of sovereignty, self-determination, and land that have always been the core of indigenous anti-colonial struggles since Europeans first arrived on our shores. Leslie Marmon Silko's first novel, *Ceremony*, was published nine years later in 1977 to critical acclaim, and that novel remains one of the most often taught and studied texts within the field. Louise Erdrich's first novel, *Love Medicine*, appeared in print in 1984. Erdrich, the Ojibwe counterpoint to William Faulkner, is the author of thirteen novels, including *The Beet Queen* (1986), *Tracks* (1988), *The Crown of Columbus* (1991, with Michael Dorris), *The Bingo Palace* (1994), *Tales of Burning Love* (1996), *The Antelope Wife* (1998), *The Last Report on the Miracles at Little No Horse* (2001), *The Master Butchers Singing Club* (2003), *Four Souls* (2004), *The Painted Drum* (2005), *The Plague of Doves* (2008), and *Shadow Tag* (2010). Erdrich has also written six young adult novels, three non-fiction books, and three collections of poetry. Her novels trace the intricacies of interrelated generations of Native and white families on a Chippewa reservation in North Dakota, and characters appear and evolve throughout the thirteen novels. Land, space, kinship, and traditional knowledges all contribute to the tribal histories her novel constructs and reimagines.

After Silko's *Ceremony* and Erdrich's *Love Medicine*, writings by American Indian women proliferated in comparison to the texts available from the nineteenth century. In the 1980s, Paula Gunn Allen published *The Sacred Hoop* as a gynocentric intervention to the stereotypes and misinformation about the status and roles of women in tribal communities, in addition to publishing collections of traditional and short stories by and about American Indian women. Janet Campbell Hale (Coeur d'Alene) published *The Jailing of Cecelia Capture* in 1985, a novel that explores in counterpoint how a successful Indian law student can still be captured by the administrative bureaucracies of the US government that police the bodies of non-white women. And Pawnee/Otoe-Missouria author Anna Lee Walters published *Ghost Singer* in 1988. Taking up issues of artifact and bone collecting that underwrote nineteenth- and twentieth-century anthropology, Walters's novel examines the implications and consequences for institutions like the Smithsonian in Washington,

DC, that house cultural patrimony and ancestors stolen from indigenous peoples.

In 1990, Chickasaw poet and novelist Linda Hogan published her first novel, *Mean Spirit*, and has since written *Solar Storms* (1995), *Power* (1998), and *People of the Whale* (2008), in addition to her poetry volumes that include *Calling Myself Home* (1978), *Seeing through the Sun* (1985), *The Book of Medicines* (1993), and *Rounding the Human Corners* (2008). Hogan's work engages the spatial through the environmental and theorizes how colonization is scored onto lands and women's bodies. In 1994, Susan Power's novel *The Grass Dancer* opened a Standing Rock Sioux conversation with Louise Erdrich's *Love Medicine* in a richly textured story that interweaves past and present, ancestors and ghosts, into the lives of Dakota Sioux characters living on a North Dakota reservation. In 1996 and 1997, Ojibwe novelist and activist Carole LaFavor published *Along the Journey River* and *Evil Dead Center* as part of an Ojibwe lesbian mystery series that features the adventures of an amateur detective who lives on the Red Lake Reservation. By the turn of the twenty-first century, Bitterroot Salish novelist Debra Magpie Earling's novel *Perma Red* appeared in print in 2002, and Choctaw novelist, poet, and scholar LeAnne Howe's first novel, *Shell Shaker*, was published by Aunt Lute Books in September 2001 and was followed by her Indian baseball novel *Miko Kings* in 2007. Howe's work troubles linear histories that assume narratives of progression from past to present and instead constructs southeastern Chickasaw and Choctaw worlds that exist in the boundaries between space and time, pre-Removal and Indian Territory, Oklahoma and a decolonized future.

Writings by American Indian women, though shaped by the historical and literary aesthetics of the moment in which they are written, disrupt the usual trajectories of multicultural narratives of progress towards inclusion and are often striking in the ways in which they enunciate the conflicts that erupt out of the cultural and political collisions initiated at the moment of colonization and transatlantic arrivals. These texts are often articulations of decolonial action situated and grounded within the central roles that women have played within their communities as leaders, activists, and outspoken critics of US federal policies that have served to strip indigenous nations of lands, culture, and language. American Indian women's writing is transnational from the start; it is concerned with identity and its discontents; it reinvents language and appropriates non-Native textualities to produce texts that, while often new and innovative, are tied to oral traditions and land. There is a certain coherency to the themes and strategies that emerge when taking a long view of the field. In 1987, Elizabeth Cook-Lynn (Crow Creek Sioux) suggests that "it is the responsibility of a poet like me to 'consecrate' history and event, survival and joy and sorrow, the significance of ancestors and the unborn" in her work ("You May Consider Speaking About Your Art," 59). In 2000, LeAnne Howe explains that

> When I write fiction, poetry, or history (at least the kind of history I'm interested in writing), I pull the passages of my life, and the lives of my mothers, my mothers' mothers, my uncles, the greater community of *chafachuka* ("family") and *iksa* ("clan"), together to form the basis for critique, interpretation; a moment in the raw world. My obligation in that critique is that I must learn more about my ancestors, understand them better than I imagined. Then I must be able to render all our collective experiences into a meaningful form. I call this process "tribalography." ("My Mothers, My Uncles," 214–15)

In 1991, Robert Warrior wrote that "we need scholars to respect the integrity and continuity of American Indian literature, both historical and contemporary, as a literature of resistance to colonialism, and to compare it to other literatures of resistance, whether African American, African, or Arab" ("A Marginal Voice," 30). The continued assumption that American Indian literatures belong to US national literature is a colonialist assumption that subverts the sovereignty and self-determination of indigenous nations.

Joy Harjo, in a poem written specifically for *English Postcoloniality: Literatures from Around the World* (1996), explains the importance of decolonization for indigenous peoples. "It was as if we were stolen, put into a bag carried on the back of a white man / who pretends to own the earth and the sky. In the sack were all the people of the world. / We fought until there was a hole in the bag / When we fell we were not aware of falling" (15). The poem explains how stories and songs "are like humans who when they laugh are indestructible" and ends with the observation that though "no story or song will translate the full impact of falling or the inverse power of rising up," it is necessary for every act of creation to try. Harjo draws upon the Iroquois creation story of Sky Woman or the Woman Who Fell from the Sky to articulate the possibilities of imagination to disrupt the violences of colonization. Whether decolonization takes its form in the struggle to restore the Hawaiian Kingdom, to return traditional lands to the indigenous nations from which they were stolen, or to write intellectually rigorous scholarship that engages seriously the implications of indigenous tribal specificities, sovereignty, and that inverse power of rising up, is the story American Indian women tell throughout their work.

Notes

1. I am indebted here to Robert Allen Warrior. In "A Marginal Voice," Warrior critiques Arnold Krupat's *A Voice in the Margin* for assuming "that American Indian literature belongs first to the *national* literature of the United States and only secondarily to itself and to the literature of other colonized people (often called 'Third World Literature'). This smacks of assimilationism, insofar as Krupat does not reveal any awareness of the sovereignty and separate political status of Native nations" (30).
2. In *Red on Red*, Womack writes, "tribal literatures are not some branch waiting to be grafted onto the main truck [of American canonical literature]. Tribal literatures are the *tree*, the oldest literatures in the Americas, the most American of American literatures. We *are* the canon" (6–7).
3. For more on non-Native assertions of replacement narratives, see O'Brien's *Firsting and Lasting: Writing Indians Out of Existence in New England*.
4. For more on how *Gardens in the Dunes* might be read in relation to captivity narratives, see Huhndorf's *Going Native: Indians in the American Cultural Imagination*.
5. The Bechdel test refers to cartoonist Alison Bechdel's 1985 *Dykes to Watch Out For* comic strip "The Rule." The rule about movies, novels, and other representations of women in popular media must satisfy three requirements. "One, it has to have at least two women in it . . . who, two, talk to each other about, three, something besides a man." See Alison Bechdel's "DTWOF: The Blog," post "The Rule" (August 16, 2005). http://alisonbechdel.blogspot.com/2005/08/rule.html.
6. For more on Native literary nationalisms, see Weaver, Womack, and Warrior's *American Indian Literary Nationalism*. Huhndorf critiques nationalist criticism in *Mapping the Americas: The Transnational Politics of Contemporary Native Culture* as it "disregards global social dynamics and colonial critique, often opposing the struggles for sovereignty to the interrogation of European ideologies and practices" (11). Additionally, she claims, nationalist criticism reifies certain histories of treaty relations over others and "neglects indigenous communities that fall outside the legal category of 'nation'" (11).

Works cited

Allen, Paula Gunn. *The Sacred Hoop: Recovering the Feminine in American Indian Traditions*. Boston: Beacon Press, 1986.

Austin, Mary. "Non-English Writings ii: Aboriginal." In *The Cambridge History of American Literature*. Vol. 4. Ed. William Peterfield Trent, John Erskine, Stuart Pratt Sherman, and Carl Van Doren. New York: G. P. Putnam's Sons, 1921.

Baym, Nina, *et al.*, eds. *The Norton Anthology of American Literature*. 7th edn. "Native American Literatures." Ed. Arnold Krupat. New York: W. W. Norton, 2007.

Bernardin, Susan. "On the Meeting Grounds of Sentiment: S. Alice Callahan's *Wynema: A Child of the Forest*." *ATQ: The American Transcendental Quarterly* 15.3 (September 2001): 209–24.

Blaeser, Kimberly M. *Gerald Vizenor: Writing in the Oral Tradition*. Norman: University of Oklahoma Press, 1996.

Callahan, S. Alice. *Wynema: A Child of the Forest.* 1891. Ed. A. LaVonne Brown Ruoff. Lincoln, NB: University of Nebraska Press, 1997.

Callahan, S. Alice. Cherokee Women's Petitions, 1817, 1818, 1821 [1831?]. *The Cherokee Removal: A Brief History with Documents.* Ed. Theda Perdue and Michael D. Green. New York: Bedford/St. Martin's, 1995.

Cook-Lynn, Elizabeth. "You May Consider Speaking About Your Art." In *I Tell You Now: Autobiographical Essays by Native American Writers.* Ed. Brian Swann and Arnold Krupat. Lincoln, NB: University of Nebraska Press, 1987.

Cushman, Horatio Bardwell. *History of the Choctaw, Chickasaw, and Natchez Indians.* Greenville: Headlight Print House, 1899.

Derounian-Stodola, Kathryn Zabelle. "Introduction." In *Women's Indian Captivity Narratives.* New York: Penguin, 1998.

Deloria, Jr., Vine. *The World We Used to Live In: Remembering the Powers of Medicine Men.* Golden, CO: Fulcrum, 2006.

Erdrich, Louise. "Captivity." In *Original Fire: Selected and New Poems.* 2003. New York: Harper Perennial, 2004.

Love Medicine. 1984. New and expanded version. New York: Harper Perennial, 2005.

Fitzgerald, Stephanie and Hilary E. Wyss. "Land and Literacy: The Textualities of Native Studies." *American Literary History* 22.2 (Summer 2010): 271–9.

Hale, Janet Campbell. *The Jailing of Cecelia Capture.* 1985. Albuquerque: University of New Mexico Press, 1987.

Harjo, Joy. "A Postcolonial Tale." In *English Postcoloniality: Literatures from Around the World.* Ed. Radhika Mohanram and Gita Rajan. Westport, CT: Greenwood Press, 1996.

Hogan, Linda. *Solar Storms: A Novel.* 1995. New York: Scribner, 1997.

Howe, Craig. "Keep Your Thoughts Above the Trees: Ideas on Developing and Presenting Tribal Histories." In *Clearing a Path: Theorizing the Past in Native American Studies.* Ed. Nancy Shoemaker. New York: Routledge, 2002.

Howe, LeAnne. *Miko Kings: An Indian Baseball Story.* San Francisco: Aunt Lute Books, 2007.

"My Mothers, My Uncles, Myself." In *Here First: Autobiographical Essays by Native American Writers.* Ed. Arnold Krupat and Brian Swann. New York: Modern Library, 2000.

Shell Shaker. San Francisco: Aunt Lute Books, 2001.

Huhndorf, Shari M. *Going Native: Indians in the American Cultural Imagination.* Ithaca: Cornell University Press, 2001.

Mapping the Americas: The Transnational Politics of Contemporary Native Culture. Ithaca: Cornell University Press, 2009.

Johnson, E. Pauline (Tekahionwake). *Collected Poems and Selected Prose.* Ed. Carole Gerson and Veronica Strong-Boag. Toronto: University of Toronto Press, 2002.

Kilcup, Karen L. *Native American Women's Writing: An Anthology, c.1800–1924.* Malden, MA: Blackwell, 2000.

LaFavor, Carole. *Along the Journey River: A Mystery.* Ithaca: Firebrand Books, 1996.

Evil Dead Center: A Mystery. Ithaca: Firebrand Books, 1997.

Mankiller, Wilma and Michael Wallis. *Mankiller: A Chief and her People.* New York: St. Martin's, 1993.

Mourning Dove. *Cogewea, The Half-Blood.* 1927. Lincoln, NE: Bison–University Press of Nebraska, 1981.

O'Brien, Jean M. *Firsting and Lasting: Writing Indians Out of Existence in New England.* Minneapolis: University of Minnesota Press, 2010.

Parker, Robert Dale. *The Invention of Native American Literature.* Ithaca: Cornell University Press, 2003.

Power, Susan. *The Grass Dancer.* New York: G. P. Putnam's Sons, 1994.

Ruoff, A. LaVonne Brown. "Early Native American Women Authors: Jane Johnston Schoolcraft, Sarah Winnemucca, S. Alice Callahan, E. Pauline Johnson, and Zitkala-Ša." In *Nineteenth-Century American Women Writers: A Critical Reader.* Ed. Karen L. Kilcup. Malden, MA: Blackwell, 1998.

Sarris, Greg. *Keeping Slug Woman Alive: A Holistic Approach to American Indian Texts.* Berkeley: University of California Press, 1993.

Schoolcraft, Jane Johnston. *The Sound the Stars Make Rushing Through the Sky: The Writings of Jane Johnston Schoolcraft.* Ed. Robert Dale Parker. Philadelphia: University of Pennsylvania Press, 2007.

Silko, Leslie Marmon. *Ceremony.* 1977. New York: Penguin, 1986.

"An Expression of Profound Gratitude." In *First World, Ha Ha Ha! The Zapatista Challenge.* Ed. Elaine Katzenberger. San Francisco: City Lights Books, 1995.

Gardens in the Dunes: A Novel. New York: Simon & Schuster, 1999.

Simpson, Audra. "From White into Red: Captivity Narratives as Alchemies of Race and Citizenship." *American Quarterly* 60.2 (June 2008): 251–7.

Walters, Anna Lee. *Ghost Singer: A Novel.* 1988. Albuquerque: University of New Mexico Press, 1994.

Warrior, Robert Allen. "A Marginal Voice." *Native Nations* 1.3 (1991): 29–30.

The People and the Word: Reading Native Nonfiction. Minneapolis: University of Minnesota Press, 2005.

Weaver, Jace, Craig S. Womack, and Robert Warrior. *American Indian Literary Nationalism.* Albuquerque: University of New Mexico Press, 2005.

Williams, John. *The Redeemed Captive Returning to Zion.* 1853. Bedford: Applewood Books, 1992.

Winnemucca, Sarah. *Life Among the Piutes: Their Wrongs and Claims.* 1883. Reno: University of Nevada Press, 1994.

Womack, Craig S. *Red on Red: Native American Literary Separatism.* Minneapolis: University of Minnesota Press, 1999.

Zitkala-Ša. *American Indian Stories, Legends, and Other Writings.* New York: Penguin, 2003.

2

Women writers and war

JONATHAN VINCENT

From its inception, feminism has not known whether to fight men or to join them;
whether to lament sex differences and deny their importance or to acknowledge
and even valorize such differences; whether to condemn all wars outright or to
extol women's contributions to war efforts . . . The story of feminism and male /
female identifications is . . . a tumult of ongoing encounters with a long, grand
genealogy – from the prototypical maternal figure, the Madonna, to the exemplary
woman warrior, Joan. As discourse, feminism is not just a series of explicit
endorsements but a cluster of implicit presumptions guiding rhetorical choices and
controlling dominant tropes and metaphors.
Jean Elshtain, "Feminism's War with War"[1]

Exclusions: *patria*, patrimony, patriarchy

In February 1676, a band of Nipmuc, Narragansett, and Wampanoag Indians
assaulted the village of Lancaster, Massachusetts. The raid was a local battle
of Metacom's (or King Philip's) War, a bloody imbroglio raging across sectors
of New England that would alter profoundly colonists' sense of New World
sanctuary and divine commission. Although largely exacerbated by English
expansion, and though the war's toll fell most adversely on indigenous Americans, the events at Lancaster that afternoon left numerous colonists dead
and many houses in ashes. The assailants, as was customary, took hostages.
Among the party of settlers abducted from the scene of that "dreadfull hour"
was Mary Rowlandson, a pious pastor's wife, who would spend the next three
fretful months traveling or encamped among her enemies: cryptic creatures
her biblically filtered optic could regard only as "hell-hounds," "ravenous
beasts," barbarous "Heathen" devils (*The Sovereignty and Goodness of God*, 69–
71). Although she was eventually ransomed and returned home, her "afflic-
tion," as she typically described the unwanted adventure, drank so deeply
of the "Wine of astonishment" as to violate the bordered integrity of her
self-comprehension (112). *"I can remember the time when I used to sleep quietly*

without workings in my thoughts," she reflects, *"but now it is other wayes with me"* (III).

Six years later, partly to restore that breached fortress of personhood, Row-landson wrote and published *The Sovereignty and Goodness of God* (1682), an account of her harrowing capture, bondage, and "redemption" for having survived such an ordeal of spiritual and cultural otherness. Literally "read to pieces," her "captivity narrative" inaugurated the only literary genre unique to the New World and, by some accounts, established its first bestseller.[2] The phenomenon of its appearance is remarkable for other reasons, however. Although they had banished women from such immodest public utterance after Anne Hutchinson's defiance of clerical authority a generation prior, the all-male ecclesiastical hierarchy not only tolerated Rowlandson's literary out-burst but heartily endorsed it. Assuaging anticipated offense at her seemingly arrogant intrusion into the "publick view" was a preface most likely written by Increase Mather, beseeching members to apprehend in "such works of God" not vain self-promotion brazenly "thrust . . . into the press" but "many passages of working providence" to "benefit" others (64–6). That a woman's war narrative was the only form of personal writing to bypass colonial censors suggests just how purposeful such accounts of "universall concernment" were in alerting congregants to mutually menacing forces and recalling them to their collective security in the body of Christ.

US war narratives typically convene that dyadic purview, socializing notions of polity and commonwealth in the mystical corpus of "the peo-ple" while arraying that harassed solidarity against both threats from without and dissociated "fifth columns" within. Persistently stalking the endangered "flock" in Rowlandson's narrative are figurations of indigenous peoples as marauding packs of "ravenous Wolves" and "roaring Lyons" that, as with Daniel in his biblical den, seek only to rend asunder the holy comity (105, 107). But inimical also to that social aggregate are ostensibly converted souls passing perfidiously among the elect: treacherous "praying Indians," but even spiritually and racially degenerated white colonists who pursue private levity at the expense of the larger Puritan errand. With its unmistakable call for personal regeneration and rededication to the life of the whole, the captivity narrative genre provided ministers with countless heuristics for community revival.

Yet Rowlandson also uses aspects of the acquiescent mode to advance fairly seditious rebukes of the order's masculine leadership, often disguising those critiques by displacing them onto the providential will.[3] Commenting on "a few remarkable passages of providence," for instance, Rowlandson relays the humor with which her captors *"derided the slowness, and dullness of the* English *army,"* scoffing at their prisoners *"as if the English* would be a quarter of a year getting ready" – which they were. Especially considering that guarantees of protection were what allegedly legitimated men's dominion over the public realm, the fact that *"so numerous"* an English army quailed in its pursuit of the enemy at the Baquag River constitutes another "marvelous" incident for which she takes "special notice" (104–5). More audaciously, in its many suggestions that the endurance of such distress and tribulation supplies the author with special, esoteric knowledge – an unfiltered glance into noumenal reality itself – the text insinuates an experiential authority unmatched by most of the community's male membership.[4]

The Sovereignty and Goodness of God thus enters the complex symbolic field both empowering and constraining women writers on war. Establishing political "legitimacy" in self-authenticating rites of violence extrinsic to the culture of everyday life, Rowlandson discloses subterranean intimacies between war participation and collective belonging, between the way self-abnegating assumptions of risk and sacrifice paradoxically levy portals of access to the public sphere and its conference of more "recognized" social stature. A century later, abjuring both theological and monarchical sovereignty and founding the liberal-republican nation, the Declaration of Independence announced the arrival of a revolutionary democratic order and the birth of the citizen as precisely that expender of sacrifice and risk. Mutually pledging "our Lives, our Fortunes, and our sacred Honor," the roll call of all-male signatories signed into being the collective "We" constituting a new "Form of Government" by dispersing sovereign power – "the Right of the People" – into the body politic.[5] It was a wildly performative act, rhetorically "self-fathering" the "abstract citizen" it ostensibly only described.[6] Banished from inclusion in that departicularized, deracinated, ungendered public body, however, were the unpropertied, slaves, and women. Their exclusion from the founding of "universal rational man" reveals the white male body as the tacit, ascriptive standard of inclusion that it was, the sole "relay to legitimation" in what Lauren Berlant calls "an erotics of political fellowship" ("National Brands/National Body," 113). Ambling forth from the Revolutionary War's self-conferring "trial by fire," the citizen-soldier – voluntarist, self-mastering, at-the-ready to defend the common good – was the only subject entrusted to represent that political compact.

As a symbol of national belonging, the citizen-soldier authenticated singularly masculine domains of partisan risk – the marketplace, the debate chamber, but especially the battlefield – as the exclusive provinces of political meaning.[7] Endemic to the very character structure of civic inclusion, then, is what Wendy Brown calls an asymmetrical division of sexual labor hinged to men's monopolization of "prerogative power," of the state's police (internal) and military (external) functions. Freshly replicating "sons of liberty" across the generations, "republican mothers" would busy themselves with reproduction in the private sphere while men would be free to pursue self-interest in the more creative, productive arenas of public life.[8] This arrangement was sustained by the relative estrangement of military episodes throughout the early nineteenth century to precincts nominally apart from domestic affairs – engagements on the frontier, between ships on the Atlantic, or on the Mexican border. Male authors, consequently, penned the majority of war fiction during this period, generally romantic tales of cavalier gallantry in the chivalric tradition popularized by Sir Walter Scott: James Fenimore's Cooper's *The Spy* (1821) or Robert Montgomery Bird's viciously racist "Injun" killer, *Nick of the Woods* (1837).

Inclusions: subjects of sacrifice and the struggle of/for representation

As the first modern "total" war, the Civil War collapsed the ideological sectioning of public and private spheres, drawing upon every sector of society for its prosecution. Fought exclusively "on United States territory," Elizabeth Young attests, it "definitively eroded the boundary between male 'battlefront' and female 'homefront'" (*Disarming the Nation*, 2).[9] Given early narrative form largely by women writers, literary expressions of the tumultuous national feud proliferated in magazine serials, omnibus volumes, published journals and memoirs, and a flourishing of war novels. In mostly sentimental and melodramatic modes, domestic fictions presented vehicles through which to comprehend the conflict's cataclysmic devastation and emotional challenges (Augusta Jane Evans's *Macaria; or, The Altars of Sacrifice* [1864]); occasions for reflection on the slavery question (Harriet Beecher Stowe's *Uncle Tom's Cabin* [1852] and Harriet Jacobs's *Incidents in the Life of a Slave Girl* [1861]); and forums to imagine a convalescent, recombinant future (Elizabeth Stuart Phelps's *The Gates Ajar, or Our Loved Ones in Heaven* [1868] and E. D. E. N. Southworth's *How He Won Her: A Sequel to Fair Play* [1869]). While women represented the largest portion of their audience, the vast swaths of leisure time afforded by distended periods of static encampment furnished soldiers with ample opportunity to consume these fictions as well.

Yet shortly after the war, a cultural remasculinization of Civil War memory overwhelmed the female market for war writing, rescuing the mythic contours of the "American *Iliad*," as one critic described it, from "the crude and mawkish pathos" of its female expositors.[10] As early as *Miss Ravenel's Conversion from Secession to Loyalty* (1867) – John William DeForest's proto-realist doxology to manly leadership, professional discipline, and the "mortal earnest" of the battlefield – a changed template for American war recollection emerged (319). This recollection elided those castrating phallic pens wielded, William Dean Howells complained, by "the young-lady writers in the magazines . . . everywhere fighting the campaigns over again."[11] Civil War narratives increasingly tapered and streamlined their scale, rendering mostly battlefield sketches, tales of "great men" in the major campaigns, and fratricidal narratives of fractured but mending (and now stronger for it) Blue and Gray brotherhood. By the late 1890s, a time of bracing imperial adventurism and frenetic capitalist expansion, Civil War stories sloughed even the formal confines of the battle romance, accumulating appeals to "adventure," as Kathleen Diffley notes, that "traded old homesteads for wider spaces and delayed romance in favor of the open road" (*Where My Heart is Turning Ever*, 125).[12]

Consequently, critical projects in recent decades have striven to recover the larger picture of the war, retrieving accounts of "women's contributions" or simply restoring, as Alice Fahs contends, female "voices that have been submerged or masked" ("The Feminized Civil War," 1462, 1494). A familiar example is Confederate Mary Chesnut's refurbished wartime diary, edited and published by C. Vann Woodward as the Pulitzer Prize-winning *Mary Chesnut's Civil War* (1981).[13] Furthermore, recent "reunion" studies show how a culture of reconciliation went to work in the confusing decades that immediately followed, suturing wounds left agape in the severed national body. Lisa Long considers the popularity of consolation literature like Phelps's *The Gates Ajar* (1868) as a kind of compensatory ontological prosthesis, rehabilitating the psychic and bodily traumas riven by the war.[14] Prominent also were serialized "romances of reunion" mushrooming up in *Atlantic Monthly*, *Harper's Monthly*, and *Lippincott's Magazine* throughout the 1860s, '70s, and '80s which, as Nina Silber, Alice Fahs, and Kathleen Diffley demonstrate, often dramatized cross-sectional marriages between Union soldiers and once-prodigal-but-now-tamed Confederate belles as restorative portraits of a healed national family.[15] As the "domestic" quarrel wreaked havoc in the "house divided," so the romance plot mended the "bonds of affection" that bitter divorce unraveled. While reunion stories typically encouraged women's sacrificial patriotism and subordination to masculine leadership, as Fahs contends, they nonetheless "focused on women's feelings and emotional struggles as a valid, indeed central, story of the war" ("Feminized," 1471).[16]

Notably dissenting exceptions to this more reparative project exist in literatures that adapted the occasion of "civil war" to intervene more dialectically in the prevailing structure of civil society and the gender ideologies buttressing it. One mostly forgotten example is Jane Goodwin Austin's *Dora Darling; or, The Daughter of the Regiment* (1865), which presents a young girl's flight from the domestic confines of an unhappy Confederate foster home to seek refuge in a Union army encampment. Accepted by the soldiers, she accompanies them on their battles and excursions as a provisioner, learning alternate models of "family" life and eventually leaving to seek an education. Another is Southworth's *How He Won Her*, which follows the disguised exploits of "man-hater" Britomarte Conyers serving as a daring and courageous soldier in a Union regiment. Reconciliation narrative that it is, Southworth's text frequently employs the trope of "civil war" to enlarge upon the antiquated nature of nineteenth-century marriage laws and to barter for a more robust conception of "woman's rights."

Recent literary critics elaborate on that contentious politics of resistance to nineteenth-century standards of feminine decorum, exhuming women's Civil War stories to explore how they challenge the regnant paradigm of public and private spheres and the legal non-personhood of the *feme covert*. Drew Gilpin Faust, for instance, considers wartime bestsellers like Evans's *Macaria* as a "paean to self-sacrifice," but one also modeling "rights of self-ownership and self-determination" for Confederate women ("Altars of Sacrifice," 1220). In a detailed analysis of women's writing by white and black authors, Elizabeth Young surveys works that seize upon the war story to reconfigure "the hierarchy that privileged white male citizenship over female civility," retaining "the more disruptive legacies of the war to foster their own ongoing incivilities." Returning "issues of gender and sexuality" to the center of national symbolization are, among others, Louisa May Alcott's *Hospital Sketches* (1863), Elizabeth Keckley's *Behind the Scenes* (1868), and Frances Harper's *Iola Leroy, or, Shadow's Uplifted* (1892), which "employ the idea of 'civil war' as a metaphor for conflicts of gender, sexuality, and race" (Young, *Disarming the Nation*, 17–18).[17]

One politically complicated, long-neglected text to confront the nation's racial symbolic is *What Answer?* (1868), a novel by abolitionist and suffrage activist, Anna Dickinson. Depicting the injustices attending the "amalgamated" marriage of Willie Surrey, a wealthy white man, and Francesca Ercildoune, a passing "quadroon," Dickinson uses the Civil War novel to attack the biological fiction of "one drop" blood logics and the persistence of racist biases held despite the many juxtaposed examples of black largesse and white ignobility her novel marshals before its audience. When the war arrives, Willie enlists, linking the fate of their relationship to the larger "cause" of the democratic struggle toward which he embarks. Counterpoint to Willie's enlistment and eventual wounding at Chancellorsville is the war service of Robert Ercildoune, Francesca's brother, who joins the famous 54th Massachusetts, procuring many injuries and losing an arm in the charge on Fort Wagner. Although Robert climbs "the mount of sacrifice," the union for which he tenders his loyalty remains principally unchanged, prohibiting him from voting upon his return (*What Answer?*, 253). Dickinson's extended portrayal of the racial subtext of the New York Draft Riots of 1863 only adds to the charge, one leveled at the north as much as the south. The ghostly conclusion, a cooptation and misprision of Lincoln's more conservative dictum of "consecrated" ground at Gettysburg, presents an announcement of unfinished war that, like the novel's inquiring title, reaches virally out into the culture. "Finish the work that has fallen from our nerveless hands," the voices of war dead speak from the ground. "Let no weight of tyranny, nor taint of oppression, nor stain of wrong, cumber the soil nor darken the land we died to save" (312).

Dickinson's novel, however, regards the war through that double-jointed lens that impugns the nation's racial betrayals while subsuming the story of black sacrifice beneath an overarching metaphysic of national coalition. Indeed, her appeals for a more expansive citizenry are coextensive with her nativist longings for a culture of obedience and loyalty, imploring the nation to constellate its unruly public. *What Answer?*, for instance, evinces little love for dissociated immigrant enclaves: the "scum of the city," "that most ignorant portion of the community" threatening the "defense of the nation's life" (260–1). Visible in the "vast moving multitudes" of the draft riot's "Reign of Terror" are a farrago of "drunken Irish tongues" and visages of the "most degraded of the German population" (268, 262, 272). Repulsed, Dickinson invites readers to "scrutinize the faces" of the "multitudes" – "deformed, idiotic, drunken, imbecile, poverty-stricken; seamed with every line which wretchedness could draw or vicious habits and associations delve" (273). Most shameful are the "ragged, frowzy, drunken women," presumably prostitutes, assembled outside the Orphan Asylum (266). "Let it, however, be written plainly and graven deeply," she writes, "that the tribes of savages – the hordes of ruffians – found ready to do their loathsome bidding, were not of native growth, nor American born" (272). Thus does her call for wider democratic recognition also resound with the exclusionary overtones of her moralistic patriotism.

As a protest venue, the war novel's interior/exterior stakes often exhibit this dichotomous exchange. While opening avenues to address the country's democratic failures, war's correlative urgency toward unanimity and collectivity often nurtures more disciplinary attitudes toward social regulation. Precisely as states of emergency like war mobilization fog the binaries of public/private, inclusion/exclusion, front/rear, they furnish occasions for political redress, to be sure, but also opportunities to corral that more "representative" social body into the common life of the state. Modeling a kind of affective transfer, to put it another way, the war novel increasingly makes "visible" a more ecumenical portrait of the nation's many interest groups, recalling democratic war aims and urging the country to make good on its most cherished egalitarian ideals. But the expansion of that more inclusive regime often incorporates countercurrents of dissent within the organizational ethos of a national security paradigm, establishing an overarching state sovereignty as the sole guarantor of that more tolerant order. While racist motives recalcitrant to Lincoln's "nigger war" certainly motivated the New York riots, for instance, the draft represented a unique intrusion of state power into the citizen's private motives and desires, impressing nationals beyond their will into duties and obligations that – like the president's suspension of habeas corpus and seizure of the railroads – violated core premises of the social contract and the presumably self-elective nature of citizen consent.[18]

By the turn of the century, surely attuned to the argument for "legitimacy" that war's collective sacrifice maintained, some women war writers participated in the increasing militarization of national ideologies, promoting the Progressive Era's "preparedness" campaign to acculturate stronger national bonds. If remanning the Civil War constituted one tributary of that ideological project, few novelists exerted more brawn than reconstructed Virginians Ellen Glasgow and Mary Johnston. As if in answer to a young Willa Cather's challenge to women writers, Glasgow channeled the war theme in *The Battle-Ground* (1902), her first bestseller, to confront "Reality with a capital R" (xvi). "I have no faith in women in fiction," a young Cather had decreed in 1895. "When a woman writes a story of adventure, a stout sea tale, a manly battle yarn, then I will hope for something great from them, not before."[19] Distinguishing the novel from the maudlin romances of male writers like Thomas Nelson Page's *Two Little Confederates* (1888) and John Esten Cooke's *Wearing of the Gray* (1867), reviewers praised *The Battle-Ground* for its "historical accuracy," cautioning readers that its "minutely realistic account of the war" might make it "too much for their nerves." Glasgow gleefully reveled in such reviews and often "bragged that military officers in Great Britain studied its descriptions of battle."[20]

Glasgow only tentatively embraced the Women's Suffrage Movement, but for Johnston, a prominent organizer in the Equal Suffrage League of Virginia, the links between war and the franchise were more obvious.[21] Although she self-identified as a socialist and stood with pacifists during World War I, her bewitchment with war and its generation of collective subjectivity were crucial aspects of her writing. In years immediately prior to the Great War, Johnston published a hulking Civil War epic spread across two highly influential volumes – *The Long Roll* (1911) and *Cease Firing* (1912). As a history of Thomas "Stonewall" Jackson's campaign and the culture of loyalty it exacted, *The Long Roll* portrays "a side of war which Walter Scott had never painted" (158). Promoting a national education in military efficiency and identity-of-interest, it focuses extensively on tactical coordination and battlefield maneuver as thrilling images of self-subordination to group loyalty.[22] Thirty years later, in the midst of operations in World War II, General Dwight Eisenhower remarked that, "If I want to read military tactics for pleasure, I choose to read Mary Johnston."[23] But Johnston's stance lent her text the very quality of historical "truth" favored by the militarist luminaries of her time, men like Herbert Croly, Theodore Roosevelt, and Leonard Wood, who offered images of the war-united nation's "strenuous life" as a blueprint for the good society and palliative to factional discord.

Mobilization for the Great War brought the dialectic of sacrifice and inclusion to the fore in unprecedented ways, enfolding women's political desire within a complex nexus of competing allegiances – between the *realpolitik* advantages of military consent and the idealism of pacifist principles, between longings for increased public agency and the compulsory loyalty to the state that self-expansion mandated. As ambulance corps drivers, Red Cross nurses, and wireless operators abroad, for instance, women fashioned a world of comparative freedom from the constrictive domestic roles of an earlier age, validating the rightfulness of such public access and discovering prospects for group solidarity. At home, women's voluntary associations aligned with the war effort in a mixture of earnest and coerced enthusiasm, uniting the huge home front "knitting army" for uniform and bandage production, channeling capital through war bond promotion, and overseeing food production and rationing. Laying claim to the civic voluntarism of the citizen-soldier tradition, they submitted an incontestable case for civic inclusion that capsized arguments denying women citizenship, arguments grounded on the fact that they "could not represent their country on the field of battle and thus make the ultimate sacrifice" (Smith, *The Second Battlefield*, 7). To do so, however, meant auguring that example of democratic participation to the socializing initiatives of an expanding governmental program. While many women remained firmly antagonistic to militarism and imperialism, advocating against intervention in anti-imperialism leagues, others became vitriolic orators in deeply repressive anti-sedition syndicates, venomously persecuting the caviling "woman slacker" most visible in the figure of antimilitarists like Alice Paul. Like Carrie Chapman Catt, however, most saw compliance with war aims ambivalently but pragmatically as a lifeline to the vote and economic equality. Correctly calibrating that rubric of sacrifice and inclusion, women won the ballot in 1920 in large part since they had "proved their trustworthiness" in war, often – reaffirming the ideological primacy of domesticity – as givers of husbands and sons (Smith, *The Second Battlefield*, 103).[24]

Women's writing reveals all the churning and shape-shifting occurring within the war's political crucible. With the advent of intervention, numerous patriotic potboilers came forth from writers like Mary Raymond Shipman Andrews and Temple Bailey, hailing a metaphysics of sacrifice and love for the flag as conduits to spiritual enrichment. Less winsomely, Frances Wilson Huard's *My Home in the Field of Honor* (1916) describes her political transition from liberal idealist to Hobbesian realist when her war work as nurse, cook, and armed sentry leads her to exalt the "wonderful national resolution to do one's duty, and to make the least possible fuss about it" (12). Living on a hillside above the Marne at the outbreak of the war, journalist Mildred Aldrich – good friend of ambulance drivers Gertrude Stein and Alice B. Toklas – published letters to American friends in volumes like *A Hilltop on the Marne* (1915) and *On the Edge of the War Zone* (1917), books the French government believed finally inspired the US intervention and for which she was awarded the Legion of Honor. Edith Wharton and Willa Cather contributed their own encomiums to the theologized nation in Wharton's *The Marne* (1919) and *A Son at the Front* (1923) and Cather's *One of Ours* (1922), winner of the Pulitzer Prize. Cather, for instance, lauds the "Olympian" nature of those men who die "for the purity of an abstract idea" (*One of Ours*, 142, 331), while Wharton trumpets a rising culture of loyalty and self-sacrifice in the militarist culture of the preparedness movement. Praising duty-bound men and women "shaken into their proper places," Wharton proclaims the providential "design" of an American empire "slowly curving a new firmament over the earth" (*A Son at the Front*, 166, 213). As Kimberly Jensen ascertains, some women's identification with the war – many of them "institutional feminists" of the New Woman movement, advocates of progressive reform, or New Women of Color like Addie

Hunton – testifies more to their affirmation of nationalist "virtues" and "loyalty" than to a contrarian troubling of the status quo. Deeply compliant with war aims, she argues, they sought mostly "access" or "recognition" rather than "to transform the paradigm of citizenship that equated full civic status with military service" ("Women, Citizenship and Civic Sacrifice," 142). As "more powerful citizens," so their argument ran, "they could offer a more powerful loyalty and patriotism to their nation" (158).

Two politically ambiguous novels to emerge from the upheaval were Gertrude Atherton's *The White Morning* (1918) and Jessie Redmon Fauset's *There is Confusion* (1924), especially given that modernism, as Janet Lyon notes, "adapted as a central tenet the disavowal of femininity, with femininity standing in for a whole host of artistic disorders including sentimentality, mystification, dissolution, optimism, and naturalized passivity" ("Gender and Sexuality," 230). Atherton's novel dramatizes the story of German women initially "flamed with patriotism" for their "great Teutonic Empire" only to arrive at a grimmer knowledge of the German military's calumny and sadism. Fortified by unpropagandized American reports, Atherton's German women are inducted into the "ghastly story" of their country's betrayals – its militarist terrorizing of the population, its oppressive patriarchy, its "lying, treachery, cruelty, brutality, [and] degeneracy" (*The White Morning*, 49, 56, 79). Since men are "hopeless as revolutionary material," Gisela Döring (once an American nanny) leads a women's uprising, violently overthrowing the Kaiser's masculinist order and establishing a "Woman's Republic," one opposed to essentialist ideologies of women's "passionate longing for completion in man, oneness . . . [in] the 'organic unit'" (133). Antithetical to a culture of militarism, *The White Morning* advocates healthier social alternatives not only to Germany's massive militarist establishment but indirectly, published during mobilization as it was, to an analogous culture of militarization fomenting in the USA. Its model of collective proto-feminist power, ascribed to German women but certainly resonating more locally for its US readership, constructed templates for political coalition and collective consciousness essential to channeling women's dissent against the state. Conversely, however, its many indictments of German villainy obliquely corroborated ideologies of US war propaganda – an unwelcome validation in a year that witnessed the massive expansion of a repressive state apparatus and passage of the Sedition Act of 1918. The women's alliance at one point, in fact, stridently devotes itself to President Wilson's "promises of deliverance" and the "irresistible almighty power" of the United States (92, 99, 110, 118). Published in 1918, furthermore, the novel both appropriates the revolutionary imaginary of the Russian Revolution for women, while deflecting that energy into celebratory expatiations on the "German race" as a more culturally deserving community for such political paroxysms, a vexing veneration from the vantage point of 1933 (192).

Much like Dickinson's *What Answer?*, Fauset's homefront-centered *There is Confusion* invokes the trope of "double battle" – against enemies abroad and racism at home – that will eventually frame the call for "Double V" advanced during World War II by the *Pittsburgh Courier* (269). Literary editor of *The Crisis*, the organ where W. E. B. Du Bois famously called for African Americans to "close ranks" with the war effort, Fauset used the occasion of black sacrifice to challenge US apartheid and the glacial pace of racial change. While black men sacrifice their lives for democracy abroad, her protagonist, Joanna Marshall, becomes a "battle-scarred veteran" in the cultural war at home. Casting her as a dancer in a wartime tribute to the democracies, Fauset controversially invokes the conceit of the black female body "standing in" for America – or passing – by having a masked Joanna metonymically portray the role of the USA in an international pageant on a New York stage. Defiantly subtracting her disguise for an astonished Greenwich Village crowd, Joanna proclaims, "I hardly need to tell you that there is no one in the audience more American than I am. My great-grandfather fought in the Revolution, my uncle fought in the Civil War and my brother is 'over there' now" (*There is Confusion*, 232). Fauset's fantasy of democratic inclusion symbolically challenges the contradictions of a white supremacist political community fighting for democracy overseas. But her idealization of domestic assimilation also employs a metaphor of "harmonious chords," a pluralism that legitimates the US nation-state as the overarching category of Joanna's political allegiance. In so doing, Fauset sublimates her call for women's visibility within a correlatively stratifying and self-regulating structure of national consent. Thus is Joanna's dissent enfolded in that "metonymic nationalism" Barbara Foley describes as intended "to combat disenfranchisement and bigotry" but which ultimately conjoins "with the nationalism of 100 percent Americanism" (*Spectres of 1919*, ix). If, as Sandra Gilbert maintains, technological modern war remade the male citizen into a "faceless being," a "symbol for the state, whose nihilistic machinery he was powerless to control or protest," the entrance of women into that same dissembling, hegemonic order seems less and less like progressive victory and more like institutional absorption ("Soldier's Heart," 198).

Renunciations: modern war and women's changing politics of resistance

World War I, however, also provided the occasion for caustic remonstrations against war's violent inhumanity and the increasingly bellicosity of US foreign policy. Galvanizing a politics of protest were advocates who argued vitally for women's right to the public commons while simultaneously defying the program of the expanding US state and its systemization of permanent war. It was an especially difficult task considering the proximity of that dissent to disabling confirmations of women's "natural" pacifism. So stunning was the travesty and waste depicted by Ellen La Motte in *The Backwash of War* (1916), her memoir of service in a French field hospital, that it was officially banned in the United States. Postmaster General Albert Burleson even prohibited copies of *The Liberator* advertising it from the US mail. Cataloging the gory and loveless scenes of "human wreckage" at her hospital, La Motte's collection of thirteen sketches also indicts the adventurism of US ambulance literati, the aesthetics of self-sacrifice, and the rabid nationalism that the war unleashed. Another long overlooked work in US literary history is Mary Lee's satirically titled *It's a Great War!* (1929). Originally named "The Farce," Lee changed the title to enter it in a contest for the best war novel publicized by the American Legion and Houghton, Mifflin, and Company. Because the Legion was reluctant to award the prize to a woman author (even though Lee was herself a member), Lee split the $25,000 award with William Scanlon, author of *God Have Mercy on Us* (1929), a pugnacious textbook on the necessity of taking of human life and the need for efficient military discipline.

Chief among Lee's themes is US war propaganda's deception of the American public, and she received hundreds of letters from veterans thanking her for at last telling "the truth" about the war. In addition to her unenviable portraits of hospital life, her account – told in elliptical, stream-of-consciousness prose patches – reveals wards of American doughboys convulsed with venereal disease, US soldiers as invading rapists, and white MPs murdering black soldiers for sport. Inverting many male writers' masculinist equations of war participation with naturalist validations of a primitivist "reality" – a trope ubiquitous in war narratives by Leonard Nason, Hervey Allen, Theodore Fredenburgh, and Theodore Roosevelt, Jr. – Lee declared that women alone could tell a true war story since men's versions were too stained with sentimentality. "Emotion blurs the picture" for them, Lee avers, but women possess the "intellectual clarity" to see through seductive images of war as a "beautiful adventure" (*It's a Great War*, vi). Lee's novel was debated for the Pulitzer Prize, and though she did not win, rumors circulated that the announcement was delayed that year – a year incidentally that saw the publication of Ernest Hemingway's *A Farewell to Arms* (1929) – due to disputes over her work.

The politics of World War II representation were understandably fraught. Unlike World War I, antifascist intervention was initially promulgated by an international Left. Beginning with the US volunteer forces that – in defiance of isolationist US policy – opposed Generalissimo Franco's fascist coup in Spain in 1936, American activists helped compose the diverse "historical bloc" of the Popular Front, a makeshift hodgepodge of Communists, Socialists, Trotskyites, Social Democrats, anarchists, and progressive liberals.[25] Militarily, the Popular Front took shape as the International Brigades, described by Lois Orr in her recently published *Letters from Barcelona* (2009), as a progressive counterpoint to the conservative politics of some women's war writing in the USA during the period. Although they denounced slavery as an outmoded feudalism, for instance, the agrarian nostalgia of Margaret Mitchell's *Gone with the Wind* (1936) and Caroline Gordon's equally backward-looking *None Shall Look Back* (1937) nonetheless plied Depression-era readers with sustentative images of an "American way of life" in the opulent bounty of a plantation past.

Once World War II was underway, the conservative position was perhaps most clearly assumed by Gertrude Stein, who bafflingly recommended Hitler for the Nobel Peace Prize in 1938 and collaborated with the Vichy regime in her occupied France. Her more enthusiastic critics understandably dismiss her war autobiographies, but recent commentators find them worthy of reconsideration. For Zofia Lesinska, they are "historically and artistically compelling" for their "centrifugal" energies, for their depiction of the "estrangement of female subjectivity" and their wavering of the "ideological certitudes" subtending "Good War" memory (*Perspectives*, 15, 21, 32). Similarly, Madelyn Detloff considers Stein's emphasis on the quotidian and "non-momentous" aspects of everyday life as "a sign of resilience and resistance to the dehumanizing purpose of war, an insistence that daily life is worth living and preserving" (*The Persistence of Modernism*, 78).

On the homefront after 1941, political authority gathered ever more trenchantly around a massive national security enterprise, a complex synergy of public and private energies bolstered by a more representative rhetoric of liberal pluralism, while justifying a strident geopolitical realism in foreign policy to defend that haven of democracy. Manifestos like Margaret Mead's *And Keep Your Powder Dry* (1942) urged the nation to embrace a more visceral "social engineering" as part of its "tremendous effort to translate permanent danger and unprecedented plenty into a newly ordered world" (xiii, 76). Her sentiment was shared by writers like Margaret Banning who urged women to link their struggle for equal rights with the "rights and privileges of democracy" defended by the US war machine (*Women for Defense*, 13). In *Women for Defense* (1942), she expounds upon the need for less sentimentally aloof, "realistic" women, urging them to discover the antidote to Nazi misogyny in sacrificial love for the "independence" of "patria." "Defense," she counsels, "must go beyond the meeting, into the home, into the job, into the mind" (13). Living in Austria from 1933 to 1936, expatriate American writer Kay Boyle was a close witness to fascism's ascent. Her novels vituperatively indict Nazi monstrosity, while simultaneously corroborating the Manichean worldview that would define Cold War liberalism's *Pax Americana* – the politically diminishing romance with the domestic idealism of the nuclear family and the consensus society of cul-de-sac USA. Bestselling novels like *Avalanche* (1946) celebrate the open society against a culture of totalitarian fear, but couch that theme in the moral certitudes of Christian allegory and, at times, a fawning adulation of masculine virility. Boyle, in fact, used her books as platforms on which to market war bonds, advertising them on the covers of works like *A Frenchman Must Die* (1939) and *Primer for Combat* (1942).[26]

One complex figure is Martha Gellhorn, a left progressive who reported from Spain for an American audience, following the struggle against fascism all the way to the liberation of Dachau. Most significantly, her *Point of No Return* (originally published as *The Wine of Astonishment* in 1948) broke a literary silence, unveiling the brutality and abomination of the concentration camps (as did Irwin Shaw's *The Young Lions* that same year). Furthermore, her figuration of Dorothy Brock as an independent personality recalcitrant to the restrictive rigidity of traditional gender roles represents a forceful interruption into the conservative ideologies galvanizing the post-war flight to the suburbs. An important forgotten work, Gellhorn's retributive, often stirring, novel is a powerful reminder of what catastrophes men – and for her it is unequivocally gendered – are capable of manufacturing "when sanctioned by the State" (*Point of No Return*, 316, 331). But its realist prescriptions were also consonant with an evolving Cold War metaphysic: that erect, hallucinatory optic surveying the planet with a stern, preemptive gaze. Wondering how to cope with a "world which had grown ugly and strange," Gellhorn surmises a universe everywhere "dangerous with a danger you did not see . . . poisoned, spreading" (323). Like her protagonist Jacob Levy, who was "blasted into a knowledge of evil that he had not known existed in the human species," Dachau's "point of no return," she acknowledges, fundamentally changed "how I looked at the human condition" (330). "I remember what I felt," she writes, "frantic, insane fear" (330). "What happened once could happen again" (323).

She was right, of course, and the memory of the Final Solution continues hauntingly to remind the world of the human capacity for orgiastic terror. But considered from a different vantage point, her narrative jibes with moods of resignation deteriorating into the post-war malaise, the "turning inward" of political life that abandoned progressive drives for social justice and institutional change for the milder consolations of the basement rec room and the backyard barbeque.[27] What else had the technocratic hubris of the bomb and the revelations of the camps shown if not that the millennial hope of history was an unwieldy utopian dreamworld unadapted to a changed and sinister universe? With economic affluence on the rise and the horizons of political life stretched to global dimensions in the global standoff with Communism, political retraction came naturally. It was a time for citizens to tend to their gardens, take stock of their own affairs, and trust the business of democracy to the experts.

As "containment" initiatives reshaped foreign policy, the "arsenal of democracy" they ostensibly insulated increasingly confirmed Americans as moral champions of an unrivaled and universally desired "way of life," guardians of simple, tried-and-tested values sustaining a basically wholesome existence in the face of global upheaval. Chief among them was the nuclear family, an institution – as the Office of War Information never tired of guaranteeing – for which the war was fought. Eager to rehabilitate and reharmonize a disrupted sexual economy, one "restructured" by nearly two decades of depression and war, national security organs hounded the country's disorganized gender relations, imploring the nation to "get itself together" and restore the "traditional gender roles" that were the building blocks of national security (May, *Homeward Bound*, 90–1). Chief among their worries was finding employment and housing for the legions of broken and maladjusted veterans returning from Europe and the Pacific, men no longer resourceful enough to persevere in a world without military routine and chain of command. Adding to their dismay were the "domineering," "independent," and, worse, "promiscuous" women who, having fled from the claustrophobic private sphere during mobilization, refused to return to the old order's domestic economy.

Because the rhetoric of mobilization appealed not to aggrandized national sentiment but to local, privatized structures of meaning, the family emerged as one of the most contested sites of post-war life. As John Limon claims, war novels increasingly worried whether or not the family was "strong enough to absorb the brunt of war without being a casualty of the war" (*Writing after War*, 210). Gordon Hutner, furthermore, shows how numerous "readjustment" novels worked to "tranquilize for the middle class the trauma from which so many returning soldiers suffered" and to urge restored belief "in a coherent comprehensible society" (*What America Read*, 243). Anticipating the psychological hardships and challenges of the healing process were "representations of adjustment" like Zelda Popkin's *The Journey Home* (1945), Gertrude Mallette's *Once is Forever* (1946), Alice Parson's *I Know What I'd Do* (1946), Betsey Barton's *The Long Walk* (1948), and Elizabeth Janeway's *The Question of Gregory* (1949).[28] But others like Marita Wolff's *About Lyddy Thomas* (1947) castigated the "domestic containment" Elaine Tyler May describes as thriving in the post-war years, indicting its constrictive zone of possibility as well as the alleged moral altruism of its returning male guardians. Erasing the divide between the war-making of the "domestic" homefront and the damage the war wreaked in the everyday lives of the "domestic" household, Wolff brings the war home in the most dramatic of ways.

Redirecting "entrapment" themes resonating through war fiction by male authors – James Gould Cozzens's *Guard of Honor* (1948), James Jones's *From Here to Eternity* (1951), Joseph Heller's *Catch-22* (1961) – *About Lyddy Thomas* relates the story of one woman's harrowing flight from her murderous, alcoholic husband, an abusive returned veteran whose "psychoneurotic" homecoming seeks to restore the prewar arrangement (131). But Lyddy's years of independence – especially the satisfaction she experienced as a riveter in an aircraft plant and in a brief affair with an affectionate, respectful admirer – leave her with a sense of "a whole world of things going on" beyond the "bottled up" compound of her home, "the kitchen sink" world Ben, her husband, expects her to resume (75, 198, 331, 387). She longs to travel, to listen to jazz, to eat in restaurants, to drink beer with friends. "I'm not even the same person that you kissed good-bye and thought about all that time over there," she tells him, "I'm so different" (76). Wolff depicts Ben's surging aptitude for brute force as a propensity quickened by the war and fostered by American military training. When Lyddy finally informs Ben that she wants a divorce, he forcefully repairs his dominion through a sequence of savage physical assaults, a vicious rape, and finally aspirations to murder her.

The bulk of the novel figures Lyddy's flight from Ben's would-be imprisonment in the same symbolic registers as the slave narrative. She is hunted by Ben as his rightful property, a claim with which the community and the legal structure seem reluctant to interfere. Assisted by a friend's money, she is secreted through a network of YWCA dormitories in a clandestine passage from city after city, a trek that finally returns her to a hidden location in her hometown. *About Lyddy Thomas* thus reveals the placidly normative order of the homefront's insulated "rear" for the crisis zone of a war front that it actually is. "The god-damned war," one character utters in the final scene, "What'd they mean, it's over? So another hunk of it ends here in an alley back of nowhere" (447). Assailing "warm hearth" ideologies of the post-war domestic revival, tropes that honored the family domicile as a "secure private nest," Wolff's acerbic proto-feminist novel anticipated critiques of suburban domesticity that would swell at least one current of the Second Wave (May, *Homeward Bound*, 3). Exploring the enlarged range of desire that war emergency presented women, it also thwarts the post-war amnesia that pulpits, marketing agencies, television, and other media outlets encouraged in their daily tributes to domestic bliss.

Bringing the war home structures the thematic resistance of much women's war writing since World War II, a domestic focus that reduces the international scale and global *ecumene* of US proxy wars to examine their more quotidian effects in the American family. "Why now?" asks Maureen Ryan, referring to the spate of Vietnam War writing by women during the 1980s: Joan Didion's *Democracy* (1984), Jayne Anne Phillips's *Machine Dreams* (1984), Sandra Crockett Moore's *Private Woods* (1988), Mary Morris's *The Waiting Room* (1989), Susan Fromberg Schaeffer's *Buffalo Afternoon* (1989), Elizabeth Ann Scarborough's *The Healer's War* (1989). "Because for the women who wait," she replies, "the war begins when the husbands, sons, lovers, and brothers return – or with the grudging recognition that their men will never come home." These are certainly the thematic topoi of Bobbie Ann Mason's *In Country* (1985), a study in Samantha "Sam" Hughes's inquest into the psychological injury the war exacted on her Uncle Emmett and quest to assume the place of her dead father, a casualty of Vietnam. Mason's work figures the damage that war enacts on participant families – the traumatizing absence and lack it effects on women's subjectivities but also the ravaged psyches of men who return, men who often enlisted under duplicitous governmental auspices to protect the family.

Accounts like Mason's enacted a particularly contrarian interruption into the hawkish ethos of her time, a moment when President Reagan and his neoconservative ideologues were pathologizing reluctance toward international adventurism as a kind of enervated cultural "impotence," the symptom of a lingering "Vietnam syndrome." But works that reinforce a narrative of women as paralyzed "outsiders" to an essentially masculine war domain, texts that reinforce their second-order role as mother, wife, sister, in relation to "their men," fail to comprehend the dynamic world of women at war taking shape in recent decades. How to address the changing politics of representation now that women are directly complicit with military power? How should we read what Zillah Eisenstein and the editors of *Feminism and War* describe as the "visibility/invisibility/hyper-visibility" problem of women in the military as inclusion becomes tangled in an oscillating and disorienting politics of democratic progress and deference (Riley, Mohanty, and Pratt, *Feminism and War*, 7)? On the one hand, the struggle for parity continues as most women are officially banned from the clout-bestowing environments of combat duty (even as terrorism, technology, and media subsume the entire human environment within a topography of potential war crisis). Furthermore, established and resentful male interests often try to reestablish their exclusive dominion over a declining sovereignty forcefully, a fact most vividly exemplified in reports on the harassment and rape of women soldiers. On the other hand, women's more "representational" entrance into spheres of prerogative power, an admission celebrated by the liberal warfare state as triumphal evidence of its universality, erodes the more clearly antagonistic confrontation with military power advocated by earlier generations.[29] In apocalyptic fiction like the Christian evangelical *Left Behind* series, an eschatological allegory of American war-making in the Middle East, women soldiers are happily included as part of the paramilitary Tribulation Force: the camo-clad Chloe Steele as a divine assassin dispensing swift and deadly cosmic judgments. And however much she may deconstruct its dominant tropes, that the first best-director Oscar awarded to a woman went to Katheryn Bigelow for *The Hurt Locker* (2009), arguably one of the most "masculine" war films in American cinema history, should at least acknowledge the structural kinship between national inclusion and collective identification with the emissaries of its generative violence. Over 300 years later, the "publick view" proffered Mary Rowlandson as a dividend consequent on her risk and sacrifice for the mystical community comes forth again anew as a parable of more vital realities extrinsic to the everyday affairs of common life.[30]

While the memory of the "forgotten war" in Korea is only recently beginning to show its afterlife in novels like Susan Choi's *The Foreign Student* (1998), very little writing by women participating in Middle East conflicts has yet to appear. One recent volume, *Powder: Writing by Women in the Ranks, from Vietnam to Iraq* (2008), explains that often this dearth exists because of "repercussions, formal and informal, that the military imposes upon those who speak their minds while on active duty" (xiii). But as blogs begin to surface, as poems appear in magazines, streams of gendered affiliation are beginning to refract. Consequently, feminist criticism in the new millennia will have a new set of interpretive cruxes to negotiate, dilemmas most likely to fracture along the fault lines of liberal and left ideals. Strands of liberal feminism frequently justify the occupation of foreign territories, occupations in which women soldiers participate, as initiatives desirous of "women's liberation" from oppressive regimes and a bestowing of universal human rights. Paradoxically, however, this project often reasserts a narrative of "female vulnerability, inadequacy, and inferiority" and legitimates a masculinist mythology of Western posse-like "rescue missions," a sexist "cowboy" or "superman" fantasia sedulously documented in Susan Faludi's *The Terror Dream* (2–3). Conversely, anti-imperial feminism, which always risks being mistaken for a kind of essentialist maternalism, labors to disassemble the military-industrial complex, "the dismantling of the military machine," as Angela Davis summarizes, "even within a struggle for 'equality'" ("Resexing Militarism for the Globe," 4). But as that struggle resists also (and rightly) the "racist targeting of immigrants and people of color domestically, along with justifying the curtailment of civil liberties and the increased militarization of domestic law enforcement and the policing of US borders," it becomes less and less easy to identify what is particularly "feminist" about it. Standing watch at the crossroads of each of these comparably new encounters is the dialectic of sacrifice and inclusion: the contract of political recognition for national loyalty and the contentious negotiation of public and private meaning within the state's increasingly flexible structure of belonging.

Notes

1. See Elshtain, *Women and War*, 231–2.
2. See Lepore, *The Name of War*, 125–6, 149; Salisbury, "Introduction," 49.
3. See Lepore, *The Name of War*, 134; Salisbury, "Introduction," 48.
4. "She feels that she has seen through the veil that covers the face of God," claim Richard Slotkin and James K. Folsom, "and the vision has made her not insane, but possessed of a sanity that makes the real world hollow, empty of meaning, vain" (*So Dreadfull a Judgment*, 310).
5. See Holland, *The Body Politic*, xix–xxi; Brown, *States of Injury*, 166–96; Nelson, *National Manhood*, 1–60; Berlant, "National Brands / National Body," 112–13.
6. On the gendered "self-fathering" of the nation, see Young, *Disarming the Nation*, 5.
7. As Simone de Beauvoir once beheld, man-as-warrior is imbued with "sacred" qualities; in his proximity to danger as self-"inventor," as "project," he "spills over the present and opens up the future." "The warrior risks his own life to raise the prestige of the horde," and thus "throughout humanity, superiority has been granted not to the sex

that gives birth but to the sex that kills" (*The Second Sex*, 73–4). For Moira Gatens, sacrifice is a patrimony providing men in particular with a more "'total' enactment of subjectivity" – dating back perhaps even to "the original covenant between God and Abraham" – providing fuller "admission to the political body being that one could make the appropriate *forfeit* [sacrifice]" (*Imaginary Bodies*, 25).

8. See Kerber, *Women of the Republic*, esp. 11–12.

9. Even as it "displaced women of all races and classes," adds Shirley Samuels, "it provided a disquieting liberation from previously rigid roles" (*Facing America*, 82). For Lee Ann Whites, concomitantly, the war over slavery set loose a correlative "crisis in gender," revealing "manhood" and "independence" as, in actuality, "relational" dependencies, "social construction[s] built upon the foundation of women's service and love" ("The Civil War as a Crisis in Gender," 3, 16).

10. The phrase "American Iliad" is David Blight's, "A Quarrel," 121. The sexist critic is Gordon S. Haight. See his "Introduction" to John William De Forest's *Miss Ravenel's Conversion*, xiii.

11. Elizabeth Young gives a full recounting of this exchange, *Disarming the Nation*, 7. She also provides an excellent analysis of the phallic challenge that women's writing represented, 1–23.

12. See Fahs, "The Feminized Civil War," 1493; Fahs, *The Imagined Civil War*, 313. For an excellent discussion on the changing politics of war narrative, see Diffley, *Where My Heart is Turning Ever*, xi–xlvii, 1–53.

13. For an incisive recent analysis of Chesnut's work, see Stern, *Mary Chesnut's Civil War Epic*.

14. See Long, *Rehabilitating Bodies: Health, History, and the American Civil War*, 58–82.

15. See Silber, *The Romance of Reunion*; Diffley, *Where My Heart is Turning Ever*, 54–79; Fahs, "The Feminized Civil War."

16. On the gender aspects of reunion, see also Fahs, *The Imagined Civil War*; Gardner, *Blood and Irony*; Whites, *The Civil War as a Crisis in Gender* and *Gender Matters*; James, *A Freedom Bought with Blood*.

17. For an excellent discussion of Iola Leroy, see also James, *A Freedom Bought with Blood*, 63–83.

18. Harris, "The New York City Draft Riots of 1863."

19. See Cather, *Kingdom of Art*, 409.

20. See Goodman, "Introduction," xviii.

21. See Scura, *Ellen Glasgow: The Contemporary Reviews*, 355.

22. The inclusion of fold-out maps as appendices furthermore teaches readers to observe domestic territories as geographical indices of collectivity, places best remembered topographically as strategic points of interest under siege.

23. See www.brtraditions.com/story_vol11_no2_johnston.htm.

24. To convolute matters even more, Wilson, although he was initially resistant to suffrage, knew that accommodating women was crucial to national security and "vital to the winning of the war" (Kennedy, *Over Here*, 284). But when he intervened in Congressional debates over suffrage to lend his support, he based his claims on the rationale that women's essentially nurturing natures made them his "natural allies" in the quest for a nonpunitive peace. On the experience of World War I for women, see Jensen, *Mobilizing Minerva*; Capozzola, *Uncle Sam Wants You*.

25. The use of the Gramscian term "historical bloc" to describe the Popular Front comes from Michael Denning's *The Cultural Front*, 6.
26. Austenfeld, *American Women Writers and the Nazis*, 57–8.
27. As William Graebner shows, linking private consumption, family "togetherness," and national loyalty, the unflinchingly "Good War" waged against a hideous and sinister global nightmare paved the road for the "turning inward" of American life, the turning "away from the public realm of politics and economics and toward the neurotic, troubled, fragmented, and 'rootless' self" (*The Age of Doubt*, 102). Crucially, the "rarification" of reformist discourse affected a political shrinkage in which "ideas of self come full circle" since "the turn inward is virtually indistinguishable from the culture of the whole," a culture in which "the self becomes largely a repository of images and values that are useful in the larger project of human integration" (118).
28. See Hutner, *What America Read*, 238–43.
29. In the modern epoch's militarization of everyday life, total war, as Michael Hardt and Antonio Negri suggest, becomes *"properly ontological,"* categorically universal and androgynous, "absolute" to the point that perhaps war's "masculinity" serves as a ubiquitous standard for men and women alike (*Multitude*, 18–19).
30. On the disparity between women in the military as "frontline feminists" and "militarist collaborators," see also Dombrowski, *Women and War in the Twentieth Century*, 23–30.

Works cited

Atherton, Gertrude. *The White Morning: A Novel of the Power of the German Women in Wartime*. New York: Frederick A. Stokes Company, 1918.

Austenfeld, Thomas Carl. *American Women Writers and the Nazis: Ethics and Politics in Boyle, Porter, Stafford, and Hellman*. Charlottesville: University Press of Virginia, 2001.

Banning, Margaret. *Women for Defense*. New York: Duell, Sloan and Pearce, 1942.

Berlant, Lauren. "National Brands / National Body: *Imitation of Life*." In *Comparative American Identities: Race, Sex, and Nationality in the Modern Text*. Ed. Hortense J. Spillers. New York: Routledge, 1991.

Blight, David. "A Quarrel Forgotten or a Revolution Remembered? Reunion and Race in the Memory of the Civil War, 1875–1913." In *Beyond the Battlefield: Race, Memory, and the American Civil War*. Amherst: University of Massachusetts Press, 2002.

Bowden, Lisa and Shannon Cain, eds. *Powder: Writing by Women in the Ranks, from Vietnam to Iraq*. Tucson: Kore Press, 2008.

Brown, Wendy. *States of Injury: Power and Freedom in Late Modernity*. Princeton: Princeton University Press, 1995.

Capozzola, Christopher. *Uncle Sam Wants You: World War I and the Making of the Modern American Citizen*. New York: Oxford University Press, 2008.

Cather, Willa. *The Kingdom of Art: Willa Cather's First Principles and Critical Statements*. Ed. Bernice Slote. Lincoln, NB: University of Nebraska Press, 1966.

One of Ours. 1922. New York: Vintage, 1991.

Clinton, Catherine and Nina Silber, eds. *Divided Houses: Gender and the Civil War*. New York: Oxford University Press, 1992.

Davis, Angela Y. "Resexing Militarism for the Globe." In *Feminism and War: Confronting US Imperialism.* Ed. Robin L. Riley, Chandra Talpade Mohanty, and Minnie Bruce Pratt. New York: Zed Books, 2008.

De Beauvoir, Simone. *The Second Sex.* Trans. Constance Borde and Sheila Malovany-Chevallier. New York: Knopf, 2010.

DeForest, John William. *Miss Ravenel's Conversion from Secession to Loyalty.* 1867. Ed. Gordon S. Haight. San Francisco: Rinehart, 1955.

Denning, Michael. *The Cultural Front: The Laboring of American Culture in the Twentieth Century.* New York: Verso, 1997.

Detloff, Madelyn. *The Persistence of Modernism: Loss and Mourning in the Twentieth Century.* New York: Cambridge University Press, 2009.

Dickinson, Anna. *What Answer?* 1868. New York: Humanity Books, 2003.

Diffley, Kathleen. *Where My Heart is Turning Ever: Civil War Stories and Constitutional Reform, 1861–1876.* Athens, GA: University of Georgia Press, 1992.

Dombrowski, Nicole Ann, ed. *Women and War in the Twentieth Century: Enlisted with or without Consent.* New York: Garland Press, 1999.

Elshtain, Jean Bethke. *Women and War.* Chicago: University of Chicago Press, 1995.

Fahs, Alice. "The Feminized Civil War: Gender, Northern Popular Literature, and the Memory of the War." *Journal of American History* 85.4 (March 1999): 1461–94.

   The Imagined Civil War. Popular Literature of the North and South, 1861–1865. Chapel Hill: University of North Carolina Press, 2001.

Faludi, Susan. *The Terror Dream: Fear and Fantasy in Post-9/11 America.* New York: Metropolitan Books, 2007.

Fauset, Jessie Redmon. *There is Confusion.* 1924. Boston: Northeastern University Press, 1989.

Faust, Drew Gilpin. "Altars of Sacrifice: Confederate Women and the Narratives of War." *Journal of American History* 76.4 (March 1990): 1200–28.

Foley, Barbara. *Spectres of 1919: Class and Nation in the Making of the New Negro.* Urbana: University of Illinois Press, 2008.

Gardner, Sarah. *Blood and Irony: Southern White Women's Narratives of the Civil War, 1861–1937.* Chapel Hill: University of North Carolina Press, 2004.

Gatens, Moira. *Imaginary Bodies: Ethics, Power, and Corporeality.* London: Routledge, 1996.

Gellhorn, Martha. *Point of No Return [Wine of Astonishment].* 1948. Markum, Ontario: Plume/New American Library, 1989.

Gilbert, Sandra. "Soldier's Heart: Literary Men, Literary Women, and the Great War." In *Behind the Lines: Gender and the Two World Wars.* Ed. Margaret Randolph Higonnet, Jane Jenson, Sonya Michel, and Margaret Collins Weitz. New Haven: Yale University Press, 1987.

Glasgow, Ellen. *The Battle-Ground.* 1902. Tuscaloosa: University of Alabama Press, 2000.

Goodman, Susan. "Introduction." In *The Battle-Ground.* Tuscaloosa: The University of Alabama Press, 2000.

Graebner, William. *The Age of Doubt: American Thought and Culture in the 1940s.* Boston: Twayne Publishers, 1991.

Hardt, Michael and Antonio Negri. *Multitude: War and Democracy in the Age of Empire.* New York: Penguin, 2004.

Harris, Leslie. "The New York City Draft Riots of 1863." *In the Shadow of Slavery: African Americans in New York City, 1626–1863*. www.press.uchicago.edu/Misc/Chicago/317749. html.

Holland, Catherine A. *The Body Politic: Foundings, Citizenship, and Difference in the American Political Imagination*. New York: Routledge, 2001.

Huard, Frances Wilson. *My Home in the Field of Honor*. 1916. Charleston, SC: BiblioBazaar, 2006.

Hutner, Gordon. *What America Read: Taste, Class, and the Novel, 1920–1960*. Chapel Hill: University of North Carolina Press, 2009.

James, Jennifer. *A Freedom Bought with Blood: African American War Literature from the Civil War to World War II*. Chapel Hill: University of North Carolina Press, 2007.

Jensen, Kimberly. *Mobilizing Minerva: American Women in the First World War*. Urbana: University of Illinois Press, 2008.

"Women, Citizenship and Civic Sacrifice." In *Bonds of Affection*. Ed. John Bodnar. Princeton: Princeton University Press, 1996.

Johnston, Mary. *The Long Roll*. London: Constable and Co. Ltd., 1911.

Kennedy, David M. *Over Here: The First World War and American Society*. New York: Oxford University Press, 1980.

Kerber, Linda. *Women of the Republic: Intellect and Ideology in Revolutionary America*. Chapel Hill: University of North Carolina Press, 1980.

Lee, Mary. *It's a Great War!* Boston: Houghton Mifflin, 1929.

Lepore, Jill. *The Name of War: King Philip's War and the Origins of American Identity*. New York: Vintage, 1998.

Lesinska, Zofia. *Perspectives of Four Women Writers on the Second World War: Gertrude Stein, Janet Flanner, Kay Boyle, and Rebecca West*. New York: Peter Lang, 2002.

Limon, John. *Writing after War: American War Fiction from Realism to Postmodernism*. New York: Oxford University Press, 1994.

Long, Lisa. *Rehabilitating Bodies: Health, History, and the American Civil War*. Philadelphia: University of Pennsylvania Press, 2003.

Lyon, Janet. "Gender and Sexuality." In *The Cambridge Companion to American Modernism*. Ed. Walter Kalaidjian. New York: Cambridge University Press, 2005.

May, Elaine Tyler. *Homeward Bound: American Families in the Cold War Era*. New York: Basic Books, 1988.

Mead, Margaret. *And Keep Your Powder Dry: An Anthropologist Looks at America*. New York: William Marrow and Co., 1965.

Nelson, Dana. *National Manhood: Capitalist Citizenship and the Imagined Fraternity of White Men*. Durham, NC: Duke University Press, 1998.

Riley, Robin L., Chandra Talpade Mohanty, and Minnie Bruce Pratt, eds. *Feminism and War: Confronting US Imperialism*. New York: Zed Books, 2008.

Rowlandson, Mary. *The Sovereignty and Goodness of God*. 1682. Ed. Neal Salisbury. New York: Bedford/St. Martin's, 1997.

Ryan, Maureen. "The Other Side of Grief: American Women Writers and the Vietnam War." *CRITIQUE: Studies in Contemporary Fiction* 36.1 (1994): 41+.

Salisbury, Neal. "Introduction: Mary Rowlandson and Her Removes." In *The Sovereignty and Goodness of God*. Ed. Neal Salisbury. New York: Bedford/St. Martin's, 1997.

Samuels, Shirley. *Facing America: Iconography and the Civil War*. New York: Oxford University Press, 2004.

Scura, Dorothy M. *Ellen Glasgow: The Contemporary Reviews*. New York: Cambridge University Press, 2009.

Slotkin, Richard and James Folsom, eds. *So Dreadfull a Judgment: Puritan Responses to King Philip's War, 1676–1677*. Middletown, CT: Wesleyan University Press, 1978.

Smith, Angela K. *The Second Battlefield: Women, Modernism, and the First World War*. New York: St. Martin's Press, 2000.

Stern, Julia A. *Mary Chesnut's Civil War Epic*. Chicago: University of Chicago Press, 2010.

Wharton, Edith. *A Son at the Front*. 1923. DeKalb: Northern Illinois University Press, 1995.

Whites, Lee Ann. "The Civil War as a Crisis in Gender." In *Divided Houses: Gender and the Civil War*. Ed. Catherine Clinton and Nina Silber. New York: Oxford University Press, 1992.

  The Civil War as a Crisis in Gender. Athens, GA: University of Georgia Press, 1995.

  Gender Matters: Civil War, Reconstruction, and the Making of the New South. New York: Palgrave Macmillan, 2005.

Wolff, Marita. *About Lyddy Thomas*. New York: Random House, 1947.

Young, Elizabeth. *Disarming the Nation: Women's Writing and the American Civil War*. Chicago: University of Chicago Press, 1999.

3
American women's writing in the colonial period

KIRSTIN R. WILCOX

Anne Bradstreet, Mary Rowlandson, and Sarah Kemble Knight: every recent textbook covering the historical span of American literature includes at least two of those three names among its colonial-era writers. Anne Bradstreet (1612–72), an immigrant to the Massachusetts Bay Colony, published *The Tenth Muse, Lately Sprung Up in America*, a collection of her poetry, in 1650, and a posthumous collection with new material in 1678. Mary Rowlandson (1637–1711) spent nearly three months of captivity with the Narragansett tribe in 1676 before returning to her settlement in Lancaster, Massachusetts; her book describing these events, *The Sovereignty and Goodness of God* (1682), is the most well-known instance of the captivity narrative genre. Sarah Kemble Knight (1666–1727) kept a journal of her journey from Boston to New York in 1704–5, describing in lively and humorous detail her adventures on the road, an account first published in 1825 as *The Journal of Madam Knight*.

The isolated voices of these three writers long sustained the myths that (1) early American women wrote little and (2) "early America" was the same thing as the present-day northeastern United States. In the past few decades, those myths have been overturned. Scholars of women's literature have identified important women's writing spanning the full range of New World experience, levels of literacy, social position, wealth, and national orientation. At the same time, those working in post-colonial and hemispheric studies have resisted the teleology of later historical developments and so redefined the terms "colonial," "American," and "writing." "Early American women's writing" is no longer limited to the literary verse and narratives penned by Anglophone women destined to die (even if they were born elsewhere) within the borders of the territory that would become the United States. Surveying the field of early American literature in 2000, David S. Shields observed that

No other field of American literary inquiry is now so free. No master narrative controls research. A minimal canon permits readers free range rather than fixation on a lineage of master texts . . . the field has become singularly fluid, with a mutable and expanding canon, an archive fat with undiscovered and unremarked works. ("Joy and Dread among the Early Americanists," 636)

The persistence of Bradstreet, Rowlandson, and Kemble Knight does not establish a revisionist canon so much as it represents a holding pattern for a literary field still coming to terms with this profound transformation. Though they are landmarks on an out-of-date geographic map, these three writers demarcate the three often overlapping generic territories that early American women's writing occupied: poetry, life-writing, and testimony.

Of these three forms, poetry was perhaps the most supple and widely recorded. Publishing a book of poetry made Bradstreet unusual in 1650, but writing poetry did not. Unlike fiction and drama, poetry could be composed, remembered, and shared, even when paper, writing implements, and leisure time were scarce. These properties made poetry available as a form of expression for people who lacked the resources necessary for prose composition (Steedman, "Poetical Maids"). For women who did have ample material circumstances for their literary endeavors, poetry was the currency of elite literary exchange and therefore the genre of first choice. Hardly surprising then that so many "firsts" in American women's literary history are poems. The first work of African American literature? "Bars Fight" (c.1746) by Lucy Terry (c.1730–1821), describing an Indian raid in Deerfield, Massachusetts. Oral transmission alone preserved this poem (part of Terry's once-extensive oeuvre) until it was published for the first time in 1855. The first literary work by a woman in the Americas? Five sonnets penned between 1574 and 1580 by Leonor de Ovando, a nun in Santo Domingo (Chang-Rodríguez, "Colonial Voices," 117). First published work of Anglophone American literature? Anne Bradstreet's The Tenth Muse. Poetry was also the medium of much of the earliest American literature, the oral literary traditions of the indigenous tribal peoples that originally populated the Americas. Women's creative endeavors are not easily isolated from the fragmentary remains that were written down and translated by nineteenth- and twentieth-century ethnographers, or from the texts that are a part of living tribal culture. They cannot be dismissed either; the issue is not the absence of women but the inadequacy of the methodological tools provided by the study of Eurocentric literary traditions.

Poetry was portable: a poem could be enclosed in a letter, copied to share with friends, cherished in a commonplace book, or read at a gathering. Some women left behind only a poem or two to document a literary bent that may well have been more extensive: examples include Mary English's (1652–94) single acrostic and Anna Hayden's (1648–1720) two elegies. Many poems were the product of sociable literary interactions that are, like Lucy Terry's poems, now lost to us, but *Milcah Martha Moore's Book*, published for the first time in 1997, reveals some of this lost world of women's verse. Milcah Martha Moore wrote little poetry herself, but she copied the verse of friends and acquaintances into her commonplace book. This modern edition of Moore's collection records the poetry of Hannah Griffitts (1727–1817) and Susanna Wright (1697–1784), most of whose writing would otherwise be now lost. It also contains the only extant fragments that the travelogue Elizabeth Graeme Fergusson (1737–1801) wrote and sent home in widely circulated installments when she traveled to England in 1764, along with a few of her poems. Unlike Fergusson, Griffitts and Wright are not known to have published any of their work; they instead let their works be disseminated by letter and manuscript from their intimate friends to broader circles of Quaker affiliation and community.

These processes of transmission were a significant feature of belletristic writing, not only in colonial American but in the wider Anglophone world. For many readers and writers of the time, circulating and copying poetry and prose in manuscript form was a common way for literary life (whether vocation or pastime) to be lived. Such manuscripts could circulate widely, but manuscript poetry was often closely tied to the social world that brought it into being. Fergusson's home, Graeme Park, was itself a well-known center of literary activity, including such prominent literary men as Benjamin Rush and Nathaniel Evans. Fergusson's friend and fellow poet Annis Boudinot Stockton (1736–1801) was similarly prominent in the colonial literary world, not because of the handful of poems she published in periodicals, but as a consequence of her literary salon at Morven in New Jersey and the extensive literary correspondence that disseminated her poems to a far-flung readership.

Dimensions of this social role of poetry carried over from manuscript culture into print. The Anglophone colonial market for print had a place for women's poetry, but in the form of contributions to periodicals, not books. Appearing usually as "Laura" (the name she also put to her manuscript poems), Fergusson published poems in *The Pennsylvania Magazine*, *The Columbian Magazine*, *The American Museum*, and *The Universal Asylum*. Fergusson's niece and literary protégé, Anna Young Smith, published in some of the same periodicals, using the pseudonym "Sylvia," though more of her verse is preserved in manuscript form in Fergusson's commonplace books (which have not been published in a modern edition). Some twenty poems by "Emilia" (Annis

Boudinot Stockton) appeared in *The New American Magazine*, *The Pennsylvania Chronicle*, *The Pennsylvania Magazine*, *The New Jersey Gazette*, *The Columbian Magazine*, *The Gazette of the United States*, and *The Christian's, Scholar's, and Farmer's Gazette*. The newspapers and magazines that published these women writers generally merged hard news with advice, almanac-style data, and *belles-lettres*. Such venues for poetry flourished through the mid- to late eighteenth century, principally for local readerships, but most were displaced in the early national period by more long-lived and narrowly conceived literary publications that had a broader national audience.

These prolific and known poets are not isolated examples. Many "A Lady," demarcated only by her hometown (if by anything), or "A Female Hand," can be remembered for verses published as far south as the *Barbadoes Gazette* or as far north as the *New Hampshire Gazette*. Their poetry flourished in all the periodicals of Boston, New York, and Philadelphia as well. Women poets designating themselves as residents of the colonies also sent their work to London to be published in the metropolitan magazines that were being imported to British North America. The rigorous anonymity of this poetry has made it easy to exclude from literary history. Ascribing any one poem with certainty to a particular author, much less an identifiable and unambiguously female author, is difficult. American magazines cheerfully (and often silently) republished copy from British magazines and newspapers, many female pseudonyms (like Benjamin Franklin's Silence Dogood in *The New-England Courant*, edited by his brother James) are clearly meant to be satiric, and some men adopted pen names with feminine endings. Moreover, the quantities of verse that were published with no authorial attribution of any gender further complicate the issue.

The full range of this body of poetry defies categorization, but a few titles can demonstrate its diversity. Through the periodical press, women poets created opportunities for communal mourning ("To the memory of . . . Mrs. Hannah Dale [Relict of Dr. Dale] who died the 9th of April, 1751, aged 29 years" by "H – S – . . . a Lady of her Acquaintance," *South Carolina Gazette* 886, May 6, 1751, 1), commented on current events ("A Poem on the late Successes of Admiral Vernon in the West Indies, by a Lady residing at Jamaica," *London Magazine* X, July 1741), moralized ("The Progress of Life" by "A Female Hand," *New England Weekly Journal*, August 23, 1731), displayed their skill in writing on fashionable themes ("A Lady's Lamentation for the Loss of her Cat," *American Magazine* II, Jan. 1745, 36), and explored the full range of aesthetic and discursive opportunities offered by this medium.

Some periodical poetry took issue with gender norms. "Newspapers had hardly started to appear in the colonies (circa the mid-1720s) when literate middle- and upper-class women began using them as venues for self-representation and public suasion on issues pertinent to themselves" points out Paula Bernat Bennett (*Poets in the Public Sphere*, 6). Poems expressing varying degrees of gender advocacy appeared in periodicals up through and beyond the American Revolution, and Bennett identifies interesting clusters of poems published on these themes in the 1720s and '30s in *The American Chronicle*, *The South Carolina Gazette*, and *The American Weekly Mercury* (Bennett, *Poets in the Public Sphere*, 6–8). The most well known of these early gender critiques is Elizabeth Magawley's satire, "The Wits and Poets of Pennsylvania," in *The American Weekly Mercury* of 1730. Little is known of Magawley, who published her poem under the name "Generosa" – only that she was sufficiently active in Philadelphia's literary circles to conclude with this poem a lengthy exchange with several male correspondents over the question of whether *The American Weekly Mercury* was unfairly representing women in its pages.

Pamphlet- or book-length works of woman-authored poetry tended to have a less secular, more devoutly religious frame. Jane Dunlap's *Poems, Upon Several Subjects, Preached by the Rev'd and Renowned George Whitefield* (1771), reflect less the literary aspirations of the writer than the celebrity of the addressee (it is worth noting that the frontispiece is a woodcut of Whitefield, not Dunlap). Longer and more widely ranging collections like the posthumous *Some Memoirs of the Life and Death of Mrs. Jane Turrell* (Boston, 1735) edited by her father, Martha Brewster's *Poems on Divers Subjects* published in 1757 in Connecticut and 1758 in Boston, and Phillis Wheatley's *Poems on Various Subjects, Religious and Moral* (London, 1774) combined biblical, devotional, and elegiac themes with the display of secular belletristic versatility.

The relationship between piety, publicity, and book publication took different forms elsewhere in the New World. Sor Juana Inés de la Cruz (1648?–95) published multiple editions of *The Castalian Inundation* [sometimes translated as *The Overflowing of the Castalian Spring*]: *by the Tenth Muse of Mexico* (1689). This collection of courtly verse was published in Spain through the intervention of Sor Juana's noble patrons, but it represents a fraction of the devotional, scholarly, occasional, and lyric verse that she produced (Paz, *Sor Juana*, 199). Nor was Sor Juana an isolated example of women's Spanish-language poetic authorship in the early Americas. Two poets writing in Spanish in Peru are known only by their pseudonyms: Clarinda, whose 1608 *Discourse in Praise of Poetry* has not yet been translated into English, and Amarilis, whose

"Epistola a Belardo" was included in Lope de Vega's 1621 miscellany, *La Filomena* (Chang-Rodríguez, "Gendered Voices," 278).

Colonial America did not supply the urban infrastructure that encouraged other conventional literary genres prevalent elsewhere at the center of the colonial empires. The few theaters had difficulty enough staging existing repertoire, much less producing new plays, and apart from Sor Juana's short sacramental plays, there remains little evidence of women's dramaturgy (Merrim, "Sor Juana Criolla"). The decentralized nature of American printing, which was concentrated in Boston, New York, and Philadelphia, coupled with poor routes of distribution, also meant that no new works of fiction got published in the American colonies. Imaginative self-expression perforce took other forms: letters, journals, and other kinds of life-writing, all of which were molded by cross-cultural encounters, distance from metropolitan centers, and the pressures of displacement and new settlement.

Women's life-writing from the colonial era documents a wide range of responses to these circumstances. Sarah Kemble Knight's travel journal is perhaps the most well-known example, but it is not geographically or generically representative of an expansive genre that varied as widely as early American women themselves. Like poetry, letters cemented social bonds and connected family and community over the distances of far-flung empires. In the process of writing them, women could come to terms with tragedy, work through spiritual concerns, solidify a sense of self being shaken by new surroundings, and affirm their religious, familial, and class orientation. At one end of the social spectrum are the letters Margaret Tyndal Winthrop (1591–1647) wrote in the 1630s, recording her journey to the Massachusetts Bay Colony to join her husband, the governor of the colony. Maria van Cortlandt Van Rensselaer (1648–89) corresponded extensively during the last twenty years of her life while seeking to retain control over a vast family estate (which now comprises most of Albany County in New York), as New Netherlands became an English title and various family members contended for their rights to its wealth. Eliza Lucas Pinckney (1722–93), born in Antigua, recorded her experiences of running three plantations and single-handedly inaugurating the cultivation of indigo in South Carolina. At the other end of the social spectrum, single letters, preserved by happenstance, are the only documentation of some women's existence, like Elizabeth Bland, an early settler in Georgia who has left to history only her 1735 petition (denied) to return to England (Harris, *American Women*, 193–5). Elizabeth Sprigs's 1756 letter to her father is one of the few known texts recording a laboring woman's experience (Harris, *American Women*, 49–50). Another otherwise unrecorded dimension of women's lives in the colonies is supplied by the letter of Mary Stafford (1711), of whom little is known, other than the privations and resilience (the struggles to "clear starch dress heads & make linen" for sustenance) documented in this single letter (Harris, *American Women*, 191).

Other concerns and other forms of authorial selfhood emerge from the letters of nuns who came from France to form convents in the New World. In New Orleans, Marie Madeleine Hachard (1704–60) navigated between the mandate granted to her Ursuline order to administer a hospital for the Company of the Indies and the Ursuline's wish to establish a school in the area. Her letters reveal "a community of women with a powerful sense of their own authority," writes Emily Clark, who has recently translated and edited the Ursuline correspondence from New Orleans ("Patrimony without Pater," 96). In Quebec, Marie de l'Incarnation (1566–1618) devoted herself to converting the indigenous tribes. Of her voluminous writing during that time, only 278 letters survive (written to the son she bore before taking holy orders) and one of the two spiritual autobiographies she wrote. Her letters remain an important resource for the history of this French colony, and, like the letters of Marie Hachard, draw attention to the limitations of the Jesuit *relations* as an accurate reflection of the role of French-speaking women in the New World.

In many cases, only thin and permeable generic boundaries separate letters from more explicitly autobiographical forms of self-expression: journals, diaries, and memoirs. Esther Edwards Burr (1732–58) kept a journal between 1754 and 1757 that takes the form of letters to her friend Sarah Prince (later Sarah Prince Gill), in which she seeks – but does not always find – spiritual solace in sharing her quotidian frustrations with a sympathetic friend. Sarah Eve (1749–74) began her journal in order to keep her sea captain father informed of her activities while he was away. Other journals that survive from the era record the range of women's experiences of the exigencies of farming and housekeeping at various life stages: Mary Wright Cooper (1714–78) did not begin her record of agrarian life on Long Island until she was in her fifties; Elizabeth Sandwith Drinker's more prosperous circumstances in Philadelphia are documented in the thirty-six volumes of the diary she kept from her early twenties on.

It is significant that while Sarah Prince's responses to Esther Edwards Burr's letter journal have not survived, the religious meditations that Prince Gill wrote at the end of her life did. Much of the women's life-writing that found its way into print in the colonial era served to preach, testify, and exhort, often drawing on personal narratives of conversion. Initially published as part of a sermon preached by her husband Moses Gill following her death in 1771, Gill's devotional exercises were also published alone, first as a separate volume titled *Devotional Papers Written by the Late Mrs. Sarah Gill* (1773) and then bundled with *The Dying Exercises of Mrs. Deborah Prince* (her sister) in Edinburgh in 1785. Quaker women like Bathsheba Bowers (*An Alarm Sounded to Prepare the World to Meet the Lord in the Way of His Judgments*, 1709) and the prolific Sophia Hume (who actively promoted the rights of Quaker women to preach) followed in the pattern of English Quaker men and women, who saw the publication of personal journals as a way to model the necessary spiritual struggles of Quaker belief. Hume's earliest publications were directed to the inhabitants of South Carolina (to whose ministry she felt divinely called) but published in Philadelphia and Bristol (*An Exhortation to the Inhabitants of the Province of South-Carolina, to Bring their Deeds to the Light of Christ*, 1748, 1750), London (*An Epistle to the Inhabitants of South Carolina, Containing Sundry Observations*, 1754), as well as Wilmington and Newport. A more complex weaving of the Quaker conversion narrative can be found in *Some Account of the Fore Part of the Life of Elizabeth Ashbridge . . . Written by Her Own Hand Many Years Ago* (1755), in which Elizabeth Ashbridge (1713–55) recounts her journey to America and her struggle to maintain her Quaker faith in spite of her husband's opposition. Devotional works by women of other denominations often took the form of deathbed maternal admonitions – even when the author recovered. Sarah Goodhue's (1641–81) *Copy of a Valedictory and Monitory Writing* first appeared in Cambridge, Massachusetts, after her death in 1681, but Mercy Wheeler (1706–96) published her *Address to Young People, Or . . . Warning from the Dead* in 1733, and *The Dying Mother's Legacy* of Grace Smith (1685–1740) appeared in advance of her death, in 1712.

A different kind of record of personal experience comes from women writers testifying in a variety of contexts (to audiences that seek the information) to their personal experience in the New World. Much of the women's writing that is taken to be paradigmatic of the early colonial experience comes to us in the form of testimony. Mary Rowlandson's *The Sovereignty and Goodness of God* was originally published in 1682 and went through multiple editions in both the American colonies and England. Rowlandson's narrative circulated widely enough to establish some conventions for the captivity narrative as a literary genre, conventions that emerge in *God's Mercy Surmounting Man's Cruelty, Exemplified in the Captivity and Redemption of Elizabeth Hanson* (1728). As Rowlandson's and Hanson's titles suggest, such narratives also offered proof of God's providence and Christ's dispensation. Consequently, many women's captivity narratives come down to us not as freestanding narratives, but as case studies and exempla in men's sermons and religious writings. Hannah

Duston's remarkable account of having murdered her captors appears in Cotton Mather's fast-day sermon, *Humiliations Follow'd with Deliverances* (1697), as well as his 1699 *Decennium Luctuousum* and his 1702 *Magnalia Christi Americana*. The voices of other American women captives also emerge from Mather's works: most notably Mary French (who wrote a poem to her sister that he included), Hannah Bradley, Mercy Short, and Hannah Swarton.

The explanatory and redemptive power of such narratives of personal experience also prompted the publication of criminal confessions, such as that of Esther Rodgers, whose account of murdering her bi-racial child appeared in *Death the Certain Wages of Sin*, a collection of such confessions compiled by John Rogers in 1701, or the Native American Patience Boston, whose *Confession, Declaration, Dying Warning, and Advice* was published in 1735 and again in 1738 as *The Faithful Narrative of a Wicked Life*. A less sensational and prescriptive account of women's experience can be found in petitions and court records that convey the oral testimony of women who had to defend themselves in court against accusations of criminality, witchcraft, or heresy. The Salem witch trials presented the evidence and petitions of women like Tituba (an enslaved woman who saved herself from execution by confessing) and Mary Easty, who avowed her innocence. One of the most prominent voices of early American women's religious authority and empowerment, Anne Hutchinson, is known exclusively through her reported testimony in the antinomian controversy of 1638, which resulted in her trial for sedition and subsequent banishment from the colony.

As these groupings of texts indicate, the boundaries of colonial American women's literature run directly through a number of vital texts that have no firm foundation within conventional genres, or even within conventional forms of gendered authorship. Even poetry, the most conventional of literary forms for colonial women, presents challenges for scholars trying to make important poets and their works available to modern audiences within the existing frameworks of literary scholarship and teaching. Pattie Cowell's unsurpassed anthology introduced a number of pre-revolutionary women poets to modern scholars, but necessarily truncated their work, lifting poems out of their prose texts that framed them and isolating individual poets from the social exchanges that brought their poetry into being. Scholarly efforts to establish the rich contexts of community and affiliation that fostered women's creativity have produced a number of much-needed books as well as painful trade-offs: an excellent biography of Elizabeth Graeme Fergusson (Osterhout, *The Most Learned Woman in American*), but no modern edition of her collected poems; a fine edition of Annis Boudinot Stockton's poems (Mulford, "Only for the Eye"), but no biography; a painstakingly accurate modern print edition of Milcah Martha Moore's manuscript commonplace book (Blecki and Wulf, *Milcah Martha Moore's Book*), from which it is difficult to lift individual poems for teaching purposes.

The issue of framing is even more complex for women's texts that stand entirely outside conventional literary frameworks. Does the reported speech of an Anne Hutchinson or a Tituba count as early American women's writing? Kathleen Donegan has advocated the generic umbrella of "the case" as a way to unite "the panoply of forms" (personal narratives, court testimony, petitions, confessions, and the like) circulating in early America. Such an approach, Donegan argues, would make possible "a new poetics . . . of instrumentality and praxis," in which works could be classified, read, and compared in terms of the cultural work they do and the colonial "I" they advance ("True Relations," 455). Her proposal of the "case" (defined by its rhetorical purposes) as a distinct literary genre already characterizes much of the most innovative recent scholarship in early American women's writing. Scholars tackling issues as diverse as infanticide (Harris, *Executing Race*) and Anne Hutchinson's role in the construction of the gendered liberal subject (Dillon, *The Gender of Freedom*) draw on specific "cases" to illuminate the experience of women, particularly non-white and working-class women, who got little representation in print otherwise.

Such texts present difficult methodological questions about how precisely to discern the authentic voice of the woman whose experience has been recorded – or even whether an authentic voice is still audible from within the institutional and literary frameworks that hold these accounts in place. How does one separate the genuine voice of a Hutchinson, Hanson, Duston, Boston, or Rodgers from that of the male editor, transcriber, or compiler through whom it is refracted into print? Lorrayne Carroll has treated these methodological questions with regard specifically to captivity narratives, particularly the editorial intervention of Cotton Mather in *Rhetorical Drag: Gender Impersonation, Captivity, and the Writing of History*. Tamara Harvey raises these issues with regard to women's criminal narratives in her work on Patience Boston. Teresa A. Toulouse, Michelle Burnham, and Tara Fitzpatrick have further explored the cultural work that women's captivity narratives performed and the role they played not as expressions of female agency and experience (as they have long been viewed) but as sites for the articulation of changing ideas of colonial American masculinity and authority.

"Cases" also require the critic to examine the relationship between print, orality, and performance. In many instances, a "case" records not a woman's considered effort to represent herself on the written page but a public performance, bound by a different set of conventions than print and responding to a different set of literary expectations. Performative acts took many forms. David Shields's *Civil Tongues and Polite Letters in British America* (1997) describes the sociable contexts of polite conversation, tea-table convention, and the literary coterie, all of which afforded some middle-class and elite women in the British American colonies culturally sanctioned opportunities for cultivating and performing their literary gifts. Expanding on the work of Joseph Roach and Christopher Looby, Sandra Gustafson has opened the field of early American literature to include women's acts and performances. In *Eloquence is Power: Oratory and Performance in Early America*, Gustafson examines how women were gradually excluded from these forms of early American oral tradition. John Demos takes a different approach to filling in the cultural meanings of acts in *The Unredeemed Captive* (1994), which explores the documents surrounding the case of Eunice (Margaret) Williams, in order to reconstruct the experience of a woman who chose to stay with her Native American captors rather than return to her family of origin.

Such reconstruction, distillation, and extrapolation may be necessary to uncover the full breadth of women's experience in early America. As Carla Mulford has argued, "By focusing exclusively on women's written literary expression . . . we can undermine apt representation of women's attitudes about and their participation in the social formation, whether we are talking about women's friendships, their domestic lives, or their roles in social and political life" ("Writing Women in Early American Studies," 114). After all, the gaps in the record of women's written literary expression are vast, even among elite and literate women. For women with less immediate access to the tools of literacy, the gaps are even more telling. "Why don't we have a substantial body of work by Native American women during the seventeenth and eighteenth centuries?" asks Hilary Wyss, a question "made all the more interesting by the fact that Native men in New England during this period produced a great deal of writing" ("Native Women Writing," 120). Rather than trace the boundaries of such abysses or await the recovery of as yet unknown archival material, Mulford proposes a disciplinary expansion: "If we would attempt to consider all forms of women's symbolic expression, whether in painting on canvases, or in stenciling verses or flowers on their household walls, or in creating quilts and clothing for members of their households, we could begin to account for the cultural work women – all women, from all relevant races and classes – were engaging in" ("Writing Women in Early American Studies," 114).

Susan Stabile has merged the study of material culture with the examination of more conventionally literary activities in order to bring to life the coterie culture of the midatlantic region in *Memory's Daughters: The Material Culture of Remembrance in Eighteenth-Century America* (2004). Yet in many cases, the material culture available for scrutiny by the literary scholar mirrors the textual evidence available: either way, the trail leads back to the inner lives of elite women. Locating the subjective experience and cultural work of less-privileged women requires different disciplinary tools than those that the literary scholar has available. Historian Karin Wulf studies tax records and demographic data as well as letters and manuscript poems to understand the experience of unmarried women in mid-eighteenth-century Philadelphia: how they understood their social position, coped with poverty in some cases, contributed to their city's urban culture, and played a role in the waning power of the Moravian and Quaker communities. Archeologists like Alexandra Chan have read physical evidence buried in the soil of former slave dwellings in order to reconstruct the lived experience of New England household slaves prior to the American Revolution. Such research provides a more complete picture of early American women's lives and the varied forms that their cultural work could take, but to be done well, it requires disciplinary tools and frameworks that lie well outside the skill set of scholars trained to examine belletristic texts.

Writing is, by its very nature, unlikely to produce the kind of knowledge of women's broader cultural work that Mulford advocates – but it is not clear that literary scholars should therefore change their disciplinary orientation to produce a more accurate historical record, particularly when so many texts remain unexplored that can yield productively to the tools of literary analysis. Conventional literary and historical scholarship continues to find new ways to illuminate the discursive and intellectual contexts in which women wrote. Catherine Kerrison identifies important ways that the intellectual lives of antebellum southern women differed from those of their northeastern counterparts, and Eve Tavor Bannet explores how the transatlantic trade in letter-writing manuals shaped the voices and discursive possibilities of literate women in the American colonies. Laurel Thatcher Ulrich, working on the diary of midwife Martha Ballard, demonstrates how close textual exegesis can be merged with broader historical inquiry to illuminate the life of a woman whose ability to tell her own story was limited. Many woman-authored texts still await the kind of scrutiny that could yield further insight into a much wider range of American women's experience: texts available in modern print editions but awaiting such study include the letterbooks of Eliza Lucas Pinckney and the diaries of Elizabeth Sandwith Drinker and Martha Cooper. Among the non-Anglophone texts that have been translated (and are even available in machine-readable form!) Maria Van Rensselaer's 1669–89 correspondence densely weaves together reflections on politics, the struggles to maintain financial control, and her household concerns to illuminate the lives of Dutch-speaking women in the northern colonies.

Another largely unexplored realm of women's textual production are the literary networks of both manuscript circulation and publication that provided a creative outlet for literate women up and down the North American Atlantic seaboard. As Karen Weyler argued in the 2009 roundtable, "Feminists Intervene in Early American Studies," published in *Early American Literature*, "we have yet to see, in studies of early American women's writing, anything like the flurry of scholarship on collaborative practices in the transatlantic nineteenth century." More comprehensive work on the connections between manuscript circulation and print and on early networks of literary women is needed to expand on the studies of individual poets and collectors like Stockton, Fergusson, and Moore. Moreover, our existing poetics is poorly equipped to cope with some of the key features of early American women's writing. Qualities like ephemerality and anonymity are generally regarded as nonliterary but made periodical writing an important literary outlet for women who lacked the resources of a Bradstreet, Griffitts, or Wheatley. Women's manuscript and periodical poetry also has the potential to productively complicate the debate about whether the political and cultural life of the colonies was lived through print (as Michael Warner, in *The Letters of the Republic*, has argued), oratorical performance (Christopher Looby, *Voicing America*), or polite sociability (David S. Shields, *Civil Tongues and Polite Letters*). The intersection of those modes – the way that the printed page made the public performance of polite sociability available and civically significant to those with little access to upper-class literary coteries – often drew women to the early American periodical. Yet before this body of women's poetry can be theorized, it needs to be more thoroughly surveyed. Despite the growing availability of online archives of periodicals and the explosion of interest in women's writing in the past four decades, J. A. Leo Lemay's *Calendar of American Poetry* (1969–70) remains the most comprehensive bibliographic guide to woman-authored periodical poetry and the identification of pseudonyms.

Collaborations between historians and literary scholars, like that which produced the 1997 edition of *Milcah Martha Moore's Book*, are another important avenue for creating a more complete knowledge of the full range of early American women's creativity. Similarly, the welcome intervention of folklorists, anthropologists, and scholars in non-Anglophone literary traditions can provide crucial global and non-European contexts against which to situate women's written experience that has been taken to be paradigmatic. The anthropologist Pauline Turner Strong, for example, situates the handful of white women's captivity narratives within the essential cultural context of cross-cultural encounters that resulted, far more often, in the capture and exploitation of far greater numbers of Native people. The recognition that America was a polyglot literary entity also means that Anglophone Americanists have much to gain from the work of scholars in other national histories and languages. The African historian Ray A. Kea, for example, navigates the realm of archival Dutch sources to bring to life the religious leadership and advocacy of Marotta/Magdalena, a West African Moravian convert who rose to prominence in St. Thomas in 1739 when she addressed the Danish–Norwegian queen on behalf of her community. The archives still await more researchers prepared to expand our knowledge of Spanish-, French-, Dutch-, and German-speaking women.

Some of the most compelling recent scholarship in early American women's writing transcends unstable early national boundaries by considering the ways that prominent early women writers confronted similar discursive situations. As Ivy Schweitzer has pointed out, "these early writers are embedded in a transnational and global flow of culture perhaps less emphasized in the early nineteenth century and certainly occluded in the later nineteenth century, where women writers were drawn into a US nationalist paradigm" ("My Body," 409). Rubrics like "Tenth Muse" have long been used to draw Anne Bradstreet and Sor Juana Inés de la Cruz into dialogue with one another, but in recent years the pan-American analysis of women's writing has become more ambitious in its scope. Rather than isolating such prominent writers as Sor Juana and Marie de l'Incarnation from the Anglophone literature of Puritan America, critics like Stephanie Merrim, Tamara Harvey, and Robert Hilliker have traced the broader currents of religious debate that shaped colonial women's writing. The comparative analysis of how these early modern women conceptualized and reconstrued dominant assumptions about the relationships between bodies, authority, and theology illuminates the history of gender formation.

Effacing the anachronistic boundaries of subsequent literary traditions opens up further possibilities for more accurately understanding the discursive situation of early American women writers. "Written in America, by an author born in America, published first in America, set in America, concerned with issues that are specifically grounded in the new country" are the "convergence of various criteria" with which Cathy Davidson settled the question of the "first" American novel (*The Power of Sympathy* by William Hill Brown, a post-Revolutionary work). Yet by these criteria, few colonial woman-authored texts would qualify as "American." Anne Bradstreet and Mary Rowlandson were born in England; Bradstreet's *The Tenth Muse*, Sor Juana's *The Castalian Muse*, and Phillis Wheatley's *Poems on Various Subjects, Religious and Moral* were all first published overseas. As Joe Snader has argued, even the familiar captivity narratives long assumed to be a conventionally American genre can be more accurately regarded as part of a circum-atlantic tradition with many English forebears. Many early American writing women saw themselves not as the pioneering voices of an emergent literary tradition, but as participants in cultural formations that they brought with them from their European homes and continued to sustain with their letters and narratives for the family left behind.

Does early American women's writing include someone like Aphra Behn (1640–89) (as William Spengemann has argued) who spent most of her life squarely ensconced in London? Little is known about her interlude in the British West Indies, and there is some doubt about whether she ever made the transatlantic crossing at all, but she had enough material for two significant works about the colonial experience: a novel (*Oroonoko; or The Royal Slave*) and a play (*The Widow Ranter*), which warranted her inclusion in Myra Jehlen and Michael Warner's anthology, *The English Literatures of the Americas*. If Canada can claim the novelist Frances Brooke (1724–89) as the first Canadian novelist, based on the publication of *The History of Emily Montagu* during her four years in Quebec (before the treaties that established Canada as a separate entity from the thirteen colonies), should the umbrella of early American literature open wide enough to include her? What about Charlotte Lennox (1730–1804), who lived in America for only four years, but turned that experience into a novel (*The Life and Adventures of Harriot Stuart*) that was one of the first fictional depictions of life in the North American British colonies?

Then there are recently rediscovered writers who, unlike Behn and Lennox, have not already been claimed by a national tradition. The "anonymous Lady" whose passionate and graceful love poems were published in *The Barbadoes Gazette* in 1732–3 remains unknown (as do the authors of other poems by anonymous women in the same periodical between 1731 and 1737), and efforts to confirm her identity as the British poet Martha Sansom Fowke (1689–1736) have been inconclusive (Guskin, *Clio*, 15; Overton, *Letter to My Love*, 27–35). Nothing in these female-authored verses gives them the geographic specificity that would guarantee their inclusion in Caribbean or American literature anthologies, but by the same token, nothing in them necessarily excludes them from those traditions, either.

And what about *The Female American*, first published in London in 1767 and recently made available in a modern edition edited by Michelle Burnham? It purports to be a found manuscript of a real woman, Unca Eliza Winkfield, half English, half Native American, who becomes a missionary on an obscure Caribbean island after being shipwrecked. The text resurfaced in Vermont in 1816, where another edition was published. There is no evidence that *The Female American* was anything other than the work of someone, not necessarily female, who read contemporary travelogues but never left the British Isles. Yet *The Female American* takes place mostly on colonial territory, and it was written before the American Revolution ran a dividing line across the British Atlantic world. The "female American" narrator is the daughter of an English father and a Native American mother and thus "American" in the terms understood by eighteenth-century readers. Perhaps most significantly, any female (or male) American wanting to publish a novel in 1757 from the colonies would have seen the benefit of sending the manuscript to London if the opportunity presented itself, as neither the press nor the routes of distribution were sufficiently well established in the colonies to make local publication preferable.

Without the teleology of subsequent historical and literary developments, colonial American women's writing threatens to dissolve into a transnational ocean of early modern texts. Under those circumstances, any pre-1776 imaginative work situated in the Americas becomes "American," and the feminist task of retooling the existing historical narratives to reflect the experience of women gets deferred indefinitely, along with the quest for national origins. But disciplinary incoherence is the price of radical inclusivity only if one grants the obsolete premise that "coherence" in the study of early American literature radiates out from a center in New England and is best defined by the work of a handful of white men. The recovery and study of colonial women's writing in the Americas should have as its goal the creation of new forms of coherence that will help us to group and understand the work of men and women alike, reflecting a complete, nuanced, and multiphonic account of life in the New World.

Works cited

Bannet, Eve Tavor. *Empire of Letters: Letter Manuals and Transatlantic Correspondence, 1688–1820*. Cambridge: Cambridge University Press, 2005.

Bennett, Paula Bernat. *Poets in the Public Sphere*. Princeton: Princeton University Press, 2003.

Blecki, Catherine La Courreye and Karin A. Wulf, eds. *Milcah Martha Moore's Book: A Commonplace Book from Revolutionary America*. University Park: Pennsylvania State University Press, 1997.

Burnham, Michelle. *Captivity and Sentiment: Cultural Exchange in American Literature, 1682–1861*. Hanover: University Press of New England, 1997.

Burnham, Michelle, ed. *The Female American, Or, The Adventures Of Unca Eliza Winkfield*. Peterborough, ON: Broadview Press, 2001.

Carroll, Lorrayne. *Rhetorical Drag: Gender Impersonation, Captivity, and the Writing of History*. Kent, OH: Kent State University Press, 2007.

Chan, Alexandra. *Slavery in the Age of Reason: Archaeology at a New England Farm*. Knoxville: University of Tennessee Press, 2007.

Chang-Rodríguez, Raquel. "Colonial Voices of the Hispanic Caribbean." In *A History of Literature in the Caribbean, Vol. 1: Hispanic and Francophone Regions*. Ed. A. James Arnold with Julio Rodriguez and J. Michael Dash. Amsterdam: John Benjamins, 1994.

"Gendered Voices from Lima and Mexico: Clarinda, Amarilis, and Sor Juana." In *A Companion to the Literatures of Colonial America*, ed. Susan Castillo and Ivy Schweitzer. New York: Blackwell, 2005.

Clark, Emily. "Patrimony without Pater: The New Orleans Ursuline Community and the Creation of a Material Culture." In *French Colonial Louisiana and the Atlantic World*. Ed. Bradley G. Bond. Baton Rouge: Louisiana State University Press, 2005.

Voices from an Early American Convent: Marie Madeleine Hachard and her New Orleans Ursulines, 1727–1760. Baton Rouge: Louisiana State University Press, 2007.

Clark, Emily and Virginia Meacham Gould. "The Feminine Face of Afro-Catholicism in New Orleans, 1727–1852." *William and Mary Quarterly* 59.2 (1992): 409–48.

Crane, Elaine Forman, ed. *The Diary of Elizabeth Drinker*. Boston: Northeastern University Press, 1991.

Cowell, Pattie. *Women Poets in Pre-Revolutionary America 1650–1775: An Anthology*. Troy, NY: Whitston Publishing, 1981.

Davidson, Cathy N. *Revolution and the Word: The Rise of the Novel in America*. New York: Oxford University Press, 1986.

Demos, John. *The Unredeemed Captive: A Family Story from Early America*. New York: Knopf, 1994.

Dillon, Elizabeth Maddock. *The Gender of Freedom: Fictions of Liberalism and the Literary Public Sphere*. Stanford: Stanford University Press, 2004.

Donegan, Kathleen. "True Relations and Critical Fictions: The Case of the Personal Narrative in Colonial American Literatures." In *A Companion to the Literatures of Colonial America*. Ed. Susan Castillo and Ivy Schweitzer. New York: Blackwell, 2005.

Fitzpatrick, Tara. "The Figure of Captivity: The Cultural Work of the Puritan Captivity Narrative." *American Literary History* 3.1 (1991): 1–26.

Guskin, Phillis J. *Clio: The Autobiography of Martha Fowke Sansom (1689–1736)*. Newark, NJ: University of Delaware Press, 1997.

Gustafson, Sandra. *Eloquence is Power: Oratory and Performance in Early America*. Chapel Hill: University of North Carolina Press for the Omohundro Institute of Early American History and Culture, 2000.

Harris, Sharon M., ed. *American Women Writers to 1800*. New York: Oxford University Press, 1996.

Executing Race: Early American Women's Narratives of Race, Society, and the Law. Columbus: Ohio State University Press, 2005.

Harvey, Tamara. *Figuring Modesty in Feminist Discourse across the Americas, 1633–1700*. Aldershot: Ashgate, 2008.

"Taken from Her Mouth: Narrative Authority and the Conversion of Patience Boston." *Narrative* 6.3 (1998): 256–70.

Hilliker, Robert. "Engendering Identity: The Discourse of Familial Education in Anne Bradstreet and Marie de l'Incarnation." *Early American Literature* 42.3 (2007): 435–70.

Horne, Field. *The Diary of Mary Cooper: Life on a Long Island Farm, 1768–1773*. New York: Oyster Bay Historical Society, 1981.

Jehlen, Myra and Michael Warner, eds. *The English Literatures of America, 1500–1800*. New York: Routledge, 1997.

Karlsen, Carol F. and Laurie Crumpacker, eds. *The Journal of Esther Edwards Burr, 1754–1757*. New Haven: Yale University Press, 1984.

Kea, Ray A. "From Catholicism to Moravian Pietism: The World of Marotta/Magdalena: A Woman of Popo and St. Thomas." In *The Creation of the British Atlantic World*. Ed. Elizabeth Manke and Carole Shammas. Baltimore: The Johns Hopkins University Press, 2005.

Kerrison, Catherine. *Claiming the Pen: Women and Intellectual Life in the Early American South*. Ithaca: Cornell University Press, 2006.

Lemay, J. A. Leo. "A Calendar of American Poetry in the Colonial Newspapers and Magazines and in the Major English Magazines through 1765. Part One: Through 1739." *Proceedings of the American Antiquarian Society* 79.2 (1969): 291–392. "Part Two: 1740 through 1759." *Proceedings of the American Antiquarian Society* 80.1 (1970): 71–222. "Part Three: 1760–1765." *Proceedings of the American Antiquarian Society* 80.2 (1970): 353–469.

Looby, Christopher. *Voicing America: Language, Literary Form, and the Origins of the United States*. Chicago: University of Chicago Press, 1996.

Merrim, Stephanie. *Early Modern Women's Writing and Sor Juana Inés de la Cruz*. Nashville: Vanderbilt University Press, 1999.

"Sor Juana Criolla and the Mexican Archive: Public Performances." In *A Companion to the Literatures of Colonial America*. Ed. Susan Castillo and Ivy Schweitzer. New York: Blackwell, 2005.

Mulford, Carla. *Only for the Eye of a Friend: The Poems of Annis Boudinot Stockton*. Charlottesville: University Press of Virginia, 1995.

"Writing Women in Early American Studies: On Canons, Feminist Critique, and the Work of Writing Women into History." *Tulsa Studies in Women's Literature* 26.1 (2007): 107–18.

Ousterhout, Anne M. *The Most Learned Woman in American: A Life of Elizabeth Graeme Fergusson*. University Park: Pennsylvania State University Press, 2004.

Overton, Bill. *A Letter to My Love: Love Poems by Women First Published in the Barbadoes Gazette, 1731–1737*. Newark, NJ: University of Delaware Press, 2001.

Paz, Octavia. *Sor Juana; Or, the Traps of Faith*. Trans. Margaret Sayers Peden. Cambridge, MA: Harvard University Press, 1988.

Pinckney, Elise and Marvin Zahniser, eds. *The Letterbook of Eliza Lucas Pinckney, 1739–1762*. Columbia, SC: University of South Carolina Press, 1997.

Roach, Joseph R. *Cities of the Dead: Circum-Atlantic Performance*. New York: Columbia University Press, 1996.

Schweitzer, Ivy. "'My Body / Not to Either State Inclined': Early American Women Challenge Feminist Criticism." *Early American Literature* 44.2 (2009): 405–10.

Shields, David S. *Civil Tongues and Polite Letters in British America*. Chapel Hill: University of North Carolina Press, 1997.

"Joy and Dread Among the Early Americanists." *William and Mary Quarterly* 3rd ser. 57.3 (2000): 635–40.

Snader, Joe. *Caught Between Worlds: British Captivity Narratives in Fact and Fiction*. Lexington: University Press of Kentucky, 2000.

Spengemann, William C. "The Earliest American Novel: Aphra Behn's *Oroonoko*." *Nineteenth-Century Fiction* 38.4 (1984): 384–414.

Stabile, Susan. *Memory's Daughters: The Material Culture of Remembrance in Eighteenth-Century America*. Ithaca: Cornell University Press, 2004.

Steedman, Carolyn. "Poetical Maids and Cooks Who Wrote." *Eighteenth-Century Studies* 39.1 (2005): 1–27.

Strong, Pauline Turner. *Captive Selves, Captivating Others: The Politics and Poetics of Colonial American Captivity Narratives*. Boulder, CO: Westview Press, 1999.

Toulouse, Teresa A. "Female Captivity and 'Creole' Male Identity in the Narratives of Mary Rowlandson and Hannah Swarton." In *Creole Subjects in the Colonial Americas: Empires, Texts, Identities*. Ed. Ralph Bauer and José Antonio Mazzotti. Chapel Hill: University of North Carolina Press, 2009.

"The Sovereignty and Goodness of God in 1682: Royal Authority, Female Captivity, and the 'Creole' Male Identity." *English Literary History* 67.4 (2000): 925–49.

Ulrich, Laurel Thatcher. *A Midwife's Tale: The Life of Martha Ballard, Based on her Diary, 1785–1812*. New York: Knopf, 1990.

Van Laer, A. J. F., ed. and trans. *Correspondence of Maria van Rensselaer 1669–1689*. Albany: University of the State of New York, 1935.

Warner, Michael. *The Letters of the Republic: Publication and the Public Sphere in Eighteenth-Century America*. Cambridge, MA: Harvard University Press, 1990.

Wulf, Karin. *Not All Wives: Women of Colonial Philadelphia*. Ithaca: Cornell University Press, 2000.

Wyss, Hillary. "Native Women Writing: Reading Between the Lines." *Tulsa Studies in Women's Literature* 26.1 (2007): 119–25.

4

Religion, sensibility, and sympathy

SANDRA M. GUSTAFSON

An important early phase in the recovery of American women's writing focused on the rich vein of sentimental fiction written in the middle years of the nineteenth century. Historian Carroll Smith-Rosenberg laid the groundwork for this recovery and revaluation in "The Female World of Love and Ritual" (1975); a decade later literary historians Jane Tompkins and Cathy N. Davidson published influential studies and new editions of sentimental fiction by American women. Soon questions arose about each of the terms defining the field: How American was it? Did men write it? Was it limited to fiction? What were the distinguishing characteristics and lineages of "sentiment"? Scholars also examined its political premises, putting less emphasis on its potential for imaginative empowerment and more on its coerciveness. Whereas in *The Feminization of American Culture* (1977), Ann Douglas had identified the rise of sentimental writing in the nineteenth century with an intellectual slackness that afflicted Protestant clergymen as well as women, another body of criticism well represented by Amy Kaplan's essay "Manifest Domesticity" (1998) pursued an ideological critique that identified different problems in the tradition. Kaplan shifted the concept of "domestic" from its principal scholarly use as an allusion to the private sphere to focus instead on its public significance in the realms of economy and nation building. Reframed in this way, the fiction that Tompkins and Davidson had celebrated for the ways it liberated middle-class white women appeared in a harsher light as part of the cultural apparatus of American empire.

Running parallel to these developments in nineteenth-century American literary history, and occasionally intersecting with them, was a second body of scholarship on the rise of sentimental writing in the eighteenth-century Atlantic world. In *Cato's Tears* (1999), Julie Ellison considered the transatlantic development of stoic sentimentality, a masculine variant of the culture of sensibility that characterized British and American political culture in the eighteenth century and remains influential today. Sarah Knott's 2009 study of *Sensibility and the American Revolution* is the closest analog in the historiography of British America to G. J. Barker-Benfield's influential analysis of sensibility's intellectual and social roots in *The Culture of Sensibility: Sex and Society in Eighteenth-Century Britain* (1992). Like Barker-Benfield, Knott stresses the importance of medical theories of the body to the rise of sentimentalism and connects it to revolutionary politics, while giving greater attention to the role of booksellers and literary coteries in fostering sentimental writing by both women and men. Periodicals also became an important outlet for women writers, and the essays collected in *Periodical Literature in Eighteenth-Century America* (2005) include sentiment-tinged discussions focused on the early republic by Lisa M. Logan and Sharon M. Harris. The pervasiveness of sentimental thinking is suggested by two studies that discuss writings by women that are only tangentially concerned with the culture of sensibility. In *Memory's Daughters*, a 2004 study of a coterie of women writers in the Philadelphia region between 1760 and 1840, Susan M. Stabile highlighted literary and material practices of memory, while Susan Scott Parrish discussed the contributions of women writers to colonial and early national transatlantic networks of naturalists in *American Curiosity* (2006). In their otherwise quite different works, Stabile and Parrish share a focus on the aspects of their environments that inspired women to write, extending the materialist conception of the self anchored in the nerve-based theories of sensibility into material domestic culture and naturalist activities. Another line of scholarship that explores the connections between sentimental theory, theology, and women's writing has been most recently developed by Abram Van Engen, who in "Puritanism and the Power of Sympathy" (2010) relates a body of Puritan theology on the emotions to Anne Bradstreet's "A Dialogue Between Old England and New; Concerning their Present Troubles, Anno, 1642." Van Engen joins other scholars in pointing to a longer and more explicitly religious lineage for literary sentimentalism.

In this essay I consider four authors whose works collectively illuminate the world in which women's writing began to flourish in colonial British North America and the early United States. Their works demonstrate that by 1750 the language of sensibility infused women's private and public writings dealing with a full spectrum of issues including religion and politics, and they point to the range of concerns and stances that sensibility helped foster. In the religious writings of Esther Edwards Burr and Annis Boudinot Stockton and in the political writings of Stockton, Phillis Wheatley, and Margaretta Bleecker Faugères, we find exemplified the multiple discursive registers and formal dimensions of women's sentimental writing. These authors worked in a variety of genres, including journals, personal meditations, essays, poetry, drama, and short fiction. They benefited from evangelical social networks, coterie culture, and political associations, as well as from the developing print marketplace of periodical publication and book circulation. Taking into account the transatlantic, multiply raced and gendered, generically heterogeneous culture of sensibility, and attending to its complex sources in religion, medicine, philosophy, and the arts, my analysis of sensibility's place in the writings of Burr, Stockton, Wheatley, and Faugères provides a fresh view of the broader context of sentimental writing that fostered the tradition of women's sentimental fiction from Susanna Rowson and Hannah Foster through Harriet Beecher Stowe and beyond.[1]

In the spring of 1755, Esther Edwards Burr read Samuel Richardson's *Pamela, or Virtue Rewarded* (1740) with her friend Sarah Prince. These young women, daughters of leading evangelical ministers, undertook a shared reading of this early sentimental novel soon after they began exchanging the letter-journal that they kept from 1754 until 1757.[2] The letter-journal recast elements of the Puritan diary in a genre that generated spiritual insight out of the interplay between the two women. Burr's entries, which alone survive, capture her emotional responses to the events of her daily life and reflect on her relationship to men and to a higher power understood in masculine terms. She incorporated the traditional themes of religious endeavor, a longing to be close to God through prayer, meditation, and devoted labor, and a failure to sustain that ideal state. The letter-journal also enacts a concept of female friendship based on intellectual and creative exchange. Produced by a woman at the center of a network of elite northeastern evangelicals, and written for a woman equally prominent in those circles, the letter-journal circulated beyond Burr and Prince to a small group of female friends, including the young Princeton-based poet Annis Boudinot Stockton. The exclusivity of this network – which they called the Sisterhood or the female freemasons – is captured in Burr's entry for January 15, 1756: "These *Hes* shall know nothing about our affairs *until they are grown as wise as you and I are.*" The exchange of writings among this group of women was intended to create a distinctively feminine spiritual, intellectual, and literary community.

Writing remained a controversial pursuit for women in British North America, even in an evangelical community that celebrated the exemplary value of holy women and supported female education. In the letter-journal Burr reflected on the conditions of writing in ways that suggest her ambivalence about her literary ability. She commented on the quality of her writing materials (vellum and quills), criticized the clarity of her penmanship and the inadequacy of her prose style, and described the physical ailments and domestic labors that made writing difficult. Despite such distractions and uncertainties, Burr clearly understood her writing as a contribution to a literary community. She employed pseudonyms, referring to Sarah as Fidelia and herself as Burrissa. In addition to Richardson, she read and commented on the works of English women writers including Mary Jones, Elizabeth Singer Rowe, and Hannah Pearsall Housman. Her insight into literary creation grew as she observed her husband Aaron prepare a sermon for publication and responded to the works that Sarah sent her. She learned from these efforts, and the later journal entries grow more vivid and direct in their language and conception. But the many demands on her time prohibited sustained endeavor, and she continued to complain of her lack of artistry and her inability to communicate effectively, writing in her entry of April 16, 1756, "'Tis impossible for one that has no better faculty of communicating than I have, to give you any Idea how full of those *peticular matters* I feel." At times her efforts at immediacy resonate with Richardson's epistolary fiction. "I don't so much as look over what I send to you," she wrote to Sarah on November 9, 1754. "You have my thoughts just as they then happen to be." Here she characterized her style in the improvisational terms that she and Richardson both drew from the evangelical Protestantism that they shared. The evangelical emphasis on spontaneity made forms of to-the-moment writing such as the letter-journal into art of the most valued kind – an exemplary and redemptive register of God's workings in the soul.[3]

The interplay of daily life, spiritual realization, and literary endeavor is central to an exchange in the letter-journal over the meaning of Solomon's good woman. Responding on December 1, 1754 to Sarah's light-hearted query whether the good woman who "kept a candle a burning all Night" did not "set up to read," Esther first asked Aaron his opinion about the scripture passage. When he responded with a jest, she began to record her own interpretation but was interrupted by guests. She did not find time to return to the question until eleven days later, and then she insisted that the good woman must sleep "unless she was made of some other sort of Matter than we be." Punning on *"Matter"* and *mater* (or mother), Burr adopted a practice common among spiritually minded women of associating her efforts to produce religious writing with the travails of Mary. Burr's descriptions of trying to write while holding or nursing a young child make this allusion particularly striking. The journal similarly registers her loneliness and sense of isolation. It served as an imperfect material substitute for Sarah's presence, as Burr noted when she wished for a *"Long Letter as long as from here to Bost[o]n"* or when she expressed envy toward her text, which would "injoy the privileges of being handled in the most free and intimate manner and I deprived!" *"In short,"* she concluded, *"I have a good mind to seal up my self in the Letter and try if I cant Rival it."*

Annis Boudinot Stockton's poetic tribute to Burr further explores the relationship between female friendship, spiritual redemption, and literary improvisation. Stockton developed her appreciation for Burr's virtue in part by reading the letter-journal, suggesting how one woman's effort at literary creation generated further literary improvisations by her friends. She wrote "To my Burrissa" on the spur of the moment, while she stood ready to depart the Burr home. Preserved in Burr's diary, the poem celebrates its subject as an object of desire and emulation. "My soul aspires / And clames a kin with yours," Stockton wrote, and she went on to celebrate "the Sacred Flame / Of Friendship rising in my Brest" (*Only for the Eyes of a Friend*, 78). Some of Stockton's first surviving poems employ the language of sensibility to defend women from newspaper satires on the female sex. These juvenile works were produced during the years when she participated with Burr and other young Princeton women in an ongoing discussion of gender roles.[4] In 1756 she offered an impromptu answer to a widely publicized "Sarcasm against the ladies" (74) that develops the metaphor of women as cheap print. "Woman [*sic*] are books in which we often spy / Some bloted lines and sometimes lines awry," the author claims, and concludes his satire with the wish that "my wife were / An almanack – to change her every year." Boudinot's response pursues the metaphor of woman-as-book, but insists that it takes a perceptive reader to "discern / The beauties of those books they attempt to learn." "Men of sense and taste" – that is, men of sensibility – are wise enough to overlook superficial defects and read more deeply. Some ten years later in her response "To the Visitant," an essay advocating education for women, Stockton praised the author as just such a "candid, gen'rous man" whose "sentiments bespeak a noble heart."[5] Sensibility provided a bond between men and women as well as among the evangelical women of her circle.

Stockton outlined the varieties of sensibility in "Sensibility, an ode," an undated poem written sometime after her marriage in late 1757 or 1758. Addressing sensibility as a "Celestial power," she conjures a sacralized realm of "altar" and "throne" within her own heart and begs the ungendered deity to "temper all my soul, and mark me for thy own." Sensibility's mark is first and foremost the tear that falls from the eyes of a devotee:

> Give me to feel the tender trembling tear
> Glide down my cheek at sight of human woe
> And when I cant relieve the pang severe
> The melting sigh of sympathy to know.
>
> (250–1, lines 1–2; 5–8)

Careful not to celebrate feeling at the expense of action, she nonetheless views sympathy as a social virtue regardless of immediate consequence. In addition to its mournful side, sensibility includes a positive, community-building dynamic that embraces social exchange, often in the service of civic life. Echoing the Latitudinarian divines who developed sentimental theory in part as a rebuttal of stoic thought, Stockton rejects "the stoics frown" which refuses "the balm that sweetens all this mortal strife" (line 24):

> May sprightly wit and true benevolence
> Give relish to each good which heaven bestows
> May cheerfulness with smiling innocence
> Increase the charms that o'er creation glows
> Nor to these only do thy laws extend
> For love and friendship claim an ample part.
>
> (lines 25–30)

This social element of sensibility dominates Stockton's civic poetry. Her patriotic works celebrate their "bright theme" in a voice untinged by the irony or ambivalence of "venal bards" who use their talents to adorn "a despots brow." Unlike these hypocritical poets, whose "every wreath" contains "a rugged thorn, / And praise a Satire proves," Stockton enjoyed the unalloyed appreciation of her subjects (160–1, lines 13–16). "We can never be cloyed with the pleasing compositions of our female friends," George Washington wrote to her in August 1788, when he had already received several of her poetic tributes, concluding that the "Ladies" were among "the best Patriots America can boast" (215–17 n. 251; esp. 216). Stockton's public poetry contributed to an emerging national role for women in the manifestation of allegiance to the state, with sensibility as the cornerstone. She defended women's intellectual abilities and justified their participation in public life; modeled the civic roles that women could play by presenting their support for the patriot cause and their enhancement of state authority; and propounded the conservative Federalist ideology of a hierarchically ordered society.

Stockton's first published poem, "To the Honourable Col. PETER SCHUYLER" (1758), celebrated a hero of the French and Indian War on the occasion of his visit to Princeton. Printed in both the *New-York Mercury* and *The New American Magazine*, the poem was praised for discovering "so fruitful and uncommon a Genius" in its "fair Author" and directed "especially to your female Readers" (84). Stockton was an early promoter of patriotic sentiment among her circle of manuscript and newspaper readers. The conservative elite of New Jersey, led by Royal Governor William Franklin, were slow to take up the patriot cause, and Richard Stockton was no exception. Annis's first surviving poem on the imperial conflict is "On hearing that General Warren was killed on Bunker-Hill, on the 17th of June 1775," which she wrote a year before her husband publicly revoked his pro-imperial position and was elected to the Continental Congress (19–22). This work marks the beginning of a series of political poems that Stockton produced between 1775 and 1793 in which she commemorates major events of the Revolutionary War and celebrates Washington's military and civic leadership.

Her political writings culminated in her poems from the 1790s in support of Washington and his administration. In works on the Genet controversy and in support of Alexander Hamilton, Stockton melded neoclassical poetic conventions with sentimental rhetoric. She sought to limit the potentially volatile emotions aroused in the post-Revolutionary "age of passions," containing them within a hierarchical society based on feeling. Defending the Federalist regime as a new natural order, Stockton both enacted and described a female role in protecting it from attack.[6] Stockton's poem in support of Alexander Hamilton's fiscal policies appeared in the *Gazette of the United States*, the newspaper that had earlier published Hamilton's essays defending himself against the attacks of his opponents. In the letter to the editor that accompanied her "Impromptu on reading the several motions made against Mr. Hamilton," Stockton offered a rationale for submitting a work on a topic of public note, which she based in sensibility. The "impromptu" nature of the poem's composition extended the evangelical trope of improvisation, while the letter worked to strike a balance of feeling and reason. "I am no politician," Stockton insisted, "but I *feel* that I am a patriot, and glory in that sensation." Sentiment was governed by "my plain judgment" which evaluated the facts of the case. After reading the motions against Hamilton, she has concluded that his opponents are driven to persecute the Secretary by their lesser talents or their personal ambition. Such individuals seek "to perplex and embarrass the effect of those talents we cannot emulate – or . . . some of desperate fortunes, chuse to make confusion, that in the bustle they may seat themselves in the chair." These considered opinions, she concludes, are not hers alone, for "I have the pleasure to find all my neighbours are of the same sentiments" (174–5).

The defense of Hamilton is Stockton's most partisan work. It monumentalizes her subject in terms similar to those she had long used to describe Washington while trivializing Hamilton's detractors as talentless aspirants to his position rather than as members of a critical public. Character, not real economic conflict or ideological difference, forms the heart of the crisis as she portrays it. This is not to say that Stockton acted from reflexive loyalty. Throughout her life she asserted the intellectual equality of men and women and formed her own political opinions. The range of civic activities that Stockton engaged in and that she portrayed for women in her work is substantial: newspaper reading, political discussion, participation in public ceremonies, armed defense of Washington, and, of course, the composition of patriotic poetry. She both practiced and promoted women's thoughtful attention to national affairs. But what her poems do not imagine for American women is a voice of dissent. Any resistance to the emerging political order falls outside the Federalist ideal of unity and hierarchy grounded on sensibility that Stockton celebrates.

Phillis Wheatley's poetic career parallels Stockton's in revealing ways. Comparing their works, which overlap in style and substance, we can better understand how the patriot discourse of sensibility shaped Wheatley's poetry. Like Stockton's, Wheatley's oeuvre includes numerous elegies and occasional poems, as well as praise poems celebrating prominent men (notably George Washington). Stockton's elegies typically cultivate the sorrowful feelings that a death evokes. By contrast, Wheatley sought to contain and direct the power of sympathy to some higher religious or civic purpose. In "A Funeral Poem on the Death of C.E. an Infant of Twelve Months" (after 1772), for instance, Wheatley worked to mitigate, and even constrain, the grief of Charles Eliot's parents. She opens with a lengthy description of the infant's soul traveling to heaven and praising God for his own youthful death, then turns to the parents to ask: "Say, parents, why this unavailing moan? / Why heave your pensive bosoms with the groan?" For several lines she presents the parents' expression of grief in sentimental terms, "Can we the sigh forbear, / And still and still must we not pour the tear?," but then closes the poem with an abrupt admonition to the parents to anticipate joining their child in heaven (*Complete Writings*, 37–9, lines 25–6; 36–7; and 44–6). Where in similar tributes Stockton cries with the grieving family, Wheatley instructs them. In a later elegy, "To Mr. and Mrs. ——, on the Death of their Infant Son" (written before 1778; pub. 1784), Wheatley abruptly directs the grieving parents to "suppress the clouds of grief that roll, / Invading peace, and dark'ning all the soul" (94–6, lines 53–4). Such strategies are not limited to her elegies. The views of heaven that she commends to fellow artist Scipio Moorhead in "To S. M. A Young *African* Painter, On Seeing His Works" (1773) are another instance of Wheatley's effort to instruct the imaginations of her readers in visions of redemption and transcendence.

In her political poetry as well, when Wheatley evokes grief she does so in order to sublimate it toward a higher, collective goal. She opens "To His Excellency General Washington" (1776) with a sentimental, if deliberately abstract, scene:

> See mother earth her offspring's fate bemoan,
> And nations gaze at scenes before unknown!
> See the bright beams of heaven's revolving light
> Involved in sorrows and the veil of night!
>
> (88–90; lines 5–8)

Rather than detailing the "sorrows" of warfare, Wheatley rapidly shifts attention away from the suffering that surrounded her (she was at the time a refugee from occupied Boston) to evoke an image of a puissant and luminous goddess Columbia commanding seemingly limitless patriot forces. Similarly, "Liberty and Peace, A Poem" (1784) brackets a short description of wartime suffering within celebratory lines on the rising glory of America, depicted as a near-transcendent realm of peace and freedom.

In "To the Right Honourable William, Earl of Dartmouth" (1772), Wheatley delineates another tableau of suffering and mournfulness, once again containing the sentimental scene in a laudatory, transcendent vision, which in this instance depicts the Earl of Dartmouth borne "upwards to that blest abode, / Where, like the prophet, thou shalt find thy God" (39–40; lines 42–3). In a rare reference to her own enslaved status, Wheatley explains that the "love of *Freedom*" and concern for "the common good" that she shares with Dartmouth spring, not directly from her personal experience of slavery, but rather from her ability to empathize with the sufferings of her parents mourning their daughter's enslavement (see lines 20–31). Wheatley displays the self-divided subjectivity characteristic of the theory of sensibility as it was developed by Adam Smith in *A Theory of Moral Sentiments* (1759). She becomes a sentimental subject, not by herself suffering in slavery, but by imagining the sorrow of her parents, who are in turn suffering partly because of what they imagine she is experiencing. Her readers are invited to imagine her trauma only through these multiple layers of mediation.

The limitations of the rhetoric of sensibility for shaping a critical public domain are marked by Wheatley's resistance to serving as an object of sentiment. Sentimentality threatens to deflect substantive discussion in favor of silent (and silencing) spectacle. While the sentimental subject constitutes her or his identity by observing another's suffering, the sentimental object merely suffers.[7] Wheatley's strongly affective passages serve a double function: they testify to her humanity, and they elicit a feeling response from the reader. She then forcefully directs the response thus stimulated to particular actions (contemplation of the divine, commitment to political liberty, heroic military leadership). She uses the language of sentiment to teach rather than for personal expression.

Wheatley's clearest expression of her own inner conflicts and grief over her enslavement appears in one variant of "Farewell to America" (1773), a poem composed as she prepared for her voyage to London. After hailing "Britannia" and taking leave of New England for "One short reluctant Space," Wheatley abruptly inserts an apostrophe to "Temptation," urging it away, and envying those protected from its "fatal Power." This cryptic address perhaps describes the temptation Wheatley felt to remain in England, where she hoped to find freedom. Eliciting the muse's sympathy, Wheatley turns away from the reader. She signals her sorrow even as she forecloses the reader's sentimental response by masking its causes. She will not be a sentimental spectacle. Unwilling to present herself as a sentimental object, Wheatley found other ways to use sentimental moral philosophy to articulate her opposition to slavery. Her strongest abolitionist stance appears in her multiply republished letter to Samson Occom (1774), where she insisted on the "natural Rights" of "Negroes" and asserted that "in every human Breast, God has implanted a Principle, which we call Love of Freedom." Wheatley takes the existence of the moral sense as proof that God will eventually liberate the enslaved. Seeking "to convince [patriots] of the strange Absurdity of their Conduct whose Words [in favor of liberty] and Actions [defending slavery] are so diametrically opposite," she calls down God's wrath on those who "countenance and help forward the Calamities of their fellow Creatures" (152–3). Here, as in her elegies and many of her political poems, Wheatley presents the scene of suffering as a temporary but necessary condition, a moment of earthly sorrow that both motivates human action and anticipates divine correction or redemption.

In striking contrast to the deliberate reticence of Wheatley, Margaretta Bleecker Faugères developed an expressive theory of radical republican sensibility in a handful of generically varied works on political themes that she composed in the 1790s. Her writings offer an early instance of the oppositional protest literature that came to prominence in the Indian rights and antislavery activism of the 1820s and '30s. Faugères's radical sensibility set her apart from other women writers, including her mother Ann Eliza Bleecker, who was a member of the elite literary and political circles of New York City and a committed participant in the culture of sensibility, whose works Faugères collected in a volume that she published in 1793. Faugères's essays, poetry, and drama blend her mother's interest in the literature of sensibility with the physiological expertise and Jacobin political leanings of her husband, French physician Peter Faugères. In works that portray the effects of injustice on the minds and nervous systems of those oppressed by monarchy, slavery, unjust debtor laws, and generalized social turmoil and malaise, Faugères illuminates the connections between medical, political, and literary understandings of sensibility in the 1790s.[8]

One of Faugères's earliest works, a satirical essay on the "Benefits of Scolding" (1790), manifests her interest in the intersections of social and psychological repression with physical illness. In a humorously clinical tone, she suggests that scolding offers both mental and physical benefits: "Scolding is not only good for the mind but the body too," she writes. "It makes respiration more free, and cures cold; and by promoting perspiration, has been known to remove complaints of long standing." Faugères then offers the tale of a woman suffering from consumption who returned to health by scolding:

> A lady of my acquaintance was in a very ill state of health some time ago, as every body thought in a consumption; but one day (as the Doctors were sitting by her) luckily something went wrong, and the poor invalid forgetting her reduced situation, gave vent to her feelings, and scolded most eloquently, and displayed her talents in such a manner as rectified the mistake, brought on a profuse perspiration, and greatly relieved her. The benefits arising from such proceedings were more than she could have expected; she, however, repeated it with the same success, and is now a hearty woman.
>
> (*The Posthumous Works of Ann Eliza Bleecker*, 267)

The therapeutic benefits of "giving vent" to one's feelings are literalized here, as the "profuse perspiration" that accompanies the lecture adjusts a physiological imbalance brought on by the effort to repress frustration. Behind the humor there is a serious message: restricting women's speech has harmful, perhaps fatal consequences.

A weightier image of liberating openness appears in Faugères's 1792 poem, "On seeing a Print, exhibiting the Ruins of the Bastille." Imagining the repressive force of the *ancien régime*, she personifies "extreme Despair" as a Bastille prisoner who "Swallow'd the earth in speechless rage, / Or phrenzied gnaw'd his iron cage, / Tore off his flesh, and rent his hair." The reader is invited to imagine the liberation of the silenced, self-consuming victim of "despotic pow'r" (*The Posthumous Works of Ann Eliza Bleecker*, 330) as a liberation of political voice. Similar images of repression and release, often with a physical dimension, inform her patriotic poems celebrating the Fourth of July. The most notable of these was written as the United States contemplated war with France. "Ode for the Fourth of July, 1798" was read as part of a commemorative celebration held by a number of radical republican groups. In his oration George Clinton, Jr., the nephew of New York's longtime governor of the same name, sided firmly with the French republicans and against war. To promote public exchange in the face of the Alien and Sedition Acts then being passed, Clinton urged the importance of a free press and "an unrestrained communication of sentiment and discussion of public measures" (Clinton, *An Oration*, 10).

In her ode, Faugères echoes Clinton's aversion to war and amplifies his message of unrestrained communication through her characteristic imagery of liberty as expansiveness: "Freeborn children of this land / Let each ardent wish expand: / Hail the hour with sacred glee, / On this day of LIBERTY" (15–16). Faugères's imagery of repression and release sought to return the body politic to health through a purgative act of speech followed by properly balanced public sensibility. Yet expression and liberation were not always therapeutic. Too rapid an oscillation between extreme states could prove deadly. In her essay "Fine Feelings Exemplified in the Conduct of a Negro Slave" (1791), Faugères sought to refute Thomas Jefferson's famous account of the deficiencies of black sensibility by relating the story of the slave Mingo, whose depraved master punished him for his low spirits with seven years of cruel tortures, until a ship's captain took pity on him, purchased him, and gave him his freedom. This is Faugères's account of Mingo's response to the captain's generous act: "Overpowered with joy, the old man clasped the captain's knees; he wept aloud – he raised his swimming eyes to heaven – he would have spoken his thanks – but his frame was too feeble for the mighty conflict of his soul – he expired at his benefactor's feet!" (*The Posthumous Works of Ann Eliza Bleecker*, 270). Rather than being incapable of appreciating his freedom, as Jefferson suggested would be the case, Mingo displays the tender feelings of gratitude to a fatal degree. In contrast to the consumptive woman who finds release and health through scolding, Mingo cannot negotiate the transition to liberty and voice. We never hear Mingo speak, even at the moment of his manumission and death. With no apparent outlet in white society, Mingo is doomed to die from "the mighty conflict of his soul" (270).

Like "Fine Feelings," Faugères's 1795 play *Belisarius* depicts the rending of a body under stress from an unbearable conflict within the soul. The story of Belisarius provided a popular locus for exploring the political dimensions of sensibility and constructing images of a civic body subject to dismemberment, notably in Benjamin Franklin's famous Stamp Act cartoon of 1766 "Date Obolum Belisario" ("Give poor Belisarius a penny"). Faugères significantly rewrote the widely read political novel about Belisarius by the French philosophe Jean François Marmontel (1767) by adding prominent female characters to the plot. In the character of Belisarius's former fiancée Julia, who has no counterpart in Marmontel's version of the tale, Faugères embodies the union of emotional and political strains in an oppressive regime. The play is filled with characters whose discordant passions threaten to tear them apart physically. Only Julia articulates the threat directly and suffers the literal consequences. While Belisarius displays a preternatural ability to suppress his rage, Julia has an explosive temperament. Her death is precipitated by an act of defiant speech directed at the Empress Theodora. In words that differ strikingly from Belisarius's consistently moderate and forgiving tone, Julia insists upon her sanity and righteousness as she speaks her rage-filled truth to power. Relating a "hideous tale / That weeping Truth pour'd in my startled ear," Julia identifies Theodora as the source of all the evil at court. After Theodora has guards force Julia offstage, Julia suffers "horrible convulsions" (*Belisarius*, 38) and dies speechless, with blood gushing from her mouth and eyes. Like the consumptive scold of Faugères's essay, then, Julia seeks relief from emotional pressures in speech; but unlike the scold, and like Mingo the freed slave, Julia's effort at psychological liberation proves to be deadly, as the abrupt shift from constraint to speech produces extreme physiological consequences.

The final instance in Faugères's work of the motif linking the psychological and political consequences of speech through their effects on the body appears in her most directly political piece, an anti-capital punishment poem entitled "The Ghost of John Young the Homicide" (1797). Written as part of a campaign to challenge the state's debtor laws and the death penalty, the poem relates the *cause célèbre* of John Young, a musician and composer who fell deeply in debt to a number of creditors while attempting to expand his musical business throughout the United States. In his prison house narrative, Young describes his futile and increasingly desperate efforts to escape from indebtedness, describing debtor's prison as "the only Bastille in this Land of Boasted Freedom" (7). After several imprisonments which only worsened his financial circumstances, Young grew reckless and fatally shot the deputy sheriff who came to arrest him.

Writing, as her title states, "with a View of rescuing [Young's] Memory from Obloquy, and shewing how inconsistent sanguinary Laws are, in a Country which boasts of her Freedom and Happiness," Faugères sets her poem in a midnight graveyard. Here the melancholy narrator wanders disconsolate until she comes upon a recent grave where she encounters a "weeping Spectre" (2). The remainder of the poem, spoken in Young's voice, criticizes the heartlessness of a justice system that would brutally execute a man, order his remains dismembered by the anatomists, and deny him a grave. Faugères does not try to defend Young's actions. Unlike Julia, who insists that her frantic words are true reason in the face of brutal oppression, Young admits to murdering his victim in a rage. But he goes on to contrast his excessively emotional behavior with the judges' unemotional exercise of legal authority. Young's judges are not Belisarius-like in their emotional balance; rather, the absence of sensibility marks the exercise of false justice. Of equal horror to Faugères is the sentence that Young's corpse was to be given to medical researchers to anatomize. As in Franklin's Stamp Act cartoon, the body of the citizen suffers dismemberment due to the misguided acts of the state. A better solution, Faugères proposes in her final stanzas, would have been to sentence Young to life imprisonment, where he would be "Shut from the blessings of Society, / And to the bonds of useful toil innur'd" (6).

Here and throughout her work, Faugères develops a pattern of imagery that links the emotional intensities of sensibility with the experience of political oppression and the figuration of civic embodiment (or dismemberment). Faugères envisioned a civic body that, once exposed to the extreme stimuli of oppression, requires careful purging, most often in the form of speech – the effective speech of the scold, or the temperate speech of Belisarius, but not the explosive speech of Julia or John Young. In an unjust social order, Faugères suggests, the repressed rage of its victims will lead them to turn murderous, either assaulting representatives of the law, as Young did, or directing their fury inward upon themselves as happens to Julia.

★★★

The trajectory that I have traced from Burr to Stockton to Wheatley to Faugères suggests how American women who wrote in literary genres after 1750 were already working at the nexus of evangelical Protestantism, race, nationalism, and reform that Jane Tompkins found to be critical to an understanding of *Uncle Tom's Cabin* (1852). Their works give a fuller picture of the sentimental milieu, including its multivalent political possibilities, than the fiction written by their contemporaries Rowson and Foster can by itself offer. Other writers – I think particularly of Judith Sargent Murray and Mercy Otis Warren – add further nuances to the portrait without fundamentally altering its central image.[9] My goal is to provide a through-line to a literary narrative about the culture of sensibility that, in becoming transatlantic and multigendered, has lost some of its interpretive power for the history of American women's writing. This is not the only story to tell, but I hope it will be a useful one.

Notes

1. Marion Rust develops a number of these contexts in *Prodigal Daughters: Susanna Rowson's Early American Women*, the first sustained intellectual and cultural biography of Rowson.

2. In *Jonathan Edwards: A Life*, George Marsden discusses this reading of Richardson and notes that Esther's father Jonathan may also have read the novel (419). For a more complete account of Burr's letter-journal, see my entry on "Esther Edwards Burr" in the *Dictionary of Literary Biography*.

3. These entries can also be read as instances of what Sharon M. Harris characterizes as *discours décousu*, or a poetics of interruptability. See Harris's introduction to *American Women Writers to 1800*, 3–4. On women's spiritual writings and their relationship to personal authority, see Scheik, *Authority and Female Authorship*, 3.

4. Burr describes her own role in the "battle of the sexes" in *The Journal of Esther Edwards Burr, 1754–1757*, ed. Karlsen and Crumpacker, 236, 256–8. For an important introduction to Stockton and the Princeton circle, see Carla Mulford's introduction to *Only for the Eyes of a Friend*.

5. The full title of the poem suggests that Stockton continued to discuss issues of women's status with other concerned women: "To the Visitant, from a circle of Ladies, on reading his paper. No. 3, in the Pennsylvania Chronicle" (*Only for the Eyes of a Friend*, 89–90). The poem was published in *The Pennsylvania Chronicle and Universal Advertiser* and reprinted by Matthew Carey twenty years later in the *American Museum* (188, n.54).

6. In *In the Midst of Perpetual Fetes*, David Waldstreicher argues that in the 1780s Federalist supporters of the Constitution developed sentimental spectacle as a form of social control. Such spectacles presented the people's deeply felt dedication to their social superiors, who in turn were required to feel deeply while displaying their worthiness to govern by holding those emotions in rational control. During this decade elite women entered the nationalist public sphere more actively than ever before as performers and spectators at these genteel celebrations. Stockton's poetry may be read as an extension of this Federalist project of sentimental social control. See pp. 74, 104–5, 107.

7. Hartman addresses the splitting of the sentimental object in *Scenes of Subjection*.

8. For a helpful reading of Faugères, see Harris, *Executing Race*, ch. 4.

9. On Murray and sensibility, see Baker, *Securing the Commonwealth*. On Warren, see Davies, *Catharine Macaulay and Mercy Otis Warren*.

Works cited

Baker, Jennifer Jordan. *Securing the Commonwealth: Debt, Speculation, and Writing in the Making of Early America*. Baltimore: The Johns Hopkins University Press, 2005.

Barker-Benfield, G. J. *The Culture of Sensibility: Sex and Society in Eighteenth-Century Britain*. Chicago: University of Chicago Press, 1992.

Burr, Esther Edwards. *The Journal of Esther Edwards Burr, 1754–1757*. Ed. Carol F. Karlsen and Laurie Crumpacker. New Haven: Yale University Press, 1986.

Clinton, George Jr. *An Oration Delivered on the Fourth of July, 1798*. New York: M. L. and W. A. Davis, 1798.

Davidson, Cathy N. *Revolution and the Word: The Rise of the Novel in America*. New York: Oxford University Press, 1986.

Davies, Kate. *Catharine Macaulay and Mercy Otis Warren: The Revolutionary Atlantic and the Politics of Gender*. New York: Oxford University Press, 2005.

Douglas, Ann. *The Feminization of American Culture*. New York: Knopf, 1977.

Ellison, Julie. *Cato's Tears and the Making of Anglo-American Emotion*. Chicago: University of Chicago Press, 1999.

Faugères, Margaretta V. *Belisarius: A Tragedy*. New York: T. and J. Swords, 1795.

"Benefits of Scolding." In *The Posthumous Works of Ann Eliza Bleecker*. Ed. Margaretta V. Faugères. New York: T. and J. Swords, 1793.

The Ghost of John Young the Homicide. N.p., 1797.

"Ode for the Fourth of July, 1798." In George Clinton Jr., *An Oration Delivered on the Fourth of July, 1798*. New York: M. L. and W. A. Davis, 1798.

"On seeing a Print, exhibiting the Ruins of the Bastille." In *The Posthumous Works of Ann Eliza Bleecker*. Ed. Margaretta V. Faugères. New York: T. and J. Swords, 1793.

Gustafson, Sandra M. "Esther Edwards Burr." In *American Women Prose Writers to 1820*. Ed. Carla Mulford *et al*. *Dictionary of Literary Biography*. Vol. 200. Detroit: Bruccoli Clark Layman and Gale Research, 1999.

Harris, Sharon M., ed. *American Women Writers to 1800*. New York: Oxford University Press, 1996.

Executing Race: Early American Women's Narratives of Race, Society, and the Law. Columbus: Ohio State University Press, 2005.

"The *New-York Magazine*: Cultural Repository." In *Periodical Literature in Eighteenth-Century America*. Ed. Mark L. Kamrath and Sharon M. Harris. Knoxville: University of Tennessee Press, 2005.

Hartman, Saidiya. *Scenes of Subjection: Terror, Slavery, and Self-Making in Nineteenth-Century America*. New York: Oxford University Press, 1997.

Kaplan, Amy. "Manifest Domesticity." *American Literature* 70 (1998): 581–606.

Knott, Sarah. *Sensibility and the American Revolution*. Chapel Hill: University of North Carolina Press for the Omohundro Institute of Early American History and Culture, 2009.

Logan, Lisa M. "'The Ladies in Particular': Constructions of Femininity in the *Gentlemen and Ladies Town and Country Magazine* and the *Lady's Magazine; and Repository of Entertaining Knowledge*." In *Periodical Literature in Eighteenth-Century America*. Ed. Mark L. Kamrath and Sharon M. Harris. Knoxville: University of Tennessee Press, 2005.

Marsden, George. *Jonathan Edwards: A Life*. New Haven: Yale University Press, 2003.

Mulford, Carla. "Introduction." In *Only for the Eyes of a Friend: The Poems of Annis Boudinot Stockton*. Ed. Carla Mulford. Charlottesville: University of Virginia Press, 1995.

Parrish, Susan Scott. *American Curiosity: Cultures of Natural History in the Colonial British Atlantic World*. Chapel Hill: University of North Carolina Press for the Omohundro Institute of Early American History and Culture, 2006.

Rust, Marion. *Prodigal Daughters: Susanna Rowson's Early American Women*. Chapel Hill: University of North Carolina Press for the Omohundro Institute of Early American History and Culture, 2008.

Scheick, William J. *Authority and Female Authorship in Colonial America*. Lexington: University Press of Kentucky, 1998.

Smith-Rosenberg, Carroll. "The Female World of Love and Ritual: Relations between Women in Nineteenth-Century America." *Signs* 1 (1975): 1–29.

Stabile, Susan M. *Memory's Daughters: The Material Culture of Remembrance in Eighteenth-Century America*. Ithaca: Cornell University Press, 2004.

Stockton, Annis Boudinot. *Only for the Eyes of a Friend: The Poems of Annis Boudinot Stockton*. Ed. Carla Mulford. Charlottesville: University of Virginia Press, 1995.

Tompkins, Jane. *Sensational Designs: The Cultural Work of American Fiction, 1790–1860*. New York: Oxford University Press, 1986.

Van Engen, Abram. "Puritanism and the Power of Sympathy." *Early American Literature* 45 (2010): 533–64.

Waldstreicher, David. *In the Midst of Perpetual Fetes: The Making of American Nationalism, 1776–1820*. Chapel Hill: University of North Carolina Press for the Omohundro Institute of Early American History and Culture, 1997.

Wheatley, Phillis. *Complete Writings*. Ed. Vincent Carretta. Harmondsworth: Penguin, 2001.

5

Women's writing of the Revolutionary era

JENNIFER J. BAKER

The American Revolution showcased women's capacities to engage in political debate and act in their support of, or opposition to, colonial rebellion. The new nation's Constitution did not, however, bring women suffrage or change their legal status. It is precisely women's new sense of their own potential, coupled with the lack of opportunities to realize that potential, which makes their writing of the era rich for study. This chapter will explore how Revolutionary-era women writers aspired to civic involvement, intellectual equality, physical liberation, and personal gratification, despite their inferior legal stature and exclusion from formal political processes. Specifically, it will show how they did so by positioning themselves in relation to two ideological strains of Revolutionary thought: classical republicanism, which enshrined male civic virtue and military service, and liberalism, which maintained that liberty, a condition variously defined, was a natural human right. These were not the only intellectual strands of Revolutionary thought (the importance of evangelical Protestantism, for example, has been well documented), and nor were these ideologies mutually exclusive so much as different in their emphases.[1] My aim is to show how these modes of thought were crucial points of reference for contemplating women's place in the new republic, as well as how the tensions between them were of particular relevance to women's attempts at self-empowerment. National independence had ushered in a "new era in female history," as Judith Sargent Murray wrote, but the exact nature of the Revolution's legacy for women remained unclear (*The Gleaner*, 703).

Since its inception three decades ago, the formal study of Revolutionary-era women's writing has centered on questions regarding women's changing status and self-assessment in the new nation. This approach took its cues from the study of women's history in the Revolutionary era, a project that began in the 1970s under the aegis of second-wave feminism and historical revisionism. At that time, the then-recent accounts of Bernard Bailyn, Gordon S. Wood, and J. G. A. Pocock viewed the Revolution as an intellectual movement led by white, propertied men and aimed at restoring an English tradition of political liberty that was allegedly being corrupted by the king and parliament; drawing from the oppositional politics of the Commonwealth of the English Civil War (which had been shaped by the Florentine Renaissance revival of the republicanism of ancient Greece and Rome), this discourse maintained that governments were susceptible to corruption, and political rights – rights to judicial proceedings, free speech, self-taxation – were always in jeopardy. This republicanism, moreover, had a moral dimension: it was the property-owning man, capable of subordinating private interests to civic welfare and willing to bear arms for the republic, who was to keep corruption in check. While these arguments of the late 1960s and early '70s had, and still have, great explanatory power, the American Bicentennial also provided an occasion to consider the more marginal players – women as well as tradesmen, laborers, free blacks, and slaves – who joined the struggle for independence.[2]

This approach entailed looking beyond the experience of elite white men, but it also required that historians revise their long-held assumption that the American Revolution was not meaningful for women. In challenging this view, Mary Beth Norton, Linda K. Kerber, Nancy Cott, Laurel Ulrich, and others showed that, although women were not legally enfranchised in the post-war era, they exhibited more confidence in their abilities, found moral, intellectual, and financial support through informal female networks, and enjoyed greater status and influence within the family and society.[3] While these historians acknowledged the possibility that women's status might have improved as a result of their visible war-time activity (as in other wars, women capably filled traditionally male jobs and ran the farms and businesses left behind when men joined the fight), their scholarship has been primarily interested in tracing out how the political and social ideals of the Revolutionary era might have prompted a fundamental reconsideration of women's capacities and social status.

In tandem with the historiographic work of the 1970s, feminist literary critics began to recover women's writing long overlooked in the formation of a mostly male literary canon. Because the study of American literature had been organized around a literary historical trajectory running from New England Puritanism to Emersonian Romanticism, women of the Revolutionary and early national era had been doubly neglected by a critical establishment that dismissed many American eighteenth-century writers as poor imitators of their British counterparts. Moreover, since its beginnings in the 1940s, the formal study of American literature had been shaped by a desire to locate a uniquely American experience in the literature of the past, and this motivation had often led to the exclusion of writings that did not explicitly engage questions of national identity. Like many writings of the Revolutionary era, women's diaries and letters often record the emotionally fraught process through which the colonies severed ties with England, not to mention the horror with which Loyalists and pacifists witnessed a civil war. Such writings also often reflect women's priorities as household mistresses rather than participants in nation-formation. In the last three decades, critical self-awareness about the ties between national identity and canon-formation has helped address this problem of exclusion, and, in addition, the recent global turn of American literary studies reminds us that the nation-state is not the only frame with which to view early American literature. Elizabeth Maddock Dillon has gone so far as to argue that "colonial, post-colonial, and transnational geopolitical formations" even inform the rhetorical construction of privacy and domesticity ("Secret History," 79).

In one of the first considerations of women's Revolutionary-era writings, published on the occasion of the Bicentennial, Wendy Martin argued for the literary and historical significance of the diaries and letters in which women recorded their "private experience" of the war; but, while Martin productively called attention to a neglected body of life-writing, she remained uninterested in women's novels, which she described as "Richardsonian" (that is, derivative) and "pious, sentimental stories" ("Women and the American Revolution," 323). Just a decade later, however, Cathy N. Davidson's field-changing *Revolution and the Word* (1986) detailed the political dimensions of the early republican novel. Although Davidson did not focus exclusively on women writers, she looked particularly at the way in which these novels addressed women and other marginalized groups overlooked in the framing of the Constitution.[4] The novels of the 1790s remain central to the study of early American women's writings, and the fiction of Hannah Webster Foster, Susanna Haswell Rowson, Tabitha Tenney, Rebecca Rush, and S. B. K. Wood are now granted aesthetic complexity and political engagement.

Taken together, Martin's and Davidson's work implies a distinction between the private world of life-writing and the public world of print. More recent studies, however, have enriched and complicated our understanding of what constituted a public literary arena. Scholarship on early republican drama, for example, has shown that some women earned publicity through performance rather than print, and that the theater was "one of a very few actual public spaces," according to Amelia Howe Kritzer, "in which the active participation of women was considered legitimate (at least, by those who considered the theater itself legitimate)" ("Playing with Republican

Motherhood," 151). Mercy Otis Warren's *Ladies of Castille* (1784), for example, uses the story of the resistance to imperial government in sixteenth-century Spain to showcase women's capacities to support the cause of popular revolt. In Susanna Rowson's *Slaves in Algiers* (1794), the enslavement of women by Barbary pirates is an occasion to decry gender inequality and celebrate the new United States as a country in which white women are rewarded for virtue. Sarah Pogson's *The Female Enthusiast* (1807), a dramatic rendering of Charlotte Corday's assassination of Jacobin Jean-Paul Marat, contemplates the rewards and risks of female political activism.

Another alternative to print was found in the coterie culture of white, urban intellectual women. Carla Mulford, David Shields, Susan Stabile, Catherine La Courreye Blecki, and Karin Wulf have shown how highly educated women circulated poetry and essays in manuscript form within small circles of like-minded men and women. Through an analysis of their material practices, for example, Stabile explains how women used authorship, compilation, and archiving to memorialize their lives and art. Whereas Stabile focuses on the creation and preservation of artifacts removed from civic life, Shields considers the quasi-public coteries in which women exchanged political ideas and commentary; of particular interest to feminist scholars is Shields's discussion of the tea table as crucial to the emerging public presence of eighteenth-century elite women. By uncovering these alternatives to print media, this scholarship has made available new methods and materials for the study of eighteenth-century female discourse.

In detailing how American women writers imagined their role in the Revolution and the Revolution's legacy for future generations of women, this essay turns to writings of a number of genres, print and otherwise. The rubric "Revolutionary" designates not simply a time period (roughly the last three decades of the eighteenth century) but a set of concerns specifically related to civic identity. While it is important to recognize that they are not wholly representative of the female Revolutionary experience, this essay concentrates on women writers who contemplated their place in civil society outside the home or the relevance of their home lives for the national polity. In doing so these writers anticipated the main discourses of women's advocacy – as well as the challenges and contradictions of those discourses – in the century to follow.

I turn first to women's writings about the war, including first-person accounts, propaganda, and post-war reflections on the nation's origins. Because women were assumed constitutionally incapable of meeting the physical demands of military service (although, in actuality, women did occasionally enlist disguised as men), these writers revise the classical republican model of male citizenship grounded in military service. To do so, they high-light alternative forms of female civic engagement as well as the limitations of military virtues. As I will show, whereas these patriotic writings stressed the obligations of citizenship, other writings highlighted the limited reach of the Revolution and called for women's inclusion in the national polity by extending the political language of emancipation to their own conditions. The multivalent term "liberty," which was an essential part of both republican and liberal vocabularies, took on new meaning in white women's writings about the constraints of a patriarchal society as well as in the writings by and about enslaved black women. Finally, I will consider how women's writing took inspiration from liberalism's emphasis on self-assertion and the pursuit of happiness but also understood that such pursuits threatened republican virtues of self-restraint, fiscal responsibility, and sexual chastity.

Women, war, civic engagement

Revolutionary-era women's writings – diaries, journals, letters, testimonies, tracts, and propaganda – are limited in scope, as they derive largely from white, literate, Anglo-American women. Nevertheless, they reveal much about the varied ways that such women experienced the war *as* women, and they express a spectrum of emotions – from apathy to dread to fervor – and political opinions. These writings indicate how women envisioned specifically female modes of civic engagement in the absence of formal means of political participation and in a republican culture that equated male military service with civic virtue.

Such civic engagement involved activities of citizenship *outside* those of political parties, elected office, governmental bodies, and other exclusively male political arenas.[5] Through these activities women forged connections to a national community, which they were obliged to serve but also from which they felt themselves entitled to special protections in return. It is worth noting that this civil arena overlaps with, but is not synonymous with, the public as it has been variously defined. Civil society does not, like the public sphere Jürgen Habermas describes, define itself in opposition to the state apparatus or necessarily see itself as a check on the excesses of state power. Nor is civil society synonymous with the public world of commerce, in opposition to which a private, woman's sphere was increasingly demarcated (if not in fact, at least rhetorically and ideologically) during the market revolution of the early nineteenth century. Because Revolutionary-era women often deployed domestic skills for national causes, "civic" is a more appropriate term in that it does not belong exclusively to a putative private or public realm.[6]

As one might expect, civic-minded sentiments fill the letters of Mercy Otis Warren, Abigail Adams, and other women closely connected to the elite inner circle of Revolutionary statesmen. Through hearsay and newspaper reports, such women kept abreast of military maneuvers and fervently discussed politics with their male and female correspondents. Warren, whose brother, James Otis, was one of the most important political thinkers in the early years of colonial agitation, looked forward to the day when America would take "her rank among the nations" ("Letter to Dorothy Quincy Hancock," 73). The dramatist and propagandist hoped the new republic might "come as near the point of perfection, as the condition of humanity will admit" ("Letter to John Adams," 70). Although Adams frequently lamented that all "domestic pleasures and enjoyments" were absorbed in her husband's duties as diplomat and statesman, she steadfastly supported independence and felt confident that God would "not forsake a people engaged in so righteous a cause" ("Letter to John Adams," May 7, 1776, 167; "Letter to John Adams," June 17, 1776, 187).

A number of women's writings record direct involvement with the war effort. Although Sarah Osborn, the wife of an army commissary guard, traveled with the troops at her husband's insistence, she came to take pride in supplying food and water to soldiers under fire. In her petition for a widow's military pension – the only known account of a woman who traveled with the army – she recalls boasting to George Washington that she never feared the bullets because they "would not cheat the gallows."[7] To suggest her service would be worthy of hanging renders it an act of political dissent rather than wifely accommodation (Osborn, *The Revolution Remembered*, 245). Another patriot, the New Jersey artist Patience Lovell Wright, lived in London and socialized at the court of King George III but quickly embraced the colonial cause at the outbreak of war and even served as a spy for the rebels. Writing to her friend, Benjamin Franklin, she declared her "honest Intention to serve [her] Contry" and her conviction that she could be serviceable "to Bring on the Glorious Cause of sivil and religious Liberty" ("Letter to Benjamin Franklin," 190). And Betsy Foote, a young woman from a Connecticut farming family, took pride in the fact that her cloth spinning would aid the colonial boycott of British manufactured goods. Coining a new adjective, she wrote in her diary that she "felt Nationly" when such domestic work took on political significance (quoted in Norton, *Liberty's Daughters*, 169).

Many women's first-person accounts avoid discussions of the war's underlying causes or political stakes, either because their religious principles

condemned the conflict or because they felt ill-equipped as women to formu-
late an opinion on war or to follow its complex military maneuvers.[8] Whatever
their political investments, however, women's life-writings all attest to the
havoc that war wrought on women's lives – through the sacrifice of husbands
and sons, inflated prices and the expropriation of goods, epidemics, the ran-
sacking or seizure of their homes, assault and even rape by soldiers, and the
enforced quartering of troops under their roofs. For those women who did
enter public conversation as propagandists and commentators, it is precisely
this trauma that justifies their decision to weigh in on the war. Writing to
Hannah Winthrop in 1774, Warren claimed that the war's risks to domestic
security qualified her for the task of political commentary:

> When I took up my pen I determined to leave the field of politicks to those
> whose proper business it is to speculate and to act at this important crisis; but
> the occurrences that have lately taken place are so alarming and the subject so
> interwoven with the enjoyments of social and domestic life as to command
> the attention of the mother and the wife who before the contest is decided
> may be called to weep over the names of her beloved sons, slain by the
> same sword that deprived of life their intrepid and heroic Father. ("Letter to
> H. F. T. Winthrop," 27)

While Warren does not challenge the distinction between women's and men's
spheres, she does indicate that the exigencies of war require more flexible
thinking with respect to gender and political opinion-making. As Angela
Vietto aptly puts it, Warren often "self-consciously announces the existence
of a discursive boundary just before crossing it" (*Women and Authorship*, 54).
Here the transgression is justified because women are participants in the
Revolution by virtue of their duty to protect the safety of home and family. If
"domestic life" and the "field of politicks" are different arenas of activity, they
are nevertheless "interwoven."

According to patriot propaganda, women experienced the trauma of war as
they might in all wars, but as American patriots they considered themselves
particularly vulnerable to a rapacious British military that did not respect
private property rights or codes of civil conduct. Esther de Berdt Reed, a
Pennsylvania woman who founded a women's organization to raise money
for soldiers, reasoned that the Continental Army was not simply protecting
women from British advances but securing a domestic peace that was under
threat. "We know that at a distance from the theatre of war, if we enjoy any
tranquillity, it is the fruit of your watchings, your labours, your dangers," she
declared in an address to soldiers in a 1780 broadside (*Sentiments of an American*

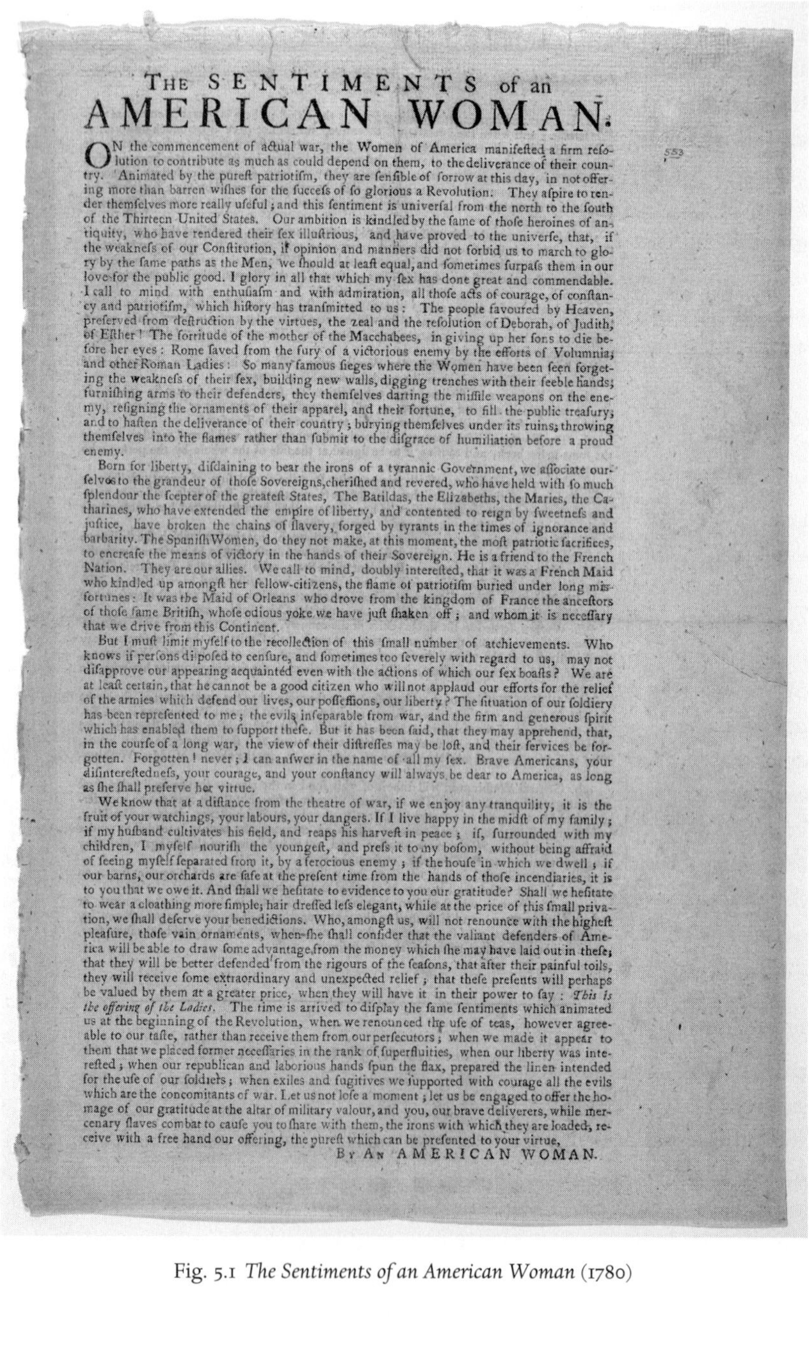

THE SENTIMENTS of an
AMERICAN WOMAN.

ON the commencement of actual war, the Women of America manifested a firm resolution to contribute as much as could depend on them, to the deliverance of their country. Animated by the purest patriotism, they are sensible of sorrow at this day, in not offering more than barren wishes for the success of so glorious a Revolution. They aspire to render themselves more really useful; and this sentiment is universal from the north to the south of the Thirteen United States. Our ambition is kindled by the fame of those heroines of antiquity, who have rendered their sex illustrious, and have proved to the universe, that, if the weakness of our Constitution, if opinion and manners did not forbid us to march to glory by the same paths as the Men, we should at least equal, and sometimes surpass them in our love for the public good. I glory in all that which my sex has done great and commendable. I call to mind with enthusiasm and with admiration, all those acts of courage, of constancy and patriotism, which history has transmitted to us: The people favoured by Heaven, preserved from destruction by the virtues, the zeal and the resolution of Deborah, of Judith, of Esther! The fortitude of the mother of the Macchabees, in giving up her sons to die before her eyes: Rome saved from the fury of a victorious enemy by the efforts of Volumnia, and other Roman Ladies: So many famous sieges where the Women have been seen forgetting the weakness of their sex, building new walls, digging trenches with their feeble hands; furnishing arms to their defenders, they themselves darting the missile weapons on the enemy, resigning the ornaments of their apparel, and their fortune, to fill the public treasury, and to hasten the deliverance of their country; burying themselves under its ruins; throwing themselves into the flames rather than submit to the disgrace of humiliation before a proud enemy.

Born for liberty, disdaining to bear the irons of a tyrannic Government, we associate ourselves to the grandeur of those Sovereigns, cherished and revered, who have held with so much splendour the scepter of the greatest States, The Batildas, the Elizabeths, the Maries, the Catharines, who have extended the empire of liberty, and contented to reign by sweetness and justice, have broken the chains of slavery, forged by tyrants in the times of ignorance and barbarity. The Spanish Women, do they not make, at this moment, the most patriotic sacrifices, to encrease the means of victory in the hands of their Sovereign. He is a friend to the French Nation. They are our allies. We call to mind, doubly interested, that it was a French Maid who kindled up amongst her fellow-citizens, the flame of patriotism buried under long misfortunes: It was the Maid of Orleans who drove from the kingdom of France the ancestors of those same British, whose odious yoke we have just shaken off; and whom it is necessary that we drive from this Continent.

But I must limit myself to the recollection of this small number of atchievements. Who knows if persons disposed to censure, and sometimes too severely with regard to us, may not disapprove our appearing acquainted even with the actions of which our sex boasts? We are at least certain, that he cannot be a good citizen who will not applaud our efforts for the relief of the armies which defend our lives, our possessions, our liberty? The situation of our soldiery has been represented to me; the evils inseparable from war, and the firm and generous spirit which has enabled them to support these. But it has been said, that they may apprehend, that, in the course of a long war, the view of their distresses may be lost, and their services be forgotten. Forgotten! never; I can answer in the name of all my sex. Brave Americans, your disinterestedness, your courage, and your constancy will always be dear to America, as long as she shall preserve her virtue.

We know that at a distance from the theatre of war, if we enjoy any tranquility, it is the fruit of your watchings, your labours, your dangers. If I live happy in the midst of my family; if my husband cultivates his field, and reaps his harvest in peace; if, surrounded with my children, I myself nourish the youngest, and press it to my bosom, without being affraid of seeing myself separated from it, by a ferocious enemy; if the house in which we dwell; if our barns, our orchards are safe at the present time from the hands of those incendiaries, it is to you that we owe it. And shall we hesitate to evidence to you our gratitude? Shall we hesitate to wear a cloathing more simple; hair dressed less elegant, while at the price of this small privation, we shall deserve your benedictions. Who, amongst us, will not renounce with the highest pleasure, those vain ornaments, when she shall consider that the valiant defenders of America will be able to draw some advantage from the money which she may have laid out in these; that they will be better defended from the rigours of the seasons, that after their painful toils, they will receive some extraordinary and unexpected relief; that these presents will perhaps be valued by them at a greater price, when they will have it in their power to say: *This is the offering of the Ladies*. The time is arrived to display the same sentiments which animated us at the beginning of the Revolution, when we renounced the use of teas, however agreeable to our taste, rather than receive them from our persecutors; when we made it appear to them that we placed former necessaries in the rank of superfluities, when our liberty was interested; when our republican and laborious hands spun the flax, prepared the linen intended for the use of our soldiers; when exiles and fugitives we supported with courage all the evils which are the concomitants of war. Let us not lose a moment; let us be engaged to offer the homage of our gratitude at the altar of military valour, and you, our brave deliverers, while mercenary slaves combat to cause you to share with them, the irons with which they are loaded, receive with a free hand our offering, the purest which can be presented to your virtue,

BY AN AMERICAN WOMAN.

Fig. 5.1 *The Sentiments of an American Woman* (1780)

Woman). The murder of Jane McCrea was a particularly gruesome reminder that women were not untouched by war. (Figs. 5.1 and 5.2.) When McCrea was scalped and killed by British-allied Iroquois on her way to see her fiancé at Fort Edwards in July 1777, British General John Burgoyne's refusal to punish the alleged attackers fueled patriot propaganda aimed at exposing the barbarity of the British military. Newspaper reports created a national myth around McCrea's murder, even going so far as to claim she was slain in her bridal gown on the day she was to wed. Tales of the incident, which played heavily to fears of Iroquois savagery, allegedly galvanized support among colonists who had previously remained neutral in the conflict. When, in what seemed a miracle, the Continental Army defeated Burgoyne at the Battle of Saratoga in October, McCrea was declared a martyr, having spilled her blood in order to inspire the victory.[9]

For two writers of the Hudson Valley, Ann Eliza Bleecker and her daughter, Margaretta Bleecker Faugères, McCrea's sad tale meshed with their own family tragedy. In 1777, Bleecker, with four-year-old Margaretta and a baby daughter, Abella, fled Burgoyne's advance, and while seeking refuge, lost Abella to dysentery. McCrea and Abella both haunt Bleecker's *History of Maria Kittle*, an epistolary novel that draws on the captivity narrative tradition to tell the story of a resilient woman who endures kidnapping and the murder of her children at the hands of Iroquois.[10] In "The Hudson," Faugères's 1793 poem about the war in upstate New York, McCrea's murder stands in for the death of Abella. As McCrea's silver-haired father bathes "his mangled daughter with his tears," the poem makes clear that Revolutionary sacrifices were not limited to the battlefield. Moreover, through such a tragedy Faugères has become personally knowledgeable about the war and is authorized to record the history of the region: "Say, shall a *Female* string her trembling lyre," she asks rhetorically in the opening stanza in an apostrophe to the river, "And to thy praise devote th'advent'rous song?" ("The Hudson," 38, lines 9–10).

When women expressed political opinions or undertook service in support of the war, they did not simply indicate their stake in the outcome but also worked to revise the classical republican notion of a masculine civic personality grounded in military service. With the rare exception of Deborah Gannett and other cross-dressing women who secretly fought with the Continental Army, women did not take up arms, and they readily assumed themselves incapable of meeting the physical demands of military service. Nevertheless, they challenged the traditional assumption that women are non-political beings, emphasizing that patriotism might take non-military forms. Reed maintained that if constitutional weakness, as well as current "opinion and

Fig. 5.2 "Murder of Miss Jane McCrea," Currier and Ives (1846)

manners," forbade women to "march to glory by the same paths as the Men," they would "at least equal, and sometimes surpass them in [their] love for the public good" (*Sentiments*). In the words of her biographer, Judith Sargent Murray felt that "women's attributes – their morality, their intellectual strength, their 'tender passions'" – were devalued and ignored in times of war, and she insisted that the willingness to sacrifice one's life in combat was "only one – and not necessarily the most important – measure of patriotism" (Skemp, *First Lady of Letters*, 92). Whereas "the road of preferment is thrown open" to men and "glory crowns the military hero," Murray lamented, the female sex could only enjoy "but *secondary* or *reflected* fame." Murray felt military vocation too emasculating for women – at the "shrine of patriotism," she wrote, Spartan women had "immolated nature" (*The Gleaner*, 452–453, 706) – but she urged her readers to recognize the non-military contributions of women.[11]

Women's writing was instrumental in galvanizing support for the war and highlighting women's capacities for political organization and activism. A poem attributed to the Philadelphia poet Hannah Griffitts and published in *The Pennsylvania Chronicle* in 1768 called on women to boycott tea in protest at Grenville's Tea Acts, boldly claiming that the feminine exercise of purchasing power might compensate for the lackluster support provided by the Sons of Liberty:

> If the Sons (so degenerate) the Blessing despise,
> Let the Daughters of Liberty, nobly arise,
> And tho' we've no Voice, but a negative here.
> The use of the Taxables, let us forebear,
> (Then Merchants import till yr. Stores are all full
> May the Buyers be few & yr. Traffick be dull.)
> Stand firmly resolved & bid Grenville to see
> That rather than Freedom, we'll part with our Tea . . .
> ("The female Patriots," 172)

Reversing the common stereotype of women as impulsive consumers, this poem calls on women to make civic-minded sacrifice. Within the poem, women are voiceless but express their patriotism through deeds. The poem itself is a means of expression, and the coterie in which this poem circulated was a forum in which women could debate ideas. As Andrew Burstein has written, the tea table fostered a form of "political criticism that classical republicanism had failed to describe" ("The Political Character of Sympathy," 619). The boycott of tea by tea-drinking elite women was an especially daring, even scandalous, form of activism. For this reason, the so-called Edenton Tea Party of 1774, in which fifty-one women in Edenton, North Carolina, banded together and signed a pledge to boycott tea, was widely satirized in British newspapers.[12]

In addition to highlighting non-military forms of civic service, women writers also emphasized that their feminine sensibilities might advantageously soften the military virtues associated with the ancient republics. In describing the sacrifices that women make when husbands and sons go off to war, for example, Warren wondered, "Who in these modern days, has arrived at such a degree of Roman virtue as not to grudge the costly sacrifice?" ("Letter to H. F. T. Winthrop," 27). In Warren's view, the fact that a woman is loathe to sacrifice a son or husband does not diminish her patriotic devotion, but, instead, modernizes the military virtues and reflects a mode of feeling that is indispensible to the social formation of the new nation.[13] Although this feminized sympathy was associated *in practice* with the male civic personality and the political oratory of men, women writers could lay special claim to it in order to emphasize their own political relevance.

Mourning the daughter she lost during Burgoyne's advance, for example, Bleecker finds that maternal grief ennobles her patriotic sentiments. In the poem "On Reading Dryden's Virgil," Bleecker likens her melancholy to that of the hero of Rome's national epic:

> Now cease these tears, lay gentle *Vigil* [*Virgil*] by,
> Let *recent* sorrows dim the pausing eye:
> Shall *Æneas* for lost *Creusa* mourn,
> And tears be wanting on *Abella's* urn?
> Like him I lost my fair one in my flight
> From cruel foes—and in the dead of night.
> Shall he lament the fall of *Illion's* tow'rs,
> And *we* not mourn the sudden ruin of *our's*?
> ("On Reading Dryden's Virgil," 230, lines 1–8)

Aeneas's departure from the ravaged city of Troy in Book Two of *The Aeneid* elicits painful memories of Bleecker's flight from Tomhanick, New York. But she finds consolation in the fact that Aeneas, too, could not help mourning the lost city and the wife who was sacrificed so he might found Rome. If Aeneas, the exemplar of duty, or *pietas*, mourns the familial sacrifice, then Bleecker's grief is warranted as well. Such mourning does not minimize her patriotism.[14] In ways relevant here, Burstein writes that such emotion made sense "as a category of political thought" in part, because the "revolutionary generation recognized the limitations of the classical model," particularly in historiography in which the values of ancient Greece and Rome might overshadow the "present, viscerally felt recollection" ("The Political Character of Sympathy,"

608). By focusing on the bereaved figure of Aeneas, Bleecker can recollect the war in classical terms but still express maternal grief.

Women writers of the Revolutionary era often felt justified to write about the war because their selves, families, and homes were at stake – and also because, despite their inability to bear arms, they felt themselves valuable contributors to the cause of independence and a positive influence on the nation's political culture. This sense of agency brought with it a sense of entitlement, and women writers were compelled to consider whether the rhetoric in which colonial agitators had framed their grievances carried implications for their own social standing. Turning to Revolutionary rhetoric, they found a language of liberty that in its rhetorical instability would prove both illusory and empowering.

Women and the language of liberty

As a gauge of women's changing self-perceptions, the literature of the Revolutionary era often works through indirection. Although the treatment of gender is conspicuously absent in female-authored histories of the war, for example, their focus on the male worlds of political negotiation and military conflict should not lead us to believe that historians like Mercy Otis Warren, Sarah Wentworth Morton, and Hannah Adams did not appreciate the event's potential to challenge the status quo. As Nina Baym observes, to write history was itself a bold claim to "know and opine on the world outside the home, as well as to circulate their knowledge and opinions among the public" (*Work of History*, 1).

The question of the Revolution's legacy for women is taken up directly, albeit with scathing irony, in the writing of wives, widows, and unmarried women protesting legal inequalities. When Mary Willing Byrd, a Virginia widow, was accused of treason and stripped of her property, her petition to governors Thomas Nelson and Thomas Jefferson drew from the vocabulary of colonial legislative representation to stress the injustice. "I have paid my taxes and have not been Personally, or Virtually represented," she noted. In the years leading up to the Revolutionary war, colonial officials had complained that the "virtual representation" of colonial interests in British parliament was not sufficient and that colonists were entitled to the direct or "personal representation" of elected representatives from the colonies themselves. Under the laws of coverture, married women's interests were said to be represented by their husbands, but, as a widow, Byrd could neither represent her own interests nor rely on a husband to do so. "This cannot be called *Liberty*" she remarked pointedly ("Letter to Thomas Nelson," 704 "Letter to Thomas Jefferson," 692).

Byrd invokes the term "liberty" in the conventional sense in which it was used by many colonial agitators who insisted that taxation without representation was an infringement on their rights as English subjects. But, as Edward Countryman notes in his study of Revolutionary rhetoric, this term meant many things to eighteenth-century Americans: in a Christian sense, for example, it referred to the freedom from sin; in a Lockean sense, it designated an individual's freedom from the encroachment of others on his private property; in a classical republican sense, it referred to, among other things, a financially independent person's freedom from debt or private interests. Moreover, in the years leading up to the Revolution, a term that was already multivalent began to take on additional meanings for disenfranchised groups: artisans, mechanics, and urban workingmen who did not own property, as well as women and enslaved blacks. For these marginalized groups, liberty meant the freedom to pursue personal autonomy and various kinds of personal gratifications, including spiritual elevation, education, economic reward, and corporeal freedom. The language of liberty was essential to both classical republican and liberal ideologies, but the pursuit of personal autonomy and gratification was associated with the latter – and, in fact, often considered antithetical to the former's emphasis on suppressing private interests.

Whether this language of liberty was determinative or illustrative – that is, whether it shaped women's sense of themselves or just provided the language to express ideas formed elsewhere – is not clear (and, in fact, a similar question has governed the study of the political rhetoric during the years of colonial agitation and war). What is clear, however, is that the Revolution is the crucial point of reference for women questioning the status quo in a patriarchal society.[15] In "Lines, written by a Lady who was questioned respecting her inclination to marry," an anonymous poem published in *The Massachusetts Magazine* in 1794, the speaker finds in colonial rebellion a powerful model and vocabulary for rejecting the institution of marriage. The poem's speaker compares the marital state to slavery, much in the way Revolutionary propagandists had likened colonial subjection to bondage: "No ties shall perplex me, no fetters shall bind, / That innocent freedom that dwells in my mind. / At liberty's spring such draughts I've imbib'd / That I hate all the doctrines of wedlock prescrib'd." Comparing her heart to a "haughty republic," she suggests that recent political events – through which she has tasted freedom at "liberty's spring" – have led her to embrace the single life ("Lines, written by a lady," 3–6, 9).

In examining how women writers invoked the term "liberty," one must bear in mind that the Revolution promoted a language of slavery and liberation that was already central to a number of colonial and early national discourses. Such language, for example, was part of the Protestant understanding of spiritual redemption as a moment of emancipation from the bonds of sin; for this reason, the language of liberation is essential to a number of prominent literary genres, such as the Indian captivity narrative and the spiritual autobiography, which were governed by Protestant concerns with spiritual regeneration. Moreover, as Countryman notes, even in a Revolutionary context, the language of liberty came to appeal to many sectors of the population, including Loyalists. Hence, it is not surprising that when Loyalist Grace Galloway's husband fled to England at the outbreak of war, this unhappily married woman used language strikingly similar to the poet of *The Massachusetts Magazine*. Despite being impoverished and separated from her beloved daughter, Galloway wrote, "I am happy & the Liberty of doing as I please Makes even poverty more agreeable than any time I ever spent since I married . . . I want not to be kept so like a slave as he always Made Me in preventing every wish of my heart" ("Diary of Grace Galloway," 59–60). One would be hard pressed to say Galloway, who abhorred the Revolution, was radicalized by national independence; rather, it is more accurate to say that she drew on a language of liberation that was popularized by the colonial conflict but also flexible enough to accommodate various meanings.

For those women who did support the war, nevertheless, the Revolution crucially furnished both inspiration and vocabulary. In a letter written during the invasion of Charlestown, for example, Eliza Yonge Wilkinson wittily suggests a link between the political liberties cherished by patriots and a woman's freedom of thought. While singing the praises of colonists' efforts to secure America as a "land of Liberty," Wilkinson introduces a telling "digression" about female intellect. After a perfunctory apology for meddling "with political matters," she declares, "I won't have it thought, that because we are the weaker sex as to *bodily* strength . . . we are capable of nothing more than minding the dairy, visiting the poultry-house, and all such domestic concerns." Wilkinson protests that men do not allow women the "liberty of thought" so that their minds "can soar aloft," forming "conceptions of things of higher nature" (*Letters of Eliza Wilkinson*, 60–1). Wilkinson's dismissal of this protest as a "digression" is coy or perhaps even sarcastic, and the implicit connection between the two themes – the war for independence and the woman's intellectual freedom – is reinforced by the repetition of the word "liberty."

Like Judith Sargent Murray and other Revolutionary-era women's advocates, Wilkinson follows Descartes in claiming that, though women and men are bodily different, the intellect is without gender.[16] This claim complemented the Enlightenment tenet that humans were universally capable of reason and lent crucial support to the reform of female education in the new republic. Accordingly, Murray reasoned that the political revolution would be followed by a revolution within female academies. Congratulating her "fair country-women" on the "happy revolution which the few past years has made in their favour," Murray rejoiced that women, whose "principle attainment" had previously been the "use of the needle," were now encouraged to devote at least some of their time "to studies of a more elevated and elevating nature" (*The Gleaner*, 702–3).

Wilkinson and Murray could focus on intellectual freedom because their physical freedom was secured. For the black woman protesting her own enslavement, the war for independence brought to mind liberty of a different kind. In an alleged petition to the Massachusetts legislature, published in *The Massachusetts Magazine* in 1787, a slave known only as "Belinda" requested that she be reimbursed for fifty years of forced labor and invoked the Revolution in support of her argument: the war, she insisted, had been a struggle for the "preservation of that freedom, which the Almighty Father intended for *all* the human race" ("Petition of an African slave," 539, my emphasis). Of course, there is no way to know the extent to which the testimony is the slavewoman's own – or that of a transcriber, magazine editor, or abolitionist fabricator – but the document shows unequivocally the tendency of antislavery discourse to apply the struggle for colonial rights to the plight of the slave. In its reference to Lockean notions of *universal* rights to freedom and private property, moreover, the petition is a remarkable claim that a black woman be duly compensated for her labor.

Belinda's petition extends the logic of colonial rebellion to the condition of the slave. But those opposed to slavery also invoked rebellion ironically to emphasize the nation's hypocrisy. Writing to her husband, Abigail Adams pointed out the contradictions of a slaveholding nation waging a war for liberty: "I wish most sincerely there was not a slave in the province. It always appeared a most iniquitous scheme to me – to fight ourselves for what we are daily robbing and plundering from those who have as good a right to freedom as we have" ("Letter to John Adams," September 24, 1774, 39). During the years of colonial agitation leading up to the war, Phillis Wheatley also noted the irony of the slaveholder's complaint about the abridgement of his liberties. In a well-known 1774 letter to Samson Occam (subsequently published in two newspapers), Wheatley wrote of the "strange Absurdity of their Conduct whose Words and Actions are so diametrically opposite," noting that the "Cry for Liberty" was commensurate with the "Exercise of oppressive Power over others" ("Letter to Samson Occam," 153).

Wheatley speaks here of civil freedom, a condition that is distinct from the spiritual freedom she believes can only come with Christian conversion. In Wheatley's view, it is possible to be enslaved physically and emancipated spiritually, and for this reason some literary critics have dismissed Wheatley as accommodating white, slaveholding culture.[17] But Wheatley also maintained that "civil and religious Liberty" were "inseparably united," and she seems to have cared deeply about the "vindication" of the civil "natural Rights" violated with the physical bondage of Africans ("Letter to Samson Occam," 153). Although sympathetic to the cause of national independence, her poetry reminds her readers that the infringement of colonial rights constitutes slavery only in the metaphoric sense of the term. In "To the Right Honourable WILLIAM, Earl of DARTMOUTH," Wheatley begins the poem with a condemnation of the abridgement of colonial liberties, but, as part of this condemnation, claims she is peculiarly poised to value freedom because she has endured corporeal bondage: "And can I then but pray," she writes, "Others may never feel tyrannic sway?" ("To the Right Honourable WILLIAM," 40, lines 30–1). As Vincent Carretta observes, Wheatley suggests here that the "reality of chattel slavery" has been "trivialized by the political metaphor" (Wheatley, *Complete Writings*, xxviii). But Wheatley also understood that such rhetoric, however metaphoric and detached from the reality of physical enslavement, offered a vocabulary that might, in a different context, be literalized in order to endorse an abolitionist cause never intended by the architects of colonial rebellion.

Sacrifice and self-assertion: woman in the new republic

Although women patriots challenged the republican enshrinement of military virtues, they did not dismiss its values altogether but, instead, worked to revise them. Many women writers – particularly those who had received some classical education – shared the republican fear that the new nation might, like ancient Rome, succumb to corruption; in addition, they endorsed a feminized version of classical republicanism, which detached civic virtue from male military prowess and economic independence and realigned it with female moral and sexual propriety.[18] It is worth considering, then, how women's writing exposed and addressed the tensions between the republican language of sacrifice and the liberal language of self-assertion.

Members of the post-Revolutionary generation worried about the suscep-
tibility of the new republic to corruption but also acknowledged that the
protection of national integrity could not be left to governmental institutions;
therefore, churches, schools, and families were entrusted with the task. In this
way, white women were to play a crucial role in training sons for citizenship
and fostering patriotism in their husbands. An excerpt from Algernon Sidney's *Maxims*, reprinted in *The United States Magazine*, made this very point:
"It is of the utmost importance, that the women should be well instructed
in the principles of liberty in a republic. Some of the first patriots of antient
times, were formed by their mothers" ("Maxims for Republics," 19). In Linda
K. Kerber's words, this American version of republican virtue "included –
hesitantly – a role for women" ("The Republican Mother," 43). But, while
this form of guardianship granted women a measure of political significance
and prompted improvements in their education, it linked that significance to
their containment within the home. In making female sexual chastity crucial
to national welfare, it also justified a sexual double standard.

Given this rhetoric of feminized republican virtue, what were women to
make of the liberal rhetoric that emphasized self-assertion and the pursuit of
liberty and property (as well as the vaguely defined goal of "happiness")? In the
post-war era, particularly after the publication of Mary Wollstonecraft's 1792
Vindication of the Rights of Woman, women's complaints about legal inequalities, the deficiencies of their education, and the constraints of marriage took
on added force as they appropriated the language of "natural rights," made
famous in Thomas Paine's *Rights of Man* and Thomas Jefferson's *Declaration of
Independence*. The Lockean notion of universal human rights, which Jefferson
extended to property-less white men (but denied to women and blacks), was
not wholly incompatible with the notion of republican motherhood and wifehood. Indeed, as Rosemarie Zagarri notes in her study of women in the early
republic, even an ardent women's advocate like Wollstonecraft focused on
rights that she believed would ultimately help women become better wives
and mothers. There were, nevertheless, undeniable tensions between these
two ideological strains, and some women were better positioned to reconcile
those tensions than others.

Consider, for example, two complaints lodged by widows against the Continental Congress, both of which passionately invoke the republican language
of civic virtue while also claiming the right to pursue wealth through financial
investment. In a remarkably bold pamphlet entitled *The Case of the Whigs Who
Loaned their Money on the Public Faith* (1783), Philadelphian Letitia Cunningham
invokes female sexual virtue in criticizing the Continental Congress for not

paying out interest on the governmental bonds she had purchased in support of the war effort. In likening a bankrupt republic among solvent nations to a "common prostitute" among "chaste and reputable matrons," Cunningham stresses the dire consequences of fiscal irresponsibility for a young republic (*The Case of the Whigs*, 26). The reference to the prostitute implies its opposite: the virtuous republican woman, with whom Cunningham is herself aligned. But Cunningham's stake in the nation's future is civic-minded *and* entrepreneurial, and the fact that she has pursued earnings by investing in war bonds does not negate her civic-mindedness. A similar assumption marks the deposition of Rachel Wells, a less educated but nevertheless eloquent New Jersey widow who petitioned the Continental Congress in 1786 when the state of New Jersey refused to pay interest on her state bonds. Wells's deposition demands the interest due her, but it also demands that her loan be recognized as civic service comparable to that of the soldier or statesman: although she could not fight, she sacrificed financially to support the nation and did "as much to Carrey on the Warr as maney that Sett now at ye healm of government" (Wells, "Petition"). In instances such as these, the potential tensions between civic virtue and the private pursuit of wealth are reconciled by the mechanisms of public finance, through which private investors serve self and nation simultaneously.[19] As Cunningham's language makes clear, republicanism's wariness of corruptive fiscal irresponsibility actually underscores her demand that the interest due to her be paid in a timely manner.

But if we literalize Cunningham's metaphoric prostitute – and talk of sexual chastity rather than republican solvency (and this is precisely the kind of corruption implied by the ideology of republican motherhood) – self-assertion and civic virtue are not so easily reconciled. In Hannah Webster Foster's *The Coquette* (1797), one of the most popular novels of the early republic, Eliza Wharton's pursuit of gratification simply will not mesh with republican standards of female virtue. At one level, the novel is a cautionary tale about the dangers of female materialism, self-interest, and seduction. A striking passage early in the novel, in which Eliza comments on the death of the man to whom her father had promised her hand in marriage, presents her pursuit of pleasure in political terms that would seem to condemn her:

> You, madam, who have known my heart, are sensible, that had the Almighty spared life, in a certain instance, I must have sacrificed my own happiness, or incurred their censure. I am young, gay, volatile. A melancholy event has lately extricated me from those shackles, which parental authority had

imposed on my mind. Let me then enjoy that freedom which I so highly prize. Let me have opportunity, unbiassed by opinion, to gratify my natural disposition in a participation of those pleasures which my youth and innocence afford. (*The Coquette*, 13)

Eliza invokes the language of slavery and filial emancipation common in Revolutionary rhetoric, but this rhetoric does not ennoble her aspirations; indeed, having tasted freedom with the death of her fiancé, she forsakes the very notion of duty and sacrifice and embraces a morally suspect pursuit of pleasure. But, at the same time, *The Coquette* is also a sympathetic portrait of a young woman admirable in her desire for autonomy and intellectual equality. When she declares, "I despise those contracted ideas which confine virtue to a cell. I have no notion of becoming a recluse" (*The Coquette*, 13), it is possible to read those lines as a valid criticism of classical republican notions of feminine virtue.

Accordingly, the criticism of this novel has divided along these lines. Some readers have taken at face value the warnings issued to Eliza about the dangers of excessive freedom. Nina Baym describes Eliza as a "spoiled and artful flirt who refuses good marriage offers" (*Woman's Fiction*, 51), and, according to Michael T. Gilmore, Eliza's death in childbirth at a roadside tavern is punishment for autonomy and pleasure-seeking (her family is to blame, too, for having not provided sufficient moral guidance). Most recently, Laura H. Korobkin argues that the novel condemns Eliza's pursuit of aristocratic luxury and confirms middle-class values of restraint and moderation.[20] While these readings would see Foster's tale as a more conventional republican novel in which coquettes symbolize some of the greatest threats to the young nation – irrationality, pleasure-seeking, consumerism – other readers find that Foster rewrites the story of the real-life Elizabeth Whitman with much more critical distance. Following the initial lead of Davidson, who claimed the novel exposes the "fundamental injustices" of patriarchal culture (*Revolution and the Word*, 144), Carroll Smith-Rosenberg, Gillian Brown, Elizabeth Maddock Dillon, Karen Weyler and others have seen Eliza as a woman who falls prey to the inherent contradictions of post-Revolutionary culture. Specifically, Eliza's decision-making is governed by political, social, and legal ideals – the pursuit of happiness, female independence, contractual consent, civil sociability, companionate marriage – that turn out to be illusory or impracticable.

Most critics agree that Foster's novel is concerned with the politics of female sexuality, but they disagree on how Eliza is finally to be judged.[21] In part, these varying interpretations are a function of the novel's formal qualities. The epistolary form and the lack of a governing narrative make it difficult to locate the moral center of the novel, particularly because some of the most significant statements about female virtue come from characters who are themselves morally suspect.[22] Another reason may be that the book is symptomatic of a culture that was itself contradictory, upholding republican values of self-restraint and sacrifice even as it felt the lure of liberal promises of personal gratification. In a relatively early reading of the novel, Kristie Hamilton argued something similar when she noted that the urban settings of the novel exposed Eliza to market culture, creating a conflict between "republican virtue and the appeal of materialism" ("An Assault on the Will," 140). So, too, did Elizabeth Barnes in claiming that the novel highlights the way sentimental culture asserts the "reality of self-determination" while yoking it to "standard norms of behavior" (*States of Sympathy*, 71).

This kind of vexed quest for self-determination is a consistent theme in many women's novels of the new United States. As Marion L. Rust notes in her assessment of *Charlotte Temple* (1791), the heroine's tragedy dramatizes the "difficulty in making contemporary theories of self-enfranchisement function in accord with equally powerful ideologies of womanhood" ("What's Wrong with *Charlotte Temple*?" 499).[23] Even the thoroughly unlikeable villain of Rebecca Rush's *Kelroy* (1812) can be seen as dramatizing the limitations of female self-liberation. In this novel, Mrs. Hammond, a widow who is impoverished by her late husband's imprudent financial speculations, seeks independence by undertaking debt to buy luxury goods in the hopes that a façade of wealth will attract a wealthy husband for her youngest daughter. Her predicament reveals how elusive independence can be in a volatile economy but also how much more so for a woman who must rely on the whims of the marriage market. Mrs. Hammond, whose cruel machinations obstruct her daughter's marriage to the man she loves, represents female ambition at its most pernicious, but ultimately this novel questions how fully women can act on any form of ambition. That Mrs. Hammond attains financial security by winning a lottery only suggests that self-determination is a function of chance.

Like many Revolutionary-era women's writing, Foster's novel contemplates whether language can be instrumental in effecting social change. In one of the most memorable lines of *The Coquette*, Lucy Freeman, in an attempt to assure her friend that a respectable marriage would not "abridge" her "privileges," writes to Eliza, "You are indeed very tenacious of your freedom, as you call it; but that is a play about words" (*The Coquette*, 30–31). While Lucy suggests that Eliza has invested the word "freedom" with undue relevance, a "play about words" is precisely what Phillis Wheatley identifies as a source of power for the disenfranchised. In a manuscript verse excised from her *Poems on Various Subjects*, Wheatley, writing of colonial rebellion, declares, "Thy Power, O Liberty, makes strong the weak / And (wond'rous instinct) Ethiopians speak / Sometimes by Simile, a victory's won" ("America," 75, lines 5–7). Perhaps the victors are the colonial agitators who deploy similes of filial relation and slavery, but perhaps victory might also belong to the African who, inspired to speak, challenges chattel slavery through a logical extension of the rhetoric of colonial protest.

Language, in other words, can make promises that do not extend to women or are not easily reconciled with prevailing moral standards, but that insta-bility, as Wheatley suggests, is promising in its own way. Accordingly, in 1848 first-wave feminists at Seneca Falls expressed their grievances through a statement modeled on Thomas Jefferson's *Declaration of Independence*. With irony, these women used the rhetoric of liberty and happiness to highlight the unfinished work of a Revolution that did not enfranchise women or change their legal status, but they also took that language at face value, deriving inspiration from the rebellion of an earlier generation and applying its logic to their own conditions.

Notes

1. See Endy, "Just War, Holy War," for an overview of the various scholarly interpreta-tions of Protestantism's role in the Revolutionary experience in New England colonies.
2. See, for example, Young, *The American Revolution*.
3. Norton argued that the 1780s and '90s "witnessed changes in women's private lives – in familial organization, personal aspirations, self-assessments" (*Liberty's Daughters*, xix). Kerber's *Women of the Republic* theorized the ideology of "republican motherhood," according to which white middle-class and elite women were made guardians of national virtue. Cott's *The Bonds of Womanhood* and Ulrich's "'Daughters of Liberty'" showed how white women of New England were empowered through, respectively, female networks and evangelical Christianity.
4. Consider that for the first two decades of the journal's existence, *Early American Literature* published regular articles on Anne Bradstreet, Phillis Wheatley, and Mary Rowlandson but only two essays on a novel by a woman: one article was a study of Sukey Vickery by Davidson; the other was a reading of *The Coquette* by Walter P. Wenska, Jr., who described Foster's novel as the exception to the rule when it came to the "weepy-creepy school of early American fiction" ("*The Coquette* and the American Dream of Freedom," 243).
5. For a useful discussion of the difference between civic society and the political arena, see Kelley, *Learning to Stand and Speak*, 5–10.
6. The dichotomy of "private" and "public," while indispensible to feminist literary stud-ies, has been heavily scrutinized. Critics have paid particular attention to the question of

women's exclusion from the rational-critical debate of the disembodied public sphere of print described by Warner's influential account of the American "republic of letters." Dillon's and Burgett's works have significantly revised Warner's argument. In *The Gender of Freedom*, Dillon concludes that privacy – what she takes to be the salient concern of modern liberalism – is, in fact, a precondition for one's participation in the public sphere. In *Sentimental Bodies*, Burgett argues that sentimentalism maintained the political dimension of the body, hence resisting its privatization.

7. See Berkin, *Revolutionary Mothers*, for accounts of these female camp followers as well as other non-elite women who supported the cause of national independence.

8. Relating details of the Battle of Brandywine, for example, Elizabeth Drinker indicated that her familial obligations made it difficult to follow the events of war: "This has been a day of Great Confusion to many in this City; which I have in great measure been kept out of by my constant attension on my sick Child" (*The Diary of Elizabeth Drinker*, 62). A young Jemima Condict noted with detachment the looming conflict when she wrote, "It seems we have troublesome times a coming, for there is great disturbance abroad in the earth and they say it is tea that caused it" (Harrison, "Excerpts from the Diary of Jemima Condict Harrison," 36). Professing an aversion to politics, an even younger Sarah Wister focused her entries largely on her prospects for romance with local soldiers. Although she recognized the horrors of war and the loneliness that women feel when soldiers enlist, her diary alludes to the conflict as an adventure that elicits dreams of "bayonets and swords, sashes, guns, and epaulets" (Wister, *The Journal and Occasional Writings of Sarah Wister*, 45).

9. For a discussion of the national myth surrounding McCrea, see Engels and Goodale, "'Our Battle Cry Will Be: Remember Jenny McCrea!'"

10. For an analysis of women's experience of the Revolutionary War in Bleecker's and Faguères's writings, see Sharon Harris, *Executing Race*.

11. See Vietto, *Women and Authorship in Revolutionary America*, for an analysis of the woman warrior in Revolutionary-era writings and the relation of that figure to discussions of the physical differences between men and women.

12. This poem, attributed to Griffitts, was copied into Martha Milcah Moore's commonplace book. Karin A. Wulf, co-editor of this commonplace book, writes that, while the collection contains political poems and draws from the tradition of salon culture, its greatest concern is friendship and humility in the face of God. Wulf concludes that it was largely shaped by the "Quaker traditions that encouraged literacy for women and created a circulating library of Quaker materials" (Blecki and Wulf, *Martha Milcah Moore's Book*, 25).

13. Burstein ("The Political Character of Sympathy") has emphasized the role of sympathy in softening the rigidity of Roman military virtues as well as facilitating collective identification among citizens and legislative representation.

14. Indeed, as Ellison has written, such "patriotic elegies" give mourning "historical meaning," positing the nation as a "figure of memory and compensation" in the absence of the cherished child ("Race and Sensibility in the Early Republic," 454, 449, 461).

15. Bernard Bailyn's *Ideological Origins of the American Revolution*, for example, argued that Revolutionary pamphlets were not mere verbal rationalizations of class warfare or economic self-interest (as Charles Beard and other "progressive" historians had argued)

but, rather, the expression of political views that structured the very way pamphleteers understood their position within the empire.

16. See Baym, "Between Enlightenment and Victorian," for a discussion of the influence in early America of Cartesian theories of genderless intellect.

17. For some examples of scholarship that uphold Wheatley's racial conscience and solidarity, see Grimsted, "Anglo-American Racism," and Erkkila, "Phillis Wheatley and the Black American Revolution."

18. See Bloch, "The Gendered Meanings of Virtue in Revolutionary America," for a discussion of this transformation.

19. This was the premise behind Alexander Hamilton's national banking scheme, which aimed to harness private entrepreneurial energies for public good. Hamilton's detractors saw nothing virtuous in the scheme and argued, in fact, that it represented the ultimate form of corruption.

20. Evans ("Rakes, Coquettes and Republican Patriarchs") argues that Rowson's and Foster's novels did not simply voice middle-class values but actually helped create them in a new nation in which class structure was still in flux.

21. Burgett (*Sentimental Bodies*) is a notable exception. He argues that the novel privatizes and effectively de-politicizes sex and the body, rendering the text far less subversive than other critics have assumed.

22. Jennifer Harris also argues that Foster deploys the epistolary form to "obscure her authorial hand" and avoid charges that she had first-hand knowledge of the kind of sexual impropriety depicted in the book. The epistolary form, Harris argues, led Foster's readers to believe that the novel was, in fact, "renderings" of the real-life Elizabeth Whitman's letters "to which readers assumed she had access" ("Writing Vice," 369).

23. Other scholars have argued similarly that Eliza's demise is the result of such contradictions but they find her predicament not uniquely feminine so much as symptomatic of post-Revolutionary culture. Robert A. Ferguson's *Reading the Early Republic*, for example, aligns Eliza with an entire generation that felt ambivalent about the place of ambition in republican culture.

Works cited

Adams, Abigail. "Letter to John Adams." September 24, 1774. In *The Letters of John and Abigail Adams*. Ed. Frank Shuffleton. New York: Penguin, 2004.

"Letter to John Adams." May 7, 1776. In *The Letters of John and Abigail Adams*.

"Letter to John Adams." June 17, 1776. In *The Letters of John and Abigail Adams*.

Bailyn, Bernard. *The Ideological Origins of the American Revolution*. Cambridge, MA: Harvard University Press, 1967.

Barnes, Elizabeth. *States of Sympathy: Seduction and Democracy in the American Novel*. New York: Columbia University Press, 1997.

Baym, Nina. *American Women Writers and the Work of History, 1790–1860*. New Brunswick: Rutgers University Press, 1995.

"Between Enlightenment and Victorian: Toward a Narrative of American Women Writers Writing History." *Critical Inquiry* 18.1 (Fall 1991): 22–41.

Woman's Fiction: A Guide to Novels by and about Women in America, 1820–1870. 2nd edn. Urbana: University of Illinois Press, 1993.

Berkin, Carol. *Revolutionary Mothers: Women in the Struggle for America's Independence.* New York: Knopf, 2005.

Blecki, Catherine La Courreye and Karin A. Wulf, eds. *Martha Milcah Moore's Book: A Commonplace Book from Revolutionary America.* University Park: Pennsylvania State University Press, 1997.

Bleecker, Ann Eliza. "On Reading Dryden's Virgil." In *The Posthumous Works of Ann Eliza Bleecker in Prose and Verse.* Ed. Margaretta Bleecker Faugères. New York, 1793.

Bloch, Ruth H. "The Gendered Meanings of Virtue in Revolutionary America." *Signs* 13.1 (1987): 37–58.

Brown, Gillian. "Consent, Coquetry, and Consequences." *American Literary History* 9.4 (Winter 1997): 625–52.

Burgett, Bruce. *Sentimental Bodies: Sex, Gender, and Citizenship in the Early Republic.* Princeton: Princeton University Press, 1998.

Burstein, Andrew. "The Political Character of Sympathy." *Journal of the Early Republic* 21.4 (Winter 2001): 601–32.

Byrd, Mary Willing. "Letter to Thomas Jefferson." In *Jefferson Papers.* Vol. 4. Ed. Julian P. Boyd *et al.* Princeton: Princeton University Press, 1951.

"Letter to Thomas Nelson." In *Jefferson Papers.* Vol. 5. Ed. Julian P. Boyd *et al.* Princeton: Princeton University Press, 1952.

Cott, Nancy. *The Bonds of Womanhood: "Woman's Sphere" in New England, 1780–1835.* New Haven: Yale University Press, 1977.

Countryman, Edward. "'To Secure the Blessings of Liberty': Language, the Revolution, and American Capitalism." In *Beyond the American Revolution: Explorations in the History of American Radicalism.* Ed. Alfred F. Young. DeKalb: Northern Illinois University Press, 1993.

Cunningham, Letita. *The Case of the Whigs Who Loaned their Money on the Public Faith.* Philadelphia, 1783.

Davidson, Cathy N. *Revolution and the Word: The Rise of the Novel in America.* Oxford: Oxford University Press, 1986.

Dillon, Elizabeth Maddock. *The Gender of Freedom: Fictions of Liberalism and the Literary Public Sphere.* Stanford: Stanford University Press, 2004.

"The Secret History of the Early American Novel: Leonora Sansay and Revolution in Saint Domingue." *Novel: A Forum on Fiction* 40.1–2 (Fall 2006 / Spring 2007): 77–103.

Drinker, Elizabeth. *The Diary of Elizabeth Drinker: The Life Cycle of an Eighteenth-Century Woman.* Ed. Elaine Forman Crane. Philadelphia: University of Pennsylvania Press, 2010.

Ellison, Julie. "Race and Sensibility in the Early Republic: Ann Eliza Bleecker and Sarah Wentworth." *American Literature* 65.3 (September 1993): 445–74.

Endy, Jr., Melvin B. "Just War, Holy War, and Millennialism in Revolutionary America." *William and Mary Quarterly.* 3rd series. 42.1 (January 1985): 3–25.

Engels, Jeremy and Greg Goodale. "'Our Battle Cry Will Be: Remember Jenny McCrea!': A Précis on the Rhetoric of Revenge." *American Quarterly* 61.1 (March 2009): 93–112.

Erkkila, Betsy. "Phillis Wheatley and the Black American Revolution." In *Feminist Interventions in Early American Studies*. Ed. Mary Carruth. Tuscaloosa: University of Alabama Press, 2006.

Evans, Gareth. "Rakes, Coquettes and Republican Patriarchs: Class, Gender and Nation in Early American Sentimental Fiction." *Canadian Review of American Studies* 25.3 (1995): 41–62.

Faugères, Margaretta Bleecker. "The Hudson." In *Women's Early American Historical Narratives*. Ed. Sharon M. Harris. New York: Penguin, 2003.

Ferguson, Robert A. *Reading the Early Republic*. Cambridge, MA: Harvard University Press, 2006.

Foote, Betsy. "Diary." October 23, 1775. Connecticut Historical Society, Hartford. Quoted in Norton, *Liberty's Daughters*.

Foster, Hannah W. *The Coquette*. Ed. Cathy N. Davidson. Oxford: Oxford University Press, 1987.

Galloway, Grace Growden and Raymond C. Werner. "Diary of Grace Growden Galloway." *The Pennsylvania Magazine of History and Biography*. 55.1 (1931): 32–94.

Gilmore, Michael T. "The Literature of the Revolutionary and Early National Periods." In *The Cambridge History of American Literature*. Ed. Sacvan Bercovitch *et al.* Vol. 1: *1590–1820*. Cambridge: Cambridge University Press, 1997.

Griffitts, Hannah. "The female Patriots. Address'd to the Daughters of Liberty in America." 1768. In Blecki and Wulf, *Martha Milcah Moore's Book*.

Grimsted, David. "Anglo-American Racism and Phillis Wheatley's 'Sable Veil,' 'Length'ned Chain,' and 'Knitted Heart.'" In Hoffman and Albert, *Women in the Age of the American Revolution*.

Hamilton, Kristie. "An Assault on the Will: Republican Virtue and the City in Hannah Webster Foster's *The Coquette*." *Early American Literature* 24.2 (1989): 135–51.

Harris, Jennifer. "Writing Vice: Hannah Webster Foster and *The Coquette*." *Canadian Review of American Studies* 39.4 (2009): 363–81.

Harris, Sharon M. *Executing Race: Early American Women's Narratives of Race, Society, and the Law*. Columbus: Ohio State University Press, 2005.

Harrison, Jemima Condict. "Excerpts from the Diary of Jemima Condict Harrison." In *Weathering the Storm: Women of the American Revolution*. Ed. Elizabeth Evans. New York: Paragon, 1975.

Hoffman, Ron and Peter J. Albert. *Women in the Age of the American Revolution*. Charlottesville: University of Virginia Press, 1989.

Kelley, Mary. *Learning to Stand and Speak: Women, Education, and Public Life in America's Republic*. Chapel Hill: University of North Carolina Press, 2006.

Kerber, Linda K. "The Republican Mother: Women and the Enlightenment: An American Perspective." In *Toward an Intellectual History of Women: Essays by Linda K. Kerber*. Chapel Hill: University of North Carolina Press, 1997.

  Women of the Republic: Intellect and Ideology in Revolutionary America. Chapel Hill: University of North Carolina Press, 1980.

Korobkin, Laura H. "'Can Your Volatile Daughter Ever Acquire Your Wisdom?': Luxury and False Ideals in *The Coquette*." *Early American Literature* 41.1 (2006): 79–107.

Kritzer, Amelia Howe. "Playing with Republican Motherhood: Self-Representation in Plays by Susanna Haswell Rowson and Judith Sargent Murray." *Early American Literature* 31.2 (1996): 150–66.

Lee, Richard Henry. "Letter to Hannah Corbin Lee." March 17, 1778. In *The Letters of Richard Henry Lee*. Vol. 1. Ed. James C. Ballagh. New York: Macmillan, 1911.

Lewis, Jan. "The Republican Wife: Virtue and Seduction in the Early Republic." *William and Mary Quarterly* 44.4 (October 1987): 689–721.

"Lines, written by a Lady who was questioned respecting her inclination to marry." *The Massachusetts Magazine*. September 1794.

Martin, Wendy. "Women and the American Revolution." *Early American Literature* 11.3 (Winter 1976/7): 322–35.

"Maxims for Republics." *United States Magazine; a Repository of History, Politics and Literature*. January 1779.

Mulford, Carla, ed. *Only for the Eye of a Friend: The Poems of Annis Boudinot Stockton*. Charlottesville: University of Virginia Press, 1995.

Murray, Judith Sargent. *The Gleaner*. 1798. Introduction by Nina Baym. Schenectady, NY: Union College Press, 1992.

Norton, Mary Beth. *Liberty's Daughters: The Revolutionary Experience of American Women, 1750–1800*. Ithaca: Cornell University Press, 1980.

Osborn, Sarah. "Deposition, 1837." In *The Revolution Remembered: Eyewitness Accounts of the War for Independence*. Ed. John C. Dann. Chicago: University of Chicago Press, 1980.

"Petition of an African slave, to the legislature of Massachusetts" By Belinda. *The American Museum, or Repository of Ancient and Modern fugitive Pieces, Prose and Poetical* 1.6 (June 1787): 537–9.

Pogson, Sarah. *The Female Enthusiast: A Tragedy in Five Acts. Charleston, 1807. Plays by Early American Women, 1775–1850*. Ed. Amelia Howe Kritzer. Ann Arbor: University of Michigan Press, 1995.

Reed, Esther de Berdt. *The Sentiments of an American Woman*. Philadelphia, 1780.

Rowson, Susanna. *Charlotte Temple*. Ed. Cathy N. Davidson. Oxford: Oxford University Press, 1987.

Rush, Rebecca. *Kelroy: A Novel*. Ed. Dana D. Nelson. New York: Oxford University Press, 1992.

Rust, Marion L. "What's Wrong with *Charlotte Temple*?" In *Charlotte Temple*. Ed. Marion L. Rust. New York: W. W. Norton, 2011.

Shields, David S. *Civil Tongues and Polite Letters in British America*. Chapel Hill: University of North Carolina Press, 1997.

Skemp, Sheila L. *First Lady of Letters: Judith Sargent Murray and the Struggle for Female Independence*. Philadelphia: University of Pennsylvania Press, 2009.

Smith-Rosenberg, Carroll. "Domesticating 'Virtue': Coquettes and Revolutionaries in Young America." In *Literature and the Body: Essays on Populations and Persons*. Ed. Elaine Scarry. Baltimore: The Johns Hopkins University Press, 1988.

Stabile, Susan M. *Memory's Daughters: The Material Culture of Remembrance in Eighteenth-Century America*. Ithaca: Cornell University Press, 2004.

Ulrich, Laurel Thatcher. "'Daughters of Liberty': Religious Women in Revolutionary New England." In Hoffman and Albert, *Women in the Age of the American Revolution*.

Vietto, Angela. *Women and Authorship in Revolutionary America.* Aldershot: Ashgate, 2005.

Warner, Michael. *Letters of the Republic: Publication and the Public Sphere in Eighteenth-Century America.* Cambridge, MA: Harvard University Press, 1992.

Warren, Mercy Otis. "Letter to Hannah Feyerwether Tolman Winthrop," 1774. In *Mercy Otis Warren: Selected Letters.* Ed. Jeffrey H. Richards and Sharon M. Harris. Athens, GA: University of Georgia Press, 2009.

"Letter to John Adams," March 1776. In *Mercy Otis Warren: Selected Letters.*

"Letter to Dorothy Quincy Hancock," April 1776. In *Mercy Otis Warren: Selected Letters.*

Wells, Rachel. "Petition to Congress May 18, 1786." Microfilm Papers of the Continental Congress National Archives, Washington, DC, microfilm M247, roll 56, item 42, vol. 8, 354–5. Excerpt in *Women's America: Refocusing the Past.* 5th edn. Ed. Linda K. Kerber and Jane Sherron De Hart. Oxford: Oxford University Press, 2000.

Wenska, Jr. Walter P. "*The Coquette* and the American Dream of Freedom." *Early American Literature* 12.3 (Winter 1977/8): 243–55.

Weyler, Karen. "Marriage, Coverture, and the Companionate Ideal in *The Coquette* and *Dorval.*" *Legacy: A Journal of American Women Writers* 26.1 (2009): 1–25.

Wheatley, Phillis. "America." 1768. In *Complete Writings.* Ed. with an introduction, Vincent Carretta. New York: Penguin, 2001.

"To the Right Honourable WILLIAM, Earl of DARTMOUTH, His Majesty's Principal Secretary of State for North-America, &c." In *Complete Writings.*

"Letter to Samson Occom," February 11, 1774. In *Complete Writings.*

Wilkinson, Eliza Yonge. *Letters of Eliza Wilkinson, During the Invasion and Possession of Charlestown, S.C. by the British in the Revolutionary War.* Ed. Caroline Gilman. New York: Samuel Colman, 1839.

Wilson, Joan Hoff. "The Illusion of Change: Women and the American Revolution." In Young, *The American Revolution.*

Wister, Sarah. *The Journal and Occasional Writings of Sarah Wister.* Ed. Kathryn Zabelle Derounian. Cranbury, NJ: Associated University Press, 1987.

Wright, Patience Lovell. "Letter to Benjamin Franklin." March 29, 1778. *The Papers of Benjamin Franklin,* Vol. 26.

Young, Alfred F., ed. *The American Revolution: Explorations in the History of American Radicalism.* De Kalb: Northern Illinois University Press, 1976.

Zagarri, Rosemarie. *Revolutionary Backlash: Women and Politics in the Early American Republic.* Philadelphia: University of Pennsylvania Press, 2007.

6

Women writers and the early US novel

ANDY DOOLEN

Recovery efforts

Not too long ago, the early American novel was one of the most maligned genres in US literary history. Regardless of the author's gender, the novel was viewed as unstructured and stylistically flawed, overloaded with silly plot contrivances, and hopelessly didactic and sentimental. In *The Columbia History of the American Novel* (1991), Jeffrey Rubin-Dorsky went so far as to insist that the genre did not really exist. Impeded by political duties and uncertainties, an overweening sense of propriety, and scarce cultural resources, the post-revolutionary generation failed to develop an "authentic American language" for "literary purposes" (Elliott *et al.*, *The Columbia History*, 11). As such, the novels of Charles Brockden Brown, William Hill Brown, Royall Tyler, and Hugh Henry Brackenridge apparently lacked the telling signs of a distinctive national voice. "While America may have proclaimed its political independence from Britain," Rubin-Dorsky concluded, "it nevertheless remained culturally subservient well into the nineteenth century" (11). In US literary history, women novelists were even further marginalized than their neglected and misunderstood male counterparts. Their novels were viewed as inferior copies of English and European models. Relegated to the domestic sphere in the prevailing critical paradigm, women novelists were not taken seriously. They were widely assumed to be disengaged from the public endeavor of constructing national identity.

Rubin-Dorsky's essay managed to sum up conventional thinking about the unremarkable origins of the American novel precisely at the moment when feminist critics were challenging the exclusion of women writers from the US literary canon. The intellectual roots of this recovery project were traceable back to the 1960s and '70s, when feminist scholars had subjected gender ideology – specifically, the doctrine of separate spheres – to a withering critique. They depicted the private sphere as an oppressive domain, restricting female agency and subjecting women to the vagaries of patriarchal authority. While women were not entirely powerless in the home, their political agency was limited to playing the roles of republican mothers and wives, cultivating patriotic virtues and practices in their children and husbands. By the 1980s and '90s, the feminist critique of separate spheres ideology had unearthed more complex forms of female subjectivity and community in the early US. Patriarchal power and gender ideology might have barred women from participating in the outside world of history and politics, but women writers constantly transgressed the boundary by interjecting their voices into public life. In Nina Baym's meticulous accounting, women published an extraordinary amount of materials that contributed to guiding the course of national affairs: fiction, religious tracts, conversion narratives, children's books, local-color stories, plays, poetry, translations, biographies, histories, textbooks, family memoirs, cookbooks, advice books for boys and girls, editorials, manifestoes, and essays (*American Women Writers*, 3). Reflecting on this impressive yield, Baym concluded that women always were conspicuously present in public life. Contrary to the theories of Habermas and his followers, the "absence of women [from the public sphere] was not mandated by the theory so much as it is a typical artifact of male myopia" (6). Correcting this defective vision, innovative scholars such as Baym, Cathy Davidson, Susan Harris, Annette Kolodny, Jan Lewis, Mary Kelley, and Jane Tompkins depicted American women writers as deeply imbricated in public life and in the production and dissemination of print culture.

This collective rethinking of gender politics reformed our understanding of the early US novel by fostering awareness of the major contributions of women authors like Susanna Rowson, Hannah Foster, Tabitha Tenney, Rebecca Rush, Lydia Maria Child, and Catharine Maria Sedgwick. Since many of their novels had fallen out of print long ago, these authors received little or no scholarly attention until feminist literary critics and editors began recovering and reintroducing their major works.[1] But the old stereotypes long deployed to belittle women writers – they wrote purely sentimental, didactic, and domestic fictions – remained intact. Twentieth-century literary criticism discouraged the study of women novelists, equating their sentimentalism with flawed and inferior literary practices, and misunderstanding their affective styles and themes, which were often clever and nuanced vehicles for social and political critique. Thus, the recovery project fixed its attention on redefining sentimentalism. Feminist literary critics faced an enormous obstacle – a prejudice Baym defines as the "longstanding invidious association of sentimentalism with foolish femininity" ("Women's Novels and Women's

Minds," 1). Yet critics such as Nancy Armstrong, Lora Romero, June Howard, Shirley Samuels, and Dana Nelson, among others, conceptualized a more complex, even subversive, literary discourse.

Developing techniques for interpreting the dynamic between literature and culture, critics demonstrated how women writers revised the dominant modes of the early American novel – sentimental, gothic, picaresque, and historical. Once dismissed as escapist romances by earlier generations of critics, sentimental fictions provided insight into how interpersonal feelings and relationships contributed to the formation of republican society. Gothic fictions were no longer copies of a superior foreign standard but expressions of the anxious feelings of American women denied civil rights and protections in the early US. Women novelists altered the conventional picaresque narrative, as Davidson observed, by introducing a female protagonist whose wanderings into regions of "hard-core realism" provided a stark picture of women's lives (*Revolution and the Word*, 190). For Joanne Dobson, *literary sentimentalism* signified a distinctive literary practice – "not a discreet literary category, as the term 'genre' might imply, but rather an imaginative orientation characterized by certain themes, stylistic features, and figurative conventions" ("Reclaiming Sentimental Literature," 266). Based in emotional and philosophical connection and commitment, literary sentimentalism focused on the experiences of personal relationships, family life, community, social responsibility and other relational modes of being. In literary sentimentalism, the principle theme is not the individual's flight from society but rather the desire for sympathy, connection, and gender solidarity. As a result, recovery scholarship not only exposed the masculinist underpinnings of the US literary canon: through critical soundings of the distinctive voices of female and male novelists alike, the recovery project also belied the truism about the feeble origins of the American novel. Rather than a barren stretch preceding the mid-century American Renaissance, the pre-1830s is now recognized as a period of distinctive literary vision.

Finally, critics have been able to delineate how literary sentimentalism also engages in cultural critique. Sentimental writing was a powerful medium for weighing in on all controversial aspects of nation-building, such as racial and social inequality, educational reform, women's rights, and the necessities for living a virtuous republican life. As a result, the old canard about sentimentalism has been debunked. The affective idiom certainly was concerned with domestic matters, but it circulated between overlapping private and public spheres and its politics were wildly unpredictable. The circulation of empathetic feeling in any given novel could be the author's conservative ploy to reinforce the hierarchies of bourgeois culture or an act of resistance against the racial and sexual violence intrinsic to the formation of those hierarchies or a hazy reflection of the novelist's personal struggles and ambivalences. Dobson points out the vast range of expression that defines sentimental writings, which "can be profound or simple, authentic or spurious, sincere or exploitative, strong or weak, radical or conservative, personally empowering or restrictive, well or poorly written; they can adhere to the strictest limitations of stereotype and formula, or they can elaborate the possibilities of convention in significant ways" ("Reclaiming Sentimental Literature," 266).

This more sophisticated understanding of literary sentimentalism, exemplified in the recent work of Elizabeth Barnes, Bruce Burgett, Nelson, Samuels, and Julia Stern, among others has transformed the study of early US literature and culture. Once the lonesome territory of Charles Brockden Brown and James Fenimore Cooper, the history of the early American novel, over the last thirty years, has expanded to include formerly excluded women authors. Yet the recovery project, which some critics rightly celebrate, remains in its early stages; one can only guess which authors and novels will be securely implanted in the literary canon in 2050. On several occasions, Judith Fetterley has cautioned literary critics about the provisional status of women writers ("Commentary," 604). While generous institutional support and visionary editors and scholars have spurred the beginning of the recovery project, the problem of doing literary history, of tearing down and reconstructing the dominant critical paradigms, remains the greatest challenge. Fifteen years ago, few critics would have predicted that Rebecca Rush's *Kelroy*, viewed as a success story of feminist recovery efforts – a novel Davidson first praised as "one of the best written in America before 1820" (*Revolution and the Word*, 234) – would, once again, fall out of print. At the same time, few could have foreseen, with any accuracy, how innovative spatial approaches to American women's fiction would serve as a catalyst for the latest stage of the recovery project. I will consider this development in the final section.

Quixotic fictions

First published in 1794, and having over 200 editions, Susanna Rowson's *Charlotte Temple: A Tale of Truth* was one of the most popular novels in early America (Cowie, *The Rise of the American Novel*, 15). The British-born Rowson was a well-known educator, a prolific writer of fiction, drama, and pedagogical texts, and the founder of a school. Equal parts thrilling entertainment and moral pedagogy, *Charlotte Temple* is a seduction novel that centers on the trials of its heroine, Charlotte, seduced and abandoned during the American Revolution. In London, a British army officer, Montraville, sweeps Charlotte off her feet and promises to marry her once they reach America, but soon after their arrival in New York, he dumps her for a more advantageous match. Montraville intends to support Charlotte, but a second villain, Belcour, never delivers the money to her in a cruel attempt to seduce her and destroy Montraville. Pregnant Charlotte finally flees the city, finding sanctuary in a poor servant's room in the outskirts, but she dies soon after giving birth to a daughter. In British and American sentimental writing, the marriage-seduction plot mapped out the moral hazards awaiting impressionable young women on both sides of the Atlantic; consequently, twentieth-century literary criticism focused on how the heroine's failure to curb personal and sexual impulses hastens her fall from grace. Contesting this view, Davidson, Jan Lewis, and other feminist critics claimed that tales of seduction were also deeply invested in the construction of national identity. They argued that the marriage-seduction plot was rooted in the specific, chaotic conditions of the post-revolutionary nation. The immensely popular seduction narratives are to be read "not merely as cautionary tales addressed to young women but also as political tracts in which men and women explored the possibilities for virtue in a corrupt world" (Lewis, "The Republican Wife," 716).

This notion of a *politicized* sentimental narrative flew in the face of the stereotypical view of the private, parlor concerns of women's fiction. While the tragedy of Charlotte Temple warned female readers about the dangers of immoral conduct, the novel could also be read as national allegory. The rhetoric of marriage and seduction resonated with the republican view that the family – husband, wife, and children bound together in an affectionate, virtuous, and voluntary union – represented the ideal model for American progress. Such a union gave women a definite political role in society, which explains why the tragedy of Charlotte Temple might have captivated a national audience: Rowson had spun an alarming tale about a blossoming republican family threatened by the enemies of innocence and virtue.

Recent criticism has delved even deeper into the operation of sympathy and sentiment in *Charlotte Temple*. For Julia Stern, Rowson probes the philosophical equation between theatricality and duplicitous social and political relations. While the moral implications of the stage made eighteenth-century philosophers like Rousseau and Diderot uneasy about the artifices inherent in political life, Rowson, having considerable experience in the theater as an actor and playwright, took a less pessimistic position on the issue of theatricality. More modern novelist and philosopher than schoolmarm in Stern's analysis, Rowson composed a novel that consists of multiple narrative frames that mediated her anxieties about the theatrical attitudes and conventions that structure society. While aware of the delusions fostered by theatrical spectacle, Rowson also envisioned her novel as an alternative site of democratic communion "through which the witnesses to the heroine's plight – characters within the novel and readers outside of it – come together and function as a unified corporate body" (Stern, *The Plight of Feeling*, 33). The loss of Charlotte instigates a shared experience of melancholy and compassion, passing from the rational and healing voice of the maternal narrator to sympathetic readers. Ultimately, the novel, and the reading experience it inspires, indicts the "unfinished business" of post-revolutionary society, making *Charlotte Temple* an "extraordinary artifact" of gendered cultural power (33).

A second novel of seduction and abandonment, *The Coquette*, has been essential to the ongoing reassessment of literary sentimentalism. Hannah Foster's 1797 epistolary novel relates the downfall of Eliza Wharton, a clergyman's daughter who spurned the marriage proposals of two reputable preachers, fell victim to her desires, and eventually died during childbirth. Based on the scandalous real-life tragedy of Elizabeth Whitman, whose mysterious death in Boston was condemned in the national press, and whose immoral life was allegorized in sermons and editorials, Foster's novel delved into the affective experiences of the heroine and discovered a nation in crisis (Davidson, *Revolution and the Word*, 111). Foster wished to send a message about the dangers of female autonomy and the need for more vigilant parenting, but the novel also reflected her ambivalence about the role of women in republican society. While the family might be the exemplary model for an enlightened republican nation, marriage did not always provide women with an ideal sanctuary. As Davidson observes, the origin of Eliza Wharton's suffering was traceable back to her narrow escape from a loveless marriage years earlier. Unwilling to surrender her independence and friendships by accepting a poor match, the thirty-seven-year-old heroine still hopes for an egalitarian partnership that obeys the just dictates of head and heart. For Davidson, it was a dilemma shared by many women in early America. Eliza Wharton hoped for an ideal partnership of equals, for a union, but she is never given anything more than a "difficult choice between unsatisfactory alternatives, a common quandary in early American sentimental novels, and a dilemma, no doubt, faced by many American young women" (143). Resistance was especially dangerous, since prolonging independence left women like Eliza increasingly susceptible to the advances of rogues like Sanford and Boyer, the two men trying to seduce her. By depicting the harsh realities and restrictions experienced by many women, Foster's novel exposed how republican attitudes toward gender "all but smothered the cry for female equality, a cry faintly but subversively heard" in *The Coquette* (135).

Recent criticism does not view the fictional rendering of social injustice as synonymous with resistance but adopts a more cautious, and often ambivalent, approach to the meaning of Eliza Wharton's downfall. On their surface, sentimental narratives were supposed to be morally instructive, to teach readers about proper conduct, but Kristin Boudreau argues that this axiom conceals a "perverse connection between sympathy and pleasure" (*Sympathy in American Literature*, 43). The danger was that the reader would identify with the wrong sentiments and experience some degree of pleasure in the spectacle of Eliza Wharton's suffering. For Boudreau, *The Coquette* presents multiple gazes, different kinds of watching, but the novel is unable to delineate clearly between the good sort of watching that leads to social reform and virtuous conduct and the bad kind of watching that leads to selfish pleasure and amusement. The novel thus calls into question, perhaps against Foster's intentions, the belief that sympathetic spectacle was a vehicle for social and sexual reform (46). Bruce Burgett also examines the contradictory cultural and political effects of *The Coquette*. Through a deft analysis of the epistolary structure, which presents indiscrete correspondence as a moral hazard, Burgett unpacks an elaborate narrative form unsure of its political aims. Sentimental novels like *The Coquette* engage in a paradoxical understanding of embodiment in which the female body is simultaneously perceived as internal and exclusive to the subject *and* open to public observation and manipulation. While Foster attempts to privatize sentiment in the female body, the letters in the novel advocate a sentimental identity politics located "within and against a republican understanding of all subjectivity as audience-oriented and publicly mediated" (Burgett, *Sentimental Bodies*, 109). In other words, the fantasy of sentimental autonomy in *The Coquette* cannot be dislocated from the public sphere, which ultimately grounds women as gendered subjects of the nation-state.[2]

Tabitha Tenney satirized sentimental fiction in *Female Quixotism* (1801), which follows the heiress Dorcasina Sheldon, "whose head had been turned by the unrestrained perusal of Novels and Romances," on a series of outlandish adventures (3). Years earlier Dorcas had rejected a suitor because he did not resemble the noble romantic hero and now her fantasy life prevented her from seeing that crooked men actually were plotting to steal her inheritance. Since the men in her novels are often noblemen in disguise, Dorcas constantly confuses reality and fiction. She blindly falls for O'Connor, believing him to be an honorable gentleman, despite the fact that everybody around her knows that the Irishman is a dangerous imposter. Subsequent dalliances with shady men arrive at the same pathetic conclusion until Dorcas, middle-aged and disheartened, concludes that a lifetime of reading novels has left her unsuitable for marriage. Linda Frost and Gillian Brown have connected the satire of *Female Quixotism* to the class anxieties experienced by Tenney and other Federalists in the wake of the Alien and Sedition Acts and Jefferson's subsequent election to the presidency. For Frost, the relentless pursuit of Dorcas articulates the novel's anti-democratic logic: she embodies the American nation; the villains, either hailing from foreign countries or the lower classes, seduce her with loose talk. Rather than being a vehicle for female agency, the seduction-marriage plot exposes how lax moral supervision could result in Dorcas marrying a rogue whose only ambition is to use her to invade the upper class and upset the social order ("The Body Politic," 118).

Brown extends this interpretation by focusing on the dynamic between quixoticism and Lockean liberal individualism. Quixotes are irrepressible spirits who create their own realities, defy social constraints, and often blaze a path to freedom and self-fulfillment (*The Consent of the Governed*, 163). While feminist criticism values the Quixote's pursuit of happiness, Brown notes that she also was a deluded reader unable to decipher the signs of life; her quixotic impulses might lead to many exhilarating transgressions but they did not automatically result in a more egalitarian vision. For instance, in some quixotic fictions, like Tenney's novel, the Quixote must be cured of her addiction to romantic conventions for the sake of social and political order. Since Dorcas remains a threat of marrying beneath her, friends and family abduct her and imprison her in a rural retreat until she recovers from her romantic delusions. By the novel's end, as Brown explains, the "post-quixotic perspective mirrors a conservative reaction to the progress of democratic values"; readers are cautioned against leaving the "common reality" of gender and class distinctions for flights into dream worlds that bear no relation to the consensual ground of national affiliation. Thus, the reformation of Dorcas reinforces the cultural construction of consent in the early US: "consent relies upon the presence of the disenfranchised, who mark the condition from which a consensual society distinguishes itself" (*The Consent of the Governed*, 14). The operation of consent demands the exclusion of specific individuals – women, slaves, the laboring classes, foreigners – whose presence on the margins affirms the narrow definition of political power in the US.[3]

Rebecca Rush's *Kelroy*, published anonymously in 1812, also explores the perilous effects of economic and social disorder. Mrs. Hammond, the widow of a Philadelphia merchant, lives frugally with her daughters, Lucy and Emily, until she orchestrates a coming-out party in the hopes of brokering advantageous marriages for her daughters. Equal parts gothic tale and novel of manners, *Kelroy* depicts the monstrous ambitions of Mrs. Hammond, who essentially trades her daughters for luxuries and commodities – the city house, country estate, handsome servants, and sundry objects of conspicuous consumption, all paid for on credit and by personal loans. When the creditors eventually demand payment, her funds plummet and a fire destroys her house and prized possessions. Yet, in a twist of fate, she plays, and wins, the lottery. Meanwhile, Emily has not followed her older sister's example by marrying rich – she has fallen in love with the penniless Wertherian Kelroy, who heads to India to make the fortune that will earn him into the family. But Mrs. Hammond sabotages the unprofitable love affair by intercepting the correspondence between Emily and Kelroy, then forging letters to each of them that end the relationship. A resigned Emily marries another man, but when a stroke paralyzes her mother at the wedding reception, Emily discovers the stolen correspondence in her mother's desk. The novel ends in tragedy: Emily dies from grief, Kelroy perishes in a shipwreck, and the evil mother suffocates on her last word. Few people had even read *Kelroy* prior to being introduced to the novel in Davidson's *Revolution and the Word*. Rebecca Rush's "grim matrimonial poker game" exposed the "mercantile basis of bourgeois 'love'" in which women were valued primarily as objects of commercial exchange (*Revolution and the Word*, 234). Mrs. Hammond's actions may be despicable, but Dana Nelson warned readers against a rush to judgment – the mother may be vicious but "so too is the situation to which she responds" ("Introduction," xvi). Her gender bars her from rational and legitimate economic advancement. She can only gamble, by playing the lottery and by trading one of the few commodities allowed to her in the patriarchal order – her daughters.

The forces of modern capitalism were rebuilding the idealized national community of the post-war years, which exacerbated widespread concerns about the effects of international trade and entrepreneurial individualism on the moral and intellectual foundations of republican society and government. For Karen Weyler, rapidly changing economic conditions decisively shaped *Kelroy*. Drawing upon the historical development of the China and East India trade, Weyler demonstrates how Rush's novel addressed these anxieties by distinguishing legitimate trade from gambling and speculation – Kelroy was engaging in international commercial practices that could serve as a virtuous foundation for the middle class (*Intricate Relations*, 26). Early US novels,

such as *Kelroy*, celebrated the rise of US commercial freedoms, which bene-
fitted individual and public interests and fostered national harmony. Yet Mrs.
Hammond's role in the marketplace is clearly limited to being a consumer.
While Rush exposed how greed and ambition could destroy social order,
her novel, like other early fictions, constructed rational economic desire as
a masculine prerogative (106). Nevertheless, critics of commodity capitalism
have investigated the role of feminine consumption in facilitating, and occasionally constricting, women's political agency. As Lori Merish observes, the
American woman as "republican consumer" – like the complimentary roles
of "republican mother" and "republican wife" – announced the emergence of
a new cultural type in the nineteenth century (*Sentimental Materialism*, 18).

The rise of the American historical novel after 1815 has been attributed to
a wide range of factors, from the phenomenon of Sir Walter Scott's *Waverley*,
the homegrown example of James Fenimore Cooper, and the emergence of
romanticism, to the patriotic demand for a distinctly national literature and
the public fascination with the western frontier. Signaling a shift in cultural
taste, the historical novel eclipsed the sentimental novel of seduction, making
the "Radcliffean Gothicism, epistolarism, seduction conventions, and rhetoric
of sensibility in these works look quite obsolete, and they sank from public
consciousness" (Baym, *American Women Writers*, 152). While the historical
novel typically is associated with the "emphatic masculinity" of Scott and
Cooper, women writers such as Harriet Foster Cheney, Eliza Cushing, Lydia
Maria Child, and Catharine Maria Sedgwick embraced the genre and the
distinctive national voice it fostered.[4] This section concludes by considering
two recovered novels – Child's *Hobomok* and Sedgwick's *Hope Leslie* – that have
greatly improved our understanding of how women novelists intervened in
public discourse during the early national period.

Published anonymously in 1824, Lydia Maria Child's *Hobomok; A Tale of
Early Times* begins with the image of an "old, worn-out manuscript" about the
founding of the Puritan colony. Yet the principal male narrator promptly puts
the manuscript aside to tell the unknown history of rebellion and cross-cultural
encounters. The stern father of the heroine Mary Conant has forbidden her
from marrying the Episcopalian Charles Brown. Hearing that Brown has died
in a shipwreck, Mary, who has also lost her mother, is consumed with grief
and inexplicably agrees to marry the friendly Indian Hobomok in a mystical
wilderness ceremony. Three years later, after Mary has borne a son, Brown
suddenly appears in Salem in search of Mary. Noble Hobomok, who has
heard Mary pray for the missing Brown in her sleep, tearfully surrenders his
beloved wife and child and disappears forever into the western wilderness.

Finally, Mary's sojourn with Hobomok has reformed her unfeeling father, who blesses the marriage between Mary and Brown, and little Hobomok is sent away to Cambridge to learn how to be a proper Englishman.

In the now classic introduction to the 1986 edition of *Hobomok*, Carolyn Karcher argued that Child's radical rewriting of Puritan history successfully contested the masculine project of creating a national literature during the 1820s. While the historical novel associated with Cooper reinforced patriarchal authority, white supremacy, and the dead-end logic of racial conflict, Child's novel envisioned alternatives that promised to foster social harmony and interracial friendship. As Karcher suggests, Charles Brown and Hobomok function as doubles in the novel's plot, providing a glimpse into Mary's deepest desires for an alternative politics and ethics. Mary's two lovers "both represent a fusion of nature and culture. Both foster the aesthetic impulses Puritan society contemns. Both fulfill the spiritual aspirations thwarted in Mary by a religion that has ruled out the feminine principle. Both embody the sexuality Puritanism seeks to repress. And both, above all, provide a means of defying patriarchal authority, as vested not only in Mary's father but in the society for which he stands" (*Hobomok*, xxix). The symbolic fusion of the two lovers appears to splinter during the novel's final resolution to the conflict – Hobomok vanishes and his mixed-race child is assimilated into Anglo-American society. Such a solution, which constitutes cultural genocide, undermines the theme of interracial unity. Yet Karcher points out that the twenty-four-year-old author was virtually alone among other novelists in offering a non-violent vision of assimilation during a decade of increasing racial conflict and Indian removal, even as she too was unable to resolve a racial contradiction at the core of American liberty.

By recasting the captivity narrative as a novel of courtship, authors of frontier romances were able to investigate the motives and desires of white women who freely married Indian men. In this context, Ezra Tawil focuses on the *internal* dynamic between desire and race in *Hobomok*. Contrary to the captivity scenario, Mary did not marry outside of her community because she was seduced, raped, or coerced; by judging the union to be a "bad marriage," Child authorizes the novel's examination of Mary's degradation and the discovery of its "true cause" (Tawil, *The Making of Racial Sentiment*, 109). The mystical ceremony that unites the two lovers is represented as a counterpart to a corrupt and ignorant society – too many obstacles have resulted in the "systematic redirection of her natural desires" (110). Her father's interdiction against her marriage to Brown constitutes the "causal link" in the plot, leading to a series of unfortunate actions, beginning with Mary's first tears and culminating in her "wayward fate" with Hobomok. Tawil notes how Child employs the language of desire and love to describe the union between Hobomok and Mary but only in "terms of the absence of precisely those feelings" (112). The prohibitions and superstitions of family and society have diverted her natural impulses so that she could never actually love Hobomok. Mary's return to the Puritan community underscores how race helps to form individual subjectivity. While religious bigotry had driven her into the wilderness three years earlier, her father now accepts, and blesses, the marriage between Mary and Brown, a union based on race as the fundamental marker of identity.

One of the most successful and respected fiction writers of the period, Catharine Maria Sedgwick also probed the history of seventeenth-century Massachusetts. *Hope Leslie* (1827) is set in the aftermath of the bloody Pequot War. William Fletcher and his wife, who had accompanied John Winthrop to Massachusetts, are entrusted with the guardianship of Hope and Faith Leslie after their mother dies during the journey to the New World. The girls join the Fletcher household, which includes younger children and two Pequot servants, Magawisca and Oneco. While Fletcher and Hope are in Boston, Indian raiders massacre the Fletcher family and capture Faith and the boy Everell. A split second before Everell is to be sacrificed, Magawisca courageously jumps in front of the hatchet, swung by her father, the vengeful Pequot chief. She loses an arm but saves the boy's life. While the valiant Hope Leslie survives on the violent frontier, she also must avoid being kidnapped by the villain Sir Philip Gardiner, who attempts to destroy her new extended family. Gardiner implicates Magawisca in an Indian conspiracy against the Puritan community, but she avoids punishment after Everell and Hope make a passionate plea for her liberty before the court. Meanwhile, Faith returns from captivity, but she is happily married to Oneco and chooses not to rejoin her sister but to remain with her Indian family. In an early and influential essay, Dana Nelson argued that Sedgwick's historicism, in *Hope Leslie; or, Early Times in the Massachusetts*, provided a more "positive cultural vision, proposing likenesses between cultures, and developing affinities and relationships between characters of different 'racial' groups" ("Sympathy as Strategy," 192). By having Magawisca tell her story of the Pequot War, and showing Everell's emotional openness to the atrocities inflicted upon her people, Sedgwick exposes the historical construction of racial difference, which establishes the continuity between colony and nation. Sedgwick's attempt to establish cross-racial understanding ultimately fails to deliver on its promise and "instead establishes a metaphor which allows the Indians to peacefully fade from the vision of her text" (199). Yet the ethic of "reciprocal awareness" that Sedgwick creates in *Hope Leslie* both rejects bigotry and confronts the savage effects of federal Indian policy.

Building upon the insights of Kelley, Karcher, and Nelson, Philip Gould has investigated Sedgwick's elaborate cultural critique of nineteenth-century America. For Gould, critics have obscured the fact that historical novels "do not merely make analogies between past and present but actually inscribe *contemporary* history" (*Covenant and Republic*, 5). In an age of Jacksonian myth-making, historical fiction by women could be a vehicle for political revision; for Sedgwick, redefining the legacy of republicanism conveyed a subtle critique of the masculinist ideals of citizenship. Sedgwick's *Hope Leslie* self-consciously redefines republican ideology via Puritanism, discovering the radical implications inherent in an ideology cognizant of female virtue, strength, and intellect (102). In the courtroom encounter between Hope and Governor John Winthrop, Sedgwick establishes the correlation between gender and political power and virtue. Pleading for mercy for Magawisca, Hope speaks in the idiom of politicized Christian benevolence, but Gould shows how Sedgwick actually is exploiting a republican language of civil rights and protections. Hope might be pleading before Governor Winthrop, but there is nothing passive about her display of feminine virtue, and selfless love is a form of political power. It can ameliorate the "viability of a narrowly masculine understanding of the public" and the "misogynistic ramifications of public, masculine citizenship" (114, 113). Yet, by the end of the novel, Sedgwick's ambivalence about miscegenation threatens to undermine the thematic of female virtue and power. While the novel has established a loving republican marriage as the democratic model for political relations, Faith and Oneco are removed to the west. And Magawisca, after giving an odd speech about innate racial differences, must leave if Hope and Everell are ever to marry.

Foreign sojourns

The feminist critique of domestic ideology may have revealed the fluid borders between private and public spheres, but the prominence given to the American nation obscured the significance of the foreign. Correcting this oversight, Amy Kaplan pointed out that the *domestic* had a double meaning: it linked family and nation, presenting the former as a microcosm for the latter, but also imagined both in opposition to foreign forces beyond the territorial and imaginary borders of the national home ("Manifest Domesticity," 183–4). Domestic ideology marked the boundaries between savagery and civilization, which unified white men and women against racialized antagonists, providing a sense of an Other essential to the US imperial project. Building upon Kaplan's analysis, spatially minded critics redrew the gendered boundaries of the domestic realm in an international setting. The emergence of Empire Studies after 1990 challenged nation-based critical paradigms and fostered awareness for how national development was tied to global and hemispheric spaces and forces.[5] To borrow Henri Lefebvre's famous metaphor of the merging of geographical scales, the home, like the nation, is produced by a nexus of spatial relations. The national home – permeated from every direction and showing linkages with global flows of capital, culture, and politics – is always contingent and changing.

By enriching our understanding of the geopolitical cross-currents of early American women's fiction, the development of spatial critical practices promises to consolidate the tenuous gains of the recovery project. For instance, Theresa Strouth Gaul speculates that our dependence on a national paradigm has failed to account for the complexities of *Female Quixotism* and *Kelroy*, "perhaps explaining why both have generated only a handful of scholarly articles and why *Kelroy* has gone out of print" ("Recovering Recovery," 276). When we position women's novels outside the narrow spatial logic of literary nationalism, the narratives belie the myths about their parochial concerns. Political violence devastated the fictional homes, picaresque heroines often fled the ruins, and the global forces at work in these novels fit poorly within the boundaries of a national paradigm. "Transnational" or "Transatlantic" or "Hemispheric" approaches provide literary critics with additional tools for analyzing the production of space in early novels and for making sense of the often expansive political and historical visions of women writers.

If the restrictive *domestic* label is still blithely attached to women novelists, the good news is that the ongoing recovery of their neglected works is revising the literary history of the early national period. Resistance to nation-based inquiry has resulted in the recent republication of Leonora Sansay's *Secret History; or, The Horrors of St. Domingo* (1808) and Susanna Rowson's *Reuben and Rachel; or, A Tale of Old Times* (1798). As Gaul has suggested, the expansive geography of Rowson's novel may explain why it clashed with the priorities of literary nationalism:

> Centering its action in the Atlantic basin and its relations, exchanges, and contacts, *Reuben and Rachel* presents a plethora of plot elements that Atlantic studies has established as significant, including water crossings, ships and shipwrecks, and port cities. The novel contains no less than fourteen journeys

by ship, at least ten of them traversing the Atlantic. Conquest, Colonialism, and religious conversion are carried out via maritime travel early in the novel, as is mercantilism in later sections. Liverpool and Philadelphia both feature in the plot near the end of volume two, registering their important status as port cities in the Atlantic basin. Philadelphia particularly emerges as a "crossroads of cultures" in the conclusion, wherein English, Irish, French, and Native American characters come into contact.[6] ("Recovering Recovery," 277–8)

Broader spatial frameworks less focused on the US make sense, since the novels clearly envisioned transnational passages, utilized foreign locations, and featured an international cast of characters. Rowson was British by birth, American by residence. While her conflicted transatlantic loyalties never meshed with the nationalist agenda of US literary history, a new generation of critics, less attached to the national model, has been redefining her career for a contemporary audience. Foremost among them, Marion Rust has shown how Rowson's protean identity, and her constant exploration of female subjectivity detached from narrow domestic or nationalist spheres, constituted the source of Rowson's extraordinary popular appeal.

Likewise, the critical trend toward wider spatial contexts partially explains both the republication of Sansay's *Secret History* and the innovative scholarship that has accompanied its release. The daughter of a Philadelphia inn-keeper, Leonora Sansay was best known as a friend, mistress, and confidant to Aaron Burr. In 1800, she married a refugee from Saint Domingue, returned with him to the island to reclaim an estate confiscated during the first years of the revolution, and wrote to Burr about her experience there. As Michael Drexler observes in his impressive introduction to the Broadview edition, Sansay's letter to Burr marked the origins of *Secret History*, an epistolary novel set in Saint Domingue during the revolt against French rule. Confounding the boundary between fact and fiction, Sansay invents an American heroine, Mary, who travels to Haiti with her newly married sister Clara and her French colonial husband, St. Louis. Like Sansay, the fictional Mary is a close friend of Vice President Burr and the letters between them detail the social and political conflicts of revolutionary Saint Domingue. Depictions of violence are interwoven with letters that record the dissolution of Clara's marriage to the villainous St. Louis, her dalliances with other men, and her husband's abuse. As the political and domestic hazards mount, Mary and Clare seek refuge in Cuba, but St. Louis follows them and, in a futile attempt to control his wife, rapes Clara. After a brief period apart, the sisters reunite and escape to other safe locations in Cuba and in Jamaica. The final letter in the novel announces their desire to return to Philadelphia.

The Caribbean setting of *Secret History* cannot be easily incorporated into the conventional framework of US literary nationalism, which typically treats Haiti not as a real place but as a terrifying metaphor for racial violence. This constricted national focus has overlooked the political, social, economic, and historical relationships between these neighboring lands, cultures, and peoples. Building upon Colin Dayan's analysis of Sansay, imaginative scholars like Drexler, Elizabeth Dillon, Gretchen Woertendyke, and Sian Silyn Roberts are helping readers to see how a transnational model can unlock the previously overlooked literary value of *Secret History*. For example, Drexler ultimately shows how the standard nationalist agenda of identity, citizenship, and democratic values prevents us from understanding how Sansay positioned her investigations of masculinity and violence in a hemisphere where colonialism remained a destructive force. A declaration of Sansay's newfound public voice, *Secret History* depicts the "affinities between the society of post-revolutionary United States and that of revolutionary Saint Domingue, where men in positions of authority are consistently portrayed as bungling, venal, malicious, or sadistic. Whether at home or abroad, in the neighborhood of the placid Schuylkill River or on the shores of the turbulent Caribbean, Sansay envisions a world in which women's happiness seems all but circumscribed by violent masculinity" (*Secret History*, 33). Drexler's insight not only rejects the artificial boundary between the US and Haiti but also severs the link between women's writing and domesticity. When positioned in a hemispheric framework, *Secret History* can be appreciated for its exploration of the shared histories of colonialism and revolutionary insurrection that build the US and Haiti together.

Elizabeth Dillon also makes a convincing case for viewing *Secret History* through a hemispheric lens. She argues that the tendency for critics to treat the early novel as a national allegory cannot account for the events in *Secret History*. Read as allegory, the novel's depiction of households ruined by patriarchal cruelty symbolize disorder located in a higher public realm; however, the novel is the obverse of the standard allegorical mode, since gender politics and sexual violence actually intervene in the masculine arena of geopolitics ("Secret History," 80). Fractured homes do not refer elsewhere – they constitute the "secret history" of colonialism and its connection to patriarchy. While the overthrow of colonial rule has left some women destitute and husbandless, the Haitian Revolution has also emancipated them, not only from the constraints and abuses of marriage but also from the racial hierarchies of colonialism. A new egalitarian community of white colonial and creole women takes shape in the crucible of revolutionary violence. Rather than asserting the differences between creole and American identities, Sansay delves into the formation of creole subjectivity in the hemisphere. Sansay, simultaneously, acknowledges racial and national differences but questions their logic, and emphasizes the creole nature of the US and the kinship of American nationals with the peoples and cultures of the Atlantic world. Once removed from the narrow logic of the national frame, *Secret History* offers a radically different understanding of the "domestic" worlds imagined by American women writers.

American women writers may have "entered literary history as the enemy," but their novels have catalyzed the rebuilding of US literary and cultural studies (Baym, "Melodramas of Beset Manhood," 130). The foreign sojourns and affective politics of novels like *Secret History* and *Reuben and Rachel* have shifted our conception of the relationship between gender and nation. The women in *Secret History* are refugees in a colonial nightmare, finding strength in sisterly love, but the novel ends before one can know for sure if they will ever return home to republican Philadelphia and find happiness – they would be returning to a patriarchal society that denied them political equality and offered few civil rights and protections. By removing the sisters from national time and space, and by refusing to send them home for inclusion into American society, Sansay issues a stinging rebuke: the sisters are trapped in a time lag in which true republicanism has not yet arrived in the hemisphere. If literary nationalism longed for a novel form that reflected the rise of democratic culture, then Sansay shows how this desire could not easily account for the political paradox being imagined by some women writers. The American Republic invested certain individuals with rights and protections, but the price of belonging was their complicity in maintaining the racial and gender relations of eighteenth-century colonialism.

Notes

1. The history of the recovery effort is now well known. Three innovative publishing series have transformed our understanding of women writers in the nineteenth century: the American Women Writers series (Rutgers University Press), the Early American Women Writers series (Oxford University Press), and the Schomburg Library of Nineteenth-Century Black Women Writers Series. On the recovery effort, see Gaul, "Recovering Recovery," and Fetterley, "Commentary."
2. Extending her 1988 analysis of *The Coquette*, Carroll Smith-Rosenberg also delves into the subversive language of the novel and examines the fraught relationship between political independence and social order. See Smith-Rosenberg, *This Violent Empire*.
3. On the interplay between consent and coercion, and the larger matrix of sexual relations, see also Haag, *Consent*.

4. An abbreviated list of their historical novels published between 1815 and 1840 includes: Cheney's *A Peep at the Pilgrims in Sixteen Hundred and Thirty-Six* (1824), Cushing's *A Tale of the Revolution* (1825), Child's *Hobomok; A Tale of Early Times* (1824) and *The Rebels* (1825), and Sedgwick's *Hope Leslie* (1827) and *The Linwoods* (1835).

5. For Americanist literary and cultural critics, Empire Studies generally commences in the early 1990s with the publication of Kaplan and Pease's *Cultures of United States Imperialism*.

6. The phrase "crossroads of cultures" alludes to Shelley Fisher Fishkin's 2004 Presidential Address to the American Studies Association: "Crossroads of Cultures."

Works cited

Armstrong, Nancy. *Desire and Domestic Fiction: A Political History of the Novel*. New York: Oxford University Press, 1987.

Barnes, Elizabeth. *States of Sympathy: Seduction and Democracy in the American Novel*. New York: Columbia University Press, 1997.

Baym, Nina. *American Women Writers and the Work of History, 1790–1860*. New Brunswick: Rutgers University Press, 1995.

"Melodramas of Beset Manhood: How Theories of American Fiction Exclude Women Authors." *American Quarterly* 33.2 (1981): 123–39.

"Women's Novels and Women's Minds: An Unsentimental View of Nineteenth-Century American Women's Fiction." *Novel: a Forum on Fiction* 31 (1998): 335–50.

Boudreau, Kristin. *Sympathy in American Literature: American Sentiments from Jefferson to the Jameses*. Gainesville: University Press of Florida, 2002.

Brown, Gillian. *The Consent of the Governed: The Lockean Legacy in Early American Culture*. Cambridge, MA: Harvard University Press, 2001.

Burgett, Bruce. *Sentimental Bodies: Sex, Gender, and Citizenship in the Early Republic*. Princeton: Princeton University Press, 1998.

Child, Lydia Maria. *Hobomok* and Other Writings about Indians. Ed. Carolyn Karcher. New Brunswick: Rutgers University Press, 1986.

Cowie, Alexander. *The Rise of the American Novel*. New York: American Book Co., 1948.

Davidson, Cathy. *Revolution and the Word: The Rise of the Novel in America*. New York: Oxford University Press, 1986.

Dillon, Elizabeth Maddock. "The Secret History of the Early American Novel: Leonora Sansay and Revolution in Saint Domingue." *Novel: a Forum on Fiction* 40.1–2 (2006): 77–103.

Elliott, Emory, *et al.* eds. *The Columbia History of the American Novel*. New York: Columbia University Press, 1991.

Fetterley, Judith. "Commentary: Nineteenth-Century American Women Writers and the Politics of Recovery." *American Literary History* 6.3 (1994): 600.

Fishkin, Shelley Fisher. "Crossroads of Cultures: The Transnational Turn in American Studies – Presidential Address to the American Studies Association, November 12, 2004." *American Quarterly* 57.1 (2005): 17–57.

Foster, Hannah Webster. *The Coquette*. New York: Oxford University Press, 1986.

Frost, Linda. "The Body Politic in Tabitha Tenney's Female Quixotism." *Early American Literature*, 32.2 (1997): 113–34.

Gaul, Theresa Strouth. "Recovering Recovery: Early American Women and *Legacy*'s Future." *Legacy* 26.2 (2009): 262–83.

Gould, Philip. *Covenant and Republic: Historical Romance and the Politics of Puritanism*. Cambridge: Cambridge University Press, 1996.

Haag, Pamela. *Consent: Sexual Rights and the Transformation of American Liberalism*. Ithaca: Cornell University Press, 1999.

Harris, Susan K. *19th-Century American Women's Novels: Interpretive Strategies*. Cambridge: Cambridge University Press, 1990.

Howard, June. *Publishing the Family*. Durham, NC: Duke University Press, 2001.

"What is Sentimentality?" *American Literary History* 11.1 (1999): 63–81.

Kaplan, Amy. "Manifest Domesticity." In *No More Separate Spheres!* Ed. Cathy N. Davidson and Jessamyn Hatcher. Durham, NC: Duke University Press, 2002.

Kaplan, Amy and Donald Pease, eds. *Cultures of United States Imperialism*. Durham, NC: Duke University Press, 1993.

Kelley, Mary. *Private Woman, Public Stage: Literary Domesticity in Nineteenth-Century America*. New York: Oxford University Press, 1984.

Kerber, Linda K. *Women of the Republic: Intellect and Ideology in Revolutionary America*. Chapel Hill: Published for the Omohondro Institute of Early American History and Culture by the University of North Carolina Press, 1980.

Kolodny, Annette. *The Lay of the Land: Metaphor as Experience and History in American Life and Letters*. Chapel Hill: University of North Carolina Press, 1975.

Lewis, Jan. "The Republican Wife: Virtue and Seduction in the Early Republic." *The William and Mary Quarterly: A Magazine of Early American History and Culture* 44.4 (1987): 689–721.

Merish, Lori. *Sentimental Materialism: Gender, Commodity Culture, and Nineteenth-Century American Literature*. Durham, NC: Duke University Press, 2000.

Nelson, Dana D. "Introduction." In *Kelroy: A Novel*. By Rebecca Rush. New York: Oxford University Press, 1992.

National Manhood: Capitalist Citizenship and the Imagined Fraternity of White Men. Durham, NC: Duke University Press, 1998.

"Sympathy as Strategy in Sedgwick's *Hope Leslie*." In *The Culture of Sentiment: Race, Gender, and Sentimentality in Nineteenth-Century America*. Ed. Shirley Samuels. New York: Oxford University Press, 1992.

Roberts, Sian Silyn. "Dispossession and Cosmopolitan Sociability in Leonora Sansay's *Secret History*." In *Early America and the Haitian Revolution: Essays on the Cultural History of Atlantic Colonialism and Modernity*. Ed. Elizabeth Maddock Dillon and Michael J. Drexler. Philadelphia: University of Pennsylvania Press, forthcoming.

Romero, Lora. *Home Fronts: Domesticity and its Critics in the Antebellum United States*. Durham, NC: Duke University Press, 1997.

Samuels, Shirley. *Romances of the Republic: Women, the Family, and Violence in the Literature of the Early American Nation*. New York: Oxford University Press, 1996.

Sansay, Leonora. *Secret History, Or, The Horrors of St. Domingo: And, Laura*. Ed. Michael Drexler. Peterborough, ON: Broadview Press, 2007.

Smith-Rosenberg, Carroll. *This Violent Empire: The Birth of an American National Identity*. Chapel Hill: Published for the Omohundro Institute of Early American History and Culture by the University of North Carolina Press, 2010.

Stern, Julia A. *The Plight of Feeling: Sympathy and Dissent in the Early American Novel*. Chicago: University of Chicago Press, 1997.

Tawil, Ezra. *The Making of Racial Sentiment: Slavery and the Birth of the Frontier Romance*. Cambridge: Cambridge University Press, 2006.

Tompkins, Jane P. *Sensational Designs: The Cultural Work of American Fiction, 1790–1860*. New York: Oxford University Press, 1985.

Weyler, Karen Ann. *Intricate Relations: Sexual and Economic Desire in American Fiction, 1789–1814*. Iowa City: University of Iowa Press, 2004.

Woertendyke, Gretchen. "Romance to Novel: A Secret History." *Narrative* 17.3 (2009): 255–73.

7

Women in literary culture during the long nineteenth century

NANCY GLAZENER

Over the past two centuries, the idea of literature has carried a lot of clout. Writers' desires and ambitions have taken shape in relation to literature: writers who longed to be literary, did not care about being literary, or thumbed their noses at literature were all affected by it. Readers have quarreled about which works and authors were truly literary. Moreover, in the USA and many other nations, understandings of literature were institutionalized within the publishing industry and in secondary and higher education, and these institutional practices remained influential even when the terms of literary value began to be called into question. The most famous controversies about literary value were the late twentieth-century canon wars, which increased the number and range of writings valued in teaching and scholarship, but these controversies did not really expand the literary canon: they dissolved it. In place of a distinction between literary writings that are important to teach and study and subliterary or nonliterary writings that are not, most academics whose field of study is still institutionally identified as "literature" care about a wide variety of writings and print texts, including but not limited to traditional literary genres such as novels and poetry.

Precisely because a strictly bounded conception of "literature" no longer adequately captures the ways in which serious readers value old and new works, we are now in a position to take stock of literature as a cultural phenomenon. And from the beginning – around the turn of the nineteenth century, as I will explain – literature was bound up with gender. Authors' accomplishments and failures were ascribed to their genders in myriad ways. Each literary genre was a gendered terrain, sometimes marked by a whole-sale gendering (so that sentimental fiction was linked to women, naturalist fiction to men) but more often marked by gender in various, even conflicting, ways. Moreover, the very idea of literature had a paradoxical relationship to women. The increased participation of women as readers and authors in the nineteenth century meant that women were sometimes associated with mass culture and commercialism, the enemies of literature: this was the gist of Nathaniel Hawthorne's mid-century complaint about "a d——d mob of scribbling women" (*The Letters, 1853–1856*, 304). However, around the same time, an ideology of "True Womanhood," predicated on the idea that bourgeois white women ought to be protected in domestic enclaves from the economic stresses and political corruptions of public life, created a symbolic association between women and literature, since literature was also supposed to be insulated from politics and economics (Welter, *Dimity Convictions*, 21–41).[1] Later in the century, renegotiating the terms on which both women and literature had been sequestered, many women took up formal or informal work involving publication, education, or cultural trusteeship, thereby becoming active promoters and arbiters of literary culture.

This essay will examine some of the ways in which literature affected women and women affected literature, moving from the late eighteenth century (before literature in the modern sense had come into view) to the early twentieth century (when literature was well established and had become the province of experts – some of them women – in departments of modern literatures and languages). I will first consider a woman author whose work helps throw into relief the importance of recognizing literature as a specific model of textual value, not an all-purpose measure. Since most of this volume explores women's work as authors, however, the rest of this essay will examine ways other than authorship in which women have contributed to literature, such as their work in promoting the study of legacy texts: works that have passed the test of time, according to literature's gatekeepers. This work has amounted to the ongoing creation of a "usable past," a context in which new writers would write and new readers would read (V. Brooks, "On Creating a Usable Past"). We know that works of literature have shaped people's understanding of what women could be and how they mattered. Now we can begin to see how women helped to determine what literature could be and how it mattered.

Reading beyond/before literature

The modern version of literature, which became the basis of departments of modern languages and literatures, was invented between about 1800 and 1850, mainly in the public cultures of the nations, colonies, and former colonies of Western Europe. Before the nineteenth century, the term "literature" referred to valued writings of many kinds, including treatises in mathematics or logic or ethics, sermons, histories, and philosophical dialogues. Literature meant letters, in the sense of "republic of letters" or "man of letters," and literature constituted the materials of instructional reading at a time when mainly elite men had the opportunity to become well educated. This older, broader sense of literature still circulates in the academic tradition of the literature search, an inventory of scholarship on a given question.

By about 1850, literature had become a more specialized category designating accomplished writings in certain imaginative genres: poetry, fiction, drama, and certain kinds of essays.[2] Only works in these genres raised the urgent question of whether they were literature or not, although sometimes works in other genres (such as histories) were admired for their literary style or literary pleasures. I characterize this version of literature as modern because it emerged as part of the specializing, rationalizing reorganization of knowledge and culture associated with modernity (Punter, *Modernity*, 13–23). The modern version of literature drew especially on aesthetic theories holding that the transformative experiences offered by art and literature could offset the alienating tendencies of capitalism. However, the modern version of literature was also developed to be a force that would form and inform citizens, an accoutrement of civil society. This version of literature – an unstable compound of aesthetic and civic republican theories – was celebrated within Euro-American imperial cultures, and it was adapted, resisted, and countered when it was exported to other parts of the world and interacted with other textual traditions.[3]

Modern literature was cosmopolitan (we might say "Euro-cosmopolitan"), insofar as the canon of modern literature consisted of a set of great writers from European nations (Shakespeare, Dante, and Goethe especially). It was also national, insofar as each nation defined its own literary tradition and began to endow the works in this tradition with national significance. And of course, it was organized by languages that were not only national: for example, the study of English literature was developed in Scotland, Ireland, India, and many other Anglophone parts of the world where readers also charted their own literary traditions.[4] Moreover, literature was simultaneously developed both as a retrospective category – a rubric for valuing legacy texts – and as a standard of value and a marketing category for new publications.

The development of literature made for a great winnowing of legacy texts, although the tendency of purist literary history to separate a very small "canon" of texts – "Literary Bibles," as one devotee put it (Snider, *Writer*, 120) – from the rest was offset by the tendency of nationalizing literary histories to include writers who were well known or linked to important episodes in national history. Whereas many women writing before the nineteenth century had had trouble in their lifetimes getting time to write, opportunities for publication, or a fair reading from the public, the development of literature meant that legacy texts by women had to navigate a new determination of value. Literary canonicity determined not just which legacy texts would be valued, but on what terms, with the result that certain kinds of writerly accomplishments were effaced or distorted.

An instructive example in this regard is Phillis Wheatley, who began to write poetry as an enslaved teenager during the 1760s and published a volume of poems in 1773. Her history also demonstrates that gender is not a uniform category but rather always operates as part of an assemblage of circumstances. Wheatley's work was shaped by neoclassicism. She wrote many poems in formal, public genres: most notably, odes to famous men (including the Earl of Dartmouth, King George III, and George Washington) or prominent groups (students at Harvard) and elegies on the deaths of public figures (such as the evangelical minister George Whitefield). Like many poems that were highly regarded during the late colonial and early national years, Wheatley's writings are strongly marked by orthodox Christian piety and neoclassical and biblical allusions, features that distinguish her work from the personal revelations, vivid natural settings, and speculative spiritual and political inquiries of the Romantic writers who followed her. Because she was African, female, and a slave, Wheatley's poetic presentations of Christian character and classical learning and her assumption of public authority were closely scrutinized: Wheatley's work challenged prejudices that Africans were inferior to Europeans and women to men.

Readers whose tastes were formed by the Romantics and later writers often find neoclassical poetry especially hard to enjoy. A tendency to privilege lyrical, verbally concentrated poetry over all other kinds gathered momentum during the course of the nineteenth century, as certain strains of Romanticism became literary orthodoxies (Jackson, *Dickinson's Misery*, 1–15). Compared to neoclassical poetry, some works written much longer ago – Shakespeare's sonnets about the slippery intimate landscape of love and desire or Spenser's chivalric allegory, *The Faerie Queene* – offer pleasures of subjective identification and wordplay that satisfy modern literary tastes better than many neoclassical poems. The poems of the American Puritan writer Anne Bradstreet, written 100 years before Wheatley's, are probably more accessible to readers today than Wheatley's poems are, since many of Bradstreet's poems – such as "Upon the Burning of Our House July 10th, 1666" and "To My Dear and Loving Husband" – take up Bradstreet's personal and domestic experiences and focus on her emotional struggles and resolutions. Criticism about Bradstreet sometimes casts her as a precursor of later poets who write about their experiences and perceptions as women (Amore, "Introduction").

Readers who look for confessional moments in Wheatley are likely to be disappointed. Especially in the case of the poem most directly addressing her experience as a slave, "On Being Brought from Africa to America" (1773; Wheatley, *Complete Writings*, 13), readers' disagreements about whether irony is at work are sometimes fueled by the fear that if irony is *not* at work, Wheatley is an apologist for her oppressors (Gates, *Trials of Phillis Wheatley*, 81):

> 'TWAS mercy brought me from my *Pagan* land,
> Taught my benighted soul to understand
> That there's a God, that there's a *Saviour* too:
> Once I redemption neither sought nor knew.
> Some view our sable race with scornful eye,
> "Their colour is a diabolic die."
> Remember, *Christians, Negroes*, black as *Cain*,
> May be refin'd, and join th' angelic train.

We may long for Wheatley's inside story: the one glimpsed in her letter to Rev. Samson Occom, in which she references every human's inborn tendency to be "impatient of oppression" (*Complete Writings*, 153). However, even if Wheatley had been willing and able to circulate a poem lamenting or resenting her own enslaved state (thereby criticizing the white Wheatley family, who allowed her to study and write poetry), it is not at all clear that her culture of poetry would have encouraged or tolerated that stance. Joanna Brooks has proposed that Wheatley effectively wrote surrogate confessional poetry for white women who were her patrons and sponsors, though: poems such as "To a Lady and Their Children, on the Death of her Son and their Brother." These poems might have been part of an implicit bargain by which Wheatley performed emotional work and constructed cultural value for white women's grief in return for their efforts to get her poetry published ("Our Phillis, Ourselves," 8–12). However, Wheatley's white supporters failed her in her efforts to publish a second volume of poetry and may even have lost the manuscript (16–17).

Brooks's scholarship underlines the extent to which gender as well as race was at stake in Wheatley's authorship: not only her gender but also the genders of the white men and women involved in her work. Some of her poems were oriented toward the world of learning, public commentary, and cultural reflection (a masculine-coded world in which women sometimes participated); other poems were oriented toward commemorating women's griefs, charting the emotional reverberations of deaths that were not publicly consequential (a feminine-coded world in which men sometimes participated). Although many of Wheatley's poems were published in periodicals or her collection, handwritten manuscripts of her poems also circulated among white women. Thus, her poems circulated in masculine-dominated print culture as well as among a coterie of women readers (J. Brooks, "Our Phillis, Ourselves," 8; Mulford, "Print and Manuscript Culture," 338–40). Moreover, her poems were published by subscription, as was common: rather than a publishing house determining that her writings deserved to be read and were likely to sell, subscribers committed in advance to buy a book. This practice marks another respect in which Wheatley's conditions of writing did not fit the ideas of literary ambition developed in the next century. Subscription publishing meant that a published volume was destined not for the great anonymous public or for posterity (often marked as the proper audience for literature) but for an identifiable set of people who wanted to own this book.

More than any other genre in Wheatley's time, poetry carried ingredients that would in the next century come to characterize literature.[5] As far back as Aristotle's *Poetics* (a key text in eighteenth-century neoclassical culture), poetry was identified with the pleasures of imitation, laying groundwork for literature's imaginative reconstruction of the world. Influential defenses of poetry, such as Sir Philip Sidney's "Defence of Poesy" (1579), justified its fictiveness – "feigning," a term that highlights its deceptive quality – because it made instruction palatable. But the poetry Sidney defended included scholarly treatises written in verse:

> So Thales, Empedocles, and Parmenides sang their natural philosophy in verses; so did Pythagoras and Phocylides their moral counsels; so did Tyrtaeus in war matters, and Solon in matters of policy; or rather they, being poets, did exercise their delightful vein in those points of highest knowledge which before them lay hidden to the world. ("Defence of Poesy," 103–4)

If we carry backward in time tastes that were shaped by the modern category of literature, we may have trouble responding to poems written when poetry could take more varied forms. Anne Bradstreet's poem "Of the Four Humours in Man's Constitution" (1650) – one of her lesser-known poems – is not a work of original research or analysis, but neither is it lyrically expressive or narrative. Rather, it's a first-person meditation on the humors, an attempt to come to terms with the literal and metaphorical power attributed to choler, blood, phlegm, and melancholy, which had for centuries been understood as physiological substances governing people's health and temperament. Bradstreet's poem is closer to the tradition of scholarly writing in verse that Sidney referenced than it is to lyric poetry. It might even be an ancestor of popular science writing, insofar as it engages contemporary medical knowledge. Like many of Wheatley's poems, it is not clearly literary: not because it is a careless or inferior work, but because it is not designed to appeal to modern literary sensibilities.[6]

The instructional potential of poetry that Sidney emphasized and that shaped some of Bradstreet's poetry is an important context for Wheatley's work. The family that enslaved Wheatley gave her an education that was unusual not only for a slave (although laws prohibiting slave literacy only became common after the 1820s, and mainly in the south) but also for a white woman, an education much closer to the kind of college preparation that privileged young white men received. Writing poetry was a well-respected outcome of education, a way of contributing to public life and reflection. In American colleges at the time, the composition of poems was a common educational exercise, closely linked to collegiate emphases on rhetoric and oratory. Commencements typically featured public performances by students in the form of orations, readings of original poems written for the occasion, and debates.[7] To be chosen as a class poet or orator was a high honor, and a surprising number of eighteenth- and nineteenth-century men of letters earned early public recognition in this way. For example, Hugh Henry Brackenridge and Philip Freneau were admired for "The Rising Glory of America," a poem that Brackenridge delivered in 1771 at commencement for the College of New Jersey (later Princeton) (Marsh, *Philip Freneau*, 25). Joel Barlow, graduating from Yale in 1778, delivered his original epic "The Prospect of Peace" (Ford, *Joel Barlow*, 17). Commencement compositions were often published and reprinted in newspapers, with the result that Timothy Dwight's valedictory address at Yale's 1776 graduation (when he was a tutor rather than a new graduate) earned him some measure of fame (Kafer, "The Making of Timothy Dwight"). Writing poetry was a form of educated participation in civic life, and Wheatley's poetry amounted to a claim that she – African, enslaved, and female – could participate. This is not to say that her poetic talent was or is irrelevant, but that asking whether her poetry is literature is not equivalent to asking whether or not she was an excellent writer.

For the better part of two centuries after her death, Wheatley was treated as a curiosity or a minor figure in literary studies: a first, or an early, African American woman poet noteworthy mainly for having existed. During the late twentieth century's contestation of the literary canon, a canonization of Wheatley was set in motion, most famously by Henry Louis Gates. Gates called attention to the gatekeeping Wheatley had endured from the very start, in the form of the "Wheatley Court," an oral examination of Wheatley conducted by the eighteen white men of standing who then signed a document attesting to Wheatley's authorship (*Trials of Phillis Wheatley*, 5–32).[8] The vision of young Wheatley being interrogated, simply to prove that she was capable of writing these poems, captured the high political stakes of her authorship as well as the steep pitch of the playing field on which she had contended. However, efforts to establish Wheatley's literary worthiness tended to value her work mainly for its intimations of the Romantic aesthetics that would cohere after her death. For example, one of Wheatley's critic-advocates supported his case for her work's literary importance by identifying in her poetry two foundational and interrelated aesthetic values, the most potent terms in Romantic literary aesthetics: the imagination and the sublime (Shields, "Phillis Wheatley's Struggle," 252–67).

In Wheatley's world, though, poetry was literature, in the broad sense that included Newton's scientific writings and Mather's sermons, and poetry (like many forms of literature) was also a form of cultivated civic participation. Imagination was important, but it did not have the prominence it would come to have in the next century. For this reason, Thomas Jefferson's oft-cited criticism of Wheatley's lack of imagination – which he couched as a generalization about "blacks," thereby fixing Wheatley as a representative of her race – is not as significant as many readers have assumed because imagination was not the *sine qua non* of poetry (*Notes on the State of Virginia*, 266–7). (Significantly, Jefferson's contemporary, the marquis de Barbé-Marbois, attributed to Wheatley's writings "imagination, poetry, and zeal, though no correctness nor order nor interest," rendering not only a contrary judgment about Wheatley's imaginativeness but also a different array of qualities relevant to a consideration of her verse [Gates, *Trials of Phillis Wheatley*, 42].) In light of the neoclassical aesthetics and civic republican ideologies of poetry that formed the landscape for Wheatley's poetic practice, the question of whether her poems count as literature might productively be replaced by the question of which texts repay our attention, and how, as we learn to read beyond the modern category of literature.

Better living through Shakespeare

Modern literature emerged partly from the long struggle in which the unified classical curriculum in higher education was replaced by the vernacular instruction and well-differentiated disciplines of the modern research university, part of a still-larger transformation in which national languages became more important in learned culture than Latin and Greek.[9] In the nineteenth century, the case for the value of modern vernacular writings was supported by widespread admiration for authors who were time-tested but much more recent than the ancient Greeks and Romans. William Shakespeare became the prototypical modern literary author.[10] His writings were venerated throughout Europe and its zone of influence, especially in Germany, the cradle of aesthetic philosophy. Critics who wrote about Shakespeare's genius, Shakespeare's ability to invent natural characters, Shakespeare's moral insights, and Shakespeare's stylistic precision all contributed to working out a platform for the cultural value of the imaginative genres that were being grouped together in a new way as "literature." As literature became the authoritative rubric for legacy writings, other works of poetry, prose, and drama from earlier eras came to be valued on the same terms as Shakespeare's works and connected with each other through the idea of literature. This retrospective development of literature also helped set the terms for deciding which new works or genres could count as literary.

Even though esteem for Shakespeare helped move higher education away from the classical curriculum, America's share in developing a Shakespeare-centered version of modern literature happened in public culture, not just (or even first) in English departments. Specialized departments of English literature and language were formed in American universities mainly after the Civil War.[11] In the late eighteenth and early nineteenth centuries, Shakespeare circulated in higher education but not as a part of literary coursework because literature courses did not exist. Excerpts from Shakespeare appeared in textbooks in rhetoric and elocution; college literary societies read and performed Shakespeare's plays; and as of the 1830s, isolated faculty members offered extracurricular lectures or a stray course on Shakespeare.[12]

These college-sponsored clubs and lecture series constituted only a small segment of the widespread public reading and study of Shakespeare in the long nineteenth century. Americans were wild about Shakespeare. They participated avidly in working out ways of enjoying and understanding his plays. Shakespeare's plays were available in countless editions, high-priced or cheap, and they were read far and wide. It should not surprise us that a Mississippi riverboat pilot, George Ealer, recited Shakespeare by the hour to the young cub pilot Samuel Clemens (later known as Mark Twain), nor that Elizabeth Cady (later Stanton) argued about *The Taming of the Shrew* with law students in her father's office (Twain, *Is Shakespeare Dead?* 15–20; Stanton, *Eighty Years and*

More, 34). In the antebellum decades, the plays were often performed before diverse audiences. Audiences in New York City even rioted over a face-off between rival performances of *Macbeth* in 1849 (Cliff, *Shakespeare Riots*). As Lawrence Levine has documented, over the course of the nineteenth century, dramatic productions of Shakespeare became more and more exclusive as Shakespearean theater came to be the preserve of elites. Similarly, over the course of the nineteenth century, the reading and interpretation of Shakespeare came gradually to be the preserve of English professors. However, it was through widespread public reading and study of Shakespeare that many of the foundations of English literary studies were laid. As a result, we can treat the circulation of Shakespeare as a diagnostic dye tracing many of the networks through which the idea of modern literature began to circulate. These networks constituted literary culture, the cultural domain composed of stakeholders in modern literature.

Merely reading Shakespeare was not necessarily a literary endeavor: people had been doing that for centuries. What was new was that, in the nineteenth century, so many people reading Shakespeare were also talking and thinking about questions that helped define what literature was and how it ought to be read and valued. For instance, in addition to reciting Shakespeare's plays by heart, George Ealer involved his cub pilot in countless discussions about whether William Shakespeare really wrote the plays attributed to him. This controversy was at its hottest between the 1850s, when Ealer was defending Shakespeare's authorship to Twain, and the early twentieth century, when Twain contributed to the controversy by publishing *Is Shakespeare Dead?* (1909). Precisely because the literary canon operated through authors, with masterworks forging an author's literary status and minor works trailing along, enormous energy went into figuring out what made Shakespeare capable of writing the plays, his most admired writings.[13] For some readers, the mystery of how a modestly educated English boy became one of the greatest writers of all time was adequately answered by the idea of Genius. In this way of thinking, Shakespeare's writings could be studied and analyzed, but how a Shakespeare came to be was a miracle or a sacred mystery (in keeping with George Bernard Shaw's later diagnosis of "Bardolatry" [Dobson, *The Making of the National Poet*, 6]). For other readers, the extraordinary knowledge of law, medicine, high life at court, and ancient sources registered in the plays made them doubt that the historical William Shakespeare could have obtained the requisite education and experience: skepticism about William Shakespeare's authorship was predicated on equal veneration of the plays but a dissenting explanation of literary authorship.

We know more today than nineteenth-century readers did about how good William Shakespeare's education was and about the opportunities he had for gaining the knowledge of the world that informs the plays.[14] However, the fact that the authorship controversy was based on historical misunderstanding should not distract us from how important it and other Shakespearean questions were to many American readers in the nineteenth century. Women were extremely active in Shakespeare studies: indeed, Twain identifies Delia Bacon's argument against William Shakespeare's authorship as an ignition point for his disputes with Ealer, and Twain's own arguments against William Shakespeare's authorship echoed many points made by Bacon (who believed Francis Bacon had a share in writing the plays but who was not his descendant).[15] Like many women who were early stakeholders in literary culture, Bacon built on the foundation of her own early education (in Catharine and Mary Beecher's school in Hartford, Connecticut) through independent study and several kinds of teaching. In the 1830s and '40s, she was teaching seminar-style classes in New Haven and New York in which she and her women students discussed writings by philosophers (Dugald Stewart, Thomas Reid, Victor Cousin) as well as by Samuel Taylor Coleridge (the best-known critic of Shakespeare) and Shakespeare himself. She also offered public lectures in New York about historical and literary topics (Hopkins, *Prodigal Puritan*, 49–57, 66–70, 154–65). Like Margaret Fuller's Conversations in the Boston area during the same period, Bacon's classes were organized for well-read women who had exhausted their formal educational opportunities.[16] However, because these informal courses had no institutional supervision, they could be much more innovative and far-reaching than official college courses. The courses led by Bacon and Fuller seem to have provided remarkably ambitious literary instruction at a time when English literature was barely taught in most American colleges.[17]

The American women's club movement was fueled by women's exclusion from higher education (and then their underrepresentation, once they began to be admitted), and in the latter decades of the nineteenth century, many women's clubs were Shakespeare societies.[18] They ranged from the Fortnightly Shakespeare Club of New York (which published the *American Shakespeare Magazine* in the late 1890s [Fleming, "The Ladies' Shakespeare," 5]) to the Shakespeare Literary Club in tiny Clarendon, Texas, in the 1880s (Seaholm, "Earnest Women," cited by Long, *Book Clubs*, 34). Most clubs required participants to prepare talks and papers on texts read in common. Many women's Shakespeare clubs were segregated: white racism and class exclusivity led to the development of separate club networks for African American women,

Jewish women, working women, and other constituencies (McHenry, *Forgotten Readers*, 180).[19] All these clubs were part of the continuing tradition of self-education and mutual education that had supported lyceum lectures (in which Shakespeare had been a favorite topic since at least the 1830s) and, beginning in 1878, Chautauqua Literary and Scientific Circles, which offered course materials and even degrees to adults who studied together in local Chautauqua circles. The majority of Chautauqua students were white women (Rieser, *The Chautauqua Moment*, 167), and Chautauqua publications included textbooks and study guides about literature.

A number of women authors took part in the work of literary clubs and informal schools: Julia Ward Howe often spoke to women's clubs on literary topics, for example (Gere, *Intimate Practices*, 59, 203). Howe was also involved in one of the more surprising educational initiatives of the late nineteenth century, the Concord School of Philosophy and Literature (1879–89). The Concord School was operated by New England Transcendentalists and St. Louis Hegelians, two groups devoted to studying philosophy and literature at a time when the two disciplines were being strictly differentiated in universities.[20] A. Bronson Alcott and William Torrey Harris, perhaps the only devotee of Hegel ever to serve as US Commissioner of Education, were the founders, and Emerson lectured. In addition to Howe, Sophia Ripley, and Ednah Cheney (a philosopher specializing in aesthetics who, as a teenager, had taken part in Fuller's Conversations), one of the women active in the Concord School was Susan Blow, a pioneer in the American kindergarten movement (McFadden, "Boston Teenagers"; Dykeman, "Ednah Dow Cheney's American Aesthetics"). A published scholar of Dante's work, Blow organized study courses on Shakespeare and other modern and ancient authors for kindergarten teachers (Snider, *St. Louis*, 317–24).

Shakespearean studies were fueled by print and reported in print, so they left many traces. Through print, their influence also extended beyond their participants. Literary lectures delivered in lyceums, Chautauqua sessions, women's clubs, and the Concord School were often reported in local newspapers, and the printed accounts sometimes offered substantive summaries. Well-received lecture series were often published as separate articles in magazines or collected into books, and the resulting books and articles might be reviewed or referenced in magazines and newspapers. Editions of Shakespeare often included prefaces, critical notes, or study guides, and a surprising number of books of Shakespeare criticism addressed to non-specialist readers were published and widely reviewed. Catalyzed especially by Coleridge's writings about Shakespeare, numerous Shakespeareans collectively worked out some of the characteristic features of literary criticism that the twentieth and twenty-first centuries would inherit. Questions of textual criticism, adjudicating among the different versions of the plays; aesthetic questions about the formal unity of the plays, relying on careful close reading to work out the crucial contribution of every interchange and scene to the overall effect of each play; philological inquiries into the etymologies, histories, connotations, and resonances of particular words and phrases; characterological and thematic criticism; and, of course, endless attempts to elaborate the nature and magnitude of Shakespeare's accomplishment – all these critical tasks were undertaken by Shakespeareans in public culture and were widely disseminated in print.

One of the most prominent Shakespearean publications was the journal *Poet-Lore*, begun in 1889 by Charlotte Porter and Helen A. Clarke to support the study of the writings of Shakespeare and Robert Browning. In its first six years, before it broadened its purview, *Poet-Lore* published critical interpretations of both authors, reviews of Shakespeare productions, and digests of the activities of Shakespeare and Browning societies at home and abroad. Porter and Clarke, jointly and separately, also published numerous critical writings about Shakespeare, Browning, and other authors, including study guides for the use of clubs and individuals. Their Shakespeare study guides drew on the best contemporary scholarship about the plays, referencing the international critics featured in the Variorum editions of Shakespeare (which had in turn been produced by Shakespearean scholars who were not academics) as well as a wide range of other criticism from the USA and Europe. Porter and Clarke practiced an intelligent version of aesthetic criticism, rooted in Coleridge's practices but pursued more thoroughly and extended. They homed in on authorial purposes (inferred from textual effects); they argued for the formal unity of each work; they encouraged readers to consider the myriad ways in which a text's construction contributed to its central effects or thematic elaboration; and they offered suggestions about the interpretive significance of allusions and source texts, which they tracked down assiduously. They also attended to female characters and gender relations. Porter and Clarke were nationally prominent and extremely prolific (as writers and editors) during the era when even Jane Addams's Hull-House had a Shakespeare club (Addams, *Twenty Years at Hull-House*, 435).

Shakespearean actresses were also active in literary authorities. Following the example of Sarah Siddons, a number of actresses offered public readings of Shakespeare that included interpretive commentary on the plays. Some of them also published Shakespearean criticism as part of their memoirs or in other forums. Siddons's niece, Fanny Kemble, was one of the best-known Shakespearean readers in the USA, but many lesser-known actresses followed suit. Abby Sage Richardson, another actress-reader, wrote a textbook based on her experience teaching informal classes "principally for young women." Her textbook polemically claimed English literature as the heritage of American readers, offering a history from *Beowulf* to Sir Walter Scott that was printed in at least eleven editions (*Familiar Talks*, v). An especially intriguing actress-critic is H. Kate Richmond-West, an actress who gave Shakespeare readings in the midwest and at some point offered a course in Shakespeare to a class of "fifty colored men and women." Drawing on that course, she published two volumes of a projected series called *The Shakespearean World*, discussions of *A Winter's Tale* and *King Lear* based on the premise that access to Shakespeare is "the privilege of humanity – not narrowed to a class, but the common heritage of all" (*Interpretation of A Winter's Tale*, 4).[21]

It is possible that many women were drawn to study and write about Shakespeare because his plays offered especially intriguing women characters and especially inviting accounts of female ambition and desire.[22] Anna Jameson's *Characteristics of Women* (1832), a British study of Shakespeare's female characters, set a direction followed by many American women who wrote about Shakespeare. Whether or not Shakespeare's works were especially hospitable to women readers, it is important that Shakespeare's works were also the most conspicuous site of literature's construction. Women who moved into Shakespeare studies were effectively staking their claim to a new cultural domain: not an exclusive claim, but a claim competing with men's. Moreover, the fact that both literature and women were symbolically relegated to private life, where they were supposed to offer antidotes to political controversy and market competition, meant that women who helped work out the nature and value of literature could address – perhaps indirectly, perhaps even unconsciously – some of their own privileges and limitations. They could also carve out a room of their own within the cultural complex of literature.

How classy is literature?

To find literature valuable was to make literature a potential marker of status. Precisely because creating literature and appreciating literature were established as crucial, especially worthy human capacities, debates over what counted as literature (and who got to say so) were also debates about who could attain the highest human qualities. By this logic, Jefferson's criticism of Wheatley was an early outcropping of the use of literary criticism to adjudicate human value. Kansas City's segregated Shakespeare clubs amply attest to the cultural work Shakespeare was not doing, in spite of the evidence that many people who were oppressed or struggling claimed literature, including Shakespeare, as their own.[23] The tradition of *belles-lettres*, derived from French salon culture, bequeathed to literature the potential to consolidate class privilege by making literature part of the polite culture that elite readers sought to monopolize (Warnick, *The Sixth Canon*, 95). In this respect, the belletristic tradition was much more openly exclusive than the two other cultural traditions converging in modern literature: civic republicanism, which emphasized literature's capacity to inform citizens and renew their moral commitments; and idealist aesthetics, which valued literature's capacity for transcendent insights and experiences. The potential for literary reading and study to count as markers of polite accomplishment – "conspicuous leisure," in Thorstein Veblen's term – meant that class was always at stake in American literary culture, along with the class privilege of whiteness.

This context is important for considering Edith Wharton's "Xingu" (1911), a biting satire of the status-mongering pseudo-intellectualism of literary club-women. Especially because of her commitment to literary professionalism, Wharton had reasons to distance herself from well-to-do women who "got up" works by authors old and new in the service of elite socializing. It is important to locate Wharton's invective in relation to the professionalization of academic literary studies, however. "Xingu" targets a women's club as an amateur organization whose members mistake superficial knowledge for the real thing. It was written after university-credentialed literary expertise had consolidated: by the 1910s, English was a core discipline for undergraduate and graduate studies, and most college English professors had completed the specialized training required for a Ph.D. Accordingly, Wharton lampoons the club's feeble simulation of a university's division into departments of knowledge: Miss Van Vluyck covers "[p]hilanthropy and statistics" (a significant pairing, hinting at the emergence of Progressive forms of managerial sociology out of late nineteenth-century club work); Laura Glyde handles literature; and Mrs. Ballinger's "province" is "the Book of the Day," which means that she knows about whatever trendy volume is held to represent the "Thought of the Day" ("Xingu," 7–8). An earlier Wharton story, "The Pelican" (1898), made a similar attack on superficial feminine learning in the person of Mrs. Amyot, who offered public lectures on Greek art, contemporary poets, Goethe (cribbed from George Lewes's work, the male narrator assures us), and science and religion. The combination's very eclecticism marks

Mrs. Amyot's amateurism, compared to the disciplinary specialization of modern universities.

Women's literary clubs could be the engines of contempt and cultural hoarding, most assuredly; Charles W. Chesnutt's "Baxter's *Procrustes*" (1904), a satire of a men's club dedicated to collecting and producing beautiful limited-edition books, shows that men's literary clubs could be as pretentious. Wharton's and Chesnutt's satires skewer literary snobbery, but they also point to what went sour when public literary culture became amateur literary culture. The clubs in these stories are stagnant backwaters, perhaps because of their fussy exclusivity but perhaps also because the elevation of academic expertise over other forms of cultural authority left no room for non-academics to participate in serious literary study and scholarship except as a form of ritual display. Before it came to be taken for granted that new literary knowledge would be published in academic venues such as *PMLA* (founded 1884), academics and non-academics alike contributed to publications such as *Notes and Queries* (founded 1849), *Shakespeareana* (1883–93), and *Poet-Lore* (founded 1889), and there were many forms of interchange between literary scholars who were professors and literary scholars who were not.[24] Porter and Clarke had collegial relations with Professor Hiram Corson of Cornell and Professor Richard G. Moulton of the University of Chicago, for example, and may have met both men through the Browning Society (Peterson, *Interrogating the Oracle*, 57, 91–2).

The Browning Society, which was much more active in the USA than in England, was in its heyday (the late nineteenth century) one of the last preserves of public literary culture that brought together academics and other serious readers. In the twentieth century, it came to be disparaged as a fan club whose stereotypically female members had had crushes on the distinguished widower Robert Browning – another caricature that combines misogyny with the shaming of amateur studies. Published papers of the Browning Society show that members were involved in characteristically literary endeavors – close reading, thematic interpretation, identification of sources and allusions – but were noteworthy for entertaining expansive interests in Browning's social and spiritual visions, in keeping with the diminishing generalist tradition in academic literary studies rather than the intense specialization and narrow disciplinarity of the newer faculty (Renker, *Origins of American Literature Studies*, 13–22). Browning's admirers valued him as a poet who addressed the complexities of "modern" – meaning contemporary – life, and Browning societies appear to have fostered hopes for social transformation and spiritual regeneration, including transformations of gender relations and intimate life. Many admiring accounts of Robert Browning's poetry lingered over his marriage to Barrett, and critical discussions of Browning's poems about love and relationships appeared to draw confidence from his well-known admiration for his wife as a fellow practitioner (indeed, a poet initially much more famous than he was). Porter and Clarke's annotated edition of Barrett Browning's poems features an illustration of Harriet Hosmer's sculpture of the Brownings' clasped hands, and Hosmer's reputation for being ambitious, talented, and independent may have amplified the sculpture's rendering of equal partnership (Browning, *Complete Works*, 1: lix–1). Browning's most active critics included a number of women who partnered with other women and may have been lesbians (including Porter and Clarke), and it is possible that their interest in his poetry was enhanced by the ways in which the Brownings' anti-patriarchal elopement and the poets' equal commitments to their writing careers could point beyond the heteronormative.[25]

Literature could be a medium of sociability, formal or informal instruction, cultural memory, collective longing, personal transformation, or vicious exclusivity: indeed, literature was invented to do all these things, and women were involved in all of them. Another way women shaped literary culture was by working in the publishing industry, in which books were marketed according to their literariness and book reviews perpetually negotiated literary questions.

As the nineteenth-century US publishing industry grew, markets for publication became more finely differentiated, and gender was an important principle of differentiation. Significantly, there were no major women's publishing houses. *Woodhull and Claflin's Weekly*, a newspaper founded in 1870 by Victoria Woodhull and her sister, was a rare and short-lived example of a publication controlled at the highest management levels by women – indeed, women who were radical suffragists. However, there were many periodicals aimed at women, such as *Godey's Ladies' Magazine* and *Ladies' Home Journal*, and there were series of books marketed to women. Many publications for children, such as *St. Nicholas Magazine* (founded 1873), were edited by women and featured mainly women as contributors. In these stretches of print culture, some women worked hard to establish the significance of women's (and girls') intellectual and cultural lives, drawing on a range of ideas about gender, even though these publications also helped to position women as a special category of consumer.

In the male-dominated stretches of print culture that counted as "general," and within the particular stretches devoted to literature, women also participated, sometimes as magazine editors (the novelist Caroline Kirkland edited *Union Magazine* and *Sartain's*; Jeannette L. Gilder co-edited *The Critic* with her brother), sometimes as reviewers (a role many authors played part-time), sometimes as press readers (as in the case of Susan M. Francis at Houghton-Mifflin [Reitt, "Editorial Occupations," 40–1]), and sometimes in other capacities. They were likely to be pressed into service as representatives of a female point-of-view whether or not they wished to be: for instance, Edmund C. Stedman wrote that he deferred to his colleague and "Junior Editor," Ellen Mackay Hutchinson, about her "fellow crafts*women*" in determining selections for the *Library of American Literature* (1889–90), the most ambitious American literary anthology of the nineteenth century (Stedman and Gould, *Life and Letters*, 2: 140). Some women had a special intellectual commitment to shaping the terms on which women writers were considered: Margaret Fuller, who made a strong case for the value of Elizabeth Barrett's work, was adamant that Barrett's poetry ought to be judged by the same standards as men's poetry.

The fact that many American women were involved in developing and promoting literature does not mean that they controlled its meaning. All their efforts took place in national and international contexts in which women in the aggregate were legally, politically, economically, and socially disadvantaged compared to men, and women's participation in literary culture was powerfully shaped by this disparity. Women of color, immigrant women, poor women, and women whose lives – including their writing and reading – departed from normative models of femininity were likely to face even greater difficulties finding a place to stand in literary culture (or to a platform from which to criticize it). Yet recognizing that literature was a cultural project invented over time by many people allows us to think in new ways about women's contributions, not only as authors but also as readers, teachers, agents of the publishing industry, and cultural trustees and stakeholders. We can also examine how literature, this powerful cultural institution, helped to structure relations between women and men and relations among different groups of women, in the days when the most important question asked about any piece of imaginative writing was "But is it literature?"

Notes

1. True Womanhood was influential, but an important later movement in feminist scholarship has complicated our understanding of the multiple ideologies of gender at work; see Davidson, *No More Separate Spheres!*.

2. I focus on fiction and poetry here rather than drama and essays, since fiction and poetry were more central to the new, narrower version of modern literature that I am tracing. Drama (Shakespeare's signature genre) was a problem for literature, especially the discipline of literary studies, precisely because it was linked to stage performance rather than private readerly encounters; see Smith, *American Drama*. The essay's literary standing was pressured partly by its becoming a genre of scholarship and journalism and partly by its becoming the fundamental genre of composition instruction. On the essay's fortunes within composition, see Lockhart, *Revising the Essay*; and Connors, *Composition-Rhetoric*, 64, 310.

3. Some of the cultural and political negotiations that accompanied Europe's attempts to impose its version of modernity – including the modern conception of literature – are analyzed in Chakrabarty, *Provincializing Europe*, especially ch. 7, "*Adda*: A History of Sociality," which discusses twentieth-century developments in Bengali literary culture that ambivalently engaged European literary texts and norms.

4. Oxford and Cambridge added chairs of English literature in the early twentieth century, much later than universities in other parts of the world and the newer English universities (University College, London and King's College, both of which offered courses in English literature when they merged in 1836) (Reid, *Wordsworth and the Formation of English Studies*, 41–2). On the importance of Scotland and Ireland in the development of English studies, see especially Court, *Institutionalizing English Literature*; Crawford, *The Scottish Invention of English Literature*; Miller, *The Formation of College English*; Rhodes, *Shakespeare and the Origins of English*; and Siskin, *The Work of Writing*. On the importance of India, see Viswanathan, *Masks of Conquest*. An important work linking the formation of English studies to the internal English apparatus of governance – the empire's internal patrolling, effectively – is Hunter, *Culture and Government*. Tracing the beginning of English literary studies is difficult in part because of the difference between locating early versions of the modern understanding of literature and locating early instances of people studying or lecturing about texts that we now consider literary. For example, some of the earliest public university-sponsored lectures about Anglophone texts that we now consider literary were Adam Smith's lectures at the University of Edinburgh in 1848–51, lectures that were retrospectively titled *Lectures in Rhetoric and Belles-Lettres* (on the model of Hugh Blair's later lectures under that rubric) but that did not substantively address *belles-lettres*, much less literature (Duncan, "Adam Smith, Samuel Johnson and the Institutions of English," 38).

5. My emphasis that "literature" is distinct from "poetry" marks a shift from many genealogical accounts of literature that treat poetry and literature as effectively continuous, so that the history of literature can go back to Aristotle's *Poetics* and beyond. For an influential example of this approach, see Wellek, *The Rise of English Literary History*.

6. Bosco and Murphy note that influential criticism about Bradstreet in the 1960s relegated her poem about the humors and other general intellectual topics to her "apprenticeship," identifying her more personal poems with her artistic "maturity" ("New England Poetry," 120).

7. These events were often attended by people who were not connected with graduates. For example, while visiting Philadelphia in 1791, Judith Sargent Murray attended a debate that was part of the commencement exercises of Pennsylvania College (Skemp, *First Lady of Letters*, 196).

8. Joanna J. Brooks has found no evidence that the oral examination occurred and thinks Wheatley may have asked the men to document her authorship for the London publishers she was approaching ("Our Phillis, Ourselves," 1–7).

9. On the relationship between the development of literature and the development of national languages in the nations, colonies, and former colonies of Europe, see Casanova, *The World Republic of Letters*, esp. ch. 2, "The Invention of Literature." Casanova treats literature as a contemporary global phenomenon whose roots can be traced in ancient texts in many parts of the world, offering in effect an extraordinarily expanded canon.

10. To some extent, the ongoing study of any canonical author contributed to the development of ideas of literature, especially before English literary studies was securely institutionalized. The story of literature can be told in relation to many authors. Two studies that argue for Shakespeare's paramount influence on the development of English literary studies are Dobson, *The Making of the National Poet*, and Rhodes, *Shakespeare and the Origins of English*. On Shakespeare's works having been reinterpreted to accord with the eighteenth- and nineteenth-century aesthetics that would characterize modern literature, see Taylor, *Reinventing Shakespeare*, and de Grazia, *Hamlet without Hamlet*.

11. Courses in English were available as early as the 1830s in University College, London and King's College (Reid, *Wordsworth and the Formation of English Studies*, 41), setting an important precedent for modern literary studies in higher education. However, even in England, the movement from English literature's being featured in the curriculum to its becoming a fundamental discipline was slow (Reid, *Wordsworth and the Formation of English Studies*, 89). On the development of English departments in the USA, see Graff, *Professing English*; Renker, *The Origins of American Literature Studies*; Shumway, *Creating American Civilization*; and Graff and Warner, *The Origins of Literary Studies in America*.

12. About Shakespeare's prominent inclusion in textbooks for elocution and oratory and other kinds of eighteenth-century anthologies, see Simon, *The Reading of Shakespeare*; Rhodes, *Shakespeare and the Origins of English*; and Lauck, *The Reception and Teaching of Shakespeare*, 9–30.

13. No wonder that Shakespeare is Michel Foucault's prime example of the "author-function" at work in "What is an Author?"

14. See, for example, Greenblatt, *Will in the World*, which addresses many questions about Shakespeare's life first formulated in the nineteenth century: the quality of his education, what he did after he left Stratford and before he joined Burbage's company, what his investment might have been in applying for a family coat of arms, etc.

15. For discussions of Bacon's theories and the ways in which her political readings of the plays anticipated recent trends in Shakespeare studies, see Baym, "Delia Bacon," and Glazener, "Print Culture."

16. Fuller expanded her initial course to include men, partly to increase her income and partly to take advantage of college graduates' training in classical languages (Capper, *Margaret Fuller*, 1: 290–306; 2: 50).

17. Some of the earliest lectures on Shakespeare by American college professors were George Ticknor's lectures at Harvard in the 1830s (of which no transcript or summary exists) and Henry Reed's lectures on British poets in 1841 at the University of

Pennsylvania; Reed may have been the first US academic to hold a title that included "English literature," since he had been appointed to a chair in Rhetoric and English Literature in 1835. By the 1850s, there were occasional courses on Shakespeare (or courses on British poets or even British literature that featured Shakespeare) at a number of colleges, under professors appointed in literature, *belles-lettres*, poetry, rhetoric, and moral philosophy (Lauck, *The Reception and Teaching of Shakespeare*, 208–21). However, many literary scholars of the later nineteenth century did not remember literature as they knew it having formed any part of their education at Yale and Harvard as late as the 1860s and '70s (Simon, *The Reading of Shakespeare*, 47–8).

18. In this way, the women's club movement built on a long history of women's reading circles and literary societies (some affiliated with academies and seminaries for young women) devoted to mutual education, although some of the groups were committed broadly to education rather than specifically to literature. See Garfield, "Literary Societies"; Kelley, "'A More Glorious Revolution'"; and McHenry, *Forgotten Readers*.

The first college in the USA to allow women to take courses with men was Oberlin College in 1837. In the following decades, more men's colleges followed suit and more female academies evolved into women's colleges. However, in 1869, fewer than 15 per cent of the recipients of bachelor's degrees in the USA were women (Connors, *Composition-Rhetoric*, 42).

19. For a comprehensive discussion of women's clubs for various constituencies in this era, see Gere, *Intimate Practices*, who also argues that the reading practices of clubwomen helped to establish public support for academic literary studies and kept alive broader traditions of reading than college English courses did (243–4).

20. The St. Louis Movement's self-appointed chronicler was Denton J. Snider, who published on Shakespeare and lectured at the Concord School, Chautauqua, and in Chicago classes aimed at kindergarten teachers and who undertook many other literary classes for adults, in addition to years spent teaching high school. Snider's *The St. Louis Movement* discusses the Concord School and along the way identifies a number of women who participated in St. Louis, Concord, and Chicago philosophical and literary circles.

21. Although the title-page lists Richmond-West as editor, the work consists of an introduction and a single essay, both apparently authored by Richmond-West.

22. A host of scholarship has explored gender in Shakespeare as well as women writers' and readers' relationship to Shakespeare's works; see Novy, *Cross-Cultural Performances*, *Engaging with Shakespeare*, and *Women's Re-Visions of Shakespeare*. Women have taken active public interest in Shakespeare and his legacy at least as far back as the "Shakespeare Ladies Club," which was organized in 1736 to promote the production of Shakespeare's plays and later lobbied for Shakespeare's memorial in Westminster Abbey (Taylor, *Reinventing Shakespeare*, 93; Fleming, "The Ladies' Shakespeare," 3).

23. Hilary Rowland's "Shakespeare and the Public Sphere," ch. 4, analyzes three unlikely nineteenth-century admirers of Shakespeare: Elizabeth Cady Stanton, Frederick Douglass, and George Wilkes, a "radical republican" who founded the *Police Gazette* and also published *Shakespeare from an American Point-of-View* (New York: Appleton, 1877).

24. The initial title of *PMLA* (Publications of the Modern Language Association) was *Transactions of the Modern Language Association*. Many college professors who did not hold a Ph.D. (and some who did) were disturbed that increased influence of faculty

Ph.D.-holders would result in unproductive levels of specialization and weakened undergraduate teaching. These professors may have had more in common with literary non-academics than with their colleagues who had a Ph.D. (Gold, *Rhetoric at the Margins*, 120–2).

25. A number of women faculty members at Wellesley College who lived in long-term relationships with women were active in Browning studies: Vida Dutton Scudder (English), who wrote about Browning's work in *The Life of the Spirit in the Modern English Poets* (1895), lived with editor and novelist Florence Converse; Margaret Sherwood (English), who wrote about Browning's poetry in *Undercurrents of Influence in English Romantic Poetry* (1934), lived with Martha Hale Shackford (English), who edited a volume of Barrett Browning's letters; Katharine Lee Bates (English) wrote a poem about Browning, "In the Poet's Corner," and with Katharine Coman (Economics) made use of Browning's work in their joint project *English History Told by English Poets* (1902). Bates and Coman lived together for decades, and Bates published a book of poetry (*Yellow Clover: A Book of Remembrance*) about Coman after her death. Palmieri, *In Adamless Eden*, offers a thorough discussion of the Wellesley faculty from this era and the many partnerships (known sometimes as "Wellesley marriages") among women faculty and students.

Works cited

Addams, Jane. *Twenty Years at Hull-House; with Autobiographical Notes*. New York: Macmillan, 1912.

Amore, Adelaide P. "Introduction." In *A Woman's Inner World: Selected Poetry and Prose of Anne Bradstreet*. By Anne Bradstreet. Ed. Amore. Lanham, MD: University Press of America, 1982.

Baym, Nina. "Delia Bacon, History's Odd Woman Out." *The New England Quarterly* 69 (1996): 223–49.

Bosco, Ronald A. and Jillmarie Murphy. "New England Poetry." In *The Oxford Handbook of Early American Literature*. Ed. Kevin J. Hayes. New York: Oxford University Press, 2008.

Brooks, Joanna. "Our Phillis, Ourselves." *American Literature* 82.1 (2010): 1–25.

Brooks, Van Wyck. "On Creating a Usable Past." *The Dial* 64.7 (1918): 337–41.

Browning, Elizabeth Barrett. *The Complete Works of Mrs. E. B. Browning*. Ed. Charlotte Porter and Helen A. Clarke. 6 vols. New York: Thomas Y. Crowell, 1900.

Capper, Charles. *Margaret Fuller: An American Romantic Life*. 2 vols. New York: Oxford University Press, 1992.

Casanova, Pascale. *The World Republic of Letters*. Trans. M. B. DeBevoise. Cambridge, MA: Harvard University Press, 2004.

Chakrabarty, Dipesh. *Provincializing Europe: Postcolonial Thought and Historical Difference*. Princeton: Princeton University Press, 2000.

Chesnutt, Charles W. "Baxter's *Procrustes*." In *Stories, Novels, and Essays*. Library of America edition. Ed. Werner Sollors. New York: Literary Classics of the United States, 2002.

Cliff, Nigel. *The Shakespeare Riots: Revenge, Drama, and Death in Nineteenth-Century America*. New York: Random House, 2007.

Connors, Robert J. *Composition-Rhetoric: Backgrounds, Theory, and Pedagogy*. Pittsburgh: University of Pittsburgh Press, 1997.

Court, Franklin E. *Institutionalizing English Literature: The Culture and Politics of Literary Study, 1750–1900*. Stanford: Stanford University Press, 1992.

Crawford Robert, ed. *The Scottish Invention of English Literature*. New York: Cambridge University Press, 1988.

Davidson, Cathy N., ed. *No More Separate Spheres! A Next Wave American Studies Reader*. Durham, NC: Duke University Press, 2002.

de Grazia, Margreta. *Hamlet without Hamlet*. New York: Cambridge University Press, 2007.

Dobson, Michael. *The Making of the National Poet: Shakespeare, Adaptation, and Authorship, 1660–1769*. Oxford: Clarendon Press, 1992.

Duncan, Ian. "Adam Smith, Samuel Johnson and the Institutions of English." In *The Scottish Invention of English Literature*. Ed. Robert Crawford. New York: Cambridge University Press, 1988.

Dykeman, Therese B. "Ednah Dow Cheney's American Aesthetics." In *Presenting Women Philosophers*. Ed. Cecile T. Tougas and Sara Ebenreck. Philadelphia: Temple University Press, 2000.

Fleming, Juliet. "The Ladies' Shakespeare." In *A Feminist Companion to Shakespeare*. Ed. Dympna Callaghan. Malden, MA: Blackwell, 2000.

Ford, Arthur L. *Joel Barlow*. New York: Twayne, 1971.

Foucault, Michel. "What is an Author?" Trans. José V. Harari. In *The Foucault Reader*. Ed. Paul Rabinow. New York: Pantheon Books, 1984.

Fuller, Margaret. "Miss Barrett's Poems." In *Literature and Art*. 2 vols. New York: Fowlers and Wells, 1852.

Garfield, Michelle N. "Literary Societies: The Work of Self-Improvement and Racial Uplift." In *Black Women's Intellectual Traditions: Speaking their Minds*. Ed. Kristin Waters and Carol B. Conaway. Burlington, VT: University of Vermont Press, 2007.

Gates, Henry Louis. *The Trials of Phillis Wheatley: America's First Black Poet and her Encounters with the Founding Fathers*. New York: Basic Books, 2003.

Gere, Anne Ruggles. *Intimate Practices: Literacy and Cultural Work in US Women's Clubs, 1880–1920*. Urbana: University of Illinois Press, 1997.

Glazener, Nancy. "Print Culture as an Archive of Dissent; Or, Delia Bacon and the Case of the Missing Hamlet." *American Literary History* 19.2 (2007): 329–49.

Gold, David. *Rhetoric at the Margins: Revising the History of Writing Instruction in American Colleges, 1873–1947*. Carbondale: Southern Illinois University Press, 2008.

Graff, Gerald. *Professing English: An Institutional History*. Chicago: University of Chicago Press, 1987.

Graff, Gerald and Michael Warner, eds. *The Origins of Literary Studies in America: A Documentary History*. New York: Routledge, 1989.

Greenblatt, Stephen. *Will in the World: How Shakespeare Became Shakespeare*. New York: W. W. Norton, 2004.

Hawthorne, Nathaniel. *The Letters, 1853–1856*. Ed. Thomas Woodson *et al.* Vol. 17 of *The Centenary Edition of the Works of Nathaniel Hawthorne*, 23 vols. Ed. William Charvat *et al.* Columbus: Ohio State University Press, 1987.

Hayes, Kevin J., ed. *The Oxford Handbook of Early American Literature*. New York: Oxford University Press, 2008.

Hopkins, Vivian C. *Prodigal Puritan: A Life of Delia Bacon*. Cambridge, MA: Harvard University Press, 1959.

Hunter, Ian. *Culture and Government: The Emergence of Literary Education*. Houndmills: Macmillan, 1988.

Jackson, Virginia. *Dickinson's Misery: A Theory of Lyric Reading*. Princeton: Princeton University Press, 2005.

Jefferson, Thomas. *Notes on the State of Virginia*. 1781. *Writings*. Ed. Merrill D. Peterson. Library of America edition. New York: Literary Classics of the United States, 1984.

Kafer, Peter. "The Making of Timothy Dwight: A Connecticut Morality Tale." *William and Mary Quarterly* 47.2 (1990): 189–209.

Kelley, Mary. "'A More Glorious Revolution': Women's Antebellum Reading Circles and the Pursuit of Public Influence." *New England Quarterly* 76.2 (2003): 163–96.

Lauck, John Hampton, II. "The Reception and Teaching of Shakespeare in Nineteenth and Early Twentieth Century America." Diss., University of Illinois, Urbana-Champaign, 1991.

Levine, Lawrence. *Highbrow/Lowbrow: The Emergence of Cultural Hierarchy in America*. Cambridge, MA: Harvard University Press, 1990.

Lockhart, Tara. "Revising the Essay: Intellectual Arenas and Hybrid Forms." Diss., University of Pittsburgh, Pittsburgh, 2008.

Long, Elizabeth. *Book Clubs: Women and the Uses of Reading in Everyday Life*. Chicago: University of Chicago Press, 2003.

Longaker, Mark Garrett. *Rhetoric and the Republic: Politics, Civic Discourse, and Education in Early America*. Tuscaloosa: University of Alabama Press, 2007.

Marsh, Philip M. *Philip Freneau: Poet and Journalist*. Minneapolis: Dillon Press, 1967.

McFadden, Margaret. "Boston Teenagers Debate the Woman Question, 1837–1838." *Signs* 15.4 (1990): 832–47.

McHenry, Elizabeth. *Forgotten Readers: Recovering the Lost History of African American Literary Societies*. Durham, NC: Duke University Press, 2002.

Miller, Thomas P. *The Formation of College English: Rhetoric and Belles Lettres in the British Cultural Provinces*. Pittsburgh: University of Pittsburgh Press, 1997.

Mulford, Carla. "Print and Manuscript Culture." In *The Oxford Handbook of Early American Literature*. Ed. Kevin J. Hayes. New York: Oxford University Press, 2008.

Novy, Marianne. *Engaging with Shakespeare: Responses of George Eliot and Other Women Novelists*. Iowa City: University of Iowa Press, 1998.

Novy, Marianne, ed. *Cross-Cultural Performances: Differences in Women's Re-Visions of Shakespeare*. Champaign: University of Illinois Press, 1993.

—— *Women's Re-Visions of Shakespeare: On Responses of Dickinson, Woolf, Rich, H.D., George Eliot, and Others*. Champaign: University of Illinois Press, 1990.

Palmieri, Patricia Ann. *In Adamless Eden: The Community of Women Faculty at Wellesley*. New Haven: Yale University Press, 1995.

Peterson, William S. *Interrogating the Oracle: A History of the London Browning Society*. Athens, OH: Ohio University Press, 1969.

Porter, Charlotte and Helen A. Clarke. *Shakespeare Study Programs: The Tragedies.* Boston: Richard G. Badger; Toronto: The Copp Clark Co., 1914.

Punter, David. *Modernity.* New York: Palgrave, 2007.

Reid, Ian. *Wordsworth and the Formation of English Studies.* Burlington, VT: Ashgate, 2004.

Reitt, Barbara B. "Editorial Occupations in the American Book Trade in the 1880s and 1890s." *Book Research Quarterly* 4.2 (1988): 33–46.

Renker, Elizabeth. *The Origins of American Literature Studies: An Institutional History.* New York: Cambridge University Press, 2007.

Rhodes, Neil. *Shakespeare and the Origins of English.* New York: Oxford University Press, 2004.

Richardson, Abby Sage. *Familiar Talks on English Literature: A Manual.* 1881. 11th edn. Chicago: A. C. McClurg, 1891.

Richmond-West, Mrs. H. Kate, ed. *The Shakespearean World* no. 1: *Interpretation of A Winter's Tale.* Chicago: Knight and Leonard, 1882.

Rieser, Andrew C. *The Chautauqua Moment: Protestants, Progressives, and the Culture of Modern Liberalism.* New York: Columbia University Press, 2003.

Rowland, Hilary. "Shakespeare and the Public Sphere in Nineteenth Century America." Diss., McGill University, Montreal, 1998.

Seaholm, Megan. "Earnest Women: The White Women's Movement in Progressive Era Texas, 1880–1920." Diss., Rice University, Houston, 1988.

Shields, John C. "Phillis Wheatley's Struggle for Freedom in her Poetry and Prose." In *The Collected Works of Phillis Wheatley. By Phillis Wheatley.* Ed. John C. Shields. New York: Oxford University Press, 1988.

Shumway, David R. *Creating American Civilization: A Genealogy of American Literature as an Academic Discipline.* Minneapolis: University of Minnesota Press, 1993.

Sidney, Sir Philip. "The Defence of Poesy." In *Selected Writings.* Ed. Richard Dutton. New York: Fyfield Books, 1987.

Simon, Henry W. *The Reading of Shakespeare in American Schools and Colleges: An Historical Survey.* New York: Simon and Schuster, 1932.

Siskin, Clifford. *The Work of Writing: Literature and Social Change in Britain, 1700–1830.* Baltimore: The Johns Hopkins University Press, 1998.

Skemp, Sheila L. *First Lady of Letters: Judith Sargent Murray and the Struggle for Female Independence.* Philadelphia: University of Pennsylvania Press, 2009.

Smith, Susan Harris. *American Drama: The Bastard Art.* New York: Cambridge University Press, 1997.

Snider, Denton J. *A Writer of Books / In His Genesis.* St. Louis: Sigma Publishing, 1910.
    The St. Louis Movement in Philosophy, Literature, Education, Psychology, with Chapters of Autobiography. St. Louis: Sigma Publishing, 1920.

Stanton, Elizabeth Cady. *Eighty Years and More (1815–1897): Reminiscences of Elizabeth Cady Stanton.* New York: European Publishing Company, 1898.

Stedman, Laura and George M. Gould. *Life and Letters of Edmund Clarence Stedman.* 2 vols. New York: Moffat, Yard, 1910.

Taylor, Gary. *Reinventing Shakespeare: A Cultural History, from the Restoration to the Present.* New York: Weidenfeld and Nicolson, 1989.

Twain, Mark. *Is Shakespeare Dead?* New York and London: Harper, 1909.

Viswanathan, Gauri. *Masks of Conquest: Literary Study and British Rule in India*. New York: Columbia University Press, 1989.

Warnick, Barbara. *The Sixth Canon: Belletristic Rhetorical Theory and its French Antecedents*. Columbia: University of South Carolina Press, 1993.

Wellek, René. *The Rise of English Literary History*. New York: McGraw-Hill Book Company, 1966.

Welter, Barbara. *Dimity Convictions: The American Woman in the Nineteenth Century*. Athens, OH: Ohio University Press, 1976.

Wharton, Edith. "The Pelican." In *Collected Stories*. Vol. 1: *1891–1910*. Ed. Maureen Howard. Library of America. New York: Literary Classics of the United States, 2001.

"Xingu." In *Collected Stories*. Vol. 2: *1911–1937*. Library of America edition. Ed. Maureen Howard. New York: Literary Classics of the United States, 2001.

Wheatley, Phillis. *Complete Writings*. Ed. Vincent Carretta. New York: Penguin, 2001.

8

Moral authority as literary property in mid-nineteenth-century print culture

SUSAN M. RYAN

The *Liberator*, which covered Harriet Beecher Stowe's 1853 tour of England in minute detail, described in its June 10 issue a London antislavery event at which Stowe had appeared as guest of honor: "The assembly filed past Mrs. Stowe, exchanging courtesies, and afterwards adjourned to supper, where a marble bust of Mrs. Stowe, by Bernard, was exhibited" ("Mrs. Stowe," 91). The sheer oddity of these attendees encountering Stowe and her marble likeness in rapid succession intensifies the contrast between the cool, white stillness of the bust – suggestive of remoteness, authority, purity, status – and the live, conversant, dare I say mildly frumpy author before them. The juxtaposition collapses time, preempting the long process of canonization that would ordinarily precede the commissioning of an author's bust, a static object calculated to signify his or her timelessness. Their coexistence also undermines the customary distance between presence and reputation, the bust reminding guests of Stowe's preeminence in the world of letters and of social reform, even as she eats her dinner among them.

This marble rendering – signifying a moment at which Stowe becomes literally iconic – both indexes and asserts the synergy among her popularity, her literary status, and her moral authority, insofar as the author's celebrity in England was, in the early to mid-1850s, inextricable from her antislavery advocacy via fiction. But the terms of those linkages, within and beyond English abolitionist circles and the *Liberator's* readership, are not entirely clear. To what extent did Stowe's popularity derive from a perception of her moral righteousness? That is, how many of the hundreds of thousands who bought and read *Uncle Tom's Cabin* did so not simply because they had heard that it offered a well-told narrative but because it tapped into their own preexisting sense of slavery's injustice? For some, including many of Stowe's English admirers, this was certainly the case. But the converse is also possible: the novel's very popularity may have endowed its author with a degree of moral authority – by which I mean an extension of personal character into the realm of influence, actual or potential – that she did not have at the outset. If, for proslavery authors, Stowe's talents as a storyteller belied her fundamental ideological corruption (and, indeed, corrosiveness), for other readers, the novel's effectiveness, its ability to engage readers, may have pointed to its underlying righteousness. But we must not lose sight of the fact that many read and enjoyed this book without acknowledging its moral force and certainly without being converted by it. A Mrs. M'Kee, for example, wrote in New York's *Christian Parlor Magazine* that "a work which can thus force admiration from the indifferent, and compel respect even from opposers, must have most extraordinary power," but then she seeks to neutralize that power by claiming to "speak . . . only of its merit as a literary work, and without reference to its moral bearings on slavery . . ." ("Literary Celebrities," 305).

Despite M'Kee's assertion, literary merit and "moral bearings" could not be so easily disentangled in the middle decades of the nineteenth century. I have begun with this meditation on Stowe because the tensions, contradictions, and alignments that permeated her reception illuminate, if they also exaggerate, more widespread phenomena. The nineteenth century saw not just a dramatic expansion of the domestic book trade, but also a significant increase in commentary on literary matters within US periodicals, in the form of book reviews, advertisements, and miscellaneous articles on literary figures, trends, and controversies. In this proliferating print culture, the moral character of mid-nineteenth-century authors, both male and female, became a key element in the marketing and reception of books and in the formation of literary reputations. Moral authority became, then, a kind of literary property that could be accumulated, squandered, overestimated, damaged, and repaired.

This essay examines the particular ways in which mid-century women authors negotiated such questions in light of mainstream gender expectations, including the pressure to fulfill domestic obligations and the perceived hazards of female publicity. Women's involvement in the great social reform projects of the day also informed the moral valences that attached to their authorial ventures. In exploring these structures, I offer three central assertions. The first is methodological: given the field's ever-expanding array of keyword-searchable digital databases, scholars now bear a responsibility to read much more widely than was possible in the days of paper- and microfilm-only archives. That is, it is no longer sufficient to consult a few well-plumbed sources (for example, canonical novels and such landmark periodicals as the *North American Review* or *Godey's Lady's Book*) in our investigations of nineteenth-century print culture. The Wright American Fiction index, for example, allows researchers to identify and access long-forgotten works that address questions central to their projects. Similarly, in researching the circulation of literary figures and texts within the era's periodical culture, we should look beyond the obvious, paying attention not just to articles trained on our objects of study – the kinds of pieces that might appear in an author's or a literary executor's clipping file – but also to passing references and off-handed remarks, which in the aggregate can tell us a great deal about how particular authors were perceived and represented. Furthermore, we now have the opportunity – and, I would argue, the obligation – to consult nonmetropolitan print sources (small-town and western newspapers and magazines) and other publications that represented the views and concerns of those outside the Anglo-American cultural establishment. To return to the example of Stowe: the *Liberator* and the *Southern Literary Messenger* played crucial roles in registering and shaping her 1850s reception for their disparate audiences, but comments in more obscure papers like the Moulton (AL) *Advertiser* or the *Maine Farmer* shed light on Stowe's resonance as a cultural figure beyond the venues that scholars have identified as important taste- and opinion-makers. Opportunities to study an author's circulation within the era's African American press have expanded as well. Not only are such well-known titles as *Frederick Douglass's Paper* more widely accessible and more easily searchable than they were even ten years ago, but so are less-often-mentioned publications such as the *Provincial Freeman* (an Ontario paper published by African American expatriates), which, incidentally, commented acerbically on the *Uncle Tom's Cabin* phenomenon.[1]

This more capacious archive tends to undermine reductive understandings of authors' reputational negotiations. Accordingly, my second claim is that women writers were not simply the victims of a sexist society that burdened them with unreasonable moral obligations and standards. On the contrary, they – like their male counterparts – often exploited these cultural constructs, using moral status as a means of shoring up a flagging literary reputation or, in some cases, putting their literary attainments and skills in the service of enhancing their moral authority. I do not mean to suggest that women were never disadvantaged, personally or professionally, by gendered expectations, but rather that they were remarkably savvy in their negotiations of this unequal field.[2]

My final claim, based on primary research in US periodicals, is that women authors' intersecting moral and literary reputations appear to have been more resilient – and their transgressions more forgivable – at mid-century than is often supposed. Rather than adhering to what we might call the "fallen woman" model, in which an author's loss of moral authority, whether through scandal or through shifting cultural attitudes, signified her literary demise, I propose instead a more elastic notion of women authors' reputational economies. Moral authority, it seems, could be diminished and later restored, with scandals and missteps effectively contained or quarantined at least for certain periods and purposes within the literary field.

Critical interventions

Scholarship on nineteenth-century US women has dealt extensively with the moral stakes of authorship, not least because those stakes were a signal feature of the era's literary culture.[3] As Nina Baym notes in *Novels, Readers, and Reviewers* (1984), "talk about morality is so characteristic of and so widely prevalent in novel reviewing in the 1840s and 1850s as to indicate that it was taken as part of the reviewer's job" (173). These judgments often extended to the author as well as to his or her text. Further, creative works themselves anticipated and in some cases invited these lines of inquiry. Registering a keen awareness of authorship as a kind of moral hazard, many women authors used their prefaces to reassure readers that they had written the book in question ultimately for the good of young people or some other deserving constituency, even as they attested that no domestic duties had been neglected during the period of its composition. Further, a number of mid-century narratives make the moral status of the author a central thematic preoccupation. Harriet Jacobs's *Incidents in the Life of a Slave Girl* (1861) is perhaps the most apt example – Linda Brent, Jacobs's pseudonymous persona, stages her own fraught sexual history as a complex interplay of apology and defiance, assuring readers that she warrants forgiveness, and thus moral redemption, while also telling them that they are in no position to judge her in the first place.

The era's faith in the power of prose to do the work of moral suasion also contributed to this concern, among both nineteenth-century reviewers and contemporary scholars, with the moral status of books and authors. Moral themes abounded in mid-nineteenth-century texts, as women authors (for example, Alice Cary, Mrs. E. N. Gladding, Caroline Lee Hentz) penned temperance tales or incorporated temperance elements into their novels (see Stowe, obviously, but also E. D. E. N. Southworth, Augusta Jane Evans, and many others); elaborated on virtuous conduct in the face of adversity (for example, Susan Warner, Maria Cummins, Louisa May Alcott), and published volumes that responded to economic crises such as the Panic of 1837 (for example, Hannah Lee, Lucy Cooper). Among the most fervent and most controversial authors were those who intervened in the slavery debates. Scholars have tended to focus on abolitionist authors: Child, Jacobs, and Stowe are the most widely discussed figures, but a number of other authors and venues warrant more focused scholarly attention, including *The Liberty Bell* (1839–58), an antislavery annual edited by Maria Weston Chapman that published works by a number of women, including Caroline Healey Dall and Eliza Lee Follen.[4] Less thoroughly studied are the mid-century women whose reformist positions contemporary scholars find especially troubling – that is, those who wrote in support of such projects as Liberian colonization (for example, Sarah J. Hale) or so-called benevolent slaveholding (for example, Mary Eastman, Caroline Lee Hentz, and others).

With so many women authors articulating their desire to effect social change through prose, it makes sense that their readers, then and now, would attempt to gauge their moral success or failure, not just in terms of direct influence in their own time, a matter that is notoriously difficult to measure, but in terms of the works' moral resonances and implications more broadly considered. Was the work in question – and by extension its author – socially useful or pernicious or some vexing mixture of the two?

The pervasiveness of these considerations is best illustrated by the fact that they shadow nearly every critical paradigm that scholars have used to study nineteenth-century US women's writing. Attention to domesticity as a critical keyword is one of many examples. Works such as Mary Kelley's *Private Woman, Public Stage* (1984), Gillian Brown's *Domestic Individualism* (1990), and Lora Romero's *Home Fronts* (1997), among many other interventions, examine (albeit with disparate methods and arguments) the moral and political stakes of authorial publicity, especially as mediated by the thematics of domestic fiction and the hostilities of the broader culture.[5] More recently, Amy Kaplan's work on "manifest domesticity" interrogates the degree to which women authors' figurations of the domestic supported variously coercive transnational projects (*The Anarchy of Empire*, 23–50), while Lori Merish considers the "affiliated emergence" of women's material consumption and the genre of domestic fiction, arguing that the latter works to endow "personal possessions . . . with characterological import" (*Sentimental Materialism*, 2).

As these instances suggest, the preoccupations and exigencies of the scholar's own critical-cultural moment complicate and inform their analyses. The effective recovery of lost, forgotten, or devalued texts by women authors, for example, often relies on an assertion of authorial merit that extends beyond the purely aesthetic (a category that arguably did not exist in the antebellum decades in any case). It makes sense, then, that claims to literary and to moral worth might intersect in scholarly arguments for the canonicity of forgotten or demoted women authors. Jane Tompkins's revaluing of sentimental literature in *Sensational Designs* (1985) is an influential example. Tompkins's attempt to shift the grounds of literary evaluation from the question of what a text is (according to predetermined, typically masculinist aesthetic criteria) to what it does necessarily engages the question of the work's – and its author's – moral valence.

The concerns of the critical present, however, sometimes lend themselves to a more ambivalent recalibration of the moral status of nineteenth-century authors. For example, Americanists launched a sustained critique of the ethical blind spots of nineteenth-century white women writers and reformers at a moment, most pointedly in the early to mid-1990s, when progressive women in the academy (and beyond) were grappling with the limitations of liberal feminism. This critique took its most sustained form in critical conversations on sentimentalists' appropriative and coercive gestures *vis-à-vis* slaves, the poor, and other disadvantaged social actors. Sentimentalism, perhaps because it so suffused reformist literature, seems especially to invite such inquiries, as is evidenced by Shirley Samuels's groundbreaking edited collection *The Culture of Sentiment* (1992), often cited as a high-water mark in the reconsideration of sentimentalism's moral economies.[6] June Howard's 1999 call for scholars to "resist positions 'for' and 'against' sentimentality" suggests how polarizing those concerns had become by the end of the decade ("What is Sentimentality?," 65).[7] In the aftermath of this intensive focus on sentimentalism, scholars have worked to embed it within – and at times to differentiate it from – broader cultural phenomena, considering, for example, where sentimentalism and the era's discourses of benevolence overlap and diverge (Ryan, *The Grammar of Good Intentions*) and examining a wider range of affects that preoccupied nineteenth-century writers (Castiglia, *Interior States*; Ngai, *Ugly Feelings*). In keeping with the so-called aesthetic (or neo-formalist) turn in US literary studies, scholars have investigated reform literature as a key genre in its own right, one that incorporates but cannot be delimited by sentimental tropes and strategies (Sánchez, *Reforming the World*; Bergman and Bernardi, *Our Sisters' Keepers*). And, perhaps shadowed by current shifts and crises in the world of print publishing, scholars have looked more carefully at how mid-century women negotiated matters of reputation, property, and professional status within the literary marketplace (Homestead, *American Women Authors*; Williams, *Reclaiming Authorship*).

In pointing to these critical alignments, I wish to suggest that such cross-fertilization of the past and the present, while inevitable and in some sense productive, can also skew our renderings of nineteenth-century authorship's moral economies. The following case study – a rereading of the ways in which moral burdens and possibilities shaped the reception of Lydia Maria Child's work and authorial identity following her 1833 publication of *An Appeal in Favor of The Class of Americans Called Africans* – will help to illustrate my claims.

Moral recuperations

Lydia Maria Child occupied a curious intersectional position within nineteenth-century print culture, insofar as she was taken seriously as a literary novelist, was beloved as a domestic advisor, and was both excoriated and praised as an outspoken abolitionist. As such, she is an apt figure for analyzing the era's circulation and revaluation of reputational property. By the summer of 1833, Child was well known in literary circles, the author of two novels (*Hobomok* [1824] and *The Rebels* [1825]) and, among other texts, a popular guide to budget homemaking (*The Frugal Housewife* [1829]). She also edited, beginning in 1826, a well-regarded periodical for children titled the *Juvenile Miscellany*, which incorporated didactic tales, riddles, illustrations, poems, and pieces on historical, scientific, and biographical topics. A long article in the *North American Review*'s July issue surveyed her career up to that point, reserving particular praise for her domestic advice books and biographical writings. "We trust," the author intoned, "that Mrs. Child will continue her useful labors, and have no doubt that they will be received with constantly increasing favor" ("Art. VI. – Works of Mrs. Child," 163). Child's marketability and respectability as a guide for youth and for wives of all ages seemed secure, even as the door remained open for her to take up once again the less remunerative and less solidly respectable role of novelist.

A month later, in August of 1833, Child published her *Appeal*, one of the US antislavery movement's earliest and most powerful polemics. Acknowledging that abolition was an immensely unpopular cause, Child used the book's last paragraph to privilege moral imperatives over social and economic status: "The expectation of displeasing all classes [by publishing the *Appeal*] has not been unaccompanied with pain. But it has been strongly impressed upon my mind that it was a duty to fulfil [*sic*] this task; and earthly considerations should never stifle the voice of conscience" (*Appeal*, 232). Child had cause to worry over the book's reception. Not only did it represent the cruelties of slavery directly and sometimes graphically, but the text also criticized northern racial prejudice and the agenda of the American Colonization Society, which was widely perceived at the time to represent temperate (and, crucially, segregationist) activism on the slavery question.

Carolyn Karcher's biography of Child, *The First Woman in the Republic* (1994), identifies the publication of the *Appeal* as a watershed in its author's professional life. According to Karcher, the book prompted "an irate public" to "cast her off" and "destroyed Child's literary popularity" (152, 192).[8] Heather Roberts, citing Karcher's biography, writes that Child was "virtually blacklisted by mainstream publishing houses" following the *Appeal*'s release ("'The Public Heart'," 770 n. 1).[9] Undeniably, Child's foray into abolitionist activism cost her in any number of ways. According to personal letters and the reminiscences of her contemporaries, family relationships and friendships were strained; elite Bostonians who had once welcomed her into their social circles now shunned her; her membership at the Boston Athenaeum was rescinded; and subscriptions to the *Miscellany* fell off markedly. Child resigned as the magazine's editor in the summer of 1834, bidding "a reluctant and most affectionate farewell to [her] little readers" ("Note," 323); subsequently, according to Karcher, "the *Miscellany* sputtered for another two years before finally expiring" (*The First Woman*, 169). It is important to keep in mind, though, that longevity was hardly the default for the era's periodicals. The fact that Sarah Hale, the *Miscellany*'s next editor (and one free of abolitionist taint), could not revive the publication suggests that Child's transgression was not the only factor in its demise.

These adverse social and professional consequences notwithstanding, I want to call into question literary histories that position Child as nineteenth-century America's abolitionist martyr, a woman whose dramatic fall from grace via antislavery activism signals, in a Huck Finnian reversal, her accession to a retrospective moral high ground, one that only radical abolitionists acknowledged at the time. On the contrary, Child's reception in the 1830s and '40s suggests that her reputation was not so much ruined as bruised and that the literary establishment had ways of cordoning off perceived taint that did not involve blacklisting an author completely. Further, I want to suggest that Child's moral authority prior to her publication of the *Appeal* was not entirely secure, either. Even then, Child had to navigate the complex moral standards (not to mention the class and gender codes) of an emerging literary marketplace. The *Appeal*'s reception made those negotiations more challenging, but did not fundamentally alter their character.

Child initially published *Hobomok* anonymously with the subtitle "by an American." Not surprisingly, many of its earliest reviewers assumed that the author in question was a man, though others refrained from identifying the author as either a man or a woman. Some early reviews were glowing: the *Boston Weekly Magazine*, for example, declared the novel "absolutely an honor to the literature of the country" and called its author's prose style "free and unaffected; – open, bold and candid" ("Hobomok," 107). The *North American Review*, more cautious in its praise, described the book "rather as an earnest of what the author can do, than as a performance from which he can promise himself much reputation" ("6. – *Hobomok, a Tale of Early Times*," 262). Among the book's defects, according to this reviewer, are its introduction of "so many characters and incidents not immediately connected with the main object" and its representation of an interracial marriage and divorce, "a train of events not only unnatural, but revolting, we conceive, to every feeling of delicacy in man or woman" (262, 263). Another reviewer, concurring with this charge of indelicacy, remarks that the author's descriptive and narrative abilities "redeem this little volume from the censure and the oblivion which the defects of the mere fable would, we fear, insure" ("Redwood," 235).

Child was soon widely identified as the book's author. While the revelation of her gender identity does not seem to have occasioned any particular backlash – that is, Hobomok's marriage to Mary Conant seems not to have been considered any worse for having been imagined by a woman – it is nevertheless the case that Child is most often characterized at this point in her career as "gifted" or "talented" rather than "good." In other words, her literary potential registers more forcefully than her moral power. References to Child (then "Miss Francis") in 1820s periodicals include the following: she is called a writer "of no ordinary talents," some of whose descriptive passages are "drawn with the hand of a master" ("Art. VII. – *The Rebels*," 402, 403); she is tagged as a "highly talented and endowed authoress" ("*Mentor*," 636) and as an author with "fine powers" ("Critical Notices," *United States Review*, 147). One early reviewer notes that Child's two 1820s novels "display an imagination rich almost to exuberance," suggesting that their author approaches the limits of decorum, though the piece remarks that her "highly wrought passages of affecting tenderness . . . would do honor to the head and heart of any writer in any age" ("Literary Success," 58). "Her faults," one reviewer (cited above) remarks more critically, "are evidently those, not of a feeble, but a misguided intellect," one apt to "attempt to move [the reader's feelings] by . . . revolting and shocking objects" ("Art. VII. – *The Rebels*," 403). The suggestion of moral risk in these remarks echoes a hint of literary promise unfulfilled that emerges in some of these early reviews. The *North American Review*, for example, consigns Child's second novel (*The Rebels*) to the stratum of a sophomore slump:

"The author has paid the usual price of an early reputation, that of being compelled to use redoubled exertions in order to prevent it from fading. We cannot venture to say, that her laurels have lost none of their freshness by the present attempt, but on the other hand, we think that her failure is only a partial one . . . " ("Art. VII. – *The Rebels,*" 401). If Child's emerging reputation was based, as I am suggesting, on ascriptions of literary talent rather than moral authority as it was conventionally understood, what might happen when her second book sparkled rather less?

It is unclear whether Child herself worried over this question on the terms I have offered here. Nevertheless, she did turn her authorial energies toward "moral" topics in the late 1820s and early 1830s, in the form of juvenile and domestic advice literature. Interestingly, the language of benevolence and moral authority began to figure more prominently in printed references to Child as she did so. This is not a stark contrast – the same author who mentions Child's nearly exuberant imagination, for example, also classes her among authors whose work is characterized by "purity and delicacy" ("Literary Success," 58). But the overlay of moral character becomes more noticeable once Child begins to be known as a more explicitly didactic author. Mentions of the *Juvenile Miscellany* attest to this shift: one commentator, who signs her piece "A Mother," combines an assertion of Child's "fine talents" with comments on her "benevolent mind" and her role as "friend and benefactress to parents and children" ("The Juvenile Miscellany," 40).[10] Child's authorship grows more explicitly gendered in some of these notices as well. A piece in the *Rural Repository* (Hudson, New York) remarks that "those females, who like Miss Francis are endowed with more than ordinary literary talents, could not consecrate the energies of their minds to a more useful or a more noble purpose, than" penning didactic literature for children ("Interesting to Juvenile Readers," 87).

Child's drift into the role of respectable advice-giver and molder of youth did not protect her entirely from reputational attacks. Most obviously, her antislavery sentiments began to suffuse her juvenile fiction before the publication of the *Appeal*, a circumstance that, as Karcher notes, probably contributed to the *Miscellany*'s demise. And the enormously popular *Frugal Housewife*, though it reified Child's position as a domestic authority, also exposed her to unflattering class-based judgments. Sarah Hale's review, published in the *Ladies' Magazine and Literary Gazette*, praises Child's efforts to prove that "learning, imagination, genius, do not unfit a lady for domestic usefulness" ("Literary Notices," 42), but also criticizes her use of "a few vulgarisms, which such a writer as Mrs. Child should not sanction" (42). More troubling than the use of downscale diction, for Hale, is Child's indecorous attention in the text to money. In a curiously barbed passage, Hale figures Child's own childlessness as an experiential limit on her moral authority, asserting that the author would be more careful "to distinguish between the spirit of that economy which is seeking to be rich, and that which is seeking to enrich or assist others" if she "had ever watched, with a mother's anxiety over the developement [*sic*] of mind and character in those she wished to train to usefulness and virtue" (43). In the absence of the sentimental education thought to accompany motherhood, crassness lapses into moral failure.

The ambivalence with which the literary establishment responded to Child is perhaps best illustrated in the *North American Review*'s long feature article on her work, the very piece that Karcher identifies as the apex of her authorial status prior to the reputational apocalypse that the *Appeal* supposedly initiated. The article does praise Child enthusiastically – this is one of at least two instances in which Child is named "the first woman in the republic," a description that Karcher adopts as her biography's title ("Art. VI. – Works of Mrs. Child," 138–9).[11] But mixed with that praise is the suggestion that Child is an author who needs guidance – even taming – in order to realize her full potential. The piece consistently elevates Child's more conventional and overtly didactic offerings over her novels, which here receive rather faint praise: In *Hobomok*, Child's "savage" is well drawn, but falls short of the example set by Charles Brockden Brown; the novel "cannot be reckoned by any means faultless, and belongs to the second class of Mrs. Child's productions" (140). *The Rebels*, according to this piece, tells a pleasing but utterly forgettable story. Though the author asserts that "we would not have [Child] desert fiction altogether," he nevertheless avers that Child's greatest "useful[ness]" lies elsewhere (163). Given the discomfort with which the *North American Review* greeted the more daring aspects of Child's fiction, this push seems unsurprising. However promising and respectable Child was said to be, she had already made mainstream readers uncomfortable, at least at certain textual moments, long before she came out, so to speak, as an abolitionist.

A careful look at reviews of Child's *Appeal* demonstrates that this supposedly career-killing text actually elicited a wide range of responses. Some reviews were vitriolic, as one might expect. A reviewer in the *Literary Journal, and Weekly Register of Science and the Arts*, a short-lived Providence, Rhode Island, paper, excoriates both Child and her publisher for putting forward "sentiments injurious to the peace, prosperity and morality of a community"; "no father or mother," the reviewer continues, "should allow a child to read it" ("Mrs. Child's 'Appeal'," 149). New Haven's *Quarterly Christian Spectator* remarks on Child's tone of "political malignity" and notes that, though the author "does not seem to be ... intentionally uncandid, her statements are exceedingly inaccurate ... " ("Art. VI. – Mrs. Child's Appeal," 445). And the *North American Review*, seemingly miffed that Child had ignored its well-intentioned advice, expressed "regret that a writer capable of being so agreeable, and at the same time so useful, should have departed from that line of authorship in which she has justly acquired a high reputation" ("Art. VIII. – Slavery," 170).[12] The "indelicacy" of *Hobomok*'s interracial marriage plot pales in comparison to the moral (insofar as abolitionists called attention to such issues as slaves' sexual coercion) and, crucially, political risks of abolitionist agitation.

At the other end of the spectrum, abolitionists praised the book, also as we would anticipate. The *Liberator*, for example, offers "a thousand thanks to Mrs. Child for this admirable work!" ("New Publication," 127) and, across the next several months, reprints a number of favorable notices from other papers. More remarkable is the fact that the work received balanced – even complimentary – comments in a number of venues whose primary purpose was not antislavery agitation. The Boston-based *Ladies' Magazine and Literary Gazette*, edited by Sarah Hale, calls the *Appeal* "a most extraordinary work": "We cannot now notice it, as it deserves; but we extract the preface, and entreat our readers – our sex, to comply with the request of the gifted author – read the book!" ("Literary Notices," 431). The *Christian Watchman*, a Baptist weekly published in Boston, expresses admiration for "the moral courage of this lady in risking her literary name by taking the stand which she does in this volume" ("Mrs. Child's New Work," 139), while the *American Quarterly Observer* (also based in Boston) calls the book "full of interesting anecdote, and of important principles, very happily illustrated" ("Article XI. Critical Notices," 337). Taking issue with the "fears and entreaties which Mrs. C. has expressed in her preface" (337), this reviewer notes that "the cause in which she is engaged is not so unpopular as she supposes it to be" (338–9). Though he goes on to defend the Colonization Society, which Child's book has attacked, he nevertheless asserts that "we are glad she has written the book" (338). The *Colonizationist and Journal of Freedom* (Boston), a paper one might expect to greet the *Appeal* with hostility, instead offers a balanced critique. While attempting to refute Child's anticolonizationist statements, the author also remarks that "the reputation previously acquired by the writer, was such as to entitle her to a fair hearing on any subject she chooses to discuss" ("Appeal for the Africans," 165). Another venue, the *American Monthly Review*, writes that Child treats her subject "with much more temperance, with far less prejudice, and with greater ability, than Mr. [William Lloyd] Garrison or Professor [Elizur] Wright," whose works the reviewer addresses with considerably more venom ("Art. III," 285). These few excerpts, while failing to provide a comprehensive picture of the *Appeal*'s reception, nevertheless suggest that Child's book was not as thoroughly despised beyond abolitionist circles as she had imagined it would be.

The aftermath of the *Appeal* bears revising as well. The evidence available indicates that Child was not thoroughly blacklisted, either by publishers or the book-buying public, after August 1833. Allen and Ticknor, the publishing house that had brought out the *Appeal* – and that would eventually morph into the influential firm Ticknor and Fields – published Child's second abolitionist text the following year, suggesting that the *Appeal*'s reception was not so vitriolic as to scare away a respectable publisher. This 1834 compilation, titled *The Oasis*, was poorly received beyond committed antislavery circles, and Child published most of her subsequent abolitionist writings in the 1830s either with the American Anti-Slavery Society or with Charles Whipple of Newburyport, Massachusetts, a small-time publisher who also traded in dubious medicinal preparations. Still, Child continued to publish other kinds of writings with more mainstream houses. Carter and Hendee, among other publishers, reprinted *The Frugal Housewife* many times through the 1830s (sometimes as *The American Frugal Housewife*), suggesting that Child was not so poisonous a brand name that the volume could not continue to sell. She published other 1830s texts with such Boston publishers as John Allen, Charles J. Hendee, and Otis, Broaders, and placed her work with New York and London houses as well. Karcher's biography notes that Child had some difficulty placing the manuscript of *Letters from New-York* due to the book's antislavery content. But when she published the work at her own expense with Charles S. Francis (a distant cousin) in New York and James Munroe in Boston, it proved to be a bestseller (*The First Woman in the Republic*, 308–10), belying the concern that abolitionist content guaranteed a market failure.

Further, to the extent that Child lost moral and literary capital among mainstream readers in the wake of the *Appeal*, her period of disfavor was relatively brief. Her 1836 novel *Philothea*, now seldom read, initiated a significant reputational recuperation, at least in literary terms. Even Karcher concedes that this novel signaled something of a fresh start for Child within literary circles (236–7). The *Knickerbocker*, for example, advises "all lovers of a pure, classical style, and of a narrative imbued with more than common power and interest, to posses [sic] themselves of a volume which reflects honor upon the taste and genius of the author" (370). The *American Monthly Magazine*, though it stops short of calling the novel a complete success, nevertheless notes that "the style of the work is polished and elegant; and the tone throughout is of that lofty and refined character, which could only be imparted by one thoroughly imbued with the beauty and refinement of classic letters" (*"Philothea: a Romance,"* 409). Interestingly, none of the reviews of *Philothea* that I have located makes any direct mention of the *Appeal* or of its reception, tagging Child instead as the author of *The Mother's Book* or *The Frugal Housewife*. Only the *North American Review* refers to any departure from a happy authorial path, expressing "our pleasure at meeting Mrs. Child again in the calm and gladsome light of literature" ("Art. V. – *Philothea, a Romance,*" 77). Even the *Southern Literary Messenger*, which just over a year earlier had expressed hostility toward Child's abolitionism, reviewed the novel favorably, discussing it as though its author had never published the *Appeal* ("Critical Notices," 659–62).[13]

This elision proved typical. In the era's periodical print culture, some authors expressed an initial outrage or displeasure at Child's publication of the *Appeal*, but such objections soon gave way to a calculated amnesia. Editors and reviewers – even those writing for southern periodicals – minimized Child's controversial elements, restoring her to the status of a respected American author. In the summer of 1834, just a year after the *Appeal* came out, Cincinnati's *Western Monthly Magazine and Literary Journal* ranked Child among a "brilliant constellation" of "female writers" that included such prominent (and uncontroversial) figures as Sarah Hale, Catharine Maria Sedgwick, and Lydia Sigourney ("Sketches. By Mrs. Sigourney," 444). By 1841, a reviewer in the Philadelphia-based *Journal of Belles Lettres* noted that Child's "name is a guarantee for a sensible and useful book" ("Notices of New Books," 3) – hardly a description one would apply to a pariah. Further, Child's troubles at the *Juvenile Miscellany* notwithstanding, she continued to matter, and to command a kind of public trust, as a children's author. One commentator went so far as to claim that "in all that pertains to young humanity . . . we consider her – and we say it with all due respect for the present Pope of Rome – infallible" ("The Book Trade," 125).

Child struggled financially in the 1830s and '40s, as extant letters and other documents attest, but that fact does not distinguish her from most other full-time authors of the era who lacked nonliterary means of economic support. Indeed, the suggestion that Child would have prospered as a professional author were it not for her abolitionist commitments – a notion implicit in some of the scholarship decrying her fall from grace – relies on assumptions about the antebellum literary marketplace that are difficult to support.

Conclusion

My attempt to muddy what had been a clear plot line *vis-à-vis* Child's career invites us to rethink an appealing, even inspiring, story about authorship's risks and triumphs. In this retelling, Child emerges less as a martyr than as a principled but also strategic author negotiating a complex and remarkably malleable literary scene. She was willing to court disapproval in pursuit of her abolitionist goals, but she also sought to repair her reputation – and put food on the table – by continuing to publish in modes that US readers and reviewers could endorse. In *Letters from New-York*, she seemed able, briefly, to do both.[14] The desire to endow Child with late twentieth- and twenty-first-century notions of moral authority – as abolitionist hero, as self-sacrificial truth-teller – should not supersede our attempts to understand the nineteenth-century cultural field in all its contradictions and complexities.

As this revisionist account of Child's reception suggests, I am arguing that scholars need to be more conscious of the ways in which their own ethical investments shape their readings of nineteenth-century literary culture. It is not that we should aim for some illusion of moral neutrality or banish any attempt to connect nineteenth-century matters to current ethical concerns, but rather that we should not allow our ethical investments and presuppositions to limit the questions we ask of primary sources or the interpretations we offer of them. In keeping with the vast range of archival material now available to scholars and students – not just those with ample travel budgets and limited domestic responsibilities – we need to develop a more expansive sense of the interpretive possibilities that antebellum authorship's reputational economies make available.[15]

In closing, I wish to suggest a few lines of inquiry that might emerge from the methods and critical dispositions I have proposed here. Most immediately, are there other instances in which scholars have overstated the extent of a scandal's damage to an author's reputation? Harriet Beecher Stowe is often said to have ruined her career by publishing an 1869 article calling out a long-dead Lord Byron for supposedly having committed incest. She was widely and viciously attacked in periodicals across the next several months – and yet her books continued to find publishers and audiences (albeit smaller ones than in the 1850s). Were Child and Stowe especially fortunate and resilient, or were such rebounds typical in the era's print culture? Along these lines, did abolitionist papers grant proslavery novelists the same amnesiac amnesty that Child enjoyed in the southern press just a few years after publishing her

Appeal? The *Liberator* accepted advertisements for Caroline Hentz's 1856 novel *Ernest Linwood*, despite her having published one of the better-known anti-Uncle Tom novels just a few years earlier – again, was this case representative or idiosyncratic? And what might we learn from the reputational negotiations that played out in the interconnected forms of book advertisements and reviews?[16] Here E. D. E. N. Southworth provides an intriguing test case: a preliminary look at her reviews and advertisements from the 1850s reveals surprisingly disparate representational strategies. Though her work elicited praise in some venues, reviews often criticized Southworth's heated prose, complex plots, and what the *Southern Literary Messenger* terms the "immorality" evident in "the tone, the coloring, [and] the general moulding of character and feeling" of her work ("Notices of New Works," 390). Conversely, advertisements commended her "vigor and purity of style" ("A New American Novel," 137) and termed her "a rising Star in the West" ("The Saturday Evening Post," 401). Was the insistent respectability of the Southworth advertisements working against or in concert with the outrage her work inspired in some quarters? In other words, when publishers downplayed an author's sensationalism in print advertisements, were they simultaneously relying on the whiff of scandal emerging from the reviews to spur curiosity-driven sales?

As these questions imply, much remains to be discovered regarding the circulation of moral authority in antebellum print culture. It would be inaccurate to claim that this is the period in which morality first found its American market – Franklin's *Autobiography*, to name just one example, tells us that such interconnections precede the middle decades of the nineteenth century. Nevertheless, literary status and moral reputation were in especially close commerce throughout this period, in ways that scholars do not yet fully comprehend. An energetic return to the archive may reveal complications and insights that our well-worn taxonomies (didactic literature, sensationalism, domesticity, reform, abolition) have failed to illuminate.

Notes

1. Keyword-searchable digital archives of the *Provincial Freeman* are available through the OurOntario.ca website (http://ink.ourontario.ca/browse/pf) and African American Newspapers: The Nineteenth Century (Accessible Archives).
2. My thinking on this point has been much influenced by Melissa J. Homestead's nuanced study of nineteenth-century women authors' interventions in matters of publishing and copyright law, which carefully balances notions of agency and constraint (*American Women Authors*).

3. Although this essay focuses on prose texts, many of the same issues arose with regard to women poets.

4. Now-obscure abolitionist novels by women include Mary Hayden Green Pike's *Ida May* (1854) and Mary B. Harlan's *Ellen; or the Chained Mother* (1855). For a thorough discussion of abolitionist literature aimed at young readers, see DeRosa, *Domestic Abolitionism and Juvenile Literature*.

5. See also Nicole Tonkovich's *Domesticity with a Difference*, which focuses on non-fiction by mid-century women authors.

6. See also Carby, *Reconstructing Womanhood*; Brodhead, *Cultures of Letters*; Sánchez-Eppler, *Touching Liberty*; Nelson, *The Word in Black and White*; and Hartman, *Scenes of Subjection*. For an astute analysis of sentimentalism's complex relationship to power, both sexual and political, see Noble, *The Masochistic Pleasures of Sentimental Literature*; on the cultural politics of male sentimentalism, see Chapman and Hendler, *Sentimental Men*; on sentimentalism and publicity, an intersection critical to this essay's concerns, see Hendler, *Public Sentiments*.

7. Thomas Augst's work on the intersection of moral and economic striving among men in *The Clerk's Tale* illuminates cultural contexts that bear on our understandings of women writers as well, especially those working outside of mainstream publishing venues. Two works focusing on the second half of the century offer important insights into this mid-century cultural field: Naomi Sofer's *Making the "America of Art"* charts late nineteenth-century women's retreat from moral reputation as a dominant authorial paradigm, while James B. Salazar's *Bodies of Reform* reenergizes "character" as a nineteenth-century keyword, tying it to discourses of embodiment and masculinity.

8. Although I take issue with one of Karcher's central interpretive claims, I also wish to acknowledge my debt to her scholarly work. Without Karcher's biography, many of the conversations we can now have about Child would not be possible.

9. For additional, if less strongly worded, versions of the claim that publishing the *Appeal* seriously harmed Child's career, see Sorisio ("The Spectacle of the Body," 45, 47) and Foster ("Grotesque Sympathy," 29 n. 10).

10. The *Christian Register*, which reprinted this piece, lists the original source (which I have been unable to locate) as the *American & Gazette*.

11. As Karcher points out, William Lloyd Garrison used the same language in reference to Child a few years earlier in the *Genius of Universal Emancipation* (*The First Woman in the Republic*, 85). The *North American Review* piece references Napoleon's use of the phrase to describe Madame de Staël as its point of departure rather than Garrison's praise of Child ("Art. VI. – Works of Mrs. Child," 138–9).

12. The *Southern Literary Messenger*, though it declined to review the *Appeal* directly, welcomed the *North American Review* piece as an instance of northern right-thinking on the slavery question ("North American Review, No. LXXXVIII" 650–1).

13. Bruce Mills argues that *Philothea* should be read as a work of antislavery fiction (*Cultural Reformations*, 55–71), but Child's contemporaries seem not to have interpreted it as such.

14. As Travis Foster has noted, Child revised the letters (originally published in the *National Anti-Slavery Standard*) in order to make them more palatable to a mainstream (not necessarily abolitionist) audience, a process that involved excising some antislavery

content. Despite these elisions, Foster maintains that the published volume presents "a radical model for sympathy and reform" ("Grotesque Sympathy," 7).

15. College and university libraries' budgets remain a significant constraint, as access to these digital archives is quite expensive.
16. These print forms were interconnected insofar as advertisements quoted from favorable reviews and reviews repeated claims (to astonishing numbers of books sold, for example) that appeared in advertisements.

Works cited

A Mother. "The Juvenile Miscellany." Rpt. in *Christian Register*, March 8, 1828: 40.
"Appeal for the Africans." *Colonizationist and Journal of Freedom*, October 1833: 165–71.
"Art. III." *American Monthly Review* [Boston and Cambridge, MA], October 1833: 282–97.
"Art. V. – *Philothea, a Romance*." *North American Review*, January 1837: 77–90.
"Art. VI. – Mrs. Child's Appeal in Favor of the Africans." *Quarterly Christian Spectator*, September 1, 1834: 445–56.
"Art. VI. – Works of Mrs. Child." *North American Review*, July 1833: 133–64.
"Art. VII. – *The Rebels, or Boston before the Revolution*." *North American Review*, April 1826: 400–08.
"Art. VIII. – Slavery." *North American Review*, July 1835: 170–93.
"Article XI. Critical Notices." *American Quarterly Observer*, October 1, 1833: 336–64.
Augst, Thomas. *The Clerk's Tale: Young Men and Moral Life in Nineteenth-Century America*. Chicago: University of Chicago Press, 2003.
Baym, Nina. *Novels, Readers, and Reviewers: Responses to Fiction in Antebellum America*. Ithaca: Cornell University Press, 1984.
Bergman, Jill and Debra Bernardi, eds. *Our Sisters' Keepers: Nineteenth-Century Benevolence Literature by American Women*. Tuscaloosa: University of Alabama Press, 2005.
"The Book Trade." *Merchants' Magazine and Commercial Review* [New York], January 1, 1848: 121–8.
Brodhead, Richard. *Cultures of Letters: Scenes of Reading and Writing in Nineteenth-Century America*. Chicago: University of Chicago Press, 1993.
Brown, Gillian. *Domestic Individualism: Imagining Self in Nineteenth-Century America*. Berkeley: University of California Press, 1990.
Carby, Hazel V. *Reconstructing Womanhood: The Emergence of the Afro-American Woman Novelist*. New York: Oxford University Press, 1987.
Castiglia, Christopher. *Interior States: Institutional Consciousness and the Inner Life of Democracy in the Antebellum United States*. Durham, NC: Duke University Press, 2008.
Chapman, Mary and Glenn Hendler, eds. *Sentimental Men: Masculinity and the Politics of Affect in American Culture*. Berkeley: University of California Press, 1999.
Child, Lydia Maria. *An Appeal in Favor of that Class of Americans Called Africans*. Boston: Allen and Ticknor, 1833.
  "Note." *Juvenile Miscellany*, July/August 1834: 323.
"Critical Notices." *Southern Literary Messenger*, September 1836: 659–62.
"Critical Notices." *United States Review and Literary Gazette*, November 1826: 144–51.

DeRosa, Deborah C. *Domestic Abolitionism and Juvenile Literature, 1830–1865.* Albany: State University of New York Press, 2003.

Foster, Travis M. "Grotesque Sympathy: Lydia Maria Child, White Reform, and the Embodiment of Urban Space." *ESQ: A Journal of the American Renaissance* 56 (2010): 1–32.

Garrison, William Lloyd. "Mrs. Child." *Genius of Universal Emancipation*, November 20, 1829: 85–6.

Hale, Sarah J. "Literary Notices." *Ladies' Magazine and Literary Gazette* [Boston], January 1830: 42–8.

Harlan, Mary B. *Ellen; or the Chained Mother and Pictures of Kentucky Slavery Drawn from Real Life.* Cincinnati: Applegate, 1855.

Hartman, Saidiya V. *Scenes of Subjection: Terror, Slavery, and Self-Making in Nineteenth-Century America.* New York: Oxford University Press, 1997.

Hendler, Glenn. *Public Sentiments: Structures of Feeling in Nineteenth-Century America.* Chapel Hill: University of North Carolina Press, 2001.

"Hobomok." *Boston Weekly Magazine, Devoted to Polite Literature, Useful Science, Biography, and Dramatic Criticism*, September 18, 1824: 107.

Homestead, Melissa J. *American Women Authors and Literary Property, 1822–1869.* Cambridge: Cambridge University Press, 2005.

Howard, June. "What is Sentimentality?" *American Literary History* 11 (1999): 63–81.

"Interesting to Juvenile Readers." *Rural Repository, or Bower of Literature*, October 25, 1828: 87.

Kaplan, Amy. *The Anarchy of Empire in the Making of US Culture.* Cambridge, MA: Harvard University Press, 2002.

Karcher, Carolyn. *The First Woman in the Republic: A Cultural Biography of Lydia Maria Child.* Durham, NC: Duke University Press, 1994.

Kelley, Mary. *Private Woman, Public Stage: Literary Domesticity in Nineteenth-Century America.* New York: Oxford University Press, 1984.

Knickerbocker, September 1836: 370.

"Literary Notices." *Ladies' Magazine and Literary Gazette*, September 1833: 428–31.

"Literary Success of Female Writers." *Harvard Register*, April 1827: 50–8.

"Mentor: or Dialogues between a Parent and Children, on some of the Duties, Amusements, Pursuits and Relations of Life." *Western Monthly Review* [Cincinnati], April 1829: 635–7.

Merish, Lori. *Sentimental Materialism: Gender, Commodity Culture, and Nineteenth-Century American Literature.* Durham, NC: Duke University Press, 2000.

Mills, Bruce. *Cultural Reformations: Lydia Maria Child and the Literature of Reform.* Athens, GA: University of Georgia Press, 1994.

M'Kee, Mrs. E. D. W. "Literary Celebrities." *Christian Parlor Magazine*, May 1, 1853: 305–8.

"Mrs. Child's 'Appeal'." *Literary Journal, and Weekly Register of Science and the Arts*, October 12, 1833: 149.

"Mrs. Child's New Work." *Christian Watchman*, August 30, 1833: 139.

"Mrs. Stowe." *Liberator*, June 10, 1853: 91.

Nelson, Dana D. *The Word in Black and White: Reading "Race" in American Literature, 1638–1867.* New York: Oxford University Press, 1993.

"A New American Novel." *Literary World*, August 17, 1850: 137.

"New Publication." *Liberator*, August 10, 1833: 127.

Ngai, Sianne. *Ugly Feelings*. Cambridge, MA: Harvard University Press, 2005.

Noble, Marianne. *The Masochistic Pleasures of Sentimental Literature*. Princeton: Princeton University Press, 2000.

"North American Review, No. LXXXVIII." *Southern Literary Messenger*, July 1835: 650–1.

"Notices of New Books." *Journal of Belles Lettres*, January 6, 1841: 3.

"Notices of New Works." *Southern Literary Messenger*, June 1851: 390.

"*Philothea: a Romance*." *American Monthly Magazine*, October 1836: 409.

Pike, Mary Hayden Green. *Ida May: A Story of Things Actual and Possible*. Boston: Phillips Sampson, 1854.

"Redwood." *Atlantic Magazine* [New York], July 1, 1824: 234–9.

Roberts, Heather. "'The Public Heart': Urban Life and the Politics of Sympathy in Lydia Maria Child's *Letters from New-York*." *American Literature* 76 (2004): 749–75.

Romero, Lora. *Home Fronts: Domesticity and its Critics in the Antebellum United States*. Durham, NC: Duke University Press, 1997.

Ryan, Susan M. *The Grammar of Good Intentions: Race and the Antebellum Culture of Benevolence*. Ithaca: Cornell University Press, 2003.

Salazar, James B. *Bodies of Reform: The Rhetoric of Character in Gilded Age America*. New York: New York University Press, 2010.

Samuels, Shirley, ed. *The Culture of Sentiment: Race, Gender, and Sentimentality in Nineteenth-Century America*. New York: Oxford University Press, 1992.

Sánchez, María Carla. *Reforming the World: Social Activism and the Problem of Fiction in Nineteenth-Century America*. Iowa City: University of Iowa Press, 2008.

Sánchez-Eppler, Karen. *Touching Liberty: Abolition, Feminism, and the Politics of the Body*. Berkeley: University of California Press, 1993.

"The Saturday Evening Post." *The Plough, the Loom and the Anvil* [Philadelphia], December 1850: 401.

"6. – Hobomok, a Tale of Early Times." *North American Review*, July 1824: 262–3.

"Sketches. By Mrs. Sigourney." *Western Monthly Magazine and Literary Journal*, August 1834: 444–5.

Sofer, Naomi. *Making the "America of Art": Cultural Nationalism and Nineteenth-Century Women Writers*. Columbus: Ohio State University Press, 2005.

Sorisio, Carolyn. "The Spectacle of the Body: Torture in the Antislavery Writing of Lydia Maria Child and Frances E. W. Harper." *Modern Language Studies* 30 (2000): 45–66.

Tompkins, Jane. *Sensational Designs: The Cultural Work of American Fiction, 1790–1860*. New York: Oxford University Press, 1985.

Tonkovich, Nicole. *Domesticity with a Difference: The Nonfiction of Catharine Beecher, Sarah J. Hale, Fanny Fern, and Margaret Fuller*. Jackson: University Press of Mississippi, 1997.

Williams, Susan S. *Reclaiming Authorship: Literary Women in America, 1850–1900*. Philadelphia: University of Pennsylvania Press, 2006.

9

The shape of Catharine Sedgwick's career

MELISSA J. HOMESTEAD

Two years before Nina Baym published *Woman's Fiction: A Guide to Novels by and about Women in America, 1820–1870* (1978), which set the agenda for the recovery of nineteenth-century women's fiction, she published *The Shape of Hawthorne's Career* (1976). More than three decades into the revival of nineteenth-century American women's fiction, however, literary historians rarely engage works by women across the range of their careers, as they do the works of their canonical male contemporaries, especially Nathaniel Hawthorne and Herman Melville. Instead, women who produced fiction for decades have entered literary history primarily through single novels, for example *Uncle Tom's Cabin* (1852) for Harriet Beecher Stowe. Furthermore, such singular works are read primarily in relation to genres (such as Baym's "woman's fiction," the "domestic novel," or the "sentimental novel") and sociopolitical contexts (such as the debates over slavery, Indian removal, and women's rights), rather than in relation to their authors' bodies of work. In addition, scholarship has focused overwhelmingly on antebellum women's *novels*, at the expense of short fiction. Literary historians have been more willing to concede that women who produced fiction mostly after the Civil War had true careers and that their works might be most productively considered in the context of an author's entire oeuvre, in part because more women, such as Edith Wharton, began self-consciously fashioning themselves as "serious" artists.[1]

Nevertheless, many women who began writing fiction in the antebellum period and continued to be productive for decades were not merely accidental or haphazard producers. Catharine Maria Sedgwick is a case in point. She published her first novel in 1822 and her last in 1857. Her productivity slackened in the 1850s, as aging weakened her eyesight and arthritis made it difficult to write clearly. However, from 1822 through the 1840s, she published multiple works of prose fiction (tales, sketches, novellas, or novels) nearly every year. Despite this extraordinary record of productivity, Sedgwick regularly appears in literary history as the author of a single work, *Hope Leslie* (1827), her historical novel about relations between the Puritans and the native inhabitants of New England. A few other women authors before and contemporary with Sedgwick had careers as long or nearly as long as hers – Susanna Rowson as antecedent and Lydia Maria Child and Lydia Huntley Sigourney as contemporaries, for example. What was unprecedented and remained unequaled until later in the century, however, was that Sedgwick maintained a focus on the craft of fiction (with occasional forays into non-fiction prose) and remained exclusively a producer, never taking up the work of editing. In contrast, Rowson wrote novels, plays, poetry, and schoolbooks; Child produced a considerable body of non-fiction prose in addition to fiction and devoted much time to editing; and Sigourney was primarily a poet and also often an editor.[2]

Despite Sedgwick's exceptional record, she is often characterized as a timid and reluctant producer of fiction who lost her ambition and drive in the mid-1830s, retreating into the writing of didactic fiction and domestic advice. Judith Fetterley, for instance, reintroducing Sedgwick and her story "Cacoethes Scribendi" to readers in her influential anthology *Provisions* (1985), writes, "After the publication of *The Linwoods* [1835], Sedgwick stopped writing fiction for twenty years, not to return to the genre until *Married or Single?* (1857), and turned her energies instead to the writing of a series of didactic tales intended to address and solve a variety of social problems." Adopting the hypothesis of another critic, Fetterley suggests that Sedgwick shifted to didacticism in 1835 because she believed that producing "such works fit more comfortably into [her] definition of appropriately feminine behavior than did success as a major novelist" (*Provisions*, 44). In *Private Woman, Public Stage: Literary Domesticity in Nineteenth-Century America* (1984), still a much cited source for biographical information about Sedgwick, Mary Kelley characterizes Sedgwick as "a bewildered, timid, and reluctant passenger" on the voyage of her own literary career who largely "regarded her literary endeavors as a pale substitute for what she believed should be the calling of a true woman. Not surprisingly, then, the woman who became a creator of culture was never able to regard herself as one" (199–200). A decade after *Provisions* appeared, Fetterley pondered the consequences of the recovery work rising concurrently "with the dismantling of the interpretive strategies developed during the 1950s and '60s to establish" the American literary canon, suggesting that "[t]hose interested in nineteenth-century American women writers may need to find ways to revitalize modes of criticism no longer fashionable" in order to secure canonical status for women's writing ("Commentary," 605).

Single-author study as practiced by Baym in *The Shape of Hawthorne's Career* represents just such a powerful old-fashioned tool for revaluing Sedgwick's oeuvre. In *Shape*, Baym protests against the then-prevailing tendency to read Hawthorne's works in isolation from one another, as "an arbitrary collection of works rather than a human sensibility." She proposes that in order to "discover this sensibility it is necessary to study everything he wrote that had a literary purpose – that is, was designed to be published – and to study those works in chronological order, in the context they provide for each other" (7–8). Having conducted such a reading, she finds in Hawthorne's career a "preoccupation . . . with defining a way of writing that could embody the imagination and justify it to a skeptical, practical minded audience." She also finds a significant "conversion" from a commonsense to a romantic approach to the power of the imagination (8). In his early career, Baym explains, Hawthorne adopted a moralizing posture in his fiction to overcome "the general American indifference to the arts, based on their supposed uselessness" (18). Hawthorne, then, "did not write in order to set out his moral beliefs; he set out moral beliefs in order to write" (74).

Five years older than Hawthorne, Sedgwick's years of productivity overlap to a high degree. Her career, however, took a far different "shape." While Sedgwick's letters and journals provide a wealth of evidence concerning her sense of herself as an author – and have provided fodder for characterizations of her as a timid and reluctant one – her fiction itself in its surprising variety and complexity provides the evidence for this essay. Sedgwick's works currently in print in modern editions reside in the first fourteen years of her career, and these works constitute only a fraction of even this fraction of Sedgwick's output. Her authorial scope and ambition appear much broader if we give equal weight to her fictions across subgenres and as they appeared in periodicals and anthologies, not just in books comprising works authored only by her. *Hope Leslie*, for example, gains new resonance in the context of Sedgwick's portrayals of Indians in short stories and episodes of longer works published shortly before and after it. Similarly, her didactic novellas of the 1830s, regarded fully as fiction rather than somehow not fiction (as Fetterley's claim that Sedgwick "stopped writing fiction" suggests), evidence not a retreat but a commitment, extending back to the beginning of her career, to write fiction for audiences across classes, ages, and literacy levels.

Unlike Hawthorne, Sedgwick was not truly anonymous, even early in her career (Homestead, "Behind the Veil?"). Her work was also always in demand, giving her a clear sense of her audience, or, more accurately, audiences plural.

She did not work her way through a series of personae and literary strategies on her way to achieving authority as a romantic artist. Instead, her motivations and fictional practices invert Hawthorne's priorities: from the beginning, she did not set out her moral beliefs in order to write; she wrote in order to promote a particular vision of morality. Indeed, she envisioned writing itself as form of benevolent action. With a clear sense of literary art as useful, she ranged across subgenres, narrative strategies, audiences, and themes.

A narrative account of her fiction of 1822 to 1835 amply demonstrates that a complex combination of consistency and variety, not decline or retreat, defined Sedgwick's career as a writer of fiction. Sedgwick's relatively short first novel, A New-England Tale, depicts the trials and triumphs of orphaned Jane Elton in a village setting and appeared in May 1822. Two months later, the New York Unitarian Book Society published as a pamphlet her short moral tale Mary Hollis, about a mother forced to raise her children alone after she loses her husband to intemperance.[3] It took Sedgwick two years to complete her first two-volume novel, Redwood (1824), an elaborately plotted novel of manners featuring another orphaned heroine in rural New England who triumphs over adversity. The next year saw the publication of two new works, one published separately as a book, the other published in a multi-author anthology. The book-length The Travellers: A Tale Designed for Young People was her first work specifically for children; its two child protagonists travel through upstate New York and French Canada, learning the value of benevolent action by observing it and then practicing it themselves. "The Catholic Iroquois" was Sedgwick's first story published in an illustrated annual literary anthology (or "gift book"), The Atlantic Souvenir, the first American volume published in this style already popularized in Europe. Sedgwick's tale features two converted Indian sisters in seventeenth-century French Canada, one of whom becomes a nun, the other of whom marries a white Frenchman. Culminating in the martyrdom of the married sister at the hands of her own father, the sisters' story is framed by the tale of an early nineteenth-century traveler in the region. In 1826, while Sedgwick was researching and writing Hope Leslie, she again published only shorter works, splitting her attention between adult and child audiences. "Modern Chivalry," a historical tale set during the era of the American Revolution and featuring a young British noblewoman who cross-dresses as a sailor, appeared in the Atlantic Souvenir, while a Boston Unitarian tract enterprise published The Deformed Boy, a pamphlet-length tale for children.

In 1827, Sedgwick began contributing to Lydia Maria Child's Juvenile Miscellany, to which she would contribute eight tales and sketches by 1834. Hope Leslie appeared in July 1827, and "Romance in Real Life" appeared in the gift book *The Legendary* at the end of the year. In the latter, a frame tale about travelers in contemporary western Massachusetts introduces a story of confused and masked identities during the Revolutionary War and its aftermath. Sedgwick published only a single *Juvenile Miscellany* story in 1828, but she published two tales in the *Miscellany* in 1829. In the same year, she began her association with an annual gift book for children, *The Youth's Keepsake*, with the publication of "The Elder Sister," a tale about the heroine's devotion to her motherless younger siblings and the deferral of romance and marriage. In the same year, Sedgwick also published two gift book stories for adults, "Cacoethes Scribendi," about the effect of gift books and the craze for authorship among the women of a New England village, and "The Country Cousin," yet another tale embedding a Revolutionary war-era romance in a contemporary frame.

Although Sedgwick lived in New York for part of every year in the 1820s, her fiction of that decade focuses insistently on her native New England, with excursions, mirroring her own touristic travel, to northern New York and French Canada. Her New York novel of manners *Clarence; or, A Tale of Our Own Times* (1830), split between New York City and rural regions north of it, marked a significant new focus in her fiction on New York and contemporary urban life. Nevertheless, Sedgwick also published two New England historical tales in gift books in 1830, "Mary Dyre," a fictionalized account of the actual seventeenth-century Quaker martyred by the Puritans, and "A Story of Shay's War," a tale embedding a fictional romance in the context of the actual late eighteenth-century post-Revolutionary conflict in Western Massachusetts. Sedgwick also published "The Canary Family," an animal parable for children, in the *Youth's Keepsake*.

If one focuses exclusively on single-authored books, Sedgwick's productivity might appear to drop off precipitously in the early 1830s; however, she published multiple tales and sketches each year in gift books and the *Juvenile Miscellany*. In 1831, she published two more gift book tales. "Berkeley Jail," set *c.*1800 in Massachusetts and based on actual events, features Sam Whistler, a solitary Oneida Indian living on the outskirts of a white village. Wrongly convicted of murdering a prominent white citizen, he is rescued from jail by a white friend whose family was also dispossessed of its land by the murdered man. Unlike the plot-driven and historical "Berkeley Jail," Sedgwick's other gift book tale of 1831, "A Sketch of a Blue Stocking," is a character sketch of a woman embodying a contemporary type, a married woman who successfully combines authorship with domesticity. In 1832, Sedgwick published "Spring in the City" in the *Miscellany*, her first fiction for children set in New York

City, as well as two works of fiction for adults. The gift book story "The Bridal Ring" tells the sad story of a poor and unprotected young woman from New England, who, persuaded to marry a southern gentleman privately and informally, dies of a broken heart when he leaves her and asks for his ring back so he can marry another. Sedgwick was the only woman solicited to contribute to the *Tales of Glauber Spa* anthology, in which her novella-length "Le Bossu," a historical romance set in the court of Charlemagne in the eighth century, appeared (the other tales were by William Cullen Bryant, James Kirke Paulding, William Leggett, and Robert Sands). Sedgwick departs from her earlier exclusive focus on American subject matter, but "Le Bossu" nevertheless returns to a favorite theme: true lovers separated by political conflict. In addition to two *Miscellany* tales, 1833 saw the appearance of two gift book stories, "Old Maids," which takes the form of a dialogue between a married woman and teenage girl about the lives of exemplary single women, and "A Reminiscence of Federalism," which, like "A Story of Shay's War," weds a romance plot to a tale of political conflict in rural New England during the early years of the American republic.

In 1834, Sedgwick published only one *Miscellany* tale and one gift book tale, "St. Catharine's Eve," a historical romance set in medieval France. However, her low productivity can be accounted for by the extraordinary number of works that appeared in 1835. The book-length *Home* appeared in July. Although considerably shorter than her two-volume novels (*Hope Leslie*, *Redwood*, and *Clarence*), *Home* is only somewhat shorter than *A New-England Tale* and is precisely the same length as *The Travellers*. Solicited by Unitarian minister Henry Ware for his series *Scenes and Characters Illustrating Christian Truths*, *Home* focuses on the Barclays, a family of modest means in New York City. *The Linwoods*, a two-volume historical novel set in New York City during the American Revolution, appeared in August, and *Tales and Sketches*, collecting eleven of her fourteen gift book tales, appeared later in 1835. Three new gift book tales also appeared late in the year. The title character of "Amy Cranstoun," set in seventeenth-century Rhode Island, is taken captive by Indians, while "New Year's Day," set in contemporary New York City, features the model conduct of Lizzy Percival, whose forbearance and benevolence make her father relent in his opposition to a marriage proposal from a man she loves. "The Unpresuming Mr. Hudson," the lead tale in the same volume of *The Gift* in which Edgar Allan Poe's "Manuscript Found in a Bottle" first appeared, moves south to Virginia and features "the trials of a pretty young girl who is chaperoned to watering-places by a silly, expecting, and credulous mother" (38). Finally, in 1835 Sedgwick published her first work for adults to appear in a magazine as opposed to a gift book, "Our Burial Place." Combining elements of the essay and the sketch, Sedgwick gives a factual account in the *Knickerbocker Magazine* of her family's burial plot in Stockbridge, Massachusetts. Clearly, 1835 marked anything but a falling off for Sedgwick as an author of fiction – indeed, it marked the most productive year of her career to that point, with her works traversing multiple themes, genres, audiences, and publication venues.

From this survey of her works published from 1822 to 1835, several thematic clusters emerge, linking Sedgwick's imagination more firmly and complexly to sociopolitical contexts than her novels treated in isolation would suggest. Carolyn Karcher's sustained attention to *all* of Lydia Maria Child's fiction in *First Woman in the Republic* (1994), her cultural biography of Child, has encouraged subsequent scholars to situate *Hobomok* (1824), Child's novel of Indian–white intermarriage in seventeenth-century Massachusetts, in relation to her short stories on similar themes. In contrast, *Hope Leslie*, which also features intermarriage, is taken to be Sedgwick's only foray into the genre, even though for more than a decade her literary imagination was preoccupied with white–Indian relations, and especially interracial marriage and friendship, in Massachusetts, northern New York, and French Canada.[4] In the 1820s, Indian characters are central to the gift book tales "The Catholic Iroquois" and "Berkeley Jail," while the longer *Travellers* features an extended inset tale of two generations of interracial romance, the marriage of a Frenchman to an Oneida woman, and the subsequent romance between their mixed-race, Europeanized daughter and a full-blood Oneida warrior. Indian captivity is central to *Hope Leslie* and Sedgwick's last Indian story, "Amy Cranstoun." Notably, *Redwood* earlier featured a variation on the Indian captivity theme: a devious white Shaker man hires Sooduck, a lone Indian living on the margins of white society, to hold as a prisoner for him the young white woman he has abducted from the Shaker community. "Berkeley Jail" and *Redwood* both include lone Indian figures in early nineteenth-century Western Massachusetts, separated from their tribes (implicitly removed west), "who," Sedgwick says in *Redwood*, "like the remnants of their sacrifice-rocks, remain among us monuments of past ages" (2: 74).

On the issue of slavery and the status of African Americans in the nation, Sedgwick and Child sometimes appear as foils to one another. Certainly, Sedgwick did not share Child's radical abolitionism, but neither did she ignore slavery. She grapples with slavery within the borders of the nation in subplots in *Redwood* and *The Linwoods*: the former features the abuse of the slave Africk in early nineteenth-century Virginia, while the latter features Rose, a slave woman in late eighteenth-century New York on the eve of the Revolution, whom the white heroine emancipates when she speaks powerfully of her longing for liberty. Sedgwick's thinking on race and slavery became increasingly conservative in the 1830s, and, arguably, despite Rose's stirring speech, Sedgwick takes a conservative position on the African American capacity for citizenship in *The Linwoods*.[5] In the 1820s and '30s, however, Sedgwick also engaged slavery outside the boundaries of the American nation through key subplots set in European colonial sites in the West Indies. In *Redwood*, Caroline Redwood brings a female slave with her from Virginia to New England, and the slave, Lilly, escapes with her lover, the slave of a "West India planter" also traveling in New England (2: 270). Caroline ultimately marries a Captain in the British Royal Navy and moves with him to an unnamed island in the West Indies. Reformed by the time she marries, her death from the West Indies climate and childbearing nevertheless is a punishment for her earlier transgressions. In *Hope Leslie*, Indian heroine Magawisca protests against the survivors of the colonists' massacre of her tribe being sent as slaves to "the Islands of the Sun, to bend their free limbs to bondage like your beasts of burden" (which was, indeed, the fate to which the Puritans consigned the wives and children of Pequot leaders) (55). The novel's villain, Sir Philip Gardiner, has a history of West Indian piracy and plans to escape there if his plot to abduct Hope Leslie, the English heroine, fails (334).

These novels reference the source of the wealth of the West Indies – plantations worked by slaves – only obliquely, but the brutality of white plantation owners in the region erupts unexpectedly into one of Sedgwick's children's stories, "Dogs" (1828). Discussing the sagacity of dogs with their mother, the child protagonists learn how the French planters in St. Domingo (later Haiti) deployed dogs to put down slave rebellion. Using dogs to pursue murderers or robbers, the mother explains, "might be excused . . . but no apology can be made for the French of St. Domingo," who used them to "pursue and devour" slaves who "carried on a war against their masters" because they were "determined to be free" (36). In a culmination of these themes, Sedgwick introduces a fully developed West Indian backstory for the American heroine's British grandfather in *Clarence* – a second son of an aristocrat, he goes to Jamaica to make his own fortune as a plantation owner and, after losing his British wife and son, takes a free woman of color, Eli Clairon, as a quasi wife, with tragic results for both Eli and the son she bears him.[6] Although in her fiction of the 1820s and '30s Sedgwick often displaced the controversy over slavery onto regions outside the nation, she also insistently represented cultural and economic ties between the USA and the Caribbean, making visible US complicity in slave enterprise there.

Sedgwick also grappled nearly obsessively in her fiction with political and military conflicts of the American Revolution and the early republic, most often intertwining historical events with tales of families split and star-crossed lovers kept apart by these conflicts. "Romance in Real Life," for example, presents an account of incidents in the life of Marie Angely, ostensibly an actual daughter of Hector St. John de Crèvecœur, author of *Letters from an American Farmer* (1782). The precise details of what happened to Crèvecœur's children when he left his Hudson Valley farm during the American Revolution and how he recovered them on his return from Europe in 1783 remain a mystery, but in a tale presented as derived from fact, Sedgwick accounts for several years Marie lived as "Mary Reynolds" on a Massachusetts farm on the other side of the Hudson River. Sedgwick's tale then jumps forward a decade to involve Marie in an elaborate transnational marriage plot. In "The Country Cousin," Yankee farmer Amos Blunt refuses to allow his daughter Anna to marry a British officer in the occupying army. His refusal leads to a clandestine marriage, the birth and eventual death of a blind son, and a host of tragedies, but ultimately families and nations are reconciled. In "A Story of Shay's War," the romantic conflict, like the historical tax revolt, is internal to the new nation: two young men with opposing political sympathies compete for the affection of one young woman. The story ends on the battlefield, combining heroic acts of friendship, romantic union, and death in rapid succession: Harry Lee, on the side of the insurgents, sacrifices his life to save his friend, militia-member Francis Graham, and with his dying breath conveys heroine Lora's hand to Graham. In the context of Sedgwick's full career, her novel-length treatment in *The Linwoods* of families and lovers divided by military and political conflict is a culmination rather than a departure.

Sedgwick's portrayals of Native Americans, slavery, and the Revolution barely begin to exhaust her thematic range from 1822 to 1835. For example, Sedgwick also repeatedly focuses on the status of women in the culture and the choice of marriage *versus* the single state for women, often intertwining these questions with other themes.[7] Her range in terms of audience is varied, but more easily mapped. Sedgwick published a significant number of works specifically designated for young audiences during this period. Her tales and sketches published in the *Juvenile Miscellany* and the *Youth's Keepsake* are explicitly marked as "children's literature" by their periodical contexts, while she and / or her publisher designated the *Travellers* as for children through its subtitle, *A Tale Designed for Young People*. Sedgwick did not, however, always distinguish between child and adult audiences. Reading against their original audience address, she anthologized two tales published in *The Youth's Keepsake*,

"The Elder Sister" (retitled "The Eldest Sister") and "The Canary Family," in *Tales & Sketches*, alongside tales originally published in gift books for adults. All of her "adult" novels of this period feature young female heroines – Jane Elton of *A New-England Tale*, Ellen Bruce of *Redwood*, the title character of *Hope Leslie*, Gertrude Clarence of *Clarence*, Isabella Linwood of *The Linwoods* – and these heroines make Sedgwick a founding figure of the genre of "woman's fiction." Notably, all of these heroines are adolescents, as are the majority of female protagonists in her gift book tales and sketches. In the concluding chapter of *Hope Leslie*, she directly addresses this intermediate class of readers, no longer children and not yet fully adults, "that large, and most indulgent class of our readers, the misses in their teens" (369).

An adult Sedgwick addresses young women of her own socioeconomic class in *Hope Leslie* (well educated and in comfortable financial circumstances), but her address in *Home* is explicitly cross-class. Identified on the title-page as "the author of 'Redwood' 'Hope Leslie,' &c." (that is, as the author of novels), Sedgwick dedicated *Home* to her target audience: "To farmers and mechanics this little volume is respectfully inscribed by their friend, the author" (n.p.). While this dedication makes a cross-class address explicit, it was implicit as far back as the beginning of her career in *Mary Hollis*, a tale in simple language about an exemplary working-class woman, designed for inexpensive or free distribution as a tract.

Indeed, Sedgwick's language and narrative strategies vary widely with audience, subject matter, and purpose – there is no one "Sedgwick voice." She is most often an "engaging narrator," to use Robyn Warhol's term, speaking in the first person, directly addressing readers, and guiding their gaze and their interpretation. For instance, in the beginning of a chapter in *Home*, the narrator explains, "As we have entered Mr. Barclay's dining-room, we are tempted to linger there, and permit our readers to observe the details of the dinner. The right ministration of the table is an important item in *home* education" (27). However, her use of the plural first person ("we") in some works and the singular first person ("I") in others produces distinctly different effects. As Susan Harris observes, the "we" narrator in *A New-England Tale* "assumes more authority" than Susanna Rowson's "I" narrator in *Charlotte Temple* (1791), because while Rowson's "I" is a "discrete individual," Sedgwick's "we" is a "representative voice suggest[ing] a diffused personality that speaks for the authority" of a broader culture (*19th-Century American Women's Novels*, 52).

Sedgwick consistently narrates as "we" in her novels, but she frequently narrates as "I" in her short fiction. In the "Elder Sister," for example, the first-person narrator presents herself as a friend and observer of the characters whose lives are the main focus of the story. In contrast, in "A Reminiscence of Federalism" the narrating "I" is an adult recalling events she participated in and witnessed as a child ("I was sent when a very young child . . . to pass the summer in a clergyman's family in Vermont" [107]). Narrating as "I" in "A Reminiscence" and other stories, Sedgwick delicately walks the blurry line between fact and fiction. Her parents did actually send her to spend a summer in Burlington, Vermont, as a girl, and she drew on her memories in "A Reminiscence"; however, the romance at the tale's center is clearly a carefully crafted fiction cum political allegory.[8] Narrating as "I," Sedgwick invites readers to engage her tales and sketches as representations of reality, but in tales such as "The Country Cousin" she also playfully draws attention to such narrative maneuvers as conventions of the craft of fiction. She first narrates the frame tale as "we," but then shifts to "I" in a sentence that both claims reality and pokes fun at the distinction as literary convention. "Somewhere between twenty and thirty years ago," she writes, "we – or rather I – for . . . we detest that reviewer in the abstract, the 'cold, and critical,' and pompous *we* – I was on a visit to a friend of my parents who resided in New York" (156).

In other gift book tales, Sedgwick is similarly playful in her narratorial comments on this publication context and its conventions. The opening of "Mary Dyre" prods readers to prepare them for a dark and serious tale about religious persecution, warning that "a Quaker Martyr, may appear to the fair holiday readers of souvenirs, a very unfit personage to be introduced into the romantic and glorious company of lords, and ladye lovers; of doomed brides; and all-achieving heroines; chivalric soldiers; suffering outlaws; and Ossianic sons of the forest" (294). "Cacoethes Scribendi," published five years into the gift book fad in the United States, is, among other things, an elaborate spoof of its own publication context. The density and range of allusion in "Cacoethes" (she references the works of authors from Juvenal to Milton to Pope to Shakespeare to Thomas Gray and more) highlight Sedgwick's own high level of learning and accomplishment (a level clearly higher than that of protagonist Mrs. Courland, whose pretensions to authorship the narrator gently mocks) and makes great demands on readers. Her other gift book tales and her novels can be similarly allusive, and in *Clarence* and *The Linwoods*, by quoting from works in multiple languages without providing translations, she positions herself as a woman of the world and a cosmopolitan novelist.[9]

Such sophistication would subvert her aims in works addressed to children, in which she narrates in the guise of a sympathetic teacher speaking in simple language. "I will not write out the moral of my story," the narrator of "Dogs" explains, because she remembers how much she "hated those formal morals to Æsop's fables" that "almost crushed the life out of" the stories. Nevertheless, she derives a moral from the actions of the child protagonist Mary, who "always set the qualities of the heart above the faculties of the mind – goodness above genius" (3). In *Mary Hollis*, her aim is to instruct adults possessing only basic literacy skills, so as narrator she assumes the guise of a benevolent lady counseling lower-class aspirants to self-improvement. Responding to the notion that Mary's full recovery from destitution after her husband's death from alcoholism was merely lucky, the narrator carefully explains that "Mary's *luck*" was not produced by "magic" or witchcraft but by her return "to her old trade" of tailoring. Mary herself "used to say," the narrator reports, "that her health and her time were her capital, and that it was her own fault, if the interest of such a stock did not support her" (21).

While the voices of Sedgwick's narrators predominate in these examples, as Charlene Avallone observes, Sedgwick "develops the narrative and instructive ends of her fiction as much through conversations among characters as through narration or exposition" ("Catharine Sedgwick," 197). Dialogue is thus a key feature in all of her fiction. Indeed, the story "Old Maids" consists of nothing but dialogue between characters who address each other as "Mrs. Seton" and "Anne" – in the absence of narrative markers or interpolations, only their words addressed to one another identify them as an older married woman and a younger unmarried one. Although Sedgwick wrote no purely epistolary novels, characters' words conveyed in letters figure prominently in all of her novels and many of her stories. In *Hope Leslie* and *Clarence*, readers learn about the true character and disguised identities of the villains (Sir Philip Gardiner and Henrique Pedrillo, respectively) through their letters addressed to off-stage co-conspirators.

Especially in her short stories of the 1820s, Sedgwick added further layers of voice and language by constructing frame tales. The frame of "The Catholic Iroquois," which nestles a frame inside a frame, is particularly elaborate. The opening frame tale narrates the hardships of a "gentleman" traveling "from Niagara to Montreal" in the early 1800s, who is forced to take shelter in the hovel of a French Canadian family (72). In conversation with the gentleman, the father of the family relates the history of a mysterious manuscript in the family's possession: in 1700 "young Bonchard" discovered in a cave a manuscript composed by Pére Mésnard (an actual Jesuit missionary priest of the mid-seventeenth century) and made the copy possessed by the father's illiterate family (79, 84). Only after the reader descends through these two frames does she encounter the contents of the found manuscript, the story of the Iroquois sisters who give Sedgwick's tale its name.

This rich variety and continuity over fourteen years complicate claims about Sedgwick's seemingly abrupt retreat from being a "major novelist" to being a writer of advice literature. The publishing chronology the year in which this seeming shift occurred is illuminating. The book marking her supposed retreat, *Home*, actually appeared before *The Linwoods* and was entirely consistent with the tone and style of many of her earlier works. *Home* and the two works that followed soon after it in a similar vein, *The Poor Rich Man, and the Rich Poor Man* (1836) and *Live and Let Live; or, Domestic Service Illustrated* (1837), are most often characterized as "didactic novellas" rather than "novels," and Sedgwick herself did not call them novels. Nevertheless, in all three she uses the same tools from the craft of fiction she used in her earlier longer fictions, such as character dialogue, an engaging narrator, and the manipulation of time in plotting the trajectories of multiple characters over extended periods of time.

Sedgwick wrote no fictional works as long as *The Linwoods* in the twenty years after 1835, but the quantity of her fictional output remained remarkably constant through the 1840s. As the gift books declined in prestige and popularity, she increasingly published short fiction in magazines, migrating as a marquee contributor from venue to venue (from *Godey's*, to *Graham's*, to the *Columbian*, and finally *Sartain's*). "Wilton Harvey," a tale of financial intrigue and murder during the financial panic of 1837 centering around the male protagonist named in the title, appeared serially in six installments in *Godey's* in 1842. Its length warranted separate book publication, but instead Sedgwick collected it in her *Tales and Sketches, Second Series* (1844). Interestingly, in the 1840s the founding figure of "woman's fiction" wrote two book-length fictions centering on the lives of male characters. Approximately the same length as "Wilton Harvey," *The Boy of Mount Rhigi* (1848) focuses on two young male protagonists who grow into manhood; in her Preface, Sedgwick directs the book to the attention of "our young people, who have been carefully nurtured" to "awaken" in them "their duty to those who are less favored" ([5]).

After *The Linwoods*, Sedgwick nearly abandoned seventeenth- and eighteenth-century American subject matter, but not historical fiction as a genre, writing several long tales set in early Europe, such as "The White Scarf" (1838), set in 1409 during the reign of Charles VI; "A Huguenot Family" (1842), depicting the persecution of French Protestants in the seventeenth century; and "Imelda of Bologna" (1846), set in thirteenth-century Italy.

Sedgwick also increasingly branched out into non-fiction prose forms. With *Letters from Abroad to Kindred at Home* (1841), she entered the popular field of travel literature, and her prose published in magazines sometimes took the form of non-fiction sketches or essays about contemporary society, particularly in New York. However, the literary craft acquired over two decades of writing fiction was equally important to her non-fiction prose – the "letters" in *Letters from Abroad* are no more unrevised documents of her 1839–40 travels in Europe than "A Reminiscence of Federalism" is a transparent account of her childhood summer in Vermont. Even in her two books that might most accurately be characterized as "conduct books" or "advice literature," *Means and Ends, or Self-Training* (1839) and *Morals of Manners; or, Hints for Our Young People* (1846), Sedgwick deploys the techniques of fiction, with dialogue and brief tales emerging in the midst of expository prose. Indeed, these books qualify as a reversion to what Sarah Emily Newton calls "conduct fiction," an intermediate form between the conduct book and the early American novel. Using Rowson's *Mentoria* (1791) and Hannah Webster Foster's *The Boarding School* (1798) as examples, Newton argues that "the use of anecdote or tale to illustrate . . . conduct topics" in these "semifictional texts bridge[s] the sermonizing didacticism of the conduct book and the dramatic structure of the early novel" ("Wise and Foolish Virgins," 149). Deploying this earlier genre decades later, Sedgwick bridges seemingly distinct genres in her own body of work, her later "conduct books" and her earlier "major novels."

In *The Shape of Hawthorne's Career*, Baym never defines "career," taking its meaning to be self-evident. However, some of her remarks in *Woman's Fiction* might seem to exclude antebellum women novelists if pretensions to artistic seriousness are taken as a prerequisite for having a literary career. "[T]hey saw themselves not as 'artists,'" she writes, "but as professional writers with work to do and a living to be made from satisfactory fulfillment of an obligation to their audience" (16). In a new introduction for a 1993 reprint of *Woman's Fiction*, Baym stands by her assessment that she found no American equivalents to George Eliot, that the women were not understood as particularly "literary" or as "major" in their own days and are best thought of as "professionals making a product desired by their clients rather than artists making an object expressing their own genius and talent," although she does add the qualification that professionalism entails the "possession of expertise" (xvi). But should writing to entertain and instruct an audience necessarily disqualify a writer from artistic seriousness? More recently, Angela Vietto has argued for the usefulness of "the concept of the literary career" for women writers of the

Revolutionary era. Defining career broadly as a "path" provides a tool, Vietto claims, that allows us "to examine the course writers followed in their pursuit of writing as a vocation – their progress in a variety of kinds of projects, both in their texts and in their performances as authors" (*Women and Authorship in Revolutionary America*, 91). Unlike Baym, Vietto divorces the concept of career from publication and commercial success, arguing for the application of the concept to authors whose works circulated only in manuscript.

Sedgwick's sense of authorial vocation, however, was defined from the start in relation to publication and broader audiences. As her literary career was drawing to a close, both Sedgwick and reviewers increasingly traced just such a long path. In the late 1840s, Sedgwick and publisher George Palmer Putnam planned a collected edition of her works. A truly complete collected edition never appeared – Putnam's repeated business failures and the lack of cooperation from Harper & Brothers, the publisher of many of her works of the 1830s and '40s, made it impossible (Homestead, "Introduction"). Nevertheless, it is clear that Sedgwick intended the edition to be comprehensive, encompassing both the novels of the first half of her career and the shorter didactic works of the second. As she explains in the preface to her revised 1849 edition of *Clarence*, "The selection of Clarence as the first in the series of republication has been accidental," and she also planned to republish "the smaller works, written for the largest classes of readers and for children" (xi). Although by the late 1840s she had not written a novel proper in more than a decade, she eagerly embraced the opportunity to revise *A New-England Tale*, *Redwood*, and *Clarence*, making substantive changes to all three. This self-reflexive labor may have inspired her to undertake at an advanced age the onerous task of novel-writing – her longest novel, *Married or Single?* (1857), appeared when she was in her late sixties.

Sarah Robbins argues that properly reading Sedgwick's didactic fictions of the 1830s and '40s in relation to her earlier fiction requires a willingness to recognize "the nineteenth-century overlap in literary categories usually dichotomized today," including "children–adult, straightforward–complex, didactic–aesthetic" ("Periodizing Authorship," 5). Critics in the 1850s easily located such "overlaps" as they looked back over three decades or more of Sedgwick's career, seeing the contour or "shape" of her career, with *Married or Single?* as a logical culmination. "Miss Sedgwick's long literary career," opined *The Merchants' Magazine*, "has been genuinely, and in the best sense, American." The reviewer recognizes a distinction between "[h]er novels [which] have reflected the various, and often incongruous, aspects of our American life and social relations" and "her didactic works [which] have taught the duties growing out of them, the true spirit of Christian Democracy." However, he immediately collapses the distinction, judging *Married or Single?* "worthy of a place in the long list of her admirable works." A reviewer in *The Christian Inquirer* (a Unitarian weekly) goes further, unproblematically conjoining Sedgwick's desire to engage an audience with a desire for artistic expression, and the role of moral instructor with the role of literary "genius." "Driven to authorship by a passionate love of sympathy and an irresistible proclivity for expression," the critic writes, "she has continued in it from an ever-growing love of usefulness, and a consciousness of power to assist in the cultivation of the domestic and social life of our young nation" ("Miss Sedgwick"). Sedgwick was first "a charming novelist" who gained an "eager and hungry" audience, the critic writes, but then she "dedicated" her "powers" "to the improvement, correction, and formation of our national manners." Having drawn this distinction between the "charming novelist" and the moral instructor, the critic immediately dissolves it by mapping a crossing in the opposite direction, describing how in her novels Sedgwick "ingeniously disguised the teacher in the novelist" and "kept . . . serious ends under . . . gay appearances." "[T]hroughout her whole literary career," the critic concludes, Sedgwick "has won [readers] to gentleness, truth, honor, purity, and piety" by using "her genius" to arouse emotion by bringing "before their minds the living characters . . . of her genial stories."

The careers of other women who also began writing fiction in the antebellum era but a decade or more after Sedgwick deserve similar attention. Both Harriet Beecher Stowe and E. D. E. N. Southworth, for instance, had careers fully as long and various as Sedgwick's. Stowe published short stories in magazines and gifts books for nearly fifteen years before writing *Uncle Tom's Cabin*, her first novel, and yet literary historians seldom pay attention to her earliest fiction as a context for reading her bestselling novel; nor have her novels and stories after *Uncle Tom's Cabin*, and especially her fiction of the 1860s and '70s, received adequate attention.[10] E. D. E. N. Southworth published fiction regularly from the late 1840s through the late 1880s, and yet twenty-first-century readers know her primarily as the author of a single novel, *The Hidden Hand* (serial publication 1859, book publication 1888). Arguably, Sedgwick's fiction and Sedgwick herself as a model for long-term dedication to the craft of fiction influenced both Stowe and Southworth, and yet their careers assumed their own distinctive shapes. Their bodies of work – and the bodies of work of many other women who began writing before the Civil War – await the attention of twenty-first-century literary historians willing to read attentively for the human sensibilities and dedication to craft they represent.

Notes

1. On primarily postbellum nineteenth-century women as aspiring to serious artistry in ways that antebellum women (ostensibly) did not, see Boyd, *Writing for Immortality*. Placing the emergence of the "serious" woman artist even later, see Ammons, *Conflicting Stories*.
2. See Rust, *Prodigal Daughters*; Karcher, *The First Woman in the Republic*; and Teed, "A Passion for Distinction," respectively, for each woman's career.
3. Full bibliographical details provided only for quoted works. Consult Damon-Bach, Homestead, and Roepsch, "Chronological Bibliography," for complete information. Smyers and Winship, "Catharine Maria Sedgwick," provides advertisement and review information that establishes chronology of publication within years for book publication.
4. Ryan, for example, in a broad-ranging analysis of Child's Indian fiction and relying on Karcher, characterizes Child as "writ[ing] Indian stories throughout her career," while she claims that Sedgwick "turned her attention to other matters" after *Hope Leslie* ("Republican Mothers and Indian Wives," 34).
5. Both Avallone ("Catharine Sedgwick's White Nation-Making") and Weierman ("'A Slave Story I Began and Abandoned'") trace Sedgwick's increasing conservatism on race and slavery during these years.
6. For a full analysis, see Homestead, "Introduction."
7. See Lubovich, "'Married or Single?'," and Foletta, "'The dearest sacrifice'," for career-spanning analyses of this theme in Sedgwick, although both miss the opportunity to analyze many short stories and her didactic novellas.
8. For her later-life account of her childhood experiences in Bennington, which notably includes no romance, see Kelley, *Power*, 79–82.
9. See Gould, "Catharine Sedgwick's Cosmopolitan Nation," on the cosmopolitanism of *The Linwoods*, focusing on Sedgwick's engagement with French language and culture. *Clarence*'s range of linguistic and cultural engagements beyond the borders of the American nation is even broader.
10. See Hedrick, *Harriet Beecher Stowe*, for this long trajectory – although, alas, even a Pulitzer Prize-winning biography of Stowe was not enough to make most literary historians look beyond Stowe's most famous novel.

Works cited

Ammons, Elizabeth. *Conflicting Stories: American Women Writers at the Turn into the Twentieth Century*. New York: Oxford University Press, 1991.
Avallone, Charlene. "Catharine Sedgwick and the 'Art' of Conversation." In Damon-Bach and Clements, *Catharine Maria Sedgwick: Critical Perspectives*. 192–208.
"Catharine Sedgwick's White Nation-Making: Historical Fiction and *The Linwoods*." *ESQ: A Journal of the American Renaissance* 55.2 (2009): 97–133.
Baym, Nina. *The Shape of Hawthorne's Career*. Ithaca: Cornell University Press, 1976.
Woman's Fiction: A Guide to Novels by and about Women in America, 1820–1870. 2nd edn. Urbana: University of Illinois Press, 1993.

Boyd, Anne E. *Writing for Immortality: Women and the Emergence of High Literary Culture in America*. Baltimore: The Johns Hopkins University Press, 2004.

Damon-Bach, Lucinda and Victoria Clements, eds. *Catharine Maria Sedgwick: Critical Perspectives*. Boston: Northeastern University Press, 2003.

Damon-Bach, Lucinda, Victoria Clements, Melissa J. Homestead, and Allison J. Roepsch, "Chronological Bibliography of the Works of Catharine Maria Sedgwick." In Damon-Bach and Clements, *Catharine Maria Sedgwick: Critical Perspectives*. 19–35.

Fetterley, Judith. "Commentary: Nineteenth-Century American Women Writers and the Politics of Recovery." *American Literary History* 6.3 (1994): 600–11.

Fetterley, Judith, ed. *Provisions: A Reader from 19th-Century American Women*. Bloomington: Indiana University Press, 1985.

Foletta, Marshall. "'The dearest sacrifice': Catharine Maria Sedgwick and the Celibate Life." *American Nineteenth-Century History* 8.1 (2007): 51–79.

Gould, Philip. "Catharine Sedgwick's Cosmopolitan Nation." *New England Quarterly* 78.2 (June 2005): 232–58.

Harris, Susan K. *19th-Century American Women's Novels: Interpretative Strategies*. New York: Cambridge University Press, 1990.

Hedrick, Joan. *Harriet Beecher Stowe: A Life*. New York: Oxford University Press, 1994.

Homestead, Melissa J. "Behind the Veil? Catharine Sedgwick and Anonymous Publication." In Damon-Bach and Clements, *Catharine Maria Sedgwick: Critical Perspectives*. 19–35.

"Introduction." In *Clarence; or, A Tale of Our Own Times*. Peterborough, ON: Broadview Press, 2011. 9–40.

Karcher, Carolyn. *The First Woman in the Republic: A Cultural Biography of Lydia Maria Child*. Durham, NC: Duke University Press, 1994.

Kelley, Mary, ed. *The Power of her Sympathy: The Autobiography and Journal of Catharine Maria Sedgwick*. Boston: Massachusetts Historical Society, 1993.

Private Woman, Public Stage: Literary Domesticity in Nineteenth-Century America. New York: Oxford University Press, 1984.

Lubovich, Maglina. "'Married or Single?': Catharine Maria Sedgwick on Old Maids, Wives, and Marriage." *Legacy* 25.1 (2008): 23–40.

"Miss Sedgwick." *Christian Inquirer*, September 19, 1857: 2.

Newton, Sarah Emily. "Wise and Foolish Virgins: 'Usable Fiction' and the Early American Conduct Tradition." *Early American Literature* 25.2 (1990): 139–67.

Rev. of *Married or Single?* by Catharine Sedgwick. *Merchants' Magazine and Commercial Review*, February 1, 1858: 267.

Robbins, Sarah. "Periodizing Authorship, Characterizing Genre: Catharine Maria Sedgwick's Benevolent Literacy Narratives," *American Literature* 76.1 (2004): 1–29.

Rust, Marion. *Prodigal Daughters: Susanna Rowson's Early American Women*. Chapel Hill: University of North Carolina Press, 2008.

Ryan, Melissa. "Republican Mothers and Indian Wives: Lydia Maria Child's Indian Stories." *ESQ: A Journal of the American Renaissance* 56.1 (2010): 33–70.

Sedgwick, Catharine Maria. *The Boy of Mount Rhigi*. Boston: Peirce, 1848.

"The Catholic Iroquois." *Atlantic Souvenir*. Philadelphia: Carey and Lea, 1826 [pub. 1825]. 72–103.

Clarence; or, A Tale of Our Own Times. Rev. edn. New York: Putnam, 1849.

"The Country Cousin." *The Token*. Boston: Carter & Hendee, 1830 [pub. 1829]. 153–93.

"Dogs." *Juvenile Miscellany* 4.1 (March 1828): 31–43.

Home. Boston: Munroe, 1835.

Hope Leslie; or, Early Times in the Massachusetts. Ed. Carolyn Karcher. New York: Penguin, 1998.

"Mary Dyre." *The Token*. Boston: Gray and Bowen, 1831 [pub. 1830]. 294–312.

Mary Hollis. An Original Tale. New York: New York Unitarian Book Society, 1822.

Redwood; A Tale. 2 vols. New York: Bliss & White, 1824.

"A Reminiscence of Federalism." *The Token*. Boston: Bowen, 1834 [pub. 1833]. 102–43.

"The Unpresuming Mr. Hudson." *The Gift*. Philadelphia: Carey & Hart, 1836 [pub. 1835]. 17–38.

Smyers, Virginia L. and Michael Winship. "Catharine Maria Sedgwick." In *Bibliography of American Literature*. Vol. 7. New Haven: Yale University Press, 1983. 380–96.

Teed, Melissa Ladd. "A Passion for Distinction: Lydia Huntley Sigourney and the Creation of a Literary Reputation." *New England Quarterly* 77.1 (2004): 51–69.

Vietto, Angela. *Women and Authorship in Revolutionary America*. Burlington, VT: Ashgate, 2005.

Warhol, Robyn. *Gendered Interventions: Narrative Discourse in the Victorian Novel*. New Brunswick: Rutgers University Press, 1989.

Weierman, Karen Woods. "'A Slave Story I Began and Abandoned': Sedgwick's Antislavery Manuscript." In Damon-Bach and Clements, *Catharine Maria Sedgwick: Critical Perspectives*. 122–38.

10

Writing, authorship, and genius
Literary women and modes of literary production

SUSAN S. WILLIAMS

In her 1988 introduction to *Alternative Alcott*, Elaine Showalter notes "a striking physical metaphor" between Louisa May Alcott's self-taught ambidexterity and her "conflicting literary impulses," which Showalter summarizes as tending toward the "genteel, domestic, and moralizing," on one hand, and toward "passion, anger, and satirical wit" on the other (left) hand (ix). Showalter's immediate focus is on the generic differences among Alcott's various literary productions and the way in which the sensation fiction, in particular, points to a powerful "alternative" to the domestic novels for which Alcott is best known. This focus has turned out to be a dominant one in Alcott studies over the past several decades, with numerous studies taking generic alternatives as their critical starting point. Yet Alcott's ambidexterity is also a striking metaphor for the various authorial modes that Alcott could assume. Showalter concludes that Alcott was, in fact, never fully satisfied with the work produced by either hand, because "she never entirely got over her awe for the masculine literary community of American Transcendentalist philosophy which her father represented, nor forgave herself for failing to measure up to his moral and intellectual standards." Showalter associates this masculine literary community, in turn, with the "godly inspiration" of genius, and she sees the masks that recur in Alcott's fiction as representing "her own perennial effort to conceal the deeper meanings of her work," including its genius, "from herself, as well as from others" (xlii–xliii).

Showalter's reading of Alcott engages three key terms that describe her literary production: *writer* of sensational fiction, *author* of juvenile and adult novels, and Transcendental *genius*. In this essay, I want to explore each of these terms and the general characteristics with which they were associated and applied to nineteenth-century literary women. Although these terms are, as Showalter notes, sometimes in conflict with each other, the fact that Alcott could move among all three suggests that it would be more accurate to describe them as occupying a general continuum of modes available to nineteenth-century women. In general, critics viewed female writers as being the most common and accessible mode, followed by authorship and genius. In an 1866 essay on "American Female Authorship," for example, one critic begins by noting that "we have no paucity of female writers" and "do not lack lady scribblers"; then concedes that "there have been and are American authoresses of marked ability," and concludes with a specific discussion of Harriet Beecher Stowe and Gail Hamilton as examples of women who have "genius" (8–9). As we will see, Alcott described herself, and her fictional author Jo March Bhaer, using all three of these terms, as did the critics who reviewed her novels. Using Alcott as a primary example, then, this essay will explore these various modes with an eye toward answering three fundamental questions. First, how were they described and valued in the nineteenth century? Second, how have they been described and valued in the various waves of contemporary scholarship that have accompanied the recovery of women's writing into American literary scholarship? And finally, what do these various discourses tell us about directions for future scholarship in this area? Addressing these questions can help us see not only the permeability of these various modes but also the terms by which we can understand the constraints and the opportunities that underlie this scholarly field.

Writer

If ambidexterity has become a central metaphor for understanding Alcott's authorship, Jo March has become its central fictional representation. Indeed, the analogy between Jo and Alcott was established almost as soon as *Little Women* appeared in 1868; by 1885, James Parton could note, in a collection of sketches entitled *Daughters of Genius*, that "Miss Louisa May Alcott, as every one who has read 'Little Women' would easily believe, is the original of her own harum-scarum 'Jo'" (78).[1] The title of Parton's book suggests that he is interested in the native talents of the women who have descended from or been possessed by genius. Yet he describes Alcott first not as a genius but as a "busy and voluminous *writer*" (89; emphasis added). In the sketch, he traces the origins of her career to a "pretty summer-house" her father had built in Concord, where she "first tried composing stories, but only to amuse her sisters and friends" (82). In doing so, he represents a "writer" as an amateur who is a novice about the workings of the marketplace; who is motivated more by personal circumstances than by professional success; and who "composes" naturally and easily, working in a summer house rather than a study. At the same time, Parton quotes an extended excerpt from an "interesting letter to the *Saturday Evening Gazette*" in which Alcott describes her early career and her particular response to beginning to receive regular payment for her stories. "The heart of the young authoress sang for joy," she writes, "and she set bravely forth along the literary lane, which for twenty years showed no sign of turning" (82). This account suggests that in Alcott's mind, she moved from writing, or composing, for pleasure to becoming an "authoress" at the point at which she began to receive regular compensation for her publications. Reaching that point, she decided to pursue a "literary lane" that equated with a definable career path. Following this "literary lane," she moved from writing for pleasure in a summer house to negotiating contracts; in doing so, she showed that a writer who is "ignorant" and "helpless" can become a seasoned professional. At the same time, this account underscores the interconnections among these various terms. Parton views Alcott as a "writer"; she views herself as an "authoress"; and the title of the overall collection identifies her as a "daughter of genius."

Parton's description of Alcott as a "writer" echoes numerous nineteenth-century fictional and prose accounts of literary women that stressed their amateurism; their dependence on direct experience and observation; and their physical, sometimes impulsive, need to write. In general, reviewers and essayists in this period came to use the term "writer" to connote literary producers who were amateurs; who focused primarily on realistic subjects to which they brought heightened properties of observation; and who associated the act of composing with scribbling and physical release rather than with artistry and difficulty. In the conclusion of *Little Women*, Alcott highlights the first of these characteristics by having Jo March decide to focus on her roles as wife, mother, and teacher. Although she has published a variety of her manuscripts, from sensation stories to a novel, Jo continues to define herself as an amateur. She is first motivated to enter a newspaper's prize competition because she and her family need the money; she writes not as a professional but as a daughter and sister who is trying to help ends meet while her father is recovering from his service as a chaplain in the Civil War. She submits her prize submission with a note that explains "that if the tale didn't get the prize, which the *writer* hardly dared expect, she would be very glad to receive any sum it might be considered worth" (*Little Women*, 293; emphasis added). In this formulation, prizes are associated with high literary accomplishment, while writers modestly hope to receive financial compensation commensurate with a "worth" determined by a publisher. In other words, they do not negotiate as professionals, but rather make a submission and hope for the best. When

Jo actually receives the prize, her physical gesture emphasizes this duality between high artistic accomplishment and financial gain. As she announces to her family that she has won the prize, she holds up a check for a hundred dollars in one hand and an "encouraging" letter from the publisher in the other. Her sisters wonder what she will do with the money, while her father advises her to "do better" and "Aim at the highest, and never mind the money" (293). As a compromise, Jo uses the money to send her mother and her sister Beth on an extended sea-side vacation, valuing the money on the grounds of its altruistic "investment" (294). Her writing is justified by her selflessness and her lack of alternative sources of support. These various conditions, as Lawrence Buell has claimed, made "literary commercialism . . . not only more prevalent among women writers than among men during the antebellum period but also more respectable as an overt intention" (*New England Literary Culture*, 414). Such commercialism was consistent with the amateur status of writers, who entered prize competitions or sent hopeful letters to editors rather than negotiating contracts and commissions with publishers.

Another second key representation of Jo as a writer comes later in *Little Women*, when her future husband, Mr. Bhaer, advises her "to study simple, true, and lovely characters, wherever she found them, as good training for a writer" (368). This advice associates women's writing with heightened powers of observation, and also establishes it as an art that can be developed through "good training" and evaluative discernment. Jo needs this advice because she has begun to learn that observation without such discernment can lead to a "premature acquaintance with the darker side of life," a darker side she has begun to see as she "studie[s] faces in the street" and "characters good, bad, and indifferent, all about her" in an effort to gather material for "thrilling tales" (367). In her letters and her fiction, Alcott frequently emphasizes the importance of writing from experience. *Hospital Sketches*, for example, opens with its main character, Tribulation Periwinkle, talking to her parents about how she needs something to do. When her father suggests that she "write a book," she replies that she does not "know enough" to do so, repeating the aphorism, "First live, then write." Importantly, Trib refers to her father as the "author of my being," immediately setting up a distinction between patriarchal production and the experience-based book that she could (and Alcott eventually does) write (*Hospital Sketches*, 9). In 1878, fifteen years after *Hospital Sketches* appeared, Alcott continued to emphasize the importance of her experience and observations as a justification for moving it into print, writing to an aspiring author that "when I wrote Hospital Sketches by the beds of my soldier boys in the shape of letters home I had no idea that I was taking the first step toward what is called fame" (*Selected Letters*, 232). Letters drawn from actual experiences became the basis for becoming a published writer. This description of private, domestic writing, frequently in the form of letters sent home and read aloud, as an origin of an authorial career is replicated in numerous fictional portrayals of women writers, as well as in the biographies of some of the best-known nineteenth-century women authors.[2] For example, Stowe's experiences presenting her work in progress to the Semi-Colon Club in Cincinnati were, as Joan Hedrick has shown, pivotal to her literary development and her conception of "parlor literature." In her journals, Alcott also points to this trajectory when she describes reading her first published story ("great rubbish") aloud to her family and proudly announcing it to be hers "when they praised it" (*Life, Letters, and Journals*, 45).

A third key characteristic of the woman writer is that of the avid "scribbler," the woman who has such a need to write that the words flow easily from the pen. When Jo March needs to enter into the "vortex" of her writing, she signals her departure by wearing a special "scribbling suit" (*Little Women*, 289). Writing in this sense is not a vocation but a physical desire and obsession. Such characteristics are particularly evident in what I have termed the *cacoethes scribendi* plot, which was replicated in numerous other stories, essays, and poems of the period.[3] The term "cacoethes scribendi" itself comes from a Roman satire by Juvenal that describes the mania of poets who "can't stop" as "the itch for writing grows / And fame secures them like a hangman's noose" (quoted in Sánchez, "'Prayers in the Market Place'," 101). The central conceit is that of excess, with the only constraint coming from self-immolation. As Oliver Wendell Holmes put it in a poem entitled "Cacoethes Scribendi," even when "all the pens and paper were used up . . . Still would the scribblers . . . Call for more pens, more paper, and more ink" (*Over the Teacups*, 93). Significantly, Holmes includes this poem in *Over the Teacups*, an account of conversations that were held at a table dominated by a family teapot that had been passed down to him – an account that therefore highlights the domestic origins of writing. One of the discussions centers on the urge to write. Although in general Holmes condemns such urges as producing too many submissions to editors such as himself, he praises the "generous instinct" of one woman who explains the value that private writing has for "a great many women . . . who write in verse from a natural instinct which leads them to that form of expression," trusting "their thoughts and feelings to verse which they never think of publishing" (86–7, 87). "Natural instinct" produces writing that is most valuable if it is kept private rather than being motivated by fame and a desire for publication.

Perhaps the most paradigmatic example of the *cacoethes scribendi* occurs in Catharine Maria Sedgwick's 1830 story of that name, first published in the *Atlantic Souvenir*. In that story, the itch overtakes a household of women after one of them, Mrs. Courland, reads a literary annual and is inspired to write similar pieces when she sees on its table of contents "some of the familiar friends of her childhood and youth" ("Cacoethes Scribendi," 53). In keeping with the domestic origins of many accounts of women's writing, Mrs. Courland sends off her first publication after initially reading it aloud to the assembled women in her family, including her daughter Alice, several sisters, and her mother. Having done so, Mrs. Courland works to convince her sisters that anything and everything in their experience is fair game for an essay or story; the itch comes both from a desire to share an observation or experience and to take pen to paper with "diligent fingers" (54). Importantly, only one generation in the household (Mrs. Courland and her sisters) succumbs to the itch; neither Mrs. Courland's mother nor her daughter, Alice, agrees to write. In Alice's case, the reluctance comes from a domestic modesty that fears exposure in print, and this modesty is repaid at the end by Alice's becoming engaged to the most eligible bachelor in town. Mrs. Courland's mother, on the other hand, has "a precious fund of anecdotes of the revolution and the French war" that she could share, but she refuses to do so because she writes "a dreadful poor hand" and "never learned to spell," as "no girls did in [her] time" (54).

Mrs. Courland taps this "precious fund of anecdotes" by making her mother a figure in three of her own tales, but her mother's comment is an important reminder of the general shift that Sedgwick's story represents: the grand-mother has lacked the training to feel confident about her ability to produce a legible and grammatically correct manuscript. In just three generations, Sedgwick points out, women's writing has gone from rudimentary letters written in a "dreadful poor hand" to a seemingly endless proliferation of manuscripts destined for print. Critics reading this story have tended to focus on Alice as a figure both of resistance and complicity; on the one hand, she resists entering a system of publication that, in Andrew Scheiber's terms, "substitutes commodity relations for other intimacies between reader and writer," while on the other she complies with domestic ideals that in the end lead her mother to relinquish her literary "calling" ("Mastery and Majesty," 49). Yet Alice's grandmother presents a similar dichotomy; she worries about being compliant with literary conventions of writing and spelling, but this very concern reminds us that for her, writing is itself a revolutionary act, a legacy of the political revolution that she has witnessed. Sedgwick implies

that if Mrs. Courland's mother has lived through a crucial political revolution, Mrs. Courland herself is leading another one in encouraging the
women in her family to write manuscripts and get them into print. Even
if these publications amount "to little more than polite cannibalization," as
María Carla Sánchez argues, the story does establish the relationship between
women and writing as "natural and idyllic" and "looks forward to the day
when women's literary vocations might be portrayed without parody or
satire" – a day that indeed came before the end of the nineteenth century, as
numerous representations of women writers attest ("'Prayers in the Market
Place'," 110, 111).

The political stakes of such writing have, in general, led to a critical focus
on its liberatory function. As we will see, current critical commonplaces surrounding authorship and genius associate those terms with a cultural and class
hierarchy that is exclusive rather than inclusive. Those surrounding women
writers, on the other hand, are more expansive. Reacting to blanket dismissals
of "scribbling women" in the nineteenth century, contemporary critics have
shown the considerable appeal of reclaiming the "scribblers" both as individuals and as a collective group. The "scribbling women" who produced the
first best sellers in the 1850s have been studied for their unique characteristics
and diversity of output, while the group as a whole has been celebrated for its
crucial place in the formation of nineteenth-century American culture. Rather
than understanding Nathaniel Hawthorne as dismissing women writers as a
"damned mob," for example, we have now come to understand the complex interactions between his art and that of certain members of the "mob"
and, furthermore, to understand his comment as coming out of frustration
that his publishers did not push his works as successfully as the publishers
of these women did.[4] At the same time, thinking of writing as encompassing a whole range of production, from unpublished letters and journals to
elegantly printed collected works, has opened up the field to allow more sustained study of women who were previously invisible in American literary
history. In this respect, contemporary critics focusing on women writers have
been motivated in part by a desire to expand the canon and historical context
in productive and multi-faceted ways.

Author

The critical move to recast "writer" and "scribbler" as empowering, inclusive
terms has sometimes obscured the degree to which many self-proclaimed
female "authors" in the nineteenth century worked to distinguish themselves

from the multitude of writers and to claim the title of "author" on their own terms. The comments of nineteenth-century male authors condemning the "mob" of scribbling women are legion and have, as indicated above, played a crucial role in motivating contemporary critics to reclaim the term. In doing so, however, critics have sometimes downplayed the efforts of some of these literary women to claim the cultural and disciplinary role of the author. In part, this is because the recovery of women writers has been accompanied by postmodern skepticism about the author function and the "death of the author." As Lisa Ede and Andrea Lunsford put it, "scholars now understand . . . that the notion of the author . . . is a peculiarly modern construct, one that can be traced back through multiple and overdetermined pathways to the development of modern capitalism and of intellectual property, to Western rationalism, and to patriarchy" ("Collaboration and Concepts of Authorship," 354). To the extent that authorship is associated with all of these qualities, it privileges what Ede and Lunsford call the "author-ity" of autonomous individuals, an authority that seems to go against feminist practices of collaboration even as it is embraced by women and minority writers who are only now claiming it (358).

Such efforts also reveal the fissures within the sisterhood of women writers, fissures that are often motivated by hierarchies of race and class. For example, Stowe scholars have struggled with the fact that when Harriet Jacobs approached Stowe to ask her assistance in producing a dictated narrative, Stowe replied that she would be interested in using the narrative in her own *Key to Uncle Tom's Cabin*. As Jean Fagan Yellin puts it, Jacobs was "devastated" and "felt Stowe had betrayed her as a woman" and "threatened her as a *writer*" (Jacobs, *Incidents*, ed. Yellin, xxvii–xxviii; emphasis added). Our own critical moment has, of course, made it possible to understand Jacobs's complexity and strength precisely as a writer. In a letter to Amy Post about the matter, Jacobs reiterated that "I wished it to be a history of my life entirely by its s[e]lf which would do more good and it needed no romance" (Belasco, *Stowe in her Own Time*, 100). She also reported that she herself wrote to Stowe twice but received no answer. This example underlines the ways in which Jacobs was attempting to exemplify the most pervasive values of the woman writer, focusing on her attempts, as an amateur, to get help in getting into print; to participate in the social network of letters; and to fulfill her desire to write her own experiences with "no romance." Jacobs concludes that Stowe "did not like my objection," but that "I cant help it" (Belasco, *Stowe in her Own Time*, 100). She needs to write her story and "cannot help" the terms under which she does so.

Stowe frames her work on *A Key to Uncle Tom's Cabin* primarily in terms of the need to prove that the novel was "more fact than fiction" and to "more than confirm every statement in it" (Belasco, *Stowe in her Own Time*, 68). Jacobs's narrative, in this view, is useful as part of what she calls the "immense body of facts" that will support the novel as realistic. This body of facts becomes a form of observation, or what she terms "examinations," although the "incredible" nature of their contents makes her "doubt the evidence of her own eyesight" (Belasco, *Stowe in her Own Time*, 68). If Jacobs wanted to tell her own story so that it would be founded in her real experience rather than in "romance," so too did Stowe want to provide enough experiential evidence that no one could discount the novel's abolitionist message.

This interaction casts a successful white author against a former slave who wants to have the rights to write her own story. As such, it indicates the tension in current criticism between recovering and recognizing writers, on the one hand, and understanding how some female authors distinguished themselves from amateur writers, on the other. In her own time, Stowe was often described as a writer with attributes similar to those I have discussed above. In *Daughters of Genius*, for example, James Parton emphasizes the fact that Stowe could write *Uncle Tom's Cabin* because she "was a quietly observant person on the banks of the Ohio" who "had been a writer from her childhood" (76, 74). Yet in her interactions with Jacobs, Stowe is not a writer but an author looking to justify and authorize her success by creating a companion volume to *Uncle Tom's Cabin* – a justification that has the unfortunate effect of silencing another aspiring writer. While referring to Stowe as a writer, Parton frames his sketch of her with the story of her payment of a hundred dollars to write the sketches that would become *Uncle Tom's Cabin* for the *National Era*. In this way, he emphasizes that she was paid for her work, and that, like Alcott, she was pursuing a literary career that would take her from childhood compositions to national and international acclaim.

Parton's sketch of Stowe points to three primary characteristics with which authors were associated in the nineteenth century: a proprietary mode of production; a personality anterior to the work of art; and an innate, original, and synthetic imagination. By emphasizing her ability to earn money from her writing, he focuses on the connection between literary labor and economic gain: a connection that would shape the emerging professionalism of female authors throughout the nineteenth century. Interestingly, in an 1867 essay on "International Copyright," Parton holds up Stowe as the poster woman of the mistreated author: "To say that Mrs. Stowe, through our cruel and shameful indifference with regard to the rights of authors, native and foreign, has been kept out of two hundred thousand dollars, honestly hers, is a most moderate and safe statement" (Belasco, *Stowe in her Own Time*, 173). Authorship involves literary and "honest" contractual rights that she has been precluded from receiving. In his *Daughters of Genius* sketch, Parton invokes the second attribute of authorship by focusing on Stowe's personality. As mentioned above, the sketch begins with the anecdote of her opening the envelope from the *National Era* and finding the "unexpected check for money in it" (73). In this way, he stresses her separation from the works that she produced; she is a celebrity in her own right. Finally, he highlights her powers of imagination and synthesis by describing her ability to make connections and see relations that link the part to the whole. Parton identifies this attribute in Stowe when he acknowledges that although she is first and foremost a good observer of the world around her, she also has the ability to absorb "a knowledge of the whole system of life in the Southern States" (76). Parton identifies this ability as innate, comparing her to Charles Dickens in possessing "the faculty of absorbing and reproducing human life" (75). Although many critics posited that women could potentially hold this innate ability, they also often found that many of them did not demonstrate it in their works. As one periodical essay on "Authoresses" concluded, "Humor and plot both depend on an author's true and just estimate of the relations borne by the various parts of his work to one another, and to the whole. And if this be so, we think it is not hard to understand why women stand in some danger of falling short as regards both" (350).

Nineteenth-century critics identified various circumstances that might explain why women often "fell short" in being able to possess this ability to see the world whole. Some recognized that their relative confinement to the domestic sphere decreased the range of experience from which they could draw. Others recognized that their strengths in observation and perception could sometimes lead to weakness in plot; they were more adept at description than action. Still others thought that their mandate to write moral tales could lead to too much sentimentality, which in turn obscured their ability to represent "true" characters and plots. In order to challenge such views, some female authors themselves assumed positions as literary gatekeepers. Specifically, authors such as Stowe and Alcott came to distinguish themselves from writers on three major grounds: their professionalism and business savvy; their discernment; and their flexibility in adapting to various audiences.

One of Stowe's clearest articulations of her role as an author appeared in a series of essays she wrote in January 1869 for *Hearth and Home*, the periodical that she edited.[5] In the essays, she urges "persons who have a natural talent for writing to cultivate themselves by sedulous and careful practice" and warns that writing is not an easy way to make a living ("How May I"). Quoting Balzac's observation that "to imagine is easy enough," and that "the real work consists in bringing out into language these airy conceptions," she stresses that "flexibility and versatility of style" require constant practice. She acknowledges that "certain gifts of expression, and certain graces and facilities of style, belong more naturally to women than to men," but she also says that such "nature" is actually the result of continued practice. She encourages women to write about commonplace objects and scenes but to do so with a practiced style and "thoughtful and careful study" ("How Shall I"). The problem with the mode of writing emblematized by Mrs. Courland is that it is not thoughtful or practiced, but rather rushed and slapdash. In this view, authorship is aligned with discipline and thought, not inspiration and spontaneity. Authors start as writers, and writers can become authors, but they cannot do so without effort and some expertise in "style."

Contemporary critics have identified the literary territorialism behind this practice of separating writers, especially those writing in private out of impulse or need, from authors who are emerging professionals. Jennifer Cognard-Black has posited that authorship, in this respect, operated under a "universal exceptionalism" that promised that it was broadly accessible – available to anyone who wished to be trained into it – while also being subject to "structural limitations on who qualified as an appropriate trainee" (*Narrative in the Professional Age*, 10). Judith Fetterley's influential early reading of "Cacoethes Scribendi" exemplifies the complexity of this universal exceptionalism. She argues that the story reflects Sedgwick's effort "to possess, define, and even police [her] own literary territory" (*Provisions*, 45). Interestingly, although Mrs. Courland feels a "call to become an author," her actual practice, as we have seen, is more aligned with the impulse to be a writer. This practice, Fetterley's reading suggests, highlights the distinction that Sedgwick makes between herself, as a published and successful author, and Mrs. Courland as a character. As in the case of Jacobs and Stowe, such territorial policing can complicate and even block the possibility of literary access. Even as female authors embraced the experiential power of observation, they also defined their own writing as being more controlled and disciplined in its use of it: a definition that sometimes excluded women who did not have their educational or class background.

As Charlotte Rich has pointed out, such definitions also frequently excluded multi-ethnic writers and others who did not have access to the disciplinary norms of middle-class white womanhood. In particular, Rich argues that progressive definitions of the "New Woman" were founded on an ethnocentrism that put a double burden on women "who wrote from positions of greater social marginality" (*Transcending the New Woman*, 32). For such women, writing became a form of social empowerment that could interrogate the racist assumptions of New Womanhood. For example, when Mourning Dove's Native American fictional protagonist Cogewea burns her copy of Therese Broderick's *Brand: A Tale of the Flathead Reservation* (1909) and considers writing her own account of the "threads in the woof of her people's philosophy," she is simultaneously condemning the romanticized racial stereotypes made by a white woman and asserting her right to "use the pen" even as she is considered a "'squaw'" (Rich, *Transcending the New Woman*, 59). Broderick was herself what one recent critic has called a "second-rate writer" who wrote about Montana after studying "her characters and her setting at first hand" (Beidler, "Literary Criticism in *Cogewea*," 63).[6] Neither Broderick nor Cogewea can become authors in the sense that Stowe or Alcott do, even as they all recognize the importance of drawing from observation and "first hand" experience.

When we return to the specific case of Louisa May Alcott, we see another sustained example of the difficulty of practicing "universal exceptionalism" as an author. On one hand, Alcott articulated the movement from writer to author as that of a journey; as we saw above, by the 1880s she could reminisce about a "literary lane" and her travels on it and emphasize to the "many young writers" who asked for her advice that there is "no *easy* road to successful authorship; it has to be earned by long & patient labor, many disappointments, uncertainties & trials" (*Selected Letters*, 232). On the other hand, Alcott's letters and journals frequently distinguish between writers and authors on the grounds of experience and effort, emphasizing points of differentiation rather than continuity. In particular, once she has become an "authoress," she describes "the ignorance and helplessness of women writers" with regard to business matters as "amazing." Furthermore, she notes that "only disastrous experience teaches [women writers] what they should have learned before. The brains that can earn money in this way can understand how to take care of it by a proper knowledge of contracts, copyrights, and the duties of publisher and author toward one another" (quoted in Parton, *Daughters of Genius*, 84–5).[7]

As we saw above, Jo March is described more as a writer than an author, although once she completes her first novel, she has to decide, as a "young authoress," whether to take her father's advice and let it continue to "ripen," or to heed her publisher's request that she cut it down by a third. She does cut it down, but with no sense of satisfaction: "in the hope of pleasing every one, she took every one's advice; and, like the old man and his donkey in the fable, suited nobody" (*Little Women*, 295). In *Jo's Boys*, Alcott refers to this novel as a "wreck" that "continued to float long" after its launch, "to the profit of the publisher at least" (46). *Jo's Boys* also depicts Jo's decision, out of financial necessity, to take up her pen again; she finds sudden and immense fame after a "certain publisher" asks her to write a "book for girls." She comes to define her celebrity as an author as her "last scrape," because the endless autograph seekers, sketch artists, interviewers, and other fans so interrupt her privacy and freedom even to write. Described as a "harassed author," she wishes for "a law to protect unfortunate authors," thinking it even more important than copyright protection (49). Jo does not equate authorship with literary quality; she describes herself as a "literary nursery-maid who provides moral pap for the young" who follows the "illustrious example" of Emerson and Whittier only in needing to decline to answer every piece of fan mail she receives (50). As such, she emphasizes the relationship between authorship and celebrity, and, correspondingly, the need for authors to claim certain rights ("laws") and privileges (putting fan mail in the waste basket). *Little Women* more subtly highlights the growing celebrity of authorship when it alludes to the fact that the March girls play the card game "Authors" with their British cousins (163). As we will see, it is particularly crucial that Jo suggests playing this "sensible game" following a discussion with Laurie in which she tells him that what she really wants most is "Genius." The card game testifies both to the growing cultural prestige of authors and to their status below geniuses.

Alcott's business negotiations with her various publishers document her efforts to assert her rights as an increasingly famous author. Consistent with the emphasis on realistic observation commonly ascribed to women writers, Alcott attributed the success of her works to their "use of real life and one's experience," as she wrote to Thomas Niles in 1886 (Stern, *Louisa May Alcott*, 236). At the same time, she understood the importance of productive partnerships with publishers. Although Jo in *Little Women* waits passively to discover whether she will win a prize story competition, Alcott was more assertive with her publishers. Her first extended partnership was with radical abolitionist James Redpath, who published *Hospital Sketches* as well as *The Rose Family: A Fairy Tale* and a collection of stories entitled *On Picket Duty and Other Tales*. Redpath valued the partnership above all for how it could contribute to his various political causes. He first wrote to her to ask for permission to reprint a poem she wrote about John Brown, along with her autograph, in a memorial volume called *Echoes of Harper's Ferry*. When he agreed to publish *Hospital Sketches*, he donated a portion of the profits to a charity supporting Civil War orphans. Although he hoped that Alcott also would commit part of her royalties to this cause, she objected, noting that she first had to care for her parents, seeming "ungenerous that [she] may be just" (Stern, *Louisa May Alcott*, 209). At the same time, she viewed this relationship as pivotal to her professional "journey." After correcting proofs for *Hospital Sketches*, for example, she wrote to Redpath that he was free to choose the binding, "'having consulted the authoress'" (Stern, *Louisa May Alcott*, 207). The fact that Alcott puts this phrase in quotation marks emphasizes her awareness that she is entering into the new role of "authoress," and also that this role carries with it certain professional conventions. As her partnership with Redpath evolved between 1862 and 1864, she became even more adamant about her rights, describing herself as "at liberty to dispose" of her manuscripts "to whom so ever will do them to suit me," and ultimately refusing to let him publish *Moods* after he insisted that the manuscript was too long and needed to be cut in half (Stern, *Louisa May Alcott*, 219).[8] Alcott later memorialized this decision in *Little Women*, when, as we have seen, Jo reluctantly decides to drastically cut her book manuscript at the request of her publisher Mr. Allen. Later, Alcott credited Redpath with helping her find her "style," even though the book "never made much money" (*Life, Letters, and Journals*, 105–6). Like Stowe, she recognized that the development of "style" is a key aspect of authorship, while also emphasizing the importance of its commercial transactions.

Alcott was commissioned to write *Little Women* by Thomas Niles, whom she later credited with "evolv[ing] the book from chaos & mak[ing] my fortune" (*Selected Letters*, 229). In her letters to him she identifies herself as a "fellow-worker" along with paid illustrators, copyright lawyers, and other authors (Stern, *Louisa May Alcott*, 231). She also bonds with him over the issue of celebrity and the demands of her fans. As we saw above, one overall attribute of authorship in the nineteenth century was the idea of there being a personality anterior to the work of art; readers' interest in authors' personalities and lives led to the kind of lionization that Jo March Bhaer faces in *Jo's Boys*. Writing to Niles about her decision to depict Jo's frustrations with this lionization, Alcott justifies her action with the observation that "in no other way can the rising generation of young autograph fiends be reached so well & pleasantly, & by a little good natured ridicule be taught not to harass the authors whom they honor with thier [*sic*] regard" (Stern, *Louisa May Alcott*, 236).

The need to produce such "good natured ridicule" is the result of shifting ideas of authorship in the later nineteenth century, from an emphasis on generalized domestic ideals of true womanhood to one on what we might term a cult of personality, an interest in authors' private and nonliterary lives as well as in their literary lives. This interest led readers to appreciate authors as commodities apart from their works, a shift seen not only in card games such as "Authors" but also in the increasingly large numbers of illustrations of authors in magazines and annuals, along with the photographs, engravings, and lithographs that were staples of the middle-class parlor. These material representations helped to distinguish authors from writers; if women writers composed letters and sketches in summer houses and sent in entries to writing contests, authors negotiated contracts and wrote to protégées whom they could not always encourage to continue to write. Such expertise and exclusivity, in turn, diminished the vision of literary access implicit in the "cacoethes scribendi" plot and other representations of scribbling women.

By establishing criteria for what constituted authorship, professional female authors – those who were paid for work that showed a particular level of expertise and talent – served as disciplinary gatekeepers. In this sense, their success was built on the failure of others to achieve what they had achieved, a position in the literary field that has not always been a comfortable one for feminist scholars to confront. The legal and territorial privilege associated with authorship is both inspiring – a point on the "literary lane" – and exclusionary, discounting the many efforts of writers whose work never made it into print or who were not properly compensated or recognized if they were. Yet authors undertook their role as disciplinary gatekeepers, I think, less to establish a "monopoly of literary legitimacy," as Pierre Bourdieu puts it, than to give a realistic sense of the distance to be traveled between experiential observation and aesthetic production (*The Field of Cultural Production*, 42). The representation of this distance, in turn, helped to consolidate authorship as a category that could be applied to women as well as to men.

The distance between writing and authorship also associates literary production with professional labor as well as with inherent ability. In the nineteenth century, critics looking to romanticize such native ability turned to another key term: "genius." On the one hand, authors like Alcott who examined the labor behind writing helped to demystify romantic ideals about genius; art does not just happen, but is constructed through effort and with the help of a complex literary market place. Although geniuses were even rarer than authors, they were also more natural. Authors received recognition in part through their savvy negotiation of the literary marketplace, while geniuses received recognition because of the sheer force of their native ability – an ability that, in its most romantic iteration, might lie completely unrecognized by the public. In this way, genius offered the highest literary position in terms of aesthetic value while at the same time being more akin to the position of writer or scribbler in its vision of egalitarian access.

Genius

As stated above, during the nineteenth century the core attributes of female genius were generally presented on a continuum with female writing and female authorship. In particular, the female genius was, like the writer and the author, associated with enhanced, and inborn, powers of observation and empathy and the power to document real life and real emotion. In 1886, for example, in an overview of popular conceptions of genius, Edmund C. Stedman identifies a "current belief that it is the privilege of genius to see the soul of things; not merely their externals, but to know, to feel, the secret meaning of all that makes up life." He calls this ability a "highest sense" that aids "observation, experience, [and] industry" ("Genius," 161). Given the widespread belief that women inherently had heightened powers of observation, critics frequently attributed this "highest sense" to literary women. A typical example of such an association is a review of Ann Stephens's *The Heiress of Greenhurst* (1857); the review cites the novel as another example of Stephens's "genius" because of the "faithfulness and force with which the characters are delineated" and "the exquisite descriptions of natural scenery" ("Review," 147). Earlier, critic William Alfred Jones had declared that the "real genius of the female mind" lies in women's ability to take note of their surroundings and assess their adherence to the "existing code of fashion" ("Female Novelists," 484). Such genius, according to another critic, is of a "better kind than that which produces the flashy blood-and-thunder romances," since "real literary value" comes from geniuses who apply their power to proper subjects ("American Female Authorship," 8). The female genius was also associated with innate qualities of a "warm and generous heart," "pure devotional spirit," and "deep, tender and womanly nature."[9]

This "heart" increased the genius's ability to empathize with others to a sometimes extreme degree; poet Louisa Chitwood was a genius, for example, because "she could almost hear the throbs of grief in the human hearts around her" ("M. Louisa Chitwood," 58).[10] This empathy, in turn, led other critics to argue that a woman of genius is "more" womanly than that one who is not, because she "understands, sympathizes with, appreciates a noble, manly soul" more than a "'simple-minded' maiden" can ("Intellectual Women"). Furthermore, such understanding required comparatively little effort; like the writer, the genius could produce work in fits of inspiration. "Ask any woman of genius why she writes, and she will tell you it is because she cannot help it," Ann Stephens wrote in 1839. "[T]here are times when a power which she can neither comprehend, nor resist, impels her to the sweet exercise of her intellect" ("Women of Genius," 48). Adah Isaacs Menken similarly emphasized genius as a mode of spontaneous intuition when she wrote, in 1868, that "Genius will find room for itself, or it is none"; as a power, "it cannot be suppressed any more than the earthquake can be smothered" ("Genius," 252). In this respect, accounts of female genius focus not on their labor or production – their work – but rather on their natural, spontaneous, and intuitive power. As Stedman put it, genius is "recognized, the world over, as a *gift*, something not quite attainable by labor" or calculated effort ("Genius," 148). Indeed, the opposite of genius in these formations is artifice. To write about something that is beyond the realm of observation, or to not be true to one's heart, requires a strategy of concealment or projection that is dangerous; as one critic put it, literary women who have "learnt the art of concealment ha[ve] lost one of the jewels of [their] sex" ("Our Female Poets, No. II: Mrs. Frances S. Osgood," 170).

In these formations, genius is represented as a higher order of writer. Writers and women of genius write because of an inner compulsion to do so; authors are emerging professionals who write in order to fulfill contracts and with an eye toward steady production. Some critics, such as Stedman, argued that the calculated effort of authors would enhance genius; its "inherent power can display its full capabilities only through industry, only by 'taking trouble'" ("Genius," 159). But in general there was a sense that the deliberate effort of authorship – what Stedman identifies as "mechanical work" – would diminish genius, particularly insofar as it was designed to increase notoriety (160).[11] As Stephens puts it, female geniuses "may gain notoriety, but that is a consequence of authorship, which must ever be painful to a woman of true genius, unless is added to it that public respect and private affection, which can never be secured by one who writes from a wish to shine, and from that wish alone" ("Women of Genius," 48–9).

Women who claimed themselves and were claimed by others as authors, such as Stowe and Alcott, did indeed often find notoriety painful. And they also struggled about whether to aspire to be viewed as geniuses. This struggle took two different forms. The first was living up to the fact that they had each written works that were seen, in accordance with the definitions above, as works of genius. The second was the extent to which the success and notoriety of these works would bar them from achieving a more traditionally masculine form of genius: one associated not only with heightened powers of observation but with individual autonomy and originality as well as with a prophetic imagination. Such masculine genius was coded as individual, misunderstood, isolated, and future-focused, the "only organ of communication with all that is beyond" that could in turn build artistic "bridge[s] . . . in the passage from period to period" (Brown, "Genius," 140; Hedge, "Characteristics of Genius," 151). It was spiritual and other-worldly, analogous to a butterfly, as one anonymous poem entitled "Genius" put it, who dies alone and unrecognized, but who "has known, and felt, and seen / A wider, larger hope, though lost / Far out at sea." Literary women who had achieved status as successful authors also realized that this very success precluded them from achieving certain romantic ideals.

Stowe's friends and reviewers frequently associated her with genius. In 1896, Elizabeth Stuart Phelps reminisced about Stowe and the "home of genius" that she had occupied in Andover, Massachusetts (Belasco, *Stowe in her Own Time*, 123). In doing so, she echoed critics who had identified Stowe as "unquestionably a woman of genius," having provided "ample proof of her genius in all her books," with *Uncle Tom's Cabin* in particular being "a work of genius, the offspring of an uncommon inspiration." At the same time, Stowe was criticized for any manifestations of that genius that were considered unwomanly: "her ablest works are pervaded by opinions from which a woman at least should hold herself aloof."[12] These public reactions required her to walk something of an artistic tightrope, living up to the success of her first book, on the one hand, without giving up the womanly attributes that had contributed to that success, on the other. In her *Hearth and Home* essays giving advice to writers, she addresses this issue in part by redefining genius as being compatible with the deliberate effort of authorship. The title of author should be reserved, she writes, for "those who have confessedly some natural gift – or what is called, for want of a better word, genius – for writing" and who then succeed because of practice and self-discipline that teach them particular techniques, such as not using unnecessary or "hifalutin" words ("How May I"). In this way, she hearkens back to a classic notion of "the real genius" as one "who shuns a hackneyed or a vulgar strain," as Juvenal puts it in his satire on the problems of *cacoethes scribendi* (quoted in Sánchez, "'Prayers in the Market Place'," 101). In particular, she identifies Nathaniel Hawthorne as an example of such an author, noting that his "industry in self-cultivation was equaled only by his genius." "[I]f Hawthorne had not had a natural genius for writing," she asks, "do you suppose keeping a journal and writing down minutely the particulars of every squirrel and walnut-shrub, and bird and leaf and flower and man and woman he saw, would have enabled him to compose the *Scarlet Letter*?" ("How Shall I"). By stressing the need both for an innate gift and for disciplined effort, such as keeping a journal, Stowe identifies a way to embrace genius as a necessary and positive characteristic of true artistry while at the same time challenging the romantic ideal of great artists expending little or no effort.

In her correspondence with her publishers and readers, Alcott was more explicit than Stowe in her desire to discount her status as a genius. She was willing to move down the "literary lane" that moved her from being a writer to being an author, but she was more ambivalent about the degree to which that lane could or should lead to her status as a genius. When she gave her mother a copy of *Flower Fables*, her first book, she called it "the first fruits of my genius," then scratched that out to say "little talent," and then copied it over to say "my first-born" (*Selected Letters*, 11, 12). In this formulation, talent is lesser than genius, but both become overly presumptuous, and Alcott settles instead on the biological metaphor of mothering. As her publishing career continued, she became increasingly consistent in explaining that this career was motivated by financial necessity rather than by innate genius. Hoping to get a story published in *The Atlantic Monthly* in 1861, for example, she wrote to Alfred Whitman that "money is the staff of life & without one falls flat no matter how much genius he may carry" (*Selected Letters*, 72). A few years later, once she began her partnership with James Redpath, she rejected altogether the idea of carrying genius. "I'll try not to be spoilt, & think ten or fifteen years of scribbling rather good training for an ambitious body," she wrote to him, "but people mustn't talk about genius – for I drove that idea away years ago & don't want it back again. The inspiration of necessity is all I've had, & it is a safer help than any other" (Stern, *Louisa May Alcott*, 213). She repeated this distinction between the inspiration of necessity and that of genius even after she had published *Little Women*. "I should very gladly write this sort of story altogether," she wrote to Mary E. Channing Higginson in 1868, "but, unfortunately, it does n't pay as well as rubbish, a mercenary consideration which has weight with persons who write not from the inspiration of genius but of necessity" (*Selected Letters*, 118). By 1878, she could write to another aspiring author, John Preston True, about an entirely different definition of genius. Like Stowe, she emphasized that any aspiring author must pay attention to "grammar, spelling, and punctuation" and "use short words" – must, in short, pay attention to the craft of writing. But she also emphasized that the work associated with this craft can take many years: "Work for twenty years, and then you may some day find that you have a style and place of your own, and can command good pay for the same things no one would take when you were unknown." Closing the letter, she wishes him "success," and gives him "for a motto Michael Angelo's wise words: 'Genius is infinite patience'" (*Selected Letters*, 231).[13] In this formulation, genius is related less to inspiration than to perspiration and effort, and having the patience to wait for the public to recognize it. By turning to a Renaissance figure, Alcott destabilizes the romantic notion of genius that emphasizes the "natural," almost effortless ability of geniuses to see art whole.

For Alcott, this romantic notion of genius was best exemplified by her Concord neighbor Ralph Waldo Emerson. Although she identified Concord as a place "popularly believed to be the hot-bed of genius," Emerson was its particular exemplar (*Selected Letters*, 127). Her father, Bronson, described Emerson as such in his book *Ralph Waldo Emerson: An Estimate of His Character and Genius*. In a verse tribute to Emerson, Bronson Alcott memorialized both the inborn qualities of his genius ("With native genius, with rich gifts endowed") and his nourishment of others through that genius ("the Age he nursed, his genius fed") (62). In her journals, Alcott reports the "great honor" she received when "Mr. Emerson invited me to his class when they meet to talk on Genius" (*Life, Letters, and Journals*, 85). Beginning in the late 1830s, Emerson had begun lecturing on the subject of genius, focusing on its "natural turn of mind," its spontaneity, and its representativeness. Importantly, he also focused on its "love" and gentleness, noting that "there is always somewhat feminine in the face of men of genius" ("Genius," 78). Despite this feminine aspect, however, Emerson's genius was coded primarily as confident, self-reliant, and masculine – qualities that a woman trying to provide for her family could not easily assume.

Even as Alcott struggled to live up to the example of genius exemplified by Emerson and, to a lesser extent, by her father, she explored other conceptions of genius in various works throughout her career. For example, in "The Freak of a Genius," published in 1866, she explores a "freak" or fraud in which a young, dashing "genius" poet named St. George is revealed to be the public front for the writings of an "ugly," introspective, middle-aged man named Kent (115). As stated above, nineteenth-century conceptions of genius were particularly suspicious of artifice, and this story highlights this point by showing the tragic consequences of posing as a genius when you are not, even as it highlights the pleasure involved in "observing the extraction of truth" (Stadler, *Troubling Minds*, 120). At the same time, the story provides an alternate definition of genius when Margaret, a painter who eventually becomes Kent's wife, notes that "a genius is one who, possessing a rich gift, regards it with reverence, uses it nobly and lets neither ambition, indolence nor neglect degrade or lessen the worth of the beautiful power given them for their own and others' good" ("The Freak of a Genius," 122). This definition encompasses the widespread conception of genius as an innate gift, but it also, like Stowe, stipulates that the gift's power is contingent on focused work and attention. It also defines the value of that power as lying in its ability to do good for others. At the end of *Work: A Story of Experience* (1873), as Victoria Olwell has recently shown, the heroine Christie exemplifies such genius when she reveals her gift for inspired, spontaneous political speech at a women's rights meeting in order to bridge the gap between the genteel reformers and the working women they are hoping to help. Olwell specifically notes that Christie disavows the speech as her own, a "lack of authorship [that] shows her disinterestedness" and desire to "galvanize women across class" ("'It Spoke Itself'," 47). In this way, "Christie's genius aspires toward a new political world in which particular bodies, desires, and experiences fuel rather than obstruct political subjectivity" (59).

If Christie in this scene shows a "lack of authorship," the very title of *Work* is itself "an emphatic reminder of the importance of 'doing,'" as Michelle Massé puts it, a "doing" that Alcott associates most with the discipline required for successful authorship. Massé points out that Christie is elsewhere described as being "moderately endowed with talents," an endowment that Alcott in *Little Women* repeatedly equates as being lesser than genius ("Songs to Aging Children," 333). Amy and Laurie, though possessing some talent in painting and music respectively, realize that "talent isn't genius, and no amount of energy can make it so" (*Little Women*, 418). Instead, they decide to support "ambitious girls" and "splendid fellows" who have "genius" (466), thereby providing a model of what Naomi Sofer terms "widespread private philanthropy" ("'Carry[ing] a Yankee Girl to Glory'," 42). Jo, too, although initially telling Laurie that what she really wants most is "Genius," ultimately does "not think herself a genius by any means" (*Little Women*, 163, 291). Although her family asks her if "genius burn[s]" when she is writing in her "vortex," she ultimately associates her writing, as we have seen, more with the work and effort of authorship (289).[14]

Scholars have frequently pointed out that Alcott did not give up on the ideals of genius as readily as does Jo; as Stadler puts it, "for Alcott, genius was a persistent if ungraspable preoccupation" (*Troubling Minds*, 106). After 1870 she continued to return to and revise her adult novels, struggling with *Work* for over a decade before publishing it in 1872 and completely rewriting the ending of *Moods*, first published in 1864, in 1882. In the last years of her life she also explored this theme in the unfinished novel *Diana and Persis* and in an idea for a manuscript entitled "Genius." Christine Doyle reads this as a dual anxiety both that *Little Women* was itself a "freak of genius" – the high point of her artistry – and also a concern with her public status as an author: "she may have been anxious lest the world that lionized her as a professional writer might not be so kind if she claimed to be an artist; it might say of her that her talent was not genius" (*Louisa May Alcott and Charlotte Brontë*, 21). Michelle Massé, on the other hand, argues that our critical desire to unpack such anxieties, both in Jo and in Alcott, is rooted in "our own ideas about authorship." Instead, Massé urges that we concede "that one can be a 'good-enough' author in the same way that one can be a 'good-enough' mother," and that "our wish to see Jo as a mute inglorious Milton . . . isn't true to the ambitions Jo herself articulates, or to her view of writing as a profession." If male genius can narcissistically "reside in the realm of possibility, basking in a potential that need never be made actual," authorship represents "compromise formations" that are more allied with doing, actuality, and interpersonal relationships ("Songs to Aging Children," 325).

Massé's call for current readers of Alcott to understand her authorship in positive terms is in direct response to earlier critics' focus on genius as both an ideal and a structural impossibility for women. As we saw at the beginning of this essay, critics like Elaine Showalter, following the important influence of Sandra Gilbert and Susan Gubar, have seen Alcott as struggling with her inability to live up to the example of Transcendental genius articulated by Emerson and by her father and therefore concealing the deeper meaning of her work from herself. As Keren Fite has recently put it, these arguments assume a "'palimpsestic' strategy" in which "unconscious rage is perceived as more subversive and authentic than conscious domesticity" ("Wrestling with the Angel in the House," 77). This rage, in turn, is directed at the patriarchal authority that has usurped female creativity to form what Christine Battersby terms "male motherhood" (*Gender and Genius*, 73). In eighteenth-century theories of genius, Battersby claims, "whatever faculty is highly prized is the one that women are seen to lack" (78).

As we saw above, nineteenth-century critics did imagine that women could be geniuses, associating the female genius with innate gifts of observation and "heart." And although an author like Alcott wanted to remind the readers that labor and effort were as important to successful literary production as were these innate gifts, she also gave multiple examples in her work of the ways in which genius could be associated not with narcissism and autonomy but with community building and "others' good," as Margaret puts it in "The Freak of a

Genius." Critics like Stadler and Olwell, in turn, are exploring the cultural and political work that such genius could provide, establishing the ways in which the eccentricities of genius could trouble established categories of class, race, and nation. Rather than focusing on lack and anger as the founding conditions of women's genius, then, current critics are examining the multiple ways in which the category of "genius" could create a counter public sphere. Genius has long been associated with prophecy or what Emerson calls the "seer," but current critics are showing how this prophecy operated not just in the aesthetic, moral, or philosophical realm but in the political and ideological one.[15]

Postmodernism has helped us understand the contingency of any literary identity, be it writer, author, or genius, and none of these terms is completely fixed or exclusive in any specific example. Indeed, in the climactic scene of "The Freak of a Genius" – the moment when Margaret identifies Kent as the true "genius" – she uses all three terms that I have been discussing in this essay. First, she reveals that she thought that Kent looked "more like the writer of that strong book" than did St. George. Then, she admits to applying "sundry little tests" that "convinced me that you were the author," including studying his "modes of expression." And finally, she describes a "fancy" that would not go away that St. George had "talent, but no genius." She concludes that "you may hide your true self from all the world, but not from me" (185). The fact that her narrative moves from describing the "writer" to the "author" to the "genius" suggests again that these three modes of production are on a continuum, or "literary lane," in which genius is the most aesthetically privileged but also most exclusive term. Yet Margaret also distinguishes these terms, casting all three as being separable from the personality, or "true self," behind them, and also revealing all three to be defined primarily in the eye of the beholder, or reader.

As stated above, Margaret herself is in some ways cast as the true "genius" in this novella, not only because she is a perceptive reader who can identify the genius in others but also because she uses her own "beautiful power," of painting and of perception, for her "own and others' good" ("The Freak of a Genius," 122). As such, she points to one way in which discussions of authorship and genius can be reframed so that they focus on the point of reception or consumption as well as that of production. Although the characteristics associated with these various terms emerge with documentable consistency throughout the nineteenth century, it is important to remember that they were not essential identities but rather fluid roles put forward in various cultural contexts. In this respect, the next step in understanding these terms may be to undertake more nuanced studies of the way in which readers responded to or consumed the various productions of writers, authors, and geniuses, self-styled or otherwise.

At the same time, this overview of the key terms associated with literary women also suggests three insights for scholars continuing to study modes of production. First, we need to acknowledge and be mindful of the historical precedents for our current uses of these three terms. If "author" is now less common in our critical and popular lexicon than "writer," we need to remember that, as the card game suggests, "author" was more common in the nineteenth century, and that the women who called themselves by that term were claiming an important cultural and professional position. Similarly, if we assume that "genius" was and is only associated with inborn, often misunderstood, prophetic giftedness, we need to remember that women in the nineteenth century were often called "geniuses" because of their heightened observation and empathy – some of the very same qualities associated with "scribbling" writers. Such historical understanding is crucial to understanding the ways in which women contributed to the literary culture of the nineteenth century.

Some of our current critical values surrounding these terms are shaped by what Elaine Showalter has termed "the twentieth-century feminist ending of separation and autonomy" (quoted in Massé, "Songs to Aging Children," 324). Authors are, as Alcott well understood, not autonomous, but rather are heavily invested in a network of publishers, lawyers, illustrators, and other literary "fellow-workers," including those who help produce promotional campaigns. Writers and geniuses, as more "natural" producers, fit well into this feminist ending to the extent that they remain autonomous; they fit less well if, like Jo March, they decide to forego autonomy in order to establish social roles such as wife and mother. Yet the first decade of the twenty-first century has witnessed some bold and exciting efforts to destabilize this particular ending in order to show the cultural and psychic power associated with collaboration and community. If genius can encompass not only romantic isolation but also productive social bonds, such as those formed by Christie in the lecture hall in *Work* or Margaret in her "reading" of Kent, then it, like authorship, can provide a means of writing a new feminist ending.

Lest such an ending seem overly utopian, we must also recognize, finally, that such an ending is contingent on a certain amount of class and race privilege. As we saw above, Harriet Jacobs and Mourning Dove's Cogewea could never aspire to authorship in the same way that Louisa May Alcott did, and if gender in some ways constrained her own view of her "literary path," her privilege as an educated white woman in Concord also facilitated her travels down it. Indeed, one of the appeals of the current critical interest in genius is that it can transcend these social constraints, uncovering the cultural history, as Stadler puts it, of a discourse that crosses "a variety of social categories in unexpected, unpredictable ways" (*Troubling Minds*, xvii). Seen this way, genius provides the same literary access accorded to "writers," although the historical use of the terms that I have been tracing points to the importance of continuing to account for the privileged aesthetic value that genius was assigned. Such explorations promise to help scholars continue to understand these various modes of literary production and their significance both to American literary history and to our ongoing critical conversations.

Notes

1. This book is a reprint of Parton's *Eminent Women* (1880); the difference in title points to the pliability of literary terms at the end of the nineteenth century, and to terms describing exceptional women in particular.

2. For more about these domestic origins, see Williams, *Reclaiming Authorship*, especially ch. 2.

3. For an extended discussion of this topic, see Williams, *Reclaiming Authorship*, 21–4.

4. See in particular Baym, "Again and Again, the Scribbling Women."

5. For an extended study of these essays, see Robbins, "Gendering Gilded Age."

6. Beidler quotes *The New York Times Book Review* of January 29, 1910 as his source for the fact that she drew from first-hand observation.

7. Parton cites his source as a letter to the *Saturday Evening Gazette*, but I have not been able to locate the original. Stern does not list it in her comprehensive account of Alcott's writings for the *Gazette* (*Louisa May Alcott*, 59). The same material is reprinted in "The Alcotts."

8. On Redpath and *Moods*, see *Life, Letters, and Journals*, 108–9.

9. See, for example, "Our Female Poets, No. II: Amelia B. Welby," 160; "Female Authors," 29; and Eanes, "Tribute to the Dead."

10. The article notes that Chitwood's genius is particularly notable because she is from the "pioneer State" of Indiana, "where the association with gifted minds could not possibly have influenced her own" ("M. Louisa Chitwood," 58). In this way, the article underscores the status of genius as an innate or natural "gift" while also chiding eastern readers for loving "to think that the West possesses no genius."

11. Stedman identifies Trollope as a particularly glaring example of such a mechanical worker, whose productions "when set against the work of true genius reenforced by purpose, physical strength, and opportunity, as exhibited by Thackeray or Hugo or Dickens, [render] comparison . . . simply out of thought" ("Genius," 160).

12. J. C. Derby, "Stowe and the Success of *Uncle Tom's Cabin*," in Belasco, *Stowe in her Own Time*, 80; "American Female Authorship," 9; Steele, "Living Celebrities of New England," 539.

13. Alcott also gives this Michelangelo quote in *Little Women*, noting that "If 'genius is eternal patience,' as Michel Angelo affirms, Amy certainly had some claim to the divine attribute, for she persevered in spite of all obstacles, failures, and discouragements, firmly believing that in time she should do something worthy to be called 'high art'" (281).

14. Stadler reads this "burning" as related to an erotics of shame and arousal that represents the ways in which both culture and genius can "victimize people in a manner alternately pleasurable and shaming, alternately self-affirming and self-negating" (*Troubling Minds*, 110).

15. See also Elfenbein, who shows how the character of genius provided "the best available metaphor for the supposed character of the homosexual" (*Romantic Genius*, 34).

Works cited

Alcott, A. Bronson. *Ralph Waldo Emerson, Philosopher and Seer: An Estimate of His Character and Genius in Prose and Verse.* Boston: Cupples and Hurd, 1888.

Alcott, Louisa May. *Alternative Alcott.* Ed. Elaine Showalter. New Brunswick: Rutgers University Press, 1988.

"The Freak of a Genius." In *Freaks of Genius: Unknown Thrillers of Louisa May Alcott.* Ed. Daniel Shealy. New York: Greenwood Press, 1991.

Hospital Sketches. Boston: James Redpath, 1863.

Jo's Boys and How They Turned Out: A Sequel to "Little Men." Boston: Roberts Brothers, 1891.

Life, Letters, and Journals. Ed. Ednah D. Cheney. New York: Gramercy Books, 1995.

Little Women. Ed. Anne Hiebert Alton. Peterborough, ON: Broadview Press, 2001.

The Selected Letters of Louisa May Alcott. Ed. Joel Myerson and Daniel Shealy. Boston: Little Brown, 1987.

"The Alcotts." *The Critic* (March 17, 1888): 129.

"American Female Authorship." *The Round Table* 4 (August 4, 1866): 8–9.

"Authoresses." *Arthur's Home Magazine* 27 (May 1866): 350.

Battersby, Christine. *Gender and Genius: Towards a Feminist Aesthetics.* Bloomington: Indiana University Press, 1989.

Baym, Nina. "Again and Again, the Scribbling Women." In *Hawthorne and Women: Engendering and Expanding the Hawthorne Tradition.* Ed. John L. Idol and Melissa M. Ponder. Amherst: University of Massachusetts Press, 1999.

Beidler, Peter G. "Literary Criticism in *Cogewea*: Mourning Dove's Protagonist Reads The Brand." *American Indian Culture and Research Journal* 19.2 (1995): 45–65.

Belasco, Susan, ed. *Stowe in her Own Time: A Biographical Chronicle of her Life, Drawn from Recollections, Interviews, and Memoirs of Family, Friends, and Associates.* Iowa City: University of Iowa Press, 2009.

Bourdieu, Pierre. *The Field of Cultural Production: Essays on Art and Literature.* Ed. Randal Johnson. New York: Columbia University Press, 1993.

Boyd, Anne E., ed. *Wielding the Pen: Writings on Authorship by American Women of the Nineteenth Century.* Baltimore: The Johns Hopkins University Press, 2009.

Brown, J. Brownlee. "Genius." *Atlantic Monthly* 13 (February 1864): 137–56.

Buell, Lawrence. *New England Literary Culture from Revolution through Renaissance.* Cambridge: Cambridge University Press, 1986.

Cognard-Black, Jennifer. *Narrative in the Professional Age: Transatlantic Readings of Harriet Beecher Stowe, George Eliot, and Elizabeth Stuart Phelps.* New York: Routledge, 2004.

Doyle, Christine. *Louisa May Alcott and Charlotte Brontë: Transatlantic Translations.* Knoxville: University of Tennessee Press, 2000.

Eanes, Elizabeth J. "Tribute to the Dead." *The New-Yorker* 11 (August 28, 1841): 370.

Ede, Lisa and Andrea A. Lunsford. "Collaboration and Concepts of Authorship." *PMLA* 116.2 (2001): 354–69.

Elfenbein, Andrew. *Romantic Genius: The Prehistory of a Homosexual Role.* New York: Columbia University Press, 1999.

Emerson, Ralph Waldo. "Genius." In *The Selected Lectures of Ralph Waldo Emerson.* Ed. Ronald A. Bosco and Joel Myerson. Athens, GA: University of Georgia Press, 2005.

"Female Authors." *Literary Messenger* 2 (September 1841): 29–30.

Fetterley, Judith, ed. *Provisions: A Reader from 19th-Century American Women.* Bloomington: Indiana University Press, 1985.

Fite, Keren. "Wrestling with the Angel in the House, Slaying the Monster in the Attic: The Artist Heroines in Louisa May Alcott's 'Psyche's Art' and *Little Women.*" In *Auto-poetica: Representations of the Creative Process in Nineteenth-Century British and American Fiction.* Ed. Darby Lewes. Lanham, MD: Lexington Books, 2006.

"Genius." *Continental Monthly* 6 (December 1864): 705.

Hedge, F. H. "Characteristics of Genius." *Atlantic Monthly* 21 (February 1868): 150–9.

Hedrick, Joan D. *Harriet Beecher Stowe: A Life.* New York: Oxford University Press, 1994.

Holmes, Oliver Wendell. *Over the Teacups.* Boston: Houghton, Mifflin, 1890.

"Intellectual Women; 'Commonplace Women'." *Saturday Evening Post* (January 2, 1864): 6.

Jacobs, Harriet. *Incidents in the Life of a Slave Girl.* Enlarged edn. Ed. Jean Fagan Yellin. Cambridge, MA: Harvard University Press, 2009.

Jones, William Alfred. "Female Novelists." *United States Magazine and Democratic Review* 14 (May 1844): 484–9.

"M. Louisa Chitwood: The Two Poems Bow to None but God." *The Ladies' Repository* 32 (January 1, 1872): 58–9.

Massé, Michelle A. "Songs to Aging Children: Louisa May Alcott's March Trilogy." In *Little Women and the Feminist Imagination: Criticism, Controversy, Personal Essays.* Ed. Janice M. Alberghene and Beverly Lyon Clark. New York: Garland, 1999.

Menken, Adah Isaacs. "Genius." In Boyd, *Wielding the Pen.*

Olwell, Victoria. "'It Spoke Itself': Women's Genius and Eccentric Politics." *American Literature* 77 (March 2005): 33–63.

"Our Female Poets, No. II: Amelia B. Welby." *Ladies National Magazine* 5 (May 1844): 160–2.

"Our Female Poets, No. II: Mrs. Frances S. Osgood." *Ladies National Magazine* 4 (November 1843): 170–2.

Parton, James. *Daughters of Genius.* Philadelphia: Hubbard Brothers, 1885.

"Review of New Books." *Peterson's Magazine* 32 (August 1857): 147–9.

Rich, Charlotte J. *Transcending the New Woman: Multiethnic Narratives in the Progressive Era.* Columbia: University of Missouri Press, 2009.

Robbins, Sarah. "Gendering Gilded Age Periodical Professionalism: Reading Harriet Beecher Stowe's *Hearth and Home* Prescriptions for Women's Writing." In *"The Only Efficient Instrument": American Women Writers and the Periodical, 1837–1916.* Ed. Aleta Feinsod Cane and Susan Alves. Iowa City: University of Iowa Press, 2001.

Sánchez, María Carla. "'Prayers in the Market Place': Women and Low Culture in Catharine Sedgwick's 'Cacoethes Scribendi'." *ATQ: American Transcendental Quarterly* 16 (June 2002): 101–13.

Scheiber, Andrew. "Mastery and Majesty: Subject, Object, and the Power of Authorship in Catharine Sedgwick's 'Cacoethes Scribendi'." *ATQ: American Transcendental Quarterly* 10 (March 1996): 41–58.

Sedgwick, Catharine Maria. "Cacoethes Scribendi." In Fetterley, *Provisions.*

Sofer, Naomi Z. "'Carry[ing] a Yankee Girl to Glory': Redefining Female Authorship in the Postbellum United States." *American Literature* 75 (March 2003): 31–60.

Stadler, Gustavus. *Troubling Minds: The Cultural Politics of Genius in the United States, 1840–1890.* Minneapolis: University of Minnesota Press, 2006.

Stedman, Edmund C. "Genius." *New Princeton Review* 5 (September 1886): 145–67.

Steele, Rev. G. N. "Living Celebrities of New England." *The Ladies' Repository* 24 (September 1864): 534–9.

Stephens, Ann S. "Women of Genius." In Boyd, *Wielding the Pen.*

Stern, Madeleine B. *Louisa May Alcott: From Blood and Thunder to Hearth and Home.* Boston: Northeastern University Press, 1998.

Stowe, Harriet Beecher. "How May I Know That I Can Make a Writer?" *Hearth and Home* 1 (January 30, 1869): 88.

"How Shall I Learn to Write?" *Hearth and Home* 1 (January 16, 1869): 49.

Williams, Susan S. *Reclaiming Authorship: Literary Women in America, 1850–1900.* Philadelphia: University of Pennsylvania Press, 2006.

11

Nineteenth-century American women's poetry

Past and prospects

ELIZABETH RENKER

The field of nineteenth-century poetry in the USA – and of women's poetry in particular – is now one of the most lively, active, and exciting areas of Americanist scholarship. A pressing need to clear out the ideological residue of twentieth-century literary criticism, which typically derided nineteenth-century women's poetry as trite, sentimental pablum, has driven innovation on many fronts. The first wave of scholarly attention to nineteenth-century US women poets grew from the related phenomena of feminist studies and the canon wars. Emily Stipes Watts (*The Poetry of American Women from 1632 to 1945* [1977]); Erlene Stetson (*Black Sister: Poetry by Black American Women, 1746–1980* [1981]); Cheryl Walker (*The Nightingale's Burden: Women Poets and American Culture Before 1900* [1982]); and Alicia Ostriker (*Stealing the Language: The Emergence of Women's Poetry in America* [1986]) all called powerful attention to the extensive and (at that time) entirely neglected body of work by women poets. Scholars today still build on the ground these pioneering scholars cleared, but are simultaneously recasting the field's fundamental terms of inquiry. In the pages that follow, I offer a brief overview of the emergence and development of nineteenth-century American women's poetry studies; I then turn to addressing the problems at the core of the field at the present time.

Separate spheres I: gender history

When, in 1915, Harvard poet and professor George Santayana lambasted the nineteenth century for what he called its "genteel tradition" as, among other things, "grandmotherly," conventional literature ("Genteel American Poetry," 73), he inaugurated an intellectual tradition that equated putatively female writing with bad art. The modernist poets would also influentially inveigh against their predecessors as "feminine."[1] And twentieth-century scholars, who were themselves historical products of modernism, repeated, as if by formula, the triumphant story in which modernism resuscitated what Pound called "the dead art / Of poetry" from the death clasp of the feminized nineteenth century ("Hugh Selwyn Mauberly," lines 2–3). This narrative became a standard feature of twentieth-century scholarship and its institutions of canon-formation. Paul Lauter shows that American literary studies, which began to consolidate as a field in the 1920s, developed a masculinist program to reclaim its literature from a degraded wussy fate. In this institutional setting, the perceived femininity of nineteenth-century American poetry was its doom. Emily Dickinson, the only female poet to escape the blanket condemnation, was construed to be far enough isolated from her own culture – and thus fully insulated from, and opposed to, the "grandmotherly" sentiment of the popular sphere – to have remained unsullied by the girly stain.[2] The few nineteenth-century poets whom scholars took seriously as aesthetic exceptions to the mass of lamentable poetic garbage were often hailed as "proto-modernists" or "precursors to modernism" who anticipated the great things to come. (The standard exceptions were Dickinson and Walt Whitman; sometimes additional poets such as Edwin Arlington Robinson and Stephen Crane received similar "proto-modernist" approval.) Twentieth-century accounts of nineteenth-century poetry explicitly or implicitly portrayed it as a culture of hacks and their benighted readers who frittered away their time while waiting for modernism to start.

Roy Harvey Pearce's influential 1961 study *The Continuity of American Poetry* refers only once to Lydia Sigourney, one of the most prolific and popular poets of the century. He reports that she and "her kind" wrote "below" the level of the Fireside Poets. "Lacking the intelligence to assume their proper responsibilities," Sigourney *et al.* "catered to and exploited the general (or generalized) reader" (197), Pearce explains. Aside from the (now) extremely obvious point that no critic who wants to work in this town ever again would compose such a sentence today, Pearce makes an array of analytical errors: he fails to engage, in any specific terms, the poets or poetry he condemns; he assumes that one popular female poet's name can stand in for the entire undifferentiated mass of scribblers (here ideologically invoking Hawthorne's famous remark about the mob of women writers, beloved *bon mot* endlessly repeated by anti-sentimental critics); and he simply assumes the value of elite poetry while devaluing the sphere of the popular. While the weakness of these assumptions is, from our own historical vantage, glaring, for Pearce, in 1961, these were simply standard elements of the field's master narrative. There was nothing at all unusual about his assumptions or his methods.[3]

Yet everything about how the field defined its terms was soon to be turned upside down. Critical tools honed during the rise of poststructuralism, social history, women's studies, and feminist theory from the late 1960s through the canon wars of the 1980s and '90s opened the institutional ideology about women's writing to rigorous analysis on a number of simultaneous fronts. Longstanding assumptions about history, conventionality, gender, and "greatness," like those we see in Pearce's account, began to crumble. Feminist historians in the 1960s and '70s, fighting to carve out intellectual and institutional space for women's history, proposed the influential paradigm of "separate spheres" to talk about woman's neglected place in accounts of nineteenth-century America. Working from the premise that men and women occupied distinct social and experiential realms, scholars like Carroll Smith-Rosenberg, Nancy Cott, Barbara Welter, and Mary Kelley explored a female world of private affiliations centered in the home and affections, in contrast to a male world of public activity centered in business, politics, and rationality. Separate spheres scholarship recovered a forgotten or otherwise denigrated women's world, arguing not only for its importance to an accurate American history, but for its cultural power in its own time – even if that power placed woman in the sphere of the home (Davidson and Hatcher, "Introduction," 11–12). In literary studies, the project of "recovering" vast numbers of female writers and redeeming ostensibly feminine spheres like the long-derided "sentimental" and the "domestic" opened a wealth of forgotten and neglected materials for critical analysis. Fired by concepts like Jane Tompkins's influential argument that a text performs "cultural work" in its own time, these new historicist approaches challenged modern readers to train themselves to perceive what might lie beyond the immediate scope of their own frequently modernist (and postmodern) aesthetic lenses.

As scholarship about women's social and literary history acquired greater institutional credibility, scholars found more readily available academic space, in the forms of course offerings; support from departments, programs, and professional organizations; and venues of publication. In short, a "field" was born. As is the case with all new fields of knowledge, the initial controversial volley to claim status was followed by gradual acceptance and support for increasingly sub-specialized research. The category of "women's writing" that had been so new and incendiary now had room to expand, deepen, and diversify. Scholars increasingly explored additional material factors of difference, such as race, class, occupation, access to literacy, region, and conditions of authorship, rendering the binary separate spheres model of men versus women – as tactically necessary as it had once been – more and more simplistic (Davidson and Hatcher, "Introduction," 11–12). Increasingly thorough interrogation of the history of gender further complicated binary sex-based models, leading to more careful distinctions between actual women as historical agents and cultural processes of feminization. Scholars began to explain, for example, the fact that men wrote a great deal of the era's allegedly "feminine" literature. As Cathy N. Davidson and Jessamyn Hatcher point out, today the field has reached a point where the model of sex-based separate spheres has "outlasted its usefulness" ("Introduction," 23) and given rise to new, and more nuanced, analyses of gender history.

Separate spheres II: genre history

Nevertheless, another "separate sphere" persists. The ideology that drives it remains mostly invisible. Remember that my institutional tale is not only about the history of attitudes toward "women's" or "feminine" writing. Indeed, my essay is not about women writers more generally, but about women poets in particular. Establishing women's writing as a scholarly field has, without question, been one of the major flashpoints, indeed major successes, of late twentieth-century scholarship, defining "success" in this case as a revolutionary advance in the state of knowledge. But poetry? What about poetry? As Joseph Harrington trenchantly argued in his 1996 essay, "Why American Poetry Is Not American Literature," American poetry has been mostly left out of literary histories of the United States, treated as if it occupies a separate sphere from prose fiction. Yet *this* problem of separate spheres is one to which the field in many ways remains blind, and it is one of the primary reasons that canon-busting studies, which opened the new field of writing by nineteenth-century American women and produced an avalanche of scholarship, have nevertheless left so much work still to be done in the arena of poetry in particular. "The identification of American *fiction* as American *literature* has persisted," Harrington argues (496). When in 2003 Sacvan Bercovitch reflected on his tenure as general editor of the new *Cambridge History of American Literature*, he singled out poetry as one of the two "most problematic areas"; poetry represents the "literary extreme" in current critical practice, he explained, and thus represents a categorically different set of problems for the integration of "formalist lines of continuity and change within a context appropriate to broad historical developments."[4] Here, once again, is poetry's separate sphere, predicated on a set of assumptions about "formalist lines of continuity and change" that somehow distinguish it, in a "problematic" way, within the larger project of writing American literary history. Harrington's polemic opposes conceptions of poetry's separate sphere, calling for a "new cultural criticism of US poetry" that would both trace the social history of the genre and delineate the ideology that undergirded the construction of "American poetry" by the professional field of American literature.

Scholars have at last begun to compile the elements of this new history. Mary Loeffelholz points out, for example, that poetry's "generic particularity" need not place it in a world apart from history, but is itself part of a fuller history of the cultural field (*From School*, 3). Paula Bernat Bennett, Michael Cohen, Virginia Jackson, Loeffelholz, Meredith McGill, Eliza Richards, Joan Shelley Rubin, Angela Sorby, and others have shown that poetry, including women's poetry, suffused American public and private cultures of the nineteenth century. While exhibiting tremendous and productive variation in method and focus, including book history, transatlantic studies, gender studies, social history, periodical studies, cultural criticism, genre sociology, and reception studies in particular, the new wave of poetry scholarship is animated generally by three common assumptions.

First, we need to account for a truly vast archive that has been neglected.[5] Second, accounting for this archive will necessitate writing a new history of American poetry, including poetry by women. Bennett's historicist study, for example, carefully tied to extensive and precise evidence about women poets "from every caste and class, region and religion," challenges "key scholarly assumptions about nineteenth-century US women and the poetry they wrote" (*Poets in the Public Sphere*, 3, 5). Loeffelholz situates women's poetry within a dense cultural field including the changing contours of women's relation to literacy and its variable social configurations "from school to salon." These are new and generative models for thinking about long-neglected material. Third, the new poetics will also require a new theory of poetry. It is important to note, with a nod to the historicity of the phenomenon of literary evaluation, that Pearce did not share even one of these assumptions in 1961. Of course, the current assumptions I here describe will also change or vanish as the field evolves.

In the pages ahead, I will address some of the core challenges facing nineteenth-century American women's poetry studies, taking my framework from the key terms of the field itself, each of which faces significant empirical and theoretical problems of definition.[6] These problems of definition, I will argue, are simultaneously the field's greatest opportunities for writing a fresh and bracing new cultural history of the genre for the twenty-first century.

Problem no. 1: Rethinking the category of "nineteenth-century" American women's poetry

One of the foundational narrative frames shaping the field of literary studies is that of the "period" itself, a concept now under pressure for its empirical and ontological flaws. As Jackson puts it, literary criticism at the present time faces a "double bind," because our academic focus on historicizing our materials coexists with a poststructuralist suspicion toward master narratives about periodicity ("Introduction: On Periodization and its Discontents," para. 3). Indeed, our age of scholarship has developed a more intense and thorough focus than ever before on the institutions of our own profession and on their ideological ideas of order. The very concept of "the period" (as any graduate student with an eye toward the job market is aware) is one of English studies' primary ways of cordoning literature into delimited conceptual units of time and nation, since "periods" in "English studies" typically distinguish not only among centuries but between "English" and "American" literature.

This nation-based institutional divide gets messier and less accurate year by year, as English studies moves increasingly to focus on such areas as Anglophone literatures, transatlanticism, and global studies. (See problem no. 2.) Gerald Graff argues that "periods erase history" because they primarily serve the quasi-bureaucratic entities of field coverage within departments of English: "I'm not the first to notice that academic departments operate on a kind of unspoken laissez-faire treaty according to which we politely agree to leave each other alone – that is, I won't mess with your century if you don't mess with mine" ("How Periods Erase History," para. 104). Caroline Levine notes that, since "periodizing time shapes the institution of English studies," interrogating our practices of periodization "should get us to the very grounds of contemporary historicist scholarship" ("Infrastructuralism," para. 64). Interrogating periodization will entail challenging its foundational status in our field narratives.

Periodic designations have in fact served to organize American literary materials since market demand for "American literature" schoolbooks grew in the late nineteenth century, in tandem with a growing system of public education and the establishment of English departments at the college level. These new schoolbooks, the forerunners of today's anthologies, faced the task of organizing selections about which there was not yet any entrenched consensus. F. V. N. Painter's *Introduction to American Literature* (1897), a widely adopted textbook, organized its materials into first and second colonial periods, a revolutionary period, and first and second national periods. Katherine

Lee Bates organized her 1897 *American Literature* into a colonial period, a revolutionary period, and a national era then further subdivided into "general aspects," "poetry," "prose thought," and "prose fiction" (vii–viii). Textbooks tended to copy one another, recirculating such designations and thereby creating, as institutional epiphenomena, the "periods" they claimed to reflect. While such retrospective classifications provide an historical narrative and heuristic template for readers, they can also imperil the very history they intend to serve. Distorting the heterogeneity of the past in order to make it conform to neat temporal boundaries or a grand romance of progressive history runs counter, as Jackson has observed, to today's intellectual temper. When the field was in its infancy, such grand narratives held great appeal because they brought order to the chaotic materials of a field seeking credibility and still logistically uncertain about its own bibliography. Order was indeed one of the major points of appeal, for example, of Vernon Louis Parrington's Pulitzer Prize-winning *Main Currents in American Thought: An Interpretation of American Literature from the Beginnings to 1920* (1927–30) which, as Howard Mumford Jones later put it, finally got all the messy data of American literary history into regimented form. He noted that his peers read Parrington with a "tingling sense of discovery" as they followed "this confident marshaling of masses of stubborn material into position, until book, chapter, and section became as orderly as a regiment on parade!" (Jones, *Theory*, 141).

The new wave of poetry studies works with and against "the nineteenth century" as a period narrative. While exploring the analytic yield of new methodologies, these new studies attend to, engage, and foreground historical heterogeneities. They do not seek to produce overarching seamless narratives at the expense of what Mary Poovey has notably called "uneven developments," that is, the actual historical currents of ideas, institutions, and ideologies that operate differently for different individuals positioned within various social formations (*Uneven Developments*, 3). Some comparative examples will make the point. Bennett frames her magisterial study of American women's poetry, *Poets in the Public Sphere: The Emancipatory Project of American Women's Poetry, 1800–1900*, as a century study. A contrast between Bennett in 2003 and Pearce in 1961 is, once again, instructive. Pearce introduces his title concept, "the continuity of American poetry," as one that operated by what he called "a simple plot" (*Continuity*, 4). Bennett, on the other hand, stresses that "no one story can be told of nineteenth-century women or their poetry" (*Poets in the Public Sphere*, 10). Instead, she carefully teases out transitions and contrasts in the content, style, and purpose of poetry by women over the course of the century, decade by decade, stressing throughout the synchronic and diachronic heterogeneity of her materials. A literary history from 1970 that remains excellent today, Jones's *The Age of Energy: Varieties of American Experience 1865–1915*, provides another useful example of the changing ideology of the literary historian's relation to the heterogeneity of the archive. Jones notes somewhat apologetically in his Preface, "I do not find any leading principle that might serve to make sense out of American development as a whole from the age of Andrew Johnson to the presidency of Woodrow Wilson. In hunting for some clue in this rich confusion, in seeking for some standpoint from which to survey the tumult, I have hit upon the idea of energy as being central" (xii). Jones implies that we should not make too much of "the continuity" he grants the idea of energy. It is a thematic convenience serving the occasion of writing about disparate materials. At present, the field has flipped that coin.

The new poetry scholars also push on the chronological frame of the nineteenth century. For example, Bennett and Walker stress the relation of women's poetry in the opening decades of the nineteenth century to eighteenth-century discourses of piety, civic duty, morality, communal ethos, reason, and (often erotic) wit. Bennett argues that, through 1825, women's poetry in the USA shares more stylistically with eighteenth-century poets than with the domestic and sentimental poets to follow. These early-century poets published actively in newspapers and periodicals, often anonymously, rather than in books, a form of publication that was a vital mode of contribution to the public sphere of the day – even though such anonymous and ephemeral publication has contributed to their erasure from a literary history so often ideologically focused on the names and biographies of "great authors." "The Young Girl's Resolution," published as a broadside some time between 1810 and 1814, presents one instance of the early nineteenth-century anonymous poem of erotic wit. Its first stanza reads:

> I am a brisk, young lively lass,
> A little under twenty,
> And by my comely air and dress,
> I can get sweethearts plenty;
> But I'd beware of wedlock's snare
> Though dying swains adore me,
> The men I'll teaze, myself to please,
> My mamma did so before me.
> (Bennett, *Nineteenth-Century*
> *American Women Poets*, 393)

Bennett stresses that the active poetic culture of the early nineteenth century was not the world of the nightingales or the Angels in the House who became stereotypes for the nineteenth-century American woman poet (*Poets in the Public Sphere*, 28, 33). Additionally, she shows that even sentimental poems by women had complex historical roots in the eighteenth century, in a specifically male tradition of sentiment. The twentieth century's institutional and ideological forgetting of sentiment's origins in a male discourse has miscast the debate about women's writing "sphere," mistaking a romanticized discourse of male subjectivity, made by male authors, for a "gender-specific female discourse" (*Poets in the Public Sphere*, 27). Addressing this male fount of sentiment, Sarah Piatt's 1872 "The Sorrows of Charlotte" staged a conversation between mother and daughter about *The Sorrows of Young Werther* (1774). Here, Piatt pushed back against its sweepingly influential vision of the domestic Angel as a culmination of male desire blind to actual women. When the daughter asks if Goethe's book is also about Charlotte's sorrows, the mother replies: "No, child, for never a man would care / To write such a long sad story, you see" (Bennett, *Palace-Burner*, 166 n. 22, 33; *Poets in the Public Sphere*, 23–4).

For Walker, too, "early national" poets, like Lydia Sigourney, come "most directly out of an eighteenth-century context" and are more historically continuous with eighteenth-century legacies than with the romantic ethos of her successors like Frances Sargent Osgood and Rose Terry Cooke, who, in poems like Osgood's "The Cocoa-Nut Tree" (1850) and Cooke's "Blue-Beard's Closet" (1861), turned instead to revel in exploring the psyche and the senses ("Nineteenth-Century American Women Poets Revisited," 232, 234). As Nina Baym argues, the Sigourney later parodied as exemplar of the "worst aspects of domestic sentimentalism," particularly for her funerary poems, is an icon of female authorship "based on only some fraction of what she wrote and published." The lesser-known Sigourney wrote vigorous commentaries on the American past and present through her history writing, enacting "womanly behavior that in many ways nullified the distinction between public and private" ("Reinventing Lydia Sigourney," 387–8, 391). The poem that Baym identifies as her longest and most ambitious, *Traits of the Aborigines of America: A Poem* (1822), written in 4,000 lines of blank verse arranged in five cantos, "made public demands," calling Christian America to account for its treatment of indigenous populations ("Reinventing Lydia Sigourney," 396, 399). For Baym, the case of Sigourney is emblematic of literary history's distortions of antebellum women's writing from what were often obvious public programs into domesticated ones (404).

At the other edge of the century, we encounter one of the hottest issues of all in studies of nineteenth-century poetry by American women; that is, their relation to the phenomenon of modernism that would try to expunge them, and succeed in doing so for many decades. In this case, the arbitrary boundary of a century (typically pushed to 1910 or 1915) has, all too conveniently, served to mark an absolute break within genre history itself. The new scholars have instead challenged the idea of the century break as a definitive break in "movements." In this recent analysis, late-century female poets are writers whose work provided the ground for modernism, rather than grandmothers thoroughly overturned by it (Walker, "Nineteenth-Century American Women Poets Revisited," 241; Bennett, *Poets in the Public Sphere*). Many female poets active in the late nineteenth century, including but not limited to Sarah Morgan Bryan Piatt, Emma Lazarus, Ella Wheeler Wilcox, Henrietta Cordelia Ray, Edith M. Thomas, Lizette Woodworth Reese, Louise Imogen Guiney, Mary Weston Fordham, Harriet Prescott Spofford, and Louise Chandler Moulton, have dropped out of literary history not only because they are female, but because they occupy this no-man's-land of periodicity: the *fin-de-siècle* era. Here, the period boundary *c.*1910 marks who really "counts" as a modern. As Alan Filreis notes, "A line is drawn between the poetries of the two centuries" ("Tests of Poetry," 28). Walker points out that the work of Reese, who published four volumes of poems prior to 1910, meets "most of Ezra Pound's rules for the new poetry of imagism" ("Nineteenth-Century American Women Poets Revisited," 241). Reese's volume *A Branch of May* (1887) centers in careful nature poems stripped of moralizing sentiment, as in "After the Rain": "a wind that blows / Wet boughs against a saffron sky; all June / Caught in the breath of one white rose" (6–8). Another poem in the same volume, "August," opens: "No wind, no bird. The river flames like brass. / On either side, smitten as with a spell / Of silence, brood the fields" (1–3). Bennett also makes compelling cases about the new poetry at the end of the century by writers such as Guiney, whose fascination with classical antiquity predates Pound's. Guiney's epigrammatic "Alexandriana" (1893), a group of thirteen poems in the volume *A Roadside Harp*, were often mistaken by her contemporaries for actual translations (Bennett, *Poets in the Public Sphere*, 196; Bennett, *Nineteenth-Century American Women Poets*, 320 n. 5). The density and allusiveness of number VI in the Alexandriana would fit seamlessly into the Pound era:

> Hail, and be of comfort, thou pious Xeno,
> Late the urn of many a kinsman wreathing;
> On thine own shall even the stranger offer
> Plentiful myrtle.

Other often ignored or dismissed woman poets of the late century include the African American writers Ray and Fordham. While Joan Sherman characterizes them as poets who sidestepped race in favor of a "benignly beautiful earth and heaven" (*African-American Poetry*, 265, 441), other scholars point out that their voices were instead coded for the complex discourse of race in the postbellum, pre-Harlem era, a crucial historical antecedent to twentieth-century developments in poetry (Walker, *American Women Poets*, 408; Bennett, *Poets in the Public Sphere*, 198–200). For example, in her 1897 volume *Magnolia Leaves*, Fordham's "The Saxon Legend of Language" overtly and immediately engages a hegemonic race category (20–1; Walker, *American Women Poets*, 408). The racial ideology of the "Anglo-Saxon" permeated American culture of the 1890s as a veritable obsession, and Fordham takes it on – in however conventional a poetic form – in a way that *de facto* interrogates its "legends." Undoing the "don't mess with my period" habit that Graff has addressed, the new scholars are building evidence that will challenge period boundaries as they currently organize the relation between "the nineteenth century" and the twentieth, modernism in particular.

Problem no. 2: Rethinking the category of nineteenth-century "American" women's poetry

The new wave of scholarship challenges the institutional habit of studying poems as if their artifactual lives are delimited by national boundaries. English departments remain largely organized around what Benedict Anderson calls the "imagined communities" of the nation-state, typically treating "English" and "American" literature in particular as its major (and separate) field subdivisions. Such an entrenched taxonomy classifies poems in ways that distort the history of what Meredith McGill memorably calls "the traffic in poems." An ontology of literary history driven by the nationality of authors distorts our understanding of the actual genesis, publication, circulation (over both the short and the long term), and cultural meaning of literary texts across a range of far more porous boundaries.

Maria Gowen Brooks (1794?–1845) provides one example of a poet who complicates national taxonomies and who has been lost to literary history until very recently in part because of them. The new poetics scholarship finds her challenge to traditional categories to be part of what makes her work compelling, but those very problems of placement contributed to the obscurity from which current scholars seek to resuscitate her.[7] Although Brooks was born in Massachusetts, a British reviewer included her among "modern English poetesses" along with Elizabeth Barrett; she lived as a slaveholder on a coffee plantation in Cuba; she donated book proceeds to benefit Polish refugees in the wake of revolution there. Edgar Allan Poe and Rufus Griswold gushed over her work; so did Robert Southey (who dubbed her "Maria of the West," a name she used as a pseudonym, along with its translation, Maria del Occidente) and Charles Lamb, leading to her reputation as what Geofrilyn M. Walker calls "a sort of 'honorary' Lake Poet." Her prestigious connections in this regard are surely part of what impressed Griswold.[8]

Kirsten Silva Gruesz suggests that Brooks has never been assimilated into literary history because neither her work nor her adopted residence in Cuba fits comfortably into literary-historical classifications to date. Indeed, even her pen name, Gruesz argues, "marks a kind of indeterminate transatlantic space between the United States and Britain" – remembering that Southey, looking across the Atlantic, gave this Massachusetts poet her "western" name – even as it also gestures at her specific location in Cuba on the western half of the island (Gruesz, "*Cafetal*," 38). Cuba was still a Spanish colony, but embroiled in the arena of hemispheric and colonial politics (37), and the United States was still a post-colonial "west" from the vantage of Southey's Britain. In addition, Brooks was a woman from the north living on a plantation worked by slaves whom she apparently came to own after her uncle's death and the bequest of his property, and she defended slavery (Groves, "Maria Gowen Brooks," 40–1). Finally, her exoticized poetry of the naturally luxurious Caribbean world presents an intense record of fiery female sexuality during the alleged era of the Angel in the House.

Recent critics have focused in particular on her epic poem *Zóphiël, or The Bride of Seven* (1833), for which Southey secured London publication (Groves, "Maria Gowen Brooks," 40–1). Groves classifies it as an "amorous angel" poem, a recognizable Romantic genre. Based on the apocryphal book of Tobit, the fallen angel Zóphiël maniacally lusts after the lush Jewish heroine Egla in six cantos of elaborately sexualized plotting. Zóphiël murders the suitors who, as Bennett puts it, meet their deaths trying to get inside her "fragrant bower" (Groves, "Maria Gowen Brooks," 43 n. 9; 41; Bennett, *Poets*, 175). Even though she rejects his physical advances, Egla is aflame with sexual passion, including passion for Zóphiël's "mortal form," which she watches "rapturously." Allegedly proffering to her a vase of gems, he "lowly bend[s]" to offer her the "reddening" ruby from his "full" vase, saying "Now on thy snowy bosom let it blaze; / 'T will blush still deeper to behold thy lip." By this point in the poem, one can hardly believe this excerpt appears in Griswold rather than, say, the late unpublished porn by Edith Wharton (Griswold, *Poets*, 149).

Nation-based categories show their limits not only in the cases of individual poets, but also in larger taxonomies. In a special issue of *Victorian Poetry* in 2005, Jackson launched the bracing polemic that the literary-critical category of "Victorian poetry" has excluded American works in a way that distorts the history of the genre. Defining "Victorian poetry" as a British national tradition has distorted the many transatlantic forms of exchange and circulation at the core of the era's poetic culture ("American Victorian," 161). Michael Cohen's essay for this special issue rightfully stresses the "striking fact" that the term "Victorian poetry" was coined by an American, the poet-stockbroker-critic E. C. Stedman whose companion volumes, *Victorian Poets* and *Poets of America*, appeared in 1875 and 1885, respectively. Challenging the twentieth-century accounts of American nineteenth-century culture as derivative and timid, Cohen argues that Stedman, largely written off today as the emblem of an outmoded genteel poetics, actually theorized and defined Victorian poetry as a field. Such instances of international circulation and influence must balance claims about national poetic traditions, Cohen argues ("Invention," 169).[9]

One particular strain of Anglo-American criticism focused specifically on nineteenth-century women's poetics is a recent energetic body of work on the idea of the "poetess." Although critics use the term differently, roughly put, it describes a particular type of popular woman poet whose career thrived on both sides of the Atlantic.[10] Except when it refers to Sappho, the idealized first woman poet, the term's semantic functions have often been negative, typically denigrating poetry by women under the sign of excessive emotion. Not surprisingly, recent studies of the poetess – including analyses of Lucretia Davidson, Elizabeth Oakes Smith, Sarah Helen Whitman, Adah Isaacs Menken, Helen Hunt Jackson, and others – have sought alternate ways of accounting for this common figure. The approach has proven analytically rich for an array of reasons: poetess culture is transatlantic in reach and influence; the poetess poses a particularly stark challenge to traditional literary-historical ways of positioning women's poetry as a debased category; and, on the most theoretical ground, she serves as a ground for a model of poetics aggressively opposed to formalist theories of poetry (see Jackson and Richards, "'The Poetess'"; Jackson and Prins, "Lyrical Studies"; Jackson, "Story"; Loeffelholz, *From School*, 23; see also Problem no. 4).

Although, as McGill points out, the ultimate "reach" of transatlantic studies remains to be worked out, it is already clear that this young field fundamentally recasts assumptions at the core of traditional literary history. Indeed, as she points out, the methodologies entailed in attending to the specifically Anglo-American transatlantic exchanges on which her volume focuses point in many directions, beyond nations, beyond the Atlantic world, beyond poems written in English, and into a fuller and more accurate history of poetry as it circulates in a far more complex network than national chronicles have allowed. McGill finds "the centrality of women poets, women's poetry, and figures of women" to be among the major insights of the transatlantic study of poems to date (*Traffic in Poems*, 3, 10). She proposes that this still young field "might well produce a literary history in which women poets are not the exception – marginal figures who need solicitously to be brought back into national canons – but figures who make legible the extranational origins of national myths and make it possible to track the shifting currents of cultural exchange" (4).

Problem no. 3: Rethinking the category of nineteenth-century American "women's" poetry

Griswold's 1843 preface to *The Female Poets of America* goes to great lengths to explain why female poets belong in a separate category. "It is less easy to be assured of the genuineness of literary ability in women than in men" (7), he begins. The hole of equivocation that he digs for himself (beginning with the uncertainty of the phrase "less easy") in fact grows deeper by the sentence:

> The moral nature of women, in its finest and richest development, partakes of some of the qualities of genius; it assumes, at least, the similitude of that which in men is the characteristic or accompaniment of the highest grade of mental inspiration. We are in danger, therefore, of mistaking for the efflorescent energy of creative intelligence, that which is only the exuberance of personal "feelings unemployed" . . . It does not follow, because the most essential genius in men is marked by qualities which we may call feminine, that such qualities when found in female writers have any certain or just relation to mental superiority. (7)

Rhetorically presented as if based in careful thought, the elaborate distinctions Griswold presents are convoluted by his inability to defend his core assertion that the mental and psychological natures of women differ essentially from those of men. As Cheryl Walker nicely puts it, Griswold "knew, or thought he knew, what the difference was between male and female poets" (*Nightingale's Burden*, 24). But his powerful institutional role as anthologist, literary

arbiter, and tastemaker fed the dissemination and repetition of his formulations about the separate sphere of emotional but mentally inferior "female
poets of America."

Walker's own *Nightingale's Burden* adopted a separate spheres model in 1982
as a strategic means to address the paucity of scholarship on the topic. She
presented a tradition of "the poetess" whose work represented "a frustrated,
renunciatory, fantasizing, conciliatory posture" (58). "My aim is to delineate
a single approach to tradition and to deal only with those poets who have
made the most significant contributions to its progress. I do not believe that
all women poets by virtue of their sex have been driven to write the kinds of
poems I describe here as belonging to this women's tradition," she explained
(x). Given her institutional situation at the time, Walker's articulation and
defense of any woman's tradition in American poetry at all constituted a
much-needed development, despite what we (and she) now see as its limitations ("Nineteenth-Century American Women Poets Revisited," 242 n. 4).
The category of "women's" poetry still serves the important goal of recovering the social history of actual women, but as part of a much more complex
picture of culture in which female poets and male poets shared networks of
influence and circulation and neither was inherently or exclusively "sentimental" in mode; instead, an array of poetic positions circulated in the culture,
including an image of the "female poet of America" that a woman (or, in fact,
a pseudonymous man) might adopt. Three important examples from recent
work on "woman poets" will serve.

First, as Walker points out in her 1998 reflections on the state of the field she
helped to create, despite the many questions still confronting scholars, "one
thing is clear": "Nineteenth-century American women poets did not function
in a world isolated from men or from male literary productions" ("Nineteenth-
Century American Women Poets Revisited," 232). As Richards's influential
study of Poe's relationship to Osgood, Sarah Helen Whitman, and Elizabeth
Oakes Smith has shown, "the gendering of poetic practices is far more fluid
and complex than has been previously portrayed" (*Gender*, 1). Richards shows
that the production and reception of poems were tied together as related
components of a social network, rather than functions of an autonomous
realm of individual thought and feeling centered in a solitary (male) genius.
Richards resituates one of literary history's highest-canonical male poets as an
active collaborator with the female poets in his coterie, heavily influencing
and heavily influenced by them. As she shows, at least some women poets
saw membership in Griswold's pantheon as good for marketing, but worthy

of sarcasm behind the scenes (*Gender*, 149–54). Individual poets variously played with, manipulated, castigated, or revered the category of the "female poet" or the "poetess" (not synonymous terms) in ways that scholarship is just beginning to trace. As Gruesz puts it, "Time and again, nineteenth-century women wrote *around*, rather than strictly into or out of, the Poetess convention; some merrily made sport of it" ("Maria," 100).

Richards wittily calls Poe "the honorary Poetess" (*Gender*, 198), which brings us to my second point. Just as women poets did not occupy a sphere separate from male poets, so is the reverse true: thus scholars have also turned with fresh force to the phenomenon of "sentimental men." For example, Mary Louise Kete's study, *Sentimental Collaborations: Mourning and Middle-Class Identity in Nineteenth-Century America* (2000), abandoned its original premise that sentiment was a "distinctly feminine aesthetic." So many sentimental practitioners were male that the "separate spheres" model was simply inaccurate (xii). Two of the poets central to her study, Sigourney and Henry Wadsworth Longfellow, were both cultural authorities whom the age revered as "secular mentors of ethics, manners, and mores." They strategically purveyed their cultural power in the public domain as well as the "seemingly private domain of personal subjectivity" (134). The "startling" similarities between the careers of these two popular poets, Kete argues, emblematize the inaccuracy of poetic separate spheres (135).

Third, scholars are challenging the category of the "woman poet" on theoretical grounds. Marion Thain poses the question: "What kind of a critical category is 'women's poetry?'" Answering this question in the post-recovery period is one of the foundational questions that current scholars face.[11] Jackson and Prins have responded with a theoretical model, arguing that the "poetess" was not a lyric "I," not a subjectivity, and not an historical woman of the kind typically at the core of recovery efforts; rather, they construe her to be a set of generic effects, which brings me to Problem no. 4.

Problem no. 4: Rethinking the category of nineteenth-century American women's "poetry"

The new wave of scholarship challenges literary history's definition of the term "poetry" itself, on both empirical and theoretical grounds. The primary empirical challenge is the archive, whose vastness and heterogeneity alone warrant that we now speak of "women's poetries" (Thain, "What Kind of a Critical Category," 582; Bennett, "Was Sigourney a Poetess?" 267).

Bennett's extensive archive of newspaper and periodical poems, for example, effectively demolishes a high-culture definition of "real" poetry as concerned with lyric subjectivity but unconcerned with material circumstance. She chronicles an undeniable body of evidence that women's poems of the nineteenth century passionately addressed public and political issues of the day, including the legal status of women, as in Maria Weston Chapman's "The Times That Try Men's Souls" (1848); domestic ideology, as in Fanny Gage's "The Maniac Wife" (1866); Indian rights, as in E. Pauline Johnson's "The Cattle Thief" (1894); racism, as in Sarah Louisa Forten's "An Appeal to Women" (1834); slavery, as in Eliza Earle's "Petitioning Congress" (1837); caste and class, as in Fanny Parnell's "To the Land Leaguers" (1880); and the status of minority cultures, as Emma Lazarus's "The Dance to Death" (1882).[12]

This empirical challenge to twentieth-century models also entails a redefinition of the genre term "poetry," and this is where the theoretical challenge emerges. The hegemonic ideology of formalist poetry that dominated English studies for most of the twentieth century, that is, from the rise of the New Criticism in the 1930s through the canon wars of the 1980s and beyond, closed down the vast and socially vital range of nineteenth-century poetic production by women (and men), lifting it out of a sphere of active public and popular discourse and situating it in privacy, on the page, as a series of solitary acts of reading and writing pitched at the level of high culture. As Filreis notes, "The formal analysis of poetry, an invention of the century in which the poetry it analyzes was written, is founded on the assumption that such work should then be performed on all poetry" ("Tests of Poetry," 29). The new poetry scholars are gradually dismantling this entrenched legacy and replacing it with new models.

Jackson and Prins, for example, have proposed the important counter-theory that they call "lyrical reading" (Prins, *Victorian Sappho*, 19; Jackson and Prins, "Lyrical Studies"). Stressing that twentieth-century formalism defined "poetry" as "lyric," and then defined "lyric" as a transcendent, ahistorical utterance of an imagined speaker about subjective states, they point to the ways that this restrictive definition effectively shut out of consideration (and literary history) the vast catalogue of poetic genres that the nineteenth century actually produced: ballads, songs, commemoration odes, recitations, anagrams, public poetic exchanges in periodicals, and so on. Their counter-theory recuperates the figure of the poetess in particular, about whom they argue that her "I" is empty because she is *not* a lyric subject, but instead a medium whose work registers the currents of transatlantic exchange and the social world of writing. Jackson and Prins write, "The question we would pose through these poetesses is whether the pathos attributed to their poetry may be traced to their outside position on subjectivity, rather than (as has been the case for the last one hundred and fifty years) to their utter absorption in their own particularly abstract selves" ("Lyrical Studies," 523). While the romantic "I" is a self focused inwardly, poetess poetry portrays states of subjectivity as themselves generic, as coins in a network of conventions that function as their own currency. The "extreme typicality" of poetess poetry, Richards argues, rendered it "most vulnerable to oblivion," despite both its importance in its own time and – as at the core of Richards' argument – its formative (albeit, until recently, invisible) influence on the poets who have lasted (*Gender*, 155).

The new archive and the new theoretical work on genre thus come together on argumentative ground: to disable the grip of formalism, as the twentieth century articulated it, over the domain of poetry. That shift is what (in part, though certainly not in whole) frees up the massive array of neglected poems for new forms of analysis. Indeed, non-modernist frameworks entirely change the assumptive ground for a study of poetic history. Two quick examples will have to serve in the short space remaining. First, the idea that a "poem" is not necessarily written for the page and the solitary reader already opens space for new interpretive approaches. The poems of Frances E. W. Harper, for example, must be read through modalities of oral performance and oral traditions, a relation to genre shaped by her demographic position as an African American woman directing her work to an audience of mixed literacies in public and community spaces. As Loeffelholz puts it, Harper often positions herself in "a middle ground of culture, mediating between elementary education and oral tradition on the one hand and high-art realms of allusion on the other," as in poems such as "The Little Builders" (1871).[13] Second, nineteenth-century poems were themselves often anti-lyric, heterogeneous in a way that formalism could not and did not account for. Karen L. Kilcup points out correctly that generic "myopia" in the twentieth century has distorted these heterogeneous writing practices ("Preface," xi). For example, Lucy Larcom's fascinating 1875 *An Idyl of Work*, which Larcom herself said "does not claim completeness either as poem or as narrative" (Kilcup, "Preface," vii), includes, in twelve sections and nearly 200 pages, both marriage and seduction plots as well as lyrics interspersed with blank verse narrative. Loeffelholz notes that "Larcom interpolates at least sixteen lyrics of her own writing into the narrative," including "various sonnets, narrative ballads, and hymns" ("Mapping," 158 n. 25). The plot of the narrative poem tells the tale of three young mill girls whose labors temporarily cease when the river floods in spring, leading to unaccustomed leisure and lengthy explicit discussions of the girls' transatlantic reading: Milton, Irving, Bunyan, Sir Walter Scott, Maria Edgeworth, Longfellow, Wordsworth, Whittier, Bryant, and others. As Loeffelholz points out, the transatlantic formal model for Larcom's text is Tennyson's *The Princess: A Medley* (1847), and her specific engagement here with a veritable library shelf of poems is part of *An Idyl of Work*'s extended exploration of the class dimensions of literary culture ("Mapping," 148–53).

A new archive, a new history, a new theory: since literally everything about the history of American poetry is currently on the table for reassessment, it is hard to imagine a more exciting prospect for scholars, particularly new scholars seeking areas of fresh research that will make a concrete, material contribution. Those of us working in this field will benefit from a community of boots-on-the-ground scholars working in all areas, from bibliography to biography to close reading to genre history to cultural studies to theory, helping to build not only larger pictures of the archive but also new domains of its meaning. Indeed, twenty-first-century literary histories of nineteenth-century women's poetry will barely resemble those of the twentieth century. That prospect of change is thrilling indeed.

Notes

1. See, for only one of many examples, Lentricchia, "The Resentments of Robert Frost."
2. This entire account of Dickinson is only one among many narratives to have been swept off the table by the current renaissance in poetry studies (see, for example, Petrino, *Emily Dickinson*; Jackson, *Dickinson's Misery*).
3. It is important to add that our own work today, including mine in this essay, will, from the standpoint of future critics, present similar ideological blind spots.
4. The other most problematic area for Bercovitch is ethnicity, which represents the "cultural extreme" ("Problems," 2) as opposed to poetry as "literary extreme."
5. Isobel Armstrong's 1995 commentary on women's poetry studies noted that, while we had discovered who the women poets were, we had not yet discovered how to talk about them ("The Gush of the Feminine," 15). Marion Thain places the turning point in the field from thinking of "women's poetry" as a recuperative term to the next phase, focused not on recuperation but on "charting the involvement of women's poetry in a wide range of discourses and debates," between 1995 and 2002 ("What Kind of a Critical Category," 575). Armstrong's work in nineteenth-century British women poets remains an important transatlantic and methodological source for scholars of American women poets.

6. I borrow my term "problem of definition" from Bell's brilliant interrogation of the idea of American "realism" (*The Problem of American Realism*).
7. See, for example, Gruesz, "Maria Gowen Brooks"; Bennett, *Poets*; Groves, "Maria Gowen Brooks"; G. Walker, "Maria Gowen Brooks."
8. Low, *Literary Protégés*; Brooks, "Preface," iii; Gruesz, "Maria Gowen Brooks," 89, 103 n. 12; Gruesz, "*Cafetal*," 37; Groves, "Maria Gowen Brooks," 38; G. Walker, "Maria Gowen Brooks," 49, 50.
9. On Stedman's dissemination of the term "Victorian" as a period indicator, see Ricks, *The New Oxford Book of Victorian Verse*, xxvi; Bristow, "Whether 'Victorian' Poetry," 90. Stedman himself claimed to have popularized the term (Bristow, "Whether 'Victorian' Poetry," 90).
10. Of course, not all women poets were poetesses, as Bennett, Anne Mellor, and others have noted. Bennett has critiqued poetess scholarship as it has evolved in recent years for reducing the woman poet to writing one type of poetry, and for transatlanticizing what was primarily a British phenomenon (Bennett, "Was Sigourney a Poetess?," 267). My account of poetess scholarship in this paragraph is indebted in particular to Mandell, "Introduction," and Davis, "Recent Criticism of the Poetess." See also Prins, *Victorian Sappho*, 3, 14; Armstrong, "The Gush"; Brown, "The Victorian Poetess," 180–2; Mellor, "The Female Poet and the Poetess," 82.
11. See Williams, *Reclaiming Authorship*, for a recent useful history of the category of the female author in the USA.
12. Bennett, *Poets*, 46, 122, 105, 57–8, 50, 95, 99–100; Bennett, *Nineteenth-Century American Women Poets*, 416–18.
13. Loeffelholz, *From School*, 120, 153; see also Walker, "Nineteenth-Century American Women Poets Revisited," 240.

Works cited

Anderson, Benedict. *Imagined Communities: Reflections on the Origin and Spread of Nationalism*. 1983. London: Verso, 1991.

Armstrong, Isobel. "The Gush of the Feminine: How Can We Read Women's Poetry of the Romantic Period?" In *Romantic Women Writers: Voices and Countervoices*. Ed. Paula R. Feldman and Theresa M. Kelley. Hanover and London: University Press of New England, 1995.

Bates, Katherine Lee. *American Literature*. Chautauqua, NY: The Chautauqua Press, 1897.

Baym, Nina. "Reinventing Lydia Sigourney." *American Literature* 62.3 (1990): 385–404.

Bell, Michael Davitt. *The Problem of American Realism: Studies in the Cultural History of a Literary Idea*. Chicago: University of Chicago Press, 1993.

Bennett, Paula Bernat. *Poets in the Public Sphere: The Emancipatory Project of American Women's Poetry, 1800–1900*. Princeton: Princeton University Press, 2003.

"Was Sigourney a Poetess? The Aesthetics of Victorian Plenitude in Lydia Sigourney's Poetry." *Comparative American Studies* 5.3 (2007): 265–89.

Bennett, Paula Bernat, ed. *Nineteenth-Century American Women Poets: An Anthology*. Malden, MA: Blackwell, 1998.

Palace-Burner: The Selected Poetry of Sarah Piatt. Urbana: University of Illinois Press, 2001.

Bercovitch, Sacvan. "Problems in the Writing of American Literary History: The Examples of Poetry and Ethnicity." *American Literary History* 15.1 (2003): 1–3.

Bristow, Joseph. "Whether 'Victorian' Poetry: A Genre and its Period." *Victorian Poetry* 42.1 (2004): 81–109.

Brooks, Maria Gowen. Pseudonym Maria Del Occidente. *Zóphiël; or, the Bride of Seven*. 1833. Boston: Hilliard, Gray, and Company, 1834.

Brown, Susan. "The Victorian Poetess." In *The Cambridge Companion to Victorian Poetry*. Ed. Joseph Bristow. Cambridge: Cambridge University Press, 2000.

Cohen, Michael. "E. C. Stedman and the Invention of Victorian Poetry." *Victorian Poetry* 43.2 (2005): 165–88.

Cooke, Rose Terry. "Blue-Beard's Closet." In *Poems*. Boston: Ticknor and Fields, 1861.

Cott, Nancy F. *The Bonds of Womanhood: "Woman's Sphere" in New England, 1780–1835*. New Haven: Yale University Press, 1977.

Davidson, Cathy N. and Jessamyn Hatcher, eds. "Introduction." In *No More Separate Spheres! A Next Wave American Studies Reader*. Durham, NC: Duke University Press, 2002.

Davis, Peggy. "Recent Criticism of the Poetess: A Review Essay." *Romanticism on the Net* 29–30 (February–May 2003). www.erudit.org/revue/ron/2003/v/n29/007712ar.html (accessed September 22, 2010).

Filreis, Alan. "Tests of Poetry." *American Literary History* 15.1 (2003): 27–34.

Fordham, Mary Weston. "The Saxon Legend of Language." In *Magnolia Leaves. Poems*. Tuskegee, AL: Tuskegee Institute, 1897.

Graff, Gerald. "How Periods Erase History." *On Periodization: Selected Essays from the English Institute*. Ed. Virginia Jackson. ACLS Humanities E-Book. University of Michigan Library Scholarly Publishing Office, 2010. http://quod.lib.umich.edu (accessed September 6, 2010).

Griswold, Rufus W. *The Poets and Poetry of America*. Philadelphia: Carey and Hart, 1843.
"Preface." In *The Female Poets of America*. Philadelphia: Carey and Hart, 1849.

Groves, Jeffrey D. "Maria Gowen Brooks." *Legacy* 12.1 (1995): 38–46.

Gruesz, Kirsten Silva. "The *Cafetal* of Maria del Occidente and the Anglo-American Race for Cuba." In McGill, *The Traffic in Poems*.
"Maria Gowen Brooks, In and Out of the Poe Circle." *ESQ: A Journal of the American Renaissance* 54 (2008): 75–109.

Guiney, Louise Imogen. "Alexandriana." In *A Roadside Harp: A Book of Verses*. Boston: Houghton Mifflin, 1893.

Haralson, Eric L., ed. *Encyclopedia of American Poetry: The Nineteenth Century*. Chicago: Fitzroy Dearborn, 1998.

Harrington, Joseph. "Why American Poetry is Not American Literature." *American Literary History* 8.3 (1996): 496–515.

Jackson, Virginia. "American Victorian Poetry: The Transatlantic Poetic." *Victorian Poetry* 43.2 (2005): 157–64.
Dickinson's Misery: A Theory of Lyric Reading. Princeton: Princeton University Press, 2005.

"Introduction: On Periodization and its Discontents." In *On Periodization: Selected Essays from the English Institute*. Ed. Virginia Jackson. ACLS Humanities E-Book. University of Michigan Library Scholarly Publishing Office, 2010. http://quod.lib.umich.edu (accessed September 6, 2010).

"'The Story of Boon': or, The Poetess." *ESQ: A Journal of the American Renaissance* 54 (2008): 241–67.

Jackson, Virginia and Eliza Richards. "'The Poetess' and Nineteenth-Century American Women Poets." *Poetess Archive Journal* 1.1 (April 12, 2007): 1–7.

Jackson, Virginia and Yopie Prins. "Lyrical Studies." *Victorian Literature and Culture* 7.2 (1999): 521–30.

Jones, Howard Mumford. "Preface." In *The Age of Energy: Varieties of American Experience, 1865–1915*. New York: Viking, 1970.

The Theory of American Literature. Ithaca: Cornell University Press, 1948, 1965.

Kelley, Mary. *Private Woman, Public Stage: Literary Domesticity in Nineteenth-Century America*. New York: Oxford University Press, 1984.

Kete, Mary Louise. *Sentimental Collaborations: Mourning and Middle-Class Identity in Nineteenth-Century America*. Durham, NC: Duke University Press, 2000.

Kilcup, Karen L., ed. *Nineteenth-Century American Women Writers: A Critical Reader*. Malden, MA: Blackwell, 1998.

"Preface." In *Nineteenth-Century American Women Writers: A Critical Reader*. Malden, MA: Blackwell, 1998.

Larcom, Lucy. *An Idyl of Work*. Boston: James R. Osgood, 1875.

Lauter, Paul. "Melville Climbs the Canon." *American Literature* 66.1 (1994): 1–24.

Lentricchia, Frank. "The Resentments of Robert Frost." *American Literature* 62 (1990): 175–200.

Levine, Caroline. "Infrastructuralism, or the Tempo of Institutions." *On Periodization: Selected Essays from the English Institute*. Ed. Virginia Jackson. ACLS Humanities E-Book. University of Michigan Library Scholarly Publishing Office, 2010. http://quod.lib.umich.edu (accessed September 6, 2010).

Loeffelholz, Mary. *From School to Salon: Reading Nineteenth-Century American Women's Poetry*. Princeton: Princeton University Press, 2004.

"Mapping the Cultural Field: *Aurora Leigh* in America." In McGill, *The Traffic in Poems*.

Low, Dennis. *The Literary Protégés of the Lake Poets*. Aldershot: Ashgate, 2006.

Mandell, Laura. "Introduction: The Poetess Tradition." *Romanticism on the Net* 29–30 (February–May 2003). www.erudit.org/revue/ron/2003/v/n29/007712ar.html (accessed September 20, 2010).

McGill, Meredith L., ed. *The Traffic in Poems: Nineteenth-Century Poetry and Transatlantic Exchange*. New Brunswick: Rutgers University Press, 2008.

Mellor, Anne. "The Female Poet and the Poetess: Two Traditions of British Women's Poetry, 1780–1820." In *Women's Poetry, Late Romantic to Late Victorian: Gender and Genre, 1830–1900*. Ed. Isobel Armstrong and Virginia Blain. New York: St. Martin's Press, 1999.

Osgood, Frances Sargent. "The Cocoa-Nut Tree." In *Poems*. Philadelphia: Carey and Hart, 1850.

Ostriker, Alicia Suskin. *Stealing the Language: The Emergence of Women's Poetry in America*. Boston: Beacon Press, 1986.

Painter, F. V. N. *Introduction to American Literature*. N.p.: Leach Shewell, and Sanborn, 1897.

Parrington, Vernon Louis. *Main Currents in American Thought: An Interpretation of American Literature from the Beginnings to 1920*. 3 vols. New York: Harcourt, Brace, 1927–30.

Pearce, Roy Harvey. *The Continuity of American Poetry*. Princeton: Princeton University Press, 1961.

Petrino, Elizabeth. *Emily Dickinson and her Contemporaries: Women's Verse in America, 1820–1885*. Hanover: University Press of New England, 1998.

Piatt, Sarah. "The Sorrows of Charlotte." In *Palace-Burner: The Selected Poetry of Sarah Piatt*. Ed. Paula Bernat Bennett. Urbana: University of Illinois Press, 2001.

Poovey, Mary. *Uneven Developments: The Ideological Work of Gender in Mid-Victorian England*. Chicago: University of Chicago Press, 1988.

Pound, Ezra. "Hugh Selwyn Mauberly: Part I." In *Poetry in English: An Anthology*. Ed. M .L. Rosenthal. New York: Oxford University Press, 1987.

Prins, Yopie. *Victorian Sappho*. Princeton: Princeton University Press, 1999.

Reese, Lizette Woodworth. *A Branch of May*. Baltimore: Cushings & Bailey, 1887.

Richards, Eliza. *Gender and the Poetics of Reception in Poe's Circle*. Cambridge: Cambridge University Press, 2004.

Ricks, Christopher, ed. *The New Oxford Book of Victorian Verse*. Oxford: Oxford University Press, 1987.

Rubin, Joan Shelley. *Songs of Ourselves: The Uses of Poetry in America*. Cambridge, MA: Harvard University Press, 2007.

Santayana, George. "Genteel American Poetry." 1915. In *The Genteel Tradition: Nine Essays by George Santayana*. Ed. Douglas L. Wilson. Cambridge, MA: Harvard University Press, 1967.

Sherman, Joan, ed. *African-American Poetry of the Nineteenth Century: An Anthology*. Urbana: University of Illinois Press, 1992.

Sigourney, Lydia. *Traits of the Aborigines of America: A Poem*. Cambridge: Hilliard and Metcalf, 1822.

Smith-Rosenberg, Carroll. "The Female World of Love and Ritual: Relations Between Women in Nineteenth-Century America." *Signs* 1 (1975): 1–29.

Sorby, Angela. *Schoolroom Poets: Childhood, Performance, and the Place of American Poetry, 1865–1917*. Durham, NH: University of New Hampshire Press, 2005.

Stedman, Edmund Clarence. *Poets of America*. 1885. Boston: Houghton, Mifflin, 1898.
   Victorian Poets. 1875. Boston: Houghton, Mifflin, 1889.

Stetson, Erlene, ed. *Black Sister: Poetry by Black American Women, 1746–1980*. Bloomington: Indiana University Press, 1981.

Thain, Marion. "What Kind of a Critical Category is Women's Poetry?" *Victorian Poetry* 41.4 (2004): 575–84.

Tompkins, Jane. *Sensational Designs: The Cultural Work of American Fiction, 1790–1860*. New York: Oxford University Press, 1985.

Walker, Cheryl, ed. *American Women Poets of the Nineteenth Century: An Anthology*. New Brunswick: Rutgers University Press, 1992.

"Nineteenth-Century American Women Poets Revisited." In Kilcup, *Nineteenth-Century American Women Writers*.

The Nightingale's Burden: Women Poets and American Culture before 1900. Bloomington: Indiana University Press, 1982.

Walker, Geofrilyn M. "Maria Gowen Brooks (1794?–1845)." In Haralson, *Encyclopedia of American Poetry*.

Watts, Emily Stipes. *The Poetry of American Women from 1632 to 1945*. Austin: University of Texas Press, 1977.

Welter, Barbara. "The Cult of True Womanhood: 1820–1860." *American Quarterly* 18 (1966): 151–74.

Williams, Susan S. *Reclaiming Authorship: Literary Women in America, 1850–1900*. Philadelphia: University of Pennsylvania Press, 2006.

12

Transatlantic sympathies and nineteenth-century women's writing

SUSAN DAVID BERNSTEIN

Despite the tradition of reading nineteenth-century American and British writers as part of an exclusively national community, more recent scholarship has attended to the robust transatlantic circulation of print that structured what Amanda Claybaugh describes as the "Anglo-American world" of social reform. As Meredith McGill's *American Literature and the Culture of Reprinting* has noted, we know that British and American writers were frequently mingled together in miscellany magazines like *Littel's Living Age*, sometimes called *The Living Age* (1844–1941). If such studies of the circulation of British writing in American print make manifest a tendency toward what Elisa Tamarkin calls "Anglophilia" (*Anglophilia*, 179), or the cultural capital of British literature for American nineteenth-century writers and readers, in fact American women writers in particular had a profound impact on Victorian culture through the transatlantic print network. The most celebrated example is *Uncle Tom's Cabin* (1851–2), the all-time bestseller in England in the 1850s, even outstripping the enormously popular Dickens. Before international copyright laws kept at bay pirated editions, some thirty or more versions of Stowe's novel were issued in Britain. Within the advertising pages that surround the fifth part issue number of *Bleak House*, released in July 1852, only a month after the last installment of Stowe's novel in *The National Era* (1847–60), ran a notice for London publications of "Uncle Tom's Cabin, or Negro Life in the Slave States of America," from a cloth gilt edition to a version in twenty-four "penny weekly numbers" to promote the novel's "circulation among all classes of the community." Positioned to the right of an advert for *Englishwoman's Domestic Magazine* (1852–79), the notice for these British editions of Stowe's novel includes snippets of reviews, one describing *Uncle Tom's Cabin* as "a deed of accusation – drawn up by a woman, inspired with such fervour and strength of imagery and language as a prophet of old . . . written in letters of fire, with a pen of iron . . . It is only after reading such a book that we can fully appreciate and realise the humanity of a principle which has annihilated slavery in the British

Colonies." Another excerpt from *Tait's Edinburgh Magazine* (1832–61) adds, "It will be read, and must be read, by everybody everywhere." But it would be a mistake to think that Stowe's novel alone generated this "humanity of a principle" of social activism.

Stowe's several reading tours in the UK also prompted connections with British women writers who engaged social issues in their fiction; both Anna Sewell's *Black Beauty* (1877), about animal abuse, and George Eliot's *Daniel Deronda* (1876), about Jewish emancipation in England, were inspired by *Uncle Tom's Cabin*. Wishing to arouse compassion for Jews much as Stowe had for American slaves, Eliot wrote to Stowe that she "felt urged to treat Jews with such sympathy and understanding as my nature and knowledge could attain to" and thus prompt "the imagination of men and women to a vision of human claims in those races of their fellow-men who most differ from them in custom and belief" (*George Eliot Letters*, vol. 6, 301). We also know that Eliot corresponded with Elizabeth Stuart Phelps, whose *The Silent Partner* (1871) on the relationship between factory owners and managers and workers bears close resemblance to Elizabeth Gaskell's *North and South* (1854–5). Yet this is but the tip of the massive wave of transatlantic sympathy through print.

Social claims of the disenfranchised and dispossessed suffering communities beset by sexual abuse, by poverty and a punitive welfare system, by working conditions that undermined health and child protection, for whom the rousing cause of the abolition of slavery became a rallying cry and a supple metaphor, crossed national divisions, something the circulation of verbal texts abundantly certifies. Sometimes the indelible and prolific figure of the dead child served to link readers across national and other social divisions; Dickens's Little Nell and Paul Dombey, Stowe's Evangeline, and Barrett Browning's infanticide of a slave child serve to cement compassion across the wrongs of poverty, child neglect, and slavery. Complementing the abundant textual echoes we can trace in Anglo-American literary culture is further evidence that writers of the Atlantic Rim participated in this shared realm; both British and American writers traveled across the ocean as they gave lectures and met other writers and activists. Former slaves Frederick Douglass, Harriet Jacobs, and William Wells Brown went on tours in Britain where they spoke about American slavery to British abolitionists, as they also learned of the impoverished classes there; Dickens, Frances Trollope, and Harriet Martineau visited American prisons, schools, and slaveholding states, and they folded their observations into published notes and articles and fiction that spurred social reform at home.

The myriad literary echoes across the ocean make manifest that reading and writing fiction and poetry traversed national borders in the nineteenth century, more than scholars and students routinely recognized, for the reason that we still read and profess along national lines of literary tradition. What kinds of surprising echoes emerge when we do read across the Atlantic, when we consider the nineteenth-century Anglophone print world of reprints and pirated editions along the lines that its original readers did? This essay examines the transatlantic collaborations of Eliot's Stowe-inspired "vision of human claims" through the wider literary circulation of social problem writing on tolerance for the marginalized and oppressed, from African American slaves to British Jews, from dispossessed Native Americans to impoverished factory workers. As I show, this network of sympathetic projection did not originate in one nation or from the pen of one particular writer. Instead, sympathetic identification emerged from the interplay of Anglo-American literature, as indeed its writers understood and practiced. There is no discrete point of origin for this circulation of compassion, social critique, and tolerance.

To offer a working definition of "sympathetic identification," I return to an earlier essay in which I first pondered this concept in relation to literary responses to Anne Frank's diaries. I approached "identification" as a process that cathects us as readers to the worlds unfolded through language, a phenomenon I understand as a kind of feedback loop: "For identification is a complex way of enacting a relationship between ourselves beyond scenes of reading and those selves fashioned out of language looping back to our apprehension of worlds beyond the text" (Bernstein, "Promiscuous Reading," 146). Where I cautioned against "promiscuous" reading as if we could fully enter into Frank's experience, I suggested instead a mindfulness about "dissonant" identification, or the limitations of such engaged reading. Yet, as many others have noted, sympathetic identification can also be a powerful social tool to promote affective connections that may have contingent political effects. Rather than the distant and necessarily superior stance of pity toward another, sympathy suggests a shared affective connection, or the ability to imaginatively enter into someone's suffering by suturing together related representations, whether ones remembered from one's own history, or other accounts read, seen, or heard. Transatlantic sympathetic identification highlights the kinds of distances that such imaginative links might productively narrow.

For instance, we know that *Uncle Tom's Cabin* had a tremendous readership in Britain, from its first reprintings and pirated editions in 1852. And we know that Dickens, Eliot, and Gaskell responded in their writing to Stowe's rousing call for the privileged to act with compassion toward their human brothers and sisters across social divisions. Stowe's Eliza, fleeing the slave catcher who pursues her with her child in her arms across the ice floes on the Ohio River, became a legendary figure, represented frequently in illustrations and separate plates, in British publications, and even brought forward into the reimagined Broadway and Hollywood versions in *The King and I* (1951, 1956). The most potent source of sympathetic identification in *Uncle Tom's Cabin* revolves around several horrific instances of mothers and children separated by death or slavery, like the story of Lucy who drowns herself after learning that her child has been sold to another trader while she sleeps (ch. 12). Stowe's maternal grief and despair can be traced to other precedents.

One powerful companion tale is Elizabeth Barrett Browning's "The Runaway Slave at Pilgrim's Point," a narrative poem of a slave who is raped, beaten for bearing a white child as a result of that violation, and then commits infanticide to spare her child the horrors of a life of servitude. The poem's power in part derives from the speaker's address to "pilgrim-souls" who had once fled across the ocean for religious freedom, while now this bondaged mother escapes "the whips of one / Who in your names works sin and woe" ("Runaway," lines 13–14). The poem also delivers a graphic depiction of the mother's infanticide, a desperate act of compassion for a child whose death is preferable to a destiny of slavery. This murder of mercy through suffocation occupies several stanzas, culminating with:

> And he moaned and trembled from foot to head,
> He shivered from head to foot;
> Till, after a time, he lay instead
> Too suddenly still and mute.   (lines 148–51)

The origins of this poem crossed the ocean, if scholars are correct that her cousin Richard Barrett, a speaker in Jamaica's House of Assembly, had provided the poet with an account of a Jamaican fugitive slave.[1] If the idea for the poem was sparked by the poet's familial ties to slaveholders in Jamaica before abolition across the British Empire in 1834, how did the poem itself move westward across the Atlantic? How would Stowe, whose novel capitalizes on sympathetic identification of bereaved mothers across racial divisions, have encountered this exquisitely painful poem?

"The Runaway Slave" was commissioned by *The Liberty Bell* (1839–58), an abolitionist magazine edited by a Boston woman's antislavery league for its special holiday edition in December 1847. Although this was a commission for a prominent British poet's work for an American audience, EBB's[2] attention to the plight of fugitive slaves may have been encouraged by the *Narrative of the Life of Frederick Douglass*, first published in 1845 with a reprint in Dublin later the same year which was widely distributed and read across Great Britain. If EBB did not read Douglass's account of slavery and flight, she surely happened upon the reviews that populated British periodicals.[3] Early in one of these reviews, the writer accounts how Douglass's father was "the white proprietor of the estate" where his mother was enslaved, and that following his birth he was "hired out to a planter." The article immediately conveys how the institution of bondage perverts or severs the bond between mother and child. The reviewer records how Douglass as a young child

> only saw her occasionally at night, when she could steal away to visit him for a brief space, in order to be back before sunrise, whipping being the penalty of any such unauthorised absence. The strength of the maternal feelings may be judged from the fact of these visits to see her child. She would lie down and clasp him to her bosom for an hour or two, and then depart long ere daybreak to renew her labour in the fields. The poor woman died when her boy was seven years old, and it was long before he knew anything about it.
>
> ("Narrative of Frederick Douglass," 56)

This emphasis on the "strength of maternal feelings" elicits the sympathetic identification that both EBB and Stowe transformed and circulated across genres around the Atlantic Rim, from Douglass's autobiography, to poetry, to fiction. Stowe's rousing call in the finale of *Uncle Tom's Cabin* to "mothers of America" – a figure elaborated upon throughout the novel and spotlighted several times in its conclusion – is but a piece in a long intertextual fabric of appeals rooted in sympathetic identification through "strength of maternal feelings."

In recent decades, scholars have begun to explore some of these surprising transatlantic print circulations, and their discoveries have provided stimulating evidence of an Anglo-American discourse of sympathy as a strategy for prompting interrelated acts of social reform. Marjorie Stone has explicitly linked "The Runaway Slave at Pilgrim's Point" with other abolitionist poetry and articles in issues of *The Liberty Bell* which EBB had received as autographed presentation copies from the Boston Female Anti-Slavery Society that produced the annual issue sold at its Christmas bazaar (Stone, "Elizabeth Barrett Browning," 39). The range of poetry, articles, and stories about American slavery that appeared in the annual magazine in the years while EBB was composing and revising "The Runaway Slave" provides a context for understanding how a British woman poet and daughter of a Jamaican slaveholder wrote a poem about rape and flogging, rebellion and infanticide. The writers EBB encountered in these pages were both British and American, women and men, black and white: Frederick Douglass, Lydia Maria Child, James Russell Lowell, William Lloyd Garrison, Harriet Martineau, and Elizabeth Pease. Martineau had established herself in the transatlantic abolitionist network through her American travels in 1834–6 and in her 1840 publication, *The Martyr Age of the United States*, in which she championed white abolitionists from Garrison to Maria Weston Chapman, editor of *The Liberty Bell*. As for EBB's knowledge of Douglass's first slave narrative of 1845, with its repeated images of families torn apart and scattered, although there is no explicit indication that the British poet read Douglass's book, there is sufficient evidence that she wrote the poem throughout the year 1846 (Stone, "Elizabeth Barrett Browning," 35) when Douglass himself traveled throughout Ireland, Scotland, and England, when he delivered speeches in the wake of the publication, and when his book was reviewed in leading British journals.

Just as Douglass achieved transatlantic notice for his 1845 narrative, EBB's 1844 *Poems* did much the same for her reputation in the United States, where it appeared the same year under the title *A Drama of Exile: and Other Poems*. As the leading woman poet of the Anglophone world, then, it is not surprising that Chapman and other women abolitionists commissioned EBB to write for *The Liberty Bell*, yet it is crucial to note the varied and multidirectional sources of her inspiration. By the same token, EBB's later collections also juxtaposed the social wrongs of American slavery and the oppression of poor children working in British factories: her 1850 *Poems* placed "The Runaway Slave" next to "The Cry of the Children" (Stone, "Elizabeth Barrett Browning," 47). Indeed, it is too narrow to claim that Stowe may have been inspired by EBB's "Runaway Slave" or that EBB was roused by Douglass's publication. "The Cry of the Children," first printed in *Blackwood's Edinburgh Journal* in August 1843, proved the efficacy of this style of sympathetic identification. Implicating factory owners and legislators for responsibility in the sufferings of child laborers, the poem opens with the powerlessness of their mothers:

> Do ye hear the children weeping, O my brothers,
> Ere the sorrow comes with years?
> They are leaning their young heads against their mothers,
> And *that* cannot stop their tears.   (lines 1–4)

This poem increased public outcry against child labor and resulted in improved working conditions under the 1844 Labour in Factories Act, which restricted the work day of women and children to ten hours. Within nine months, the poem appeared, reprinted from *Blackwood's*, in an American periodical.[4] When both poems appeared in her 1850 collection *Poems*, EBB switched the chronology of the compositions and positioned "The Cry" immediately after "The Runaway Slave" so that the arrangement would, as she put it, "appear impartial as to national grievances."[5] The project of sympathetic identification cut across experiences of gender, race, class, and nation, often revolving around the anguish of mothers for the varied afflictions of children under different forms of oppression and injustice. Although EBB published over a dozen poems in the New York paper *The Independent* (1848–1921), she did not supply the journal with their request for a story in prose about Italian liberation (Chapman, "'Vulgar Needs'," 73, 89). Yet the placement of her own poems on the Risorgimento cemented the association between American bondage and Italian oppression too, expanding the network of sympathy across the Atlantic to Britain and Italy.

If the spatial trajectory of a transatlantic "vision of human claims" has no single geographical origin, the temporal route of influence is equally difficult to fasten. Some scholars, like Tricia Lootens, dip back into earlier decades of the nineteenth century to demonstrate these transatlantic literary passages of sympathy and compassion by women writers. British Romantic poet Felicia Hemans's "Landing of the Pilgrim Fathers in New England," which appeared in the *New Monthly Magazine* in November 1825, was quickly reissued in book form in the United States and even anthologized in *The Best Loved Poems of the American People* over a century later (Lootens, "States of Exile," 16). "Landing" foregrounds the experience of pilgrims as aliens from elsewhere seeking a new homeland. Yet the poem's colonists assert what Lootens calls an "aggressive apologia" (26) by claiming to American Indians, "See how we, not you, finally render this land fertile." In this way, as Lootens shows us, "Landing" opens up space for the "Pilgrim Fathers" as participants in the dispossession of subject peoples, and it complicates the construction of transnational sentimentality and sympathy as selective and partial.

Where Lootens considers the subdued or insinuated traces of colonized Native Americans in a British woman's poem, Kate Flint's *The Transatlantic Indian* takes this figure as the subject of her study of imaginative renderings in Anglo-American print culture. Recasting Paul Gilroy's 1993 groundbreaking work, Flint extends this scholarly journey into what she calls "the Red Atlantic." The chief focus of *The Transatlantic Indian* is the array of complex circulations of the American Indian in British culture of the nineteenth century, from canonical writers like Hemans, Dickens, Eliot, and Gaskell, to memoirs, biographies, poems, paintings, journalism, and travel writing by, as one example, Nahnebahwequay, also named "Catherine Sutton" and "Nahnee," a Credit Indian who appealed to Queen Victoria in her poems and in person for Indian land rights in Canada (*The Transatlantic Indian*, 269–75).

Of particular interest to us, Flint includes a chapter titled "Sentiment and Anger: British Women Writers and Native Americans," in which she examines the uses of representations of Native Americans in Charlotte Brontë's *Shirley* (1849), Hemans's poems, Frances Trollope's novel *The Old World and the New* (1849), Eliza Cook's poem "Song of the Red Indian," and Emily Pfeiffer's poem "Red or White?" Flint demonstrates the range of sentiment and sympathy as "tools of personal, and national, literary advancement" (89) surrounding the American Indian through British women's eyes across the century. Pfeiffer's late Victorian poem, from her 1889 collection *Flowers of the Night*, assails the logic behind the displacement and dispossession of Native Americans, and juxtaposes "territorial ambitions and racial arrogance" of both American colonialism and British imperialism (110). In another chapter, "Indians and the Politics of Gender," Flint shows how British women writers employed American Indians to spotlight gender oppression. Gaskell's short story "Lois the Witch," set in Puritan New England of 1691 and published in 1859, offers a tale about an English woman settler who obtains native knowledge through a servant in her uncle's Salem home, an elderly Indian woman called Nattee, a name echoing Cooper's celebrated pioneer Natty Bumppo. For her first fiction publications that appeared in *Howitt's Journal* in 1847–8, Gaskell used the pen name "Cotton Mather Mills," also the name of a Puritan minister who knew some of the judges in the Salem witch trials (180). Although Flint's primary interest in *The Transatlantic Indian* is from the eastern shores of the ocean, she does situate British constructions of American subject peoples through some of the American counterparts that also circulated in Britain, from Lydia Maria Child's *Hobomok* (1824) and Cooper's *The Last of the Mohicans* (1826) to Longfellow's *The Song of Hiawatha* (1855). Flint demonstrates with compelling and fresh evidence that British women writers were avid transatlantic readers.

This transnational "vision of human claims" sometimes produced startling trajectories of inspiration. If scholars have been attuned to the language of slavery and bondage that punctuates *Jane Eyre* (1847), only recently has circumstantial evidence emerged to link Frederick Douglass's 1845 slave narrative with Charlotte Brontë's novel of female empowerment. Julia Sun-Joo

Lee assembles the historical details that support this alignment, and so she asserts, "I would go so far as to argue that *Jane Eyre* can be read as Brontë's revision of Douglass's narrative, with the white English governess uncannily paralleling the emancipatory quest of an American fugitive slave" ("The [Slave] Narrative of *Jane Eyre*," 318). Although Jamaica has a cameo role in the back story of Rochester's money through colonial property, Bertha Mason Rochester figures as the novel's powerful "portable property," the mad wife whom Rochester transported across the Atlantic and lodged in the attic of Thornfield. Lee also links Gaskell's short fiction "The Grey Woman," first published in London in 1861, with Harriet Jacobs's *Incidents in the Life of a Slave Girl* (1861) and William and Ellen Crafts's *Running a Thousand Miles to Freedom* (1860). Speculating that Gaskell may have met Jacobs during Jacobs's second trip to England in 1859, Lee argues that "The Grey Woman," although set in revolutionary France, recycles plights of American female slaves subject to sexual abuse and maternal estrangement (*American Slave*, 78–9). To complement Lee's work, we might consider Jacobs's slave narrative in its transatlantic traffic and reception since the book was published in London in 1862 under the title *The Deeper Wrong; or, Incidents in the Life of a Slave Girl*. In this light, Linda Brent's address to "ye free men and women of the north" (*Incidents*, 28) might have a more expansive range including British readers.

Where Brontë's attention to slavery as metaphor for female oppression in *Jane Eyre* likely seems motivated by Douglass's circulation in person and print in Britain just before she wrote the novel, for Jacobs *Jane Eyre* may have served as a model.[6] In *Subjects of Slavery, Agents of Change*, Kari Winter has elaborated on resemblances between Bertha Mason's attic imprisonment and Jacobs's hiding from slave owners. However we trace these networks of intertextuality, crosscurrents in many directions attest to a robust transnational reading community attuned to the distress of subjugated peoples, with women and children often the focus of vulnerability and abuse. John Plotz's *Portable Property*, a study of cultural portability, theorizes moveable objects, especially the novel, with dual properties of literal and metaphorical circulations, material form and verbal content. By the same token, we can trace the circulating networks of social problems in which sympathizing "human claims" unfold in nineteenth-century Anglo-American literature.

Although slave narratives clearly were circulated and imaginatively assimilated into EBB's poems, Brontë's novel, and Gaskell's story, to name three of many such nodes in the transatlantic print network, no American writer demonstrates this reach as profoundly as Harriet Beecher Stowe. *Uncle Tom's*

Cabin, serialized in *The National Era* in 1851–2, became the most celebrated abolitionist novel on both sides of the ocean; her repeated use of bondswomen ripped apart from their children and subject to sexual violence, along with the pathos of death of the virtuous white child Evangeline, ignited a firestorm. Stowe appealed to readers implicitly through harrowing incidents and explicitly with reflexive appeals such as this one in the novel's conclusion: "and you, mothers of America, is this a thing to be defended, sympathized with, passed over in silence?" (*Uncle Tom's Cabin*, 384).

Stowe's influence on British women writers has been well documented. For instance, Monika Mueller devotes a chapter in her book *George Eliot US: Transatlantic Literary and Cultural Perspectives* to Eliot's *Daniel Deronda* and its "quite a few affinities with contemporaneous American literature," ties that are most evident with Stowe's novels about race, *Uncle Tom's Cabin* and *Dred* (151). Mueller is less interested in the proliferations of transatlantic literary traffic than in how Eliot's speculations about national identity in her last novel both borrow and depart from Stowe's construction of race. As a whole, Mueller's study traces the bilateral reverberations of Eliot's novels and American literature. Jennifer Cognard-Black likewise places Eliot in the company of Stowe and Elizabeth Stuart Phelps to investigate "Victorian professionalism and feminine aesthetics" (*Novel of Purpose*, 4). Interested in the narratives of women as artists, Cognard-Black includes these writers together because of their prominence and correspondence with each other. Taking a different tack is Audrey Fisch's *American Slaves in Victorian England*, a study that attempts to gauge the huge cultural impact of Stowe's abolitionist fiction. Like Claybaugh's interest in social reform across Anglo-American print, Fisch looks to the fascination with American slavery in British popular culture, with attention to what the *Spectator* dubbed "Uncle Tom-mania" as many pirated versions of Stowe's novel were sold in Britain along with various other commodities such as songbooks, wallpaper, Topsy dolls, card games, paintings, and traveling performances of scenes from the novel (13). As Fisch documents, this industry of Tom-mania products merged politics and capitalism together; even so, the British press effused over the ubiquitous emotional punch of Stowe's story: "In the palace, the mansion, and the cottage, it has riveted attention. The sons of toil as well as the children of opulence have wept over its pages," wrote a reviewer in the *Eclectic Review* (quoted in Fisch, *American Slaves in Victorian England*, 14).

For many writers around the Atlantic Rim, Stowe's fiction offered one of many imaginative touchstones for a transnational trajectory of promoting sympathetic identification through literature. As I have shown, Stowe's abolitionist novels cannot be the singular source, but a flashpoint in this proliferating process of print, reading, and feeling. Eliot had reviewed *Dred* in the *Westminster Review* (1824–1914), the periodical she edited in the 1850s when *Uncle Tom's Cabin* and Stowe herself made such a spectacular entry into British print culture and Britain through her lecture tours. Although Stowe and Eliot never did meet in person, they corresponded for a decade. In *Westminster's* column "Belles Lettres," Eliot in 1856 introduces Stowe's *Dred* by underscoring the affective accent of sympathetic identification: "At length we have Mrs. Stowe's new novel, and for the last three weeks there have been men, women, and children reading it with rapt attention – laughing and sobbing over it . . . and glowing with indignation at its terrible representation of chartered barbarities" ("Belles Lettres," 571). Referring to Stowe's "genius," Eliot concludes that Stowe "attains her finest dramatic effects by means of her energetic sympathy" (574). The same year in which she reviewed *Dred*, Eliot contributed two reviews to the journal in which she articulated what became her trademark genre of psychological realism. Read in the context of her review of Stowe's novel, Eliot's call for a new art form, something she began to practice a few months later when she published her first fiction, seems to emerge from a transatlantic engagement. In "The Natural History of German Life," Eliot asserts, "Art is the nearest thing to life; it is a mode of amplifying experience and extending our contact with our fellow-men beyond the bounds of our personal lot" (54). Whether Eliot formulated her theory of realism as a consequence of her transnational reading, including Stowe, the connection is evident in her pronouncement in this essay:

> The greatest benefit we owe to the artist, whether painter, poet, or novelist, is the extension of our sympathies. Appeals founded on generalizations and statistics require a sympathy ready-made, a moral sentiment already in activity; but a picture of human life such as a great artist can give, surprises even the trivial and the selfish into that attention to what is apart from themselves, which may be called the raw material of moral sentiment. (54)

What has become a landmark of Victorian realism, namely Eliot's fiction, was forged through the interplay of her transatlantic and trans-European reading that sparked a commitment to what she later qualifies as the "vision of human claims." Despite such support for the prodigious impact of Stowe's compassionate voice on Eliot's "extension of our sympathies" through "a picture of human life" that stimulates in readers "the raw material of moral sentiment," we must view as a transnational chorus the unfolding of this textual vision encompassing a panoply of human rights that traversed national and oceanic boundaries.

Recently, scholars – using such concepts as the Black Atlantic, hemispheric reading, or the Atlantic Rim – have called for a more fully integrated approach to nineteenth-century literature that truly crosses national and geographical boundaries, just as its initial readers consumed these poems, stories, and novels. Yet the tradition of reading within national borders persists. As Jonathan Elmer has noted, "In the wake of Gilroy, there has of course been a good deal of impressive and original work, but the scope of the task has also resulted in the regular iteration of questions of method that underscore the ways in which we continue to fall short" ("Question of Archive," 252). By tracing both the material circulation of print and by following the reverberations of sympathetic identification that indeed structure nineteenth-century literature of social protest, we too can begin to reformulate how and what we read. I have only grazed the surface of the legions of women writers whose words contributed to this compelling discourse of humanitarian suffering and human rights.

The pathways to this exploration of a ranging reader are multiple, the evidence of transatlantic connections in the nineteenth century ubiquitous and still to be mined. Some crosscurrents may appear obliquely through the paratextual framing of literature. For instance, E. D. E. N. Southworth's novels make manifest the presence of EBB for American women writers through epigraphs from the British poet's verse to chapters in *The Mother-in-Law, or, The Isle of Rays* (1851), *The Lost Heiress* (1854), and *The Missing Bride, or, Miriam the Avenger* (1855). To chart the transatlantic sisterhood voicing of "human claims" here would require juxtaposing the shard of a poem with the fuller narratives of wronged women, often racialized too, like Miriam whose "form and face were of the eastern type" (*The Missing Bride*, 588).

Reading nineteenth-century Anglo-American women writers transatlantically illuminates surprising echoes for us today. A review of Rebecca Harding Davis's *Waiting for the Verdict* (1868), a novel about miscegenation, appeared in the American periodical *The Round Table: A Saturday Review of Politics, Finance, Literature, Society, and Art* (1863–9) in 1867: "Mrs. Davis is one of our most vigorous and thoughtful writers, not only among the best of living American novelists, which is not saying much, but (which is saying a great deal) worthy to tank with that brilliant English sisterhood of talent wherein Mrs. Lewes pre-eminently, and, *longo intervallo*, Mrs. Gaskell, Mrs. Riddell, Miss Thackeray, and Mrs. Edwards are foremost names" ("Reviews: *Waiting for the Verdict*," 433). The reviewer especially aligns Davis and Eliot, and even the use of "Mrs. Lewes," the proper name Eliot preferred but under which she never published in Britain because she and her partner George Henry Lewes were not legally married, is remarkable in this American article.[7] Like Eliot's own identification with Stowe's "vision of human claims," the reviewer affiliates Davis with the most exemplary member of "that brilliant English sisterhood" through the commitment to social redress:

> With Mrs. Lewes, indeed, she seems nearly akin both in the quality of her genius and her intellectual bent. We find in her the same fondness for discussing social problems, the same preference and much of the same skill for portraying the scanty joys and manifold miseries, the fierce unrest and wild temptations of the poor; the same leaning toward the darker side of life and character. (433)

Davis's earlier novel *Life in the Iron Mills* (1861), with its mill worker who constructs a sculpture of a woman out of factory waste, also might be read profitably in relation to Elizabeth Barrett Browning's sonnet, "Hiram Powers' Greek Slave." This statue of the American sculptor Hiram Powers had many transatlantic exhibits including in London in 1845, the same year Douglass and his slave narrative circulated in Britain. In 1847 EBB met Powers in Florence where she viewed the sculpture in his studio. A British art magazine remarks a few years later about Powers's statue exposing the practice of selling female slaves in Turkey, and that the beauty of its form coupled with the degradation of enslavement is meant to appeal "to the sympathies and sensibilities of our nature" ("The Greek Slave," 56). The sonnet first appeared unsigned in Dickens's *Household Words* in October 1850, and it was reprinted five weeks later in the American *International Monthly Magazine of Literature, Science and Art* (1850–2). After the sculpture was displayed at the Crystal Palace Exhibition in London in 1851, a *Punch* cartoon by John Tenniel and titled "The Virginian Slave," offered a parody where the white marble of Powers's nude statue was darkened to suggest an American female slave (Kasson, *Marble Queens*, 65–6). While scholars, such as Joy Kasson in *Marble Queens and Captives: Women in Nineteenth-Century American Sculpture* or Mary Hamer in *Signs of Cleopatra*, have examined representations in visual arts of race and gender, further research of the multiple transatlantic circulations generated by the traveling exhibition of Powers's "Greek Slave" could also align EBB's sonnet of sympathy to "confront men's crimes in different lands" (line 7) with other poems that appeared in the American press. Kasson does begin this work as she points to "the revolutionary implications" (*Marble Queens*, 69, 70) of EBB's poem in the broader scope of her project, representing female bodies in American sculpture. While she does juxtapose Lydia Sigourney's poem, "Powers's Statue of the Greek Slave" (1860) with EBB's sonnet, we might expand significantly on how these poems contribute to a transatlantic "vision of human claims" in multiple directions as they cross borders of nation and genre. Indeed, EBB's 1850 poem, like Powers's sculpture, and Stowe's novel, all qualify as interconnected examples of social protest through – as EBB puts it in the volta of her sonnet – "Art's fiery finger!" (line 9).

Using Claybaugh's Anglo-American world of social reform provides another route for tracking these transatlantic intersections. If EBB's contributions to the Boston Female Anti-Slavery Society, along with all the attention to Stowe's novels across the Atlantic, prompt us to understand this kind of multidirectional movement, there are many other instances in which women appealed to women on the other side of the ocean. British reformer Josephine Butler extended her campaign to end female "white slavery" in her "Appeal to the Women of America" (1888), where she asserts that "thousands" of those sold into sexual slavery are "children in age and knowledge" (18). This document, circulated through the New York publication *The Philanthropist* and pitched to the International Council of Women, asks for political support from American women:

> You in America are happily free from the State regulation of vice; but undoubtedly there is an extensive traffic in white slaves in your midst, and a constant importation of poor foreigners to your shores who are destined to moral and spiritual destruction. I trust you will, from your Congress, put out strong hands for the abolition of this traffic. (17–18)

Much like Stowe did decades earlier, Butler's appeal turns on the human rights of these children, whether living or dead, as "victims, voiceless and unable to plead their own cause, seem to make their ceaseless and mute appeal from their scattered, unknown graves and from out those dark habitations of cruelty where they are now helplessly imprisoned" (20). Butler's transnational activism is but another instance of women converging across the Atlantic through assorted discourses, whether fiction, poetry, or political address, to promote reforms spanning the abolition of black and white slavery to women's suffrage. To knit together in other ways the rhetorical uses of children in ratifying a humanitarian "vision of claims," we might bring into conversation, as another example, Karen Sánchez-Eppler's *Dependent States: The Child's Part in Nineteenth-Century American Culture* with Sally Shuttleworth's *The Mind of the Child: Child Development in Literature, Science, and Medicine, 1840–1900* to bridge the research gap of the Atlantic. By doing so, we can better gauge the affective power of literary children torn from their mother's arms through the auction block, or from life, even by a distraught mother's hand.

Such expansive reading practices stimulate more considerations such as Cecilia Morgan's "question of whose transatlantic world we choose" ("Rethinking Nineteenth-Century Transatlantic Worlds," 258). Elmer raises the difficulty of scope by asking, "Is it possible for a genuinely transatlantic perspective to restrict itself to an Anglophone archive? Can it really neglect the southern hemisphere? Does a transatlantic perspective not risk losing sight of all the stateless actors on the scene?" ("Question of Archive," 252). I am promoting this particular pairing of American and British women writers of the nineteenth century because of the ample evidence that they themselves read and wrote within this transatlantic context that forged "a vision of human claims." This integrated print world facilitates more readily than other creative ways of rendering such visions where emotions affiliated with suffering the loss of a child, say, circulate as common ground despite the gulf of an ocean.

Notes

1.. See the introduction to the poem provided by Stone and Taylor in Barrett Browning *Selected Poems*, 190–2.
2. I follow a convention of using "EBB" for this poet who had published under the names "Elizabeth Barrett Barrett" and, following her marriage in 1846, "Elizabeth Barrett Browning."
3. See, for instance, a review of Douglass's book that appeared in the *Spectator* on November 29, 1845. Other reviews appeared in *Chamber's Edinburgh Journal* on January 24, 1846 and in the *London Journal* on July 17, 1847.
4. "The Cry of the Children" was reprinted in *The Phalanx* (May 4, 1844): 130–1, and again in *New York Evangelist* 16.4 (January 23, 1845): 16.
5. See the head note provided for "The Cry of the Children" by Stone and Taylor in Barrett Browning, *Selected Poems*, 148–50.
6. Lee cites Jean Fagan Yellin's biography in which Yellin notes that *Jane Eyre* was one of the books in the library of the home of Cornelia Grinnel Willis, where Jacobs worked as a nursemaid (*American Slave*, 153 n. 31).
7. Eliot signed herself "M. E. Lewes" in her letter to Stowe about "a vision of human claims."

Works cited

Barrett, Elizabeth B. "The Cry of the Children." *Blackwood's Edinburgh Journal* 54.334 (August 1843): 260–2.

Browning, Elizabeth Barrett. "The Runaway Slave at Pilgrim's Point." In *Elizabeth Barrett Browning: Selected Poems*. Ed. Marjorie Stone and Beverly Taylor. Peterborough, ON: Broadview Press, 2009.

[Browning, Elizabeth Barrett]. "Hiram Power's [*sic*] Greek Slave." *Household Words* 2.31 (October 26, 1850): 99.

"Hiram Powers's Greek Slave." *International Monthly Magazine of Literature, Science and Art* 2.1 (December 1, 1850): 88.

Bernstein, Susan David. "Promiscuous Reading: The Problem of Identification and Anne Frank's Diary." In *Witnessing the Disaster: Essays on Representation and the Holocaust*. Ed. Michael Bernard-Donals and Richard Glejzer. Madison: University of Wisconsin Press, 2003.

Butler, Josephine. *Mrs. Butler's Appeal to the Women of America*. New York: The Philanthropist, 1888.

Chapman, Alison. "'Vulgar Needs': Elizabeth Barrett Browning, Profit, and Literary Value." In *Victorian Literature and Finance*. Ed. Francis O'Gorman. New York and Oxford: Oxford University Press, 2007.

Claybaugh, Amanda. *The Novel of Purpose: Literature and Social Reform in the Anglo-American World*. Ithaca and London: Cornell University Press, 2007.

Cognard-Black, Jennifer. *Narrative in the Professional Age: Transatlantic Readings of Harriet Beecher Stowe, George Eliot, and Elizabeth Stuart Phelps*. New York and London: Routledge, 2004.

Dickens, Charles. "Bleak House Advertiser." *Bleak House* 5 (July 1852): 5.

Elmer, Jonathan. "Question of Archive and Method in Transatlantic Studies." *Victorian Studies* 52.2 (Winter 2010): 249–54.

Eliot, George. "Letter to Mrs. Harriet Beecher Stowe (29 October 1876)." In *George Eliot Letters*. Vol. 6. Ed. Gordon S. Haight. New Haven: Yale University Press, 1954–78.

[Eliot, George]. "Belles Lettres." *Westminster Review* 66.130 (October 1856): 566–82.

"The Natural History of German Life." *Westminster Review* 66.129 (July 1856): 51–79.

Fisch, Audrey A. *American Slaves in Victorian England: Abolitionist Politics in Popular Literature and Culture*. Cambridge: Cambridge University Press, 2000.

Flint, Kate. *The Transatlantic Indian, 1776–1930*. Princeton: Princeton University Press, 2008.

Hamer, Mary. *Signs of Cleopatra: History, Politics, Representation*. London and New York: Routledge, 1993.

Jacobs, Harriet. *Incidents in the Life of a Slave Girl*. Ed. Nellie Y. McKay and Frances Smith Foster. New York: W. W. Norton, 2001.

[Jacobs, Harriet]. *The Deeper Wrong; or, Incidents in the Life of a Slave Girl Written by Herself.* London: W. Tweedie, 1862.

Kasson, Joy S. *Marble Queens and Captives: Women in Nineteenth-Century American Sculpture*. New Haven: Yale University Press, 1990.

Lee, Julia Sun-Joo. "The (Slave) Narrative of *Jane Eyre*." *Victorian Literature and Culture* 36 (2008): 317–29.

The American Slave Narrative and the Victorian Novel. New York and Oxford: Oxford University Press, 2010.

Lootens, Tricia. "States of Exile." In *The Traffic in Poems: Nineteenth-Century Poetry and the Transatlantic Exchange*. Ed. Meredith L. McGill. New Brunswick and London: Rutgers University Press, 2008.

McGill, Meredith L. *American Literature and the Culture of Reprinting, 1834–1853*. Philadelphia: University of Pennsylvania Press, 2003.

Morgan, Cecilia. "Rethinking Nineteenth-Century Transatlantic Worlds: Within and Through 'Indian Eyes.'" *Victorian Studies* 52.2 (Winter 2010): 255–62.

Mueller, Monika. *George Eliot US: Transatlantic Literary and Cultural Perspectives*. Madison and Teaneck: Fairleigh Dickinson University Press, 2005.

Mueller, Monika. "Narrative of Frederick Douglass." *Chambers's Edinburgh Journal* 108 (January 24, 1846): 56–9.

Plotz, John. *Portable Property: Victorian Culture on the Move*. Princeton: Princeton University Press, 2008.

"Reviews: *Waiting for the Verdict*." *The Round Table: A Saturday Review of Politics, Finance, Literature, Society, and Art* 6.153 (December 28, 1867): 433–4.

Sánchez-Eppler, Karen. *Dependent States: The Child's Part in Nineteenth-Century American Culture*. Chicago: University of Chicago Press, 2005.

Shuttleworth, Sally. *The Mind of the Child: Child Development in Literature, Science, and Medicine, 1840–1900*. Oxford and New York: Oxford University Press, 2010.

Sigourney, Lydia. "Powers's Statue of the Greek Slave." In *Poems*. New York: Leavitt and Allen, 1860.

Southworth, Emma Dorothy Eliza Nevitte. *The Missing Bride, or, Miriam the Avenger*. Philadelphia: T. B. Peterson, 1855.

Stone, Marjorie. "Elizabeth Barrett Browning and the Garrisonians: 'The Runaway Slave at Pilgrim's Point,' The Boston Female Anti-Slavery Society, and Abolitionist Discourse in the *Liberty Bell*." In *Victorian Women Poets*. Ed. Alison Chapman. Woodbridge: Boydell and Brewer, 2003.

Stowe, Harriet Beecher. *Uncle Tom's Cabin*. Ed. Elizabeth Ammons. New York: W. W. Norton, 1994.

Tamarkin, Elisa. *Anglophilia: Deference, Devotion, and Antebellum America*. Chicago and London: University of Chicago Press, 2008.

"The Greek Slave." *The Art-Journal* (February 1850): 56.

Winter, Kari J. *Subjects of Slavery, Agents of Change: Women and Power in Gothic Novels and Slave Narratives, 1790–1865*. Athens, GA: University of Georgia Press, 1995.

13

Nineteenth-century African American women writers

JOHN ERNEST

"O, ye daughters of Africa, awake! awake! arise!" (Stewart, *Productions*, 6). So wrote Maria Stewart in an 1831 pamphlet titled *Religion and the Pure Principles of Morality*. Stewart is today celebrated as a pioneering black feminist writer and activist, a woman who not only awoke and arose but also was so critical of African American women and men of her time that she soon found herself frustrated and isolated as a woman who spoke beyond her station in life. After publishing her pamphlet, Stewart presented four lectures in Boston that were then published in white abolitionist William Lloyd Garrison's antislavery newspaper *The Liberator*. Garrison's support aside, Stewart's work did not meet with an especially warm reception, and she soon moved to New York, where she published her complete work, *Productions of Mrs. Maria W. Stewart* (1835) and became a school teacher. Her teaching continued through the Civil War – at that time, located in Washington, DC, and devoted to children of families that had escaped from slavery. Later, she became the matron of the Freedmen's Hospital and Asylum in Washington, DC. Throughout her life, Stewart pressed against the restrictions that African Americans faced in the nineteenth century, and promoted especially the cause, and the responsibilities, of African American women. "How long," she asked, "shall the fair daughters of Africa be compelled to bury their minds and talents beneath a load of iron pots and kettles?" (16). The answer to this question, she believed, depended on the development of a new sense of community and common cause among African Americans. To promote that cause, African American women and men needed to disinter their minds and talents from beneath the racist detritus under which an oppressive culture tried to bury black potential. "The Americans," Stewart wrote, referring to white Americans, "have practiced nothing but head-work these 200 years, and we have done their drudgery. And is it not high time for us to imitate their examples, and practice head-work too, and keep what we have got, and get what we can?" (17). Stewart devoted herself to that head-work and in the process established herself as one of the most important of nineteenth-century African American women writers.

If we take Stewart as a foundational figure among nineteenth-century African American women's writers, how might we characterize the body of work that followed from such efforts? What is it, in other words, that identifies nineteenth-century African American women's writing as a body of work distinct from that produced by other writers at the time – be it the work of white women writers or of African American male writers? Is the history of African American women writers during the 1800s simply a record of publications produced by African American women, or should that history account for the communities of women from which these writers emerged, the "fair daughters of Africa" whose minds and talents remained buried as well as those who devoted themselves to the head-work of writing? As she does in the quotation above, Stewart often chastised her readers for either sustaining or accepting the great discrepancies between white American achievement and black. "I have been taking a survey," she notes at one point, "of the American people in my own mind, and I see them thriving in arts, sciences, and in polite literature. Their highest aim is to excel in political, moral, and religious improvement" (11–12). Stewart understood, of course, that white Americans guarded the access to the venues in which such accomplishments might be pursued and recognized, including the historical record itself. "How very few are there among them," she laments, "that bestow one thought upon the benighted sons and daughters of Africa, who have enriched the soils of America with their tears and blood: few to promote their cause, none to encourage their talents" (12). Still, Stewart is critical of black Americans as well for accepting this state of affairs: "I am rejoiced to reflect that there are many able and talented ones among us, whose names might be recorded on the bright annals of fame. But, '*I can't*' is a great barrier in the way. I hope it will soon be removed, and '*I will*' resume its place" (12).

But while Stewart was addressing an oppressive social system that bound African Americans to the laboring class, she certainly recognized that not all black women who said to themselves and others "I can" and "I will" were interested in the sort of achievements that "might be recorded on the bright annals of fame." Indeed, Stewart argued for the importance of the behind-the-scenes work associated, in the nineteenth century, with women's spheres of influence, with the ideals of womanhood then current in American culture. "Did the daughters of our land possess a delicacy of manners," she asserted, "combined with gentleness and dignity; did their pure minds hold vice in abhorrence and contempt, did they frown when their ears were polluted with its vile accents, would not their influence become powerful?" (7). But would such "daughters of our land" be recorded in the history books – or, more to the point, are they recorded in the writings of nineteenth-century African American women writers? Are African American women writers of the nineteenth century to be appreciated primarily for their ability to beat the odds and produce lasting works of literature, or are they to be appreciated as writers who give voice to African American women – a collective shaped and affiliated by similar conditions and experiences? Is the body of writing they produced a tradition of exceptional or of representative women? What history do we find recorded in the poems, pamphlets, orations, and books they produced, and how should we approach their work to determine any significant tradition of nineteenth-century African American women writers?

Too often, the history we look for in the literature is that which we already knew, so that the individual literary text does more to confirm than to expand or revise our historical understanding, beyond identifying women who distinguished themselves. By and large, the histories of African American women produced thus far have identified those who wrote and published as exceptional women – albeit women whose writings offer a glimpse into the experiences and perspectives unique to African American women. Texts are read within the context of historical scholarship on African American women, and African American women writers are presented, much like I present Maria Stewart above, as commentators on that history or as pioneers struggling towards new historical possibilities. But something is lost in the negotiation of the relation between text and context. Part of the problem, of course, is that we still know relatively little about black women's history beyond the levels of event and experience – that is, we lack a strong understanding of the range and diversity of the black women's perspectives on history or of their historical consciousness. Some time ago, Cheryl Townsend Gilkes looked back on James Harvey Robinson's comment that "history books are a poor place to look for history," adding that history books are "an even poorer place to search for African-American history and African-American women's history" ("The Politics of 'Silence',"107). With some notable exceptions, Gilkes's judgment is still sound.[1] But even beyond the misrepresentations and omissions that have defined black women's place in a great deal of historical scholarship, we can hardly claim an understanding of nineteenth-century African American women until we have some sense of how they themselves contended with fundamental challenges in understanding historical process and agency. This is the subject of this chapter – the ways in which African American women who were under the radar of the protocols of historical notice defined the terms of historical agency and significance. My central claim is that *the context is in the text* – that the texts produced by African American women are best understood as operating within a historical realm that can be accessed only by way of these texts. When African American women writers looked back to gather experience into workable narratives, they represented, often scrupulously, the conditions, the ideological frameworks, and the perspectival dynamics of African American women's experience that make of their combined writings a distinct, and highly accomplished, literary tradition, a tradition that is less exceptional than representative of African American women's history generally.

Part of the challenge of approaching the history both in and of nineteenth-century African American women's writing is that, by the usual standards, so much of it seems uncrafted. Indeed, very few literary critics have treated the writings produced by nineteenth-century African American women as great literary achievements.[2] Of course, much the same could be said of the critical response to American women's writing generally, but the problems are especially pronounced concerning the black literary tradition, for very few scholars have read even a bare majority of the texts published by nineteenth-century African American writers. The relatively few African American women writers of the 1800s who have risen to sustained critical notice passed first through a period in which the literary quality of their work was questioned. Scholars have pronounced, sometimes in print and often in conversation, Harriet Wilson's *Our Nig* a subliterary text or certain autobiographical narratives woefully uncrafted, and some have felt obligated to ask of Frances E. W. Harper's *Iola Leroy* and other texts, "Is it good enough to read?"[3] Indeed, for many readers even of those few texts that have received significant critical notice, what makes the early writers representative of African American women generally are the conditions under which they lived – and what makes them remarkable is that they reached a level of achievement that meets the standards even of those who have enjoyed the benefits of education and a privileged life. As John Reilly observed in 1986, "Despite other variety, the most prevalent assumption among those who think about Afro-American literary history – whether in articles, books, or classroom presentations – is that the success of literature can be discerned in its utility as social documentation, an assumption to which is sometimes joined severe judgment of works composed, it is presumed, before Afro-American authors had the option to choose art over combative writing. In other words, works of literature are dissolved into their referents" ("History-Making Literature," 89). In effect, many scholars of this literature have at least started – and for many writers, have continued – to judge this work in much the same way that Harriet Jacobs, in her pseudonym as Linda Jacobs, asks white readers to judge her character in *Incidents in the Life of a Slave Girl*. Commenting on her decision to take a white lover, Brent states, "I know I did wrong," but adds, "I feel that the slave woman ought not to be judged by the same standards as others" (*Incidents*, 56). In much the same way many texts produced by African American women writers of the 1800s (with Jacobs's *Incidents* a notable exception) are judged – that is, viewed as failing to meet certain standards of literary elegance, craft, or even coherence, but understandably so.

But perhaps what is needed is not to avoid the process that Reilly describes but rather to extend it – that is, to identify the referents of these works of literature so as to understand the crafted response to those referents that reveals these texts to be accomplished literary performances. Perhaps the artistry of nineteenth-century black women's writings is not simply a veil under which might be found the events or attitudes of a familiar if incomplete history; perhaps instead the artistry of these texts captures the dynamics of black women's interactions with their social and cultural environment, the means by which they asserted control over a world that defined and delimited the significance of their lives, the acts by which they responded to the pressures of their position as women and as African Americans so as to (re)create themselves as *African American women*. Instead of listening to, say, Miles Davis performing "Surrey with the Fringe on Top" and concluding that he has a poor sense of melody and structure compared to those who starred in Rodgers and Hammerstein's musical, perhaps we should consider that there is something significant both in Davis's choice of this song and in his jazz rendering of it. Similarly, we should be open to a range of performative strategies and techniques when we attend to the ways in which African American women addressed the structured social order that threatened to contain and define them, a world that other writers might address in more familiarly structured ways.

In searching for this more dynamic literary history, the history of improvisations within and on delimited spheres of engagement, one should of course begin by questioning the implicit homogeneity in the category of African American women's writing so as to identify the terms of commonality in the great diversity of writings African American women produced. African American women writers of the nineteenth century emerged from different regions, different backgrounds (including that most determining of differences, slave and free), different social classes, and different literary backgrounds, and in some cases they operated within different forums for defining the purpose and audiences of their writings. By accounting for that diversity, we might be able to identify common artistic gestures, a developing library of improvisational possibilities, that would help us determine the shared features or family resemblances distinct to African American women's writings.

Perhaps the most basic fact relating to the tradition of African American women writers is the broad range of possible relationships to the pen suggested by the word *writers*, a word that can refer, at one end of the spectrum, to an ongoing activity that never leads to publication or, at the other end, to ongoing publication and public recognition. Some black women were known as prolific and influential writers in their time – for example, Frances E. W. Harper or Pauline Hopkins, both of whom published numerous texts in various genres over a broad span of time. Others were almost completely unknown, and they are known now only for the singular texts that emerged from their experiences, as is the case with Harriet E. Wilson, whose fictionalized account of her experiences in New Hampshire, *Our Nig: or, Sketches from the Life of a Free Black*, was published virtually unnoticed in 1859; or Ann Plato, whose *Essays; Including Biographies and Miscellaneous Pieces, in Prose and Poetry* (1841) emerged from her experiences as a student in Hartford, Connecticut; or Eliza Potter, whose savvy autobiographical account of her entrepreneurial experience, *A Hairdresser's Experience in High Life*, met with some degree of local notoriety in Cincinnati, Ohio, when it was published in 1859. Elizabeth Keckley also produced a book that was viewed as sensational, but at a national level, when she published her account of her experience as Mary Lincoln's modiste in *Behind the Scenes, or Thirty Years a Slave, and Four Years in the White House* (1868).

Just as the recognition of writers might range from the narrowly local to the national, so African American women wrote from and to a broad geographical range. Some writers emerged from the northeast, the region often taken to be the hub of nineteenth-century African American literary production, but other writers either emerged from or became associated with such western locales as Ohio (the eventual home of magazine editor Julia Ringwood Coston), Illinois (the birthplace of poet, novelist, playwright, essayist Katherine Davis Chapman Tillman), and California (where Jennie Carter wrote for the *San Francisco Elevator*). In many cases, particularly involving slave narratives and other autobiographies, the tests produced by African Americans resist any neat regional identification. After all, many women born in slavery had little hope, before the Civil War, of returning to their homes, and their narratives accordingly take readers on a journey of found homes and essential homelessness, of families lost and communities abandoned, and of families partially reunited and new communities forged. In such narratives, the local, national, and often the international political environments and cultural spheres of influence are in constant interaction, complicating any narrative impulse that might lead simply from slavery to freedom or from one home to the next. In all cases, geography is of signal importance, sometimes demarcating the boundaries of expanding, concentric circles of liberty and possibility – with artistry following the journey so as to map out the topographies of experience and of shifting subjectivity.

And in many texts produced by African American women of the nineteenth century, responding to those shifting contingencies of locale and social environments was the generative impulse of both the actual and the narrative journeys. Some women, for example, wrote specifically to document and promote their religious callings – as in *The Life and Religious Experience of Jarena Lee* (1836); *Memoirs of the Life, Religious Experience, Ministerial Travels and Labors of Mrs. Zilpha Elaw* (1846); and Julia A. J. Foote's *A Brand Plucked from the Fire* (1886). Some wrote specifically in the cause of political activism and social reform, as did Ida B. Wells-Barnett in her series of publications on lynchings and mob rule, including *Southern Horrors: Lynch Law in All Its Phases* (1892) and *A Red Record: Tabulated Statistics and Alleged Causes of Lynchings in the United States* (1895). Some writers offered scholarly commentary on a wide range of subjects, as did Anna Julia Cooper in *A Voice from the South* (1892), and others offered more simple moral tales geared towards families, as did Mrs. A. E. Johnson in such works as *Clarence and Corinne; or, God's Way* (1890).

The community of African American women writers becomes even larger and more complex when we consider the collaborations central to black women's literary activities. It is hard to imagine, for example, any understanding of nineteenth-century African American women's rhetorical power that does not include Sojourner Truth, but Truth herself could not write. Her most famous speeches were preserved by others and her life's story, *Narrative of Sojourner Truth*, was published in parts, the first written by Olive Gilbert and published in 1850 and the second composed (including a selection from other writers) by Frances Titus and published in 1875 and enlarged in 1883. Both Gilbert and Titus were white, as were the writers of other important narratives of black women's lives, including *Louisa Picquet, the Octoroon: A Tale of Southern Slave Life* (1861), *Memoirs of Elleanor Eldridge* (1843), and *Harriet [Tubman]: The Moses of her People*. A more intimate collaboration was that between William and Ellen Craft in William's rendition of their journey to the north and then to England, *Running a Thousand Miles for Freedom; or, The Escape of William and Ellen Craft from Slavery* (1860). Although William assumes authority over the narrative, speaking in the first person and differentiating the narrator's perspective from that of Ellen, still the narrative includes scenes that William did not witness, and readers can easily feel Ellen's presence behind the scenes of every episode. Even the narrative of one of the most celebrated of black women writers, Harriet A. Jacobs's *Incidents in the Life of a Slave Girl* (1861), was produced in collaboration with a white woman, Lydia Maria Child, who edited Jacobs's text. Some of these collaborations were intimate and balanced, others suffered from an unequal distribution of authority joined with cultural biases never noticed by either the white writer or the narrative's white readers. In all cases, the voice of the black female subject, rising from the narrative of a black woman's experience, emerges from the collaboration obscured by cultural static but still strong, a valuable part of the expressive culture of nineteenth-century African American women.

The collaborations central to the production, dissemination, and preservation of texts came to a point in the numerous literary societies and other community associations African Americans formed before the Civil War – organizations whose influence extends throughout the nineteenth century and to our own time. When Sarah Mapps Douglass called for more active participation in antislavery efforts in 1832, she did so before the recently formed Female Literary Society of Philadelphia, addressing her audience as "my sisters." When Maria Stewart announced that same year that "the frowns of the world shall never discourage me," she did so before The Afric-American Female Intelligence Society of America. When Lucy Stanton delivered her 1850 address "A Plea for the Oppressed," she did so as president of the Oberlin Ladies Literary Society. And when Sara G. Stanley spoke before the all-male Convention of Disfranchised Citizens of Ohio in 1856, she did so as a representative of the Ladies Anti-Slavery Society of Delaware, Ohio. Such societies provided a great many African Americans, female and male, with forums for honing their skills as public speakers; they provided access to educational resources for many African American children and adults; and they provided a wide range of communities with the means by which they might *realize* themselves as communities. Some societies were informal groups, and others were highly organized associations; some were large enough to support libraries and reading rooms, while others involved simply choosing a time and place where members could gather to discuss books. Many societies offered a program of lectures at which both members such as Sarah Douglass or important guests could speak to a thoughtful and interested audience – and often these speeches were then published either in supportive newspapers, such as *The Liberator*, or in pamphlets. Indeed, many orations – probably the most central and influential of all African American writings from the nineteenth century – are still available because of literary societies.

When we recognize the importance of such societies to the inspiration and dissemination of black women's literary efforts, we can better identify what it means to talk about African American women's writing. Such organizations were havens for African American women – a refuge from the layered forms of oppression they experienced for their race, gender, and class status in a white supremacist and patriarchal culture. At such societies, women could gather both to discover and define the common experiences and concerns that affiliated them as a group. Rather than accept the broader world's sense of what it means to be black and a woman, they could read and write their way towards individual and collective agency. As Elizabeth McHenry has observed in her authoritative study of African American literary societies, members of women's literary societies could function "alternately as producers, distributors, and consumers of texts whose variety ranged from the religious to the poetic to the political. One self-conscious objective of their reading was to refine their sensibilities by producing emotional expressions of sympathy for those less fortunate. Another was to give active form and voice to the social and historical contexts in which they lived and to their own burgeoning political perspectives" (*Forgotten Readers*, 61). Importantly, these benefits were not necessarily limited to women who could read and write, for readings within and beyond the literary societies could be enjoyed by a broad range of women. Part of what is distinctive about African American women's writing, in other words, has to do with the distinct social and literary environment in which women learned to read, found encouragement and occasion to write, and shared the experience of writing and reading.

African American women's writing, in short, emerged from a wide range of locales, collaborations, and forums, and the history (or histories) of this tradition should similarly be diverse and complex. What connects this body of writing as an identifiable tradition is not biography (much less biology) but rather the experiences shaped by cultural position, the perspectives that result from those experiences, and the rhetorical methods needed to account for lives thus positioned and delimited. Regardless of region or social class, African American women were positioned at birth within certain (limited) spheres of activities, certain social roles, certain realms of possibility that they could imagine for themselves. In a patriarchal and white supremacist world, they did not have the luxury of playing any role they wished to play; and when individual women worked to break beyond their conventional roles, they did not have the luxury of doing so entirely on their own terms. African

American women's history is best understood as the multiple and interrelated stories that emerge from the interplay of experience and perspective, and African American women's writings are the best entrances into that history. What we will find when we enter into this body of writing are histories we have barely begun to recover – not simply events involving black women and stories joining individual women to a generalized collective, but interrelated experiential and perspectival sites that map out the means and effects of black women's agency in the nineteenth century. And because no individual or collective history operates in a vacuum, we will find as well different ways of viewing and understanding the many other histories (of white men, of black men, or white women) related to those of black women. The history we will find, in other words, is not simply the story of what happened to black women in the nineteenth century or the story of what black women did, but rather the story of certain modes of agency in dynamic and contingent interactions with others, and certain ways of understanding the world shaped by those interactions. The history we will find can thus provide us with significantly new ways of approaching not only the past so long ignored but also the past we thought we knew.

Since the history we will find is also one that contains multitudes and great diversity, a case study might be useful for identifying the central questions of this quest. One of the most fundamental, unavoidable challenges faced by African American women writers of the nineteenth century, I am suggesting, was that of relocating themselves historically, away from being historical afterthoughts or side-notes and toward a historical realm in which their experience and agency as black women could be understood and appreciated. Because such work emerges in response to the dynamic contingencies of period and locale, I will devote the rest of this chapter to a specific field of such efforts – African American women's attempts to (re)locate themselves historically in autobiographical writing after the Civil War. Certainly, such relocations were needed. As Elizabeth Young has argued, "black men's representations of the Civil War conformed to what Patricia Morton has analyzed as the primary project of black historiography in this period, that of 'restoring black men to a man's world'" (*Disarming the Nation*, 198). Examining a wide range of women's writings from and about the Civil War, Young observes that "for black women writers excluded from national discourse by virtue of both race and gender, 'civil wars' involve battling not only the dominant national culture but also alternative iconographies – including those constructed by white women and African-American men – that would exclude them as well" (111). Indeed, the last four decades of the nineteenth century in many ways constituted a golden age of African American historical writing, much of which positioned, implicitly or explicitly, black men as the primary agents of African American collective self-determination. Of the many important African American military, religious, and social histories and collective biographies published during this time, very few locate black women at the center of historical struggle and advance, the most prominent examples of which are Monroe Adolphus Majors's *Noted Negro Women: Their Triumphs and Activities* (1893), Lawson Andrews Scruggs's *Women of Distinction: Remarkable in Works and Invincible in Character* (1893), and Gertrude Mossell's *The Work of the Afro-American Woman* (1894).

I will focus in the remaining pages on four autobiographies that address different historical situations and possibilities, in terms of both historical time and social space: *The Story of Mattie J. Jackson* (1866), Elizabeth Keckley's *Behind the Scenes* (1868), Lucy A. Delaney's *From the Darkness Cometh the Light or Struggles for Freedom* (c.1891), and Kate Drumgoold's *A Slave Girl's Story; Being an Autobiography of Kate Drumgoold* (1898). Jackson (c.1846–?) was born in slavery in St. Louis, Missouri sometime around 1846. Her mother had seen two husbands escape from slavery, but could not manage it herself with her children, despite various attempts. Mattie managed to escape in 1863, and her mother, sister, and half-brother soon followed, though they were never able to locate her sister afterwards. After the Civil War, Mattie and her mother returned to St. Louis, and her mother remarried. Eventually, her mother's second husband discovered his former family and invited Mattie and her half-brother to join him in Lawrence, Massachusetts, where he lived with his new wife. Keckley (c.1818–1907), easily the most famous of the four writers, tells the story that led her from a life in slavery in Dinwiddie County, Virginia, to a successful career as a dressmaker to, eventually, a life in the White House, where she served as modiste to Mrs. Lincoln. Delaney (1830?–c.1890s) tells the story of her mother's legal attempts to establish her status as a free woman in St. Louis, Missouri, and then the story of her life following her and her mother's successful suits. Drumgoold (c.1858–?) tells the story of her enslavement in Virginia, her eventual education at Wayland Seminary in Washington, DC and in Harpers Ferry, West Virginia, and her subsequent life as an educator. I cannot provide definitive birth and death dates for three of these women. Keckley has received the most attention from scholars, and Eric Gardner has done archival work on Delaney that gives us more insight on her life than Delaney herself provides, but Jackson and Drumgoold remain known only through the autobiographies they left behind.

Yet the four narratives together offer an outline of a history beyond the assumed certainties of biography. Together, the four autobiographies range from the 1860s to the end of the century, from slavery and the Civil War to the post-Reconstruction era, from Brooklyn to West Virginia, Washington, DC, to Illinois, though with strong St. Louis ties, and from a "slave mother's house" to the White House. The authors were born in different times, ranging from 1818 to 1856, and they had vastly different experiences, drawing us into the law, dressmaking, and teaching, among many other concerns. In many ways, these narratives demand that we attend to Laura Edwards's warning, in her important study of the "gendered strife and confusion" that attended Reconstruction, that "rooted in middle-class culture, notions of sharply differentiated spheres of life inevitably misrepresent the ways African Americans, other ethnic groups, and working-class whites organized their worlds" (*Gendered Strife and Confusion*, 6). Examining a more complicated configuration of differentiated spheres, I want to explore the ways in which these women organized their worlds through narrative self-representation – all of them following the advice of Mattie Jackson and her black female narrative collaborator Dr. L. S. Thompson: "Manage your own secrets, and divulge them by the silent language of your own pen" (*The Story of Mattie Jackson*, 29). Addressing these writers' narrative strategies for "organizing their worlds" by differentiating among different levels and understandings of historical process, I want to look at the rhetorical devices by which "the silent language" of an alternative model of history, one centered on black women's experience, is represented as the historical understanding that encompasses all others.

All four narratives deal with the Civil War, so it is perhaps inevitable that black and white masculine history plays a prominent role in each text. Delaney's, for example, is dedicated to "The Grand Army of the Republic." Jackson writes about Lincoln, by whose "martyred blood" the enslaved had been set free, and includes a poem on Lincoln's death, and Keckley refers to Lincoln as Moses, an idol, and a demi-god (Thompson, *The Story of Mattie Jackson*, 30; Keckley, *Behind the Scenes*, 140–1). Drumgoold offers "three cheers for this great Emancipator" (*A Slave Girl's Story*, 35), and follows with praise for a gathering of men, including John Brown, Ulysses S. Grant, "Father Charles Sumner," and Frederick Douglass. And both Keckley and Delaney reserve some of their highest and most poetic rhetoric for those moments when they address the Civil War. "Oh, the front," Keckley writes, "with its stirring battle-scenes! Yes! oh, the front, with its ghastly heaps of dead!" (*Behind the Scenes*, 66). Delaney echoes, "The river of tears shed by us helpless ones, in captivity, were turned to lakes of blood! How often have we cried in our anguish, 'Oh! Lord, how long, how long?' But the handwriting was on the wall, and tardy justice came at last and avenged the woes of an oppressed race!" (*From the Darkness*, 14–15). The rhetoric of such moments, joined with expressions of profound gratitude and loss, draws into these narratives a "great man" approach to history, the masculine struggle of war by which a river of tears is channeled into lakes of blood, the history inscribed on the memory of great leaders and the untold numbers of men who joined the ghastly heaps of dead on the front lines of battle. Where, then, does the story of a black woman fit into this grand story, and what chance might she have of shifting or even expanding the narrative priorities that she herself endorses?

In many ways, the claims these women make for their autobiographical productions are quite modest. Jackson, for example, expresses her desire to "gain sympathy from the earnest friends of those who have been bound down by a dominant race in circumstances over which they had no control," adding that in the wake of "our beloved martyr President Lincoln," she feels "a duty to improve the mind" and thus publishes her story to raise funds for her education (*The Story of Mattie Jackson*, 3). Keckley's motives for publishing her book were, of course, controversial, though she still presents the book as an essentially private story. In her defense, she states, "Had Mrs. Lincoln's acts never become public property, I should not have published to the world the secret chapters of her life" (*Behind the Scenes*, 7), but more interesting is her attention to the actual writing of the narrative. Bringing us to the scene of writing, she states, "As I sit alone in my room, my brain is busy, and a rapidly moving panorama brings scene after scene before me, some pleasant and others sad; and when I thus greet old familiar faces, I often find myself wondering if I am not living the past over again. The visions are so terribly distinct that I almost imagine them to be real" (9). We enter not only her room but her consciousness, a consciousness altered by memories, and she returns us to this intensely private scene at the narrative's end. Delaney apologizes for any "want of unity or coherence" in her narrative, and she presents her own role in the larger historical story as decidedly small, suggesting that "although we are each but atoms, it must be remembered, that we assist in making the grand total of all history, and therefore are excusable in making our affairs of importance to ourselves, and endeavoring to impress them on others" (*From the Darkness*, viii). Drumgoold, like Jackson, devotes her story to the privileged who have been and remain in a position to help those less fortunate, stating, "This sketch is written for the good of those that have written and prayed that the slaves might be a freed people, and have schools and books to learn to read and write for themselves" (*A Slave Girl's Story*, 3). But she also invokes the presence of God in these affairs, asserting that African Americans have "ever found favor in His sight," and that God intervened in human events to deliver the enslaved "out of the Land of Egypt" (3). Drumgoold's point here, of course, is that there is a larger historical process to consider, the course of divine providence, and it is not saying too much to suggest that she presents the oppressed as the driving force of that larger process, which is a common thread in all four narratives.

To a great extent, these stories operate in that providential realm, and in a historical process where infinitesimal atoms discover their essential role in the progress toward a more just world. Jackson, for example, makes a point of quoting her mistress's response to Lincoln and race: "I think it has come to a pretty pass, that old Lincoln, with his long legs, an old rail splitter, wishes to put the Niggers on an equality with the whites; that her children should never be on an equal footing with a Nigger. She had rather see them dead" (Thompson, *The Story of Mattie Jackson*, 14). In its shift from first- to third-person address, this quotation accounts for Jackson's mediation in relating these events, her presence in this scene, preparing us for the sequel to this incident some twenty pages later. "My mother," Jackson relates, "met Mrs. Lewis, her old mistress, with a large basket on her arm, trudging to market. It appeared she had lived to see the day when her children had to wait upon themselves, and she likewise." "The Yankees," Jackson adds, "had taken possession, and her posterity were on an equality with the black man" (37). The process of history, in effect, has deracialized social positions that are shaped by economics and social power. To be on an equality with the black man, in this case, is simply to feel the effects of poverty and disempowerment. The perfect justice of these joined episodes sets the tone for the penultimate chapter of Jackson's account, the chapter titled "Summary" that precedes the chapter titled "Christianity," a chapter on worldly justice leading into one on its providential framework. This dynamic is even more pronounced in Drumgoold's narrative. Drumgoold, like Jackson, was hoping to sell books for self-support, and she is most aggressive about her historical importance in her plea for patronage. "Dear public," she states, "I am sure that if you have any love for the God of heaven you can not fail to find a love for this little book, and I hope you will find a fullness of joy in reading this life, for if your heart was like a stone you would like to read this little life" (*A Slave Girl's Story*, 14). Her belief in the compelling interest of the book that she is, at the time of this statement, in the process of writing, is a statement on her importance both morally and historically. "No subject," she states somewhat later in the narrative, "can surely be a more delightful study than the history of a slave girl, and the many things that are linked to this life that man may search and research in the ages to come, and I do not think there ever can be found any that should fill the mind as this book" (24). Few authors feel so assured about the reception and value of their efforts, but in this case the apparent insignificance of the subject is precisely the reason why it should come to be the center of future research.

For each of these writers, Jackson's maxim – "manage your own secrets" – does not simply mean keeping your own secrets, highlighting the second part of Jackson's maxim: "divulge them by the silent language of your own pen" (Thompson, *The Story of Mattie Jackson*, 29). The management here involves controlling the narrative principles by which not only oneself but also one's world might be made visible and valued as a realm of concerns of central importance. Jackson herself is looking to acquire that power – that is, to earn enough money from her book to further her education – but in her narrative, she reveals the principles that will inform her future as a writer. When her mistress leaves a switch for her husband to use on Mattie, Mattie bends the switch in the shape of a W, which, she informs the reader, was the first letter of the mistress's husband's name (15). As DoVeanna Fulton has insightfully observed, the W of the switch is also an inverted M, the first letter of Mattie's name and, therefore, "indicates the power reversal involved in her assertion of agency" (*Speaking Power*, 57). And when she tries to escape, she ties her "whole wardrobe" under her hoop skirt "to hide the fact" from her mistress (Thompson, *The Story of Mattie Jackson*, 27), thereby using the conventions of white women's fashion to enable the priorities of a black woman's agency. Keckley's approach to managing secrets similarly turns tragic realities to pointed commentaries. After a long discussion of the death of the Lincolns' son Willie, including a reprinted poem and a presentation of a tableau of "genius and greatness weeping over love's idol lost" (*Behind the Scenes*, 74), Keckley mentions the death of her own son on the Civil War battlefields in a quick paragraph. Perhaps this sharp contrast is in the background when, later in the narrative, she discusses the early literacy trials of young Tad Lincoln. After a lengthy discussion of Tad's insistence that "A–P–E" spells "monkey," Keckley comments, "Had Tad been a negro boy, not the son of a President, and so difficult to instruct, he would have been called thick-skulled, and would have been held up as an example of the inferiority of the race" (160) – a lesson she underscores by devoting an additional paragraph to bringing home the point. Such lessons in literacy – cultural as well as print – abound in Keckley's narrative, with the tensions between public and private history that have defined the narrative breaking out in the pages of confidential letters and public reports that she includes at the end of her narrative, allowing her world to spell itself out in ways that she has prepared the reader to understand, though Keckley herself makes a point of concluding the narrative in the privacy of the room where she did the writing (235).

Delaney similarly returns the reader to the scene of the narrative's writing, contrasting public history with private. "There are abounding in public and private libraries of all sorts," she states, "lives of people which fill our minds with amazement, admiration, sympathy, and indeed with as many feelings as there are people, so I can scarcely expect that the reader of these episodes of my life will meet with more than a passing interest, but as such I will commend it to your thought for a brief hour" (*From the Darkness*, 61–2). But Delaney expects a lot to happen in that brief hour, and even positions herself as, in effect, a reader of her own narrative – stating at one point, "I seemed to be another person – an onlooker – and in my heart dwelt a pity for the poor, lonely girl, with down-cast face, sitting on the bench apart from anyone else in that noisy room. I found myself wondering where Lucy's mother was, and how she would feel if the trial went against her; I seemed to have lost all feeling about it, but was speculating what Lucy would do, and what her mother would do, if the hand of Fate was raised against poor Lucy!" (47). As with Keckley's private-room viewing of the panorama of her life, we are drawn not just into a life but a state of consciousness, one that models for us the deep emotional and ethical response we should bring to the story. And from that realm, we can envision a different sort of history, as Delaney does when talking of her mother, someone then far from those lives contained in public and private libraries. Speaking of her mother's life and sacrifices, Delaney states, "Never would an ordinary observer connect those virtues with aught of heroism or greatness, but to me they are as bright rays as ever emanated from the lives of the great ones of earth, which are portrayed on historic pages" (51). And in this way her mother's daughter finds her context, for while she ends by disclaiming any thought that we might feel a lasting interest in her story, she adds, "but if this sketch is taken up for just a moment of your life, it may settle the problem in your mind, if not in others, 'Can the negro race succeed, proportionately, as well as the whites, if given the same chance and an equal start?'" (63–4). Not bad work, one might say, for a modest narrative, to settle such a question at one of the most deeply racist times in American history, but it is a problem, Delaney suggests, that will be settled precisely because of the apparent insignificance of her story.

All four writers make a similar case, a similar inversion of the proto-cols of historical recognition. Going out of their way to downplay their significance – even Keckley, who positions herself in a lonely room far from the White House – they argue for the encompassing significance of their stories. I do not mean by this to downplay the more public and recognizably historical achievements of the black women's era, particularly as all four women were involved in or led organizations which were centers of black women's achievements. Instead, I mean to highlight the history that remains beyond the public face of black women's history, the management of secrets by which black women took the experiences that defined black women's cultural and historical positions and argued for an alternative model for evaluating and narrating history. This is the history one encounters in the biblical rhythms of Drumgoold's style, in Keckley's narrative play on the tensions between the private and the public, in the interplay of oral and print modes of narration in Jackson's collaboration with her stepmother, and in Delaney's belief that "the grand total of history" can best be found in atomic fields of energy. This is the history that one encounters in any number of sentences in these narratives – sentences that move from the individual to the divine, from the momentary to the eternal, a comprehensive sweep of contingent historical events in sharp contrast to the scope and pace of the rest of the narrative. In short, this is the history we might discover when we look *at* the narrative form and style of these autobiographies and not *through* them to the facts of an individual life, when we learn not to apologize or make allowances for narrative form and style in these texts but understand that the history we seek is represented in their narrative form, when we read these narratives in search of a poetics of black female experience, consciousness, and affiliation. The history in and of African American women's writing – both the prominent and the obscure – is the foreground of the most visible manifestations of black women's history of this time, the silent and isolated sympathies that led to private and public col-laborations, to club movements and educational activism, church collectives and post-emancipation aid organizations. Through these and other narratives as well as through records of oral culture, perhaps we can follow the process by which women learned to manage the dynamics of historical consciousness by attending to the "silent language" they have inscribed in their life stories.

To piece together an understanding of nineteenth-century African American women's history, I am suggesting, we need to become better readers – readers attentive to the dynamics of the written records of black women's expressive culture. Rather than noting that the artistry we know how to look for is not there, we should read the artistry that connects the rhythm of a narrative to the rhythms of life; that attunes the conventions of ballads and other poetic forms to the distinctive music heard by the black woman as she stands aside from what we have taken to be the main field of action; that gives purpose and point to orations delivered in the ritual discourse of the school-room, the church hall, or the women's literary society; and that negotiates the difficult dynamics of privacy and publicity, submission and transgression, social roles and social activism, so central to black women's lives in the nine-teenth century. By way of case studies, of the kind I have offered here, we might attune our ears and train our eyes to the history related by way of such artistry, a history of black women understood not as static identities in the social landscape but as active agents in a diverse and ever-shifting historical field, artists of the improbable, and authors of a history defined by an ongoing improvisational performance by many voices – a history extensively recorded but still largely unread.

Notes

1. I do not mean to undervalue the pioneering work of such important scholars as Deborah Gray White, Jacqueline Jones, and Darlene Clark Hine, whose work has provided both the foundation and the inspiration for a great many scholars. And the scholarship on black women's history has developed considerably, ranging from studies that offer an essential focus on specific communities and historical forums – for example, Higginbotham's influential *Righteous Discontent* – to studies that account for black women's presence upon a broader historical stage – for example, Dunbar's *A Fragile Freedom*. Still, we are not far removed from the situation at the beginning of the 1980s when scholarship on African American women could be captured so acutely by the title of a book edited by Hull, Scott, and Smith: *All the Women Are White, All the Blacks Are Men, But Some of Us Are Brave*.

2. There is a strong body of scholarship on nineteenth-century African American women writers, but this remains a field known mainly to those who are in it – and those who write about nineteenth-century American literature more broadly have not always attended to this scholarship with the care it merits. A foundational study was Barbara Christian's *Black Women Novelists*, and the field was defined considerably by Frances Smith Foster's *Written by Herself*. Recent studies that both represent the development of the field and identify new paths to explore are Foreman's *Activist Sentiments* and Santamarina's *Belabored Professions*. Finally, while not specifically a literary study, immensely important – both as a mark of the work behind and as a guide to the work ahead – is Waters and Conaway's edited collection, *Black Women's Intellectual Traditions*.

3. On *Our Nig*, see Buell, *New England Literary Culture*, 301; on *Iola Leroy*, see Lauter, "Is Frances Ellen Watkins Harper Good Enough to Teach?".

Works cited

Buell, Lawrence. *New England Literary Culture: From Revolution through Renaissance*. Cambridge: Cambridge University Press, 1986.

Christian, Barbara. *Black Women Novelists: The Development of a Tradition, 1892–1976*. Westport, CT: Greenwood Press, 1980.

Delaney, Lucy A. *From the Darkness Cometh the Light or Struggles for Freedom*. In *Six Women's Slave Narratives*. Ed. William L. Andrews. The Schomburg Library of Nineteenth-Century Black Women Writers. New York: Oxford University Press, 1988.

Drumgoold, Kate. *A Slave Girl's Story, Being an Autobiography of Kate Drumgoold*. In *Six Women's Slave Narratives*. Ed. William L. Andrews. The Schomburg Library of Nineteenth-Century Black Women Writers. New York: Oxford University Press, 1988.

Dunbar, Erica Armstrong. *A Fragile Freedom: African American Women and Emancipation in the Antebellum City*. New Haven and London: Yale University Press, 2008.

Edwards, Laura F. *Gendered Strife and Confusion: The Political Culture of Reconstruction*. Urbana and Chicago: University of Illinois Press, 1997.

Foreman, Gabrielle P. *Activist Sentiments: Reading Black Women in the Nineteenth Century*. Urbana: University of Illinois Press, 2008.

Foster, Frances Smith. *Written by Herself: Literary Production by African American Women, 1746–1892*. Bloomington: Indiana University Press, 1993.

Fulton, DoVeanna S. *Speaking Power: Black Feminist Orality in Women's Narratives of Slavery*. Albany: State University of New York Press, 2006.

Gilkes, Cheryl Townsend. "The Politics of 'Silence': Dual-Sex Political Systems and Women's Traditions of Conflict in African-American Religion." In *African-American Christianity: Essays in History*. Ed. Paul E. Johnson. Berkeley: University of California Press, 1994.

Higginbotham, Evelyn Brooks. *Righteous Discontent: The Women's Movement in the Black Baptist Church, 1880–1920*. Cambridge, MA: Harvard University Press, 1993.

Hull, Gloria T., Patricia Bell Scott, and Barbara Smith. *All the Women Are White, All the Blacks Are Men, But Some of Us Are Brave: Black Women's Studies*. New York: The Feminist Press, 1982.

Jacobs, Harriet A. *Incidents in the Life of a Slave Girl, Written by Herself*. Ed. Jean Fagan Yellin. Cambridge, MA: Harvard University Press, 2000.

Keckley, Elizabeth. *Behind the Scenes, or Thirty Years a Slave, and Four Years in the White House*. Ed. Frances Smith Foster. Urbana: University of Illinois Press, 2001.

Lauter, Paul. "Is Frances Ellen Watkins Harper Good Enough to Teach?" *Legacy* 5.1 (1988): 27–32.

McHenry, Elizabeth. *Forgotten Readers: Recovering the Lost History of African American Literary Societies*. Durham, NC: Duke University Press, 2002.

Reilly, John M. "History-Making Literature." In *Studies in Black American Literature, Volume II: Belief vs. Theory in Black American Literary Criticism*. Ed. Joe Weixlmann and Chester J. Fontenot. Greenwood, FL: Penkevill, 1986.

Santamarina, Xiomara. *Belabored Professions: Narratives of African American Working Womanhood*. Chapel Hill: University of North Carolina Press, 2005.

Stewart, Maria W. *Productions of Mrs. Maria W. Stewart*. In *Spiritual Narratives*. Ed. Sue E. Houchins. The Schomburg Library of Nineteenth-Century Black Women Writers. New York: Oxford University Press, 1988.

Thompson, L. S. *The Story of Mattie Jackson; Her Parentage – Experience of Eighteen Years in Slavery – Incidents During the War – Her Escape from Slavery. A True Story. In Six Women's Slave Narratives.* Ed. William L. Andrews. The Schomburg Library of Nineteenth-Century Black Women Writers. New York: Oxford University Press, 1988.

Waters, Kristin and Carol B. Conaway, eds. *Black Women's Intellectual Traditions: Speaking Their Minds.* Burlington, VT: University of Vermont Press, 2007.

Young, Elizabeth. *Disarming the Nation: Women's Writing and the American Civil War.* Chicago: University of Chicago Press, 1999.

14

Local knowledge and women's regional writing

STEPHANIE FOOTE

Critical concerns

Regional fiction, though often associated with the short stories published in the highbrow magazines of the late nineteenth century, has proven to be an enduring genre in US fiction, especially for women writers who were among its first and most accomplished practitioners. Regional fiction's fortunes in the canon of US literature – that selected group of texts thought to be most important to the story that scholars tell about the nation's coherence – have been a barometer of the rise and fall of women's place in that canon. The canon debates around what constitutes great literature were in part spurred by the contemporary political and social debates about who counted in American culture, about whose opinions and knowledge could be understood as both disinterested and distinctive, about who was capable of addressing everyone in the nation while also expressing their own powerfully individualistic and autonomous point of view. In the 1970s and '80s, when feminist activists and feminist literary historians (such as Susan Gubar and Sandra Gilbert, Elaine Showalter, Mary Poovey, Nina Baym, Judith Fetterley, and Marjorie Pryse) recovered the work of women writers who had been consigned to the dust heap of history, they opened up the canon of US literature to perspectives that challenged the dominant narrative of how literature helped to maintain national unity and coherence, and, by doing so, they revealed a literary and cultural history in which the contests over what counted as literature, culture, and citizenship were pressing concerns for a range of writers and readers.

Indeed, the feminist critics of the 1970s and onward who were responsible for recovering women's writing made, in the very act of recovery as well as in their deliberate yoking of their work with the debates circulating around women's writing, an argument about how literature and other forms of aesthetic expression were inherently political. That is, they revealed how the operations of what I have elsewhere called the narrative fascination with remembering and forgetting, two of the engines of regional narratives, was not simply a property of a text. Rather, the dynamic of remembering and forgetting structured the entire life cycle of women's literary production.

In the case of regional writing in the late nineteenth century, women could thus be widely read, often critically acclaimed writers, even as their thematic concerns and formal innovations were diminished. And as feminist critics also pointed out, even those regional women writers who had sold well and had achieved literary status and prestige suffered the same fate as their more popular sisters who wrote vastly more sentimental or sensational literature; they were written out of the record of who and what counted as American literature once the field of American literary criticism began to solidify in the first part of the twentieth century. Critics who sought to identify a "national tradition" argued that even the most critically esteemed among them like Mary Wilkins Freeman and Sarah Orne Jewett saw deeply from a too-narrow compass, and so excluded them from the ranks of the great practitioners of literature. By resuscitating and reprinting many of the forgotten though once-loved regional texts written by women, feminist critics revived a genre that had fallen into obscurity, and identified in its constitutive parts not the slight, precious literature of nostalgia or the careful, minor representation of the narrow compass of local life that many critics of the early twentieth century had identified. They identified the genre's doubled interest in place, and argued that its interest in that category put pressure on the idea of social and geographic place, by using the dominant realist genre's focus on rich, descriptive prose and faithful depictions of social worlds and interior states in order to make a place for locations and voices that were out of the mainstream. And perhaps most importantly, they illuminated the process by which an emergent literary criticism did not ratify but created a tradition in which women's writing could be measured by standards that virtually ensured that it would be seen as local and small, and thus forgotten by later generations.

Part of the process of both recovering and replacing this genre in the long history of US literary culture involved finding ways to get individual texts back into print, into scholars' hands, and into the classroom. Part of the work of feminist critics thus centered on trying to pay attention to the entire life of a text – its production, publication, circulation, and consumption, as well as the reviews it received. Feminist critics connected these elements to pressing social concerns about whose voices counted in decisions about what literature did, how culture worked, and how social actors made use of literature as readers and writers to understand their worlds. Indeed, in some ways the recovery of women's writing was exactly the right project for feminist scholars attempting to find their own place in an academy that seemed throughout much of the twentieth century to produce scholarship about and by men; the work of early feminist critics intentionally paralleled the arguments they saw nineteenth-century and twentieth-century women regionalists like Jewett, Freeman, Cather, and Austin making about who counted in a professional literary sphere.

And yet the neat parallels between the work of women regional writers and the scholarship of feminist critics who saw in them both a challenge to and a yearning for the professional rewards and status of a literary career cannot quite answer a central question about the connection between women's writing and regional literature, a literature after all, that was not just about small domestic places, rural communities, or isolated villages, but that was about the idea of place itself. In that sense, there is no inherent connection between women and the idea of place, just as there is no intrinsic connection between the genre of regional writing – or any literary representation of geographic places – and actual, material spaces. The connections between place, space, gender, and literature that have structured much feminist recovery of women writers, as well as helped women writers to enter the literary field, rely on changing historical definitions of how place can be represented, and how its stories can be told to an audience with a range of different investments in the meaning of local places and cultures.

In this essay, I shall ask what regional writing can tell us not only about the women who wrote and read it, but about how feminism opened up the canon not only to women writers, but also to all subjects whose view seemed too narrow, whose place too definite, whose concerns too local, to really count in a public sphere that valued a putatively more detached way of seeing and narrating the nation. Some of the questions that examine regional writing's relationship to gender more broadly – an analysis indebted to its recovery by feminist critics – include the following: Why has regional writing by women been virtually synonymous with the later nineteenth-century writing? What would happen if we expanded our understanding of what constitutes regional writing, and our interpretation of how women writers and readers have engaged with its signal concerns? What can we see about gender if we stand in "the region," and what do we see about "the region" when we ask how it figures gender? What is the place of gender in literary history and in the literary market, and how did writing about specific locations help women writers find a place in public? To approach these questions, it is crucial that we examine the print history of regional writing by women, as well as its changing reception among audiences and critics, to understand why the genre has been especially hospitable to women writers. Although I describe some of the debates among the feminist critics who brought it to scholarly attention, debates that reflect the changing commitments and shape of feminism more broadly in US culture, I spend much of my time here describing the evolution of the genre throughout the twentieth century, paying special attention to the idea of the local as a way to tell these two stories about gender and regionalism together.

In some senses, women regionalist writers were assumed to have a special knowledge of the local – the world of the village, the small town, and the household – and they coordinated their work to that assumption in order to find a larger audience than the village or the household and to elevate the meaning of what local knowledge was and could do. From a prescribed position, that is, they changed the way that the partial knowledge they were assumed to have might signify. Their local ways of knowing and seeing became the narrative position that distinguished them, allowing them to question the very provincialism and shortsightedness associated with the local. Thus the story of women's regional writing is about how what were once considered "partial" or "local" ways of seeing and knowing became central to the literary tradition. These concerns are currently central to critics who focus on ethnicity and race, globalization and cosmopolitanism, for they too challenge regnant definitions of what counted as important literature and who is in a position to see what Annette Kolodny called "the lay of the land."

If feminist critics made it possible to rethink the tradition of literary history to include women's writing about place and local knowledge, they perhaps overstated the work of such women writers, many of whom can be understood as at least as desirous of critiquing mainstream literary culture as they were of joining it (and we can note as a corollary that many men writing fiction cannot in contrast be mechanically associated with a knee-jerk nationalism or complicity). No matter what privileges accrued to women writers of a certain race or class, they were limited in part by publishers and by readers' expectations to write local color or regional fiction, and it is often in the tension between this generic expectation and the ambition of the women in question that gives women's regionalism its ability to see the world aslant.

I close my essay by suggesting that claiming the local and the local's particular epistemology can change our understanding of the women regional writers in the twentieth century and in particular in the present. As I show, we might consider how feminist critics have collaborated with nineteenth-century regional writers in the revaluation of local knowledge, and that collaboration has made it possible to see a range of women writers in the twentieth century as the inheritors of a project of narrating their place in the literary field as the masters of local knowledge assumed to be common and valueless.

This project gives us a way to see local knowledge as the place where affiliations can be made with other socially marginalized groups, and where the production and reproduction of literary value in the academic world and in the literary market are inflected by the powerful reworking of conventional women's reproductive functions by women writers of the nineteenth century. Far from merely being narratives of communities closed off from the wider world, women's regional writing was in the vanguard of cultural work that took seriously the shifting dynamics of what counted as community, and who counted as a member of it. Their ability to manage their positions as outsiders and insiders in the publishing world – as practitioners of a genre of writing marketed as, on the one hand, intrinsically slight and minor and, on the other hand, aesthetically rare and refined – gave them an unparalleled position from which to observe the mechanisms that governed admission to a given community, as well as a surprising ability to see the value in how seemingly marginal social actors could enliven and enrich them.

Women's writing, women's criticism

Women, as literary critics have long known, have historically formed the majority of the readership of fiction, and they have thus been central to long-standing debates about the moral and emotional effects of reading. By the late nineteenth century, debates about how the reading of novels could damage women's morals and lead them into laziness, recklessness, and debauchery – charges that feminist critics have linked not to the scenes of seduction depicted within the novel but to the novel's power apparently to seduce women away from their household duties by offering them privacy and time to themselves – had all but disappeared. But if by the end of the nineteenth century, fiction – and the novel in particular – was not seen to be the road to female debauchery, as it had been in the eighteenth century, for example, it was not because debates about the effects of fiction had stopped. Rather, it was because those debates had moved elsewhere, now concentrated in the merit of various kinds of novels, and the kind of cultural work they could do. Thus, arguments about the danger of fiction transformed into arguments about what kind of fiction could be seen to advance moral uplift, emotional exaltation, or political change. We might see this as a debate about the relationship between literary value and genres, and in the late nineteenth century, it had repercussions for how women writers were valued. Indeed, the first concerted achievement of women regional writers was brokered by a literary sphere that was national in scope, but which paid special attention to the needs of different readers.

In the late nineteenth century, when the literary field began to assume a shape in which the editing, production, circulation, and reviewing of literary fiction were parts of a coordinated industry that, among other things, made the writing of fiction into a profession available to a surprising number of people, the ability to assess both the readership of fiction as well as the generic rules of fiction itself helped women to enter the literary marketplace not only as readers, but as editors, reviewers, and writers. Women in the late nineteenth century, for example, published literary reviews in such venues as *Harper's* and *Vogue*, singling out some novels and genres as more uplifting and worthy than others, weighing in on debates about the merits of realism and the complexities of Henry James's style, and thus helping to shape a conversation about that literature. Yet despite their enormous power as consumers, they were not, by and large, in control of what we might call the means of production of literature – there were not many women magazine editors, and those who had editorial responsibilities at national or regional magazines were generally (though not always) associated with women's magazines. The most powerful brokers of national literary reputations were the editors of the major highbrow magazines, such as *The Atlantic Monthly*. Those editors were, as Nancy Glazener has argued, extraordinarily powerful tastemakers, and publication in their magazines could profoundly affect a writer's career (*Reading for Realism*, 20–35). Being selected to appear in a nationally circulated magazine with a reputation for addressing the educated elite could spell the difference between whether a writer would find a publisher for later work as well as make writers visible to a cadre of like-minded readers. Of these editors, none was more powerful, and none more committed to helping emerging writers, than William Dean Howells.

Howells, who edited *The Atlantic Monthly* from 1871 to 1881, and wrote the column "From the Editor's Study," an extremely influential survey of the literary field for *Harper's Monthly* from 1886 to 1892, was one of regional writing's biggest fans, and, in turn, he was important to the careers of a great many writers. The regional fiction that Howells tended to most value was the fiction that could, to paraphrase one of his columns, introduce all corners of the nation to one another, reveal the diversity of what it meant to be an American, and faithfully portray the folkways of a rural life seen to be fading away. Although in retrospect, this might seem to be a failsafe recipe for what we might now imagine to be a patchwork quilt of American democracy, a multiculturalism *avant la lettre*, Howells's imagination of this literary symphony of cultural difference was underwritten by inequalities in access to the literary market that intersected in surprising ways with the dominant inequalities at play in culture at large. It was not only a project reliant on gender inequality, but racial inequality too. For example, the local villages and rural areas much in demand by readers were precisely those that seemed to have been abandoned by young men who had either migrated to the cities or to the big industrial towns of New England. These villages thus appeared to be women's spaces, inhabited by rustics who lived their lives according to commonly held beliefs and traditions, organized and governed as they had been for generations. They appeared to be out of the regular progression of time, caught in an eternal and golden past. Immune from the structuring forces of urban life like immigration, alienation, vice, and crime, the rural village that was the staple of regional fiction was an icon of the values that modernity seemed to have lost on its rapid forward march, a repository of the fantasies of how life used to be and perhaps should be again.

As Raymond Williams has argued about the turn toward nostalgic depictions of rural life in an era of increasing industrialization, the countryside became the repository of all of the values that seemed most challenged by urban relationships. A country life that seemed rapidly to be fading away, he argues, seemed to privilege face-to-face relationships over legal, contractual obligations. It was, as he goes on to argue, the repository of what was felt to be most authentic and important, most real in human relationships because rural life was organized around "knowable communities" whose richness was not a product of variability and diversity, but of the long history of shared traditions and experiences. The region as the site of what was most authentic, most in danger of being lost, most imperiled by modernity was, according to many critics, what made the genre so popular among readers in the late nineteenth century.

And yet a close look at regional fiction from this era, especially that written by women, reveals that at every turn the nostalgia that structured memories of village life was in competition with the hard facts of modern life. Indeed, it was one of the signal achievements of regional writing that it managed to balance the nostalgic tone that seemed to drive ideologies of the region with the contemporary material and political concerns to which the region was assumed to be impervious. Women's regional writing, formally and thematically, often demonstrated that face-to-face communities failed because they inevitably excluded some people in the name of preserving a particular way of life. In other words, women regionalist writers often understood that the countryside as the location of utopian "knowable communities" in

Raymond Williams's phrase (*The Country and the City*, 165–6) was a fantasy of people who did not have to struggle for recognition within them. Regions, for women writers of the genre, were microcosms, not escapes from modernity, structured by economic and social inequalities between members and often subtly structured by class, ethnicity, and racial differences. We might think here of a few of the well-known examples: Sarah Orne Jewett's 1900 story "The Foreigner," set in the coastal Maine town of Dunnet Landing in which her 1896 *The Country of the Pointed Firs* was set, and which tells the story of a Creole woman of indeterminate race who remained a stranger to her new townsfolk until the day she died; Kate Chopin's 1893 "Désirée's Baby," which tells the story of a young woman in the Louisiana Bayou who gives birth to a baby who is thought to be of mixed-race, and is cast out by her husband, who himself turns out to be of mixed parentage; or virtually all of Mary Wilkins Freeman's regional short stories, in which impoverished and aging spinsters fight daily for both sustenance and respect in the communities they help to anchor.

As they show, story by story, women regional writers paid special attention to the role of social difference in the construction of community, arguing that social marginality and local knowledge provided a paradoxically more comprehensive way to understand the broadest role of individuals in community. This paradoxical method of narrating the value of local knowledge is in no small part a critical way of understanding women regionalists' understanding of themselves as professional writers who were addressing a broad national audience and participating in a national literary culture; it was also the engine of women's regional literary texts. And finally, as I discuss, this shrewd understanding of the place of the local and the marginal, their ability to broker what might be considered common and provincial into a marketable commodity, came to influence women writers who followed them. Marjorie Pryse characterizes her work with Judith Fetterley as proposing that regional fiction is a counterdiscourse or a resistant discourse to local color, and enjoins the reader to look with, not at, local subjects: "Regionalism creates a fictional space to contest the ruling relations that subordinated rural people and other groups who possessed limited power in mainstream US society and did so by developing the subjectivity of regional persons" ("Linguistic Regionalism," 86).

Among the great women regional writers of the late nineteenth century, we can count Sarah Orne Jewett, Mary Noailles Murfree, Mary Wilkins Freeman, Zitkala-Ša, Sui Sin Far, Celia Thaxter, Rose Terry Cooke, Kate Chopin, Grace King, Mary Hallock Foote, and Alice French. There are, of course, many more; regional writing was popular, and almost every geographic location of the United States could be understood in literary terms as part of an identifiable region. It is important to understand, therefore, that the material locations used by women regional writers were not identical to the geographic places on a map; they were representations of places, and no representation, not even a map, is accurate or faithful. The regional writers did not, therefore, faithfully represent a real place for readers, even if the place they wrote about could be found by a traveler or be visited by a tourist. Instead, they created and interpreted the place they seemed to be representing, and they did so using conventions with which urban readers were already familiar. For example, they balanced the omniscient, sympathetic narrative voice with the carefully rendered dialect of a regional visitor; presented nature as in part a retreat from the urban; focused on "simple" rural pastimes while invoking the labor that rural life demanded of everyone from women to children; and they focused on face-to-face communities while often undermining their superiority by rendering vicious local conflicts with heart-rending fidelity.

Writers' ability to present the region from the position of both outsider and insider made them successful yet made it easy for later critics to waive away their achievements. Writing in the genre of realism, they were perfectly comprehensible to readers accustomed to realism's thick descriptions of places, objects, and people, but they were writing about isolated places far from urban centers, and about villages and towns that appeared to have escaped the problems of modernity, they were easy for later critics to categorize as minor. Their very strength – their ability to see how social difference structured local life – was considered their shortcoming by critics like Fred Lewis Pattee, who began in the early twentieth century to try to construct a history of "great" American literature. But certainly, as the women regional writers themselves might have argued, one surveys such a tradition from a given place, and we ignore how place shapes narratives and subjects at our peril. Indeed, from the recovery of women's regional writing by feminist critics who used it to find a place for women in the canon, regional women's writing has become an exceptionally rich genre for critics who look at the way that late nineteenth-century literature narrated the relationship between the particular and the global or cosmopolitan (Lutz, "The Cosmopolitan Midland"; Joseph, *American Literary Regionalism*), between social and ethnic difference and normative US identity (McCullough, *Regions of Identity*; Totten, "Zitkala-Ša"), and between materiality and the abstractions of nature and place (Alaimo, *Undomesticated Ground*; Comer, "Taking Feminism").

Futures and women's regional writing

Scholars who study regional writing often remark that as a genre it seemed to decline in the twentieth century. It is true that the genre that we call regional writing became less popular in the early decades of the twentieth century, but even the genre narrowly defined as part of the world of the highbrow magazine did not disappear completely. Women writers in the first half of the twentieth century often followed many of the basic conventions of the regional writing that had been developed as a subset of realism in the last part of the nineteenth century, and many of them successfully adapted those conventions, finding critical praise and a loyal audience. Indeed, some of those writers, such as Willa Cather, recognized a link with earlier women regionalists, and she in particular understood her writing as extending that project. Just as writers like Freeman and Jewett critiqued representations of women, place, and community in their work, so too did writers like Zona Gale, Willa Cather, Flannery O'Connor, and Eudora Welty use the generic conventions of regional representation to critique a narrow provincialism by grounding it in the local customs and cultures of discrete places.

Even now, we can see the inheritance of regional fiction in how the intense focus on the lifeways of particular places has informed the work of a great many women writers working today. Women writers working in the conventional regional mode, like Annie Proulx, Caroline Chute, Sharyn McCrumb and Cathie Pelletier, set their fiction in locations that they understand to be central to the development of their characters, their worldviews, their personalities, and the arc of those characters' lives. Their work, like that of Jewett, Freeman, Gale, or Cather, demands that readers take seriously how place, itself a complex network of intersecting narratives about who belongs and who does not, about who is valuable and who disposable, is among the central ways we can understand the shape of a character's life.

Such mid-list, middlebrow regional fiction, especially by women, has thus never really gone away, and it has always had a respected – if sometimes tenuous – hold on the critical goodwill lavished on contemporary realist writers. It is well reviewed, and often commands a loyal readership. It is often, as in the case of McCrumb, informed by a great deal of scholarly research about the folk tales of Appalachia, or in Pelletier's or Chute's case, by a life spent in a specific location. Pelletier and Chute write about Maine (though as readers who are familiar with their work will doubtless know, in very different ways) and are very conscious of the perils of attempting to represent an authentic regional otherness to an audience who might wish to reduce regional life to a stereotype, or who might use it, as Richard Brodhead has argued about late nineteenth-century audiences, to fulfill an acquisitive curiosity about regional folk (*Cultures of Letters*, 133).

Yet it is also true that the genre *did* decline, despite the fact that its basic narrative conventions were adapted by other writers well into the twentieth century, and despite the fact that women's writing about local places and customs continued to be a powerful way for them to enter the literary market, and to create an identifiable authorial persona for themselves. Fiction set in a particular place, or that paid attention to the particular ways in which place helped to shape community and local cultures, really *did* disappear. By this I mean that the particular genre of regional writing that first introduced specific places as cultures to urban readers, many of whom began to understand rural communities as bastions of conformity and conservatism, and who favored literature that reflected this view (the well-known "revolt of the provinces" literature). In some sense, as Gordon Hutner has recently argued, this shift was a matter of taste; the so-called high realism of James, Wharton, Jewett, and Freeman began to seem a little archaic and out of touch, and the interests of readers shifted to a more conventionally plotted realism that paid closer attention to the daily struggles of the middle classes (*What America Read*, 1–35). But although the genre of regional fiction waned, interest in place, especially the relationship between gender and place, did not.

How, then, do we account for both the decline and the endurance of regional fiction in general, and regional fiction by women in particular all throughout the twentieth century? Is there another way to approach the literary-critical truism about regional fiction's fortunes in the twentieth century apart from a narrative of decline or supersession? To understand these problems, we need to ask a different set of questions, and to define regional fiction in different terms, for part of the narrative of regionalism's decline can be traced to the way that literary critics have conflated writing about regions with the specific genre of regional realism in the late nineteenth century that was published in nationally distributed periodicals and marketed to an urban elite. That is, the conventional way literary critics discuss that particular genre has sometimes obscured how writers have understood and made legible the idea of geographic place in their work, limiting different definitions of "the region" and women's relationship to it in the literary sphere. In the name of making sure that readers have understood the important point that the region as it is represented by a writer is not "real," and that regional writing in the late nineteenth century was not merely an anthropological enterprise that sought to preserve and record, but was an artistic enterprise, critics have unwittingly helped to create the conditions under which "the region" can be conflated with "regionalism."

If, in the first half of this essay, I provided an overview of how and why women writers worked in that specific historical moment and particular literary marketplace that made regional writing such an important genre for their professional development, in this section, I ask what we might see if we survey a range of ways that contemporary women writers have tried to define ideas of place, geographic location, and local cultures in new contexts. How have contemporary women writers tried to represent the specificity of material place in genres other than the "regional literatures" of the late nineteenth century? Can we see any coherence between their project and that of the late nineteenth-century regional writers? If the overriding questions in the first section of the essay were organized around how women writers and the critics who resuscitated them used the idea of the region in order to make a place for social difference, to demonstrate the value of local ways of knowing and seeing, the questions of the second part of this essay are somewhat different. What does attention to place itself help women writers to see? What is the pay-off of trying to think about space and place – the apparently fundamental components of regional writing – for contemporary literary culture? What is the future of regional literature by women?

This last question might perhaps be the most critical, for the regional writing that we read under the sign of "regional literature" is very often oriented toward the past; it seems lyrical, remote, and its plots seem as though they are in some sense out of regular time. The places represented by women regional writers have seemed to be on the verge of disappearing, and the regional text often seems to be directed to a reader who will be a sympathetic witness to a culture that cannot survive in the future. But the regions I describe for the women writers in this section are regions that are not so easily identified with a culture, no matter how richly limned; they are vital, polyvocal, and in all cases they are presented as the objects of competing histories and representations, competing versions of "the real" of the region. I shall look at two areas where contemporary women writers have paid attention to the idea of place, organizing their texts in part to put special pressure on the idea of space and how women seek to make it legible, how they seek to know it and to come to knowledge through it. As a thought experiment, we might look at two genres, mass-market mysteries and environmental non-fiction. These are proving popular with very different kinds of writers and readers because they reconfigure place and gender together.

Each of these genres appeals to very different audiences, is published by different kinds of publishing houses, and carries different kinds of cultural prestige. And yet, each of these genres shows us the wide variety of ways that women writers have found a place in the literary establishment, as well as how they have used an idea of place in order to create particular ways of seeing and writing contemporary culture.

Perhaps the liveliest contemporary examples of regionalism are those written by authors who are working in genre fiction, and often publishing with trade presses. In particular, we can see that a great deal of contemporary mystery fiction written by women is at least as easily categorized as "regional fiction" as it is as "mystery fiction." And no wonder. If, as I have argued, the narrative of regional fiction privileges particularly local, or insider ways of knowing, and yet must be sufficiently connected to the world to express those ways of knowing the world to a broad reading audience, the mystery novel would seem to be its logical outcome.

It may seem counterintuitive to see in mass-market mysteries by and about women the truest heirs to the tradition of genteel regional writing with which this essay began. Formulaic, mass-produced, critically derided or ignored, often published in cheap disposable paperbacks and sold in airports and drugstores, mysteries seem to have nothing in common with the jewel-like short stories published in highbrow venues and enjoyed by a select group of upper-middle-class connoisseurs. And if the differences in their print cultural status is not enough, the difference in their critical reception seems to seal the deal of their difference. Mysteries are generally parts of series, follow certain generic principles, and are heavily plot-driven, ending in neat resolutions and moral certainties.

A brief – and by no means complete – bibliography of such work would include the work of Sharyn McCrumb, who writes historical thrillers set in Appalachia; Linda Barnes, who writes about a Boston private investigator; Laurie King, the author of many series, including a series of lesbian mysteries set in San Francisco; Judith Van Gieson, who created Claire Reynier, an amateur detective who is also a rare books librarian in New Mexico; Sara Paretsky, who created VI Warshawski, a private investigator working in Chicago; Joan Hess, whose Arly Hanks is a police chief in the fictional town of Maggody, Arkansas; Nevada Barr, the creator of Anna Pigeon, a park ranger in the national parks service; and Dana Stabenow, whose female PI is based in Alaska. There are dozens more, and each of the series has a dedicated fan base. But why should we imagine them as the heir to women's regional fiction? In part, they continue the earliest regional writers' concern with how women make a place for themselves, both professionally and socially, how they become members of a place and help to regulate it and imagine its futures. But women's regional mysteries also pay attention to specific locales and argue that those places demand specific forms of knowledge, specific and highly local ways of seeing and perceiving community. The mystery in these novels is not merely about what someone does, nor about the commission of a single crime; it is about a particular narrative of how places operate. Indeed, all of the crimes rely on regional writing's familiar attempt to balance community and difference in a single coherent narrative. The texts link the particular perspective of women to the ways of knowing and seeing that are tied to place, and thus extend the formal and thematic concerns of the women regionalists of the late nineteenth century.

Similarly, we might think of the genre of nature writing by women as being as much indebted to the work of the women regional writers of the late nineteenth century as it is to the work of late nineteenth- and twentieth-century male naturalists like John Muir. We might think of a writer like Mary Austin as perhaps the most famous incarnation of a writer influenced by both the understanding of "place" as mutually constituted by both culture and nature; yet we can extend the reading of women's relationship to place as an idea to current environmental writers like Annie Dillard, Diane Ackerman, Barbara Kingsolver, and Terry Tempest Williams. Although not working in fiction, all of these women employ narrative strategies that would be recognizable to the readers of late nineteenth-century women's regional writing. Indeed, the tradition of women's nature writing has made it possible for readers to challenge the putatively intrinsic link between "women" and "nature" by paying attention, in the tradition of Rachel Carson, to the politically sponsored despoliation of a natural world that has thus been compromised by a larger culture of consumerism. The emerging field of ecocriticism has paid special attention to the various implications of nature, culture, race, and gender, and women nature writers, working in the essay mode to understand the natural world and the local cultures it shapes and that shape it, have become an important voice for helping to see links between nature and gender that go beyond, as critics like Stacy Alaimo and Kristen Comer have argued, the merely romantic or domestic.

Conclusion

If looking at how women writers are rethinking how to articulate place and gender in politically charged ways helps to reveal new directions in how we can think of women and "the region," it also demands new archives, new definitions of place, and new ways to see gender and place in the literary fields. In a context in which economic globalization is often invoked as a threat to local cultures, and in which the movement of refugees across borders is among the most common ways that local cultures travel and take root in new places, mapping place in literature must become more central to academics, essayists, and fiction writers.

From the perspective of literary historical analysis then, it remains to critics to look at the different ways that literary texts have tried to map place by looking beyond how writers choose their topics, identify with distinct places or the idea of place itself, and begin to look at production and consumption as well. Literary critics must thus pay attention not just to writers who publish on "minor" issues with major presses, but must take seriously the emergence of small or regional presses that specialize in local writers, as well as those university presses that take seriously the cultural and geographic histories of their locations. We might therefore turn our attention to what Emily Satterwhite has called "reception geography," which takes seriously the social meaning of the regional popularity of different kinds of texts (*Dear Appalachia*). Both how the local is represented, and the point of view that the local allows readers and writers to take, have historically been a story that cannot be told from the center of literary history alone; it is a story that demands that center and margin be put into a new relationship both in a given historical moment as well as across history. Women writers, as I have argued, are especially skilled at the kind of binocular vision this demands, and paying attention to how they have defined place, how they have worked against and within it, how they have made a world of small places and stepped out of places to enter the wider world of print, has both shaped the field of American literature and provided a way for women critics, essayists, and fiction writers to challenge their location within it.

Works cited

Alaimo, Stacy. *Undomesticated Ground: Recasting Nature as Feminist Space*. Ithaca: Cornell University Press, 2000.

Armitage, Susan H. "From the Inside Out: Rewriting Regional History." *Frontiers: A Journal of Women Studies* 22.3 (2001): 32–47.

Brodhead, Richard. *Cultures of Letters: Scenes of Reading and Writing in Nineteenth-Century America*. Chicago: University of Chicago Press, 1993.

Campbell, Donna. *Resisting Regionalism: Gender and Naturalism in American Fiction, 1885–1915*. Athens, OH: Ohio University Press, 1997.

Comer, Krista. "Taking Feminism and Regionalism Toward the Third Wave." In *Blackwell's Reader in Regional Literatures of the United States*. Ed. Charles L. Crow. London: Blackwell, 2003.

Dobson, Joanne. "Reclaiming Sentimental Literature." *American Literature* 69.2 (1997): 263–88.

Fetterley, Judith. "'Not in the Least American': Nineteenth-Century Literary Regionalism." *College English* 56.8 (December 2004): 877–95.

Fetterley, Judith and Marjorie Pryse. *Writing out of Place: Regionalism, Women, and American Literary Culture*. Urbana, IL: University of Illinois Press, 2003.

Fetterley, Judith and Marjorie Pryse, eds. *American Women Regionalists*. New York: W. W. Norton, 1992.

Foote, Stephanie. "The Cultural Work of American Regionalism." In *Blackwell's Reader in Regional Literatures of the United States*. Ed. Charles L. Crow. London: Blackwell, 2003.

Regional Fictions: Culture and Identity in Nineteenth-Century American Literature. Madison: University of Wisconsin Press, 2001.

Glazener, Nancy. *Reading for Realism: The History of a US Literary Institution, 1850–1910*. Durham, NC: Duke University Press, 1997.

Hsu, Hsuan L. "Literature and Regional Production." *American Literary History* 17.1 (Spring 2005): 36–69.

Hutner, Gordon. *What America Read: Taste, Class, and the Novel, 1920–1960*. Durham, NC: University of North Carolina Press, 2009.

Joseph, Philip. *American Literary Regionalism in a Global Age*. Baton Rouge: Louisiana State University Press, 2006.

Kaplan, Amy. "Nation, Region, and Empire." In *The Columbia History of the American Novel*. Ed. Emory Elliott *et al.* New York: Columbia University Press, 1991.

Kolodny, Annette. *The Lay of the Land: Metaphor as Experience and History in American Life and Letters*. Chapel Hill: University of North Carolina Press, 1984.

Lutz, Tom. "The Cosmopolitan Midland." *American Periodicals: A Journal of History, Criticism, and Bibliography* 15.1 (2005): 74–85.

McCullough, Kate. *Regions of Identity: The Construction of America in Women's Fiction, 1885–1914*. Stanford: Stanford University Press, 1999.

Pattee, Fred Lewis. *A History of American Literature since 1870*. New York: D. Appleton and Century Co., 1915.

Pryse, Marjorie. "Linguistic Regionalism and the Emergence of Chinese American Literature in Sui Sin Far's 'Mrs. Spring Fragrance'." *Legacy* 27.1 (2010): 83–108.

Satterwhite, Emily. *Dear Appalachia: Readers, Identity, and Popular Fiction since 1878*. Lexington: University Press of Kentucky, 2011.

Totten, Gary. "Zitkala-Ša and the Problem of Regionalism: Nations, Narratives, and Critical Traditions." *The American Indian Quarterly* 29.1–2 (Winter/Spring 2005): 84–123.

Williams, Raymond. *The Country and the City*. New York: Oxford University Press, 1977.

Zagarell, Sandra. "Narrative of Community: The Identification of a Genre." *Signs* 13.3 (Spring 1988): 498–527.

15

Women and children first

Female writers of American children's literature

CAROL J. SINGLEY

Although we can imagine an oral tradition of children's literature by indigenous women of North America, there is scant to no record of these compositions. The written record of American female writing for children begins
with the first American poet, Anne Bradstreet (1612–72). Arriving in the New
World with the first generation of English settlers, Bradstreet speaks directly
from female experience in poetry and letters addressed to her offspring. The
tradition of children's literature continues through diverse voices in every
genre, from traditional folk and fairy tales, to historical fiction, realism, fantasy, picture books, and young adolescent fiction. Multi-dimensional and
enduring, this literature begins in the seventeenth century with the Puritans
and reaches full creative flowering in the early to mid-nineteenth century, in
concert with the development of American literature generally. It continues
to flourish today. Following its arc from the colonial period to the present,
we see aesthetic and social forces that helped to shape various understandings
of American children and the literary visions of women who wrote for them.

Anne Bradstreet is a germinal figure whose life and writing exemplify
the tensions facing women who both care for children and write for them.
Provided with a Renaissance education in England, she boarded the *Arbella*
with her husband, Simon Bradstreet, preacher and soon-to-be-governor John
Winthrop, and other English Puritans seeking relief from religious persecution. She arrived in Salem in 1630. Bradstreet did not set out to be a writer.
On the contrary, Puritans were suspicious of human creative expression that
might be considered to rival the powers of God, the supreme creator; women,
in particular, were discouraged from entering the public realm. Bradstreet's
poems became known only because her brother-in-law brought them to England and issued them under the title, *The Tenth Muse, Lately Sprung Up in
America* (1650). Her publication history serves as a touchstone for challenges

facing women writers. Bradstreet writes from the perspective not only of author but also of mother and daughter. She inserts into a highly regulated patriarchal society the concerns of a woman who is deeply religious yet wrestling with her faith and with duties to family and self.

Bradstreet writes in a letter, "To My Dear Children," about the hardship of settlement in a virtual wilderness and her struggle to reconcile her will to that of God: "I found a new world and new manners at which my heart rose." In a poem entitled "Here Follows Some Verses upon the Burning of our House," she describes in detail the anguish of losing her home and possessions in a fire that tested her faith: "Adieu, Adieu, all's vanity / . . . my hope and treasure lies above" (lines 36, 54). She also describes the experiences of marriage and motherhood. A mother of eight children, Bradstreet is a forerunner of the nineteenth-century domestic writers who celebrate mother–child bonds and invest women with the authority to guide the spiritual paths of children, the family, and the nation.

Bradstreet's writings reflect a truism in much of women's literature for children, that is, the importance of home, the strength of maternal love, and the need to balance human relationship with the mandate to honor the self in all of its manifestations: through communion with nature, through connection to the divine, and through solitude. Much of children's literature follows an archetypal pattern – home-away-home – but girls are traditionally more tied to home than are boys, especially in the nineteenth century. American literature written for children reflects, and sometimes subverts, social expectations that constrain females to home and hearth. Bradstreet helped to define a feminine domain for literature by treating subjects such as fear of childbirth and concern for children's welfare under a stepmother's care; the untimely death of children; and maternal affections that rival her spiritual devotion. Bradstreet's address to her children also speaks to a perennial issue in children's literature regarding how or even whether such literature can be defined. Her work has been read primarily by adults, not by children, drawing attention to the frequently blurred lines between literature for mature audiences and literature for juveniles. Children play key roles in determining a text's popularity or longevity, but literature aimed explicitly at children is created by adults and reflects not what children want to read but what adults expect them to read (Lesnik-Oberstein, *Children's Literature*; Rose, *The Case of Peter Pan*; Nodelman, "The Case of Children's Fiction"; Gubar, "On Not Defining Children's Literature").

Bradstreet speaks directly to her children in a short poem prefacing a letter and establishes a close connection between speaker and audience. "To My

Dear Children" begins with reference to her two most valued productions, her writing and her children: "This book by any yet unread, / I leave for you when I am dead, / That being gone, here you may find / What was your living mother's mind" (lines 1–4). In the final two lines she expresses hope that her writing will endure and her children will thrive: "Make use of what I leave in love, / And God shall bless you from above" (lines 5–6). The poem demonstrates a central aim of children's literature: that it not simply entertain but also instruct. The two dominant genres of the period were the sermon and the spiritual autobiography. Bradstreet exemplifies the latter in the letter that follows the poem and, in so doing, sets the foundation for moral qualities found in juvenile literature through the nineteenth century and into the twentieth. Wishing that her children will profit from her example, including her shortcomings, she exhorts them to strive for piety. She also imbues her work with an abiding optimism and hope for the future, a quality that critics have identified as defining American as opposed to English children's literature (Avery, *Behold the Child*).

Bradstreet interjects another feature of children's literature, especially of the modern period: that is, a sense of the developmental nature of childhood. She writes in a religious context in which the child's identity is considered fixed and, like all of humankind, fallen or sinful. Her letter follows the discourse of the day in admonishing her children to search their souls "to see what wickedness are in me" ("To My Dear Children," 45). This sense of innate depravity contrasts with a later, more romantic view of childhood innocence inherited from John Locke and Jean-Jacques Rousseau. While far from viewing children as pure or innocent, Bradstreet intuitively, and in opposition to prevailing discourse that focuses on children's flaws, demonstrates faith in the maturing process. This developmental approach to childhood, with an emphasis on learning from experience, becomes a cornerstone of the coming-of-age story, or *Bildungsroman*, prevalent in mid-nineteenth-century literature and beyond.

The deeply held Calvinist beliefs that inform Bradstreet's work affected children's literature for centuries and account for children's literature being equivalent, as Anne MacLeod writes, to the "moral tale." Puritans placed a high value on literacy, as evidenced by a large corpus of primers as well as sermons. Primers, their authors usually anonymous, were small books that instructed children in ABCs as well as catechism; they remained popular through the nineteenth century and reappeared in the twentieth century in the form of picture books and basal readers. Juvenile literature in the late eighteenth and early nineteenth centuries, in addition to primers and religious texts, included imports by British women writers such as Anna Barbauld,

Hannah More, Elizabeth Turner, and Jane and Ann Taylor. English writer Maria Edgeworth (1768–1849), in particular, greatly influenced American writers with fiction that conveyed a moral message but also introduced more pleasurable, secular models. Significant among this early literature is Susanna Rowson's *Charlotte Temple* (1791, 1794), a bestselling tale of seduction that articulated the need for moral virtue in young women at the same time that it entertained readers with its sensationalized melodrama. *Charlotte Temple*, Holly Blackford argues, is a forerunner of the modern novel about the female adolescent character forging an identity separate from that of parents and also served as a pedagogical tool in the post-Revolutionary promotion of American democratic culture and governance. Developments in children's literature from the eighteenth to the nineteenth centuries reflected a gradual shift in the perception of childhood, from children as rational beings with minds that must be cultivated to romantic innocents aligned with imagination.

Fiction for children began to be produced in volume in the early to mid-nineteenth century, when creative fiction appeared generally in the United States. Lydia Maria Child (1802–80) and Catharine Maria Sedgwick (1789–1867) led the way with historical romances, a popular genre of the period. Child's groundbreaking *Hobomok* (1824) portrays a Puritan girl who takes the unprecedented step of marrying an American Indian in this first portrayal of miscegenation between an Indian and a white. Sedgwick's *Hope Leslie* (1827), set in the 1630s during the Pequot War, provides a critique of Puritan religious intolerance and aggression toward Indians. Two heroines capture the reader's imagination in this novel: the noble Indian girl Magawisca, who sacrifices her right arm and loses connection to her father and tribe in order to save the life of a young Puritan man, Everell Fletcher; and the unflappable, resourceful Hope Leslie, who with spirit and courage manages to free imprisoned Indians, rescue the hapless Everell, and defy Puritan authority. Magawisca and Hope form the center of this well-plotted, adventure-filled tale, but even the compliant Puritan girl, Esther Downing, rings true. Sedgwick's portrayal of Hope signals the emergence of the self-sufficient American girl and models a nineteenth-century plot that Nina Baym outlines: that of the orphaned or homeless girl who with a combination of plucky individualism and conventional piety makes her way in the world and ends her journey with a secure home and an acceptable marriage, often to a solid but less dazzling counterpart (*Woman's Fiction*, 11–12).

A strong tradition of children's literature evolved with the popularity of the domestic writers of the mid-nineteenth century. The American heroine was born at this time, as Gillian Avery notes (*Behold the Child*, 173–83).

Susan Warner and Susanna Maria Cummins portray girls, usually orphaned, who first endure callous or indifferent caretakers but ultimately thrive with the solicitous maternal attentions of adoptive figures whose kindness reflects the growing cult of motherhood of the period. In this fiction, women or their feminized male counterparts serve as spiritual and emotional centers of the family, and implicitly of the nation (Singley, *Adopting America*). Their benevolent engagement serves as antidote to the impersonal threats of an increasingly urbanized and industrialized society. Domestic fiction valorizes home and hearth, with Ellen Montgomery in Warner's *The Wide, Wide World* (1850) and Gerty Flint in Cummins's *The Lamplighter* (1854) ending their adventures in marriages to men who reflect, in their combination of authority and good will, the changes taking place in the family as a whole as the nation moved from a model of patriarchal authority to one of democratic idealism that credited the young.

Women entered the literary field in growing numbers and in various ways in the nineteenth century. They became editors as well as authors. Lydia Maria Child addresses girls directly in *The Girl's Own Book* (1833), in the tradition of Anne Bradstreet, and served as founding editor of the *Juvenile Miscellany*, the first US children's magazine (1826). Pioneering newspaper columnist and novelist Fanny Fern (Sara Payson Willis) (1811–72) enjoyed commercial success, including with her bestselling collection of stories and sketches for children, *Little Ferns for Fanny's Little Friends* (1853). Caroline Howard Gilman (1794–1888) started *Rose-Bud, or Youth's Gazette* (renamed *Southern Rosebud*) in 1832. Harriet Beecher Stowe combines social reform with fiction and sentimentality to advance the cause of abolition in her phenomenal *Uncle Tom's Cabin* (1852), read by all ages. Alcott edited the popular, moderate children's magazine, *Robert Merry's Museum* (1863). Mary Mapes Dodge founded *St. Nicholas Magazine* (1873). By the time of the Civil War, women were producing a range of literature, including Civil War literature. Notable is Jane Goodwin Austin's *Dora Darling, the Daughter of the Regiment* (1864), which as James Marten notes, "goes against the usual portrayal of girls fighting their wars behind the lines" (*The Children's Civil War*, 46). The semi-orphaned, twelve-year-old Dora is the daughter of a drunken southern farmer and Unionist mother. When her mother dies, she is adopted by a northern regiment, finds herself behind the Confederate lines, and eventually reunites with her extended family.

Children had been reading and authors had been supplying them with material from the early colonial days. However, a flowering of children's literature took place in the mid- to late nineteenth century, with a proliferation of writing for and about children. These publications coincided with the growth of children's culture, encouraged by a democratic spirit in the new republic and the corresponding image of the United States as a youthful, developing nation. A golden age of children's literature began around 1865, with the publication in England of Lewis Carroll's *Alice in Wonderland* (1865), which portrayed children in playful ways rather than overtly moralistic or didactic ones. Yet this demarcation must be tempered by understanding that, during this time, as Jerry Griswold, quoting Henry Commager, notes, majors wrote for minors; literature had yet to be classified according to the age of the reader (*Audacious Kids*, viii). More commonly, magazines and newspapers arrived in American homes with poems, stories, and essays that were read and enjoyed by all members of the family. Only in the twentieth century did children's literature acquire an exclusive identity, become marginalized in the American literary canon (Clark, *The Cultural Construction*), and become rigidly classified according the reader's age.

The success of the nineteenth-century domestic writers was facilitated by a confluence of factors that included a more literate middle class with sufficient resources to devote to literature; an industrialized economy that supported a burgeoning publishing industry; an incipient women's rights movement that gradually moved women from their assigned roles as homemakers into the public arena; and a growing emphasis on children and the importance of nurture. The history of children's literature follows the history of literature in the United States generally, which is to say that it is first influenced by patriarchal, Calvinist culture and religion and then reflects a gradual feminization of culture in the mid- to late nineteenth century, with gentler, more sentimental forms of Christianity, as Ann Douglas has outlined (*The Feminization of American Culture*). Along these lines, the work of Louisa May Alcott (1832–88) permanently changed representations of family and girlhood. Reform-minded with regard to women's rights as well as temperance and abolition and highly attuned to children's needs and interests, Alcott created in the beloved *Little Women* (1868) a new form of fiction for girls that inspired generations of readers.

Louisa May Alcott, the daughter of a devoted, genteel mother and downwardly mobile, Transcendentalist father, began by writing fairy tales (*Flower Fables*, 1854) and continued to pen fiction for adults and children not only out of creative ambition but also out of financial exigency. Her family depended upon her earnings, and this dependence played a role in her decision, after the immensely popular *Little Women*, to write sequels that met the demand for more stories about the March girls and their peers. Alcott thus became a model of the professional woman writer who negotiates the realities of the marketplace and balances them with her own aesthetic aspirations. It is telling that Alcott pseudonymously wrote and published Gothic thrillers – many about pursued, drugged, or confined girls and women – at the same time that she published lighter fare for children. Her dual career – one secret, one open – reveals a writer in uneasy relation to social norms. She was unable to forego the market for wholesome children's literature, but she was also unwilling to jettison totally the desire to write candidly about women's emotions and experience.

While acknowledging the separate spheres ideology for men and women that was in place until the early twentieth century, Alcott expands roles for girls, and by association for boys who, like Laurie in *Little Women*, enjoy the arts and genteel culture as well as more typically masculine enterprises such as business. In many of her fictions she portrays unconventional families. For example, "My Girls" (1878), in the collection *Aunt Jo's Scrap-Bag*, describes seven young women, one of whom becomes a doctor and, unmarried, adopts a daughter, whom she likewise educates to pursue a vocation. In the novel *Eight Cousins* (1875), Rose is raised by six aunts and an uncle. In other fictions, Alcott depicts families who thrive with an absent father and the loving guidance and example of a strong mother such as Marmee. In *Little Women*, Father March is away at the Civil War for most of the narrative, and although he is missed, his wife and daughters manage by relying on their own resources and one another. Alcott affirms family bonds, especially those between siblings and between mothers and children. With fathers deceased or preoccupied with business, mothers play prominent roles, not only as managers of the home but also as spiritual and emotional caregivers. Alcott elevates the position of the mother and the bonds between mother and daughter to a new height with her portrayal of Marmee and the four March sisters.

The mother–daughter relationship, which Roberta Trites terms "the most complex form of relationship in feminist [children's] literature," is the subject of divergent critical views. Trites notes the passionate love between Jo March and her mother but finds such love replicated in few modern fictions, with the exception of Jamaica Kincaid's *Annie John* (1983). Adrienne Kertzer describes the silencing of the mother in many picture books (*The Quiet Lady*). Traditional fairy tales abound with missing mothers and malevolent stepmothers. Trites draws on feminist theorists such as Adrienne Rich, Barbara Johnson, Gayle Greene, and Carol Gilligan to outline two plot lines frequently encountered in children's and adolescents' novels: stories in which the daughter achieves independence from the mother in a classical Freudian manner (as in Judy Blume's *Deenie* [1973]) and stories which allow the heroine to develop without sacrificing the mother–daughter bond (as in Pam Conrad's *Prairie Songs* [1987] and Virginia Hamilton's *Plain City* [1993]) (*Waking Sleeping Beauty*, 103). Sensitive to the dearth of representations of the mother's story, she cites Sharon Creech's *Walk Two Moons* for its affirmation of mothers' lives and Crescent Dragonwagon's *The Year it Rained* (1985) for its portrayal of mother and daughter bonds that also recognizes difference (118, 104–6).

The most memorable character in Alcott's fiction, and perhaps the best-known female character in all of American children's literature, is the outspoken Jo March, whose triumphs and struggles have inspired as well as frustrated readers. All of the March girls are convincingly drawn: the domestic Meg; the artistic, fashion-conscious Amy; the gentle Beth; but Jo stands out for the sheer power of her intelligence, ambition, and ideals. Each sister must confront and overcome a unique flaw – for Meg materiality; for Amy vanity; and for Beth passivity – in the tradition of didactic children's literature in which children are expected to reach moral milestones on paths to self-improvement. Jo's challenge is to quell her anger, which she holds both against herself for failing to conform to feminine norms and against society for restricting her choices simply because she was born female. Jo aspires to be not only wife and mother but also writer and teacher, a heady combination for her time. Alcott resolves the conflict in favor of the domestic, marrying Jo not to the playful, charming, and affluent Laurie Laurence, with whom she is temperamentally suited, but to the steady, thoughtful, and supportive Professor Bhaer, with whom she founds Plumfield School, an academy for orphaned and needy children. Jo sublimates her literary ambitions in her performance of maternal and teacherly duties, but Alcott's genius is that she neither sugarcoats nor dismisses her heroine's desire for autonomy and self-expression.

Little Women and the domestic fiction with which it is kin establishes features that appear in generations of American children's books, as Gillian Avery notes. These include the virtuous orphan or semi-orphan, the "abrasive spinster aunt" (*Behold the Child*, 177), and a fluid sense of class not found in English counterparts. Novels of the late nineteenth and early twentieth centuries that portray intelligent and adventuresome girls include *The Five Little Peppers and How They Grew* (1881) by Margaret Sidney, *Rebecca of Sunnybrook Farm* (1903) by Kate Douglas Wiggin, *Anne of Green Gables* by Canadian author Lucy Maud Montgomery (1908), *Pollyanna* (1913) by Eleanor H. Porter, and *Caddie Woodlawn* (1935) by Carol Ryrie Brink. A close cousin of this genre is the school story, popular in England during the 1920s and '30s and featuring a rompish heroine, often in conflict with an unyielding headmistress, who triumphs over her studies and wins approval of peers. The genre endures today, with its key element of friendship, as readers of J. K. Rowling's *Harry Potter* series will attest. Cynthia Voight's *Tell Me If the Lovers are Losers* (1982), set in 1961 at the fictitious Stanton College, is a contemporary example of the female school story genre. It explores the dynamics among three friends from different parts of the country who relate to one another from different social, moral, and economic frameworks.

The early twentieth century saw an expansion of the market for children's literature, with books published more cheaply than before and therefore more accessible to children of the lower or lower-middle classes. A renewed focus on children, exemplified by the founding of organizations such as the Boy Scouts of America in 1910 and the Girl Scouts of America in 1912, as well as advocacy of good citizenship, sound minds, and strong bodies by such leading figures as President Theodore Roosevelt, resulted in emphasis on children's need for play and for refreshment in the outdoors. *The Secret Garden* (1911) by Frances Hodgson Burnett is salient in this regard. English-born but resident in the United States, Burnett is claimed on both sides of the Atlantic. She tells the story of orphaned Mary Lennox, who comes to live with her widowed uncle and invalid cousin, Colin Craven. Led by a robin to an abandoned garden on the estate, Mary takes the lead to bring the plants back to life. As they cultivate the soil, she and Colin reap physical and emotional benefits from their restorative work. The garden becomes the children's secret domain until, with Colin cured, they reveal the garden to Mary's grieving uncle, reviving his spirits as well as their own. The impact of positive thought, the healing powers of nature, and children's special place in the outdoors, form the center of this tale, which borders on fantasy, so emphatic is it about the immortal gifts of nature. Mary is the clear heroine of the tale; however, the ending of the story reveals its reliance on traditional gender roles and an English emphasis on heredity and primogeniture, with Mary playing a somewhat secondary role to the now healthy heir, Colin.

Nature of a different kind preoccupies the heroine in a major early twentieth-century achievement in children's literature: Laura Ingalls Wilder's autobiographical *Little House in the Big Woods* (1935) and its sequels. Wilder describes daily life on the American frontier in her chronicles of Laura and her family as they encounter Indians and wild animals, grow their own food, complete chores, and enjoy simple pleasures of rural life. Her books are studies of settlers in relationship with the wilderness and are a tribute to the pioneers who embarked on the exciting, grueling, and dangerous task of westward migration. The ever-present Ma, evocative of Marmee in *Little Women*, turns crude shelters and cabins into homes and keeps the family intact; the restless, storytelling, fiddle-playing Pa, with more than a passing resemblance to Bronson Alcott, exemplifies one aspect of the American frontier spirit. Wilder blends realism and romanticism with her stories and songs drawn from folk literature and culture, giving her tales a distinctly American character. Laura, who pursues a profession in teaching, often stands at the crossroads of desire and the marketplace; but Wilder, who composed the series during the Great Depression, makes it clear that family, not money, is the chief good. The *Little House* series has held its appeal, with the appearance of reprints, a line of commercial products, and a television series based on the books, all demonstrating the interrelationship of children's literature and material culture (Bernstein, "Children's Books").

Women writers have also made their mark in the important category of fantasy literature. In a book for young readers, *Catwings* (1988), Ursula LeGuin (1929–) portrays winged kittens that talk, fly, and discover human kindness. A major writer of science fiction, a traditionally male domain, LeGuin explores the permeability of gender in her groundbreaking *The Left Hand of Darkness* (1969), the first in a series of books about the fictional planet Hain and its universe. Her work is notable for its feminist and sociological aspects; her *Earthsea* novels explore the complex workings of art, nature, myth, and magic. Madeleine L'Engle's immensely popular *A Wrinkle in Time* (1963) depicts two siblings who with a friend solve the mystery of their parents' disappearance by traveling into the cosmos. L'Engle writes a scientifically engaging story that is also warm and approachable; her writing integrates feminine images and structures with traditionally masculine rationality. Natalie Babbitt's superb *Tuck Everlasting* (1975) explores immortality in a story about a family that will never die. Lois Lowry offers a haunting portrait of a futuristic society in *The Giver* (1993), a science fiction allegory about the challenges of balancing freedom and security. A prolific author, she writes realistic fiction about families and relationships as well as fantasy.

Women writers also employ fantasy in their retellings of traditional fairy tales, folk tales, and myths. Robin McKinley in *The Blue Sword* (1982) and Jane Yolen in *Twelve Impossible Things before Breakfast* (2001) explore the intersections of gender and power, correcting for male bias and investing female characters with autonomy. Yolen tells a haunting story of the Holocaust through the lens of the classic fairy tale, "Sleeping Beauty," in *Briar Rose* (1992), and she reflects on centuries of traditional literature for children in her collection of essays, *Touch Magic* (1981).

Female authors made significant contributions to the outpouring of realism that characterizes children's literature from the mid- to late twentieth century and deals with such topics as sex, drugs, divorce, racial discrimination, and death. Realistic fiction, which presents opportunities for authors to grapple with social and moral issues, has been particularly fertile ground for female writers who wish to address issues of gender. Louise Fitzhugh's *Harriet the Spy* (1964) portrays a spunky, eleven-year-old aspiring writer – an echo of Jo March – who freely expresses her feelings, at one point saying, "I'll be damned if I'll go to dancing school." The novel resists an overly neat resolution of the conflict that ensues when Harriet's personal journal is made public. Also noteworthy is Patricia MacLachlan's Newbery Award-winning *Sarah, Plain and Tall* (1985). A perceptive character study, it addresses children's yearnings for an intact home with two parents, somewhat in the tradition of the domestic fiction a century earlier. Anna and Caleb, whose mother died after Caleb's birth, are delighted that Sarah, who is from Maine, will marry their father and stay with them on the prairie. Set in the late 1800s, this realistic historical novel conveys female agency in two ways: the independent and competent Sarah makes her own decision to stay with the family, and the tale is narrated by Anna. Phyllis Reynolds Naylor's *Shiloh* (1991), set in rural West Virginia, is about a gentle boy's struggle to save a dog from its abusive owner and cope with the moral dilemmas that ensue from his efforts. Naylor is well known and sometimes criticized for her "Alice" books, realistic narratives about the adventures of the motherless Alice McKinley, who grows up in an all-male household.

A writer who serves as a lightning rod for questions about the appropriateness of explicit subject matter in realistic children's literature is Judy Blume (1938–). A prolific author renowned for her portrait of a boy nicknamed Fudge in *Tales of a Fourth Grade Nothing* (1972) and its sequels, she inspired widespread controversy with her groundbreaking *Are You There God? It's Me, Margaret* (1970). This now-classic novel broaches the subjects of menstruation, masturbation, religious differences, and peer pressure. One of the most banned authors in the United States, Blume has been attacked for her moral relativism and trendy adherence to "values clarification," but millions who read her fiction would disagree with her detractors. Blume has helped generations of girls to assert identities separate from those of parents and peers, value their feelings, explore their spirituality, and feel comfortable about their unique developmental paths. Blume's willingness to address formerly taboo subjects aligned with the goals and strategies of the women's movement of the 1970s and helped to give young female readers a voice and sense of their own power. A focus on realistic fiction also ushered in children's literature that addresses formerly taboo subjects of homosexuality, for example, Lesléa

Newman's *Heather Has Two Mommies* (1989), and has led to contemporary critical interest in intersections of children's literature and queer theory.

In addition to realism, a major development of the twentieth century involves multicultural children's literature. This focus on diversity is now in the twenty-first century extending beyond national boundaries to global and comparative aspects of children's literature (Beckett, *Reflections of Change*). Children of color, in particular African American children, benefited little from the golden age of literature that admirably served their white, middle-class counterparts in the late nineteenth century. Lacking adequate access to education, editors, and presses as well as economic opportunities to pursue literary careers, African American women struggled to be heard. Although it is not explicitly a children's book, *Our Nig* (1859) by Harriet Wilson deserves mention as the first female African American novel. Autobiographical, it charts the brutal mistreatment of a young mulatta who is abandoned by her impoverished mother and subjected to years of abuse in the home of an ostensibly abolitionist northern white family, where she labors as a servant. Frado Smith's experience contrasts starkly with that of fictionalized, white orphaned girls who find loving middle-class families and reap the benefits of Christian benevolence. Frado's efforts to become a writer place her in a tradition of American heroines who aspire to become literary, autonomous, and self-supporting, but unlike her white counterparts, Frado encounters insurmountable obstacles born of racism.

In the twentieth century, African American female writers have produced outstanding works in every genre, from folk tales and fantasy to historical fiction and realism. This literature informs as it entertains by promoting cultural pride, correcting inaccurate histories, and countering stereotypes and prejudices. Virginia Hamilton (1936–2002), a bestselling and prolific writer for children of all ages, was the first African American to win the Newbery Medal for *M. C. Higgins the Great* (1975), which caters to middle-grade readers. Her first book, *Zeely*, published in 1967, was a departure from books published during a time of civil rights and black consciousness, which frequently emphasized urban racial problems in the United States. Hamilton chooses a rural setting for her tale and interweaves folklore and realism to tell the coming-of-age story of a young girl who believes a local woman to be a Watusi queen.

Hamilton is also a distinguished author of traditional literature. The title story in her collection of folk tales, *The People Could Fly* (2004), expresses longing for escape from slavery. Hamilton also retells familiar stories, including the trickster tale, from an African American perspective. Like Charles Chesnutt, who wrote in the late nineteenth and early twentieth centuries, Hamilton challenges sentimental depictions of plantation life under slavery, such as those popularized by Joel Chandler Harris in his *Uncle Remus* tales. She writes with authentic, moderate dialect and a sure voice, infusing her characters and plots with the theme of freedom. She chose *American Black Folktales* as the subtitle for her collection, *The People Could Fly*, rather than the more conventional *Black American Folktales* in order to emphasize the nationality and universality of her fiction rather than its specifically racial content. As she says, "American first and black second" (quoted in Fox, "Virginia Hamilton"). Hamilton also rewrites fairy tales and folk tales, empowering women by giving them active rather than passive roles. For example, in "Catskinella," a revision of the classic "Cinderella" in the collection, *Her Stories* (1995), the heroine wears a form-fitting cat suit that emphasizes her beauty and connection to nature, runs away from her betrothed, and confidently takes steps to assure her own happiness.

Working in the realistic tradition, African American novelist and playwright Alice Childress (1916–94) breaks new ground in *A Hero Ain't Nothin' but a Sandwich* (1973), the first young adult novel to depict heroin addiction. The story of a thirteen-year-old boy, Benjie Johnson, is told from multiple points of view, including Benjie's friends, his drug dealer, his mother, and his grandmother. Also in the realistic tradition is African American writer Mildred Taylor (1948–), who draws on family history in Mississippi for her trilogy about the Logan family and their encounters with racial hostility during the 1930s. Her Newbery Medal-winning second book, *Roll of Thunder, Hear My Cry* (1976), in which the Logans fight for their rights, is narrated by Cassie, the eldest daughter, who is nine years old when the story begins and who learns the risks and rewards of asserting herself in a climate of bigotry. Realistic elements can also be found in books for very young readers. Mary Hoffman's picture book, *Amazing Grace* (1991), is an engaging story about a girl who proves that she can be the best Peter Pan in spite of the fact that she is female and black.

Among Latina writers who have made major contributions to children's literature, Julia Alvarez stands out for her bestselling *How the Garcia Girls Lost their Accents* (1991) and its sequel, *¡Yo!* (1997). Born in the Dominican Republic, she infuses her work not only with the revolutionary politics of her father, which inspired her 1994 *In the Time of Butterflies*, but also with the experience of being female and immigrant, and with the process of cultural assimilation. Innovative with its reverse chronological order and multiple viewpoints, *Garcia Girls* is a *Bildungsroman* that tells the story of four sisters. Another major achievement in Chicana literature is Sandra Cisneros's *The House on Mango Street* (1984), a sensitive, evocative, and poetic account of an adolescent girl and her family and community. Esperanza, whose name means hope, lives with loving parents and siblings in run-down neighborhoods and suffers not from lack of ambition but from lack of access to material goods and opportunities that define the American Dream. Esperanza resembles her nineteenth-century literary forebears, such as Ellen Montgomery in *The Wide, Wide World* (1850) and Gerty Flint in *The Lamplighter* (1854), in her wish for a house that is truly a home. Cisneros transforms the *Bildungsroman* by telling a story not only about individual growth but also about community. Esperanza aspires not just for herself but for others who are similarly disenfranchised. For example, she vows that if she is fortunate enough to acquire a home of her own, she will invite the "passing bums" from the neighborhood into the attic because she "know[s] how it is to be without a house" (*House on Mango Street*, 87).

Cisneros delivers a social critique of institutions such as the Catholic Church that ostensibly support the family but in practice denigrate it. When Esperanza points out her rented apartment to a nun from her school, the nun remarks insensitively, "You live *there?*" Cisneros conveys the experience of childhood on the cusp of puberty with its incipient curiosity and naïveté. For example, the girls delight in feeling like Cinderella when they wear high-heeled shoes and parade in the neighborhood, but they are chagrined by the unexpected attention they receive from men on the street. Cisneros links Esperanza's hopes and struggles to those of other female characters, including her friend Sally, who is abused by her father. She creates powerful, mythic mentors called The Three Sisters, who read Esperanza's fortune and predict her success in the world but who also, in a challenge to Anglo American individualism, remind her that she must go away in order "to come back." The novel is a testament to community as well as selfhood. The reader finishes the story confident that Esperanza will achieve her goal to become a writer and will create not only a home that is a physical space but also a home in the heart. Another writer sensitive to the difficulties of dislocation and immigration is Amada Irma Pérez, whose bilingual picture book, *My Diary from Here to There* (2002), tells of a girl's anxiety and excitement when her family moves from Mexico to the United States. Poet, essayist, and novelist of adult literature Ana Castillo draws on Aztec and Nahuati cultures to provide instruction for youths in two long poems that comprise *My Daughter, My Son, The Eagle, The Dove* (2000).

The tradition of American children's literature written by women is as deeply rooted and varied as the American literary tradition itself. Female writers play foundational roles in creating literature for children and lead the way in its development and innovation. Perhaps because women and children are historically linked in Western culture, female writers of children's literature have not met with skepticism or opposition in the same way that women writing exclusively for adult audiences have. They do not, for example, suffer the same anxiety of influence that Sandra Gilbert and Susan Gubar outline in their pivotal study of nineteenth-century female writers of adult literature (*The Madwoman in the Attic*). Women have been granted at least partial share of the domain of children's literature, and their participation in this realm is assumed, despite its essentialist pitfalls, to be normal or natural.

This is not to deny the obstacles that face the path of female writers of literature for children. Women confront the ambivalence that originates from the fact that language evokes "conflicting feelings of anxiety and empowerment in women," and they have been challenged to "manifest this 'anxious power' in various ways" (Singley and Sweeney, *Anxious Power*, xiii). Female writers have, for example, revised literary genres, especially the romance plot; imagined fluid or communal notions of self as alternatives to the individualistic portraits typically found in patriarchal culture; created meta-fiction and embedded narratives that complicate linearity and articulate communal rather than singular decision making; experimented with multiple voices and new sources of agency; encoded feminine imagery and structures; and directly opposed social, political, and economic conditions that place limits on the female children represented in their literature. These strategies might be deployed overtly in the interest of feminism or more generally in the interest of equality among individuals regardless of gender and other markers of difference such as race, class, ethnicity, religion, or sexual orientation; or they might emerge organically from aesthetic considerations of content and form.

Female writers of children's literature have faced challenges that affect the field of children's literature as a whole. Children's literature has been marginalized rather than accorded full literary status in the academy. Courses in children's literature have been relegated to "service" courses, paralleling perhaps a traditional understanding of women's importance in service roles as wives, mothers, and homemakers. Relatively recently, children's literature has been supported as an area of critical study. Through programs and advocacy of organizations such as the Children's Literature Association, the Modern Language Association has sponsored sessions about children and children's literature at annual conventions. Literary critics and theorists have in the last decades subjected children's literature to the same intensive analysis they give adult literature (Hunt, *Children's Literature*; May, *Children's Literature and Critical Theory*; Rudd, *The Routledge Companion to Children's Literature*); and children's history, culture, and literature have been represented in significant numbers in graduate and undergraduate programs at colleges and universities, including in Childhood Studies as well as English programs. Not all children's literature by women is feminist or aims to be feminist. However, as Peter Hunt writes, given the importance in children's literature of "questions of control, and other techniques through which power is exercised over, or shared with, the reader" (*Criticism*, 81), examining American women's creative visions in terms of social contexts as well as aesthetic qualities can only enhance understanding of the important role women play in the development of American literature for children.

Works cited

Avery, Gillian. *Behold the Child: American Children and their Books, 1621–1922.* Baltimore: The Johns Hopkins University Press, 1994.

Bader, Barbara. *American Picturebooks from Noah's Ark to the Beast Within.* New York: Macmillan, 1976.

Baym, Nina. *Woman's Fiction: A Guide to Novels by and about Women in America, 1820–1870.* Ithaca: Cornell University Press, 1978.

Beckett, Sandra L., ed. *Reflections of Change: Children's Literature since 1945.* Westport, CT: Greenwood, 1997.

Bernstein, Robin. "Children's Books, Dolls, and the Performance of Race; or, The Possibility of Children's Literature." *PMLA* 126.1 (January 2011): 160–9.

Blackford, Holly. "Daughters of the Revolution: Democracy and Didacticism in Susanna Rowson's *Charlotte Temple* (1974)." *Transatlantic Sensations.* Ed. Jennifer Phegley, John Cyril Barton, and Kristin N. Hudson. Burlington, VT: Ashgate, 2012.

Cisneros, Sandra. *The House on Mango Street.* New York: Vintage Random House, 1984.

Clark, Beverly Lyon. *The Cultural Construction of Children's Literature in America.* Baltimore: The Johns Hopkins University Press, 2003.

Commager, Henry Steele. "When Majors Wrote for Minors." *Saturday Review* 10 (May 1952): 10–11.

Douglas, Ann. *The Feminization of American Culture.* New York: Knopf, 1977.

Griswold, Jerry. *Audacious Kids: Coming of Age in America's Classic Children's Books.* New York: Oxford University Press, 1992.

Fox, Margalit. "Virginia Hamilton, Writer for Children, is Dead at 65." *New York Times* February 20, 2002, a19.

Gilbert, Sandra and Susan Gubar. *The Madwoman in the Attic: The Woman Writer and the Nineteenth-Century Literary Imagination.* New Haven: Yale University Press, 1979.

Gubar, Marah. "On Not Defining Children's Literature." *PMLA* 126.1 (January 2011): 209–16.

Haviland, Virginia and Margaret N. Coughlan, eds. *Yankee Doodle's Literary Sampler of Prose, Poetry, and Pictures.* New York: Crowell, 1974.

Hunt, Peter. *Criticism, Theory, and Children's Literature.* Cambridge: Basil Blackwell, 1991.

Hunt, Peter, ed. *Children's Literature: An Illustrated History.* New York: Oxford University Press, 1995.

Literature for Children: Contemporary Criticism. New York: Routledge, 1992.

Johnson, Dianne A. *Telling Tales: The Pedagogy and Promise of African American Literature for Youth*. Westport, CT: Greenwood, 1990.

Kertzer, Adrienne. "This Quiet Lady: Maternal Voices and the Picture Book." *Children's Literature Association Quarterly* 18 (1993–4): 159–64.

Lesnik-Oberstein, Karin. *Children's Literature: Criticism and the Fictional Child*. Oxford: Clarendon Press, 1994.

Lystad, Mary H. *From Dr. Mather to Dr. Seuss: 200 Years of American Books for Children*. Boston: G. K. Hall and Co., 1980.

May, Jill P. *Children's Literature and Critical Theory: Reading and Writing for Understanding*. New York: Oxford University Press, 1995.

MacLeod, Anne Scott. *American Childhood: Essays on Children's Literature of the Nineteenth and Twentieth Centuries*. Athens, GA: University of Georgia Press, 1994.

   A Moral Tale: Children's Fiction and American Culture, 1820–1860. Hamden, CT: Archon, 1975.

Marten, James. *The Children's Civil War*. Chapel Hill: University of North Carolina Press, 1998.

Nodelman, Perry. "The Case of Children's Fiction; or, The Impossibility of Jacqueline Rose." *Children's Literature Association Quarterly* 10.3 (1985): 98–100.

Rogers, Katharine M., ed. *The Meridian Anthology of Early American Women Writers: From Anne Bradstreet to Louisa May Alcott, 1650–1865*. New York: Meridian, Penguin, 1991.

Rose, Jacqueline. *The Case of Peter Pan; or, The Impossibility of Children's Fiction*. 1984. Philadelphia: University of Pennsylvania Press, 1993.

Rudd, David. *The Routledge Companion to Children's Literature*. New York: Routledge, 2010.

Singley, Carol J. *Adopting America: Childhood, Kinship, and National Identity in Literature*. New York: Oxford University Press, 2011.

Singley, Carol J. and Susan Elizabeth Sweeney, eds. *Anxious Power: Reading, Writing, and Ambivalence in Narrative by Women*. Albany: State University of New York Press, 1993.

Trites, Roberta Seelinger. *Waking Sleeping Beauty: Feminist Voices in Children's Novels*. Iowa City: University of Iowa Press, 1997.

16

US suffrage literature

MARY CHAPMAN

On Valentine's Day 1916, US suffragists sent more than 1,000 illustrated rhyming poems to legislators in an effort to court congressional support for a federal woman's suffrage amendment. One, sent to Congressman William Cary (R-Wisconsin) and reprinted in *The Suffragist* magazine, depicted a woman watering a flower in a pot and was accompanied by a parody of a well-known nursery rhyme (see Fig. 16.1):

> Cary, Cary, quite contrary
> How does your voting go?
> With pork barrel bills
> and other ills
> And your suffrage vote
> so – slow.

Another, sent to Congressman Edward Pou (D-North Carolina) and reproduced in *The Suffragist* magazine, depicted a chivalrous man presenting flowers to a charming woman; the caption read (see Fig. 16.2):

> The rose is red
> The violets blue
> But VOTES are
> Better Mr. Pou

Suffragists were prompted to try this literary stunt because, as the valentine campaign organizer conceded, the "eloquence of the soap box, cart tail, and back of an automobile variety" had little impact on legislators: "We hope that rhymes may influence the politicians where the other forces did not" ("Suffragists Use," n.p.).

These witty rhyming valentines represent only a fraction of the extensive archive of literary works written in the service of the US suffrage campaign. From the early 1850s, when an organized national women's rights movement

Fig. 16.1 "Cary, Cary," SB001822, National Woman's Party Archives, Sewall-Belmont House and Museum, Washington, DC

emerged, to 1920, when the Nineteenth Amendment enfranchising women was ratified, US women writers from a variety of racial, ethnic, and class backgrounds published hundreds of short stories, novels, poems, plays, essays and conversion narratives in support of woman suffrage. Suffrage history, however, has focused almost exclusively on the influential role played by oratory and other documentary polemical forms.[1] It credits the charismatic orators – for example, Susan B. Anthony, Elizabeth Cady Stanton, Anna Howard Shaw, and Carrie Chapman Catt – with the eventual success of the eighty-year campaign. However, suffrage organizers from the very beginning recognized how creative literature played a critical persuasive role. In an essay entitled "The

Fig. 16.2 "The rose is red," SB0001823, National Woman's Party Archives, Sewall-Belmont House and Museum, Washington, DC

Truth of Fiction, and Its Charms," published in the first issue of the very first American journal devoted to women's rights, *The Una* (1853), an anonymous editor argued that popular fiction was a valuable rhetorical form for the emergent movement. "[Fiction] brings the truth of nature – the probable, the possible and the ideal – in their broadest range and utmost capabilities into the service of a favorite principle," and demonstrates its force and beauty, and practicability, in circumstantial details, which like a panorama, presents an image so like an experience that we realize it for all the purposes of knowledge, hope and resolution" (quoted in Petty, *Romancing the Vote*, 4). In 1892, Stanton, the president of the newly formed National American Woman Suffrage Association, reiterated this appreciation of literature's ability to move people to embrace a "favorite principle": "I have long waited ... for some woman to arise to do for her sex what Mrs. Stowe did for the black race in 'Uncle Tom's Cabin,' a book that did more to rouse the national conscience than all the glowing appeals and constitutional arguments that agitated our people during half a century" (Stanton, *Pray, Sir*, vi–vii). Many suffrage supporters responded to Stanton's call, particularly in the final two decades of the campaign.

For every woman who dared to stand on a podium to address a mixed audience about the importance of enfranchising women, there were many more who expressed their political views through literary works. Popular literature was, in fact, the primary rhetorical mode available to American women because political oratory, even into the twentieth century, was considered unwomanly. In contrast to oratory, literature allowed the female suffragist "speaker" to control the visibility of her gendered body: to be strategically less visible, her voice potentially less gendered and hence less controversial. In print, particularly if she published anonymously or pseudonymously or took advantage of text's performative opportunities, a suffragist speaker's voice could be rhetorically persuasive while her literal body remained invisible and, therefore womanly and unassailable. Acoustically silent, popular literature could serve disenfranchised women as "voiceless speech."

An astonishing number of canonical and popular US writers voiced their support of woman suffrage through literary works. Sara Parton Willis, for example, wrote pro-suffrage essays such as "Independence" and "Shall Women Vote?" under the pseudonym "Fanny Fern." Harriet Beecher Stowe, more famous for supporting abolition than suffrage, published serialized fiction such as *My Wife and I* and fictional dialogues such as the *Chimney Corner* that expressed moderate support for suffrage. Louisa May Alcott and Elizabeth Stuart Phelps authored suffrage literature for children. Twentieth-century author Gertrude Atherton wrote *Julia France and her Times* (1912), a novel based on a play she had written about the British suffrage campaign. Popular Virginian novelist Mary Johnston published *Hagar* (1913), a novel about a southern woman's move to embrace suffrage. Middlebrow author Zona Gale published numerous short stories collected in *Friendship Village* and *Peace in Friendship Village*; another middlebrow author, Edna Ferber, wrote a popular novel, *Fanny Herself* (1917), that describes a New York suffrage parade in moving detail. The narrator of Mary Austin's acclaimed novel *A Woman of Genius* (1912) also mentions participating in a suffrage parade. Expatriate dramatist and actress Elizabeth Robins wrote a frequently performed play entitled *Votes for Women* (1907). Many early twentieth-century poets – Frances Harper, Charlotte Perkins Gilman, Marianne Moore, and Edna St. Vincent Millay to name just a few – wrote poetry in support of suffrage or in praise of suffragist leaders. Modernist and stunt-girl journalist Djuna Barnes wrote a shocking piece of creative journalism, "How It Feels to be Forcibly Fed" (1914), for the cause.

Even avant-gardist Gertrude Stein considered the suffrage theme when she wrote an opera libretto memorializing Susan B. Anthony, *The Mother of Us All* (1946), twenty-six years after the ratification of the Nineteenth Amendment. In addition to these more canonical figures, many popular women writers, including sensation fiction author Lillie Devereux Blake, satirical poet Alice Duer Miller, and Western novelist Abigail Scott Duniway – while less familiar to contemporary readers – also made significant contributions to the suffrage literary tradition.[2] Although no one text rivals the now-canonical status of *Uncle Tom's Cabin*, many of these works are literarily and politically moving, and performed important cultural work.

This extensive archive of literary works about suffrage complicates the common perception of US suffrage rhetoric as a primarily oratorical phenomenon; rather, this archive suggests that US women writers generated a rich rhetorical tradition beyond stump-speaking and other traditional rhetorical forms by taking advantage of the persuasive power of popular literature. At the same time, this archive complicates our understanding of the tradition of US women's writing, making evident that in addition to writing on behalf of other oppressed classes – most notably, enslaved African Americans and displaced Native Americans – US women writers also wrote on their own behalf, enacting the voicing of women's political views in a public forum in order to campaign for permission to voice those views at the polls. In addition, the modern works in this archive in particular share a concern for voice and for experiments in voice with modernist literary texts, suggesting in fact that radical political texts may also showcase modernist experiment. Taking inspiration from other recovery projects that have complicated US literary history (for example, Jane Tompkins on nineteenth-century US women's sentimental fiction and Paula Bernat Bennett on nineteenth-century US women's poetry), this essay traces a tradition of literature written as a form of suffrage rhetoric. Like popular sentimental fiction that articulated the aims of the anti-slavery and temperance movements, protested the policy of Indian Removal, or campaigned against the death penalty, suffrage literature also performed important "cultural work" (Tompkins, *Sensational Designs*, 2), from the antebellum period right up through the Progressive Era.

By adapting strategies in response to changing political and social realities over the course of a long and multi-faceted campaign, the contributors to this literary tradition succeeded in "redefin[ing] the social order" (Tompkins, *Sensational Designs*, xi) of the United States quite dramatically, by persuading voters to support state suffrage referenda, by convincing the US Congress to adopt a Constitutional Amendment that would enfranchise women in

1919, and by moving state legislatures to ratify this amendment in 1920. In effect, the literary tradition succeeded in demanding a "voice" for women. But even more importantly, writers in this literary tradition reimagined this "voice." In the process of campaigning for the vote, suffragists (paradoxically) came to recognize the limitations of those forms of voice that democratic cultures had associated most closely with active citizenship: the individual, transparent model of the orator who used his acoustical voice to express his personal, individual, unencumbered political perspective, *and* the distilled version of that acoustical voice, the Vote. By contrast, popular literature enabled suffragists to access alternative forms of "voice" that were much less individualist and monologic and much more populist and dialogic; they found that popular poetry, drama, and fiction could stage productive, consensus-building debate; that an anonymous or pseudonymous "voice" could more freely imagine women (and other interest groups) as a united collective; and that suffrage autobiography – rather than oratory or polemic – could assume a more intimate form of address. Through experiments in character, setting, tone, and trope, US suffragist authors mapped in literary form the ways in which they were reimagining participation in a democratic public sphere. In effect, what began in the nineteenth century as a strategy for dodging proscriptions against women speaking in public evolved into new models of the ways in which a group of affiliated individuals could contribute to the public conversation while also anticipating modernist experiments in voice.

Although suffrage literature from its inception featured occasional orator figures (for example, women characters who dared to counter gender norms to speak publicly about their political views), many suffrage texts mock orators whose elitism separates them from the common people or whose illogical anti-suffragist views can be readily skewered. Other suffrage texts give narrative voice over to constituencies not often represented in literature or in the political sphere. Some suffrage literature also imagines spokespeople beyond the individual orator: for example, the folksy female gossip; writers and other print cultural workers; and secretaries whose job is to "collaborate" with other speakers/writers. In more modern suffrage literature in particular, "speakers" are assisted by emergent communication technologies such as telephony, telegraphy, typewriting, and stenography. Whereas an oration might be capable of presenting only one perspective on a complex issue, in suffrage literature characters can engage in debate, providing multiple perspectives on complex issues, including women's enfranchisement. Thematically, then, suffrage literature routinely celebrates the finding of "voice" within a conversational community. Formally, suffrage literature celebrates the dialogic: it explores the potential of collaborative forms of authorship, for example, epistolary novels, composite novels, song, and documentary drama. It also uses intertextuality to produce dialogism within texts through, for example, quotation and parody. In all of these ways, suffrage literature imagines a utopian public sphere in which debate happens between democratic citizens. Although all women's writing in some way takes up the feminist theme of women's self-expression, suffrage literature takes the subject of women's achievement of political self-expression as an opportunity to experiment with literary voice.

Nineteenth-century male oratory and its literary alternative

By definition, oratory was understood in nineteenth-century America – the golden age of oratory – as a "means of securing and exercising political rights" (Karafilis, "Oratory," 126). Republican oratorical traditions were the primary means of participating in the political processes and institutions of the USA. Indeed, one's oratorical talent functioned as a linguistic marker of one's fitness for citizenship and one's subscription to the republican ideals of "Americanness." However, the model orator – the independent-thinking individual who expressed an opinion and spoke in order to persuade others of the wisdom of that opinion – was, in antebellum America, presumed male and his audience was also primarily male. Women were not typically welcome in the public oratorical sphere. "Quite simply," as rhetoric historian Karlyn Kohrs Campbell writes, "in nineteenth-century America, femininity and rhetorical action were seen as mutually exclusive. No 'true woman' could be a public persuader" (*Man Cannot Speak for Her*, 9). Although women had preached in America since the mid-eighteenth century and many antebellum benevolent associations encouraged women's participation in their meetings, women were mostly excluded from the oratorical realm, particularly the realm of political oratory.[3] Public speaking "threatened female character with widespread and permanent injury – the vine usurps the role of the elm" ("Pastoral Letter"). If a woman attempted oratorical rhetorical action, she risked losing her "claim to purity and piety" (Campbell, *Man Cannot Speak for Her*, 191). Standing up in public and demanding the attention of an audience, particularly a mixed (or "promiscuous") audience, for rhetorical purposes was regarded as unwomanly and "beyond" woman's sphere. So, too, were asserting an opinion and arguing a position.

Because of these widely held beliefs about women's proper sphere, the earliest American women's rights orators were pelted with rotten eggs, hymnbooks, tobacco plugs, and pepper when they took to the podium in the 1830s. The hall in which antislavery and women's rights orator Angelina Grimké spoke was burned to the ground by an angry mob (Catt and Shuler, *Woman Suffrage and Politics*, 114). An editorial in the *New York Tribune* labeled the series of orations presented at the 1852 National Women's Rights Convention at Syracuse "a farce" involving a lunatic fringe of "badly mated" "mannish women" and "old maids" who threatened to overturn society by consigning men to housekeeping duties while women legislators interrupted their professional duties to give birth on the "floor of Congress"! (quoted in Kraditor, *Up from the Pedestal*, 189). Even as the women's rights movement gained momentum and more women took to the podium, giving speeches to state legislatures and the public and demonstrating their tremendous oratorical talent, the majority of women, even supporters, feared that public speaking on behalf of a crusade to obtain greater civil rights for women risked making them appear "unsexed"!

Female orators provoked opposition as much because of their embodied, gendered presence in physical public spaces traditionally reserved for men as because of the revolutionary content of their orations. By their very appearance on podia, women were asserting their equal claim with men to citizenship. As a consequence, suffrage oratory was not entirely effective. Therefore, the nineteenth-century campaign for women's rights had a conundrum at its core: how to persuade others to accept the political equality of women without violating reigning gender norms that located women's sphere in the private realm of domesticity and the family. One solution to this conundrum was for female orators to adopt what was understood as a more "feminine" style of oratory.[4] By affiliating themselves and their project more closely with preaching than with politicking, orators such as Sojourner Truth grounded their rhetorical authority in women's religious or moral authority, produced a credible ethos, and assuaged fears that woman suffrage would turn women into men. Female orators also advanced a style of public speaking – less oratory than conversation – that was personal in tone, relied more on personal experience, anecdotes, and examples, and was structured inductively, inviting audience participation and identification with the speaker. These orators affiliated their rhetorical appeal with womanly influence. Others adopted a modest, feminine style of dress that compensated for the threat they posed; for example, instead of wearing controversial "bloomers," Angelina Grimké made her message more palatable by wearing modest Quaker dress that evoked both the domestic and the religious sphere (see Mattingly, *Appropriate[ing] Dress*).

Another response was to use an alternative rhetorical form that could persuade the broader public about women's rights without compromising women's femininity: popular creative literature. Unlike oratory, women's creative contributions to aesthetic genres such as sentimental and even sensational literature did not contravene nineteenth-century gender norms. Through her literary works, the nineteenth-century woman writer performed a role similar to the Republican mother, guiding readers in the skills required of the nation's citizens. Authorship was accepted as a woman's profession, particularly if she, like Louisa May Alcott, Lillie Devereux Blake, and "Fanny Fern," publicly emphasized that her earnings supported her family. Women wrote domestic novels, sentimental novels and poetry, as well as literature for children – all subgenres that focused on the domestic sphere, on families rather than individuals, and on interior emotions rather than public reason. However, by examining public issues through these putatively domestic literary forms, the popular, bestselling woman author could remain a "private woman" while occupying a "public stage," exercising a kind of indirect womanly influence over her readers.[5] Creative literature was an ideal form of persuasion for nineteenth-century women to deploy because it could be coded as private (and womanly) since it was consumed in the home, while simultaneously being public (and influential) because it could address controversial public topics such as Indian removal, slavery, the death penalty, and women's rights. Harriet Beecher Stowe is the paradigmatic example of the nineteenth-century woman who influenced readers' perspectives on a controversial issue through her literary writing. *Uncle Tom's Cabin* (1852) moved hundreds of thousands of readers, particularly in northern states, to "feel right" about slavery; by encouraging them to identify sympathetically with black characters with whom they shared a love for family, nation, and God, the novel persuaded readers to recognize African Americans' humanity and to advocate abolition. The power of Stowe's novel to effect a "radical transformation of society" (Tompkins, *Sensational Designs*, 145) through sentiment made clear that popular literature could be as effective a form of persuasion as oratory.

Between 1848 – when a national women's rights movement was inaugurated at a historic meeting at Seneca Falls, New York, organized by Elizabeth Cady Stanton and others – and 1907 – the date most scholars consider the start of the "modern" suffrage campaign, US women writers produced scores of novels, works of serial fiction, short stories, poems, and plays about the "woman question," many of which were published in the emergent women's periodicals: earlier on in women's journals such as *The Lily* (1849–56) and *The Una* (1853–5); and later in explicitly pro-suffrage journals such as *The Woman's Journal* (1870–1917), the more radical *The Revolution* (1868–70), and the western paper *The New Northwest* (1871–7). Many literary works, like Laura Curtis Bullard's sentimental novel *Christine, or Woman's Trials and Triumphs* (1856), Elizabeth Harbert's sentimental novel *Out of her Sphere* (1871), and Lillie Devereux Blake's sensational novel *Fettered for Life, or, Lord and Master* (1874), emulated Stowe's moral appeal and her examination of political questions through a narrative focus on a sphere that was womanly and domestic. In the same way that *Uncle Tom's Cabin* encouraged readers to empathize with enslaved African families, nineteenth-century suffrage texts moved their readers to identify with female characters who suffer because they lack the protection of the vote. Readers who might be disposed to dismiss suffrage supporters as "mannish women" or "hens that crow" were encouraged to identify with a range of pro-suffrage characters: the eponymous suffrage orator who is disowned and institutionalized by her autocratic father and aunt in Bullard's *Christine*; the self-supporting art student Laura, who is kidnapped and poisoned by a lascivious and corrupt judge in Blake's *Fettered for Life*; the loving wife (and mother) Verena, who is abandoned by her reactionary husband Basil in Celia ["Henrietta James"] Whitehead's parody, "Another Chapter of *The Bostonians*" (1887); the eponymous Native American heroine whose western community suffers from the effects of alcoholism in S. Alice Callahan's *Wynema: Child of the Forest* (1891); and the abused wife of a gambler and drunkard in Abigail Scott Duniway's serialized western novel *Edna and John* (1876–7). In contrast to contemporaneous negative depictions of suffragists in cartoons and newspapers, all of these texts portray suffragists as sympathetic, womanly heroines who plan to use the vote to promote legislation to protect themselves from autocratic patriarchs, unfaithful and abusive husbands, drunken, violent and lascivious acquaintances, and corrupt politicians.

Some of the earliest nineteenth-century suffrage novels, such as *Christine* and *Out of her Sphere* (and several anti-suffrage novels like Sarah Josepha Hale's *The Lecturess* [1839] and Henry James's *The Bostonians* [1886]), feature female orators asserting their right to the franchise by displaying oratorical prowess. Many nineteenth-century suffrage texts, however, offer a contrast to the citizen-ideal of the self-expressive, authoritative "voice" cultivated by the male orator as a sign of citizenship. Instead of an assertive oratorical voice that, if exercised by a woman, might limit its popularity and rhetorical effectiveness, many nineteenth-century suffrage authors adopt the more modest persona of the folksy woman gossip. For example, in her pro-suffrage poetry, African American author Frances Harper speaks through the voice of the elderly former slave Chloe; similarly, humorist Marietta Holley uses the rustic, church-going Samantha as the narrator of several pro-suffrage books. Both Chloe and Samantha assume a non-threatening style of speaking in public in their texts; paradoxically, their plain-speaking analyses of corruption among men in politics have more effect because they claim so little authority for themselves. Although their non-standard English dialect signals their racial and class differences from respected male orators, their style of communication, each suggests, may be more trustworthy than what Chloe terms the "honey-fugling" speeches of more accomplished orators, preachers, and politicians. Indeed, "honey-fugling" ("Aunt Chloe's Politics") abstractions such as "freedom," "liberty," and "independence" – ubiquitous in nineteenth-century US political oratory – come across in these plain-spoken texts as just that: abstractions yet to be achieved in the US polity. Sara Parton Willis's slang-slinging persona "Fanny Fern," for instance, voices suspicion of high-blown rhetoric in her essay "Independence" when she invokes a one-word touchstone of US democratic thought – "Free!" – only to follow it with an expressive expletive: "Humph!" (Fern, *Ruth Hall and Other Writings*, 315).

In addition to featuring speakers whose folksy style addresses a more populist audience than that of elite orators, many nineteenth-century suffrage texts challenge the self-expressive model of voice typically exercised in oratory by asserting pro-suffrage claims more dialogically through conversations between characters. Alice Sophia Callahan's novel *Wynema*, Frances Harper's poem "John and Jacob," Stowe's popular pro-suffrage novel *My Wife and I; or, Harry Henderson's History* (1871) and *Atlantic Monthly* series "The Chimney Corner" (1865–6), and Emma Ghent Curtis's Western *The Administratrix* (1889), for example, all stage extended conversations about suffrage that present different sides of the "woman question" without appearing to favor a position, or they ventriloquize extreme pro- and anti-suffragist positions in order to advance a more moderate stance. The lively encounter between the aggressive suffrage magazine editor and suffragist Audacia Dangereyes and the mild-mannered narrator Hal in Stowe's *My Wife and I*, moreover, distinguishes Stowe's moderate pro-suffrage stance from the more controversial elements of the movement advocated by her stepsister Isabella Hooker and her associate, Free Love advocate Victoria Woodhull, and thereby increases sympathy for it, especially when Hal's later discussions with an aspiring doctor, Ida Van Arsdel, generate a much more gradualist timeline for the women's franchise. Similarly, in

Alcott's children's story "Cupid and Chow-Chow" (1872), exchanges between the independent young Chow-Chow, whose humorless, emotionally distant suffragist mother has taught her to have no time for "love, domestic life, [and] feminine accomplishments," and the more affectionate Cupid, whose mother exemplifies those "trifles," produce a valuable domestic feminist compromise.

Other nineteenth-century texts cultivate dialogue intertextually by taking up canonical texts or discourses in order to insist on women authors' parity with male authors or to challenge dominant male authors' assumptions, just as Elizabeth Cady Stanton *et al.* took up the Founding Fathers' "Declaration of Independence" in their "Declaration of Sentiments" (1848). "Another Chapter of *The Bostonians*," a privately published pamphlet penned by "Henrietta James" (Celia B. Whitehead) quotes and extends James's anti-suffragist novel in order to follow up the unexplored aftermath of its problematic closure – the unlikely marriage of a suffrage orator to a violent anti-suffragist. In "A Divided Republic: An Allegory of the Future" (1885), a publicly recited text later published in a short story collection, Lillie Devereux Blake rewrites Aristophanes' *Lysistrata* – a classical drama about women who withhold sex until their lovers negotiate peace – as a utopian fantasy in which disenfranchised Eastern US women relocate, *en masse*, to western territories and states where women are enfranchised until their lovers agree to enfranchise women. In Elizabeth Stuart Phelps's children's story "Trotty's Lecture Bureau" (1877), published in *St. Nicholas Magazine for Boys and Girls*, Trotty's anti-suffrage "lecture," which makes "queer work with the long words," is represented comically as a verbal collage of parroted anti-suffrage diatribe and formulaic French phrases because the young boy has written his speech in the blank spaces of a French grammar book; in this way, Phelps tropes anti-suffrage discourse as an inherited grammar bound by tradition more than logic or nature.

The effect of this widespread dialogism in nineteenth-century US suffrage literature was the introduction of an alternative model of rhetoric that was more participatory than one-sided, thereby encouraging readers' involvement in the broader debate, regardless of their class, race, or politics. However, publishing opportunities were still incredibly limited; women's magazines had limited circulations and were, as a consequence, short-lived while more mainstream publications had not yet begun to target women readers. All of this changed dramatically in the early years of the twentieth century when developments in printing technology inaugurated a mass-print culture that suffragist New Woman writers were quick to capitalize on.

Twentieth-century suffrage literature

In the first decade of the twentieth century, the rhetorical tactics of the US suffrage campaign were dramatically transformed by two developments: first, the involvement of a new generation of suffragists, many of whom were college-educated and/or self-supporting, and working in journalism, advertising, publishing, and other relevant fields; and second, technological improvements in the publishing industry which made a variety of print cultural forms of propaganda suddenly much more affordable and available to suffrage organizations. In reaction to these developments, modern suffrage organizations took a much more active role than nineteenth-century suffrage organizations had in encouraging the production and distribution of literary works that could serve as propaganda. Organizations such as the Progressive Woman Suffrage Union, the New York Woman Suffrage Party, and the National Woman's Party founded new suffragist magazines – *The American Suffragette* (1909–11), *The Woman Voter* (1910–17), and *The Suffragist* (1913–21) respectively – that regularly published literary works.[6] Organizations such as the National American Women's Suffrage Association (NAWSA) offered prizes (and publication) for the best poems, essays, and other literary works written in support of suffrage, while regional suffragist parties introduced suffragist columns and articles to mainstream newspapers and magazines or arranged special "Suffrage" or "guest-edited" issues of mainstream publications in advance of suffrage referenda (see Chapman and Lamont, "Suffrage Print Culture"). NAWSA even inaugurated its own joint-stock suffrage publishing company, the National Woman Suffrage Publishing Company, which commissioned works such as suffrage writer and organizer Marjorie Shuler's epistolary novel *For Rent – One Pedestal* (1917) to coincide with important suffrage events such as the 1917 New York State referendum. Perhaps the biggest literary suffrage commission was *The Sturdy Oak* (1917), a composite novel commissioned by New York's Empire State Campaign communication committee to influence the same referendum campaign; Empire State Campaign organizer Elizabeth Jordan convinced fourteen of the era's most popular writers – including Fannie Hurst, Mary Austin, Dorothy Canfield, and Alice Duer Miller – each to contribute a chapter to a middlebrow modern campaign story whose plot had been drafted by Austin; the chapters were published serially in *Collier's* and then republished in novel form after the New York State referendum declared a victory for woman suffrage.

Like the earliest suffrage texts, some twentieth-century suffrage texts emphasized female oratory as one means of cultivating feminist community: the protagonist of Gertrude Atherton's *Julia France and Her Times* (1912), for example, is a popular American orator for a British suffrage organization and the heroine of Elizabeth Robins's play *Votes for Women*, likewise, becomes a successful suffrage orator. However, many modern suffrage texts move away from an investment in monologic oratory toward more dialogic means. Indeed the modern orator is often mocked as an elitist figure insulated from the desires of the general public, as in *The Sturdy Oak* when a privileged suffragist attempts to address a crowd of factory workers as "sisters" without recognizing how dramatically her class interests differ from theirs. The anti-suffragist orator is also mocked: the speaker of Alice Duer Miller's "Recollections of Anti-suffrage Speeches Heard in Early Childhood (with apologies to Wordsworth)" (1915), for example, is a petty, self-contradictory anti-suffragist orator oblivious to the internal contradiction of lecturing publicly about how women's place is "in the home." The speaker of Marie Jenney Howe's "Anti-suffragist Monologue" is similarly illogical and self-contradictory in her assertions. Instead of investing in the figure of the elite orator, modern suffrage texts celebrate the persuasive conversation of folksy women gossips like the small-town organizer Calliope Marsh of Zona Gale's *Friendship Village* stories and the strong-willed African American woman of Dorothy Dix's "Mirandy Stories," both of whom recall the nineteenth-century examples of Harper's Chloe and Holley's Samantha. Several texts celebrate the diversity of first-person voices that have not typically held the suffrage podium: for example, the outspoken Irish immigrant laundress in socialist writer Ethel Whitehead's play "The Arrest of Suffrage" (1912) and the African American man in Rosalie Jonas's poem "Brother Baptis' on Woman Suffrage" (1912).[7]

More important in modern suffrage texts than these single speakers, however, are the broad communication networks to which early twentieth-century suffragists contribute. Whereas in nineteenth-century suffrage texts, conversations are most likely to occur in intimate spaces, between family members and friends, modern suffrage texts reflect the modern reality of urban women brought together by a shared commitment to the campaign. Through conversations with absolute strangers, orphans in *The Sturdy Oak* (1917), *For Rent* (1917), and Edna Ferber's novel *Fanny Herself* (1917), as well as a childless widow in Marion Hamilton Carter's conversion narrative *The Woman with Empty Hands: Evolution of a Suffragette* (1913), are moved to think of themselves as members of collectives other than those provided by family ties: as suffragist members of unions, women's clubs, assembly districts, political parties, or suffrage organizations, as marchers in parades, even as citizens.

These collectives produce a suffragist voice in excess of the monologism of the orator. Instead, suffragist collective "voice" is coordinated and enhanced by modern communication technology. For example, typewriting and stenography produce a collaborative voice that combines the voices of the male employer who dictates and the female employee who transcribes. Through typewriting and stenography, the "typewriter girl" can revise her employer's private thoughts for public circulation, sometimes in the process reworking his message to better suit suffragist values. Telephony in suffrage texts is also represented as enabling conversation between strangers about an issue of shared concern. These modern technologies complicated the idea of a singular authoritative voice associated with nineteenth-century oratory and authorship. As a consequence of their early adoption of emergent technologies, suffragists are able to redefine the modern suffragist voice. The savvy stenographer Betty in *The Sturdy Oak*, for example, produces an anonymous collective voice for the suffragist campaign when she designs large printed placards to use in a voiceless speech demonstration, a job at which she excels because of her experience preparing smaller documents on the typewriter in her workplace. Similarly, the fragmentary multi-tasking patter of the chatty switchboard operator in Oreola Williams Haskell's story "Switchboard Suffrage" (1920) appears to single-handedly coordinate the operation of a vast (and talkative) public sphere.

Like telephony and stenography, mass-print culture – a recent development in US publishing – is also celebrated in many modern suffrage texts as a means through which suffragists can generate a collective voice that can reach – and potentially persuade – large audiences. In Edna Ferber's middlebrow novel *Fanny Herself* (1917), for example, the protagonist, emotionally moved by a New York suffrage parade, sketches a cartoon of one of the marchers and convinces an editor to feature it on his mass-circulating newspaper's front page. In Whitehead's "The Arrest of Suffrage," Mary Alden Hopkins's literary sketch "Women March" (1912), and Carter's *The Woman with Empty Hands*, suffrage "newsies" engage both supporters and detractors in conversation when they distribute suffrage publications. In all of these texts, women exercise "voices" that are more print cultural, more collective, and more diverse.

Although nineteenth-century suffrage texts often "wrote back" to foundational democratic documents, modern mass-print culture enables more sustained intertextuality by making recent anti-suffragist public statements quoted in the newspapers more available for suffragist critique. For example, Alice Duer Miller's weekly suffrage column *Are Women People?*, which ran in the *New York Tribune* (1914–17), was inspired by frequent anti-suffrage statements by President Woodrow Wilson and other public figures quoted in the news. In addition to quoting these statements directly, Miller's poetry also used more literary forms of "quotation," i.e. parody of canonical and popular poems and poetic forms, to assert her poetic and political parity with male poets. Ventriloquism, like quotation, also enabled suffragist authors to voice dominant anti-suffragist positions in order to reject them. For example, Miller's "Unauthorized Interview between the Suffragists and the Statue of Liberty" and "Campaign Material from Both Sides," as well as Charlotte Perkins Gilman's poem "The Socialist and the Suffragist" (1911), staged debate between ignorant anti-suffragist speakers and more informed suffragist speakers and swiftly reduced the "anti" perspective to shreds. Like *Are Women People?*, Brooklyn suffragists' pamphlet *Mother Goose as a Suffragette* (1912) puts "new" suffragist ideas in familiar poetic containers – in this case, suffrage ideas in familiar nursery rhymes (Fig. 16.3). For all of these writers, quoting – borrowing another's language – and ventriloquizing – speaking for or being spoken for by another – both reflected the historical conditions of feminine expression *and* served as elements of women's resistance to these conditions.

Modern suffrage literature also imagines new forms of utterance: particularly forms that revise traditionally private forms and genres to access a rhetorically persuasive form of feminine public speech. In the same way that nineteenth-century suffrage texts worked to expand the domestic sphere to encompass sites traditionally associated with the public sphere, modern suffrage texts worked to politicize literary genres traditionally associated with domesticity or intimacy, capitalizing on the activist potential of private conversations made public. Suffragist authors playfully combine forms focused on private, intimate relationships (such as melodrama and romance) with political fiction to shape narratives of attractive suffragist heroines who successfully balance personal, professional, and civic roles. Like many silent suffrage films and plays of the period, several modern suffrage novels feature attractive heroines who update nineteenth-century "womanly influence" by using both sentiment and logic to convert their anti-suffrage politician lovers to the cause.[8] Many early twentieth-century texts appropriate forms of utterance typically associated with the private sphere and turn them into forms of propaganda that mediate between the private sphere of emotion and the public sphere of politics and, by so doing, achieve more rhetorical force than a more univocally public text (like an oration) might do. For example, the valentines sent by National Woman's Party members with which I began this essay drew on the influence women exert in courtship to "woo" Congressmen to support a woman suffrage amendment, but when these valentines were reproduced

Fig. 16.3 "Disenfranchisement" cartoon from *Mother Goose as a Suffragette*

in the advocacy journal *The Suffragist* as well as in mainstream newspapers, they also "wooed" male voters to consider suffragists and the suffrage cause in a new and attractive light. Thus, the most private of conversations was turned to public ends. The valentines' reversal of the usual romantic trope of man pursuing woman's favor also reflects the potential that some modern suffragists found in flirtation and sex appeal to market their cause. These texts work to persuade not only the individuals to whom they are addressed but also a broad segment of the population who encounter these "private" texts in the public contexts of the periodicals in which they appeared.

Perhaps most significantly, many of modern suffrage literature's aesthetic innovations in voice anticipate and approximate the signature tropes of what literary scholars define as "high modernism." Cultural critics have read the twentieth-century suffrage movement in relation to the development of the various cultures of modernity (democratic, aesthetic, visual, advertising, and commodity cultures), and the existence of a feminist literary culture in relation to the emergence of literary modernism. Recent criticism has noticed a number of historical and formal connections between British suffrage literature and modernism.[9] What modernist scholar Janet Lyon has claimed about British literary modernism also applies to US literary modernism: that the "rhetoric and tactics of the militant women's movement were enfolded into the foundations of modernism" (*Manifestoes*, 94). Through quotation, ventriloquism, collaborative authorship, and tropes of communication technologies, many modern US suffragist texts anticipate the rich innovations in voice that marked literary modernist experiment. By the time high-modernist poet T. S. Eliot attempted to escape the pretensions of more oratorical Victorian poetry by exploding the form of the dramatic monologue through a collage of quotation, multiple speakers, etc. in *The Waste Land* (1922), suffrage writers had already begun to investigate the possibilities of multi-vocal literary forms in a heterogeneous public sphere.

Recovering this tradition

Although feminist scholars began to recuperate popular US fiction by women twenty-seven years ago, when Jane Tompkins published *Sensational Designs: The Cultural Work of American Fiction, 1790–1860*, the recovery of the innovative creative literature of the US suffrage campaign has begun only recently. In 1987, Bettina Friedl collected an impressive range of US suffrage drama in *On to Victory*, but that volume went quickly out of print. Reprints of popular suffrage novels such as Johnston's *Hagar*, Blake's *Fettered for Life*, Jordan's edited *The Sturdy Oak*, Abigail Scott Duniway's *Edna and John*, and Bullard's *Christine* have been issued in the past fifteen years, but many other popular and inspiring suffrage novels, including Stowe's popular *My Wife and I* and Shuler's epistolary *For Rent*, have not been republished.[10] Short fiction, poetry, and autobiographical sketches originally published in mainstream and advocacy journals remain buried in non-indexed microfilm.

Scholarly work focusing on the literary and print cultural aspects of the US suffrage campaign has emerged in the last fifteen years, most notably in Leslie Petty's *Romancing the Vote* (2006), a study of literary portrayals of the women's rights heroine in US fiction, in Caroline Levander's *Voices of the Nation* (1998), in Margaret Finnegan's *Selling Suffrage* (1999), and in articles on specific suffrage texts, at the same time that the homogeneous narrative of the US woman suffrage movement's genealogy has also been recently complicated by feminist scholars working in many disciplines.[11] Much more, however, remains to be done.

Most urgent is the establishment of a suffrage literary tradition that scholars can examine and interpret. In response to this need, Angela Mills and I recently collected over sixty literary texts in *Treacherous Texts: US Suffrage Literature 1846–1946* (Rutgers University Press, 2011). Introducing a twenty-first-century audience to texts that were popular and persuasive in their day but have been, by and large, relegated to archival obscurity requires an argument for reframing the very structures of literary critical evaluation that dismissed them in the first place, particularly the New Critical paradigm that has policed the boundary between propaganda and literature. The critical propensity for valuing only particular kinds of formal experimentation has tended to elide the strategic thinking behind many women writers' conscious deployment of more traditional forms. Many suffrage texts defy conventional understandings of genre and of literary period; others' seeming lack of ambiguity confounds usual approaches to close reading; all have been undertaken with an overt political agenda which chafes against the persistent presumption that politics makes poor art. Yet closer scrutiny reveals that suffrage literature is neither simplistic nor aesthetically deficient. Mills and I followed the lead of recent scholarship that has exposed the rich affinities between literature and propaganda (cf. Wollaeger, *Modernist Media and Propaganda*; Lyon, *Manifestoes*). *Treacherous Texts* attempts to chronicle the shifting strategies of suffragists determined to have a "say" in the public sphere, whatever the limitations of artistic or political form that compounded their political voicelessness. However, many more works of suffrage literature remain to be found and collected, particularly texts that address the complex experiences of women marginalized from the mainstream campaign by class, race, religion, or region.

In *Hard Facts*, literary scholar Philip Fisher argues that *Uncle Tom's Cabin* is an example of a text in which a method encounters its "fated, primary subject" (101); that is, the identificatory strategies of sentimentality – its extension of sympathy to the down-trodden, its recognition of commonality between the reader and the subject of the fiction – work in Stowe's text as a corrective to the worldview that tolerates slavery by reading a human being as an object, because the sentimental method assigns humanity to its subjects. Like sentimental literature, many nineteenth- and twentieth-century US women's texts more generally meet their "fated and primary object" in suffrage, because the theme of suffrage concerns both literary and political self-expression for women. Although suffrage was only one aspect of the complex stage of feminism known popularly as the "first wave," the literary works that it generated are the richest of all texts within this feminist tradition because the movement's focus on "voice" permitted authors to investigate the powerful relationship between literary and political self-expression.

Notes

1. For examples of suffrage oratory, see Waggenspack, *The Search for Self-Sovereignty*; Campbell, *Man Cannot Speak for Her*; Leeman, *"Do Everything" Reform*; Kraditor, *Up from the Pedestal*; Logan, *"We are Coming"*; Zackodnik, *"We must be up and doing"*; and Doress-Worters, *Mistress of Herself*. For analyses of women's rights orators, see Yoakum, "Pioneer Women Orators of America"; O'Connor, *Pioneer Women Orators*; Linkugel and Solomon, *Anna Howard Shaw*; Zink-Sawyer, *From Preachers to Suffragists*; Buchanan, *Regendering Delivery*; Johnson, *Gender and Rhetorical Space*; and Peterson, *"Doers of the Word."*

2. A full bibliography of US suffrage literature is included as an appendix in Chapman and Mills (*Treacherous Texts*, 320–3). For examples of suffrage novels, see Bullard, *Christine, or the Trials of Womanhood*; Stowe, *My Wife and I: or Harry Henderson's History* and *Uncle Tom's Cabin*; Harbert, *Out of her Sphere*; Blake, *Fettered for Life*; Holley, *Josiah Allen's Wife as a PA and PI: Samantha at the Centennial*; Curtis, *The Administratrix*; Callahan, *Wynema: A Child of the Forest*; Garland, *The Spoils of Office*; Duniway, *Edna and John*; Robins, *The Convert*; Stevens, *The American Suffragette*; Atherton, *Julia France and her Times*; Herrick, *One Woman's Life*; Forman, *The Opening Door: A Story of the Woman's Movement*; Price, *The Closed Door*; Johnston, *Hagar*; Ferber, *Fanny Herself*; Shuler, *For Rent – One Pedestal*; and Jordan, *The Sturdy Oak*. For examples of suffrage short fiction, see Cary, "The Born Thrall"; Blake, "Divided Republic"; Celia Whitehead, "Another Chapter of 'The Bostonians'"; Eaton, "The Inferior Woman"; Alcott, "Cupid and Chow-Chow"; Phelps, "Trotty's Lecture Bureau"; Erwin, "The Australian Ballot System"; Gale, "Friday," *Friendship Village*, *Mothers to Men*, and *Peace in Friendship Village*; Sminck, "American Clothes"; Martin, "Mrs. Gladfelter's Revolt"; and Haskell, "Switchboard Suffrage." For examples of suffrage poetry, see Harper, "The Deliverance" and "Aunt Chloe's Politics"; Fordham, "Atlanta Exposition Ode"; Gilman, *In This Our World*; and Alice Duer Miller, *Are Women People?* Suffrage dramas have been collected in Friedl, *On to Victory*. See also Selina Solomon, *The Girl From Colorado, or The Conversion of Aunty Suffridge*; Jakobi and Howe, "Telling the Truth at the White House"; Lewis, *Election Day: A Suffrage Play*; Ethel Whitehead, "The Arrest of Suffrage"; and Robins, *Votes for Women*. For examples of suffrage autobiography, consider works by Carter, *The Woman with Empty Hands*; "One"; Havemeyer, "The Suffrage Torch: Memories of a Militant"; and Day, *The Long Loneliness: The Autobiography of Dorothy Day*.

3. For an account of over 100 white and black women who preached in the United States between 1740 and 1845, see Brekus, *Strangers and Pilgrims*.

4. See Buchanan, *Regendering Delivery*; Mattingly, *Appropriate[ing] Dress*; and Johnson, *Gender and Rhetorical Space in American Life*.

5. This phrase is borrowed from historian Mary Kelley's study of nineteenth-century women fiction writers, *Private Woman, Public Stage*.

6. On suffrage periodical culture, see Finnegan, *Selling Suffrage*; Bennion, *Equal to the Occasion*; Cane and Alves, "The Only Efficient Instrument"; Russo and Kramarae, *The Radical Women's Press of the 1850s*; Martha Solomon, *A Voice of their Own*; and Ward, "*Yours for Liberty*." On cartoons, see Clark, *My Dear Mrs. Ames*; and Sheppard, *Cartooning for Suffrage*.

7. Of course, suffragist print culture makes audible some voices more than others; although Jonas's poem asserts a solidarity between women and African Americans, the stereotyped representation of African American women on trial in "Telling the Truth at the White House" belies this solidarity by dramatizing the racism of the pre-dominantly middle-class white organization that made racially marginalized women feel their needs were less important to the campaign.

8. For an analysis of suffrage cinema, see Sloan, "Sexual Warfare in the Silent Cinema."

9. See Howlett, "Writing on the Body?" and "Femininity Slashed"; Lyon, *Manifestoes*; Miller, *Rebel Women*; Green, "Advertising Feminism" and *Spectacular Confessions*; and Joannou, "Suffragette Fiction and the Fictions of Suffrage."

10. See recent editions of Jordan's 1917 edited composite novel *The Sturdy Oak*; Johnston's 1913 novel *Hagar*; Blake's 1874 novel *Fettered for Life*; Duniway's *Edna and John*; and Bullard's 1856 novel *Christine, or the Trials of Womanhood*. Digitization projects such as Project Gutenberg and Google Books are making other out-of-print texts more readily available.

11. See Hewitt, *No Permanent Waves*; Stansell, *The Feminist Promise*; Ginzberg, *Untidy Origins*; and Des Jardins, *Women and the Historical Enterprise in America*.

Works cited

Alcott, Louisa May. "Cupid and Chow-Chow." In *Aunt Jo's Scrap Bag*. Vol. 3. Boston: Roberts Brothers, 1880.

Atherton, Gertrude. *Julia France and her Times*. New York: Macmillan, 1912.

Bennion, Sherilyn Cox. *Equal to the Occasion: Women Editors of the Nineteenth-Century West*. Reno: University of Nevada Press, 1990.

Blake, Lillie D. "A Divided Republic: An Allegory of the Future." In *A Daring Experiment and Other Stories*. New York: Lovell, Coryell, 1892.

Fettered for Life, or, Lord and Master. New York: Sheldon & Co., 1874.

Brekus, Catherine A. *Strangers and Pilgrims: Female Preaching in America, 1740–1845*. Chapel Hill: University of North Carolina Press, 1998.

Buchanan, Lindal. *Regendering Delivery: The Fifth Canon and Antebellum Women Rhetors*. Carbondale: Southern Illinois University Press, 2005.

Bullard, Laura Curtis. *Christine, or the Trials of Womanhood*. Lincoln, NB: University of Nebraska Press, 2010.

Callahan, Sophia Alice. *Wynema: A Child of the Forest*. Lincoln, NB: University of Nebraska Press, 1997.

Campbell, Karlyn Kohrs, ed. *Man Cannot Speak for Her: A Critical Study of Early Feminist Rhetoric*. Vol. 1. New York: Greenwood Press, 1989.

Cane, Aleta Feinsod and Susan Alves, eds. *"The Only Efficient Instrument": American Women Writers and the Periodical, 1837–1916*. Iowa City: University of Iowa Press, 2001.

Carter, Marion Hamilton. *The Woman with Empty Hands: The Evolution of a Suffragette*. *Saturday Evening Post* (January 25, 1913): 13–16.

Cary, Alice. "The Born Thrall." In *The Revolution*. Serialized and incomplete, beginning 5.1–18 (January 6, 1870–May 5, 1871): 1–273.

Catt, Carrie Chapman and Nettie Rogers Shuler. *Woman Suffrage and Politics: The Inner Story of the Suffrage Movement*. Seattle: University of Washington Press, 1970.

Chapman, Mary and Angela Mills, eds. *Treacherous Texts: US Suffrage Literature, 1846–1946*. New Brunswick: Rutgers University Press, 2011. 253–76.

Chapman, Mary and Victoria Lamont. "Suffrage Print Culture." In *American Popular Print Culture*. Ed. Christine Bold. Oxford: Oxford University Press, 2011.

Clark, Anne Biller. *My Dear Mrs. Ames: A Study of Suffragist Cartoonist Blanche Ames*. New York: Peter Lang, 2001.

Curtis, Emma Ghent. *The Administratrix*. New York: John B. Alden, 1889.

Day, Dorothy. *The Long Loneliness: The Autobiography of Dorothy Day*. New York: Harper & Row, 1952.

Des Jardins, Julie. *Women and the Historical Enterprise in America: Gender, Race and the Politics of Memory*. Chapel Hill: University of North Carolina Press, 2003.

Dix, Dorothy. "'Mirandy' on 'Why Women Can't Vote'." *Good Housekeeping*. 54.1 (February 1912): 285–7.

Doress-Worters, Paula, ed. *Mistress of Herself: Speeches and Letters of Ernestine L. Rose, Early Women's Rights Leader*. New York: Feminist Press, 2008.

Duniway, Abigail Scott. *Edna and John*. Pullman: Washington State University Press, 2000.

Eaton, Edith [Sui Sin Far]. "The Inferior Woman." *Hampton's* 24 (May 1910): 727–31.

Erwin, Mabel Clare. "The Australian Ballot System." In *As Told By The Typewriter Girl*. New York: E. R. Herrick and Co., 1898.

Felski, Rita. *The Gender of Modernity*. Cambridge, MA: Harvard University Press, 1995.

Ferber, Edna. *Fanny Herself*. New York: Frederick A. Stokes Company, 1917.

Fern, Fanny. *Ruth Hall and Other Writings*. Ed. Joyce Warren. New Brunswick: Rutgers University Press, 1986.

Finnegan, Margaret. *Selling Suffrage: Consumer Culture and Votes for Women*. New York: Columbia University Press, 1999.

Fisher, Philip. *Hard Facts: Setting and Form in the American Novel*. New York and Oxford: Oxford University Press, 1987.

Fordham, Mary Weston. "Atlanta Exposition Ode." In *She Wields a Pen: American Women Poets of the Nineteenth Century*. Ed. Janet Gray. Iowa: University of Iowa Press, 1997.

Forman, Justus. *The Opening Door: A Story of the Woman's Movement*. New York: Harper and Brothers Publishers, 1913.

Friedl, Bettina, ed. *On to Victory: Propaganda Plays of the Woman Suffrage Movement*. Boston: Northeastern University Press, 1987.

Gale, Zona. "Friday." *Century Magazine* 88.4 (August 1914): 521–4.

Friendship Village. New York: Macmillan, 1908.

Mothers to Men. New York: Macmillan, 1911.

Peace in Friendship Village. New York: Macmillan, 1919.

Garland, Hamlin. *The Spoils of Office*. Boston: Arena, 1892.

Gilman, Charlotte Perkins. *In This Our World*. New York: Arno Press, 1974.

Ginzberg, Lori. *Untidy Origins: A Story of Woman's Rights in Antebellum New York*. Chapel Hill: University of North Carolina Press, 2005.

Green, Barbara. "Advertising Feminism: Ornamental Bodies/Docile Bodies and the Discourse of Suffrage." In *Marketing Modernisms: Self-Promotion, Canonization, Rereading*. Ed. Kevin J. H. Dettmar and Stephen Watt. Ann Arbor: University of Michigan Press, 1996.

"Femininity Slashed: Suffrage Militancy, Modernism and Gender." In *Modernist Sexualities*. Ed. Hugh Stevens and Caroline Howlett. Manchester: Manchester University Press, 2000.

Spectacular Confessions: Autobiography, Performative Activism, and the Sites of Suffrage. New York: St. Martin's Press, 1997.

Hale, Sarah Josepha. *The Lecturess, or Woman's Sphere*. Boston: Whipple and Damrell, 1839.

Harbert, Elizabeth B. *Out of her Sphere*. Des Moines: Mills & Co., 1871.

Harper, Frances W. "Aunt Chloe's Politics." In *Sketches of Southern Life (1871)*, in *A Brighter Coming Day: A Frances Ellen Watkins Harper Reader*. Ed. Frances Smith Foster. New York: Feminist Press, 1990.

"The Deliverance." In *Sketches of Southern Life*. Philadelphia: Ferguson Bros. & Co., 1893.

Haskell, Oreola Williams. "Switchboard Suffrage." In *Banner Bearers*. Geneva, NY: W. F. Humphrey, 1920.

Havemeyer, Louisine. "The Suffrage Torch: Memories of a Militant." *Scribner's* 71 (1929): 528–39.

Herrick, Robert. *One Woman's Life*. New York: Macmillan, 1913.

Hewitt, Nancy, ed. *No Permanent Waves: Recasting Histories of US Feminism*. New Brunswick: Rutgers University Press, 2010.

Holley, Marietta. *Josiah Allen's Wife as a PA and PI: Samantha at the Centennial*. Hartford, CT: American Publishing Company, 1888.

Hopkins, Mary Alden. "Women March." *Collier's: The National Weekly* 49.9 (May 18, 1912): 13, 30–1.

Howlett, Caroline J. "Writing on the Body? Representation and Resistance in British Suffrage Accounts of Forcible Feeding." In *Bodies of Writing: Bodies in Performance*. Ed. Thomas Foster, Carol Siegel, and Ellen E. Berry. New York: New York University Press, 1996.

Jakobi, Paula and Marie Jenney Howe. "Telling the Truth at the White House." *Pearson's Magazine*. 38.3 (September 1917): 129, 140–6.

James, Henry. *The Bostonians*. New York: Penguin, 2000.

Joannou, Maroula. "Suffragette Fiction and the Fictions of Suffrage." In *The Women's Suffrage Movement: New Feminist Perspectives*. Ed. Maroula Joannou and June Purvis. Manchester: Manchester University Press, 1998.

Johnson, Nan. *Gender and Rhetorical Space in American Life, 1866–1910*. Carbondale: Southern Illinois University Press, 2002.

Johnston, Mary. *Hagar*. Richmond: University Press of Virginia, 1994.

Jonas, Rosalie. "Brother Baptis." *The Crisis* 4.5 (September 1912): 247.

Jordan, Elizabeth Garver, ed. *The Sturdy Oak*. Athens, OH: Ohio University Press, 1998.

Karafilis, Maria. "Oratory, Embodiment and US Citizenship in Sutton E. Griggs's *Imperium in Imperio*." *African American Review* 4.1 (March 2006): 125–43.

Kelley, Mary. *Private Woman, Public Stage: Literary Domesticity in Nineteenth-Century America*. Chapel Hill: University of North Carolina Press, 1984.

Kraditor, Eileen S., ed. *Up from the Pedestal: Selected Writings in the History of American Feminism*. Chicago: Quadrangle Books, 1968.

Lee, Mary Ashe. "Afmerica." In *Nineteenth-Century American Women Poets*. Ed. Paula Bernat Bennett. Oxford: Blackwell, 1998.

Leeman, Richard, ed. *"Do Everything" Reform: The Oratory of Frances E. Willard*. New York: Greenwood Press, 1992.

Levander, Caroline. *Voices of the Nation*. Oxford: Oxford University Press, 1998.

Lewis, Emily Sargent. *Election Day: A Suffrage Play*. 1912. Alexandria, VA: Alexander Street Press, 2007.

Linkugel, Wil A. and Martha Solomon, *Anna Howard Shaw: Suffrage Orator and Social Reformer*. New York: Greenwood Press, 1990.

Logan, Shirley Wilson. *"We are Coming": The Persuasive Discourse of Nineteenth-Century Black Women*. Carbondale: Southern Illinois University Press, 1999.

Lyon, Janet. *Manifestoes: Provocations of the Modern*. Ithaca and London: Cornell University Press, 1999.

Martin, Helen Reimensnyder. "Mrs. Gladfelter's Revolt." In *Between Mothers and Daughters: Stories Across a Generation*. Ed. Susan Koppelman. Old Westbury, NY: Feminist Press, 1985.

Mattingly, Carol. *Appropriate[ing] Dress: Women's Rhetorical Style in Nineteenth-Century America*. Carbondale: Southern Illinois University Press, 2002.

Millay, Edna St. Vincent. "Upon this marble bust that is not I." In *The Buck in the Snow*. New York: Harper and Brothers, 1928.

Miller, Alice Duer. *Are Women People? A Book of Rhymes for Suffrage Times*. New York: George H. Doran and Co., 1915.

Miller, Jane Eldridge. *Rebel Women: Feminism, Modernism and the Edwardian Novel*. London: Virago, 1994.

Mother Goose as a Suffragette. New York: Woman Suffrage Party, 1912.

O'Connor, Lillian. *Pioneer Women Orators: Rhetoric in the Antebellum Reform Movement*. New York: Columbia University Press, 1954.

"One" [Raymond Brown]. *How It Feels to be the Husband of a Suffragette*. *Everybody's Magazine*. 30.1 (January 1914).

"The Pastoral Letter of the General Association of Congregational Ministers of Massachusetts" (1837). In Stanton, Anthony, and Gage, *History of Woman Suffrage*.

Peterson, Carla. *"Doers of the Word": African-American Women Speakers and Writers in the North (1830–1880)*. New York: Oxford University Press, 1995.

Petty, Leslie. *Romancing the Vote: Feminist Activism in American Fiction, 1870–1920*. Athens, GA: University of Georgia Press, 2006.

Phelps, Elizabeth Stuart. "Trotty's Lecture Bureau (Not a Trotty Story, but a Trotty Scrap. Told for Trotty's Friends.)." *St. Nicholas Magazine* 4.7 (May 1877): 454–5.

Price, Hannah. *The Closed Door.* Tennessee: Knoxville Lithographing, 1913.

Robins, Elizabeth. *The Convert.* New York: Feminist Press, 1980.

    Votes for Women. In The New Woman and Other Emancipated Woman Plays. Ed. Jean Chothia. London: Oxford University Press, 1998.

Russo, Ann and Cheris Kramarae. *The Radical Women's Press of the 1850s.* New York: Routledge, 1991.

Sheppard, Alice. *Cartooning for Suffrage.* Albuquerque: University of New Mexico Press, 1994.

Shuler, Marjorie. *For Rent – One Pedestal.* New York: National American Woman Suffrage Publishing Company, 1917.

Sloan, Kay. "Sexual Warfare in the Silent Cinema: Comedies and Melodramas of Women Suffragism." *American Quarterly* 33.4 (Autumn 1981): 412–36.

Sminck, Kathryn. "American Clothes." *Plainfield Daily Press* (May 2, 1914): 8.

Solomon, Martha, ed. *A Voice of their Own: Woman Suffrage Press 1840–1910.* Tuscaloosa: University of Alabama Press, 1991.

Solomon, Selina. *The Girl from Colorado, or The Conversion of Aunty Suffridge: A Playlet with a Purpose.* San Francisco: Votes-for-Women Publishing Company, 1911.

Stansell, Christine. *The Feminist Promise: 1792 to the Present.* New York: Random House, 2010.

Stanton, Elizabeth Cady. "Introduction." In Helen Gardener, *Pray, You, Sir, Whose Daughter?* Boston: Arena Publishing Company, 1892.

Stanton, Elizabeth, Susan B. Anthony, and Matilda Joslyn Gage. *History of Woman Suffrage.* Vol. 1. Rochester: Fowler and Wells, 1889.

Stein, Gertrude. *The Mother of Us All. In Last Operas and Plays.* Ed. Carl Van Vechten. Baltimore: The Johns Hopkins University Press, 1977.

Stevens, Isaac. *The American Suffragette.* New York: William Rickey, 1911.

Stowe, Harriet Beecher. *My Wife and I: or Harry Henderson's History.* New York: J. B. Ford and Company, 1872.

    Uncle Tom's Cabin. New York: Penguin, 1986.

"Suffragists Use Valentines in the Campaign for the Ballot." *Worcester Post* (February 14, 1916). n.p.

Tompkins, Jane. *Sensational Designs: The Cultural Work of American Fiction, 1790–1860.* New York: Oxford University Press, 1985.

"The Truth of Fiction, and Its Charms." *The Una* 1.1 (1853).

Waggenspack, Beth M., ed. *The Search for Self-Sovereignty: The Oratory of Elizabeth Cady Stanton.* New York: Greenwood Press, 1989.

Ward, Jean M., ed. *"Yours for Liberty": Selections from Abigail Scott Duniway's Suffrage Newspaper.* Corvallis: Oregon State University Press, 2000.

Whitehead, Celia B. ["Henrietta James"]. "Another Chapter of 'The Bostonians'." Bloomfield, NJ: S. Morris Hulin, 1887.

Whitehead, Ethel. "The Arrest of Suffrage." *The Progressive Woman* 7.64 (October 1912): 14, 16.

Wollaeger, Mark. *Modernist Media and Propaganda: British Narrative from 1900 to 1945.* Princeton: Princeton University Press, 2006.

"The Woman's Rights Convention – The Last Act of the Drama," *New York Herald* (September 12, 1852). In *Up from the Pedestal*. Ed. Aileen S. Kraditor. Chicago: Quadrangle Books, 1968.

Yoakum, Doris G. "Pioneer Women Orators of America." *Quarterly Journal of Speech* 23 (April 1937): 251–9.

Zackodnik, Teresa, ed. *"We must be up and doing": A Reader in Early African American Feminisms*. Peterborough, ON: Broadview Press, 2010.

Zink-Sawyer, Beverly Ann. *From Preachers to Suffragists: Woman's Rights and Religious Conviction in the Lives of Three Nineteenth-Century Clergywomen*. Louisville: Westminster John Knox Press, 1989.

17

American women playwrights

BRENDA MURPHY

The standard historical narrative of American drama and theater tends to privilege male writers even more than the narratives of fiction or poetry do. In the historical narrative, the important aesthetic developments and cultural moments tend to be linked to the careers of playwrights, almost exclusively male, who have achieved fame, fortune, and critical acclaim, principally in the last 100 years. Thus Eugene O'Neill is linked with early realism and modernism; Clifford Odets with the leftist theater of the 1930s; Tennessee Williams with post-World War II psychological realism; Arthur Miller with politically minded realism; Edward Albee with absurdist drama; Sam Shepard with hyperrealism and postmodernism; David Mamet with a tough dialogic realism characterized by the pseudonymous "Mametspeak"; Tony Kushner with an open, epic theater that addresses issues of politics, identity, and religious myth; August Wilson with African American history, myth, and identity. A similar list of female writers and their cultural moments might include Rachel Crothers with the social realism of the Progressive Era and the society comedy of the Jazz Age; Susan Glaspell with feminist realism and modernism; Lillian Hellman with the social melodrama of the 1930s and '40s; Lorraine Hansberry with the social realism of the Civil Rights movement; Adrienne Kennedy and Alice Childress with experimental hybrid dramatic forms in the 1950s and '60s; María Irene Fornés, Ntozake Shange, and Megan Terry with feminist experiments in the 1970s; Marsha Norman, Wendy Wasserstein, and Beth Henley with a neo-realism that emphasizes women's issues in the 1970s and '80s; and, into the twenty-first century, Paula Vogel with an open dramatic form and a focus on family, gender, and identity; Suzan-Lori Parks with remaking both dramatic structure and American history and myth; Anna Deavere Smith and Eve Ensler with a new, socially aware monologic theater.

The reasons why the lists of playwrights are not better synthesized and why the second list of names is not as generally well known as the first are many and complex. They have been addressed from a number of points of view by feminist critics, many of whom will be cited in the discussion that follows. The main purpose of this essay, however, is to tell the second narrative, emphasizing the contributions that women have made to the body of American drama and to the interaction between theater and the larger culture that makes drama a living and socially relevant art form.

The earliest playwrights

Colonial America suffered unduly from the anti-theatrical prejudice that Jonas Barish has detailed in Western culture since Plato wrote his *Republic*. In the northern colonies, with their Puritan origins, the prejudice against theatrical performance was particularly strong, and many of the colonies had laws against the exhibition of plays. The Continental Congress passed a resolution in 1774 discouraging "every species of extravagance and dissipation," including horse-racing, gaming, cock-fighting, shows, and plays (Hewitt, *Theatre USA*, 30). The Virginian George Washington was an enthusiastic theater-goer, however, and he encouraged the performance of plays that would not only divert the troops of his Revolutionary army, but improve morale by articulating the new nation's values, rallying the emotions of patriotism, and ridiculing the enemy. The best-known playwright of the Revolutionary period was Mercy Otis Warren, who was also the sister of prominent Boston patriot James Otis. Although she publicly acknowledged only *The Group*, a satire on the group of men appointed to govern Massachusetts under the Intolerable Acts which was produced in Boston in 1775, she wrote several other popular satires of the Tories in New England, including *The Adulateur* (written 1772),[1] and possibly *The Defeat* (1773) and *The Blockheads; or, The Affrighted Officers* (published 1776), a response to General Burgoyne's *Blockade of Boston* (performed 1776), a farce making fun of the revolutionaries. Although her plays focus on politics and armies, and therefore men, Warren's position on women may be gleaned from the fact that the character with the central soliloquy in *The Group* is a woman, who comes out of the shadows to impart her patriotic truth-telling about the coming Revolution to the petty, venal, and cowardly group of men who have been placed in power by the British.

Other early American playwrights include Judith Sargent Murray, the first American-born woman to have her plays produced professionally; Susanna Haswell Rowson, who wrote the popular and much-imitated comedy *Slaves in Algiers* (1794); Louisa Medina, one of the most popular melodramatists of the early nineteenth century, who often adapted her own novels for the stage;

Mary Carr Clarke, who wrote the popular comedy *The Fair Americans* (1815); and the most successful of all the early women, Anna Cora Mowatt Ritchie, a writer and actor whose social comedy *Fashion, or Life in New York* (1845) is the most anthologized play of the period and has had a number of revivals well into the twentieth century, including a hit production in Greenwich Village by the Provincetown Players in 1924. *Fashion* is part of a tradition of early American literature that contrasts the decadent values and mores of Europe with the new, plain-spoken, and healthy American values of the Republic. It contrasts the urban social climbing and status seeking of the Tiffany family with the plain rural values of their friend Trueman and of Gertrude, a servant of the Tiffanys who, in good comedy-of-manners tradition, turns out to be Trueman's granddaughter and the heir to great wealth. Of course the young women in *Fashion* are paired up with suitable mates at the end, through the agency of Trueman, and his plain republican values prevail. As Amelia Kritzer has pointed out, however, the comedy makes a fundamentally conservative statement about American society and women's place in it. The republican ideals that Trueman brings to the family are a return from the edgy risk-taking of the Tiffanys' way of life to a traditional pastoralism. Rather than achieving any independence or agency in the new social organization, the women's futures are dictated to them by this benevolent patriarch (Kritzer, "Comedies," 16–17).

As this brief survey shows, women were active as playwrights from the very beginning of what might be called an American theater, and several achieved a good deal of success and even made a living with their playwriting, a rare thing in the early nineteenth century. Kritzer has edited a collection of their plays, and most of the scholarly and critical work on this period has focused on recovering the work of the women playwrights and placing it in its theatrical, cultural, and historical contexts. There is also a substantial body of critical writing on several of them, however. Warren, who was a poet and historian of the Revolution as well as a playwright, is the subject of several books and a number of articles, as is Anna Cora Mowatt, who has garnered interest as an actor and autobiographer as well as a playwright. A good deal of attention has been given to Susanna Rowson's novel *Charlotte Temple*, but not much to her plays, which would reward more intense feminist and cultural analysis, as would those of Mary Carr Clarke and Judith Sargent Murray.

Another important line of inquiry is related to the development of melo-drama, the dominant dramatic genre of the nineteenth century. The work of recent critics and historians, such as Bruce McConachie and Jeffrey Mason, has shown that the development of melodrama in the USA was a natural response to a deeply unsettled post-revolutionary political and social order. In this context, it is not surprising that in the nineteenth century, melodrama was a particularly successful genre for women. Not only was Harriet Beecher Stowe's *Uncle Tom's Cabin*, in numerous adaptations for the stage, by far the most-produced play of the century, but many women found access to professional production by writing or adapting melodramas. Louisa Medina and Frances Hodgson Burnett were particularly prolific and popular writers of melodrama, but they were by no means unique. Critics such as Sarah Blackstone and Sherry Engle have made a good beginning in historical research, but this is a field that would reward a great deal of further study from many perspectives.

The Progressive Era

In general, the late nineteenth and early twentieth centuries were a time of great productivity for women playwrights. Several made a very comfortable living from the theater, and many plays by women were produced in New York, which had by then become the center of American theatrical activity, as well as in theaters throughout the country. According to Sherry Engle, between 1890 and 1920, more than fifty women dramatists achieved two or more productions in New York. Her *New Women Dramatists in America, 1890–1920* provides a long list of plays by women that were produced between 1885 and 1925. Engle analyzes the work of five very successful women playwrights who, for various reasons, had been lost to history: Martha Morton, Madeleine Lucette Ryley, Evelyn Greenleaf Sutherland, Beulah Marie Dix, and Rida Johnson Young. Her work of recovery builds on the earlier work of Yvonne Shafer and Sally Burke, who have identified dozens of playwrights from the early twentieth century whose work would reward analysis from a number of perspectives. Besides the recovery of playwrights, most criticism to date focuses on the feminism that some of these playwrights brought to the theater of the Progressive Era, a theater that for a number of years welcomed the discussion of social issues.

During the Progressive Era, Rachel Crothers succeeded better than anyone else at bringing the issues of first-wave American feminism into the theater in plays that were commercially viable, if not runaway hits on the Broadway stage. Her most anthologized play, *A Man's World* (1909), directly attacked the issue of the double sexual standard, provoking a good deal of controversy with her twist on the typical "problem play" ending in which a man chooses either to forgive or not to forgive an erring wife and take her back.

Crothers has her female protagonist Frank Ware reject her suitor because he refuses to take responsibility for an earlier love affair that has produced a son, and he condemns the boy's mother as immoral for having sex with him. Frank decides to reject the father and raise his child. Crothers's most important feminist statement came in *He and She* (1912/20), a multi-plotted examination of the problems surrounding the issue of combining a career with marriage and raising a family. The various women characters in the play decide that the combination is not feasible. One decides not to marry because her career means so much to her. Another gives up her career to marry. And the protagonist, who is, tellingly, more successful in her career as a sculptor than her husband, cedes an important commission to him in order to pay more attention to her daughter. Crothers, a very successful playwright who remained single all her life, and whose mother had left home for several years during the 1880s while Rachel was a child in order to go to medical school and become a physician, insisted that a choice had to be made between marriage and career. This issue was of course hotly debated both in 1912 when the play was first produced and in 1920 when it was revived with Crothers in the lead role.

During the 1920s and '30s, in keeping with the taste of the theater audience, Crothers retreated from such direct issues-based Shavian "dramas of discussion" into a witty social comedy, but she maintained her interest in feminist issues, especially in relation to such middle-class concerns as marriage, divorce, sexuality, economic independence, class and generational conflict, materialism, and spirituality. Her most successful Broadway play, *Susan and God* (1937), satirized the attempts by rich, idle women to import meaning into their lives by latching on to spiritual fads and enthusiasms. When it was revived by the Mint Theater in 2006, it was a critical success, and audiences found it surprisingly witty and contemporary.

In the retrospective view of literary criticism and history of this period, it has not been the Broadway theater that has emerged as most significant and influential, but the Art Theater or Little Theater movement that flourished in the first two decades of the twentieth century. The exciting development of modernism in all the arts that fueled Greenwich Village's Little Renaissance found a focus in theater groups such as the Washington Square Players and the Provincetown Players, where artists, writers, and intellectuals inspired by modernism, feminism, Progressive Era politics, and avant-garde activity of all kinds came together to create a new kind of theater that reflected their forward-thinking worldview. Women were central to the founding and running of these groups, and, as Cheryl Black has shown, women artists of all kinds found an opportunity to work there. Of the 145 plays produced by the Provincetown Players between 1915 and 1922, sixty were by women (Black, *The Women of Provincetown*, 165). A number of these plays have been reprinted in anthologies, notably in collections by Barbara Ozieblo and Judith Barlow.

A number of well-known women writers wrote plays for the Art Theaters, among them Djuna Barnes, Edna St. Vincent Millay, Alice Brown, Edna Ferber, and Neith Boyce. The most significant playwright to emerge from the Little Theater movement was Susan Glaspell, who has been the subject of two recent biographies by Barbara Ozieblo and Linda Ben-Zvi and the most extensive critical study of any American woman playwright. Among her plays, the best known is the much-anthologized *Trifles* (1916), a one-act play that is distinguished by its imaginative use of the conventions of theatrical realism, its elegantly simple construction, and its feminism. Linda Ben-Zvi has analyzed Glaspell's use of her reportage on an Iowa murder case as a basis for *Trifles* and the later short story, "A Jury of her Peers," and several critics, including J. Ellen Gainor, Artem Lozynsky, Karen Alkalay-Gut, and Brenda Murphy, have written about Glaspell's innovative use of the conventions of detective fiction in the play. Inspired by her vivid memory of a 1900 court case she had covered as a reporter in Iowa, in which a physically abused Iowa farm wife was convicted of killing her husband with an axe, Glaspell created a situation in which several women have been brought to the house of Minnie Wright, who is accused of strangling her husband, to take care of some domestic details while the sheriff and the district attorney investigate the house for clues to the murder, and, significantly, the motive for it.

The play takes the form of a detective story, although, as J. Ellen Gainor has noted, it manipulates the conventions of detection in order to convey Glaspell's feminist point of view, implying that both male and female viewers must "learn to see as the women do, to become feminist spectators, and realize that this kind of seeing is different from, and in this case superior to, the men's way" (*Susan Glaspell*, 49). The women discover the motive for the murder precisely by concerning themselves with the "trifles" of housekeeping in the kitchen. They find that Minnie's canary, the only source of life or joy in her home, has been killed, its neck broken, revealing the immediate motive for the murder of her abusive husband. Having uncovered the reality of Minnie's desperately unhappy life through the domestic "trifles" of her kitchen, the women tacitly agree not to show their evidence to the men, who, they agree, would not take them seriously anyway.

In a brief span of six years following *Trifles*, Susan Glaspell embarked on an extraordinary career of theatrical experimentation, which included *The*

Outside (1917) and *Bernice* (1918), culminating in her unique synthesis of modernist aesthetics and feminist ideology in the startlingly original play *The Verge* (1921). While it maintains a hold on the illusion of objective reality that is fundamental to realism, this highly personal representation of the Nietzschean female artist pushes through the conventional boundaries of realism to encompass a subjective and abstract dramatic idiom as well, using expressionistic techniques that were just arriving on the American stage from Europe. Although her own experimental plays were performed on the small stage of the Provincetown, Glaspell's work paved the way for Sophie Treadwell, another member of the Provincetown Players, to have her modernist expressionistic play *Machinal* (1928), which like *Trifles*, was based on a sensational real case of a woman killing her husband, successfully produced on Broadway.

The mid-twentieth century

Following quickly upon the Art Theater movement, another development that received little attention at the time but has figured significantly in retrospect is the theater of the New Negro movement of the 1920s. An important part of the New Negro movement, the theater had a clear agenda that was articulated by W. E. B. Du Bois in four simple principles: the drama must be about, by, for, and near "ordinary Negro people." While Du Bois favored and occasionally wrote didactic "race plays," meant to educate African Americans about their history and the contemporary issues facing them, Alain Locke and Montgomery T. Gregory, two members of the Howard University faculty who founded the theater program there in 1921, dissociated themselves from didacticism and promoted folk drama. Encouraged by Locke and Gregory, playwrights such as Willis Richardson, Zora Neale Hurston, Mary P. Burrill, May Miller, Georgia Douglas Johnson, and Eulalie Spence produced a substantial body of folk drama that was widely disseminated and produced in amateur venues throughout the African American community, although only two of Richardson's plays were produced on Broadway in the 1920s. In 1991, *Mule Bone*, a folk comedy by Hurston and Langston Hughes that was recovered through the efforts of Henry Louis Gates and George Bass, finally received a Broadway production, to enthusiastic reviews. The more serious immediate agenda of the New Negro theater was the eradication of lynching, the focus of a number of plays that were produced in high school auditoriums, church basements, libraries, and other venues, if not in theaters. Some of the best of these are Angelina Weld Grimké's *Rachel* (1916), Mary

Burrill's *Aftermath* (1919), and Georgia Douglas Johnson's *A Sunday Morning in the South* (1925). *Strange Fruit*, a collection of these plays, has been edited by Kathy Perkins and Judith Stephens, occasioning a growing body of scholarly work.

In the commercial theater, the 1920s was by far the most productive period in American history. In the 1927–8 season, the peak year of activity, there were 264 new productions in the Broadway theater, as compared with 115 in 1915–16 (Poggi, *Theater*, 47) and twenty-eight in 2000–2001 (IBDB). In the prosperous Jazz Age, much of this activity was unabashed entertainment aimed at audiences with money to spend, but the general prosperity made for a wide range of theater, from the most serious literary endeavor to the wildest revue, which was unprecedented and never to be repeated. Most of this drama was not overtly political or socially minded, but as a body it makes a substantial representation of American life, values, attitudes, and ideas in the early twentieth century. Many of the Progressive Era playwrights were active throughout the 1920s, and a number of women, including Rachel Crothers, Clare Kummer, Zoë Akins, Anita Loos, Mae West, and Frances Hodgson Burnett, produced a steady stream of plays for the Broadway theater. In the 1930s, the Great Depression brought a swift end to Broadway's prosperity, severely reducing the opportunities for playwrights. While escapist entertainment dominated the theater of the 1920s, there was also a new, more serious tinge to theater that had any kind of literary aspirations. A new socially conscious drama whose patron saint was Clifford Odets replaced the sentimental domestic comedy and chic society plays of the 1920s as the fashion on Broadway, and in alternative theater, the Art Theaters and the Little Theater movement gave way to the leftist workers theaters of the 1930s.

The most significant woman playwright of the 1930s and '40s was Lillian Hellman, who has been a controversial figure since her first play, *The Children's Hour*, was produced on Broadway in 1934. This play, which hinges on a child's lie that she has seen the two women who run her boarding school engaged in sexual activity, was shocking to some contemporary audiences for its exposure of the myth of childhood innocence and for its allusions to lesbianism. It was banned in Boston and Chicago and censored by the Lord Chamberlain's office in London. Nevertheless, it achieved great critical and popular success, running for twenty-one months and 691 performances on Broadway. Despite Hellman's consistent insistence that the play's focus was the lie and its consequences, the major focus of the play's critics has continued to be its treatment of lesbianism. In recent years, Hellman has been criticized by Anne Fleche and Mary Titus for treating lesbians as "abnormal" and endorsing the dominant heteronormative ideology of her time. In 1952, when Hellman was called to testify before the McCarthyist House Committee on Un-American Activities, she took the Fifth Amendment in answer to questions that might lead to recrimination against others as well as herself. She also made a much-quoted statement in a letter to the committee that she "would not cut [her] conscience to suit this year's fashions" (Hellman, "Letter," 3545). In the same year, Hellman directed a production of *The Children's Hour* that put the lie and the damage it caused to the women clearly at the center of the play. Since then, another important line of criticism, exemplified by Jenny Spencer and Clayton Delery, has focused on the lie and its thematic, cultural, and political implications.

As is typical in unsettled times, melodrama took on a new life during the 1930s. It was used by playwrights such as Hellman and Clare Boothe to establish a simple moral framework for advocating a particular position on an issue facing the country, such as joining the European war against fascism in Boothe's *Margin for Error* (1939) and Hellman's *Watch on the Rhine* (1941). Other plays aim to establish a moral framework for the times. Hellman used *The Little Foxes* (1939) and *Another Part of the Forest* (1947) to condemn both the capitalists who "eat the earth" and those who stand around and watch them do it. In later years, Hellman's plays became more personal and psychological, with *The Autumn Garden* (1951), *Toys in the Attic* (1960), and *My Mother, My Father and Me* (1963).

In the mid-twentieth century, from the seeds planted during the Harlem Renaissance and the New Negro Movement, grew an African American theater movement that nourished two generations of playwrights. While this theater was mostly run by and focused on men, in theaters such as the American Negro Theater (ANT), the Negro Ensemble Company, and the Black Arts Repertory Theater run by Amiri Baraka, several significant women playwrights were nurtured there. Alice Childress was an early member of the ANT, and acted in several important productions in the 1940s before she began writing plays. The younger playwrights Adrienne Kennedy and Lorraine Hansberry, however, pioneered different paths to the New York theater for African American playwrights, helping to make mainstream theater available to the generation that followed. Kennedy studied at the American Theater Wing and at the Circle in the Square School with Edward Albee, and her best-known play, *Funnyhouse of a Negro*, was first produced by the mainstream Off-Broadway theater Circle in the Square in 1962. Hansberry went directly to Broadway with *A Raisin in the Sun* (1959), the first play by an African American woman to be produced there.

A straightforward realism was the mode of choice for a playwright like Lorraine Hansberry, whose very popular *A Raisin in the Sun*, with its Broadway run of 530 performances, makes a clear statement about the economic forces and social attitudes arrayed against a black family in contemporary Chicago. Childress and Kennedy produced more experimental work, exhibiting an interest in creating new forms of theater to represent their perception of the world as African Americans and as twentieth-century women. As a result, neither playwright has garnered a great deal of popular recognition or success, but their plays have received substantial attention from academic critics. Childress was first produced in the 1950s, but her plays *Trouble in Mind* (1955), *Wedding Band* (1966), and *Wine in the Wilderness* (1969) reflect her evolving feminist consciousness. Beginning with plays like *Funnyhouse of a Negro*, *The Owl Answers* (1963), *A Rat's Mass* (1967), and *A Movie Star Has to Star in Black and White* (1976), Kennedy has shown herself to be one of the most aesthetically ambitious American playwrights of the twentieth century. Although she has occasionally been pigeonholed as postmodern, her avant-garde feminist aesthetics defy such labels. Her early plays make use of many of the techniques of expressionism to represent the fragmented subjectivities of her characters. As the audience gradually comes to understand them through the jazz technique of repetition and revision, the characters become at the same time intensely individual and representative of the universal experience of African American women. In a sense, the object of these early plays is the integration of the fragmented black female subject, a task, it becomes clear, that can never be accomplished under the conditions in which she lives.

The late twentieth century

Adrienne Kennedy was part of the explosion of playwriting in the 1970s that accompanied the second-wave feminist movement. The goal of expressing a feminist ideology through a feminist theater aesthetics motivated many drama groups such as Jo Ann Schmidman and Megan Terry's Omaha Magic Theater, the feminist theater collective At the Foot of the Mountain, and the lesbian theater ensemble Split Britches, to start theaters and produce their own plays. In these theater groups, which have theatrical roots in the alternative theater movement of the 1960s, a collaborative and anti-hierarchical feminist theatrical aesthetic gradually emerged. Many of the plays of these groups, developed collaboratively by the playwright with the actors, directors, and scenic artists, paid particular attention to issues of power in relation to gender and ethnicity, and rejected the linear plot and integrated characterization of traditional realism as phallocentric. In plays like Terry's *Approaching Simone* (1970) and María Irene Fornés's *Fefu and her Friends* (1977), the playwrights in this movement explored techniques such as transformational gender-crossing characterization and multi-sequential scenes to produce a drama that expressed their feminist vision.

The author of more than forty plays, Fornés has had a playwriting career that spans more than forty-five years. Since the late 1970s, Fornés has been involved with the Hispanic American Arts Center in New York, and her work in the 1980s and '90s turned particularly to themes inspired by her native Cuba, and the experience of Hispanic Americans. Her first play, *Tango Palace* (1964), had clear roots in the Theater of the Absurd, and she has acknowledged the direct influence of her seeing the original French production of Beckett's *Waiting for Godot* and Burgess Meredith's 1958 production of the adaption from Joyce's *Ulysses*, *Ulysses in Nighttown*. Fornés became a fixture in the avant-garde Off-Off Broadway movement of the 1960s and '70s, producing other playwrights' work as well as her own at New York Theater Strategy. It was there that *Fefu and her Friends*, still her best-known play, was produced in 1977. Ruby Cohn has suggested the unique aesthetic of Fornés's early plays: "Floating away from realism, they offer an oblique critique of reality" (*New American Dramatists*, 69). Set in 1935, *Fefu* is anchored in the realism of the mid-twentieth century, particularly through its setting, which includes several living spaces in the kind of upper-middle-class country house that would be featured in the social comedy of Rachel Crothers, Philip Barry, or S. N. Berhman. Fornés plays with the idea of the audience's relationship with the setting by having the audience move from one set to another rather than changing the sets for the living room, the lawn, the study, the bedroom, and the kitchen. The characters are a group of women who meet at Fefu's country house to discuss raising funds for the use of art as a tool for learning. In the course of the conversations, most of the characters become individualized, leading the audience into empathy with them. At the end of the play, however, Fefu berates the wheelchair-bound Julia, insisting that she can walk. She takes a gun outside, a shot is heard, and Julia's forehead begins to bleed. Fefu comes in with a dead rabbit and stands behind Julia, saying that she had just shot and killed "it . . . Julia." The shock of the ending, its departure from the cause-and-effect expectations of realism, and its underdetermined but insistent symbolism, throws all of the comfortably mimetic action that has come before into another aesthetic realm, and the play becomes a self-reflexive commentary on realism.

The gifted poet Ntozake Shange, born in 1948, is from a younger generation than Kennedy, Childress, Terry, and Fornés, who came of age in the 1950s and '60s, and worked to create a feminist theater during the throes of the Civil Rights, anti-war and early feminist movements. Shange has an MA in American Studies from UCLA, and worked with the Women's Studies program at Sonoma State College while she was developing a self-conscious feminist theater idiom in *For Colored Girls Who Have Considered Suicide When the Rainbow is Enuf* (1976). An unplotted "choreopoem" with minimalist staging, which combines music, dance, and dialogue spoken by characters individuated only by the colors they wear, *For Colored Girls* was brought into being through a long process of collaboration among Shange, who is a poet and dancer, a protean group of dancers, particularly Paula Moss, and eventually director Oz Scott. It moved from bars and other improvised venues in San Francisco to similar places in New York, eventually arriving on Broadway, where it was a surprising hit in 1976. Shange's play is a prime example of feminist theatrical aesthetics and themes. Her later plays *Spell #7* (1979), a deconstruction of the minstrel show, and *Boogie Woogie Landscapes* (1979) are similarly experimental.

During the last two decades of the twentieth century, feminist drama criticism focused mainly on the analysis of and application of feminist theory to the new feminist drama, on feminist analysis of canonical texts, and on the issue of whether realism was an appropriate or possible mode for feminist drama. Feminist critics such as Sue-Ellen Case, Lynda Hart, Jeanie Forte, and Jill Dolan argued from a materialist point of view that realism naturalizes "the master's way of seeing" (Hart, *Making a Spectacle*, 4), its mimetic transparency obscuring the author's patriarchal ideology and involving the audience as unwitting collaborators in its reinforcement. The rallying cry of this position was Audre Lorde's "the master's tools will never dismantle the master's house." Elin Diamond suggested that the gestic theater of Brecht, with its insistence on historicization rather than essentialism, was a more appropriate way to present feminist conceptions of women than traditional realism.

As Janet Brown has pointed out, realism and the Brechtian approach to theater are not mutually exclusive, as was demonstrated by director Anne Bogart's 1993 production of Clare Boothe's *The Women* (1936), a realistic play that has been criticized for its apparently misogynistic representation of women. Using Brechtian alienation techniques, Bogart's production introduced a narrator who commented on the action and music that interrupted the characters and mood rather than reinforcing them. Brown suggested that "Bogart's production highlighted the class differences that divide the female characters and the societal constraints that smother them, resulting in a clearly feminist performance" ("Feminist Theory and Contemporary Drama," 169). Using a number of feminist playwrights from the Progressive Era, the New Negro movement, and later, as examples, Patricia Schroeder responded directly to the feminist critique of realism in *The Feminist Possibilities of Dramatic Realism* (1996), pointing out that realism is not an ahistorical mode with an essentialized point of view, but exists in history itself, and has been written from the point of view of the feminist subject as well as the patriarchal one.

The realism debate colored much of the critical response to the women playwrights of the 1980s and '90s, causing some critics to question the feminist credentials of playwrights like Marsha Norman, Wendy Wasserstein, and Tina Howe, who wrote primarily realistic plays, while valorizing playwrights like Kennedy, Terry, Fornés, and Shange, who eschewed realism in favor of an antirealistic, experimental feminist aesthetic. Norman won kudos from feminist critics for *Getting Out* (1977), a play that splits the consciousness of a woman who is being released from prison into two characters, Arlene, the character in present time who has been "rehabilitated" in prison and is trying to make a conventional life for herself, and Arlie, the repressed younger self who keeps invading both Arlene's consciousness and the performance space, demanding that the pain and rage, as well as the resistance and strength, that have been part of her life experience be recognized. Norman was criticized for the realism of her Pulitzer Prize-winning *'Night, Mother* (1983), however, with critics like Forte and Dolan arguing that, despite the feminist thematics of the play, Norman's very use of realism "ultimately reinscribes the dominant ideology" (Forte, "Realism," 117). Other critics, such as Schroeder, Janet Haedicke, and Laurin Porter, defended the choice of realism as, in Porter's words, "a tool, not an ideology," which can be put to use in the hands of a feminist playwright as well as a patriarchal one (Porter, "Contemporary Playwrights," 206).

Into the twenty-first century

As the years have gone by, the focus on realism as a contested issue has diminished, and feminist critics, like feminist playwrights, have turned their attention to broader aesthetic and cultural issues. In the wake of Judith Butler's work, a good deal of attention has been paid to the performance of gender on stage, and women playwrights have addressed all aspects of women's experience, from the complexities of sexuality and gender identification to the social, political, and economic realities of American life. In keeping with the general cultural trend, women playwrights turned a good deal of attention to the exploration of race and ethnicity during the 1990s. Toward the turn of the twenty-first century, a number of well-known women playwrights were writing plays that spanned the gamut from the most avant-garde experimental playwriting to the most straightforward realism and addressed the broadest range of subjects. A suggestion of the range from many possible texts might include Paula Vogel's *How I Learned to Drive* (1998), which dramatizes the effects of sexual abuse by her uncle on a young girl; Suzan-Lori Parks's meditations on American history, *The America Play* (1994), *Venus* (1996), and *Topdog/Underdog* (2002); Anna Deavere Smith's unique performances of the many conflicting subjectivities that make up any social crisis in *Fires in the Mirror* (1991) and *Twilight Los Angeles* (1992); and Theresa Rebeck's comic takes on contemporary social issues such as political corruption, sexual harassment, and the collapse of American culture in the entertainment industry in *View of the Dome* (1996), *Spike Heels* (1992), and *The Family of Mann* (1994).

At the turn of the twenty-first century, the situation of women playwrights in the American theater was in some ways depressingly similar to that of their forebears at the turn of the twentieth, and in some ways worse. Contemporary playwrights do not have access to a vibrant popular theater the way writers of popular melodrama and sentimental comedy like Louisa Medina and Frances Hodgson Burnett did. And the production of plays by women still lags badly behind that of men, both on Broadway and in the regional and Off-Off Broadway theaters where women hold positions as artistic directors and managers, and one assumes there would be more openness to plays by women. In 2002, Susan Jonas and Suzanne Bennett's report on the status of women, which was commissioned by the New York State Council on the Arts, reported that in the 2001–2 season, only 17 per cent of the plays produced by the 460 member theaters of the Theater Communications Group (TCG), the league of professional not-for-profit American theaters, were written by women, better than the 8 per cent of the plays on Broadway, but still far from parity with men. The dismal situation described in this report was confirmed in 2009 by Emily Glassberg Sands's study of gender discrimination, in which she found that only 18 per cent of plays in non-profit subscription houses with more than ninety-nine seats were written by women. The surprising elements in Sands's study were that only 32 per cent of playwrights submitting plays were women, that women playwrights submitted fewer plays on average than men, and that, in a study in which four plays, all written by women, were submitted to theaters, half under a male pseudonym and half under a female pseudonym, male respondents rated the plays with male and female pseudonyms the same, while female respondents rated the scripts with female pseudonyms lower. A number of explanations for these factors have been offered, but the bottom line is that plays by women are still produced far less often than plays by men, and simply putting more women in the decision-making positions has not changed this.

There has been progress on some fronts, however. Jonas and Bennett report that among the ten most-produced plays nationally by TCG members in 2000–1, five were by women: *Art* by French playwright Yasmina Reza, *Spinning into Butter* by Rebecca Gilman, *Fully Committed* by Becky Mode, *Wit* by Margaret Edson, and *Dirty Blonde* by Claudia Shear. As a fairly reliable barometer of middlebrow American culture, in the sixty years between 1921 and 1980, the Pulitzer committee awarded the prize for drama to only five women as sole authors: Zona Gale for *Miss Lulu Bett* (1921), Susan Glaspell for *Alison's House* (1931), Zoë Akins for *The Old Maid* (1935), Mary Chase for *Harvey* (1945), and Ketti Frings for *Look Homeward, Angel* (1958). In the ten years between 1998 and 2009, it awarded the prize to four: Paula Vogel for *How I Learned to Drive* (1998), Margaret Edson for *Wit* (1999), Suzan-Lori Parks for *Topdog/Underdog* (2002), and Lynn Nottage for *Ruined* (2009). Among the finalists during that period were Theresa Rebeck and Alexandra Gersten-Vassilaros, Gina Gionfrido, Sarah Ruhl, Dael Orlandersmith, Quiara Alegria Hudes, Suzan-Lori Parks, Deirdre Murray, and Amy Freed. Although in one sense, this is simply further evidence of Emily Sands's claim that women have to write better plays than men in order to get them produced, it is also evidence of a wealth of playwriting by women, and this list does not include such significant playwrights as Emily Mann, Tina Howe, Beth Henley, Eve Ensler, Kia Corthron, Wakako Yamauchi, Griselda Gambaro, Melissa James Gibson, Velina Hasu Houston, Amy Herzog, Jessica Goldberg, Kristen Childs, Diana Son, Elena Garro, Maritza Wilde, and Susana Torres Molina, among many others. Against the odds, as always, it seems, women continue in the twenty-first century to write plays and to find ways to get them produced. The responsibility of critics is to find out about these plays and write about them.

Note

1. Dates of plays are for the first New York production unless otherwise noted.

Works cited

Alkalay-Gut, Karen. "Murder and Marriage: Another Look at *Trifles*." In *Susan Glaspell: Essays on her Theater and Fiction*. Ed. Linda Ben-Zvi. Ann Arbor: University of Michigan Press, 1995.

Barlow, Judith, *ed. Women Writers of the Provincetown Players: A Collection of the Shorter Works.* Albany: State University of New York Press, 2009.

Barrish, Jonas. *The Anti-Theatrical Prejudice.* Berkeley: University of California Press, 1981.

Ben-Zvi, Linda. "'Murder She Wrote': The Genesis of Susan Glaspell's *Trifles.*" In *Susan Glaspell: Essays on her Theater and Fiction.* Ed. Linda Ben-Zvi. Ann Arbor: University of Michigan Press, 1995.

Susan Glaspell: Her Life and Times. New York: Oxford University Press, 2005.

Black, Cheryl. *The Women of Provincetown, 1915–1922.* Tuscaloosa: University of Alabama Press, 2002.

Blackstone, Sarah J. "Women Writing Melodrama." In *The Cambridge Companion to American Women Playwrights.* Ed. Brenda Murphy. New York: Cambridge University Press, 1999.

Brown, Janet. "Feminist Theory and Contemporary Drama." In *The Cambridge Companion to American Women Playwrights.* Ed. Brenda Murphy. New York: Cambridge University Press, 1999.

American Feminist Playwrights: A Critical History. New York: Twayne, 1996.

Case, Sue-Ellen. *Feminism and Theatre.* New York: Methuen, 1988.

Case, Sue-Ellen, ed. *Performing Feminisms: Feminist Critical Theory and Theatre.* Baltimore: The Johns Hopkins University Press, 1990.

Cohn, Ruby. *New American Dramatists: 1960–1980.* New York: Grove Press, 1982.

Delery, Clayton J. "The Politics of Lies in Lillian Hellman's *The Children's Hour.*" *Xavier Review* 17.1 (1997): 36–46.

Diamond, Elin. "Brechtian Theory / Feminist Theory: Toward a Gestic Feminist Criticism." *The Drama Review* 32.1 (Spring 1988): 82–94.

"Rethinking Identification: Kennedy, Freud, Brecht." *The Kenyon Review* 15.2 (Spring 1993): 86–99.

Dolan, Jill. *The Feminist Spectator as Critic.* Ann Arbor: UMI Research Press, 1988.

Presence and Desire: Essays on Gender, Sexuality, Performance: Critical Perspectives on Women and Gender. Ann Arbor: University of Michigan Press, 1993.

Engle, Sherry D. *New Women Dramatists in America, 1890–1920.* New York: Palgrave Macmillan, 2007.

Fleche, Anne. "The Lesbian Rule: Lillian Hellman and the Measures of Realism." *Modern Drama* 39.1 (Spring 1996): 16–30.

Forte, Jeanie. "Realism, Narrative, and the Feminist Playwright: A Problem of Reception." *Modern Drama* 32.1 (March 1989): 115–27.

Gainor, J. Ellen. *Susan Glaspell in Context: American Theater, Culture and Politics, 1915–48.* Ann Arbor: University of Michigan Press, 2001.

Hart, Lynda, ed. *Making a Spectacle: Feminist Essays on Contemporary Women's Theatre.* Ann Arbor: University of Michigan Press, 1989.

Hellman, Lillian. "Letter to John S. Wood." May 19, 1952, recorded in House Committee on Un-American Activities, Public Hearings, Communist Infiltration of the Hollywood Motion-Picture Industry, Part 8, May 21, 1952: 3545–6.

Hewitt, Barnard. *Theatre USA: 1665 to 1957.* New York: McGraw-Hill, 1959.

IBDB: Internet Broadway Database. http://www.ibdb.com.

Jonas, Susan and Suzanne Bennett. "Report on the Status of Women: A Limited Engagement?" Prepared for the New York State Council on the Arts Theatre Program, January 2002.

Kritzer, Amelia Howe. "Comedies by Early American Women." In *The Cambridge Companion to American Women Playwrights*. Ed. Brenda Murphy. New York: Cambridge University Press, 1999.

Kritzer, Amelia Howe, ed. *Plays by Early American Women, 1775–1850*. Ann Arbor: University of Michigan Press, 1995.

Lozynsky, Artem. "The Case of the Missing Canary: A New Look at Glaspell's *Trifles*," *Feminist Studies in English Literature* 7.2 (Winter 2000): 141–58.

Mason, Jeffrey D. *Melodrama and the Myth of America*. Bloomington: Indiana University Press, 1993.

McConachie, Bruce. *Melodramatic Formations: American Theatre and Society, 1820–1870*. Iowa City: University of Iowa Press, 1992.

Murphy, Brenda. *Congressional Theatre: Dramatizing McCarthyism on Stage, Film, and Television*. New York: Cambridge University Press, 1999.

The Provincetown Players and the Culture of Modernity. New York: Cambridge University Press, 2005.

Ozieblo, Barbara. *The Provincetown Players: A Choice of the Shorter Works*. Sheffield: Sheffield Academic Press, 1994.

Susan Glaspell: A Critical Biography. Chapel Hill: University of North Carolina Press, 2000.

Perkins, Kathy A. and Judith L. Stephens, eds. *Strange Fruit: Plays on Lynching by American Women*. Bloomington: Indiana University Press, 1998.

Poggi, Jack. *Theater in America: The Impact of Economic Forces, 1870–1967*. Ithaca: Cornell University Press, 1968.

Porter, Laurin. "Contemporary Playwrights/Traditional Forms." In *The Cambridge Companion to American Women Playwrights*. Ed. Brenda Murphy. New York: Cambridge University Press, 1999.

Ritchie, Anna Cora Mowatt Ogden. *Autobiography of an Actress; or, Eight Years on the Stage*. Boston: Ticknor, Reed, and Fields, 1854.

Sands, Emily Glassberg. "Opening the Curtain on Playwright Gender: An Integrated Economic Analysis of Discrimination in the American Theater." Diss., Princeton University, 2009.

Schlueter, June, ed. *Feminist Rereadings of Modern American Drama*. Rutherford, NJ: Fairleigh Dickinson University Press, 1989.

Schroeder, Patricia R. *The Feminist Possibilities of Dramatic Realism*. Rutherford, NJ: Fairleigh Dickinson University Press, 1996.

Shafer, Yvonne. *American Women Playwrights, 1900–1950*. New York: Peter Lang, 1995.

Spencer, Jenny S. "Sex, Lies, and Revisions: Historicizing Hellman's *Children's Hour*." *Modern Drama* 47.1 (Spring 2004): 44–65.

Titus, Mary. "Murdering the Lesbian: Lillian Hellman's *The Children's Hour*." *Tulsa Studies in Women's Literature* 10.2 (Fall 1991): 215–32.

18

Turn-of-the-twentieth-century transitions

Women on the edge of tomorrow

STEPHANIE SMITH

Introduction

In the United States at the end of the nineteenth century, well-documented changes in daily life opened new horizons for women. During the first two decades of the twentieth century, as Jo Ann Argersinger writes, "the forces of industrialization transformed American society with an intensity that shattered traditions and stirred imaginations" (*Triangle Fire*, 2). The labor force swelled with thousands of new immigrants; the Great Migration of African Americans from rural to urban areas began around 1912; and while many American women had been working for decades, housebound middle-class women also began to go to work. As Jean-Michel Rabaté wrote, "urban America changed more between 1890–1910 than in the whole previous century" (*1913*, 16). One of the largest industries to which women flocked was the ready-to-wear clothing industry. New modes of production, improved technologies like the steam-powered sewing machines of the 1870s, marketing, advertising, and distribution made for increased consumption. Consumption mirrored class aspiration, allowing for "the working class's 'dream world' of bourgeois consumption" to parallel "the bourgeoisie's 'dream world' of aristocratic forms," argues Nancy L. Green in *Ready to Wear, Ready to Work: A Century of Industry and Immigrants in Paris and New York*. Sweatshop worker Sadie Frowne wrote in 1902, "a girl must have clothes if she is to go into high society at Ulmer Park or Coney Island or the theatre . . . a girl who does not dress well is stuck in a corner, even if she is pretty, and Aunt Fanny says that I do just right to put on plenty of style" (Argersinger, *Triangle Fire*, 55).

The twentieth century promised new choices for many American women, from what they did to what they wore, and, of course, who they were. A new word entered the American vocabulary at this time, originating in a place called Greenwich Village according to Christine Stansell: the word "feminist" (*American Moderns*, 43). Although they would not have the vote until 1921, suffragettes and feminists regained some of the political steam lost by the earlier Women's Movement. In Vienna, Sigmund Freud would ask the infamous question "what does a woman want?" in response to new patients showing symptoms of "neurasthenia" and "hysteria." In the United States, physician Silas Weir Mitchell developed new therapies for men and women suffering from "American nervousness," a condition attributed to the increased speed of life, according to Isaac G. Briggs (*Epilepsy, Hysteria, Neurasthenia*). As critic Nancy Bentley says, "modernity is less an epoch than a tempo" (*Frantic Panoramas*, 220).

Women of this era were restless, wrote F. Scott Fitzgerald describing Zelda Fitzgerald's post-World War I generation in *The Jazz Age*, but this restlessness was often without aim; Jennifer Fleissner prefers the "more nuanced" term "compulsion" to describe the situation that modern women wrote about, in an "attempt to narrate the modern woman's bodily story" (*Women, Compulsion, Modernity*, 13). Many works written by women at this time record and reflect upon feelings about themselves that ranged from vague dissatisfaction (or what a much later generation would call the "problem with no name") to hopelessness. In 1913, both Thea Kronberg of Willa Cather's *The Song of the Lark* and Undine Spragg of Edith Wharton's *The Custom of the Country* are physically described as restless, as if a compulsion to move had been inscribed in their flesh, part of the "strange new energy" that emerged in the 1890s (Fleissner, *Women, Compulsion, Modernity*, 23). Women authors began to explore hitherto taboo choices or silenced miseries. Emily Dickinson, Kate Chopin, Nella Larsen, along with the aforementioned Cather and Wharton come to mind, but as Elizabeth Ammons argued in 1992 in her ground-breaking study *Conflicting Stories: American Women Writers at the Turn into the Twentieth Century*, this period marked a flowering of women's voices that had been, in the past, left out by most critical paradigms of American literature, such as realism and naturalism. Indeed, Henry Louis Gates, Jr. noted that 1890 through 1910 could also be called "'The Black Woman's Era'" for the burst of African American women's narratives published then, as Claudia Tate also explores (*Domestic Allegories of Political Desire*).

Indeed, the literature written at the turn of the century provides an invaluable window onto gender, race, class, and life in the United States, as critics since Ammons, such as Nancy Bentley, Richard Brodhead, Wai Chee Dimock, Ann duCille, Julia Ehrhardt, Rita Felski, Jaime Harker, Gordon Hutner, Judith Fetterley, Barbara Freeman, Sandra Gunning, Barbara Hochman, and Paula

Treichler, to name only a few, have explored in a variety of ways. As Ammons writes

> between 1892 and 1929 there appeared "The Yellow Wall-Paper," *Iola Leroy*, *The Country of the Pointed Firs*, *The Goodness of St. Roque*, *The Awakening*, *Contending Forces*, *The Land of Little Rain*, *The House of Mirth*, *Ethan Frome*, *Three Lives*, *O Pioneers!*, *A Woman of Genius*, *The Custom of the Country*, *Mrs. Spring Fragrance*, *Herland*, *The Song of the Lark*, *Summer*, *Virginia*, *My Ántonia*, *The Age of Innocence*, *A Lost Lady*, *There is Confusion*, *Weeds*, *Barren Ground*, *Bread Givers*, *Plum Bun*, *Death Comes for the Archbishop*, *Cogewea*, *Quicksand* and *Passing*. (*Conflicting Stories*, 4)

Yet still this list represents a fraction, should one widen the frame to include letters, diaries, travel narratives or popular but neglected forms such as the penny dreadful and the dime novel. And while women authors did celebrate freedoms and choices, many sought also to come to terms with a historical legacy of physical slavery or psychological enslavement – as female characters from Nathaniel Hawthorne's tortured Puritan, Hester Prynne, to Nella Larsen's confused Harlem Renaissance heroine Helga Crane might attest.

In fact, women as *characters* in American literature have been bedeviled by the question "what constitutes freedom, for a woman, in America?" as they tried to break (or in some cases, reconnect) the legal, social, familial, financial, or romantic bonds that held them. If American letters sprang, at least in part, from eighteenth-century captivity and nineteenth-century slave narratives, then one could say that women remained indebted to those genres right through the late twentieth century.[1] The last popular version of the white female captivity narrative, the story of Mormons Olive and Mary Ann Oatman, whose family was killed in a Yavapai raid and who were adopted and tattooed by the Mohaves, was published in 1858, but it continued to be reprinted well into the twentieth century. Certainly the famous 1892 tale by sociologist, poet, novelist, and social activist Charlotte Perkins Gilman, "The Yellow Wall-Paper," recounts a captivity; Edna Pontellier in Kate Chopin's 1899 *The Awakening* does not escape the twin bondage of New Orleans social expectations and sexual appetite; and Nella Larsen's African American protagonists in both *Quicksand* and *Passing* are trapped by society, race, and desire. Similarly, Edith Wharton's novels comment on the cage of social rules, but Wharton, like Gertrude Stein, does not see how working is an improvement because most who did, entered the market as unskilled laborers, a vision shared by Theodore Dreiser's novel *Sister Carrie* (1900). One major hurdle for those who sought to work was the idea that a woman must be a lady and being a lady was a benchmark of respectability. If a woman was not a lady, she was vulnerable to abuse.

The picture that emerges from this transition from one century to the next tends to be a disturbing one, or as Ellen Glasgow wrote of the blasted southern landscape facing her protagonist in *Barren Ground*, the horizon was "bare, starved and desolate" (*Barren Ground*, 4). Even though some women wrote fantastic tales of brave new worlds like the *Angel Island* (1914) by Inez Haynes Gilmore, which chronicles the fate of five shipwrecked men who meet and fall in love with winged women, a story that literalizes the figurative wings of freedom longed for by characters from Edna Pontellier in 1899 to the Russian-Jewish immigrant Shenah Pessay in Anna Yeziereska's 1920 *Hungry Hearts*, the dominant image that emerges is of blighted lives, vanquished hopes, and pain. Even in *Angel Island*, the men, frightened that their angel-women will fly away, shear off the women's wings, leaving them with useless "wing stumps" (*Angel Island*, 347). Rather than finding cause for celebration in rapid change, many women saw upheaval, distress, or stasis. Whether grappling with the legacy of slavery, as did Frances Harper in *Iola LeRoy* (1892) and Pauline Hopkins in *Contending Forces* (1900), or experimenting with narrative form, as did Gertrude Stein in *Three Lives* (1909), women authors broke new ground writing about gendered experiences once forbidden. While I cannot, by any means, attend to the whole territory of writings sketched out here, I will offer a chronological overview, from the Gilded Age to the 1929 Crash.

End-of-the-nineteenth-century traumas

The years after the Civil War to the turn of the century are often dubbed "The Gilded Age," due to the roller-coaster economy that would collapse in October 1929. The term "Gilded Age" was coined by Mark Twain and Charles Dudley Warner in their 1873 satire *The Gilded Age, A Tale of Today*, which chronicles those economic times, but also features a lobbyist-turned-murderer, Laura Hawkins, who kills her married lover and is acquitted. Later, in 1916–17, the prolific journalist, playwright, and author Susan Glaspell, founder of the Provincetown Players theater group in 1915, wrote two of her best-remembered works about an infamous murderess, also acquitted. "A Jury of her Peers" and the one-act play *Trifles* recount the murder of John Hossack, whose wife, Margaret, was convicted of killing him with an axe. She received a life sentence, but the decision was overturned by the Iowa Supreme Court a year later. Her second trial hung the jury and she was freed.

These works testify to the resilience of the idea that a lady could *not* commit brutality, even when it was clear that she probably did.

Still, horizons were expanding, sometimes literally, as women also began to write about the west. In 1884, Helen Hunt Jackson, who became an advocate for the rights of American Indians, published *Ramona: A Story*, a realist-romantic novel about the fortunes of a half-Indian, half-Scottish woman raised among the California-Mexican aristocracy, but cruelly treated by her stepmother. Ramona Ortegna is a docile, beautiful girl who grows into a woman of courage. Falling in love with an Indian man, she leaves her pampered life and experiences the genocidal tragedy that had become the lot of the Indian in America. A Cinderella-like tale that had both political and literary impact in a way similar to Harriet Beecher Stowe's *Uncle Tom's Cabin* (1852), *Ramona* influenced short-term political reforms with respect to the Indian peoples, such as the Dawes General Allotment Act of 1887. Like Jackson, Gertrude Atherton also wrote about the west; in *Patience Sparhawk and Her Times: A Novel* Atherton penned a story so controversial in its treatment of sex that it was banned by San Francisco's Book Committee of the Mechanical Library as "vulgar" (*New York Times*, May 17, 1897). Author Charles Chesnutt, reviewing the novel, called it "unpleasant" but pointed out that Atherton was hardly alone in exploring the ground of sexuality in daring ways that paralleled sociopolitical and cultural shifts. For one thing, education was expanding. By 1900, all but three state universities admitted women on the same terms as men. Going to college signified being a modern woman; because white, middle-class women now regularly joined the labor force, women were to be found in the domains of the male professions. By the 1890s, the Civil War was the past and the United States began to flex its international muscle.

Yet, as Nathaniel Hawthorne wrote in *The Scarlet Letter*, "the past was not dead" (15). The lingering traumatic effects of slavery and the Civil War still echoed. Mark Twain's *Puddin'head Wilson* (1894) re-examines the legal fiction of slavery, while Stephen Crane's *The Red Badge of Courage* (1895) records a soldier's eye view of the war's terror. As Jennifer Travis writes, American male writers at the turn of the century tried to reimagine a masculinity shaken by "irritable heart" or "soldier's heart," the language used by physicians trying to understand what we would now call PTSD (*Wounded Hearts*, 23–4). Women writers also took up this legacy of trauma, but women's history had been shaped as well by a struggle for female emancipation that had roots in the abolitionism of the 1840s and '50s, yet extended into other realms: women sought dress reform, filled the ranks of the Temperance movement, and advocated various civil rights denied to them in the past on the sole basis of gender, despite the fact that doing so on the public stage often threatened their status as ladies.

Thus, as the new century dawned, American women writers would explore these changing expectations, while also being mindful of the past. I want to examine here three oft-cited fictions that grapple with these issues: Charlotte Perkins Gilman's 1892 "The Yellow Wall-Paper," Frances Harper's *Iola LeRoy, or, Shadows Uplifted* of the same year, and Kate Chopin's 1899 *The Awakening*. All three deal with the conflict between public and private; the ongoing effects of the past; the yearning for new freedoms that would answer to unspoken desire, as all three deal with women's "claim to physical self-definition and self-possession" (Ammons, *Conflicting Stories*, 34), although that self-possession could also easily turn into self-obsession or solipsism. "The Yellow Wall-Paper," first published in *The New England Magazine* in January 1892, became a rallying fiction for feminist scholars in the 1970s, or as Elaine Hedges's Afterword to the 1973 Feminist Press edition claims, the story seemed "one of the rare pieces of literature we have by a nineteenth-century woman which directly confronts the sexual politics of the male–female, husband–wife relationship" (*Yellow Wallpaper*, 39). The unnamed female protagonist suffers from "a temporary nervous depression – a slight hysterical tendency" (10) that will clear up so long as she quits trying "to write a word" (13). Her physician-husband, John, rents a house in the country, where he installs his wife in a top-floor nursery, but the room sounds like a torture chamber: the bed is nailed to the floor, odd metal rings are bolted to the walls which are covered with a "revolting" wall-paper, "a smoldering, unclean yellow" "lurid orange," and "sickly sulphur" (13) – gothic characteristics, as Jennifer Fleissner points out, that can also be associated with both aging and with "extremes of idiosyncrasy, hysterical femininity, 'savagery' and sex" (*Women, Compulsion, Modernity*, 81). The word revolting takes on more meaning, as the doctor's wife begins to read into the wallpaper a story about imprisoned women. After becoming, in her own mind, one of the wallpaper's "prisoners," she escapes. "I've got out at last . . . And I've pulled off most of the paper, so you can't put me back in!" (*Yellow Wallpaper*, 36) she says to John, who promptly faints, in a nice twist of gender roles: she is free and in total command, while he passes out. The diagnosis of the story is grim: when an imaginative woman is confined to the domestic, she will direct energy inward and go crazy. Gilman had been a patient of S. Weir Mitchell, so this story is often read as an indictment of his "rest cure" for nervous women, although Jennifer Fleissner's recasting of naturalism adds a nice critical double twist when she argues that the equally famous Mitchell cure for disturbed men, his camping-out cure, shared such a similar psychic terrain with literary naturalism *and* with the rest cure that "we might consider calling this re-masculinizing therapy 'the west cure'" adding "naturalism constitutes a kind of literary west cure" (*Women, Compulsion, Modernity*, 83). Fleissner notes that Gilman's story, rarely understood as part of naturalism, in fact indicts the domestic sphere fully as much as naturalism did.

On the face of it, Gilman's dark little tale does not appear to have much in common with *Iola LeRoy*; as Elizabeth Ammons says, when you put the two side by side, "crucial historical and contextual differences obviously separate the two texts" (*Conflicting Stories*, 34). Indeed, "The Yellow Wall-Paper" is more akin to Kate Chopin's *The Awakening* because Edna Pontellier also yearns to be an artist, and she ends her own life when she realizes she hasn't the strength. Both stories have sad, ambiguous conclusions: the doctor's wife is crazy, if triumphant; Edna swims out in the ocean to her death, but instead of a drowning, the story ends on a dream sequence about her childhood: "Edna heard her father's voice and her sister Margaret's. She heard the barking of an old dog that was chained to the sycamore tree. The spurs of the cavalry officer clanged as he walked across the porch. There was the hum of bees, and the musky odor of pinks filled the air" (*The Awakening*, 109). *Iola LeRoy* tells, instead, how the shadows of the past can be put to rest. Following an almost century-long pattern of near-white tragic mulatta characters, Frances W. Harper's Iola suffers but also survives: "young in years, but old in sorrow; one whom a sad destiny had changed from a light-hearted girl to a heroic woman" (*Iola LeRoy*, 59). Iola's journey from pampered southern planter's daughter to "an article of merchandise" (115) to a Union nurse, teacher and finally bride to a doctor who might have passed for white, but refuses to do so, is a tale woven "from threads of fact and fiction" designed to "add to the solution of our unsolved American problem" (282). Iola LeRoy becomes a symbol of honesty, purity, and achievement. Unlike earlier tragic mulatta figures, Iola not only survives, but Harper suggests she has the talent to write the very novel in which she is the heroine. There is no hint of tragedy or suicide here. However, as noted earlier, all three tales, no matter how different, deal with the conflict between public and private – the doctor's wife wants more stimulus; LeRoy is thrown into a private abyss of slavery but, once freed, she takes a public role; Pontellier wants to lead an artistic life as she sees fit, irrespective of social mores. All three also address the effect of the past – the doctor's wife sees many women entrapped by the wall-paper; Iola provides an example for those formerly enslaved; Edna would strip away the demands of marriage as easily as she sheds her wedding rings. All three seek new freedoms that take into account the past but forge a new future for a new century.

By 1912, Charlotte Perkins Gilman had become a prolific author (*Women and Economics* [1898] and *The Home* [1903]) and poet (*Suffrage Songs and Verses*, 1911) and had also become a member of The Heterodoxy Club of Greenwich Village, a group of women who met for the purpose of exploring their individual freedoms. The term "the New Woman" had already been coined for a growing number of women like these, who were pursuing more public lives than their mothers. By 1915, Gilman published another fictional version of woman's lot, *Herland*, which envisions a lost land, ruled and inhabited by women, a land she returned to in the 1916 novel, *With Her in Ourland*. Compared to "The Yellow Wall-Paper," both novels recast entirely how a woman's life might be lived, and both are utopian in their hopes, while relying on a dystopian logic of eugenics. As the nineteenth-century turned into the twentieth, American letters would be awash in a wave of both utopian dreams and dystopian speculation, from the empire-building view of technology that shapes Garrett P. Serviss's American version of H. G. Wells's popular *War of the Worlds*, titled *Edison's Conquest of Mars* (1898), in which the invention of radio plays a role, to the novel *Futility, or Wreck of the Titan* by Morgan Robertson (1898) which eerily predicts the sinking of the Titanic, fourteen years later.

But the legacy of slavery and ongoing sociopolitical conflicts over race continued to be at issue, often intertwined with questions about technology, science, and pseudo-science, from Darwin's theory of evolution to scientific racism or eugenics, a language that Pauline E. Hopkins also uses in *Contending Forces* and in her novel *Of One Blood: or, the Hidden Self* (1903) in order to examine "theories of genetics, heredity and racial difference, documenting the political appeal and social consequences of such popular science" (Rohy, *Anachronism and its Others*, 74). Emerging discourses like feminism, naturalism, realism, Marxism, psychoanalysis, and even theosophy, shaped the literature of the late 1890s, from Henry James's anti-feminist *The Bostonians* or his ambiguous *Turn of the Screw* to Frank Norris's bleak *McTeague*. The "New Woman," the feminist and later the flapper, restless and eager for new experiences, had arrived, and, despite ambivalences, she was not going away.

Lost ladies and laboring women

On March 25, 1911 at around 4:45 in the afternoon, a fire broke out on the eighth floor at the Triangle Waist Company. Within a short thirty or so minutes, 146 people, mostly women and girls, died, either in the fire or from jumping out the windows, a tragedy due not only to poor labor conditions, about which some of these same women had joined the 1909 shirtwaist workers strike called the "Uprising of the Twenty Thousand," but also due to inadequate safety. Those victims who chose to jump rather than to burn often jumped in groups, holding on to one another (Argersinger, *Triangle Fire*, 18). The weight and velocity of the falling women broke through the fire-fighters' nets. This public trauma galvanized labor union activists, reformers, and politicians to reconsider the relationship between owners, management, and workers, which had been, for years, adversarial and exploitative. As the fire demonstrated, women, mostly Jewish immigrants, bore the brunt of this exploitation. In the fictional 1909 *The Diary of a Shirtwaist Striker*, activist Theresa Malkiel tried to both chronicle the real life of one such worker, using the diary as a form to enhance the appeal of her tale, and also to make a case for unionization, socialism, and egalitarian marriage. This novel is often regarded as propaganda, but the fervent, dedicated voice of the character, her desire for respect in both her working and her personal life, put the novel ahead of its time.[2]

To go to work, especially for an immigrant woman at the turn of the century, was often not a choice but a necessity that could cost a woman her self-respect, and, in response, women became more active members of labor unions like the International Garment Workers Union. Despite the appalling conditions of most factories, women went to work in numbers, and, being young and full of hope, they managed to squeeze in both education and fun, despite the grueling work. They learned English, read newspapers, magazines and dime novels such as those written by American Laura Jean Libbey, who, in the course of her career, wrote some eighty-two novels and short stories all with the same plot: a young but beautiful factory girl attracts the love of an upper-class man; complications ensue, but in the end the girl marries her beau. "So popular and ubiquitous were her stories, that working girl romance novels became known as 'Laura Jean Libbeys' by the early twentieth century."[3] Another favorite dime-novel writer was British Charlotte Brame, who was published in the United States as "Charlotte M. Brame (or alternately Braeme, as it was often misspelled in the United States), Bertha M. Clay, Dora Thorne, By the Author of Dora Thorne, Florence Norton, CMB and Caroline M. Burton)."[4] Sadie Frowne, quoted earlier, wrote, "she's a grand writer and makes things just like real to you. You feel as if you were the poor girl yourself going to get married to a rich duke" (Argersinger, *Triangle Fire*, 55). Or as the fictional Shenah Pessah says of Brame, "[w]hen I only begin to read, I forget I'm on this world. It lifts me on wings with high thoughts" (Yezierska, *Hungry*

Hearts). To the newly Americanized girls of the early twentieth century, upward class mobility may have been a dream, but it was also possible; they might never marry the factory owner's son, as Coralie Harding does in *The Master Workman's Oath: Or, Coralie, the Unfortunate, A Love Story, Portraying the Life, Romance and Strange Fate of a Beautiful New York Working-Girl*, but they could climb out of abject poverty into the middle class.

However, the term "working girl" remained a euphemism for a prostitute, as Edith Wharton's Lily Bart knows only too well. Published in 1905, *The House of Mirth* mirrors in some interesting ways many of the same issues found in the dime novels and penny-dreadfuls. Lily Bart may have been born into a New York society family, but she has no secure familial or financial base. Like the factory girls, Lily's fortune is in her face. But also like the girls of the dime novels, she is adrift, trying to make a suitable marriage. She certainly cannot maintain her upper-class status without a marriage, but, as *The House of Mirth* shows, marrying was a tricky business. Lily Bart is also fickle and she has a desire for a partner, rather than an owner-husband, which she glimpses in Lawrence Selden. But her desire does not prove useful in the face of social power and money; Lily Bart's descent from aristocratic New York circles to failed hat-maker shows that if one's most useful talent is beauty, then it might prove fatal. Marriage here is portrayed as a loveless arrangement; everyone cheats, and the smooth performance of social decorum prevails. Lily is cast overboard. She becomes dependent on chloral and finally takes an inadvertent overdose – "if sleep came at all, it might be a sleep without waking. But after all that was but one chance in a hundred: the action of the drug was incalculable, and the addition of a few drops to the regular dose would probably do no more than procure for her the rest she so desperately needed" (*The House of Mirth*, 322).

Marriage, in fact, was under new pressures. Gertrude Stein's *Three Lives* is, in part, a commentary on that institution. And although it is hard to find three texts as disparate in style and execution as Edith Wharton's 1905 *House of Mirth*, Gertrude Stein's 1909 *Three Lives*, and Theresa Malkiel's *The Diary of a Shirtwaist Striker* of the same year, all three offer pictures of marriage as dismal; each demonstrates how class resists a quest for mobility; and finally all three attempt to give voice to baffled, unexamined states of desire, such as same-sex desire, the desire for an equal companion in marriage, or desires *not* to have children, all of which challenged the status quo. *Three Lives* is the most formally complex of these novels and arguably the most critical of the social rules. Formally, the novel is structured like a triptych, a work of visual art, which is divided into three sections, or panels. "The Good Anna" and

"The Gentle Lena," the first and last tales, both of which recount the lives of white servants, frame the middle tale about a light-skinned black woman, "Melanctha." In "The Good Anna," the repeated word "good" stands in for Anna's version of morality, a refusal to abide open expressions of female sexuality – men are just going to be naughty so girls should be on their guard. Anna prefers large, soft, and ineffective women as employers because they are easy to manage; meanwhile, she herself is ambivalent toward heterosexuality and generally hostile to marriage. The "only romance Anna ever knew" was for Mrs. Lehntman, "a woman other women loved" (*Three Lives*, 12), who, it turns out, works for an abortionist because she wants to "deliver young girls who were in trouble" (13). Anna spends her whole life managing other lives and dies after she wears herself out in service to others. Like Anna, Lena, a German immigrant, spends her life doing for others, first as a servant and then as a wife, although her role as a wife is more like that of a slave: she repeatedly bears children until she dies. As uninterested in her husband as he is in her, the two procreate because it is expected; she yearns for her days as a girl among other girls, just as he prefers the company of men. These two sad tales, which both indict heterosexual marriage, frame "Melanctha, or Each One a She May," which is frank about the pitfalls of sexuality. Although Stein uses a language of racism that now grates on the ear – "Melanctha Herbert was a graceful, pale yellow, intelligent, attractive negress" (*Three Lives*, 48) – this middle portrait is a powerful representation of interiority. Melanctha is intelligent, inquisitive, and introspective; she forms several strong attachments: a friendship with Rose Johnson "who had a strong sense of the proper conduct" (49); a mentor in Jane Harden who "was not afraid to understand" and "wandered widely" (59); an attachment to a doctor, Jefferson Campbell, who is both attracted to her and repelled by her; and finally an attachment to Jem Richards, a gambler. What the story says Melanctha needs is a strong, good man to make her content, but she never finds this paragon and eventually dies of consumption. All three stories chronicle the lives and deaths of ordinary people which, taken together as a triptych, paint a portrait of female sexuality that challenges the norm by emphasizing a lack of happiness, as her characters struggle against, as Melanchta puts it, being so blue as to think that killing "herself would really be the best way for her to go" (48).

By 1913, Parisian designer Paul Poiret had begun to alter the way young women wanted to dress, one response to their desire for change. The boyish look he pioneered, which raised the hemline, ditched the corset, and required a breast-flattening device called a brassiere would define the Jazz Age, flapper look. Flappers were, in large measure, post-World War I women who were willing to take risks; some of them would have called themselves "feminists," as had the "New Women," but the majority were more or less apolitical, so the flapper was a kind of cousin to the "New Woman," interested in herself, her freedom and her pleasures, and less concerned for sociopolitical commitments. In 1913, Edith Wharton created an American girl who embodied certain aspects of the flapper, and in writing *The Custom of the Country*, gave us perhaps one of the most awful American heroines ever: Undine Spragg. Undine seems to be named after the ondine, a mythological water nymph, but her mother explains that she was actually named after a hair-waver. As Jean-Michel Rabaté says, Undine is a "protean figure" (1913, 185), described as full of "youthful flexibility. She was always doubling and twisting on herself, and every movement she made seemed to start at the nape of her neck, just below the lifted roll of reddish-gold hair, and flow without a break through her whole slim length to the tips of her fingers and the points of her slender restless feet" (*The Custom of the Country*, 5). This flexible creature has an insatiable appetite for "everything" (55). Money and social prominence are her chief desires; her father provides her with a fortune, so Undine goes social climbing rapaciously. Indeed, Rabaté argues that in this respect she resembles an hysteric, ripe for a rest cure: "Like most hysterics, she produces desire all the time, without being interested in the enjoyment that possession is supposed to bring" (1913, 192). *The Custom of the Country* also explores a legal recourse heretofore forbidden to most married American women, but one Wharton herself experienced: divorce. Undine is bold, brash, decidedly unladylike, and willing to stop at nothing, not even the social disgrace of divorce, to get a higher social position. By the end of this satiric novel, she has been divorced three times. Undine Spragg may be awful in some respects, but also must inspire a certain respect because she embodies the modern: bold, headstrong, independent, determined to get what she wants, irrespective of tradition or ethics.

Caught in between: Willa Cather, Mourning Dove, and Nella Larsen

In the summer of 1914, in the wake of the assassination of Archduke Franz Ferdinand of Austria, Europe took fire. As aristocratic and government alliances broke down across Germany, Russia, England, and France, America stood back, pursuing President Woodrow Wilson's policy of non-interference, but, in 1917, the United States entered what was one of the most devastating conflicts ever staged; World War I, like the Civil War before it, redefined warfare, especially trench warfare. In her book *Not Under Forty*, Willa Cather said "the world broke in two in 1922 or thereabouts," referring to the aftereffects of World War I. In this last section I want to concentrate on three women writers caught in-between worlds: Willa Cather, Mourning Dove, and Nella Larsen.

An editor and author, Cather achieved what eluded most American female fictive characters: she was a *successful* artist and wrote one of the first American novels about a wholly successful female artist in 1915, *The Song of the Lark*, which recounts the life of opera diva, Thea Kronborg, from her childhood in a small Colorado town to the Metropolitan Opera House in New York City. But "when Willa Cather made the heroine of *The Song of the Lark* an artist, she was not making an unusual choice" (Ammons, *Conflicting Stories*, 121) because many women writers – including most of the authors already mentioned – wrote about female artists. As early as the middle of the nineteenth century, prolific and popular author Fanny Fern's *Ruth Hall* (1855) featured a female artist, as did southern writer and Confederate Augusta Evans's 1866 *St. Elmo*. Rebecca Harding Davis's *Earthen Pitchers* (1874), Elizabeth Stuart Phelps's *The Story of Avis* (1877), and Mary Austin's *A Woman of Genius* (1912) are all about women artists. Like these counterparts, Thea Kronborg faces long odds but her success mirrored Cather's own. It also points to a troubling aspect of the novel: Kronborg is a *white* woman, whose pioneering forebears stole from Native people, the same "ancient people" from whom Thea derives inspiration in Panther Canyon. As Ammons notes, "[a]lmost all of the experience open to Thea is open to her because she is white" (*Conflicting Stories*, 139), and although Cather's novel often takes note of women of color, that note bespeaks white privilege. As Stein does in *Three Lives*, Cather took up the question of same-sex attraction; but, also like Stein, leaves racism unquestioned; that racism is most clear in her last novel, *Sapphira and The Slave Girl*, Cather's only novel about her southern roots. Set before the Civil War, the novel tries to diagnose the sexualized nature of slavery, yet endorses "standard stereotypes" of African Americans and reinforces "sentimental racist myths" (*Conflicting Stories*, 135).

Caught between a past she revered and a future that seemed mechanized and artless, Cather captured that sense of being in between in *A Lost Lady*. Told from the point of view of Niel Herbert, the novel chronicles the fading days of a western pioneer, Captain Forrester, and his wife, Marian. Younger than her husband, Marian is caught between the romantic, if violent and cruel, past and the pragmatic future, represented by Ivy Peters, a grasping, cruel, exploitative man. The crucial thing about this novel is how the narrative makes clear that change is inevitable and can bring with it new freedoms; for example, unlike her priggish narrator, Niel, who wants her to remain, forever, the Captain's wife, Marian seeks new sensations and desires change. Most of all, she wants a sexual freedom that her position as wife prohibits. But Marian, like Thea, is a white woman, a position rendered normative. The ethnic other, in Cather's texts, is often an invisible yet necessary other.

Cogewea, The Half Blood: A Depiction of the Great Montana Cattle Range, published in 1927, is one of the first known novels by a Native American woman and serves as a corrective, in a sense, to normative whiteness. Mourning Dove, Hum-ishu-ma, Christine Haines, or Christine or Chrystal Quintasket was an Okanogan of eastern Washington who was a migrant farm-worker; *Cogewea* is the story of a mixed-blood girl caught between the conflicting worlds of Indian and whites. Like Helen Hunt Jackson did in *Ramona*, Mourning Dove used a combination of popular romance and history in an attempt to breach the gap between English, the language of the conquerors, and the rhythms of once daily, familiar Okanogan talk. Helped by – and no one really knows how much – Lucullus Virgil McWhorter, a white student of Indian history, Mourning Dove used the folklore of her tribe to craft a plea for the Indian people that also records the destructiveness of modernity for those women of color not as privileged as a Thea Kronborg or Marian Forrester.

Like Mourning Dove, Nella Larsen wrote two novels in the late 1920s that face class and race privilege head on. Both *Passing* and *Quicksand* focus on the social and ethical problems that race prejudice and class caste raise for a nation in which equality is the ideal, inequality the reality. Both novels chronicle the acute paradoxes of being of African descent in white America in the 1920s; *Passing* takes a close look at what the title names: some people of African descent who, because of the way they looked, could "pass" as white did so. Clare Kendry is a cold, beautiful, charming, and erotic woman who passes and has married a racist white man, John Bellew; she reconnects with a childhood friend, Irene Redfield, who can also pass, but who has chosen not to. Wishing for the privileges and freedom of whiteness, but loyal to her family and her race, Irene feels "caught between two allegiances, different, yet the same. Herself. Her race" (*Passing*, 152). The tension between these friends/enemies drives the novel. Each woman is, in fact, fascinated by the other, with ultimately fatal consequences for Clare, who either accidently tumbles or is pushed (by Irene? Bellew?) out of a window during a Harlem house party, where Bellew has finally discovered she is not lily white but in reality a "nig" which ironically was a nickname he used for his wife. In *Quicksand*, the dilemma for Helga Crane is different: born of a Danish mother and a father of African descent, Helga embodies duality and so is caught not only between worlds but desires; like Irene, she craves the security of the black middle class but finds its decorum suffocating. Both protagonists have difficulty with erotic desire as well, feeling socially driven to marry, but finding their desires more free-floating than marriage typically allows. If Irene is fascinated by Clare and vice versa, Helga is fascinated by Audrey Denney, a beauty who seems to bewitch everyone. Thus, like Cather, Larsen shows her characters trying, and often failing, to negotiate the liminal space between past and present, hetero- and homosexuality, black and white.

Conclusion

In October 1929, the fall of the stock market sharply changed the sociopolitical landscape of most Americans, ushering in the Great Depression. Austerity, if not out-and-out poverty, replaced the booming economics of the 1920s; the literary landscape accordingly changed as well, as the publishing industry, like most industries in the United States, took a hit. But at the turn into the twentieth century, women took as much advantage of these changes as they could: by 1921 they had achieved full citizenship, with the vote; had freed themselves of the corset and eighty-odd pounds of dress; advocated for legalizing birth control; and helped to expand the middle class. This period, as I have tried to demonstrate, marked a flowering of women's voices. Once left out by critical paradigms about "American" literature, this burst of American women's narratives by American women authors was an ample one, with narratives spanning the geographical continent as well as re-examining domestic, interior spaces in which hitherto taboo choices or silenced miseries had once been closeted. Critics in the 1980s, like Judith Fryer, whose *Felicitous Space: The Imaginative Structures of Edith Wharton and Willa Cather* (1986) began to remap this ignored territory, have now turned their attention not only to the literary but also to sociology or journalism, like pioneering Ida B. Wells or the later 1930s novelist/journalist Josephine Herbst, in order to speak truths. As more and more of these voices are either re-covered or reinterpreted, the field expands and older paradigms shift; for example, Amy Kaplan's *The Social Construction of American Realism* (1988) restructured an understanding of realism, while Jennifer Fleissner's 2004 revision of naturalism reorients that movement with respect to feminism.

Where will this field go? Perhaps critics will go on to forge links with the authorial daughters to come. How, for example, do these earlier texts speak to or influence a sometimes overlooked woman writer like Jean Stafford, whose 1935 novel *The Catherine Wheel* is a frightening examination of a female solipsism that can arise from a too-insistent engagement with one's desires? One intriguing direction literary criticism has taken of late, for instance in Valerie Rohy's *Anachronism and its Others: Sexuality, Race, Temporality* (2009), is a drive toward undermining ruling paradigms of new historicism and a re-examination of how time functions in American narratives. The turn-of-the-century outrush of woman-authored literature that took the measure of the past but reached out to the edge of tomorrow might also be revisited by an examination of another outpouring of women's voices in the late twentieth century: African, Asian, and Indian voices such as Toni Morrison, Alice Walker, Maya Angelou, Louise Erdrich, Leslie Marmon Silko, or Joy Kogawa, or new immigrant voices from Jamaica or Haiti or Puerto Rico, as well as future-oriented voices of feminist science fiction writers such as C. L. Moore, Ursula K. LeGuin, Joanna Russ, or Vonda McIntyre and/or to an examination of the cusp of the twenty-first century, to see how far American women have dared or will dare to go.

Notes

1. Castiglia, *Bound and Determined*; Derounian-Stodola, *Women's Indian Captivity Narratives*; Faery, *Cartographies of Desire*.
2. For a fuller discussion of this novel, see also my chapter on the word "scab" in *Household Words*.
3. From *The Master Workman's Oath*, 1022; see also the American Woman's Dime Novel project at http://chnm.gmu.edu/dimenovels/about.html
4. American Woman's Dime Novel Project at http://chnm.gmu.edu/dimenovels/authors/brame.html

Works cited

Ammons, Elizabeth. *Conflicting Stories: American Women Writers at the Turn into the Twentieth Century*. New York and Oxford: Oxford University Press, 1992.

Argersinger, Jo Ann. *The Triangle Fire: A Brief History with Documents*. Boston and New York: Bedford/St. Martin's, 2009.

Baxandall, Rosalyn and Linda Gordon. *America's Working Women: A Documentary History – 1600 to the Present*. 2nd edn. New York: W. W. Norton, 1995.

Bentley, Nancy. *Frantic Panoramas: American Literature and Mass Culture, 1870–1920*. Philadelphia: University of Pennsylvania Press, 2009.

Briggs, Isaac G. *Epilepsy, Hysteria, Neurasthenia: Their Causes, Symptoms and Treatment*. 1921. New York: Bibliobazaar, 2007.

Castiglia, Christopher. *Bound and Determined: Captivity, Culture-Crossing and White Womanhood*. Chicago: University of Chicago Press, 1996.

Cather, Willa. *A Lost Lady*. Boston: Houghton Mifflin, 1983.

The Song of the Lark. Boston: Houghton Mifflin, 1983.

Chopin, Kate. *The Awakening.* New York: W. W. Norton, 1994.

Derounian-Stodola, Kathryn Zabelle. *Women's Indian Captivity Narratives.* Harmondsworth: Penguin, 1998.

Dove, Mourning. *Cogewea, The Half Blood: A Depiction of the Great Montana Cattle Range.* Lincoln, NB: University of Nebraska Press, 1981.

Enstad, Nan. *Ladies of Labor, Girls of Adventure: Working Women, Popular Culture and Labor Politics at the Turn of the Century.* New York: Columbia University Press, 1999.

Faery, Rebecca Blevins. *Cartographies of Desire: Captivity, Race, and Sex in the Shaping of an American Nation.* Norman: University of Oklahoma Press, 1999.

Fitzgerald, F. Scott. *The Jazz Age.* New York: New Directions, 1996.

Fleissner, Jennifer. *Women, Compulsion, Modernity: The Moment of American Naturalism.* Chicago and London: Chicago University Press, 2004.

Friedan, Betty. *The Feminine Mystique.* New York: Dell, 1963.

Gates, Henry Louis. "Foreword: In Her Own Write." In *Contending Forces* by Pauline Hopkins. New York: Oxford University Press, Schomburg Library of Nineteenth-Century Black Women Writers, 1988.

Gillmore, Inez Haynes. *Angel Island.* New York: Plume-NAL Penguin Inc., 1988.

Gilman, Charlotte Perkins. *The Yellow Wallpaper.* Afterword by Elaine R. Hedges. New York: The Feminist Press, 1973.

Glasgow, Ellen. *Barren Ground.* New York: Harcourt Brace Jovanovich, 1985.

Green, Nancy L. *Ready to Wear, Ready to Work: A Century of Industry and Immigrants in Paris and New York.* Durham, NC and London: Duke University Press, 1997.

Gutjahr, Paul C., ed. *"The Master Workman's Oath: Or, Coralie, the Unfortunate, A Love Story, Portraying the Life, Romance and Strange Fate of a Beautiful New York Working-Girl"* in *Popular American Literature of the Nineteenth Century,* New York and Oxford: Oxford University Press, 2001.

Harper, Frances E. W. *Iola LeRoy, or, Shadows Uplifted.* New York and Oxford: Oxford University Press, 1998.

Hawthorne, Nathaniel. *The Scarlet Letter.* New York: W. W. Norton, 1988.

Jackson, Helen Hunt. *Ramona: A Story.* New York: Signet, 1988.

Jones, Ernest. *Sigmund Freud: Life and Work.* New York: Basic Books, 1953.

Jones, Jacqueline. *American Work: Four Centuries of Black and White Labor.* New York and London: W. W. Norton, 1998.

Larsen, Nella. *Passing.* New York: The Modern Library, 2002.
  Quicksand. Ed. Thadious Davis. New York: Penguin, 2002.

McGinty, Brian. *The Oatman Massacre: A Tale of Desert Captivity and Survival.* Norman: University of Oklahoma Press, 2005.

Mifflin, Margot. *The Blue Tattoo: The Life of Olive Oatman.* Lincoln, NB, and London: University of Nebraska Press, 2009.

Newman, Louise. *White Women's Rights: The Racial Origins of Feminism in the United States.* New York: Oxford University Press, 1999.

Peiss, Kathy. *Cheap Amusements: Working Women and Leisure in Turn-of-the-Century New York.* Philadelphia: Temple University Press, 1986.

Rabaté, Jean-Michel. *1913: The Cradle of Modernism.* London: Wiley-Blackwell, 2007.

Rohy, Valerie. *Anachronism and its Others: Sexuality, Race, Temporality*. Albany: State University of New York Press, 2009.

Smith, Stephanie A. *Household Words: Bloomer, Sucker, Bombshell, Scab, Nigger, Cyber*. Minneapolis and London: University of Minnesota Press, 2006.

Stansell, Christine. *American Moderns: Bohemian New York and the New Century*. Princeton: Princeton University Press, 2009.

Stein, Gertrude. *Three Lives*. New York: Dover Publications, 1994.

Tate, Claudia. *Domestic Allegories of Political Desire: The Black Heroine's Text at the Turn of the Century*. New York and London: Oxford University Press, 1996.

Trachtenberg, Alan. *The Incorporation of America: Culture and Society in the Gilded Age*. New York: Farrar, Straus and Giroux, Hill and Wang, 1982.

Travis, Jennifer. *Wounded Hearts: Masculinity, Law and Literature in American Culture*. Chapel Hill: University of North Carolina Press, 2005.

Von Drehle, David. *Triangle: The Fire that Changed America*. New York: Grove Press, 2003.

Wharton, Edith. *The Custom of the Country*. New York and Oxford: Oxford University Press, 2001.

House of Mirth. New York: Penguin, 1993.

Yezierska, Anzia. *Hungry Hearts* http://digital.library.upenn.edu/women/yezierska/hearts/hearts.html

19

Accidents, agency, and American literary naturalism

JENNIFER TRAVIS

Kate Chopin's "The Story of an Hour" (1894) pivots on the report of a railroad accident. Concerned that Brently Mallard's wife may be critically wounded by the news of her husband's death, the victim's friend Richards rushes to Louise Mallard's home to protect her from accident reports by "less careful" acquaintances.[1] Readers learn from the first sentence of the story that Mrs. Mallard is "afflicted with heart trouble." Could news of the fatal accident inflict another mortal blow? At once, the story links physical vulnerability with a psychological counterpart, both corporal and emotional trauma can kill. Mrs. Mallard does not experience the deleterious shock that her friend and family fear, however, at least not initially. After a brief "storm of grief" over the loss, Louise Mallard is far from "paralyzed with inability"; in fact, her troubled heart awakens. The report of her husband's accidental death does, indeed, cause a shock. What overcomes and overwhelms Louise Mallard is not grief and loss but rather the startling recognition as she gazes out the window at the burgeoning spring that with her husband's death comes new life. Anticipating Chopin's most well-known heroine, Edna Pontellier, Louise realizes that for the first time "she would live for herself." Aware too that this recognition and the joy that it brings might seem "monstrous" to some, she tries in vain to suppress this revelation, to "beat it back with her will," but against its force she is "powerless." While Josephine pounds on the bedroom door, certain that her sister is dangerously ill with grief, Louise, it turns out, is "drinking in a very elixir of life."

Through the industrial accident, "The Story of an Hour" brings together the potentially deadly consequences of technological expansion in the late nineteenth and early twentieth centuries – the explosion of accidental injuries and deaths – with the psychological trauma of gendered social relations. Responding to the growing nexus of culture, technology, and gender, Chopin evokes technological violence and the public trauma of the railroad accident in order to illuminate another genus of wounds, wounds that often proliferate in private. The railroad accident and the unexpected loss of her husband shock Louise Mallard into an awareness of her loss of self: her life has been defined by her husband's "right" to impose his "private will" on her. The accident that reportedly takes Brently Mallard's life reveals to Louise Mallard the sustained and pervasive injury of her own social station as a woman and a wife; indeed, it is the accident of her birth and her gender that has sealed her own social death. It is little wonder that her heart is "troubled." For Louise, however, the industrial accident incites new ways of thinking about subjectivity and identity and presses her to reject earlier and injurious gender constructions. As the shock of the accident jolts her from a personal and social stupor, her weak heart gains strength. When she reaches the height of her felicity, she opens the door to her room and stands at the top of the stairs "feverish triumph in her eyes" as if she has just conquered death; she is "a goddess of Victory." Almost.

In this story, feminist subjectivity is fashioned through a wounding event and, in the brief space of an hour, destroyed. At the moment Louise emerges from her room, in effect, reborn, her new-found life is quickly extinguished. Her husband, who missed his train and therefore escapes the accident that would have taken his life, walks in the front door, very much alive. For less than one hour, Louise grasps the "possession of self-assertion," but her revelations merely lead to a literal dead end. Her husband's turn of the key and with it the shock of a return to her former life swiftly kills Louise Mallard. Family, friends, and the medical community report that staggering surprise at her husband's unexpected appearance cause Mrs. Mallard's death; hers is a "joy that kills." With the death of the story's protagonist, however, the narrative replicates the painful shock that it portends. Against the public event of the railroad accident, the trauma in the official lexicon, readers are left with an invisible victim. Chopin's readers know that Louise's injuries are not simply physical or mechanical, her shock not "joy" but rather a very different kind of mental blow. With her husband's arrival home, Louise Mallard's heart stops, unable to accept the painful knowledge of a return to her former condition and the eradication of subjectivity such a confinement entails.

Kate Chopin was one among many women writers in the nineteenth and early twentieth centuries, from Elizabeth Stuart Phelps and Edith Wharton to Ellen Glasgow and Willa Cather, to see the growth of technological modernity and the threat of technological violence as vehicles through which to reimagine the gendering of injury, to assemble, moreover, an etiology of wounds less visible to the naked eye. The velocity of the railroad in Rebecca Harding Davis's short story "Anne" (1889), for example, offers Nancy Palmer a rapid escape from a life of "uneasy" safety. Its parlor cars welcome her into the "company" of "Immortals," the romanticized title she gives the famous painter and female reformer who happen to take seats nearby. The train journey also occasions a chance meeting with a former paramour with whom Anne has daydreamed a more vibrant life and the expression of her truest self. Tucked anonymously away in a seat, the ignoble conversation she overhears between the "Immortals" in the parlor car begins to unsettle her ideal; indeed, the recognition of her restive fantasy comes with a crash, quite literally, as the parlor car goes black and she is pinned between two beams listening in its place to the "shrieks of women in mortal agony" (Davis, "Anne," 749). In Davis's story the railroad encapsulates manifold risk, including the thrill of her break from social routine, her breach, both physical and spiritual, of a threshold of danger. Although the story ends with Mrs. Palmer once again safely ensconced at home among her children – she has physically survived the crash – she is left with her recurrent and still haunting question unanswered, if Anne is "dead here, will she ever live again?" Willa Cather's Paul, in her story by that title, would rather die than return to a life of enforced gender norms (Cather "Paul's Case," 750). His answer to the nagging question that Anne asks is to throw himself in front of an oncoming train. The high-speed accident, Nancy Bentley argues in *Frantic Panoramas*, is a literary trope which "signifies the tremendous powers and desires, seductive as well as menacing, generated by the velocities of twentieth-century life" (222). Chopin's use of this trope in "The Story of an Hour" implores readers to ask just what constitutes a traumatic event – the accident, her awakening, the reversal of circumstance, the fatality – and articulates other ways of framing human vulnerability in the face of technological expansion. Although the wound that Louise suffers remains misread by family, friends, and physicians, narratives like Chopin's, Davis's, and Cather's illustrate a more capacious terrain of psychic damage. In fact, Chopin exploits nervous shock, which routinely came to be associated with the railroad, that "icon of modern technology," as a way to draw critical attention to other forms of cultural violence often too "subtle and elusive to name" but nonetheless "reaching" for recognition (Micale and Lerner, "Trauma, Psychiatry, and History," 12; Chopin, "The Story of an Hour," 194).

Scholars of historical trauma studies look to the period between 1870 and 1930 as a time of expansion in the meaning and significance of the concept. New knowledge about the central nervous system and fields such as neurology meant the recognition that "weak hearts," to recall Chopin's protagonist, were often far more closely linked to fragile minds than previously thought. Roger Luckhurst in *The Trauma Question* locates the emergence of trauma in nineteenth-century industrialism and a new "accident cosmology" in which danger and catastrophe threatened to become the cultural norm (213–14), the dawn, in other words, of what Mark Seltzer has dubbed in another context America's "wound culture." The railroad was not only an agent of accident, its impact occasioned a host of new and bewildering disorders and fueled a heated medico-legal debate; with the swift pace of industrial and technological growth came new pathologies of the body and mind. John Eric Erichsen's *On Railway and Other Injuries of the Nervous System* (1866) established that the train crash could result in a series of aftershocks, injuries to the nerves which he labeled "railway spine." Erichsen's account helped shift post-accident symptomology from the body to the mind as a "key pathological site."[2] Soon neurologists and surgeons were articulating a host of invisible wounds from "fright" and "psychic harm" to "emotional shock" and "terror," all, as Eric Caplan and Ralph Harrington have argued, decades before Freud's and Breuer's work in *Studies on Hysteria* (Harrington, "The Railway Accident," 32). Erichsen's case histories included accounts of melancholia, fitful dreams, disordered memory, impotence, and a "sudden loss of business sense," among its symptoms (Luckhurst, *The Trauma Question*, 22). The very public railroad accident, and the new and surprising face of some of its earliest victims – men like Brently Mallard – required an innovative vocabulary through which to understand physical vulnerability as well as the psyche and its capacity for harm.[3] With the rapid pace of industrial and technological modernity the traditional understanding of space and time shattered, creating a "type and tempo of living that seemed detrimental to the mind and nervous system" (Micale and Lerner, "Trauma, Psychiatry, and History," 10). Walter Benjamin called this the "human sensorium": the busy streets of the nineteenth-century city with its crowds, street cars, telephones, and advertisements subjected its inhabitants to a "complex kind of training" (*Illuminations*, 171). Benjamin's accounts relied upon Freud's earliest descriptions of hysteria and trauma, descriptions that were themselves inspired by the debates over railway accidents in which passengers walked away from the scene of an accident only to be haunted in the weeks, months, and years to follow, much like Davis's protagonist "Anne," by various psychological symptoms, most invisible to the naked eye. The railroad accident, a recurring image in Freud's work, does not simply represent technological violence; it also conveys, as Cathy Caruth argues, "the impact of its very incomprehensibility" (*Unclaimed Experience*, 6). Beyond the mechanical blow and at the very heart of traumatic experience is a crisis of representation: "what returns to haunt the victim, these stories tell us, is not only the reality of the violent event but also the reality of the way that its violence has not yet been fully known" (6). Strikingly, stories like Chopin's and Davis's exploit a version of this cognitive dissonance: their narratives use shock, fright, and a new sensibility – collective human frailty in the face of technological change – as a crucial challenge to their protagonists' invisibility and that of other women like them.

The emergence of feminist subjectivity at a moment of technological crises – one of the shocks that Chopin's "The Story of an Hour" deals its readers – complicates what Donald Pizer, one of the most influential scholars on American literary naturalism, has argued are the genre's "deep roots": "the failings of the nation's industrial system." Naturalism, Pizer has argued recently, threatened the "established order" because writers like Stephen Crane, Theodore Drieser, and Hamlin Garland "boldly and vividly depicted the inadequacies of the industrial system which was the foundation of that order" ("Late Nineteenth-Century American Literary Naturalism," 201). Women writers also reveal what Wolfgang Schivelbusch has called "industrialized consciousness," not only because they expose the risks of industry and technology but also because their works allow these potential dangers to unsettle hegemonic notions of masculine force and biological determinism and to articulate new avenues for understanding self, psyche, community, and nation (*The Railway Journey*, 159). Within a genre and cultural moment perhaps best known for its fetishization of virility, scholars like Donna Campbell and Jennifer Fleissner have drawn important critical attention to women's naturalist writings.[4] This essay considers how women writers have helped to narrate a crucial change in America's cultural ethos in the late nineteenth and early twentieth centuries: from lauding muscular manhood and his aspirations to invulnerability to acknowledging collective risks and new communal hazards.[5]

Which wounds will command cultural cognition? Whose injuries heard? Edith Wharton's *The Fruit of the Tree* (1907), the follow-up to her success with *The House of Mirth* (1905), asks precisely this question and, as its title suggests, knowledge of the answers may bring with it peril and pain. Writing about two members of the professional-managerial class at the turn of the twentieth century, each seeks a cure for social injuries, John Amherst as an engineer and Justine Brent as a nurse. They meet at the start of the novel over the wounded body of Dillon, a mill operative, but quickly go their separate ways, Amherst marrying Bessie the widowed mill owner and Brent following her vocation as a visiting nurse dedicated to social and physical healing. Brent and Amherst are reunited in the novel just as it becomes clear that Amherst and his wife see social injury and injustice quite differently; she does not share his passion for industrial reform. The novel repeatedly ponders what it means to make suffering cognitively intelligible and at what cost. These problems reach their climax when Bessie herself suffers a debilitating spinal injury in a riding accident. Her wounds and subsequent "mercy killing" at the hands of Justine Brent not only allow Amherst to redistribute his wife's wealth as he sees fit, but they also crucially underscore how modern threats and vulnerabilities are themselves redistributed. By the end of the novel every character from mill hand to manager has staked their claim: "'Suffering!' [Amherst] echoed ironically" at Justine Brent's own declaration of wounds, "as though she had presumed to apply to herself a word of which he had a grim monopoly" (*The Fruit of the Tree*, 521). Just as technological violence instigates social reform in Wharton's novel, the threat of injury, what Nancy Bentley calls the "possible crash" (*Frantic Panoramas*, 246), implores the characters as well as Wharton's readers to reexamine the thresholds of physical as well as psychic harm. The discourse of injury imagined in novels like Wharton's, debated in medicine, and litigated in law courts, remade, often in surprising ways, the politics of victimhood.

Bathos and the brute: on male wounds and the woman artist

Cautioning readers about the injury and cultural upset wrought in the late nineteenth century by emancipation and increasing pressure for women's rights, Elizabeth Stuart Phelps's father, Austin Phelps, predicted a swift return to white male supremacy in his essay "Woman-Suffrage as Judged by the Working of Negro-Suffrage" (1882). Although American culture, he argued, has raised ignorance, inherited debasement, and the traditions of slavery to the top: "Society will not stay thus upset. It inevitably turns over again into its natural condition, stands on its natural feet . . . The head comes uppermost, let the hands do what they will" (*My Portfolio*, 96–7). Phelps's address registers anger and anxiety about the socio-economic changes brought about by the end of slavery, new waves of immigration, and the women's movement. White men were increasingly vulnerable not only to competition from the once invisible and marginalized – women, blacks, immigrants – but also, as we have seen, to technological violence. From the rapid-fire assault rifle employed on the Civil War battlefield to the accidents redoubling on the railroad, the instruments and industries that promised progress might deliver up little more than injury and pain. These cultural developments challenged robust notions of manhood, especially the emblem of the white male body as a symbol of political power.

Elizabeth Stuart Phelps – with little sympathy for her father's ideas – recognized that the meaning of pain and injury was pliable and its value culturally fashioned. *The Story of Avis* (1877), written a few years before the publication of her father's diatribe, and one of Phelps's most successful novels, seizes the nation's most substantial wounding event, the Civil War, pitting public trauma against private wounds, mechanized warfare and physical injuries, largely male, against other forms of cultural violence.[6] The technological violence that Phelps writes about as a feature of factory life in her reform literature is refigured as a narrative about a woman who fails to live up to her creative promise when she succumbs to the compromises of marriage, motherhood, and the repair of masculine wounds. Like Chopin and Davis, Phelps uses the idiom of injury to explore women's social entrapments; Phelps, however, writes a cautionary tale about an unconventional woman and ambitious artist whose life is ruined by her lover upon his return, dangerously wounded, from the Civil War battlefield. In the novel the very public face of Philip Ostrander's war injuries eclipse Avis's autonomy and agency. His wounds come to overshadow her artistry and her ambition. When *The Story of Avis* begins, Phelps's protagonist has already embraced what Chopin calls Louise Mallard's "brief moment of illumination" (*The Story of Avis*, 194). As a young girl Avis watched the toll that the relinquishing of artistic freedom had on her mother, who gave up a life in the theater for the commonplace responsibilities of marriage and motherhood. Avis, recalling a heroine like E. D. E. N. Southworth's Britomarte in *Fair Play* (1868) – who refuses marriage through two long volumes and several catastrophes – has vowed that she will not do the same. Avis's "ideals of art are those with which marriage is perfectly incompatible" (69). Recently returned from an apprenticeship abroad, Avis meets Philip Ostrander, a promising young scholar who fancies her beauty and, to a lesser degree, her artistic ambitions. Against her own erasure as an artist, Avis rejects Philip's appeals of love and marriage. As he sits for a portrait, however, Avis is charmed by her own artwork; as she paints Philip's portrait the beauty of the subject on the canvas quite literally seduces her. For Avis, her desire for romantic love apart from the institutionalization of marriage (and housewifery and motherhood) is her "Civil War" battle, one, she believes, which can only lead to her "death" (106). Sadly, Avis does not heed her own extended metaphor. Philip, on the other hand, convinced that Avis will not submit to his entreaties, joins the Union Army and goes off to battle. Within months, he returns, a "mutilated body" and near death; with news of his injury Avis's will begins to waver: "It was his physical ruin and helplessness which appealed to the strength in her" (90, 99–100). Beguiled by

Philip's prostrate body and "the appeal of his physical wreck and disordered future," Avis fantasizes of remaking him; she likens the healing of his wounds to the completion of his portrait (105). His woundedness attracts her – not solely from a caregiving impulse but also in light of her artistry – she believes that she can make "the poor wreck of a wounded soldier" picturesque once again (112).

Unlike writers such as Louisa May Alcott and Southworth, for whom the Civil War, as Shirley Samuels writes, "provokes risks [and] releases women from ordinary social roles" ("Women at War," 148) – even Britomarte, the "man-hater," softens to marriage at the conclusion of two long volumes and a Civil War – Phelps's protagonist does not gain strength or cultural force with her charge; she becomes what she loathes. Indeed, in Phelps's novel, the figure of the prostrate male and the female custodian is anything but a source of power. To emphasize this in the narrative, the novel is replete with near-fatal accidents and naturalist tropes like the wounded bird. Avis's dreams, moreover, are crowded with images of pain and injury, "panorama[s] of agonies," the "suffering of animals" as well as "dead and dying soldiers" with "wounded faces huddled in corners," all of which terrorize her (*The Story of Avis*, 83). Even during a romantic encounter, Philip sees Avis as a "creature whose throbbing heart was torn out of her live body" (101). Phelps uses the language of violent physical injury to underscore the threats Avis faces to her artistry and autonomy; these threats, however, remain culturally opaque in the face of Philip's more legible physical wounds. Avis convinces herself that physical pain and emotional violence are the price she must pay for romantic love: "If this be love," she responds at one such moment, "I am afraid I love you now."[7] Repairing the prostrate male body, Avis soon learns, provides an empty promise of power in the face of the loss of her artistic productivity, what is for her the most profoundly traumatic harm. Along with the burden of ameliorating Philip's wounds, Avis soon bears the financial responsibilities of the household as well as the care of their two children: "All that was weakest of him leaned upon her" (214). Driven into debt and poverty, Philip, a once-promising scholar, becomes a social outcast. He loses his job, is mired in debt, and chases other women while Avis struggles to keep the household afloat. Philip transforms from merely bathetic into a brute. In fact, as a tale of masculine degeneracy, the novel rivals the later Frank Norris's *McTeague* (1899), but Phelps never gives Philip the destructive physical power of the brutish and "stupid" McTeague – Philip Ostrander is physically weak and his intellectual strength also dissipates (*McTeague*, 5). His injury, at first a heroic war wound and a subsequent scar that preys upon Avis's "strength," becomes an anchor for them both; it pulls him down, quite literally, toward his death in the Florida muck (*The Story of Avis*, 214).

Against the privileging of hypermasculinity and the depiction of "celebratory masculinism," Jennifer Fleissner has urged a reevaluation of characters such as Hurstwood in Theodore Drieser's *Sister Carrie* and Norris's McTeague, reading them as chronicles of "male impotence," an underexamined chapter in canonical naturalist fiction (*Women, Compulsion, Modernity*, 19). Indeed, competing with the brute in American naturalism is the bathetic and wounded male; Phelps replaces Avis's aesthetically pleasing canvas with a portrait of his tyranny. By engaging the question of naturalism's wounded men, Phelps implores a more capacious understanding of the scope of woundedness and the meaning of victimhood for men and women alike. Although Philip dies and Avis survives, *The Story of Avis* ends with an image of Avis's promise arrested rather than her potential fulfilled. What is notable in Phelps's novel is how the narrative of male virility and male impotence is complemented by another masculine type, one who fashions his physical and even at times his emotional incapacity for his own reward. Male bathos, as Phelps's novel shows, hardly immobilizes masculine power. I have written elsewhere about how a discourse on injury and woundedness became a fluent language through which white middle-class men asserted power in the face of vast cultural changes in the post-Civil War years. As Austin Phelps's remarks vividly remind us, the grounds of masculine power and privilege were of necessity being redrawn. Against narratives of the degenerate brute, Phelps's novel makes visible how the rhetoric of robust masculinity might thrive through the very language that appeared to announce its demise, how, for instance, expressions of woundedness might not diminish men's agency and power, although this has been an argument often made about the function of women's spheres of sentiment.[8] *The Story of Avis* urges caution: mistaking the power of the wound and misreading the gendering of injury is its own danger.

Wounds and wombs: Ellen Glasgow's *Barren Ground*[9]

The cultural upheaval wrought by technological violence and the nascent discourse on wounds, physical and psychic, inspired in women's writing new possibilities for narrating what might once have seemed inexpressible. Like Kate Chopin's "The Story of an Hour" and Rebecca Harding Davis's "Anne," Ellen Glasgow's *Barren Ground* (1925) seizes the mechanical accident in its exploration of the technology of wounding and its expression of a unique female economy of pain. The blow that awakens Louise Mallard – contrary to the wounds that ensnare Avis – frees Dorinda Oakley from the naturalist brute and the reproduction, through marriage and motherhood, of the same. In *Barren Ground*, like "The Story of an Hour," the industrial accident shocks the female psyche and allows her to imagine herself outside the dictates of convention. When Ellen Glasgow published *Barren Ground*, she departed from her earlier work in *The Descendant* (1893) and *The Wheel of Life* (1906), which featured male protagonists and the environmental forces that sealed their successes or failures. Glasgow was thoughtful about a different fate for her more modern female protagonist: "For once, in Southern fiction," she wrote, "the betrayed woman would become the victor instead of the victim. In the end she would triumph through that deep instinct for survival, which had ceased to be a negative quality and had strengthened into a dynamic force" (Glasgow, *A Certain Measure*, 160). When the novel begins, Dorinda is stuck in a Virginia community that seems only to sow failure; she perceives herself "caught like a mouse in the trap of life," held hard by "circumstances as by invisible wires of steel" (*Barren Ground*, 56) about which she can change "nothing" (Glasgow, *A Certain Measure*, 160). As Donna Campbell has observed, *Barren Ground* is a novel "filled with epiphanies about the brutal nature of the world," a naturalist narrative to its core ("'Where are the ladies?'," 162). As a young woman Dorinda embraces a conventional hope that marriage will rescue her from a bleak cultural and economic inheritance. When her fiancé Jason jilts her for a woman with "a pile of money," however, Dorinda, alone and pregnant, boards a train for New York City; she swaps "invisible wires of steel" for an urban metropolis (*Barren Ground*, 16). In Broomsedge, Virginia, where the novel begins, and in New York City where it leads, industry and technology appear dangerous and potentially deadly. The agrarian critique of modernity and industrialization with which the novel begins reaches its climax in the collision and traumatic injury that Dorinda suffers after a short time in New York City.

Glasgow's Dorinda Oakley is a Benjaminian subject, a country girl escaping to the city whose first steps in New York quite literally recall Benjamin's description of nineteenth-century Paris as a "series of shocks and collisions" (Luckhurst, *The Trauma Question*, 20). Dorinda walks the city streets "exhausted," "sick," and in search of work. Overcome by "winking" lights, loud noises, and endless streams of traffic, she is far from her agrarian home (*Barren Ground*, 210). "As one among many tides of nausea" subside, she steps forward into the traffic and is hit by something "so swiftly that it felt as if an earthquake had flung the pavement up against the back of her head" (210).

Dorinda is struck by a cab, and the accident puts her in the hospital under the care of a celebrated surgeon named Dr. Farraday. Not only has Dorinda suffered a head injury with the collision, but the impact also causes her to miscarry. When she awakes in her hospital bed, she is informed in oblique language of the loss. The nurse, with little comfort, suggests to Dorinda that the accidental miscarriage is a misfortune waiting to be reread: "I thought you would take it sensibly," she says to Dorinda (214). The nurse implies that the chance collision actually saves Dorinda from another and perhaps more damaging fate: that of the "ruined woman." Yet this argument need scarcely be made. Dorinda already perceives motherhood as grotesque and a source of pain. She recalls with disgust, for example, the "mulatta woman" in Broomsedge with her "half breed swarm," and later she watches as Geneva, Jason's wife, loses a child, leading to her suicide (63). As the collision that causes Dorinda to miscarry puts an end to an unwanted pregnancy and one potential source of social ruin, her head injury leaves her scarcely able to remember it: "all at once she had forgotten what she wanted to know . . . there was something I wanted to ask the doctor . . . I don't seem to be able to remember what it was" (214). The nurse, in fact, instructs her to forget, and Dorinda, the dutiful patient, observes that "Relief and regret faded together" (215). Dorinda awakens from the accident stitched up and sore, but, also like Louise Mallard, "monstrously" renewed.

Dorinda recovers and thrives, but not through the vehicle she originally thought: marriage. With Dorinda's bodily injury the novel abandons its attention on conjugal affection in favor of a focus on harm. The accident leaves her with noted "revulsion" at the thought of physical intimacy and, for a long while, marriage (232). As an "innocent victim" of a random accident, she is permitted this idiosyncrasy, one which is substantially different from how Dorinda would be perceived as a fallen woman. Once again recalling cultural debates about accidents and their aftereffects, Dr. Farraday believes that her revulsion to marriage is one such aftershock, her delayed traumatic response to a violent impact. The novel connects Dr. Farraday to the medico-legal debate about such injuries; he considers Dorinda's case "unusual" and declares himself "very much interested" in its outcome (213). Of course, such accidents, as we have seen, were far less "unusual" and far more commonplace in the nineteenth century. The vehicles that provided the catalyst for mobility and freedom of movement – allowing Dorinda to escape rural Virginia for New York City – also transformed accidental injury from what legal historian Barbara Welke has described as discrete individual events into a "shared American experience" (*Recasting American Liberty*, 80). With the revolution in mobility and the increase in industrial tragedies, physical and emotional wounds were suffered by men and women alike. Not only was personal safety beyond individual control, on the railroad, in a trolley car, or on the street itself, people needed to rely on the judgment and expertise of others, to trust strangers with their own welfare, much as Dorinda does with Dr. Farraday. In fact, tort or injury law emerged at this time in response to industrialization and the growing dangers of a congested and mechanized public sphere. It also began to articulate the legal obligation that persons had to one another, even complete strangers, calling it "duty of care." The responsibilities for reasonable standards of care toward others were considered legally binding between individuals whether or not there was a direct relationship (familial, contractual, or otherwise) to unite them. Indeed, with women's increased mobility and, subsequently, their growing role as protagonists in accident cases, tort law began to acknowledge, however reluctantly, something quite different from its institutionalized patriarchal conventions. As injury law began to recognize its duty of care to women and its obligation to accommodate their accounts of accidental injury, it also came to feature women's private pain and suffering as public narrative.

Through the accident, the suddenness of impact, and what Nan Goodman has described in another context as the changing nature of "liability and human agency under negligence," Glasgow reimagines Dorinda's place in a new technological modernity and with it a more radical expression of feminist subjectivity (Goodman, *Shifting the Blame*, 4). Surviving her bodily injuries and limitations, Dorinda Oakley is given a fresh capacity for change. The physical wound that leaves her "barren" inspires other forms of fulfillment: she returns to Broomsedge and restores the family farm to its "true fertility" (Campbell, "'Where are the ladies?'," 162). Like Chopin, Glasgow challenges readers to reconsider what constitutes the narrative's traumatic event. The accident, the sudden impact, is not solely a literary metaphor, but it is also part of an official language through which to implore what was previously invisible and seemingly impossible, the cultural recognition of women's physical and emotional integrity. Accidents, as well as attending questions about responsibility and negligence that such accidents inspired, have played a crucial role in the fiction of some of the nation's most celebrated male writers, from James Fenimore Cooper to Mark Twain, as Nan Goodman has argued. Fiction written by women also imagined the real and growing risk of accident and injury as they too ventured far beyond the boundaries of the family farm. Glasgow's novel reflects the medico-legal debate in which such accidents and injuries were increasingly widespread. Collisions of the sort Dorinda suffers were among the most prominent medical and legal cases, adjudicated through-out law courts in the late nineteenth and early twentieth centuries. Reading these legal narratives, narratives resonant with Dorinda Oakley's case, historian Barbara Welke argues that it was especially "through the minds and bodies of women" that law courts came to "recognize a right to recover for injury" resulting from shock and other seemingly less tangible "emotional" harms (*Recasting American Liberty*, 202). These cases were deeply normative: women's physical vulnerability and her reproductive body provoked state intervention and protection, but, perhaps even more striking, they became emblematic; the connections the courts made between a woman's mental state and her physical symptoms would come to apply to all injured persons. Characteristics and sensations attributed to her, her vulnerability as well as her demand for physical and psychic integrity, in other words, prevailed. While Dorinda's accident and its aftermath sparks a rejection of biological determinism, it also invites readers to envision how the cultural recognition of women's wounds might, in turn, shape modern sensibilities.

Anticipating the pulse of modernity, women's narratives made accident and injury a central feature. The theme of the "disasterous wreck," as Nancy Bentley notes, would become crucial to modernist and postmodernist fiction, the "process of redirecting risk, of displacing, exaggerating, or transforming a sense of threat . . . one of the activities that characterize the modern crash culture" (*Frantic Panoramas*, 231). American women writers not only seized but also helped shape the tropes that would become critical to this modern cultural vocabulary. The new dangers associated with technology increased collective vulnerability, setting the stage for enhanced recognition of what Jane Thrailkill calls "interior corporeal states," the literary and cultural mapping of an "experiential terrain between private bodies and public events" that worked to "authenticate and bring to consciousness bodily feelings" (*Affective Fictions*, 12). Critics such as Bentley and Thrailkill demonstrate that literature, in concert with developments in science, technology, and industry, produced socially vital and shared feelings, chief among them, as Susan Mizruchi has recently argued about contemporary American literature, a collective sense of risk. How women's narratives inhabited this sensibility and, in turn, deployed cultural anxieties about "human powerlessness" toward a wider recognition of social injuries demands greater attention ("Risk Theory," 111). So too does the culture of accident suggest the importance of cultivating "counterunits" of literary study that trace uneven, messy, even accidental phenomena and their effects (Castronovo and Gillman, "The Study of the American Problems," 4). Focusing on literary depictions of accidents and injury, Sandra Macpherson, for example, sets forth what she labels a "countertradition" of the English novel, one that focuses on "harms rather than rights, accident rather than will and its analogues (intention, consciousness, sovereignty, freedom)" (*Harm's Way*, 4). Both Macpherson and Ravit Reichman, in *The Affective Life of Law*, ask how novels embrace an alternative language of agency and responsibility against the seemingly axiomatic sense that modernity progresses from "status to contract [and] from a feudal to a liberal-democratic society organized around the freedom of persons to choose their associations" (Macpherson, *Harm's Way*, 4). In reading the deployment of accidents and the language of injury in the work of the writers joined together here, we might be said to trace a version of this countertradition; with these writers' vocabulary in mind, literary critics must continue to question the constitutive structure of harm, as well as chart the cultural impact of woundedness as it is expressed in women's literary work.

Notes

1. Chopin, "The Story of an Hour." All quotes are from pp. 194–5.
2. With railway spine "post traumatic symptoms were first brought together, given a unitary diagnostic label, and granted a single etiology" (Micale and Lerner, "Trauma, Psychiatry, and History," 12). In *Affecting Fictions*, Jane Thrailkill traces the work of psychophysiology and debates over railway spine to argue that the role of narrative was "to elucidate the train of events that led from trauma to symptom, and to determine the structure of the nervous system that provided the physiological 'track' for exterior impressions to become registered in interior corporeal states" (86). For more on the cognitive effects and "transformation of the human sensorium by modernization," see Nicholas Daly, "Railway Novels," 472, and *Literature, Technology, and Modernity*. For more on the crisis of modernity as an "inexorable and mysterious trauma," see Moglen, *Mourning Modernity*, 3–25. For a philosophical history of accident, see Ross Hamilton, *Accident*.
3. For a discussion of "male hysteria" and its connections to industrial injuries, see Mark Micale's *Hysterical Men*, 49–70.
4. Recent studies by literary critics such as Donna Campbell and Jennifer Fleissner have opened the door to include more women writers of naturalism and have complicated the genre's gender politics as well as its narrative techniques and concerns. Fleissner, in particular, refrains from reading naturalism's plots of decline or determinism, what many other critics have taken as the genre's most salient features, and argues that placing women at the center of the naturalist project allows us to see the genre's most characteristic plot, "neither the steep arc of decline nor that of triumph, but rather by an ongoing, nonlinear, repetitive motion . . . a 'stuckness in place'" (30–1).
5. The language of wounds is not new to women's literature; however, the medico-legal debate of the late nineteenth and early twentieth centuries gives new meaning to what

Marianne Noble has called the "sentimental wound," the notion, as Elizabeth Barnes astutely observed that "I hurt therefore I am" ("The Epistemology of the 'Real'," 321).

6. Although Phelps often falls through the cracks of literary periodization and feminist history, as Lisa Long has noted, Phelps's fiction, which features the technology of wounds from the Civil War battlefield to the factory floor, ties her to a very specific cultural-historical milieu (267).

7. Phelps, *The Story of Avis*, 101. For a discussion of Phelps's images of sexuality, see Bauer, "Blood, Sex, and the Ugly Girl," in *Sex Expression*, 54–69.

8. Wendy Brown, in *States of Injury*, for example, cautions against "formulations of identity rooted in injury."

9. I borrow the phrase "wombs and wounds" from Jane Thrailkill's *Affective Fictions*, 12.

Works cited

Barnes, Elizabeth. "The Epistemology of the 'Real': A Response to Marianne Noble." *The Yale Journal of Criticism* 10.2 (1997): 321–6.

Bauer, Dale M. *Sex Expression and American Women Writers, 1860–1940*. Chapel Hill: University of North Carolina Press, 2009.

Benjamin, Walter. *Illuminations*. New York: Shocken Books, 1939.

Bentley, Nancy. *Frantic Panoramas: American Literature and Mass Culture, 1870–1920*. Philadelphia: University of Pennsylvania Press, 2009.

Brown, Wendy. *States of Injury: Power and Freedom in Late Modernity*. Princeton: Princeton University Press, 1995.

Campbell, Donna. "'Where are the ladies?' Wharton, Glasgow, and American Women Naturalists." *Studies in American Naturalism* 1 (2006): 152–69.

Caplan, Eric. "Trains and Trauma in the American Gilded Age." In *Traumatic Pasts: History, Psychiatry, and Trauma in the Modern Age, 1870–1930*. Ed. Mark Micale and Paul Lerner. Cambridge: Cambridge University Press, 2001.

Castronovo, Russ and Susan Gillman. "The Study of the American Problems." In *States of Emergency: The Object of American Studies*. Ed. Russ Castronovo and Susan Gillman. Chapel Hill: University of North Carolina Press, 2009.

Cather, Willa. "Paul's Case: A Study in Temperament." In *Willa Cather Early Novels and Stories*. Ed. Sharon O'Brien. New York: The Library of America, 1987.

Caruth, Cathy. *Unclaimed Experience: Trauma, Narrative and History*. Baltimore: The Johns Hopkins University Press, 1996.

Chopin, Kate. "The Story of an Hour." In *Literature: Reading, Reacting, Writing*. Ed. Laurie G. Kirszner and Stephen R. Mandell. Boston: Thomson/Wadsworth, 2007.

Daly, Nicholas. *Literature, Technology, and Modernity, 1860–2000*. Cambridge: Cambridge University Press, 2004.

"Railway Novels: Sensation Fiction and the Modernization of the Senses." *English Literary History* 66.2 (1999): 461–87.

Davis, Rebecca Harding. "Anne." *Harper's New Monthly* 78 (1889): 744–50.

Erichsen, John Eric. *Railway and Other Injuries of the Nervous System*. London: Walton and Maberly, 1866.

Fleissner, Jennifer. *Women, Compulsion, Modernity: The Moment of American Naturalism.* Chicago: University of Chicago Press, 2006.

Glasgow, Ellen. *Barren Ground.* New York: Doubleday, 1925.

   A Certain Measure: An Interpretation of Prose Fiction. New York: Harcourt, Brace, and Co., 1938.

Goodman, Nan. *Shifting the Blame: Literature, Law, and the Theory of Accidents in Nineteenth-Century America.* Princeton: Princeton University Press, 1998.

Hamilton, Ross. *Accident: A Philosophical and Literary History.* Chicago: University of Chicago Press, 2007.

Harrington, Ralph. "The Railway Accident: Trains, Trauma, and Technological Crises in Nineteenth-Century Britain." In *Traumatic Pasts: History, Psychiatry, and Trauma in the Modern Age, 1870–1930.* Ed. Mark S. Micale and Paul Lerner. Cambridge: Cambridge University Press, 2001.

Long, Lisa. "The Postbellum Reform Writings of Rebecca Harding Davis and Elizabeth Stuart Phelps." In *The Cambridge Companion to Nineteenth-Century American Women's Writing.* Ed. Dale M. Bauer and Philip Gould. Cambridge: Cambridge University Press, 2001.

Luckhurst, Roger. *The Trauma Question.* London: Routledge, 2008.

Macpherson, Sandra. *Harm's Way: Tragic Responsibility and the Novel Form.* Baltimore: The Johns Hopkins University Press, 2009.

Micale, Mark S. *Hysterical Men: The Hidden History of Male Nervous Illness.* Cambridge, MA: Harvard University Press, 2008.

Micale, Mark S. and Paul Lerner. "Trauma, Psychiatry, and History: A Conceptual and Historiographical Introduction." In *Traumatic Pasts: History, Psychiatry, and Trauma in the Modern Age, 1870–1930.* Cambridge: Cambridge University Press, 2001.

Mizruchi, Susan. "Risk Theory and the Contemporary American Novel." *American Literary History* 22.1 (2010): 109–35.

Moglen, Seth. *Mourning Modernity: Literary Modernism and the Injuries of American Capitalism.* Stanford: Stanford University Press, 2007.

Norris, Frank. *McTeague.* 1899. New York: Penguin, 1994.

Phelps, Austin. *My Portfolio: A Collection of Essays.* New York: Charles Scribner's Sons, 1882.

Phelps, Elizabeth Stuart. *The Story of Avis.* 1877. New Brunswick: Rutgers University Press, 1985.

Pizer, Donald. "Late Nineteenth-Century American Literary Naturalism: A Re-Introduction." *American Literary Realism* 38 (2006): 189–202.

Reichman, Ravit. *The Affective Life of Law: Legal Modernism and the Literary Imagination.* Stanford: Stanford University Press, 2009.

Richter, Amy G. *Home on the Rails: Women, the Railroads, and the Rise of Public Domesticity.* Chapel Hill: University of North Carolina Press, 2005.

Samuels, Shirley. "Women at War." In *The Cambridge Companion to Nineteenth-Century American Women's Writing.* Ed. Dale M. Bauer and Philip Gould. Cambridge: Cambridge University Press, 2001.

Schivelbusch, Wolfgang. *The Railway Journey: The Industrialization of Time and Space in the 19th Century.* 1977. Berkeley: University of California Press, 1986.

Seltzer, Mark. "Wound Culture: Trauma in the Pathological Public Sphere." *October* 80 (1997): 3–26.

Southworth, Emma Dorothy Eliza Nevitte. *Fair Play; or, The Text of the Lone Isle*. Philadelphia: T. B. Peterson & Brothers, 1868.

How He Won Her; A Sequel to Fair Play. Philadelphia: T. B. Peterson & Brothers, 1869.

Thrailkill, Jane F. *Affecting Fictions: Mind, Body, and Emotion in American Literary Realism*. Cambridge, MA: Harvard University Press, 2007.

Travis, Jennifer. *Wounded Hearts: Masculinity, Law, and Literature in American Culture*. Chapel Hill: University of North Carolina Press, 2005.

Welke, Barbara. *Recasting American Liberty: Gender, Race, Law, and the Railroad Revolution, 1865–1920*. Cambridge: Cambridge University Press, 2001.

Wharton, Edith. *The Fruit of the Tree*. 1907. Boston: Northeastern University Press, 2000.

20

The geography of ladyhood

Racializing the novel of manners

CHERENE SHERRARD-JOHNSON

As early twentieth-century Anglo-American women writers such as Edith Wharton, Kate Chopin, and Zona Gale used their writing to create new audiences and explore how the figure of the New Woman was changing American perceptions of gender roles, several African American women novelists worked to revamp the contested image of the New Woman into the New Negro woman. Their artistic activism linked the ideology of racial uplift with the recuperation of the image of African American woman from the dehumanizing and degrading stereotypes that went hand in hand with slavery and its aftermath. As black women writers struggled to fuse their political and aesthetic aims, they often felt frustrated by the claims of both. The proto-feminist journalist Mary Church Terrell, who is far better known for her political writings than her fiction, believed that "the Race Problem could be solved more swiftly and more surely through the instrumentality of the short story or novel than in any other way" (Terrell as quoted in McHenry, "Towards a History of Access," 234).

Terrell's frustration with her inability to place her fiction in mainstream venues such as *Harper's, Atlantic Monthly,* or *Scribner's Magazine* may have prompted writers like Pauline Hopkins to persist in serializing her novels in African American periodicals, like the *Colored American Magazine,* a publication that ensured her an audience. Despite discouraging odds, several early twentieth-century African American woman writers pioneered major literary innovations. One such endeavor was the revision or racializing of the modernist novel of manners popularized by writers like Henry James and Edith Wharton. Readers may assume that the typical novel of manners was a genteel genre of fiction that revolved primarily around the courtship exploits of young, marriageable, upper-class women. This point of view is not necessarily incorrect, and many of the plot trajectories of books that fit the template for the novel of manners do take up this subject matter; however, some authors penned novels of manners that exceeded the popular expectations of the genre by using it as a strategy for delving into ethnographic spheres of social interaction, performance, and behavior in a way that was refreshing, modern, and appealed to both popular and more discriminating audiences. The novel of manners typically examined the conventions governing social life of a particular class or category of people. Wharton's novels focused on the insular "tribes" of old New York and the new money upstarts hoping to break into their rarefied circles; Henry James frequently wrote about the adventures of Americans abroad and the complications of a cosmopolitan and/or expatriate existence.

Interior spaces in novels of manners function as sites of subtle power plays that have dramatic (and occasionally melodramatic) consequences for the characters that inhabit them. Nancy Bentley's *The Ethnography of Manners: Hawthorne, James, Wharton* observes that "the exchanges of drawing-room culture" are "indistinguishable from acts of coercive force" (70). This essay examines how an interior space that exists in the private/public frontier of social life becomes the site of a particular racialized and gendered performance that has severe ramifications for the African American novel of manners. To this end, I analyze three key scenes staged in various drawing rooms imagined in Pauline Hopkins's *Of One Blood* (1902–3), Nella Larsen's *Passing* (1929), and Dorothy West's *The Living is Easy* (1948). By illustrating how the setting of the drawing room amplifies these moments of heightened social performance and reading them alongside companion scenes from prototypical novels of manners, I argue that black women writers saw their writing as creatively engaging an interracial literary tradition as they portrayed the African American heroine as a modern American heroine.

The novels of manners that provided the best template for African American writers were those that had an ethnographic aspect. Nancy Bentley examines novel writing as a social practice: "When social manners are recast as ethnographic data, then, a notable transformation has taken place. Manners are able to encode an identity that has the ontology of a race and the holism of a prehistoric tribe" (*The Ethnography of Manners*, 76). Novels of manners, then, pay close attention to all elements of the social world; they examine the habits, behavior, and relationships of their characters and the spaces in which their characters stage and perform their social rites. The subtitle of this essay is somewhat of a misnomer because the novel of manners was already informed by the racialized discourse that governed social life in turn-of-the century United States. The distinction is relevant, however, because writers like Pauline Hopkins, Nella Larsen, Jessie Fauset, Marita Bonner, and Dorothy West consciously took on the task of reimagining the genre in a manner that underscored its relevance to both their aesthetic and political desires. Manners primarily indicate that one has mastered the accepted social conventions governing modes of behavior in a specific place and time. As Sarah Luria explains: "they confer social status by showing that the mind has brought one's physical urges under control" ("The Architecture of Manners," 7). For turn-of-the-century African American writers, especially those like Terrell and Hopkins, who believed their writing could transform the social, political, and economic status of blacks, manners were important because they were part of a strategy some upper-class blacks believed would protect them from race-based discrimination, persecution, and disenfranchisement. Proponents of racial uplift understood that manners alone were not sufficient armor, but combined with capital, color and education, they made a formidable shield. The flipside of this strategy was that the same shield could also be used to discipline and police those who did not conform. Such is the case in Frank Webb's *The Garies and Their Friends* (1857), a novel Samuel Otter considers as an "historical novel of urgent manners" that "evaluates the post-independence promise that free African-American discipline and virtue would secure legal rights and economic success" ("Frank Webb's Still Life," 731).[1]

On the surface, the concept of an African American drawing room in the public imagination at the turn of the century might seem elitist and far-fetched; however, such images did exist within early African American photography. Philosopher/activist W. E. B. Du Bois collaborated with black studio photographers to develop albums that prominently featured African American families in tasteful, well-decorated drawing rooms replete with markers of high culture and education: pianos, books, and other ornamentation. These images were designed for the Exhibit of American Negroes at the 1900 Paris Exposition; the purpose was to showcase, if not forecast, racial progress since emancipation.[2] If we read novels of manners from an ethnographic perspective, the decoration of the drawing room, an interior space within the home that is also a public space since it is where one formally receives visitors, becomes, as Bentley argues, "an object lesson for reading the ethnological materials that will disclose the origins of civilization" (*The Ethnography of Manners*, 81).

While Du Bois's albums were creating a visual argument for the diversity and accomplishment of the black subject at the turn of the century, the literary heroine and cultural icon known as the New Woman was taking shape within the novel of manners. The New Woman was a contested figure, as marked by contradictions as she was by definitive features. While her initiative, fashionable attire, and enhanced mobility signaled her status as a new icon of modern femininity, the plot trajectories with which she was associated frequently reinscribed Victorian expectations of ideal womanhood with regard to marriage and occupation. Black women writers who imagined the New Negro womanhood faced a similar conundrum: how to envision a modern, liberated heroine without falling victim to the pathologies associated with slavery that read the black female body as promiscuous and sexually vulnerable? The novel of manners provided an opportunity to write the black woman as a New Negro woman heroine, but balancing these representational strategies with the authors' individual artistic desires was a complicated endeavor.

In addition to the New Woman, other character types familiar to readers of Whartonesque and Jamesian fiction found themselves in the pages of Hopkins's, Larsen's, and West's novels, specifically the figures of the invalid and the sensualist. The invalid, as Susan Tomlinson argues in her analysis of Zona Gale's *Faint Perfume* (1923), "exposes the stark realities behind the New Woman ideal" ("'Curiously Without Body'," 584). By making the heroine of her novel an invalid whose disability prevents her from achieving her artistic potential or financial independence, Gale offers a complex critique of "the popular discourse of New Womanhood as a response to the True Woman paradigm that had cornered the narrative market on illness and confinement" ("'Curiously Without Body'," 572). More familiar examples of the invalid character include the narrator of Charlotte Perkins Gilman's "The Yellow Wall-Paper" and Henry James's characterization of Ralph Touchett in *Portrait of a Lady*. Early African American authors like William Wells Brown, the amanuensis for *Running a Thousand Miles for Freedom* (1860) by William and Ellen Craft, also made use of the figure of the invalid: Ellen Craft's disguise as a disabled, effeminate, male slaveholder allows her and her husband to seize their freedom and garner support for the abolitionist cause through public speeches recounting their daring and dramatic escape. Pauline Hopkins also represents her character Dianthe Lusk as an invalid in order to reveal and contest the complications of New Womanhood as a viable category for black women. In West's *The Living is Easy* one of the protagonist's sisters is essentially agoraphobic after she becomes morbidly obese following the loss of her husband.

The figure of the sensualist, which is often juxtaposed with the invalid, presented a representational problem for African American novelists hoping to combat the image of the black female body as an oversexed Jezebel. Some authors addressed this problem by suppressing the sexuality of their heroines by sublimating romantic or sexual desire beneath a commitment to uplift and service. If a character's sensual nature is revealed, the deviation must be violently contained. A case in point is the spectacular death of the alluring Clare Kendry in Larsen's *Passing*. The compelling literary architecture that shaped the African American drawing rooms imagined first by Hopkins, and later by Larsen and West, illustrates how early twentieth-century black women novelists transformed the modernist novel of manners and responded to the figures of the New Woman, the invalid, and the sensualist – all key figures within the genre – in order to suit their own political and aesthetic desires.

Pauline Hopkins's mesmerizing, diasporic, gothic drawing room

Although Nella Larsen's and Dorothy West's novels better fit the conventions of the ethnographic novel of manners, I begin with Pauline Hopkins because she was, quite simply, a writer ahead of her time; she revolutionizes African American fiction by incorporating "all the fire and romance which lie dormant in our history" (Hopkins, *Of One Blood*, 14). She was not afraid to experiment and drew heavily on the interracial literary tradition that she advanced. Through her serial novels Hazel Carby asserts that Hopkins undertook a "sustained attempt to develop Afro-American popular fiction" (Introduction to *Of One Blood*, xxxvii). I would add that *Of One Blood* is possibly the first example of African American speculative fiction, a sub-category of science fiction/fantasy later popularized by writers like Octavia Butler, the author of *Kindred* (1979). Just as several of Wharton's novels were written for and published in *Scribner's*, much of Hopkins's fiction was serialized in the publication the *Colored American Magazine*, a journal she also edited.[3] In her diasporic novel *Of One Blood: Or, The Hidden Self*, Hopkins brings together science and the occult, politics and romance into a sweeping adventure novel that is at times perplexing and always experimental.

Of One Blood follows the adventures of Reuel Briggs, a Harvard medical student of mysterious origin – readers familiar with Hopkins would immediately intuit that he is passing for white – whose quest for knowledge takes him from Cambridge, Massachusetts, to an ancient city in Ethiopia. His destiny is intertwined with a mysterious singer named Dianthe Lusk whom he apparently resurrects; the novel is replete with psychological and anthropological referents. Many critics have studied Hopkins's conscious integration of the psychologist William James's 1890 essay "The Hidden Self" into her novel; *Of One Blood* also draws on Henry James's representation of the mesmerized heroine in *The Bostonians* (1886) and the gothic, narrative elements of the tale within a tale format of James's psychoanalytical ghost story – also published first as a serial in *Collier's Weekly* – *The Turn of the Screw* (1898).[4] Though Hopkins thinly disguises William James's essay by attributing it to Alfred Binet, his essay actually provides her novel's subtitle. *Of One Blood* sought to address "the mystery emerging from what William James hailed as the 'ascertain[ment] that the secondary self, or selves, coexist with the primary one, the trance-personalities with the normal one, during the waking state'" (Brown, *Pauline Elizabeth Hopkins*, 394). The idea of a bifurcated self is also at the heart of W. E. B. Du Bois's psycho-sociological study *The Souls of Black Folk* (1903), specifically his articulation of "double consciousness" and the idea that the African American psyche contained "two warring ideals in one dark body" (5). Hopkins liberally draws from James in order to shape the philosophical and scientific practices employed by her hero and the broader, metaphysical themes of the novel.

For the purposes of this essay, Chapter 6 contains the critical drawing room scene. Thomas Otten notes *Of One Blood*'s abrupt shifts from "genteel settings" to "adventure romance" are not as random as they seem. In fact, such shifts are necessary for Hopkins to take "the images, themes, and historical framework common to black nationalist writing and, via a Jamesian conception of the psyche, transforms them into an interior structure" (Otten, "Pauline Hopkins and the Hidden Self of Race," 248). Because *Of One Blood* is in dialogue with both William's psychological studies and Henry's fictional portrayals of mesmerism, it is not surprising that this chapter uses a story-within-a-story format that echoes the *"amusette* to catch those not easily caught" that Henry James's narrator tells his guests in *The Turn of the Screw* (Preface, 125). The story centers on Mira: a suggestive bondwoman under mesmeric influences. Yet, as the teller reveals, while Mira's body and mind are seemingly controlled by her owner, her prophesies relay a horrific revenge upon those who have used her for malicious purposes. The storyteller, Aubrey Livingston, removes his audience from the enlightened drawing rooms of Cambridge, Massachusetts, where science accounts for unexplained phenomena, to a haunted parlor in the south in an atmosphere evocative of Edgar Allan Poe's gothicism.

Chapter 6 opens in the "long drawing-room of the Vance house" "one well-calculated to remove all gloomy pessimistic reasoning" (*Of One Blood*, 481). It is Christmastime and the hostess is dressed classically in a "gray plush tea-gown, with her hair piled picturesquely on top of her small head, and fixed there with a big tortoise-shell pin, it would have been difficult to find a more delightful object for the gaze to rest upon" (482). But the hostess, Molly Vance, is not the central heroine of this episode, nor is the mysterious patient Dianthe Lusk, who the hero Reuel Briggs famously brings out of a comatose state in front of an audience of doubting medical students. Briggs's scientific experiments are of interest to the party, but before he can relate them he is interrupted by Aubrey Livingston, who proposes to tell a story about mesmerism that supplants Reuel's recounting of how he woke Dianthe from her mesmeric sleep.

Aubrey hails from a large plantation in the south prior to the Civil War, where it was his father's practice to mesmerize his mother's maid Mira. He recounts to his captivated audience: "Many a time I have known him to call her into the parlor to perform tricks of mind-reading for the amusement of visitors, and many wonderful things were done by her as the record given in his books shows" (486). On a particular evening, during a dinner party much like the one occurring as Aubrey relates the story, Mira is called forth. At the father's prompting she transforms from "a serious, rather sad Negress" "to a gay, noisy, restless woman, full of irony and sharp jesting" (486). There is no way to determine if Mira's "metamorphosis" is a false performance or a self-protective minstrel act designed to derive some agency from the uses to which she is being put. Mira's melancholia can be attributed partially to the sexual advances of her owner, which result in the birth of three mixed-race children – Aubrey, Reuel, and Dianthe – who the reader learns of later in the novel.

When prompted by her mesmerist/owner, who she calls "Captain," Mira offers a bloody vision of the coming Civil War:

> All the women will be widows and the men shall sleep in early graves. They come from the north, from the east, from the west, they sweep to the gulf through a trail of blood. Your houses shall burn, your fields be laid waste, and a downtrodden race shall rule in your land. For you, captain, a prison cell and a pauper's grave. (487)

Naturally, the guests are horrified, and as punishment for her ominous fortune-telling, Mira is sold. Aubrey concludes his story by relating that what Mira prophesied that night did indeed come to pass, and "there is only too much truth in the science of mesmeric phenomena" (487).

The action in *Of One Blood* moves through many different locales and domains, from the concert hall, to the medical school classrooms, to the Vance estate, the Livingston family plantation, and the hidden kingdom of Meroe in Ethiopia, but it is Aubrey's drawing-room tale – his invocation of Mira – that holds the keys to unlock the puzzle of the title: how everyone came to be "of one blood." Throughout the novel, Hopkins uses the female body as a conduit for both her critique and exploitation of women's vulnerability. Her treatment of Mira as both a victim of mesmeric influence and a soothsayer of emancipatory justice typifies the dual roles of several of her female characters. Similarly, her characterization of Dianthe Lusk as an invalid whose hidden self contains both her African ancestry and her haunting artistry as a gospel singer illustrates the complexities of positioning the African American woman as a modern heroine. As Hannah Wallinger observes, "the predominant image of Dianthe" is as a "victim at the hands of powerful men" (*Pauline Elizabeth Hopkins*, 221). Given that her previous novel *Contending Forces* (1900) aggressively critiqued the sexual exploitation of black women as she sought to create a new definition of virtue that could be applied to formerly enslaved women, it is puzzling that Hopkins places Dianthe at the mercy of her two brothers. Using a fusion of medical and occult science, Briggs reanimates her presumably dead corpse only to hide the racial and artistic identity she had prior to their marriage. Over the course of the novel, she is forced to pass for white, duped into thinking Reuel is dead, commits incest first with Reuel, and, then again, with Aubrey. Finally, her attempt to kill Aubrey backfires when she is coerced into drinking the poison she intended for him. Lois Brown argues that Dianthe's death is an "entirely public and almost apocalyptic moment of transition" that allows her to be reclaimed as a daughter of Africa, but it is difficult to overlook what even Brown considers Dianthe's "savage sexualization" (*Pauline Elizabeth Hopkins*, 398, 397).

As a self-taught student of anthropology and history, Hopkins aspired to provide creative works enriched by her own readings of African American canonical studies of Africa and contemporary accounts of archeological expeditions and social Darwinism (Brown, *Pauline Elizabeth Hopkins*, 402). Hopkins unexpectedly relegates the story of American slavery to the periphery of her novel in order to weave a genre-defying, pan-African speculative novel. Yet the drawing room scene reveals that although she has imagined an adventure novel of epic proportions, the dynamics wrought by American slavery are still at the heart of the story, and its horrors still haunt and influence current events. The story-within-the-story holds the key to Dianthe's identity and a way out of her situation through a reconnection with her African ancestry. Unfortunately for Dianthe, the release and reclamation come at the cost of her life.

Nella Larsen's "decorative" "rage"

Whereas *Of One Blood* drew on the gothic tradition, melodrama, archeology, mesmerism, and the supernatural, Nella Larsen placed her novel firmly within the social geography of her own time: that of the Harlem Renaissance. In *Passing* (1929), the two main protagonists find themselves in a tension-filled relationship hinging on their desire to maintain their class privilege. Irene Redfield wishes to preserve her image as the ideal New Negro woman, mother, and wife – a lifestyle threatened by the sudden reappearance of her childhood friend Clare Kendry, who has been passing for white. Clare sees Irene as an intermediary that will allow her to reclaim her birthright as a black woman, eschew her responsibilities as a wife and mother, and still maintain the privileges accorded to her as a woman of leisure.

The critical drawing room scene in *Passing* occurs in Chapter 1 of Section III, which is entitled "Finale." This is one of several scenes that foreshadow Clare's impending fall to her death and Irene's conscious or unconscious decision to precipitate it. Just as important as the action that takes place is the setting of the tea party, like "so many other tea-parties" Irene has hosted:

> There were the familiar little tinkling sounds of spoons striking against frail cups, the soft running sounds of inconsequential talk, punctuated now and then with laughter. In irregular small groups, disintegrating, coalescing, striking just the right note of disharmony, disorder in the big room, which Irene had furnished with a sparingness that was almost chaste, moved the guests with that slight familiarity that makes a party a success. On the floor and the walls the sinking sun threw long, fantastic shadows. (91)

Edith Wharton's novels were known for their similar attention to interior design and décor; Nancy Bentley observes: Wharton "analyzes interiors as maps to the local cosmology of a people . . . rooms and furniture are codes that call for a translation into writing" (*The Ethnography of Manners*, 83). Such details are also important to Larsen. In her first novel, *Quicksand*, she situated her mixed-race protagonist in lush orientalist settings and attire to emphasize her status as an exotic Other in the various interracial communities she inhabits. In *Passing*, she brings a similar sensibility to her depiction of Clare Kendry, whom Irene views as primarily decorative. In response to her husband's query: "d'you mean that you think Clare is stupid?" Irene replies: "No, I don't. She isn't stupid. She's intelligent enough in a purely feminine way. Eighteenth-century France would have been a marvelous setting for her, or the old South, if she hadn't made the mistake of being born a Negro" (88). This conversation about Clare's aesthetic appeal, her "decorative qualities," just prior to the party have unhinged Irene's otherwise carefully guarded veneer. At the soiree she makes a series of social *faux pas*, like committing to three dinners "all on the same evening and at almost the same hour" (93).

Finally, Irene decides that Clare is having an affair with her husband. With this realization, or hallucination, comes the thought of herself as "an obstacle" to their liaison. Her response:

> Rage boiled up in her.
>
> There was a slight crash. On the floor at her feet lay the shattered cup. Dark stains dotted the bright rug. Spread. The chatter stopped. Went on. Before her, Zulena gathered up the white fragments. (93–4)

While this crack in Irene's perfect visage is startling, it is her performance afterwards to account for the breach to a witness, Hugh Wentworth, that reveals that she has mastered the correct performance of New Negro ladyhood necessary to smooth over and police both her dramatic emotions and control the situation at hand. In this she has help; Wentworth immediately offers her an excuse by apologizing: "Must have pushed you. Clumsy of me. Don't tell me it's priceless and irreplaceable" (94). In this scene Clare *is* the cup: the white fragments are her bones which will soon shatter offstage upon impact with the sidewalk; and the dark stains clearly reference blood. Indeed, contrary to Wentworth's dismissal, something priceless and irreplaceable has been broken. Also broken is Irene's marriage – not so much by Clare's interference, but by her own false performance and control of the relationship. The Redfields' marriage is a sexless union between a doctor and a socialite; they are New Negro royalty, but their position comes at a high price. Ultimately, Irene eschews Wentworth's apology and offers instead an implausible explanation: she broke the cup on purpose.

Larsen's drawing room scene cogently captures the painful strain of Irene's performance of ideal New Negro ladyhood and the resulting psychosis that results first in rage and then in the murderous impulse to rid herself of the sensualist threat that resides both within Clare and herself. In her analysis of the class dynamics of *Passing*, Jennifer Brody charts Clare's descent in relationship to Irene's ascent within their intersecting social spheres. Brody writes: "the spatial and ideological positions held by Clare and Irene are revealed in several scenes in which they interact. These scenes occur in the most 'civilized' of places – tea rooms, parlors, boudoirs and ballrooms – but, as in Virginia Woolf's novels, these genteel settings turn out to be the arenas of the most brutal and biting behavior" ("Clare Kendry's 'True Colors'," 1056).

To amplify the sinister atmosphere of New Negro society, Larsen's novel – which is organized into three sections entitled "Encounter," "Recounter," and "Finale" – mirrors the narrative structure of Edith Wharton's *House of Mirth*, which follows Lily Bart's descent from the pinnacle of the social hierarchy to the abyss. Lily is neither an invalid nor truly a sensualist, though she loves fine things and has excellent taste. Rather, she is an icon of a dying culture, emblematic of its best and most condemning aspects. As such, a viable New Womanhood remains out of reach. Unlike Irene, Lily's impulsive acts do not rid her of her enemies. In fact, one might say that her impulse is to uphold the social order, even at her own expense. And like Clare, a speculative gaze follows Lily throughout her descent.[5]

Because *House of Mirth* was originally written as a serial, there are several concise scenes that mark Lily's descent. The scenes that I find best illuminate the type of performance required to uphold and maintain the social order occur in rapid succession. First, at the close of an Italian dinner party, with a single sentence social leader Bertha Dorset manages to disparage Lily's character. Her announcement – "Miss Bart is not going back to the yacht" – is simple enough. Yet her implicit accusation that Lily and her husband are having an affair is masterfully communicated and underscored by her husband George's protest that "this is some misunderstanding" (*House of Mirth*, 229). Lily, an instructress for others in how to rise through the social hierarchy, shows herself to be outmatched when it comes to managing her own welfare. Not only does she surrender the field to Bertha, she assuages the consciences of witnesses who may be able to help her by concurring, "I am joining the Duchess to-morrow" and that "it seemed easier for me to remain on shore for the night" (229).

The next chapter reveals the ramifications of this deceptively simple interaction. Back in New York we find Lily in her aunt's drawing room, where the blinds "were drawn down against the oppressive June sun, and in the sultry twilight the faces of her assembled relatives took on a fitting shadow of bereavement" (232). Once again society has gathered in a drawing room, not for a dinner or a tea, but for the reading of Mrs. Peniston's will, which proves to be an equally entertaining social event. Just as Bertha's succinct dismissal is met with discomfort, Lily's disinheritance is met with a "subdued gasp of surprise" which again she sacrificially rushes in to ease by holding out her hand to her cousin and saying, "Dear Grace, I am so glad" (235). Then, amidst whispers and innuendos, the drawing room transforms from a site of social negotiation to what it really is, a wake for Lily's dream of financial independence: "Miss Bart and Gerty found themselves almost alone in the purple drawing-room, which more than ever, in its stuffy dimness, resembled a well-kept family vault in which the last corpse had just been decently deposited" (235). Gerty is a financially independent New Woman, but her pleasant, though meager, apartment is not a substitute for the splendid interiors that Lily was "made for" (25). Without money, Lily, like the funerary flowers she is named for, is destined to adorn a corpse.[6]

Lily does offer a rationale for her reluctance to defend herself. When Gerty asks why Lily does not tell her friends the whole truth, she replies, "What is truth? Where a woman is concerned, it's the story that's easiest to believe. In this case it's a great deal easier to believe Bertha Dorset's story than mine, because she has a big house and an opera box, and it's convenient to be on good terms with her" (237). Similarly, because on the surface Irene Redfield is the proper New Negro wife, mother and social hostess, her side of the story, like Dorset's, is more believable: "She just fell, before anybody could stop her," Irene explains to the investigators who ultimately pronounce the cause: "death by misadventure" (114). The misadventure is, of course, Clare's transgressive behavior, her racial passing, her ambiguous sexual appeal, and her eschewing of wifehood and motherhood: all behaviors that violate both black and white social codes of conduct. Like Hopkins, Larsen offers a study on New Negro womanhood that questions its viability and the high costs of its maintenance within the social order.

Dorothy West's "indoor novel"[7]

Drawing on its predecessors, Dorothy West's *The Living is Easy* introduces a uniquely Machiavellian heroine who perfects the genteel performance of the New Negro lady to such a degree that her mask, her performance, is almost undetectable. In *The Living is Easy*, West draws on Zora Neale Hurston's ethnographical approach to folk culture and emulates Edith Wharton's dissection of old New York into various tribes. Although many critics read *The Living is Easy* as an autobiographical novel, what makes it an ethnographic novel of manners is how successfully she represents the lives of Boston's black Brahmins and the homes and neighborhoods they inhabit. Yet, her novel is not a sociological study; as James Clifford describes "the making of ethnography is artisanal, tied to the world work of writing" ("Introduction: Partial Truths," 6). West's artistry is evident in the realism she brings to her characters and settings as well as the satirical perspective she brings to her representation of class stratification among the black bourgeoisie. Like Wharton, West employs a "double strategy" that both critiques and preserves "the authority of the turn-of-the-century leadership class" (Bentley, *The Ethnography of Manners*, 102). As such, challenges to the old system of manners and class privilege inevitably "accommodate the very changes that class appeared to oppose" (102). West laces her narrative with satire, and her portraits of black middle-class socialites are simultaneously reverent and derisive. Mary Helen Washington aptly identifies one of the central complexities of reading West: she is "both a fierce critic of the bourgeois life and a loyal daughter upholding the values of family and class" (xiii). *The Living is Easy* is the most consistent example of the African American novel of manners, but the double strategy and the unevenness of her satire leave readers unsure of the exact target of her critique.

Cleo Judson models how a lady navigates the perils of the drawing room through an exercise in restraint and deviousness that is wholly innate to her complex persona. The scene is a party hosted ostensibly for a dean from the south who has come to raise support for a wrongfully accused southern black man. As soon as Cleo extends a warm welcome to her guests, it is clear that she has perfected the performance of New Negro ladyhood. In addition to her stunning appearance, "when she spoke, her accent and inflection showed no detectable flaws. Her silvery chatter, her lovely, lovely laugh were bright threads weaving her guests together in a comforting assurance that this party might be taking place in a white lady's parlor" (*The Living is Easy*, 244). The table set with boiled lobster "enchanted" her guests, and the "parlor and dining room hummed with well-being" (252).

One of the first impressions Cleo's guests remark upon, after praising the lavish spread of delicacies, is her décor. The furniture in the Judson's "drawing room" – West does not use this exact term here but it is the space in which the guests find themselves – has a tarnished and recognizable history. In the course of the evening a judge remarks: "Dear Mrs. Judson, I've the oddest feeling that I've been here before. What is the magic you exercise that makes me feel completely at home in your charming house?" It is a sign of Cleo's successful penetration of the privileged spheres of the black Brahmins that they feel immediately at home in her house. Yet the reason for this familiarity has a pernicious undertone. When asked "Did you have a decorator or is your own taste your wonderful talent?" Cleo has a decision to make. Does she affirm what some of her male guests have deduced, that they recognize the furniture from a gambling den on the West end, and risk the enmity of their wives with their "expressions of innocent envy" (248)? It is a testament to her social prowess that Cleo reveals the truth, announcing that "'I am sure that all of you' – she surveyed them with a gentle smile – 'knew Lenore Binney before I met her as Simeon's fiancée. With her generous nature she was good enough to give me the benefit of her exquisite taste when I began to furnish my house'" (248). Thus Cleo reveals that she is well aware that the judge and his ilk have visited the Duchess's infamous sporting house and dares them to confess the reason for their familiarity with her acquired décor: a challenge from which the men, in the face of their women, back away from.

Thus triumphantly Cleo commences her elaborate buffet, which consists of an abundant table that notably does not include the southern fare typically associated with black food culture. Instead:

> creamed mushrooms and welsh rarebit, and plates of the startling white of turkey breast and the dark breast of wild duck. There were thin round crackers spread with a spiced mixture of cream cheese and whipped white of egg, toasted bread of triangle and diamond shapes spread with snappy cheese sprinkled with paprika, and caviar, and minced sardine, and baskets of buttered tea rolls. For the ices that were to follow were little cakes and ladyfingers. (252)

The excessive luxury of the food extracted at the high cost of her husband's invisible labor is part of the elaborate décor. It sets the stage for Cleo's *coup d'état* by invoking an atmosphere that is as distant from the south as possible. In Cleo's drawing room, removed from both the rural poverty of southern blacks or the urban challenges of the southern migrants, the Brahmins feel insulated and secure from the policies and practices of racial injustice.

Despite the alienating environment, however, Dean Galloway's story is so poignant that it still manages to evoke some support. "Against their will" the guests are moved to feel a connection with "their Southern brothers as themselves. They waited for a straw in the wind" (263). Cleo is that straw in the wind. She enacts a performance, which she has rehearsed in several mini-acts of manipulation throughout the night, that sways public opinion away from Dean Galloway and condemns her invalid brother-in-law and ultimately the Judson's fortunes, though at the time she is unaware of the connection. This act cements Cleo's status as a true Bostonian and severs all ties from the region of her birth. It is an exceptional drawing-room performance. Moreover, like the scenes from the preceding novels discussed, it has severe consequences for the witnesses as well as the targets.

In 1930 Eugene Gordon, journalist and founder of the Saturday Evening Quill, a literary society of Boston writers, penned an article entitled "Negro Society" for *Scribner's*. The article provides a detailed overview of the class stratifications of African Americans in a variety of geographic locales. At one point, he comments on color prejudice and hair straightening among upper-class black women: "It is a question of survival, not one of simple imitation; as a matter of fact, it is not imitation at all, but conformity to the customs of their country" ("Negro Society," 141). Is Gordon's reference to Wharton's novel *The Custom of the Country* coincidental? Perhaps not, but the echo is a rich one. *Scribner's* serialized the novel in 1913. West had originally hoped that her novel would be serialized in *Ladies' Home Journal*, but the editors ultimately decided against it for fear of losing advertising revenue. Cleo's single-minded quest for social advancement and influence is reminiscent of *The Custom of the Country*'s Undine Spragg, whose talent for reinvention and surface sensuality, like Cleo, hides a cold heart. Also like Cleo, Undine is famously dissatisfied, even at the apex of her social ascendance, she pathologically wonders: "she had everything she wanted but she still felt, at times, that there were other things she might want if she knew about them" (362). Unlike Undine however, Cleo does have a heart and, at the end, realizes what damage her machinations have wrought, though her anger is directed vaguely at society, rather than herself. What makes Undine a unique character is that by following the customs of the country, her performance, her false self attains her desires. As Bentley writes, the novel attributes "extraordinary mobility to a figure who is at the same time a literal poseur, a factitious model self" (*The Ethnography of Manners*, 197). In other words, Undine is a successful passer who is undisturbed by her divided self, whereas the bifurcation that draws Clare Kendry back across the color line and that masks Dianthe Lusk's African heritage is fatal.

The question of imitation has plagued racialized novels of manners and early African American women's fiction for decades. It influenced the critical reception of their fiction, which was often described as sentimental, melo-dramatic, or Victorian, and its exclusion from early literary histories of black literature. The purpose of this essay has been to show how these early black female fiction pioneers were deeply engaged in an *interracial* tradition of American writing. They foresaw diverse audiences for their fiction and wrote both within and outside of expected genres, ideologies, and styles. In following how they reshaped the novel of manners, we gain an enhanced understanding of the multiple narrative techniques they drew upon to craft their scenes and characters, and a new vantage point through which to understand the literary and ethnographic strategies deployed by the writers with whom they were in intertextual dialogue. By mapping the geography of ladyhood for African American women, these novelists also explored the advantages and pitfalls endemic to the role of the New Negro woman. By staging these imaginative explorations within the space of the African American drawing room and the genre of the novel of manners, they also propelled forward the tradition of black woman's writing by introducing complex heroines who navigate a changing racial landscape.

If Claudia Tate's and Ann duCille's foundational studies have illustrated how black women authors used the conventions of the sentimental novel to create "domestic allegories of political desire," following black women writers' transformation of the novel of manners illustrates how a distinctive African American literature emerged from an intertextual, interracial exchange of narrative strategies and representations. In shifting the novel of manners to new terrains, the writers analyzed here illuminated how class stratification worked within African American communities. Their efforts presage works like Ann Petry's *The Street* (1946), Gwendolyn Brooks's *Maud Martha* (1953), and Gloria Naylor's *Linden Hills* (1985) – all texts that pay similar attention to how social geography and location influence gender and class dynamics within American culture. Whether in Petry's uneasy marriage of literary realism and naturalism, Brooks's experimental prose-poem, or Naylor's reimagining of Dante's *Divine Comedy*, each work highlights tensions between the cultural desire for respectability and the freedom for self-expression within a society constructed to restrict and marginalize communities of color. Paying close attention to the interplay of intertextual exchange in the multiethnic spectrum of American literature illuminates the evolution of the African American heroine over the twentieth century and into the twenty-first.

Notes

1. In his analysis of Frank Webb's *The Garies and Their Friends*, which was published in London but set in Philadelphia, Otter seeks to uncover what he sees as the "intricacy and recalcitrance of these novels of racial manners" ("Frank Webb's Still Life," 729).
2. Sherrard-Johnson, "Transatlantic Collaborations"; Smith, "Second-Sight: Du Bois and the Black Masculine Gaze."
3. Pauline Hopkins served as an editor for the *Colored American Magazine* from 1900 until 1904 when she was essentially forced out by agents of Booker T. Washington, who had moved the magazine headquarters from Boston to New York.
4. Claudia Tate also notes that *Of One Blood*'s "psychic allusions invoke not only Du Bois but William and Henry James as well" in her analysis of the novel as domestic novel in which "political optimism" has "gone awry" (*Domestic Allegories of Political Desire*, 205). See also Susan Gillman's analysis of how "occult science" and forms of syncretized Western and African knowledge are "central to Hopkins's racial vision in *Of One Blood*" in "Pauline Hopkins and the Occult," 62.
5. In her comparative treatment of Hopkins's *Contending Forces* and Wharton's *House of Mirth*, Kristina Brooks reads Lily's performance as part of a *tableaux vivant* as an example of how "Wharton illustrates the extremity of Lily's self-staged social mis-step by associating her with the black slave woman, whose self was publicly and wholly commodified by others at the slave auction" ("New Woman, Fallen Woman," 103).

6. Jennie Kassanoff's excellent essay reads Lily Bart as Wharton's example of how class decline leads to racial extinction. In her final scene, which the comparison of the drawing room to a mausoleum has already foreshadowed, Lily's "final death tableau thus transforms her into the period's quintessential museum piece – the perfectly preserved taxidermic specimen" ("Extinction, Taxidermy, Tableaux Vivants," 70).

7. Seymour Krim's review "Boston Black Belt" refers to *The Living is Easy* as "an indoor novel in which the look at life is from the kitchen and the parlor" (*New York Times*, May 16, 1948).

Works cited

Baker Jr., Houston A. *Modernism and the Harlem Renaissance*. Chicago: University of Chicago Press, 1988.

Bentley, Nancy. *The Ethnography of Manners: Hawthorne, James, Wharton*. Cambridge: Cambridge University Press, 1995.

Brody, Jennifer DeVere. "Clare Kendry's 'True Colors': Race and Class Conflict in Nella Larsen's *Passing*." *Callaloo* 15.4 (Autumn 1992): 1053–65.

Brooks, Kristina. "New Woman, Fallen Woman: The Crisis of Reputation in Turn-of-the-Century Novels by Pauline Hopkins and Edith Wharton." *Legacy* 13.1 (1996): 91–111.

Brown, Lois. *Pauline Elizabeth Hopkins: Black Daughter of the American Revolution*. Chapel Hill: University of North Carolina Press, 2008.

Clifford, James. "Introduction: Partial Truths." In *Writing Culture: The Poetics and Politics of Ethnography: A School of American Research Advance Seminar*. Ed. James Clifford and George E. Marcus. Berkeley: University of California Press, 1986.

Du Bois, W. E. B. *The Souls of Black Folk*. 1903. New York: Penguin, 1989.

duCille, Ann. *The Coupling Convention: Sex, Text and Tradition in Black Women's Fiction*. New York: Oxford University Press, 1993.

Gordon, Eugene. "Negro Society." *Scribner's Magazine* 88 (August 1930):132–42.

Gillman, Susan, "Pauline Hopkins and the Occult: African American Revisions of Nine-teenth Century Sciences." *American Literary History* 8.1 (Spring 1996): 57–82.

Gillman, Susan, Alys Eve Weinbaum, and W. E. B. Du Bois, eds. *Next to the Color Line: Gender, Sexuality*. Minneapolis: University of Minnesota Press, 2007.

Hopkins, Pauline. *Of One Blood: Or, The Hidden Self. The Magazine Novels of Pauline Hopkins.* 1902–3. Introduction by Hazel Carby. New York: Oxford University Press, 1988.

James, Henry. *Turn of the Screw*. 1886. New York: W. W. Norton, 1998.

Portrait of a Lady. 1881. New York: W. W. Norton, 1995.

Kassanoff, Jennie. "Extinction, Taxidermy, Tableaux Vivants: Staging Race and Class in *The House of Mirth*." Special Topic: Rereading Class. *PMLA* 115.1 (January 2000): 60–74.

Larsen, Nella. *Passing*. 1929. New York: Penguin, 1997.

Luria, Sarah. "The Architecture of Manners: Henry James, Edith Wharton and the Mount." *American Quarterly* 49.2 (June 1997): 298–327.

McHenry, Elizabeth. "Towards a History of Access: The Case of Mary Church Terrell." *American Literary History* 19.2 (Summer 2007): 381–401.

Otten, Thomas. "Pauline Hopkins and the Hidden Self of Race." *English Literary History* 59.1 (Spring 1992): 226–57.

Otter, Samuel. "Frank Webb's Still Life: Rethinking Literature and Politics through the Garies and Their Friends." *American Literary History* 20.4 (Winter 2008): 728–52.

Sherrard-Johnson, Cherene. "Transatlantic Collaborations: Visual Culture in African American Literature." In *A Companion to African American Literature*. Ed. Gene Andrew Jarrett. Oxford: Wiley-Blackwell, 2010.

Smith, Shawn. "Second-Sight: Du Bois and the Black Masculine Gaze." In *Next to the Color Line: Gender, Sexuality and W. E. B. Du Bois*. Ed. Susan Gillman and Alys Eve Weinbaum. Minneapolis: University of Minnesota Press, 2007.

Tate, Claudia. *Domestic Allegories of Political Desire: The Black Heroine's Text at the Turn of the Century*. New York: Oxford University Press, 1992.

Tomlinson, Susan. "'Curiously Without Body': The Hidden Language of Zona Gale's *Faint Perfume*." *Modern Fiction Studies* 52.3 (Fall 2006): 570–87.

Wallinger, Hanna. *Pauline E. Hopkins: A Literary Biography*. Athens, GA: University of Georgia Press, 2005.

Washington, Mary Helen. *Preface* to Dorothy West, *The Richer, the Poorer*. New York: Doubleday, 1995.

West, Dorothy. *The Living is Easy*. 1948. New York: The Feminist Press, 1975.

Wharton, Edith. *The Custom of the Country*. 1913. New York: Penguin, 2006.

   The House of Mirth. 1905. New York: Penguin, 2000.

21

Self-made women

Novelists of the 1920s

JEAN M. LUTES

The so-called "Roaring Twenties" opened with American women getting the right to vote and went on to produce that enduring icon of female freedom, the flapper, who tossed her bobbed hair and kicked up her heels, beads flying. But when it came to serious women's fiction, the decade, according to literary historians, left us with little to celebrate. Critics have argued both that the era failed to nurture women's literary talents and that the academic establishment grew increasingly dismissive of women's writing after World War I. "In the 1920s, American women writers were demoted and degraded by a nation taking pride in its military victory," Elaine Showalter concludes in her sweeping history of American women's writing. "In the years following the armistice, women writers were gradually but systematically eliminated from the canon of American literature as it was anthologized, studied, and taught" (*A Jury of her Peers*, 294).[1] Certainly Showalter is right to observe that most women novelists of the 1920s suffered from critical neglect. Yet that neglect – as distinguished critics like Showalter have repeatedly demonstrated – is not proof positive of the insignificance of those novelists. In fact, the 1920s was a decade of intense professional success and intellectual achievement, not only for literary stars like Edith Wharton and Willa Cather, but also for a whole range of women novelists, including Dorothy Canfield Fisher, Edna Ferber, Jessie Redmon Fauset, Ellen Glasgow, Fannie Hurst, Nella Larsen, Julia Peterkin, and Anzia Yezierska. Their novels reached a broad audience of readers and achieved considerable recognition; women received five of the nine Pulitzer Prizes for fiction awarded in the 1920s.[2]

In some ways, the very visibility of these novelists contributed to their subsequent devaluation: Pulitzer Prizes and blockbuster sales created contemporary buzz but did not guarantee literary staying power; indeed, women writers' ability to attract publicity could be and was turned against them, cited as a sign of their lack of artistic integrity. The enshrinement of high literary modernism as the most important literary movement of the early twentieth century helped to make women's novels of the 1920s seem unimportant. That movement was defined, at least in part, by its rejection of the earnestness and emotionality associated (often inaccurately) with women's fiction.[3] This essay – which focuses on the high-profile Wharton and Cather but also refers to a range of other authors – builds on three decades of feminist work that has resisted such dismissals. I argue that women's fiction of this decade responded in influential and innovative ways to modernity, particularly to the rising tide of consumerism, emergent systems of publicity and celebrity, and new ideas about emotion and individuality. Women novelists creatively manipulated the vibrant mass culture of the United States and experimented in the representation of the female psyche. Adapting to the changing literary marketplace with energy and flair, many of these writers cultivated public lives as celebrity-authors, even as they offered their readers intimate portraits of the private lives of characters ranging from high-society belles to immigrant tenement-dwellers.

Why flappers had no monopoly on being modern

Despite literary history's dim view of their work, success stories for women novelists in the 1920s are easy to find. Publicists labeled Anzia Yezierska "the sweatshop Cinderella" to call attention to her spectacular rise to celebrity author from a poor Jewish immigrant community in New York City. Yezierska's first short-story collection, *Hungry Hearts*, achieved acclaim in 1920, and she quickly followed that success with another story collection and two novels, *Salome of the Tenements* (1923) and *Bread Givers* (1925). Edna Ferber – who had already attracted a large group of loyal readers with her brisk stories featuring divorced mother and traveling saleswoman Emma McChesney – found even more success in the 1920s with the publication of bestselling novels *So Big* (1924) and *Show Boat* (1926). Fannie Hurst, also already famous for the hugely popular short stories she published in magazines in the teens, attracted even more attention when her second novel, *Lummox* (1923), achieved both critical and popular success. Hurst was a well-known public figure, often quoted and pictured in newspapers. Screenwriter Anita Loos created an international sensation with her 1925 bestseller, *Gentlemen Prefer Blondes*, a hilarious satire that both promoted and mocked the flapper's status as youthful icon. The now-obscure Viña Delmar sailed to early fame with her bestselling first novel, *Bad Girl* (1928), an explicit treatment of courtship, premarital sex, abortion, and childbirth. Yet writers like Yezierska, Ferber, Hurst, Loos, and Delmar have never been considered part of American modernism in the manner of, say, Ernest Hemingway and Gertrude Stein, whose work still defines early twentieth-century American literature for most educated readers. The dominant narrative of American literary history tells us that modern women writers, with very few exceptions such as Stein, were, quite simply, not all that modern.

From the perspective of the era's glitzy, youth-centered mass culture, part of the problem was at the top of women's fiction. Even the early twentieth century's two most accomplished and recognizable women novelists, Wharton and Cather, could appear dismayingly matronly and old-fashioned, sometimes defiantly so.[4] Their age itself was not in their favor; it was a sign of the times that in promotions for *Gentlemen Prefer Blondes*, Anita Loos downplayed her age; she was in her late thirties when *Blondes* came out, but she appeared and acted much younger. By 1920, both Wharton (in her late fifties) and Cather (in her late forties) had already published several novels and achieved critical and popular recognition, Wharton mostly for her incisive depictions of the complex machinations of high-society New York, Cather mostly for her powerful narratives of the men and women who settled the west. But their relatively non-experimental approaches to narrative, combined with their status as well-established authors and their evident distaste for signature modern phenomena – such as the sexual liberation associated with the flapper and the mass-market advertising circulated by the newly powerful mass media – led many twentieth-century critics to downplay or ignore their contributions to literary modernism. Even groundbreaking feminist interpretations such as Elizabeth Ammons's "Cool Diana and the Blood-Red Muse: Edith Wharton on Innocence and Art" (1982) read Wharton as an extender of the realist tradition of women's fiction that Nina Baym had traced in the nineteenth century, rather than a vital contributor to the post-war literary ferment (216).

In the last two and a half decades, however, scholars have begun to see both Wharton and Cather as modernist authors whose work influenced the upcoming generation of literary innovators, including some of the best-known male modernists. Wharton "was writing fiction that was as 'advanced' as anything modernism produced," according to Robert A. Martin and Linda Wagner-Martin. "[Ernest] Hemingway would have been sitting at Wharton's feet, had he had the opportunity. He didn't. He did, however, read her, and owned more than half a dozen of her books" (Martin and Wagner-Martin, "The Salons of Wharton's Fiction," 108, 104). After *The Great Gatsby* was published in 1925, F. Scott Fitzgerald wrote to Cather "to explain an instance of apparent plagiarism," since he had read Cather's 1923 novel *A Lost Lady* while writing *Gatsby*, and he recognized significant similarities between the titular figure of

Cather's novel, Marian Forrester, and his own lost-generation heroine, Daisy
Buchanan (Rosowski, "Historical Essay," 225). Increasingly, critics have read
both Wharton's and Cather's fiction as definitively modernist in theme and
style.[5] Throughout her career, Wharton delighted in narrative ironies, and she
repeatedly took up taboo topics, including divorce, extramarital sex, out-of-
wedlock pregnancy, incest, and a mother who leaves her child to pursue her
own sexual satisfaction. She was also influenced by the intellectual ferment
that fueled modernist thought. Wharton's *The Age of Innocence*, which won the
Pulitzer Prize in 1921, has been read as an illustration of her deep engagement
with Henri Bergson and Albert Einstein's new theories of memory and time
(Klimasmith, "Salvaging History"). Critics have argued, likewise, that Cather's
fiction reveals significant affinities with modernist aesthetics, including a fascination with acts of meaning-making and moments of everyday witnessing
(Rose, "Modernism"; Millington, "Willa Cather's American Modernism").
Cather's *A Lost Lady* has been interpreted as "a distinctly modernist text" that
explores the cultural conflicts that shaped the emergent modernist aesthetic
after World War I (Trevitte, "Cather's *A Lost Lady* and the Disenchantment
of Art," 183).[6]

Cather's essay on the art of the novel, "The Novel Demeuble" (The Unfur-
nished Novel), was first published in *The New Republic* in 1922 and went on
to become her most important and widely read article (Woodress, *A Literary
Life*, 342). Cather makes a graceful, original argument for writerly restraint
very much in line with a high-modernist ethos, urging authors to "leave the
room bare for the play of emotions, great and little." "Whatever is felt upon
the page without being specifically named there – that, one might say, is created," Cather wrote: "It is the inexplicable presence of the thing not named,
of the overtone divined by the ear but not heard by it, the verbal mood, the
emotional aura of the fact or the thing or the deed, that gives high quality to
the novel or the drama, as well as to poetry itself" ("The Novel Demeuble,"
41–2). Cather's essay also condemns the mass-produced novel and carefully
distinguishes worthy fiction from the commercialized work that she saw as
a threat to great art. Here Cather takes a position that fits nicely into the
high-modernist disdain for writers – many of them women – who courted
masses of readers. That disdain was not uniform or complete, however, as
David M. Earle's *Re-Covering Modernism* has demonstrated. Earle shows that
William Faulkner and Ernest Hemingway both benefited from their association with the decidedly populist venue of pulp magazines. A close look at
Wharton's and Cather's own negotiation of the high-stakes game of literary
publicity shows that they, too, profited from their association with more

popular forms of mass-print culture. Predictably, however, the reputations of male writers proved more impervious to the perceived taint of mass culture than the reputations of female writers. In part because mass-print culture was already feminized, inextricably linked to the growing importance of female consumers as a key audience for advertising, the stigma of mass culture attached all the more firmly to the women writers who forged their careers in a dynamic relationship with it. Wharton's and Cather's deep ambivalence about the mass-print phenomenon reflects their awareness of this problem.

Doing away with the awning?: Wharton

Despite their discomfort with consumer culture, both Wharton and Cather manipulated advertising and publicity to their advantage. Scholars are just beginning to explore the commercial magazine context in which many of their novels were serialized before being published as books, but biographers of both women have already offered ample evidence that Wharton and Cather negotiated a volatile literary marketplace with remarkable success. Wharton (1862–1937) – born into a wealthy, socially prominent family in which women were expected to dress well and get married, not to read and write – transformed herself into a well-respected, prolific professional, aided in part by her father's early tolerance for (and indulgence of) her passion for reading. Wharton was attentive to the advertising used to promote her books, and she did not hesitate to complain directly to her publishers when she felt her work was being neglected. "Certainly in these days of energetic and emphatic advertising, Mr. Scribner's methods do not tempt one to offer him one's wares a second time," Wharton concluded in an April 1899 letter to her publisher after expressing her disappointment in the minimal advertising for her short-story collection, *The Great Inclination* (Bell, "Lady into Author," 296–8). Wharton complained again in 1911 after the slow sales of *Ethan Frome* (Lewis, *Edith Wharton*, 311), and she negotiated hard for higher royalties as her work became more popular.[7] Although she did not leave the genteel Scribner's as immediately as she threatened in 1899, she did use bids from rival publishers to get better deals, and she eventually switched for good to Appleton in the 1920s, when Scribner's publishing house was unable to keep up with the broad audience and the large profits offered by the slick, newer (and less explicitly literary) magazines, which targeted a mostly female readership (Bell, "Lady into Author," 305–6; Lewis, *Edith Wharton*, 395–6).

    The Age of Innocence was serialized – appearing alongside advertisements for complexion powder, corsets, brassieres, and antiperspirant – in the women's magazine *Pictorial Review* in 1920 and then published by Appleton to great fanfare, including "lavish advertising," pronouncing Wharton "the greatest woman novelist in America" (Lewis, *Edith Wharton*, 429). In 1905, Wharton had objected to scandal-mongering advertisements when Scribner's promoted *The House of Mirth* by promising that it would share never-before-told secrets of high society (Lee, *Edith Wharton*, 201). By 1920, however, Wharton voiced no objections when Appleton promoted *The Age of Innocence* with an advertisement headlined, "WAS SHE JUSTIFIED IN SEEKING DIVORCE?" The advert continued, "Why was this American girl forced to leave her brutal Polish husband? Why did Ellen, Countess Alenska [*sic*], return to New York, seeking to forget? . . . All the glamor of the society life of the original Four Hundred is the background for this story, the nights at the opera, the balls, the intimate amusements of the society leaders of the day" (quoted in Lee, *Edith Wharton*, 588). *Pictorial Review* promoted its serialization of the novel with a letter competition for readers, inviting them to share their thoughts about marriage and asking directly, "Does Your Husband Really Love You?" (quoted in Lee, *Edith Wharton*, 593). *Age of Innocence* sold extremely well, outpacing Fitzgerald's and Hemingway's sales and making Wharton nearly $70,000 in a two-year period (Klimasmith, "Salvaging History," 581; Lewis, *Edith Wharton*, 429–30).[8]

Wharton did not always enjoy publishing in venues like *Pictorial Review*, no matter how remunerative it was; she expressed outrage when an editor told her they planned to cut the installments to make space for illustrations and advertisements, responding haughtily, "I cannot consent to have my work treated as prose by the yard" (Benstock, *No Gifts from Chance*, 361–2). Still, she was more than pleased by the novel's popularity, and she followed with the runaway bestseller *Glimpses of the Moon* (1922), also serialized in *Pictorial Review* and published by Appleton. On the inside flap of the jacket for *Glimpses of the Moon* appeared a formal portrait of Wharton in furs with seed pearls in her hair, photographed in Paris in 1920 (Benstock, *No Gifts from Chance*, 369). Two decades earlier, in a dialogue published in *Scribner's* when she was on the brink of attaining literary fame, Wharton revealed her own fascination with literary celebrity and with the ways that private lives become public through an imagined reunion between ex-lovers, a famous female novelist, and a famous male poet. At one point, the famous novelist observes, "I died years ago. What you see before you is a figment of a reporter's brain – a monster manufactured out of newspaper paragraphs, with ink in its veins" ("Copy," 658). By the 1920s, Wharton had become, in some sense, one of those monsters, but she somehow found ways to manage the role without being subsumed by it. And she had already explored, in fiction like *The Custom of the Country* (1913), the psychic consequences of living in a media-saturated world.

The narrator's ironic references to publicity in *The Age of Innocence*, set in the "old New York" of the 1870s and published in 1920, suggest that Wharton had some fun calling attention to the striking changes in attitudes toward media exposure that occurred in the fifty years that elapsed between the novel's setting and its time of publication. One of the novel's most memorable figures, Catherine Manson Mingott, the eccentric, enormously overweight matriarch of the society family into which Newland Archer is marrying, is usually housebound. As her granddaughter's wedding to Archer approaches, however, Mrs. Manson Mingott horrifies her relatives by expressing interest in attending the nuptials, threatening her family, the narrator tells us, with a "monstrous exposure of her person." She even considers having the church awning dismantled to make room for her wheelchair, but, as the narrator explains:

> The idea of doing away with this awning, and revealing the bride to the mob of dressmakers and newspaper reporters who stood outside fighting to get near the joints of the canvas, exceeded even old Catherine's courage, though for a moment she had weighed the possibility. "Why, they might take a photograph of my child *and put it in the papers!*" Mrs. Welland [the bride's mother] exclaimed when her mother's last plan was hinted to her; and from this unthinkable indecency the clan recoiled with a collective shudder. (*The Age of Innocence*, 156–7)

The narrator invites us to chuckle at the expense of these publicity-shy socialites, who shudder at the thought of a bride's picture appearing in the newspaper. As the ironic tone of this passage intimates, the novel does not celebrate this bygone era as an innocent age. At other moments in the novel, Wharton reminds her readers, in effect, that an audience-oriented subjectivity could easily co-exist with a pronounced tendency to shun public exposure. At one point, the Countess Ellen Olenska, the intellectually free, independent-minded, Europeanized heroine of the novel, complains to her would-be lover, Archer, about the lack of privacy in American households: "I always feel as if I were in the convent again – or on the stage, before a dreadfully polite audience that never applauds" (114). Ellen expresses her recognition that she is always on stage, even when she is supposedly most protected from the public glare, when she unexpectedly yokes the protected private sphere of the convent to the unprotected public sphere of the theater: in both cases, she suggests, she is performing for others. Indeed, most of *Age of Innocence*'s ethnographic description of society rituals involves precisely that: the characters are always performing for each other, perhaps most determinedly for their closest intimates. After May Welland and Newland Archer are married, their exchanges are described as carefully scripted, determined by conventions in place long before they ever met each other. When, toward the narrative's conclusion, May hosts an elaborate farewell dinner for Ellen as an unspoken sign of her triumph over her rival for her husband's affection, Archer recognizes himself as a participant in "a conspiracy of rehabilitation and obliteration" (288), even as he feels his love for Ellen more powerfully than ever before. In the novel's final chapter, set in Paris twenty-six years after that farewell dinner, Wharton contrasts Archer's emotional restraint (he's now a widower) with the frankness of his son, who has learned of his father's long-ago love for Ellen and arranged a reunion. As Archer sits on a bench outside Ellen's apartment building (he has sent his son up in his stead), he contemplates another awning, perhaps an echo of the church awning that shielded Archer's bride on their wedding day. Until darkness falls, Archer gazes at the awning that is located over the balcony of Ellen's apartment (305–7). As a contemplative spectator of an event he cannot actually see, Archer finds that despite his yearnings for freedom, he, like Mrs. Manson Mingott, cannot do away with the awning. Wharton's final vision of Archer in the dusk adopts a modernist attitude towards the performance of intimacy, even as it acknowledges some of the rewards of being shielded from public view.

In touch with her time: Cather

Unlike Wharton, Willa Cather (1873–1947) was employed for years as a journalist and editor before she began to support herself as a full-time author, and in those various positions, she became intimately acquainted with some of the editorial processes that shaped the changing literary marketplace.[9] One critic has argued that Cather "was so well-grounded in the business of marketing fiction that she felt compelled to defend an autonomous ideal of art even as her awareness of economic realities would have compelled her to recognize the limits of such an ideal" (Trevitte, "Cather's A Lost Lady," 204). Cather's early work as a newspaper drama critic and her well-known fascination with famous actresses and opera singers exposed her to the culture of celebrity that emerged in the late nineteenth century and drew her, while she was still in college, into the process by which artists became not just public figures but commodities, consumed by a mass public (Schueth, "A Portrait of an Artist," 33–7). From 1906 to 1911, Cather's editorial work at *McClure's*, a magazine known for its visual appeal, educated her in the impact of new technologies for mass-producing images. She dramatized the vexed relation between celebrity status and artistic achievement directly in her 1920 story "Coming, Aphrodite!," in which an artistically committed male painter falls in love with an ambitious young opera singer who betrays him when she fails to understand why he prizes artistic integrity over commercial success. At the story's conclusion, the singer returns to New York in a triumphant production of "Coming, Aphrodite!" and goes out of her way to learn that her former lover has had an influential career in art, although he has never earned popular acclaim. In the last paragraph, the singer's face becomes "hard and settled, like a plaster cast; so a sail, that has been filled by a strong breeze, behaves when the wind suddenly dies. Tomorrow night, the wind would blow again, and this mask would be the golden face of Aphrodite. But a 'big' career takes its toll, even with the best of luck" ("Coming, Aphrodite!" 101). Like Wharton's "monster" with ink in her veins, Cather's brittle mask of Aphrodite reflects a disturbing vision of an artist whose fame threatens her humanity. And like Wharton, Cather sought ways to wear the mask herself while mitigating its more negative consequences.

Although Cather deflected attention from her own involvement in the machinery of mass culture and sought to protect herself and her books from commercial imperatives (Rosowski, "Historical Essay," 178), critics have shown that Cather demonstrated "a shrewd ability" to fit her authorial persona – which often seemed so *anti*-modern – into a decidedly modern celebrity culture. A 1926 typescript shows that a short interview with Cather, published in the *Nebraska State Journal*, was actually a bit of fiction Cather manufactured, presumably to promote her own work; she wrote both parts of the Q-and-A article herself (Porter, "Cather on Cather II," 53). Cather worked closely with publicity departments of her publishing houses and sent out photographs for magazine and newspaper profiles. Although she remained famously protective of her privacy and ambivalent about her status as a public figure, she left behind a substantial legacy of photographic portraits, including one by celebrity photographer Edward Steichen published in *Vanity Fair* in 1927. As Michael Schueth suggests, the many photographic portraits of Cather reveal that she collaborated with other artists to create and control her authorial persona, and she carefully "managed her career in the increasingly celebrity-driven literary marketplace" ("Cather and her Stars," 47–9). Cather proved to be a skillful businesswoman and publicist, and in the 1920s she was working especially hard to assure her reputation and shape her public image.

Concerned about the critical reception of her war novel, *One of Ours* (1922), Cather reached out to potential reviewers – not only her friend Dorothy Canfield Fisher, but also Carl Van Doren, H. L. Mencken, and William Allen White – before the novel was published, hoping to enhance the book's appeal (Stout, "Willa Cather and her Public in 1922," 29–32). Her efforts, for the most part, failed to generate positive reviews; *One of Ours* was widely panned by critics for its unconvincing characterization of its soldier-hero. It sold well, however, and it was awarded the Pulitzer Prize.

Overall, the decade was an immensely productive one for Cather. Several of her most highly regarded novels – *A Lost Lady*, *The Professor's House* (1925), and *Death Comes for the Archbishop* (1927) – were published in the 1920s. Cather paid careful attention to book advertising and, like Wharton, she changed publishers when she felt her professional interests were not being well served. In 1921, Cather told her editor at Houghton Mifflin that she was publishing her next novel, *One of Ours*, with Alfred Knopf, mainly because Knopf's publicity strategies were better: Knopf's advertisements were more aggressive than the reserved, formal promotional copy Houghton Mifflin had used to publicize Cather's previous work (Hamilton, "Advertising Cather," 13). Cather's business acumen is also evident in her profitable association with the Book-of-the-Month Club, which began in 1926. That association had complex effects on her literary reputation: Mark Madigan argues that although the Book-of-the-Month Club expanded her readership significantly, it also reinforced a vision of Cather as a "highly skilled but conventional novelist who was out of touch with her time" ("Willa Cather and the Book-of-the-Month Club," 80). This conclusion suggests the paradoxical results of popularity and the curse of the so-called middlebrow novelist, whose ability to appeal to a large group of readers could become, oddly, a vulnerability – a sign that she was not on the cutting edge of literary innovation. Cather appeared "out of touch with her time" because she was out of touch with the most influential literary tastemakers of the day, not with the majority of readers themselves.

Cather thematized her preoccupation with time – not with timeliness, but rather with the passage of time itself – in many of her novels of the 1920s. The problem of time is central to the elegiac *A Lost Lady*, which was serialized in the *Century* and provided Cather's first major critical success of the 1920s, a welcome triumph after the disappointing reviews of *One of Ours*.[10] Like Wharton's *Age of Innocence*, *A Lost Lady* looks backward: in the opening sentence, the narrator locates the novel's time frame as "thirty or forty years ago" (the 1880s or 1890s) and its setting as "one of those grey towns along the Burlington railroad, which are so much greyer today than they were then" (*A Lost Lady*,

3). Thus the decline of the small town is forecast from the very beginning, and the sense of generational loss (which would also be strong in Ferber's *So Big*) is palpable immediately. The novel recounts the fate of a small-town boy's admiring attachment to a pioneering railroad man, Captain Forrester, and his beautiful wife, Marian Forrester, the "lost lady" of the title. From the opening pages, Marian, who is twenty-five years younger than her husband, is represented as irresistibly charming. The novel represents both Marian's struggle to deal with Captain Forrester's decline, death, and loss of fortune and the struggle of Niel Herbert, the boy who idolizes her, to maintain his faith in his womanly ideal even as Marian's drinking, adultery, and dissolution challenge that faith. Cather rewrote the manuscript three times, as she sought to find "the right balance between the objectivity of her third-person narration and the intimacy of her controlled limitation of perspective to the mind of a young boy" (Schroeter, *Willa Cather and her Critics*, 23). Although the narrative obviously honors the bygone heroism of male pioneers like Captain Forrester and mourns the rise of money-grubbing "new men" like Ivy Peters, a nasty character who blinds a woodpecker for fun in the book's opening pages, Cather also manages to represent the emotional complexity and vitality of Marian, the woman whose choices so disappoint her young male admirer. When Marian tumbles off her nineteenth-century domestic pedestal and accepts Ivy Peters as a lover, the narrative documents not only Niel Herbert's feelings of betrayal, but also the persistence of Marian's will to live in the modern world of commerce and publicity that Niel finds so distasteful. Like Wharton in *The Age of Innocence*, however, Cather reminds her readers that even in the flush times of Captain Forrester's successes, social conventions exerted a powerful – and sometimes distorting and stultifying – effect. Niel repeatedly remarks upon the rigid rituals that govern the Forresters' interactions, and throughout the novel he is intrigued by Marian's status as a charismatic public figure; his musings position her as a carefully constructed persona whose ability to create a sense of privileged intimacy (especially with men) is critical to her husband's own social status.

The managed heart: psychic interiority in women's novels

The tremendously varied narratives produced by women novelists did not, as a rule, reimagine narrative conventions in the overt way practiced by some of the best-known modernist innovators such as Stein and Faulkner. Yet their work was influential and formally innovative nonetheless. They created new narrative models for depicting psychic interiority, devoted to disclosing women's new realities in the early twentieth century. Those realities were shaped by broad social changes such as the rise of women working outside the home, increased openness about female sexuality, expanding educational opportunities for women, the explosion of mass culture in print and film, and changes in domestic technologies and products designed to minimize the work of homemaking. These changing conditions for women were accompanied by fundamental changes in ideas about where individual feelings come from and how women's (and men's) emotional lives were best understood. Unlike the emotional realism associated with the nineteenth-century sentimental tradition, the new representations of psychic interiority were influenced by ideas about the sources of emotion generated by the scientific discipline of psychology, which grew in power and prominence in the late nineteenth and early twentieth centuries. Psychologists circulated two contradictory notions at the same time: on the one hand, they believed that emotions could be managed and controlled; on the other, they believed that emotions were biomechanical, produced spontaneously within the body and thus uncontrollable. This split vision, as feminist psychologist Jill G. Morawski has shown, represented emotions "as natural, organic states *and* as artificial, malleable, and indeed correctable ones. Humans were rendered both natural and artificial simultaneously" ("Educating the Emotions," 234). Many women's novels offered intensely fractured characterizations of women's inner lives, featuring characters caught in this very tension.

In Dorothy Canfield Fisher's 1924 bestseller, *The Homemaker*, for instance, a wife and mother who keeps a perfect house is consumed by rage and despair because she hates housework and resents the way her young children inevitably disrupt domestic order. Her psychological state manifests itself not only in violent outbursts of temper but also in a painful, embarrassing skin condition. Yet when her husband loses his job and she is forced to work outside the home, she finds meaning, purpose, and calm: her skin condition disappears and she is able to enjoy her family's company again. In Fisher's novel, emotions are both organic (determined by forces outside the character's control) and correctable (subject to change based on the character's choices). Emotional management proved crucial to the culture of consumption created by mass-market advertising in the decades leading up to the 1920s.[11] It is not surprising, then, that Fisher's homemaker finds professional success and personal fulfillment as the retail manager for a large department store. Advertisers promoted consumption as a mode of self-expression and an emotional outlet, helping to create a culture in which inner lives and retail purchases were assumed to be inextricably intertwined. Arguably, the more radical element of Fisher's novel is found in her characterization of the father whose career founders: when he has to quit work after he is paralyzed in an accident, he discovers a passion for childrearing.[12]

In a somewhat more conventional "bootstraps" narrative, Anzia Yezierska's *Bread Givers* (1925) depicts its Jewish immigrant heroine as deeply divided in her struggle to become educated: she is both strikingly disciplined in her pursuit of the American dream and still subject to psychic fracture and loss of emotional control. Notably, Yezierska depicts respect for retail goods as a key aspect of the heroine's Americanization. When her mother dies, she earns the scorn of her community when she challenges the Jewish mourning ritual by refusing to tear the good clothes she has purchased with her own hard-earned money. Even at the end of the novel, when her years of work and determination have been rewarded with a steady teaching job and a loving boyfriend, the heroine continues to feel a deep conflict between her American successes and the harsh judgments of her father, an Orthodox rabbi: "I felt the shadow still there, over me. It wasn't just my father, but the generations who made my father whose weight was still upon me" (*Bread Givers*, 297). Yezierska portrays the female psyche riven by competing demands of Old World traditions shaped by religious institutions and New World expectations shaped by a secular consumer society. Her emotional destiny is simultaneously a bodily one, formed by her ethnic heritage, her environment, and the personal desires that emerge in response to those influences.[13]

Other novelists explored female emotion and consumerism without giving readers even the measured happy ending that Yezierska allowed her heroine. Nella Larsen's *Quicksand* (1928) – a first novel which was well reviewed when it appeared and has since been celebrated as a signal modernist achievement – suggests an intricate relation between consumer environments and psychological states as it follows its mixed-race heroine's search for identity. Larsen's fiction imagines the female psyche as both natural and artificial, susceptible to management but never wholly controllable. Even as the heroine, Helga, finds herself stifled by racial prescriptions and assumptions, she cultivates a sense of personal style in clothes and domestic accessories, always seeking to express an interiority she is hard pressed to define. Toward the end of the novel, the narrator represents Helga's pseudo-conversion experience in an African American revival meeting – which leads to her final entrapment in the "quicksand" of marriage and childbearing – as both a choice and a physical collapse: "as Helga watched and listened, gradually a curious influence penetrated her; she felt an echo of the weird orgy resound in her own heart; she felt herself possessed by the same madness; she too felt a brutal desire to shout and to sling herself about . . . She had eaten nothing since yesterday. She fell forward against the crude railing which enclosed the little platform. For a single moment she remained there in silent stillness . . . And in that moment she was lost – or saved" (*Quicksand*, 114). Helga's "moment" is caused by her own sense of emotional loss *and* her biological drives for both food and sex; in the days that follow, she surrenders her sense of self not just to the call of the spirit, but to her sexual desire for the minister himself, whom she promptly marries. Larsen's grim ending leaves little doubt that Helga is, in fact, lost in that moment. As the novel concludes, Helga – overwhelmed by one pregnancy after another, alienated from her husband and from the Christian community – recovers from a deep postpartum depression only to become pregnant immediately with her fifth child.

Larsen's second novel, *Passing* (1929), again represents women caught in a byzantine matrix of racial assumptions, consumer culture, and sexual desire, their emotions emerging from a jumble of physical imperatives and artificial constraints.[14] Jessie Redmon Fauset's presentation of color- and class-conscious African American heroines in *There is Confusion* (1924) and *Plum Bun* (1929) takes up similar issues; Fauset depicts women torn by misdirected desires, stymied by a racist and sexist environment where the pursuit of artistic aspirations seems to require a (misguided) separation from the black community that has nurtured them.[15]

In a very different vein, Julia Peterkin created a primitivist fantasy of maternal power through the African American protagonist of her Pulitzer Prize-winning novel, *Scarlet Sister Mary* (1928). Unlike Larsen's Helga, Peterkin's heroine finds renewal and meaning in childbearing. As a white southern author who expressed her own emotional conflicts through the perspective of black characters, Peterkin requires us to consider complex questions about authorship and authenticity. Yet through Mary, the sinner of the novel's title, Peterkin offers a compelling portrait of a woman whose rich inner life is made possible by both her biological imperatives and her self-conscious decisions, particularly her ability to shrug off social censure and find her own way within a racially defined community.

Even Willa Cather, who tended to take a more mythic approach to her narratives, representing her characters from the outside rather than detailing their inner thoughts, devised methods for imagining the tension between biology and culture that characterized the modern approach to interiority. In *The Professor's House* (1925), the narrator's description of Tom Outland's revelatory experience on the Blue Mesa posits the source of his emotion as *both* internal and external, a state that emerges from within a dynamic relationship between his physical body and his material surroundings. When Tom returns to the Mesa alone, as he watches the sun set and the stars come out, he finds himself connected to the Mesa in a way he had never felt before:

> in a sense, that was the first night I was ever really on the mesa at all – the first night that all of me was there. This was the first time I ever saw it as a whole. It all came together in my understanding, as a series of experiments do when you begin to see where they are leading. Something had happened in me that made it possible for me to co-ordinate and simplify, and that process, going on in my mind, brought with it great happiness. It was possession. The excitement of my first discovery was a very pale feeling compared to this one. For me the mesa was no longer an adventure, but a religious emotion. (*The Professor's House*, 250–1)

In its direct declarative sentences, its restrained use of adjectives, its repetition of "first," even its crystal-clear pattern of referents for pronouns, the narrative style of this passage coordinates and simplifies, echoing the mental process that Tom apparently achieves on the Mesa. In a novel that bemoans the distractions of material excesses, Tom's claim to "possession" is both striking and worrisome; he cannot actually own the Mesa, obviously, so what does possession mean in this context? It is possible to read Tom's revelation as a troubling instance of Euro-Americans appropriating the ancient history of the continent's original inhabitants as their own. Yet it is also possible to read this moment as a redefinition of possession itself; "possession" becomes an expression of physical and emotional connection to the landscape. Tom describes the impact of his possession-inspired religious emotion as physical:

> It was my high tide. Every morning, when the sun's rays first hit the mesa top, while the rest of the world was in shadow, I wakened with the feeling that I had found everything, instead of having lost everything. Nothing tired me. Up there alone, a close neighbour to the sun, I seemed to get the solar energy in some direct way. And at night, when I watched it drop down behind the edge of the plain below me, I used to feel that I couldn't have borne another hour of that consuming light, that I was full to the brim, and needed dark and sleep. (251–2)

Tom's transcendent experience, linked to the natural cycle of the rising and setting sun, energizes his mind and body. To put it baldly, the sunlight enables his intellectual enlightenment. Cather links biology and culture here, since Tom uses his "high tide" for studying: "It was the first time I'd ever studied methodically, or intelligently. I got the better of the Spanish grammar and read the twelve books of the Æneid" (251).

Despite the frequent focus on psychic interiority, the emotional excess often negatively associated with women's fiction is, strikingly, *not* in evidence in the 1920s. Edna Ferber's *So Big* (1925), a bestseller which won a Pulitzer Prize, is a case in point. It chronicles the life of the enterprising Selina DeJong, left destitute first by her gambler-father and again by her husband, who turns her husband's struggling vegetable farm into a thriving business. Ferber's rollicking narrative – packed with period-specific details about turn-of-the-century Chicago and the surrounding region – centers on Selina's energy and love of beauty, rather than her interior life; her inner desires manifest only as they are channeled into tireless efforts to ensure that her son's future is secure. Selina's only real failure is the generational decline she is unable to forestall: the novel's second half shows how her son, for whom she has provided all the opportunities denied to her, fails to find a meaningful vocation and instead leads a privileged, empty, consumerist existence; the narrative ends with the son realizing he has become "nothing but a rubber stamp" (*So Big*, 358). In service of Ferber's critique of contemporary materialism, the narrator describes the son's corrupted psyche in far greater detail than Selina's healthier one.[16]

We find another work-obsessed farmer-heroine in Ellen Glasgow's *Barren Ground* (1925), a woman who denies all sexual desire when, as a young woman, she is jilted by her lover and essentially freezes her emotional life, creating her own numbness. When the heroine's mother dies, she reacts conventionally – "For a few minutes she broke down and wept, less from grief than from the knowledge that grief was expected of her" (*Barren Ground*, 266) – but her own interior life remains a mystery to her, and her work on the farm functions as her primary expression of self. Even Fannie Hurst, the popular novelist who was called a "sob sister" because of the emotional and stylistic excesses in her fiction, offered a relatively restrained depiction of her heroine's emotion in *Lummox* (1923). A major critical and commercial success for Hurst, the novel tracks the path of a long-suffering, large-bodied cleaning woman who is impregnated by the son of one of her employers. Hurst's emphasis on her heroine's physical size is significant here as a reflection of the biomechanical approach to psychic interiority. Throughout, the novel stresses the disjunction between the character's intense bodily experience (the organic source of her emotion) and her inability to translate that experience into language. Hurst's fiction is full of such intermingling of body and emotion; her plots return almost obsessively to physical manifestations of psychic pain. Her characterizations repeatedly depict bodies and psyches intermingled, so that her literary vision straddles modern psychology's competing commitments to biological determinism and individual control. These novels demonstrate that the supposedly banal appeal to heart-wrenching emotion is, in fact, not a primary characteristic of women's fiction of the 1920s. Implicitly, these novelists do ask their readers to identify with their protagonists, yet the complexity of their depictions of psychic interiority belies the application of any single, reductive narrative formula.

Against a female tradition?

The caption under a photograph of Cather published in the 1927 *Vanity Fair* called her "An American Pioneer" and announced that "Today, after twenty-two years of scrupulous craftsmanship, she is the heir apparent to Edith Wharton's lonely eminence among America's women novelists" (*Vanity Fair*, July 1927, 30). Neither Wharton nor Cather, it is worth noting, aspired to attain such eminence among American *women* writers. Wharton's friend Henry James probably influenced her at least as powerfully as any woman novelist did, and Cather's spare aesthetic had more in common with Hemingway than either Cather or Hemingway would have liked to admit.[17] In many ways, Wharton and Cather did not see themselves as writing in a female literary tradition; as if to prove their detachment, both slipped dismissive references to wildly popular novels from that tradition into their own novels. In *Summer* (1917), Wharton's heroine kills time in a musty small-town library by knitting lace, which she keeps wound around "a disintegrated copy" of Maria Cummins's 1854 bestseller, *The Lamplighter*. In *A Lost Lady* (1923), Cather's narrator characterizes her male protagonist's incommodious home life by noting the slovenly habits of the family's housekeeper, "who liked to sit down after breakfast and read murder trials, or peruse a well-worn copy of *St. Elmo*" (*A Lost Lady*, 29–30), August Jane Evans's smash hit of 1866. In Wharton's and Cather's vision, these widely circulated and influential women's novels – which have since been taken up by feminist literary historians as compelling objects of study in their own right – are rendered inert, better used as coasters or doorstops than for their intended purpose. Such gestures, of course, acknowledge the ongoing power of the very legacy they denigrate. Despite their own ambivalence toward the category of women's writing, reading Cather and Wharton *as* women writers has immeasurably enriched our appreciation for the complexity of their work. Attending to the ways that gender intersects with their other defining themes – which are as varied as the nature of desire, the emergence of national identity, the landscape's effect on individual consciousness, and the imprisoning but often comforting strength of social convention – reveals both the impressive nature of their achievement and the broad social impact of their work. At least as important, acknowledging the significance of their gender explains their uncertain place in literary history far more effectively than their perceived lack of stylistic and thematic innovation. Given the variety of powerful (and popular) narratives produced by women novelists in the 1920s, it is telling that the 1927 *Vanity Fair* promotion for Cather argued that she was in line to succeed Wharton in "lonely eminence." The line implies not just that most woman-authored fiction was not very good, but also that there was limited room at the top for women writers, anyway.

Of course, Wharton and Cather do not need to be "recovered" at this point. Even if their precise place (as realists or modernists, as formal innovators or highly skilled conventionalists) is still subject to debate, their work has been, and continues to be, studied with enthusiasm and meticulousness by feminist and non-feminist scholars alike. But the ambivalence that Wharton and Cather themselves manifest toward their female contemporaries and precursors remains a dominant strand in American literary history. As new scholarship emerges on novelists such as Canfield Fisher, Ferber, Hurst, Larsen, Fauset, and Yezierska, these writers continue to be unevenly and incompletely integrated into the broad narrative of literary modernism – a narrative that demands our attention because it organizes the way most readers still understand early twentieth-century literature. The tremendous outpouring of critical studies on mass culture and literary modernism has done an excellent job of exploring the significance of the most popular, "lowbrow" forms of culture. But the vast middle ground of print culture – in which formal innovations in narrative style were less confrontational, and in which women's magazines and serialized fiction played such a large role – remains largely unaccounted for in these repositionings. Loren Glass's fine study of modern literary celebrity, *Authors Inc.*, which includes only one woman writer (Gertrude Stein), is a good example. Glass argues that women writers were, by and large, excluded from the mode of literary celebrity that allowed writers "to straddle elite and mainstream audiences" (*Authors Inc.*, 17). Glass's astute analysis of the masculinist bias of celebrity authorship in the modern era, however, cannot help us to understand a popular figure such as Fannie Hurst. Even as his book tells us why writers like Hurst were necessarily excluded from membership in the elite realm of literary authorship, it raises a different question: What impact did writers like Hurst have? Tracing the process of these writers' marginalization is not equivalent to articulating the significance of their writing – in the history of ideas, the history of aesthetics, and the history of women. This work remains to be done. Until it is, American literary history will not fully appreciate the 1920s, a decade that roared with the voices of women novelists.

Notes

1. In "Cool Diana and the Blood-Red Muse: Edith Wharton on Innocence and Art," Elizabeth Ammons asserts that women's literary work in this decade was, by and large, not distinguished: "The twenties, as even the most cursory literary survey will show, did not generate women writers in the United States. New talent was not nurtured" (223).
2. Wharton in 1921 for *Age of Innocence*, Cather in 1923 for *One of Ours*, Margaret Wilson in 1924 for *The Able McLaughlins*, Edna Ferber in 1925 for *So Big*, Julia Peterkin in 1929 for *Scarlet Sister Mary*.
3. For an early version of this argument, see Suzanne Clark's *Sentimental Modernism* (1991).
4. Wharton, for instance, chose to set her 1920 triumph, *The Age of Innocence*, in the 1870s, fifty years in the past, leaving her open to accusations of nostalgia, and she titled her 1934 memoir *Looking Backward*. Cather, for her part, "increasingly fell into the habit in the twenties of regarding herself as radically removed from her time" (Schroeter, *Willa Cather and her Critics*, 22), and she appeared to deliberately exclude younger readers from the intended audience of her 1936 essay collection, pointedly titled *Not Under Forty*.
5. Amy Kaplan's analysis of Wharton as a literary professional immersed in consumer culture is a good early example of such work ("Edith Wharton's Profession of Authorship"). For more studies of Wharton's modernism, see Klimasmith, "Salvaging History"; Singley, "Bourdieu, Wharton, and Changing Culture in *The Age of Innocence*"; Bauer, *Edith Wharton's Brave New Politics*; and essays collected in Joslin and Price (eds.), *Wretched Exotic: Essays on Edith Wharton in Europe*, and Bell (ed.), *The Cambridge Companion to Edith Wharton*; on Cather's modernism, see Wilson, *Melting-Pot Modernism*; Millington, "Where is Cather's Quebec?," and "Willa Cather's American Modernism"; Reynolds, *Willa Cather in Context*; Urgo, *Willa Cather and the Myth of American Migration*; and Rose, "Modernism: The Case of Willa Cather."
6. In another compelling reading of *A Lost Lady* as modernist, Janis P. Stout suggests that the gaps in Cather's narratives "are perhaps the most visible manifestation of Cather's affinity with modernism"; Stout calls these gaps "vacancies that fracture the text, opening it to indeterminacy and leading us to ask questions for which answers are not supplied" (Stout, *Willa Cather*, 192). Hermione Lee writes that *A Lost Lady* is "as teasing and elusive as more ostentatiously modernist narratives" (207).
7. For more instances of Wharton's attempts to manage the advertising and promotion of her novels – as well as a thoughtful discussion of how mass-market print culture shaped Wharton's literary vision – see Paul Ohler's forthcoming essay in *English Studies*

in Canada, "Forms of Ambivalence to 'Tabloid Culture' in Edith Wharton's *The Custom of the Country*."

8. For more details on *Pictorial Review's* advertising, see Lee, *Edith Wharton*, 587–93. For illuminating studies of *Pictorial Review* as a consumer-oriented context for Wharton's serialized fiction, see Thornton, "'Innocence' Consumed," and "Selling Edith Wharton."

9. For details about Cather's editorial work and the commercial context of magazine fiction, see Bradley, "To Entertain"; Bucker, "'That Kitchen with the Shining Windows'"; and Lavin, "Intellectual Warfare."

10. *A Lost Lady* was an unqualified success: it was published to near-universal acclaim and it sold well (Gerber, *Willa Cather*, 31; Robinson, *Willa: The Life of Willa Cather*, 239; McFarland, *Willa Cather*, 62). In 1934, it also became the only one of Cather's novels made into a film; the adaptation was so disastrous that Cather never again allowed any of her novels to be made into films (Schueth, "Taking Liberties"; Rosowski, "Historical Essay," 223–5).

11. In a 1983 study, sociologist Arlie Russell Hochschild coined the phrase "the managed heart" to describe the emotional labor required by the profit imperatives of twentieth-century commerce.

12. For commentary on Canfield Fisher, see Harker, *America the Middlebrow*; Parchesky, "The Business of Living and the Labor of Love" and "'You Make Us Articulate'"; and Ehrhardt, *Writers of Conviction*.

13. For commentary on Yezierska, see Mikkelsen "From Sympathy to Empathy"; Botshon, "The New Woman of the Tenements"; Piper, "The Making of an American"; Friedman, "Marriage and the Immigrant Narrative"; Xavier, "Decontaminating the Canon"; and Botshon and Goldsmith, *Middlebrow Moderns*.

14. For commentary on Larsen, see Harrison-Kahan, "'Structure Would Equal Meaning'"; Scheper, "The New Negro Flâneuse in Nella Larsen's *Quicksand*"; Hutchinson, *In Search of Nella Larsen*; Jenkins, "Decoding Essentialism"; Zackodnik, "Passing Transgressions"; and Davis, *Nella Larsen, Novelist of the Harlem Renaissance*.

15. For commentary on Fauset, see Garcia, "Jessie Redmon Fauset Reconsidered"; Harker, *America the Middlebrow*; Botshon and Goldsmith, *Middlebrow Moderns*; Tomlinson, "Vision to Visionary"; Wall, *Women of the Harlem Renaissance*; and Allen, *Black Women Intellectuals*.

16. In her earlier Emma McChesney series, Ferber also imagined a son who failed to live up to his mother's radical example. Emma's son, Jock, chooses a career in modern advertising, a business that his mother – a highly successful saleswoman herself – sees as insincere and overly detached from the lives of its middle-class audience. Jock dismisses his mother's ideas as old-fashioned, but Ferber's narrator suggests that Emma's promotional strategies are both more effective and more honest. For a thoughtful analysis of these stories, see Reeser, "'She believed her ballyhoo'."

17. Despite their differences in age, gender, and career paths – and despite Hemingway's well-known mockery of *One of Ours*, Cather's war novel – the two authors share some thematic and aesthetic preoccupations. Cather's famous description of "the thing not named" as the distinguishing characteristic of the great novel, for instance, is strikingly similar to Hemingway's theory of omission, in which he suggested that he eliminated everything except what was absolutely necessary, so that his writing was like an iceberg

in which nine-tenths of the meaning was not visible. For discussions of such similarities, see Trout "Antithetical Icons?," and Love, *"The Professor's House."*

Works cited

Allen, Carol. *Black Women Intellectuals: Strategies of Nation, Family and Neighborhood in the Works of Pauline Hopkins, Jessie Fauset, and Marita Bonner.* New York: Garland, 1998.

Ammons, Elizabeth. "Cool Diana and the Blood-Red Muse: Edith Wharton on Innocence and Art." In *American Novelists Revisited: Essays in Feminist Criticism.* Ed. Fritz Fleischmann. Boston: G. K. Hall and Co., 1982.

Bauer, Dale M. *Edith Wharton's Brave New Politics.* Madison: University of Wisconsin Press, 1994.

Bell, Millicent. "Lady into Author: Edith Wharton and the House of Scribner." *American Quarterly* 9.3 (Fall 1957): 295–315.

Bell, Millicent, ed. *The Cambridge Companion to Edith Wharton.* Cambridge: Cambridge University Press, 1995.

Benstock, Shari. *No Gifts from Chance: A Biography of Edith Wharton.* New York: Charles Scribner's Sons, 1994.

Botshon, Lisa. "The New Woman of the Tenements: Anzia Yezierska's *Salome.*" *MFS: Modern Fiction Studies* 56.2 (Summer 2010): 233–61.

Botshon, Lisa and Meredith Goldsmith, eds. *Middlebrow Moderns: Popular American Women Writers of the 1920s.* Boston: Northeastern University Press, 2003.

Bradley, Jennifer L. "To Entertain, To Educate, To Elevate: Cather and the Commodification of Manners at the *Home Monthly.*" In *Willa Cather and Material Culture: Real-World Writing, Writing the Real World.* Ed. Janis P. Stout. Tuscaloosa: University of Alabama Press, 2005.

Bucker, Park. "'That Kitchen with the Shining Windows': Willa Cather's 'Neighbour Rosicky' and the *Woman's Home Companion.*" In *Willa Cather and Material Culture: Real-World Writing, Writing the Real World.* Ed. Janis P. Stout. Tuscaloosa: University of Alabama Press, 2005.

Cather, Willa. *A Lost Lady.* Ed. Charles E. Mignon and Frederick M. Link with Kari A. Ronning. Lincoln, NB, and London: University of Nebraska Press, 1997.

"Coming, Aphrodite!" In *Collected Stories.* New York: Vintage Books, 1992.

"The Novel Demeuble." In *On Writing: Critical Studies on Writing as an Art.* New York: Knopf, 1949.

The Professor's House. New York: Knopf, 1925.

Clark, Suzanne. *Sentimental Modernism: Women Writers and the Revolution of the Word.* Bloomington: Indiana University Press, 1991.

Davis, Thadious M. *Nella Larsen, Novelist of the Harlem Renaissance: A Woman's Life Unveiled.* Baton Rouge: Louisiana State University Press, 1994.

Earle, David. *Re-Covering Modernism: Pulps, Paperbacks, and the Prejudice of Form.* Burlington, VT: Ashgate, 2009.

Ehrhardt, Julia. *Writers of Conviction: The Personal Politics of Zona Gale, Dorothy Canfield Fisher, Rose Wilder Lane, and Josephine Herbst.* Columbia, MO: University of Missouri Press, 2004.

Ferber, Edna. *So Big*. New York: Grosset & Dunlap, 1924.

Friedman, Natalie. "Marriage and the Immigrant Narrative: Anzia Yezierska's *Salome of the Tenements*." *Legacy: A Journal of American Women Writers* 22.2 (2005): 176–86.

Garcia, Claire Oberon. "Jessie Redmon Fauset Reconsidered." In *The Harlem Renaissance Revisited: Politics, Arts, and Letters*. Ed. Jeffrey O. G. Ogbar. Baltimore: The Johns Hopkins University Press, 2010.

Gerber, Philip L. *Willa Cather*. New York and London: Twayne Publishing, 1995.

Glasgow, Ellen. *Barren Ground*. New York: Sagamore Press, 1957.

Glass, Loren. *Authors Inc.: Literary Celebrity in the United States, 1880–1980*. New York and London: New York University Press, 2004.

Hamilton, Erika. "Advertising Cather during the Transition Years (1914–1922)." *Cather Studies 7: Willa Cather as Cultural Icon*. Ed. Guy Reynolds. Lincoln, NB: University of Nebraska Press, 2007.

Harker, Jaime. *America the Middlebrow: Women's Novels, Progressivism, and Middlebrow Authorship between the Wars*. Amherst: University of Massachusetts Press, 2007.

Harrison-Kahan, Lori. "'Structure Would Equal Meaning': Blues and Jazz Aesthetics in the Fiction of Nella Larsen." *Tulsa Studies in Women's Literature* 28.2 (Fall 2009): 267–89.

Hochschild, Arlie Russell. *The Managed Heart: Commercialization of Human Feeling*. Berkeley: University of California Press, 1983.

Hutchinson, George. *In Search of Nella Larsen: A Biography of the Color Line*. Cambridge, MA: Belknap Press, 2006.

Jenkins, Candice M. "Decoding Essentialism: Cultural Authenticity and the Black Bourgeoisie in Nella Larsen's *Passing*." *MELUS: The Journal of the Society for the Study of the Multi-Ethnic Literature of the United States* 30.3 (Fall 2005): 129–54.

Joslin, Katherine and Alan Price, eds. *Wretched Exotic: Essays on Edith Wharton in Europe*. New York: Peter Lang, 1993.

Kaplan, Amy. "Edith Wharton's Profession of Authorship." *English Literary History* 53.2 (1986): 433–57.

Klimasmith, Betsy. "Salvaging History: Modern Philosophies of Memory and Time in *The Age of Innocence*." *American Literature* 80.3 (September 2008): 555–81.

Larsen, Nella. *Quicksand*. New York: Penguin, 2002.

Lavin, Matt. "Intellectual Warfare in Collier's Magazine: Art versus Advertising in Cather's Serialized Novel *The Professor's House*." *Willa Cather Pioneer Memorial Newsletter* 49.2 (October 2005): 31–2.

Lee, Hermione. *Edith Wharton*. New York: Knopf, 2007.

    Willa Cather: Double Lives. New York: Pantheon, 1989.

Lewis, R. W. B. *Edith Wharton: A Biography*. New York: Harper & Row, 1975.

Love, Glen A. "*The Professor's House*: Cather, Hemingway, and the Chastening of American Prose Style." *Western American Literature* 24.2 (1990): 295–311.

Martin, Robert A. and Linda Wagner-Martin. "The Salons of Wharton's Fiction." In *Wretched Exotic: Essays on Edith Wharton in Europe*. Ed. Katherine Joslin and Alan Price. New York: Peter Lang, 1993.

Madigan, Mark J. "Willa Cather and the Book-of-the-Month Club." *Cather Studies 7: Willa Cather as Cultural Icon*. Ed. Guy Reynolds. Lincoln, NB: University of Nebraska Press, 2007.

McFarland, Dorothy Tuck. *Willa Cather*. New York: Ungar, 1972.

Mikkelsen, Ann. "From Sympathy to Empathy: Anzia Yezierska and the Transformation of the American Subject." *American Literature: A Journal of Literary History, Criticism, and Bibliography* 82.2 (June 2010): 361–88.

Millington, Richard H. "Where is Cather's Quebec? Anthropological Modernism in *Shadows on the Rock*." *Cather Studies* 4 (1999): 23–44.

"Willa Cather's American Modernism." In *The Cambridge Companion to Willa Cather*. Ed. Marilee Lindemann. New York: Cambridge University Press, 2005.

Morawski, Jill G. "Educating the Emotions: Academic Psychology, Textbooks, and the Psychology Industry, 1890–1940." In *Inventing the Psychological: Toward a Cultural History of Emotional Life in America*. Ed. Joel Pfister and Nancy Schnog. New Haven and London: Yale University Press, 1997

Parchesky, Jennifer. "The Business of Living and the Labor of Love: Dorothy Canfield Fisher, Feminism, and Middle-Class Redemption." *Colby Quarterly* 36.1 (March 2000): 29–47.

"'You Make Us Articulate': Reading, Education, and Community in Dorothy Canfield's Middlebrow America." In *Reading Acts: US Readers' Interactions with Literature, 1800–1950*. Ed. Barbara Ryan and Amy Thomas. Knoxville: University of Tennessee Press, 2002.

Piper, Kevin. "The Making of an American: Counternarration in Louis Adamic's *Laughing in the Jungle* and Anzia Yezierska's *Bread Givers*." *MELUS: The Journal of the Society for the Study of the Multi-Ethnic Literature of the United States* 35.1 (Spring 2010): 99–118.

Porter, David H. "Cather on Cather II: Two Recent Acquisitions at Drew University." *Willa Cather Newsletter and Review* 46.3 (Winter/Spring 2003): 49, 53–8.

Reeser, Alanna L. "'She believed her ballyhoo': Women and Advertising in Fiction by Edna Ferber, Jessie Redmon Fauset, and Fannie Hurst." M.A. thesis. Villanova University, 2007.

Reynolds, Guy. *Willa Cather in Context: Progress, Race, and Empire*. New York: St. Martin's Press, 1996.

Robinson, Phyllis C. *Willa: The Life of Willa Cather*. Garden City, NY: Doubleday, 1983.

Rose, Phyllis. "Modernism: The Case of Willa Cather." In *Modernism Reconsidered*. Ed. Robert Kiely. Cambridge, MA: Harvard University Press, 1983.

Rosowski, Susan J., with Kari A. Ronning. "Historical Essay." In *A Lost Lady* by Willa Cather. Ed. Charles E. Mignon and Frederick M. Link with Kari A. Ronning. Lincoln, NB, and London: University of Nebraska Press, 1997.

Ryder, Mary R. "Looking for Love in All the Wrong Places: Voyeurism in Cather's 1920s Fiction." *Willa Cather Pioneer Memorial Newsletter* 49.1 (2005): 3–8.

Scheper, Jeanne. "The New Negro Flâneuse in Nella Larsen's *Quicksand*." *African American Review* 42.3–4 (Fall 2008): 679–95.

Schroeter, James, ed. *Willa Cather and her Critics*. Ithaca: Cornell University Press, 1967.

Schueth, Michael. "A Portrait of an Artist as a Cultural Icon: Edward Steichen, *Vanity Fair*, and Willa Cather." In *Cather Studies 7: Willa Cather as Cultural Icon*. Ed. Guy Reynolds. Lincoln, NB: University of Nebraska Press, 2007.

"Cather and her Stars: Negotiating a Culture of Celebrity." *Willa Cather Newsletter and Review* 45.2 (Fall 2001): 33–7.

"Taking Liberties: Willa Cather and the 1934 Film Adaptation of *A Lost Lady*." In *Willa Cather and Material Culture: Real-World Writing, Writing the Real World*. Ed. Janis P. Stout. Tuscaloosa: University of Alabama Press, 2005.

Showalter, Elaine. *A Jury of her Peers: American Women Writers from Anne Bradstreet to Annie Proulx*. New York: Knopf, 2009.

Singley, Carol. "Bourdieu, Wharton, and Changing Culture in *The Age of Innocence*." *Cultural Studies* 17 (May 2003): 495–519.

Stout, Janis P. "Willa Cather and her Public in 1922." In *Cather Studies 7: Willa Cather as Cultural Icon*. Ed. Guy Reynolds. Lincoln, NB: University of Nebraska Press, 2007.

Stout, Janis P. *Willa Cather: The Writer and her World*. Charlottesville: University Press of Virginia, 2000.

Thornton, Edie. "Selling Edith Wharton: Illustration, Advertising, and *Pictorial Review*, 1924–25." *Arizona Quarterly* 57.3 (Autumn 2001): 29–59.

Thornton, Edith. "'Innocence' Consumed: Packaging Edith Wharton with Kathleen Norris in *Pictorial Review* magazine, 1920–21." *European Journal of American Culture* 24.1 (2005): 29–45.

Tomlinson, Susan. "Vision to Visionary: The New Negro Woman as Cultural Worker in Jessie Redmon Fauset's *Plum Bun*." *Legacy: A Journal of American Women Writers* 19.1 (2002): 90–7.

Trevitte, Chad. "Cather's *A Lost Lady* and the Disenchantment of Art." *Twentieth-Century Literature* 53.2 (Summer 2007): 182–211.

Trout, Steven. "Antithetical Icons? Willa Cather, Ernest Hemingway, and the First World War." *Cather Studies 7: Willa Cather as Cultural Icon*. Ed. Guy Reynolds. Lincoln, NB: University of Nebraska Press, 2007.

Urgo, Joseph R. *Willa Cather and the Myth of American Migration*. Urbana and Chicago: University of Illinois Press, 1995.

Wall, Cheryl A. *Women of the Harlem Renaissance*. Bloomington: Indiana University Press, 1995.

Wharton, Edith. "Copy." *Scribner's* 27.6 (June 1900): 657–63.

The Age of Innocence. New York: Barnes and Noble Classics, 2004.

Summer. New York: Bantam, 2008.

Wilson, Sarah. *Melting-Pot Modernism*. Ithaca: Cornell University Press, 2010.

Woodress, James. *Willa Cather: A Literary Life*. Lincoln, NB: University of Nebraska Press, 1989.

Yezierska, Anzia. *Bread Givers*. New York: Persea Books, 2003.

Xavier, Silvia. "Decontaminating the Canon: The Case of Anzia Yezierska and Patronage in Early-Twentieth-Century American Fiction." *New Literatures Review* 43 (April 2005): 23–36.

Zackodnik, Teresa. "Passing Transgressions and Authentic Identity in Jessie Fauset's *Plum Bun* and Nella Larsen's *Passing*." In *Literature and Racial Ambiguity*. Ed. Teresa Hubel and Neil Brooks. Amsterdam: Rodopi, 2002.

22

Recovering the legacy of Zara Wright and the twentieth-century black woman writer

RYNETTA DAVIS

The December 25, 1920, *Chicago Defender* features a "New Book on Market" review that praises Chicago-based writer Zara Wright's *Black and White Tangled Threads*, labeling it "a most remarkable book," noting that "[t]o read this story will be a convincing proof that as a writer Mrs. Wright is unexcelled" (8). This review was not the only glowing endorsement of Wright's literary debut. Positive reviews marketing Wright's novel continued to appear in the *Chicago Defender* throughout the 1920s. A December 3, 1921 review titled "Gift Book Supreme" acknowledges that *Black and White Tangled Threads* had been "Endorsed by press, pulpit and public," and that the book's author tells a "story that will stand as a monument of greatness in the future years" (5). Similarly, an advertisement in the December 10, 1921, *Chicago Defender* boasts that the novel is "Unquestionably the best book ever written by one of our own authors . . . No home should be without this wonderful book" (4). Moreover, *Black and White Tangled Threads* appears on a "Survey of Negro Life in Chicago: Books You Should Know and Read" list that promotes the most important books by "Negro" and white authors (Fig. 22.1). Wright's name appears alongside prominent black writers such as Phillis Wheatley, Sojourner Truth, Paul Laurence Dunbar, W. E. B. Du Bois, Jessie Fauset, and Angelina Weld Grimké. Wright's portrait also appears in John Taitt's 1925 *Souvenir of Negro Progress*. The photograph documents the achievements of eleven successful Chicago blacks; Wright is the only author, and one of two black women featured.

Black and White Tangled Threads was published in 1920 by Barnard and Miller, a private publishing house in Chicago; the novel sold for $2.50. The novel was reissued twice under the same cover with its sequel, *Kenneth*: once in 1975 by the AMS Press, and in 1995 as part of the African American Women Writers, 1910–1940 series edited by Henry Louis Gates, Jr. Since 1995, Wright's novels have languished in obscurity, and her literary legacy remains obscured despite

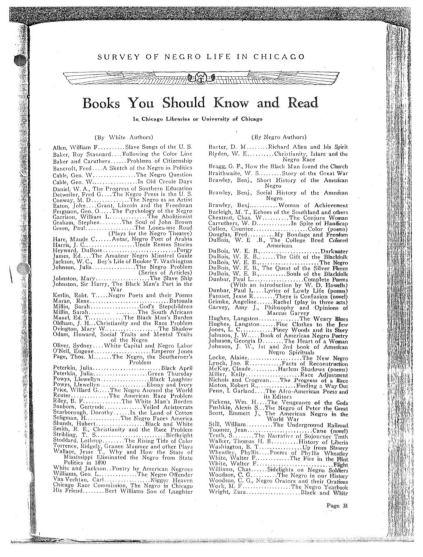

SURVEY OF NEGRO LIFE IN CHICAGO

Books You Should Know and Read

In Chicago Libraries or University of Chicago

(By White Authors)

Allen, William F.........Slave Songs of the U. S.
Baker, Roy Stannard....Following the Color Line
Baker and Caruthers......Problems of Citizenship
Bancroft, Fred....A Sketch of the Negro in Politics
Cable, Geo. W................The Negro Question
Cable, Geo. W................In Old Creole Days
Daniel, W. A., The Progress of Southern Education
Detweiler, Fred G...The Negro Press in the U. S.
Conway, M. D................The Negro as an Artist
Eaton, John....Grant, Lincoln and the Freedman
Ferguson, Geo. O....The Psychology of the Negro
Garrison, William L................The Abolitionist
Graham, Stephen......The Soul of John Brown
Green, Paul................The Lonesome Road
        (Plays for the Negro Theatre)
Hare, Maude C......Antar, Negro Poet of Arabia
Harris, J. C................Uncle Remus Stories
Heyward, DuBose................................Porgy
James, Ed....The Amateur Negro Minstrel Guide
Jackson, W. C., Boy's Life of Booker T. Washington
Johnson, Julia................The Negro Problem
        (Series of Articles)
Johnston, Mary................The Slave Ship
Johnston, Sir Harry, The Black Man's Part in the
        War
Kerlin, Robt. T.....Negro Poets and their Poems
Maran, Rene................................Batouala
Millin, Sarah................God's Stepchildren
Millin, Sarah........The South Africans
Manel, Ed. T............The Black Man's Burden
Oldham, J. H..Christianity and the Race Problem
Ovington, Mary W................The Shadow
Odum, Howard, Social Traits and Mental Traits
        of the Negro
Oliver, Sydney....White Capital and Negro Labor
O'Neil, Eugene................Emperor Jones
Page, Thos. M................The Negro, the Southerner's
        Problem
Peterkin, Julia........................Black April
Peterkin, Julia................Green Thursday
Powys, Llewellyn................Black Laughter
Powys, Llewellyn................Ebony and Ivory
Price, Willard G...The Negro Around the World
Reuter................The American Race Problem
Riley, B. F................The White Man's Burden
Sanborn, Gertrude........Veiled Aristocrats
Scarborough, Dorothy......In the Land of Cotton
Seligman, H............The Negro Faces America
Shands, Hubert................Black and White
Smith, R. E., Christianity and the Race Problem
Stribling, T. S................Birthright
Stoddard, Lothrop........The Rising Tide of Color
Torrence, Ridgely, Granee Maumee and other Plays
Wallace, Jesse T., Why and How the State of
        Mississippi Eliminated the Negro from State
        Politics in 1890
White and Jackson..Poetry by American Negroes
Williams, Geo. L................The Negro Offender
Van Vechtan, Carl................Nigger Heaven
Chicago Race Commission, The Negro in Chicago
His Friend........Bert Williams Son of Laughter

(By Negro Authors)

Barter, D. M........Richard Allen and his Spirit
Blyden, W. E.........Christianity, Islam and the
        Negro Race
Bragg, G. F., How the Black Man found the Church
Braithwaite, W. S........Story of the Great War
Brawley, Benj., Short History of the American
        Negro
Brawley, Benj., Social History of the American
        Negro
Brawley, Benj..........Woman of Achievement
Burleigh, M. T., Echoes of the Southland and others
Chestnut, Chas. W.........The Conjure Woman
Carruthers, W. D................In Spite of Handicap
Cullen, Countee................Color (poems)
Douglas, Fred.........My Bondage and Freedom
DuBois, W. E .B., The College Bred Colored
        American
DuBois, W. E. B................Darkwater
DuBois, W. E. B......The Gift of the Blackfolk
DuBois, W. E. B........................The Negro
DuBois, W. E. B., The Quest of the Silver Fleece
DuBois, W. E. B........Souls of the Blackfolk
Dunbar, Paul L................Complete Poems
        (With an introduction by W. D. Howells)
Dunbar, Paul L....Lyrics of Lowly Life (poems)
Fausset, Jesse R........There is Confusion (novel)
Grimke, Angeline......Rachel (play in three acts)
Garvey, Amy J., Philosophy and Opinions of
        Marcus Garvey
Hughes, Langston................The Weary Blues
Hughes, Langston......Fine Clothes to the Jew
Jones, L. C................Piney Woods and its Story
Johnson, J. W....Book of American Negro Poetry
Johnson, Georgia D................The Heart of a Woman
Johnson, J. W., 1st and 2nd book of American
        Negro Spirituals
Locke, Alaine................The New Negro
Lynch, Jno. R........Facts of Reconstruction
McKay, Claude........Harlem Shadows (poems)
Miller, Kelly................Race Adjustment
Nichols and Crogman....The Progress of a Race
Moton, Robert R................Finding a Way Out
Penn, I. Garland....The Afro-American Press and
        its Editors
Pickens, Wm. H....The Vengeance of the Gods
Pushkin, Alexis S...The Negro of Peter the Great
Scott, Emmett J., The American Negro in the
        World War
Still, William........The Underground Railroad
Toomer, Jean........................Cane (novel)
Truth, S........The Narrative of Sojourner Truth
Walker, Thomas H. B.........History of Liberia
Washington, B. T................Up from Slavery
Wheatley, Phyllis....Poems of Phyllis Wheatley
White, Walter F................The Fire in the Flint
White, Walter F................................Flight
Williams, Chas....Sidelights on Negro Soldiers
Woodson, C. G.........The Negro in our History
Woodson, C. G., Negro Orators and their Orations
Work, M. E................The Negro Yearbook
Wright, Zara................Black and White

Page 31

Fig. 22.1 Frederic H. H. Robb's "Books You Should Know and Read" in *Survey of Negro Life in Chicago – The Intercollegian Wonderbook* (1922–7)

the positive reviews her novel received upon publication. Although much of this acclaim appeared in the black periodical press, primarily the *Chicago Defender*, Zara Wright's name is excluded from contemporary discussions of African American literature and black Chicago-based writers.

447

Zara Wright's novels were reviewed and advertised repeatedly in the *Chicago Defender*, a well-respected Chicago-based black periodical with a national readership. This coverage suggests that she was not only well known, but also well respected in Chicago's black community. While most of the novel's first (black) readers found much to admire in Wright's works, the few twentieth-century scholars familiar with her texts responded less enthusiastically.[1] For example, Ann Allen Shockley argues that *Black and White Tangled Threads* is a "rambling melodramatic romantic novel" (*Afro-American Women Writers*, 380) and that Wright's novels are "fairy tales created by a fanciful imagination building on nineteenth-century models and adding a few twists of her own" (382).[2] Wright's texts draw heavily on a rich tradition of black women's writings that recast black female sexuality as empowering and noble. As Shockley argues convincingly, *Black and White Tangled Threads* and *Kenneth* are strikingly similar to 1890s and early twentieth-century black women's fiction including Frances E. W. Harper's *Iola Leroy* (1892) and Pauline Hopkins's *Contending Forces* (1900).[3] Like the works of Harper and Hopkins, Wright's fiction addresses the precarious social position of the "tragic" mulatta, particularly the mixed-race heroine's response upon discovering that she is "contaminated with African blood," and thus legally black according to the one-drop rule (*Black and White Tangled Threads*, 25).[4]

The striking resemblance to nineteenth-century race melodramas may account for the scant contemporary critical attention to Wright's fiction.[5] As Maggie Sale explains, "Although Zara Wright published in 1920, her treatment of racial injustice is often more in keeping with her nineteenth-century female predecessors than with her twentieth-century male contemporaries. Thus twentieth-century shifts in literary, cultural, and political values until recently have relegated Wright's works . . . to underserved obscurity" ("Introduction," xx). Careful reconsideration of Wright's body of work, and her social milieu, reveals a more nuanced treatment of recurring nineteenth-century themes such as racial passing, miscegenation, and "illicit" interracial sexual relations.

Wright's fictions participate in what literary scholar Claudia Tate calls "literary interventionism" (*Domestic Allegories of Political Desire*, 11). Like her nineteenth-century predecessors, who "reaffirmed in novels their belief that virtuous women like themselves could reform their society by domesticating it" (Tate, *Domestic Allegories of Political Desire*, 19), Wright's virtuous, near-white protagonist in *Black and White Tangled Threads* uses the domestic sphere to agitate for blacks' political and civic rights. Ultimately, Wright revises the nineteenth-century black family romance narrative by eliminating both the formerly enslaved black mother and the white father, positioning their mixed-race progeny to mediate intra-familial racial strife within the white family.[6] Unlike many nineteenth-century heroines such as Iola Leroy, Wright's protagonist, Zoleeta, is neither remanded to chattel slavery, nor is she forced to protect herself from white men's sexual advances. Instead, she inherits her father's wealth and struggles to claim her white paternal kinship rights.

To date, details about Wright's personal life and literary career are scant. Indeed, when Wright is mentioned in seminal anthologies such as Ann Allen Shockley's *Afro-American Women Writers, 1746–1933* (1988) and Emmanuel S. Nelson's *African American Authors, 1745–1945* (2000), analysis of her works typically begins with the claim that she is "A rarely mentioned novelist" (Shockley, *Afro-American Women Writers*, 380), or that "very little is known about the novelist Zara Wright" (Woodard, "Zara Wright," 508). Wright is not mentioned in the *Norton Anthology of African American Literature*. Archival materials found in Chicago, Illinois, namely the Newberry Library and the Vivian G. Harsh Research Collection of Afro-American History and Literature at the Carter G. Woodson Branch of the Chicago Public Library, as well as the Schomburg Center for Research in Black Culture in Harlem, New York, tell the story of a remarkable, race-conscious twentieth-century black woman writer. Specifically, these collections hold heretofore unknown details about Wright's civic activities, as well as her birthplace, birth date, and death. An obituary dated November 1, 1930, published in the *Chicago Defender* under the heading, "Mrs. Zara[h] Wright, Author of 'Black and White Tangled Threads,' Dies," reveals that she was born in Cincinnati, Ohio in 1865, that she moved to Chicago approximately in 1895, that she died on October 22, 1930, and that she was "active in civic and welfare movements" until a few years prior to her death. The obituary acknowledges that "Mrs. Wright was an outstanding personality in her community. And while she devoted some time to her public service work after the demise of Mr. Wright most of her time was taken up with writing" (4). Most of the archival sources that mention Zara Wright note her civic participation in Chicago's black community, and they note that she is the author of *Black and White Tangled Threads*. Taken together, these archival discoveries uncover previously unknown details about Wright's life that will help scholars better understand the role of a twentieth-century African American woman writer in American literary history and culture beyond period-defining traditions such as the Harlem Renaissance.

This essay repositions Zara Wright as a pivotal figure in the African American Women's literary tradition at a crucial moment in the field of African

American Studies, as evidenced by the ongoing recovery of "lost," forgotten, and underappreciated literary texts by nineteenth- and twentieth-century African American women writers. Consider, for example, the Schomburg Library of Nineteenth-Century Black Women Writers, edited by Henry Louis Gates, Jr. This forty-volume collection has made several out-of-print black women's texts accessible. Henry Louis Gates, Jr. also rediscovered and republished Harriet. E. Wilson's *Our Nig* (1859). Moreover, in 1994, literary historian Frances Smith Foster republished three of Frances E. W. Harper's nineteenth-century novels, which were originally serialized in the *Christian Recorder*. Henry Louis Gates, Jr. and Frances Smith Foster's exemplary archival research has significantly enhanced the study of nineteenth-century African American literature and paved the way for more discoveries, as evidenced by the rediscovery and subsequent 2006 republication of Julia Collins's 1865 novel, *The Curse of Caste*, which was also serialized in the *Christian Recorder*. This archival discovery by literary scholar William Andrews and historian Mitch Kachun challenges earlier assumptions about the origins of the African American literary tradition. Moreover, it prompts us to revisit non-traditional "literary" spaces such as serial publications, black clubwomen's meeting records, and the black periodical press in search of undiscovered literary texts and contextual documents that help scholars to understand authors and their historical milieu.[7] In addition to the republication of Harper's three novels, *Minnie's Sacrifice, Sowing and Reaping*, and *Trial and Triumph*, as well as Collins's *The Curse of Caste*, the 2010 republication of Jessie Fauset's last novel, *Comedy: American Style* (1933), edited by Cherene Sherrard-Johnson, further underscores the need for revisionist readings and new scholarly editions of underappreciated black women's literary texts.

To remedy the exclusion of writers such as Wright from the African American literary canon, like literary scholar Maggie Sale, I argue that we must expand our focus beyond Harlem to other geographic and cultural sites of black literary and political expression such as Chicago, Washington, DC, St. Louis, and northern California. In his recent study, *Unexpected Places: Relocating Nineteenth-Century African American Literature*, Eric Gardner cautions that "Because of limits on authors, genres, subjects, and locations drawn by previous scholars (and by the larger academy) nineteenth-century African American literature has often been reduced to southern stories told in bound books that were written by blacks in the urban Northeast" (12). These geographic and thematic limitations are certainly applicable to discussions of twentieth-century African American literary study as well. As scholars, we must widen the scope of our literary and cultural archive to include urban spaces that have been marginalized by period-defining locales such as Harlem. As Maggie Sale argues persuasively in the introduction to the 1995 edition of Wright's novels, *Black and White Tangled Threads* and *Kenneth* have not "received the attention they would have had they been published in New York. While Harlem certainly was a hotbed of cultural activity, the narrow geographical focus of most African-American criticism on the Harlem Renaissance obscures the cultural and literary developments of other urban black communities" ("Introduction," xxi).

Chicago should have offered Wright a ripe geographic space for black literary and civic expression since, as historian Nicholas Lemann explains, "[t]he black population of Chicago grew from 44,000 in 1910 to 109,000 in 1920, and then to 234,000 in 1930" (*The Promised Land*, 16). Despite this concentrated black population, as well as the rise of black women's clubs that emphasized the value of black history and literature, Wright's works have not received the attention they deserve (Knupfer, *Toward a Tenderer Humanity*). Like Harlem, 1920s Chicago offered its black citizens a wealth of social, political, and economic opportunities in the form of black women's clubs, as well as a prominent black print culture as evidenced by the wide circulation and political force of such newspapers as the *Chicago Defender* and the *Chicago Sunday Bee*. As Ann Meis Knupfer explains, Chicago was also a prominent geographic space for black clubwomen's activist work. Indeed, black clubwomen and activists worked collectively to challenge racial and gender oppression, as well as poor housing conditions. Race riots in Chicago in 1919 threatened not only to disrupt black racial progress, but also to undermine interracial reconciliation and collaborative political work efforts in the city.

In *Black and White Tangled Threads*, Wright highlights the interconnectedness of blacks and whites to demonstrate the absurdity of racial classification as many of Wright's black characters remain largely unaware of their racial identity. By forcing virulent white racists to confront and, in most cases, live with their previously unacknowledged black relatives, Wright suggests the inevitability of interraciality (as did her literary and social activist predecessor Pauline Hopkins in *Contending Forces* in 1900). In a passage that highlights the "tangled threads" that the title of Wright's novel invokes, Hopkins's mixed-race matriarch, Ma Smith, underscores the inevitability of black and white race mixing, noting that "There are strangely tangled threads in the lives of many colored families – I use the word 'colored' because these stories occur mostly among those of mixed blood" (*Contending Forces*, 374–5).[8]

Set in the upper-class worlds of Italy, England, and primarily Louisville, Kentucky, Wright's novel, which is aptly titled *Black and White Tangled Threads*, examines the "tangled" racial threads and legacy of the Andrews family; the novel contains multiple themes including racial passing and racial misrecognition, miscegenation, as well as race consciousness and pride. The novel's heroine, Zoleeta Andrews, is the product of a consensual interracial union; her mother, Mildred Yates, who was a slave, and her father, Harold Andrews, the son of a slaveholder, fall in love and eventually abscond to England to marry; the couple then moves to India. Because both of Zoleeta's parents die when she is a child, she is adopted by her uncle Paul, her father Harold's older brother, and raised on the plantation where her mother and father met. Much of the novel focuses on Zoleeta's Aunt Claretta's efforts to prohibit Zoleeta from marrying Lord Blankleigh, a wealthy Englishman; Claretta despises Zoleeta's beauty and, most of all, her blackness. Claretta has Zoleeta abducted and imprisoned by a man she pays to pose as Zoleeta's uncle, and Claretta ultimately teaches her daughter Catherine to hate Zoleeta as well. Their efforts to ruin Zoleeta's life and to thwart her marriage are unsuccessful; Zoleeta does marry Lord Blankleigh and moves to England where she lives briefly before returning to the United States, against her husband's will, to agitate for blacks' civic equality. Lord Blankleigh forces Zoleeta to leave their son Allen in England with him. Allen remains unaware of his mixed-race identity until he reads a letter from his mother as he is preparing to visit her at novel's end. While living in the United States, Zoleeta gives birth to a daughter that Lord Blankleigh does not meet until they are reunited at novel's end. The novel ends happily with the Blankleighs returning to England.

Wright emphasizes Zoleeta's virtuousness from the very beginning of *Black and White Tangled Threads*. She explains in her Introduction that "The heroine of this story portrays a type of womanhood so often sought for, so rarely found." Zoleeta is noble and self-sacrificing, despite Claretta's efforts to ruin her life and marital prospects. Consider, for example, that Zoleeta is forced to leave a northern boarding school because her cousin Catherine, Claretta's daughter, exposes her racial identity. Even after this revelation, Zoleeta willingly uses her generous allowance to cover Catherine's tuition. Despite her unselfishness, Zoleeta's character is not flawless. At one point in the novel, she asks her uncle Paul Andrews,

> why are the Colored people ostracised [*sic*] and scorned by the whites? History teaches us that American Negroes are descended from the Ethiopians of Africa. Now there are various colors. Is not the Caucasian race responsible for their mixed blood? Is it not inhuman and cruelly unjust to mistreat anyone on account of his color? If a person is known to have Negro blood in their veins they are placed beyond the pale of respectability. It is true that I am

well received for it is not known that my ancestors were once slaves and sold on the auction block. I feel that I am living a terrible, deceitful life, there are times when I am receiving so much homage my eyes flash with scorn when I think of how my friends and admirers would fall away from me if they knew me to be the offspring of the despised race of blacks, and it is only my love for my father's people that prevents me from proclaiming to the world this secret. (*Black and White Tangled Threads*, 144)

Zoleeta's "love for [her] father's people . . . prevents" her from openly acknowledging her blackness (140). Wright's text reveals a deep ambivalence about this white bourgeois desire; indeed, the novel does not extol the virtues of whiteness. Unlike her nineteenth-century literary heroines, including Harper's Iola Leroy and Hopkins's Dora Smith, both of whom embrace their blackness by expressing their desire to identify with their black mothers and what they perceive to be a more virtuous community, for Wright's heroine, the paternal body compels her to identify as white. By choosing to identify with white patriarchal authority, Zoleeta makes a strategic choice that is inextricably linked to property rights and inheritance.

Zoleeta's husband and his family are aware of her racial identity, a theme that Wright's contemporary Nella Larsen would address in her novel, *Passing* (1929), through the character of Gertrude Martin, whose husband and family know that she is a black woman passing for white. Zoleeta's daughter, however, is totally unaware of her mother's racial heritage and, thereby, her own. Agnes boasts proudly, "that if she had a drop of Negro blood in her, she would cut herself and let it flow out. And if she married a man that had Negro blood and she had not been aware of it before that she would leave him" (310). Agnes's disdain for blackness recalls a scene in Harper's *Iola Leroy* (1892) in which the eponymous heroine defends the southern slaveholding system before she is remanded to slavery after the revelation of her blackness. Similarly, Agnes's condemnation of black blood anticipates Jack Bellew's racist diatribe that there are "'No niggers in [his] family. Never have been and never will be'" in Larsen's *Passing* (1929). Jack Bellew discovers that he has been duped when he learns at novel's end that his wife is a "'damned dirty nigger!'" (*Passing*, 111). Agnes, however, remains unaware of her black heritage because her parents withhold this knowledge. Like Harper, Wright and Larsen disrupt whites' racial superiority claims, even as their fictions challenge white supremacists who assume that they can distinguish racial difference visually. In contrast to Agnes's racist sentiment, Wright portrays another character's overt acceptance of racial difference. In response to Agnes's overt denunciation of blackness, Dian argues, "'If my husband had Negro blood and only two drops, I would puncture his breast and drink one drop so I would feel that we were equal and feel proud of it'" (310).

Black and White Tangled Threads is full of dramatic twists. One of the most compelling storylines involves Catherine's marriage to Guy Randolph, a young painter. While living in Italy, Guy discovers that his childhood nurse, Hebe, was actually his mother. She escaped slavery and posed as his nurse. The revelation of her husband's mixed-race heritage prompts Catherine to abandon him and their son, Kenneth, and return to the United States. *Kenneth*, the sequel to *Black and White Tangled Threads*, traces the storyline involving Catherine's mixed-race former husband, Guy Randolph, and their son Kenneth, as well as the life of Kenneth's friend, Dr. Philip Grayson, a dark-skinned medical doctor. Wright continues to build on the theme of interracial interdependence in *Kenneth*. The novel begins with Dr. Philip Grayson, a dark-skinned black man, rescuing individuals after a railroad disaster near Frankfort, Kentucky. Among the many individuals he rescues is a beautiful nineteen-year-old white woman, Alice Blair, the daughter of a wealthy banker. Alice falls in love with Dr. Grayson, and she becomes deathly ill after he rejects her marriage proposals; he even refuses to marry her to save her life. Blair repeatedly visits Grayson's office to pursue him; she does not relent to his efforts to "'discourage'" her (*Kenneth*, 258). Dr. Grayson does not desire Alice. Indeed, he intends to marry a black woman, Odene, yet Alice "threaten[s] to publicly accuse [him] of trying to dishonor her" (258) if he doesn't agree to marry her. Here, as Sale points out, Wright recasts the stereotype of the black male oversexed beast by depicting the white woman as the sexual aggressor. According to Sale, "this scenario challenges the stereotypical notions that black men always desire white women, that relations between black men and white women are always created by black men pursuing white women, and that black men are aggressors and white women are passive victims" ("Introduction," xxvi). On the one hand, Dr. Philip Grayson refuses Alice's marriage proposals because he loves Odene; on the other hand, he also recognizes the potential physical threat he would face should he attempt to marry a white woman. Indeed, upon learning of Alice's desire for the dark-skinned black doctor, her father becomes ill and dies. Although Wright does not explicitly name the potential consequences of intermarriage between blacks and whites in the south, she invokes Dr. Philip Grayson's fears of being lynched despite his consistent efforts to reject a white woman's sexual advances.

Perhaps Wright's radical reconsideration of black–white sexual relations in the 1920s was too incendiary – as was Lillian Smith's representation of consensual sexual/interracial desire in 1920s Georgia between a black woman and a white man in *Strange Fruit* (1944). To be sure, Wright's fiction had its detractors precisely because her novels addressed these "taboo" issues. Indeed, the November 5, 1927 *Chicago Defender* featured a book review of two novels published seven years prior. In the *Defender's* "Bookshelf" column, Warren Brown reacquainted the newspaper's readers with *Black and White Tangled Threads* and its sequel, *Kenneth*, at precisely the moment that Georgia state legislators had enacted a law prohibiting "the intermarriage of the races" ("Way Down in Dixie," 13). Brown's review acknowledges that potentially incendiary topics such as racial passing, miscegenation, and consensual interracial unions, what he refers to as themes "having such an acid taste" (13), no doubt contributed to the scarcity of publishing venues available to a twentieth-century midwestern black woman writer like Wright. A "publisher catering to the popular reading public would not welcome such a manuscript," Brown argues (13). Moreover, Wright's works appeared ten years prior to the rise of the Chicago Black Renaissance which may also account for the lack of scholarly discussion about her works. When compared to local Chicago writers such as playwright Lorraine Hansberry, Wright's fiction may have been considered decidedly less political. Although *Black and White Tangled Threads* and *Kenneth* may have been overlooked or dismissed by twentieth-century literary scholars, these novels add substantially to our understanding of other black women writers' literary texts such as Larsen's *Quicksand* (1928) and *Passing* (1929), as well as Fauset's *There is Confusion* (1924), *Plum Bun: A Novel without a Moral* (1929), *The Chinaberry Tree* (1931), and *Comedy: American Style* (1933). Indeed, reading Wright both complicates and deepens our understanding of canon formation in African American literary studies.

To date, archival research shows that Zara Wright only published two literary texts, *Black and White Tangled Threads* and *Kenneth*. However, the genre-specific titles "Novelist and Dramatist" appear under Wright's name in the photograph of her featured in John Taitt's *Souvenir of Negro Progress*. Moreover, Knupfer notes that Wright, along with other black clubwomen, read their poetry aloud at a Phillis Wheatley black women's club meeting (*Toward a Tenderer Humanity and a Nobler Womanhood*, 118). Evidence that Wright wrote poetry and plays in addition to her novels demonstrates that the archival work necessary to uncover the totality of Wright's legacy has only just begun. Indeed, although Wright dedicates her novels to the "memory" of her deceased husband, J. Edward Wright, details about his life are still unknown. Recovering Wright's "midwestern" literary texts also raises questions about other black women's writings published in underrepresented geographic spaces and on the margins of period-defining movements such as the Chicago and Harlem Renaissances.

Notes

1. Contemporary scholarship on Wright's novel is scant. To date, I have only found two twentieth-century discussions of her text: Ann Allen Shockley's critical analysis included in her seminal anthology, *Afro-American Writers, 1746–1933*, and Maggie Sale's "Introduction" to the 1995 edition of Wright's novels.
2. See Shockley, *Afro-American Women Writers, 1746–1933*, 280. Shockley acknowledges that the "uniqueness" of Wright's first novel "lay in its mulatto story with a different twist; it showed the effects of miscegenation upon a white antebellum southern family who acknowledges a mulatto as a legitimate family member" (280). However, the praise stops here. Shockley contends that "Wright, like the rest of her female contemporaries, was more concerned with spinning propaganda than presenting a story with a valid plot and characters. This was the weakness in their fiction" (280).
3. See Hopkins's *Hagar's Daughter* (1901–2) and *Of One Blood* for similar novelistic treatments of themes such as racial passing and miscegenation by a black woman writer at the turn of the century.
4. In the "Introduction" to the 1987 Beacon Press edition of Harper's *Iola Leroy*, Hazel V. Carby notes that "It is no historical accident that the mulatto figure occurs most frequently in Afro-American fiction at a time when the separation of the races was being institutionalized throughout the South" (xxi). See also Carby, *Reconstructing Womanhood*.
5. Missing information about Wright's personal life may also account for scant discussions of her novels. As well, erroneous census reports may have made it more difficult to find accurate details about her life. For example, the 1920 United States Federal Census Report classifies Zara Wright as "Sara Wright."
6. Zoleeta's father, Harold Andrews, defies his slaveholding parents and marries their former slave, Mildred Yates. While Harold's mother eventually forgives her son for this social transgression, his father dies without forgiving him (*Black and White Tangled Threads*, 11). This plot line draws heavily on a similar story of disinheritance and attempted filicide in Julia Collins's serialized novel, *The Curse of Caste* (1865).
7. See Elizabeth McHenry, *Forgotten Readers*. See also Frances Smith Foster, "A Narrative."
8. Maggie Sale argues that Wright "makes her connection to [turn-of-the-century literary] culture explicit by taking her title from *Contending Forces*" ("Introduction," xviii).

Works cited

"Black and White Tangled Threads." *Review of Black and White Tangled Threads*, by Zara Wright. *Chicago Defender* (June 10, 1922): 3.

Brown, Warren. "Way Down in Dixie." *Review of Black and White Tangled Threads and Kenneth*, by Zara Wright. *Chicago Defender* (November 5, 1927): 13.

Carby, Hazel. "Introduction." In *Iola Leroy*. By Frances E. W. Harper. Boston: Beacon Press, 1987.

——. *Reconstructing Womanhood: The Emergence of the Afro-American Woman Novelist*. New York: Oxford University Press, 1987.

Foster, Frances Smith. "A Narrative of the Interesting Origins and (Somewhat) Surprising Development of African American Print Culture." *American Literary History* 17.4 (Winter 2005): 714–40.

Gardner, Eric. *Unexpected Places: Relocating Nineteenth-Century African American Literature*. Jackson: University of Mississippi Press, 2009.

Glasque, Thias. "Gift Book Supreme." Review of *Black and White Tangled Threads*, by Zara Wright. *Chicago Defender* (December 3, 1921): 5.

Hopkins, Pauline. *Contending Forces*. 1900. New York: Oxford University Press, 1988.

Knupfer, Anne Meis. *Toward a Tenderer Humanity and a Nobler Womanhood: African American Women's Clubs in Turn-of-the-Century Chicago*. New York: New York University Press, 1996.

Larsen, Nella. *Passing*. 1929. New York: Penguin, 2003.

Lemann, Nicholas. *The Promised Land: The Great Black Migration and How It Changed America*. New York: Vintage Press, 1992.

McHenry, Elizabeth. *Forgotten Readers: Recovering the Lost History of African American Literary Societies*. Durham, NC: Duke University Press, 2002.

Nelson, Emmanuel S., ed. *African American Authors, 1745–1945: A Bio-Bibliographical Critical Sourcebook*. Westport, CT: Greenwood Press, 2000.

Nelson, Emmanuel S. "New Book on Market." *Chicago Defender* (December 25, 1920): 8.

Robb, Frederic H. H., ed. *The Negro in Chicago: 1779 to 1927*. Chicago: Washington Intercollegiate Club of Chicago, Incorporated and International Negro Student Alliance, 1929.

Sale, Maggie. "Introduction." In *Black and White Tangled Threads and Kenneth*. By Zara Wright. New York: G. K. Hall and Co., 1995.

Shockley, Ann Allen. *Afro-American Women Writers, 1746–1933: An Anthology and Critical Guide*. Boston: G. K. Hall and Co., 1988.

Taitt, John. *Souvenir of Negro Progress*. Chicago: De Saible Association of Chicago, 1925.

Tate, Claudia. *Domestic Allegories of Political Desire: The Black Heroine's Text at the Turn of the Century*. New York: Oxford University Press, 1992.

Woodard, Loretta. "Zara Wright." In *African American Authors, 1745–1945: A Bio-Bibliographical Critical Sourcebook*. Ed. Emmanuel S. Nelson. Westport, CT: Greenwood Press, 2000.

Wright, Zara. *Black and White Tangled Threads*. 1920. New York: G. K. Hall and Co., 1995.

——. *Kenneth*. 1920. New York: G. K. Hall and Co., 1995.

23

Jewish American women writers

HANA WIRTH-NESHER

The most well-known work of Jewish American literature can be found on the Statue of Liberty. Written by Emma Lazarus in 1883 and affixed to the pedestal in 1903, "The New Colossus" puts these words in the mouth of America's most famous icon as she welcomes newcomers at her gates. "Give me your tired, your poor, / Your huddled masses yearning to breathe free, / The wretched refuse of your teeming shore. / Send these, the homeless, tempest-tost to me, I lift my lamp beside the golden door!" (*Selected Poems*, 58). The denial of human rights and the physical violence to which Jews were subjected in Russia as reported in the international press moved Lazarus to write this poem, and to lend her efforts to the cause of the refugees who began to stream into the United States. Within days of composing these stirring words, Lazarus wrote another poem entitled "1492" where she brings together her pride in being both American and Jew. Her dual identity is encapsulated in the fateful date itself, 1492, that she addresses as "Thou two-faced year," and that she imagines as weeping "when Spain cast forth with flaming sword, / The children of the prophets of the Lord" (87). Referring to the expulsion of the Jews from Spain at the time of the Inquisition and to Columbus setting sail that same year for what would become the Americas, Lazarus recounts that although her people were "hounded from sea to sea, from state to state," and "Close-locked was every port, barred every gate," a new door did open for them, "A virgin world where doors of sunset part" (87). America became a haven where "falls each ancient barrier that the art / Of race or creed or rank devised." As her biographer points out, "not since the Puritans envisioned New England as a 'New Jerusalem' was there as compelling a vision of the spiritual destiny of the nation" (Schor, *Emma Lazarus*, 193).

Lazarus's credentials as an American in the nineteenth century were derived not only from her belief in its spiritual destiny, but also from her lineage. She could trace her own family back to the origins of the nation, for they were prominent Sephardic Jews, descendants of those who were expelled from

Spain and who took leadership roles in the establishing of the two largest Jewish congregations in the colonies. Her great grand-uncle, Moses Seixas, wrote the famous letter of welcome to George Washington, which the president voiced in his address to Jews in the new Republic, that "the Government of the United States . . . gives to bigotry no sanction, to persecution no assistance." Moreover, she had impeccable literary credentials, as her work had been praised by the likes of Henry and William James, Emerson, and James Russell Lowell, who claimed that her poem "The New Colossus" was so noble that it surpassed the Statue itself as an achievement.

The story of Jewish American women authors begins with Lazarus not only historically, but also conceptually; she expressed her Jewish identity in the four broad areas that would engage subsequent writers: ethnicity, religion or religious culture, language, and gender. My criterion for inclusion in this essay about Jewish American women authors is that they themselves acknowledged Judaism or Jewishness as significant for their writing, which was also aimed at a broad, universal audience. By ethnicity, I mean the sense of being a member of a people with a shared history and culture that entails collective identity and responsibility. Her outrage and pain at the persecution of those she considered her brethren prompted her to write "The New Colossus." Her commitment to them was not confined to pen and ink. She labored philanthropically and politically on their behalf, advocating a Jewish homeland as a solution to their plight and greeting Russian Jewish refugees at the overflow shelter constructed at Ward's Island. Furthermore, she was outspoken about her Jewish identity, publishing a collection of poems entitled "Songs of a Semite" that proclaimed her ethnicity, or in her own period, as one reviewer put it, "a champion of her race." By religion, I mean observance of rituals or other commandments for spiritual or cultural reasons, or engaging with Judaism's liturgy and holy texts. Emma Lazarus invoked the Hebrew scriptures in her poetry, she wrote a regular column for the *American Hebrew*, and she studied Hebrew, observing that the intensive verb form *piel* could serve as an analogy for the Jewish people themselves, who are "the intensive form of any nationality whose language and customs they adopt." Her sense of herself as an American poet encompassed her awareness of a Hebrew literary tradition, demonstrated by her translations of medieval Hebrew poetry into English, albeit from the German translations of a great precursor for both Jewish and American poetry, Heinrich Heine. If we take a closer look at her sonnet on The Statue of Liberty, her voice as American, Jew, and woman will become audible. Before Liberty sounds her call to the huddled masses, Lazarus describes the statue as a woman and mother:

> Not like the brazen giant of Greek fame,
> With conquering limbs astride from land to land;
> Here at our sea-washed, sunset gates shall stand
> A mighty woman with a torch, whose flame
> Is the imprisoned lightning, and her name
> Mother of Exiles.

America's Colossus, in contrast to the brazen wonder of the ancient world, is not the male sun-god Helios or Apollo. Masculine paganism has been superseded in the New World by a "mighty woman with a torch," who is a "Mother of Exiles." In a work by Lazarus written at the same time as "The New Colossus," she writes, "Hark to the cry of the exiles of Babylon, the voice of Rachel mourning for her children," a characterization of Rachel from Jeremiah where the Lord, moved by Rachel's weeping for her children, comforts her, "thy children shall come again to their border" (Marom, "Who is the 'Mother of Exiles'?" 250). Moreover, the figure of Deborah in the Book of Judges bears the name Lapidot, which would mean a woman with a torch (Wolosky, "An American-Jewish Typology"). In either case, Lazarus has substituted a female figure from Judaic sources for a male figure in Hellenistic mythology.

If the immigrants arriving at America's shores are actually exiles returning to their motherland, then America is the new Israel as envisioned by the Puritans. This rhetoric posed a problem for many Jews in the New World, who retained the age-old yearning for the ingathering of exiles in ancient Israel, but many others, like Lazarus, saw America as their genuine Promised Land. The Reform Rabbi Isaac Mayer Wise declared the Fourth of July, for example, to be the second greatest redemption of mankind after the exodus from Egypt (1858). For Lazarus in her celebrated poem, it is the Hebraic woman who safeguards the port of entry to America, where the "wretched refuse" from Czarist Russia's pogroms are universalized into every immigrant who would ever sail into New York harbor.

One of those immigrants at the turn of the century was Mary Antin, whose memoir *The Promised Land: The Autobiography of a Russian Immigrant* (1912) became immensely popular for decades, topping the *New York Times* bestseller list, receiving an enthusiastic reception from coast to coast. It was published in special educational editions with teaching manuals in civics classes as late as 1949, and went into thirty-four printings. Written when Antin was twenty-nine, *The Promised Land* depicts her former life in the Pale of Settlement, her voyage to the United States at the age of twelve, and the stages of her Americanization in Boston. The first part documents details of her life in Russia, from the forbidding boundaries between the Jewish and Gentile worlds, the fear of pogroms, and the religious customs that regulated her world, to the taste of cherries and the sight of poppies. The second part traces her education as a patriotic American inspired by Washington, Lincoln, and the English language, hailing America as the apex of human achievement. "I am the youngest of America's children, and into my hands is given all of its priceless heritage . . . Mine is the whole majestic past, and mine is the shining future" (*The Promised Land*, 364).

What accounted in large part for the popularity of this book was Mary Antin's unqualified embrace of the melting-pot ideology, willingly and fervently remaking herself in order to assimilate into America. For Americans troubled by immigrant multitudes whose non-Protestant and non-Nordic profile raised fears about the survival of America's ethnic and religious culture, Antin's devout submission to her Promised Land allayed those fears. The unusual publicity blurb from the *Springfield Republican* on the book's cover illustrates this concern, for it advertises a memoir in terms of the future rather than the past. "It is long since we had so cheering a word on the future of the country." Her patriotic adaptation to America made her so attractive to mainstream Gentile readers that they extended it to her physical as well as mental being, as in this headline from the *Christian Science Monitor* – "Tales of Race Characteristics Altered by Residence in America." Perhaps the most reassuring line in *The Promised Land* for non-Jewish readers was this assertion from the prologue: "I was born, I have lived, and I have been made over . . . I am as much out of the way as if I were dead, for I am absolutely other than the person whose story I have to tell" (xi).

Insofar as Antin was praised as an exemplary immigrant willingly transformed by America, and insofar as she herself recorded her life story as one of death and rebirth, it is surprising to come across this sentence midway through the book: "In after years, when I passed as an American among Americans . . . I thought it miracle enough that I, Mashke, the granddaughter of Raphael the Russian, born to a humble destiny, should be at home in an American metropolis, be free to fashion my own life, and should dream my dreams in English phrases" (197). Antin admits that she can "pass" as an American, a notion that implies performance and deception. If she is passing, then some essence of her former self has survived her transformation. The substance of that remainder appears to be language, for if she dreamed her dreams in English phrases, then she must have spoken those dreams in a slightly accented English. Only in the disembodied medium of writing could accent be transcended. Only on the printed page could she pass as an American, for as she herself summarized at the end of the autobiography, "I learned at least to think in English without an accent."

Arriving in America at the age of twelve, Antin applied herself to learning English with a passion. She describes the obstacles for Yiddish speakers like herself, the dreaded "th," which she dubbed "an almost insurmountable obstacle," and the "w," that required inventive mouth exercises for her to get "my stubborn lips" to pronounce "village" and "water" in rapid alternation (207). Antin is proud of her talent for acquiring languages, which she attributes to her polyglot Jewish heritage. Since only boys were instructed in Hebrew in religious Jewish communities in Europe, Antin recalls that her parents hired a private tutor for Hebrew, whose alphabet she doodles onto the pages of her manuscript. In fact, Antin's first published work was her own translation of a long letter in Yiddish that she had written to her uncle upon her arrival in America, *From Plotsk to Boston*, with a preface by Israel Zangwill. As an immigrant dedicated to mastering English, it soon became the holy language that displaced Hebrew. "It seems to me," she wrote, "that in any other language happiness is not so sweet, logic is not so clear . . . I could almost say that my conviction of immortality is bound up with the English of its promise" (208).

For this Jewish immigrant writer, passing as an American was a linguistic matter. To become an American for Antin meant writing flawless and unaccented prose. It meant transcending her accented speech, that accent inscribed on her mouth and tongue as the body remembering its initiation into language. In short, it meant erasing her corporeal self in her writing, the woman's body that had formerly spoken Yiddish and read Hebrew, in order to become the male voice that she associated with American literature. Her models were Emerson and Whitman, and she read them as transcendental minds concerned only with matters of the spirit. In the cerebral finale of this memoir, the young woman writer is perched above the crowd at the elevated entrance to the Boston Public Library, her temple of culture, the heir of the writing that it enshrines. Only on the appended acknowledgments page, detached from the rest of the autobiography, does her woman's body, which she has been at great pains to efface in the work, make a fleeting appearance as she thanks the child she bore, "to my daughter, who enlarged me."

Although Lazarus was a poet from a distinguished and affluent Sephardic family and Antin was a prose writer from an impoverished but well-educated immigrant family from Russia, both regarded being Jewish as a spiritual legacy that strengthened their claim to being American. Since Lazarus regarded herself as a Semite whose family was expelled from Europe by Catholics, she considered her Hebraic culture to be compatible with the Puritan and Hebraic origins of America. Antin, in contrast, minimized the significance of her Jewish origins, which she strategically portrayed as just another form of Protestantism. "The Judaism of the Pale," she wrote, "stripped of its grotesque mask of forms . . . was simply the belief that God was, had been, and ever would be, and that they, the children of Jacob, were His chosen messengers . . . the Jew was conscious that between himself and God no go-between was needed" (38). Despite their difference in social class, both of these writers benefited from the education available to them in America. Antin lost no opportunity to criticize the Jewish community of the Pale for excluding women from formal classroom study, and she extolled America most for making it possible for women like herself to learn. Another celebrated immigrant author and contemporary of Mary Antin, Anzia Yezierska, saw her Jewishness as ethnic rather than spiritual and, therefore, inescapable not only because of her personal history but also because of her blood.

Known briefly as "the Cinderella of the slums" for her rags-to-riches short-lived success story when her story collection *Hungry Hearts* was filmed in Hollywood, Anzia Yezierska immigrated to the United States as a child from the Pale of Settlement and settled with her family on New York's Lower East Side. In her best-known novel, *Bread Givers* (1925), Sara Smolinsky tells the story of her struggle to escape poverty and patriarchy in the New World. Formerly a Talmud scholar, her father Reb Smolinsky expects his daughters to be his bread givers in the New World, where traditional Jewish scholarship is not highly valued, and to submit to his choice of husbands. Witness to the disastrous marital choices foisted on her three sisters by her father's selfishness, she leaves home to liberate herself from the patriarchal culture that prevents her Americanization. Her strategy for upward social mobility is to become a schoolteacher, one of the few options available to the daughters of immigrants. Finding that fluent and unaccented English is a prerequisite for such a position, Sara Smolinsky, like Antin, turns to diction with a passion. Yet her education is marked by privation stemming from being both immigrant and woman. She envies the style, refinement, and privilege of the Gentile students in her college, while she suffers from discrimination, learning that even when it comes to ladling out soup in cafeteria lines, the men always receive the choicest morsels of meat. True to America's promise, however, dedication to her studies pays off, as Sara graduates valedictorian of her class, earns her teacher's license, and returns to an immigrant classroom to teach children like herself. She drills them into speaking American.

Having rejected suitors who belittle her professional ambition, Sara finds a Prince Charming who is also an educator, Hugo Seelig, principal of her school. In a Jewish American version of Pygmalion, English diction inspires romance. During an elocution class for her pupils, Sara backslides, mispronouncing the word "sing." When she notices that she has been observed by her principal, her anxiety causes her to repeat the mistake. "You try it again, Rosy. The birds sing-gg." Mr. Seelig interrupts her softly as he enunciates "Sing." In her embarrassment she fails again, this time rescued from further humiliation by the man destined to become her husband. "The next moment he was close beside me, the tips of his cool fingers on my throat. 'Keep those muscles still until you have stopped. Now say it again,' he commanded. And I turned pupil myself and pronounced the word correctly" (*Bread Givers*, 272). In contrast to Antin who evaded faulty pronunciation through disembodied writing, Yezierska emphasizes her character's body as a site of warring identities. Proper diction may be seductive, but enduring love requires racial bonding. "You and I," says Seelig well into their courtship, "we are of one blood" (280). The price paid by Sara for this ethnic Jewish affirmation is that Hugo brings Old World values to his New World achievements, which translates into literally bringing the patriarch back into the household. In the name of honoring parents, Reb Smolinsky, now a widower, is reinstated as the autocratic voice that drowns out the voice of woman. Although Hugo's reverence for English combined with his memories of Poland make him the ideal mate for Sara, his equal reverence for Hebrew and orthodox Jewish values makes him complicit in eclipsing Sara's hard-earned light. The last words of the book undermine the otherwise happy ending of this novel of education and courtship. "Then Hugo's grip tightened on my arm and we walked on. It wasn't just my father, but the generations who made my father whose weight was still upon me" (297).

Two years earlier Yezierska had already explored an immigrant girl's desperation to escape the ugliness of her neighborhood for the refinement that she associates with Gentiles in her first novel, *Salome of the Tenements* (1923). *Salome* is an abortive fairy tale and harsh critique of uptown philanthropists and reformers who romanticized poverty in the Settlement Houses aimed at Americanizing immigrants. Inspired by her own short-lived romance with the philosopher John Dewey and the fairy-tale wedding of her politically radical friend Rose Pastor to the millionaire philanthropist Graham Stokes, *Salome of the Tenements* both exposes and reinforces the ethnic stereotypes of her time. Sonya Vrunsky is the exotic Russian Jewess reviving the enervated high-born John Manning, who sees "the naked soul of her race shining in her eyes" (*Salome of the Tenements*, 32). Her marriage to Manning ends in disaster when he can no longer tolerate her feisty behavior and unmannered family and friends. She finds his upper-class world to be chilling: "I could never choke myself into the form of your society friends" (131). Like Sara Smolinsky, Sonya marries, if not the man of her dreams, then the man of her heart and blood, who will cherish her – Jacques Hollins, self-made Fifth Avenue fashion designer, formerly Jaky Solomon of the Lower East Side. He recognizes her vibrant beauty at a glance and is "shaken by a sharp personal thrill that came straight from the racial oneness of the two of them" (25). Her love of beauty is redirected from Manning's palatial estates to the more practical calling of fashion design. Both Sonya and Sara are passionate about their vocations, which form the basis of their marriages to men who share their aspirations as well as their Jewish ethnicity. The heavy weight of immigration itself, that compounded the weight of childbearing and housework for women's bodies, is literalized by the Yiddish writer Celia Dropkin. In her story "A Dancer," a young mother grown heavy in body and spirit becomes so obsessed with memories of herself as an agile girl in dance slippers in Warsaw that she repeatedly tries to leap across rooms and window ledges until, like a "mournful bird" ("A Dancer," 200), she is confined.

The works published during the first half of the twentieth century, whether by immigrants or by their children, were fraught with anxiety about acceptance by Gentile Americans, whether in voice, manners, clothing, décor, or cultural capital. Since Jews were regarded as racially Other in this period, it is no wonder that Jewish women writers identified with African Americans who crossed the color line by passing as white. Edna Ferber's novel *Showboat* (1926) dramatizes the risks and price of a light-skinned African American woman who passes, and Fannie Hurst's *Imitation of Life* (1933) also explores the effects of the color line on women passers subject to financial and emotional dependency. As Susan Gubar observed, "That Jewish American women authors produced two popular texts in the genre of the passing novel puts their achievements into a conversation with African American modernists" ("Jewish American Women Writers," 234). American racism continued to concern Jewish American women writers well into the twentieth century, most notably among writers like Hannah Arendt and Lore Segal, both refugees from Nazi Germany. When Arendt was criticized for claiming, in her essay "Reflections on Little Rock" (1959), that marriage laws in twenty-nine states that prohibited what they termed miscegenation were a more flagrant breach of the

Constitution than school segregation, she replied that "as a Jew I take my sympathy for the cause of the Negroes as for all oppressed or underprivileged peoples for granted and should appreciate it if the reader did likewise" (492). In *Her First American* (1985), Segal traces the parallels and differences between African American and Jewish American collective trauma, and the bitter descent into competing martyrdom.

In the decades after World War II, Jewish American women writers projected bolder, more secure voices, exemplified by Grace Paley and Cynthia Ozick, both the children of immigrants who grew up in New York in Yiddish-speaking families. According to Paley, "Two ears, one for literature, one for home, are useful for writers" (*The Collected Stories*, x). One of Paley's debut stories, "The Loudest Voice" (1959), mocks the stereotype of Jewish voices as loud, as the narrator Shirley Abramowitz reaps the benefits of her strong vocal chords when she is chosen to be the voice of Jesus in the public school Christmas pageant. The story hones in on the most highly charged event for Jewish children in Christian culture, Christmas, and reads it from a secular and cultural perspective, "It was a long story and it was a sad story" (*The Collected Stories*, 39). Shirley's father, a Russian immigrant, takes pride in his daughter's achievement, dismissing the harmful effects of performing in a Christmas play by regarding the holiday anthropologically: "this is a holiday from pagan times also, candles, lights, even Chanukah . . . So if they think it's a private holiday, they're only ignorant, not patriotic" (38). Far from keeping a low profile at a season that showcases Christianity, Shirley exudes the confidence that comes from having her loud voice validated as an asset in a meritocracy where Jewish children can excel at Christian events. Paley's voice is humorous and ironic as Shirley, unintimidated by Christian symbols, feels sorry for the Christmas tree on the street corner "decorated for us by a kind city administration" that placed it in a Jewish neighborhood. "On the way to school, with both my hands I tossed it a kiss of tolerance. Poor thing, it was a stranger in Egypt" (38). Shirley's final action comically exemplifies America as a tolerant hodge-podge of practices, beliefs, and languages. "I climbed out of bed and kneeled. I made a little church of my hands and said, 'Hear, O Israel' . . . " (40). The gestures are Christian, the prayer Jewish. "Then I called out in Yiddish, 'Please, good night, good night. Ssh'," to her parents and their friends who "debated a little in Yiddish, then fell in a puddle of Russian and Polish." Self-assured after her starring role as Christ in the pageant, Shirley "had prayed for everybody: my talking family, cousins far away, passersby, and all the lonesome Christians. I expected to be heard. My voice was certainly the loudest" (40). Just as Paley herself expected to be heard not by God, but by her American readers, in this new buoyant voice authored by a Jewish woman.

If Shirley Abramowitz's voice is a social triumph, Paley's story "A Conversation with My Father" is a Jewish woman writer's manifesto. The conversation takes place between the narrator and her eighty-six-year-old father in his hospital room where his heart "will not do certain jobs anymore" (*The Collected Stories*, 232). He makes a deathbed request to his writer daughter, that she produce a story for him that conforms to his idea of great literature, "a simple story . . . the kind Maupassant wrote, or Chekhov, the kind you used to write. Just recognizable people and then write down what happened to them next" (232). She recognizes that lurking behind this innocent request is a plea to return to traditional values that would limit the possibilities for women, but she also wants to please him. "I *would* like to try to tell such a story, if he means the kind that begins: 'There was a woman . . .' followed by plot, the absolute line between two points which I've always despised. Not for literary reasons, but because it takes all hope away. Everyone, real or invented, deserves the open destiny of life" (232). She humors him by making up parodies of stories with tragic endings. He demands more realistic social texture to identify characters by the determinants of lineage and class. She recoils from conventional action yet serves up plots with tragic endings. Before he can revel in their poignance, she retracts the closure, granting her women characters another chance. His tragic outlook stems as much from his generation's worldview as from his failing heart, and he accuses her of evading life's truths: "Tragedy! Plain tragedy! Historical tragedy! No hope. The end" (237). She has to decide between letting him have the last word, or rescuing her women characters from the deterministic fate that has awaited them in classic literature and life. "She's my knowledge and my invention. I'm sorry for her. I'm not going to leave her there in that house crying" (237).

In this conversation between father and daughter, Paley stakes out a poetics for women that echoes the humor of Yiddish literature as a survival strategy, but also serves as a harbinger of the voices of Jewish women who would be forerunners in the feminist movements of the 1960s and '70s, such as Betty Friedan and Gloria Steinem. On stage, Wendy Wasserstein's witty scripts, with their ethnic accent and topical barbs at middle-class propriety, made room for women who refused to limit themselves to prescribed roles. "Do you know what the expression 'good ga davened' means?" asks Holly in *Uncommon Women and Others*, performed in 1977: "It means someone who davened, or prayed, right . . . They marry doctors and go to Bermuda for Memorial Day weekends. These girls are also doctors, but they only work part-time because of their three musically-inclined children and weekly brownstone renovations" (*The Heidi Chronicles and Other Plays*, 62). In her Pulitzer Prize-winning *The Heidi Chronicles* (1990), a feminist character, disappointed in the rhetoric and choices of her peers, admits: "It's just that I feel stranded. I thought the whole point was that we were all in this together" (*The Heidi Chronicles and Other Plays*, 233).

Unlike Antin and Yezierska, who strove to erase any traces of Yiddish in their prose, and Paley, who retained Yiddish as inflection and syntax, Ozick is steeped in Yiddish literature, which she has translated into English, as well as Jewish religion and history that serve as her imaginative matrix. In her artistic credo, "Toward Yavneh," she writes, "Jewish literature is always writing that touches on the liturgical . . . When a Jew in Diaspora leaves liturgy . . . literary history drops him and he does not last" (1993). Her novel, *The Puttermesser Papers* (1997), is an intriguing allegory of the Jewish female writer in the Hebraic intertextual tradition. Single, middle-aged, childless lawyer Ruth Puttermesser returns from work one day to find a female golem on her bed in her New York apartment, and, having studied Jewish mysticism, she knows exactly how to breathe life into its clay mold: she must carve the Hebrew word *emet* (truth) on its forehead and utter God's name aloud. As she gives birth through language and art rather than through the female body, Puttermesser discerns a white patch with nearly invisible letters floating to the surface, "a single primeval Hebrew word, shimmering with its lightning holiness, the Name of Names, that which one dare not take in vain. Aloud she uttered it" (*The Puttermesser Papers*, 40). At this critical moment, Ozick reproduces the word uttered by Puttermesser, the Hebrew letters isolated and untranslated on the page: "השם Hashem." The informed reader knows better, for this Hebrew word is actually "The Name," a euphemism for God rather than the tetragrammaton whose utterance is prohibited in Judaism.

To clear space for herself as a Jewish woman writer in a Hebraic world of text that has been almost exclusively male, Ozick brings to life a female golem who will assist her creator in becoming Mayor of New York City, and she overturns tradition by making the golem's creator a woman as well, whose favorite pastime is studying Hebrew letters. As the female creator of a female golem, and as a woman who longs to give birth to a daughter, Ruth distinguishes between similar Hebrew letters by imagining them as pregnant women facing in different directions. For Puttermesser the letters are fertile, as they are also the means of breathing life into clay. According to legend, when the golem's unchecked growth results in a gargantuan being, he must be deadened by the erasure of the letter *aleph* on the forehead, turning "truth" (*emet*) into "death" (*met*). In the deathbed scene that hovers between intertextual allegory and mother/daughter drama, the mute golem begins to speak in a bleating childish voice when she realizes that she is about to be reduced to soulless clay as this fantasy of female creativity is also subject to Jewish tropes of the limits of human invention. *The Puttermesser Papers*, therefore, is both an allegory of the Jewish female writer in the Hebraic intertextual tradition, and a tale of maternal desire and creation.

Ozick's female golem is not the only imagined gender reversal in writing by Jewish women. In a mirror image of this work Anna Margolin (pseudonym for Rosa Lebensboym), modernist Yiddish poet, dons the mask of a speaker who is neither Jewish nor female in her poem "I Was Once a Boy" (or Lad or Youth) since the word "yingling," according to Anita Norich, was coined by Margolin and is indeterminate in gender. In the poem, the speaker imagines herself empowered and decadent at the center of two pagan civilizations, in Socrates's inner circle and as Caesar: "Rose-garlanded, drinking wine all night / In high spirits, heard tell the news / About the weakling from Nazareth / And wild tales about Jews" (trans. Kathryn Hellerstein in Chametzky, *Jewish American Literature*, 265). In this provocative cross-gender fantasy with both homoerotic and incestuous references, Margolin impersonates the voice of the center as projected from the margins of Jewish, and early Christian, civilizations.

In contrast to the woman's voice as modernist persona or folkloric reversal, female perspective in Holocaust narrative requires historical accuracy and an empathic imagination, which Ozick brings to her novella *The Shawl*, informed by the testimonies of survivors. Isabella Leitner's *Fragments of Isabella: A Memoir of Auschwitz* (1978) was among the first memoirs to document the particular sufferings of women. Packed into cattle cars with barred windows, no air, no toilets, and no doctors, Leitner recalls: "I was menstruating. There is no way for me to change my napkin . . . no room to sit . . . no room to stand . . . no room to breathe. This is no way to die. It offends even death" (*Fragments of Isabella*, 28). With women separated from their husbands, fathers, and brothers, they are left to care for themselves, and Leitner describes the death of her mother, her grief at not being able to save her infant sister, the devastating scene of women giving birth to babies: "how good of you to come before roll call though, so your mother does not have to stand at attention while you are being born . . . Your mother has no rights. She only brought forth fodder for the gas chamber. She is not a mother. She is just a dirty Jew who has soiled the Aryan landscape with another dirty Jew" (41). Leitner married a veteran of the war in America, as did Gerda Weissmann Klein, who recalls the American soldier who first spoke to her in the barracks by referring to the emaciated and sick inmates as "ladies" in *All But My Life* (1957). Klein cradles the head of her friend Ilse, who whispers to her before she expires, "If my parents survive, don't tell them I died like this" (*All But My Life*, 205). Years before taped Holocaust testimonies, these two writers exposed a woman's perspective on life in the camps: menstruation, sterilization, birth, rape, humiliation of a woman's body. Subsequent recorded testimonies served as the basis of Holocaust fictions like *The Shawl*, where survivor Rosa Lublin, traumatized by the murder of her infant daughter hurled against an electrified barbed-wire fence, continues to address her dead child by writing Polish letters to the grown woman she would have become. Since Rosa's breasts have dried from malnutrition, her daughter Magda sucks on a shawl that her mother deems a miracle of maternity, "it could nourish an infant three days and three nights" (Ozick, *The Shawl*, 5). But when Magda is murdered, her mother denies the very fact of her maternity and her daughter's birth by stuffing the same shawl into her own mouth, an act that muffles her cries and that devours her daughter and returns her to the womb. In the attempt to swallow that remnant of her maternity, she too becomes a lost child in the act of sucking it. Silenced voices are also the subject of the Yiddish poet Kadya Molodowsky, who immigrated to the United States in 1935. Gazing at the last mail she received from Nazi Europe in "Letters from the Ghetto," she wrote "Your brief letters – Three lines on a card, nothing more. / As if every mile added a stone – / That is how heavy they are." In 1945 she begins her poem with "God of Mercy / Choose – another people" (*The Penguin Book of Modern Yiddish Verse*, 330). American-born Muriel Rukeyser, for whom Jewishness was a matter of choice, regarded her identity in the war years as an ethical gift that the Jew dare not refuse: "If you refuse / Wishing to be invisible, you choose / Death of the spirit, the stone insanity" ("To be a Jew in the Twentieth Century," 538).

Ethical questions have continued to preoccupy Jewish American women writers in their representation of the Holocaust. Rebecca Goldstein turns to brutal choices faced *in* the camps in "The Legacy of Raizel Kaidish" (1985), where the tension between a survivor mother and her daughter dramatizes two moral philosophies, idealism and logical positivism. In her novel *The Mind/Body Problem* (1983), the infertility, miscarriages, and menstruation of Jewish women in America are shadowed by the countless unborn of those women who perished in the Holocaust. In "A Letter to Harvey Milk" (1988) Leslea Newman brings the persecution of gays to her story about a young American lesbian who becomes the confidante of an aging survivor. She is the first person to whom he can tell of the love of two men in a camp and the terrible price exacted by the Nazis for this last shred of human intimacy. New perspectives on the period of World War II have been produced recently by immigrants to the United States from the former Soviet Union, exemplified by Lara Vapnyar's collection *There are Jews in My House* (2003) where a Gentile Russian woman must make a moral decision whether to continue hiding her Jewish friend and daughter under German occupation. The horrors committed by Nazism have profoundly affected the writings of Jewish women in genres other than fiction. Apart from Hannah Arendt's controversial essay on American racism, Susan Sontag traced her influential work on the ethics of viewing in *On Photography* (1973) to what she called her "negative epiphany" when she first encountered photographs of Bergen-Belsen and Dachau in a bookstore in Santa Monica when she was twelve: "When I looked at those photographs something broke ... I felt irrevocably grieved, wounded ... something went dead, something is still crying" (*On Photography*, 20).

For a younger generation of women writers after the war, Jewish identity has revolved around memory and innovation. What aspects of tradition can sustain them as American women intent on remaining Jews without compromising their freedom as women? Many of these works focus on either historical memory (often of the Holocaust as discussed above), Jewish languages, or religious practice and spirituality, or some combination of all three.

What immigrant grandparents surrendered in the New World and what their children chose to forget, the grandchildren remember. Secure in English and in America, contemporary women writers are importing languages whose inscription on the tongues of their forebears was a source of frustration and dismay. This reflects both the renewal of interest in Yiddish, Ladino, and Hebrew within the Jewish community and the evocation of languages other than English in ethnic and minority writing in the United States in general. Access to these languages ranges from scattered memories of grandparents' speech to acquiring these languages and their literature through study. Having earned a doctorate in Yiddish literature, Dara Horn weaves both Yiddish and Hebrew into English prose. For example, Marc Chagall and the Yiddish writer Der Nister, a victim of Soviet anti-Semitism in the Gulag, are central characters in her novel *The World to Come* (2006). Rebecca Goldstein's novel *Mazel* (1995) spans three generations of Jewish women from Warsaw to New York: Sasha, the daughter of a Polish rabbi who abandons the shtetl for a career as a Yiddish actress in Warsaw and New York; her daughter Chloe, a professor of classics at Columbia; and her granddaughter Phoebe, a mathematician who returns to the traditional Judaism and domesticity that her mother and grandmother rejected. Jacqueline Osherow addresses and echoes Yiddish poets of the past, like Yankev Glatshteyn, whose acrid post-Holocaust "Dead Men Don't Praise God" (*Dead Men's Praise*, 79) is the point of departure for her poem, as she gingerly asks when it might be possible to reintroduce praise without being heartless. In Nicole Krauss's *The History of Love* (2005), a Holocaust survivor's lost love named Alma is also an analog for the lost manuscript of his Yiddish novel that survived only in translation into Spanish, where Alma means soul. Krauss's novel is a saga of circulating manuscripts, ghost writers, and translation. By the end of the book, the Yiddish original that has been destroyed in a flood takes on the mystery and power generally reserved for Hebrew, as its absence becomes the sacred site out of which all writing emanates.

Alongside the Yiddish remainder in contemporary works by women authors' depictions of their family history, immigration, American Jewish popular culture, and the legacy of European Jewish civilization, Hebrew continues to leave its mark as well. The dramatic rise of Conservative and Reform Judaism in America during the post-war years created a liberal environment for Jewish women, who were welcomed to participate in religious rituals, in sharp contrast to the dogmatic exclusions that writers like Antin and Yezierska had been subjected to previously. Whereas Sara Smolinsky in *Bread Givers* refused to let her rabbi rend her hard-earned tailored garment at her mother's funeral as the practice of *kria* requires, Mary Antin refused to submit to her "atavistic" revulsion when she downed her first ham sandwich in the inner sanctum of her revered English teacher's parlor, and Tillie Olsen's matriarch refused to bless the Sabbath candles in *Tell Me a Riddle* because they are "mumbo words and magic lights to scare away ghosts" (*Tell Me a Riddle*, 81), women in contemporary Jewish American literature often derive their inspiration from religion and adapt Judaic practice rather than abandon it, with exceptions such as Pearl Abraham's exposé of the Hasidic community in *The Romance Reader*. In contrast to Yezierska's railing against her patriarchal father, two recent works have portrayed observant fathers with tenderness as they embody lost cosmopolitan worlds for their daughters: Havana for Achy Obejas in *Days of Awe* (2001) and Cairo for Lucette Lagnado in her memoir *The Man in the White Sharkskin Suit* (2008). Post-colonial in their vantage point, these books also romanticize the polyglot (Spanish, Arabic, French, English, Hebrew) sites of empire where Jews usually fared better than in ethnic nationalist states.

In the spirit of laying claim to Judaism, E. M. Broner insists on her right to recite the Kaddish for her mother, traditionally required only of sons, and she records her daily experience during her year of mourning, as she encounters resistance along with respect and empathy. Allegra Goodman, secure in her right both to choose from among American Judaism's movements and to contribute to the forging of religious practice, satirizes the incursion of contemporary politics into ancient rituals in *The Family Markowitz* (1996), brings Jane Austen's wit and wry moralizing to the role of women in the Orthodox Jewish community in *Kaaterskill Falls* (1998), and sets a young heroine on a global spiritual journey in *Paradise Park* (2001) that takes her to Israel and back to New England. Only there, in the biblically named town of Sharon, can she realize the American egalitarian and traditional Jewish practice that she has been seeking. Other Jewish American women writers, like the poet Shirley Kaufman, found their new home in Israel, where they have continued to write in English about their new landscape of jacarandas, jasmine, stone, sealed rooms, and desert vistas. "We know what we want / before we know who we are," writes Kaufman in her poem "Reasons" (99). "That's why I came down / out of the air, unsure / as each of us in the first / departure, everyone telling me / this is home." The English poet Shelley's warning in the mouth of the ruined statue of an Egyptian Pharaoh – "Look on my works, ye Mighty, and despair!" – resonate for Kaufman as she contemplates "the Temple Mount / Haram al-Sharif . . . when I lay the palm of my hand on pitted history" ("Sanctum," 130).

Hebrew as a repository of Jewish culture has permeated the poetry of Jewish American women in recent years. Scenes of acquiring Hebrew literacy, ubiquitous in the works of male writers, convey women's sentiments about their ancestral language. When Jacqueline Osherow invokes the Bible in "Eight Months Pregnant in July, High Noon, Segesta" it is for its sound as well as its content: "I liked, in other words, to hear true stories – / A woman laughing at the child she carries, / A twin embezzling blessings from a twin . . . , / I luxuriated in their lulling Hebrew / Unraveling in my ears as they were sung / With the murky splendor of a holy tongue" (*Conversations with Survivors*, 61–2). In her poem "A Footnote for Perets Markish," Osherow concedes to the Yiddish poet Markish, who was executed by the Stalinist regime, that despite her freedom of expression in America, he always had a poetic edge simply by using the Hebrew alphabet. "I just want to talk to you," she writes, "And I could never get this language to convey / What yours manages to give off just by virtue / Of squeezing into an ill-suited script / Obsolescent two thousand years ago, / Though our stubborn ancestors continued to adapt / Its rococo crowns and stems to any sound . . . They meant the things they had to say to last, / And used the eternal *aleph-bet*" (*Dead Men's Praise*, 39–40).

One of the most interesting developments has been women's poetry in a meditative mode that artfully blurs the line between poetry and prayer. Maeera Shreiber has observed that Marcia Falk's collection *The Book of Blessing* "constitutes the first wholesale effort to reconceive prayer radically from a feminist theological perspective" (*Singing in a Strange Land*, 185). The point of departure for Falk's poetry is the challenge to male priesthood in the Bible itself, the figure of Hannah in the Book of Samuel addressing God in silent unmediated prayer, "Now Hannah she spoke in her heart." For further proof of Judaism's respect for Hannah's voice, Falk then draws on a Tractate from the Talmud that celebrates Hannah's private supplication. Marge Piercy's collection *The Art of Blessing the Day* offers prayer-poems at traditional seasons, holiday cycles, and rites of passage, as well as private occasions. "Bless whatever you can / with eyes, hands, and tongue. If you / can't bless it, get ready to make it new" (*The Art of Blessing the Day*, 5). In "A Candle in a Glass," Piercy describes the memorial *yahrtzeit* candle on the anniversary of a loved one's death as a "little low light . . . you couldn't read by it or even warm / your hands. So the dead are with us only / as the scent of fresh coffee, of cinnamon, / of pansies excites the nose and then fades, / with us as the small candle burns in its glass. / We lose and we go on losing as long as we live, / a little winter no spring can melt" (*The Art of Blessing the Day*, 49). Women have treasured the Book of Ruth, she claims, for its portrayal of the cherished bond between Ruth and Naomi: "Show me a woman who does not hide / in the locket of bone that deep / eyebeam of fiercely gentle love / she had once from mother, daughter, / sister" (*The Art of Blessing the Day*, 101).

None of these writers can represent the full range of experience that Jewish American women have voiced in their works. I would like to conclude with Grace Paley, an ardent Jewish secularist, and Marge Piercy, an ardent Judaic writer of liturgical and spiritual poems. Paley dedicated her *Collected Stories* to the memory of a friend, "my colleague in the Writing and Mother Trade. I visited her fifth-floor apartment on Barrow Street one day in 1957 . . . After that we talked and talked for nearly forty years. Then she died. Three days before that, she said slowly, with the delicacy of an unsatisfied person with only a dozen words left, Grace, the real question is – how are we to live our lives?" Each of the Jewish American woman writers in this brief survey has asked that question, regardless of whether she located the Jewish dimension of her life in ethnicity, religion, collective memory, languages, culture, marginality, social responsibility, or a shared sense of destiny. "A woman and a Jew," writes Marge Piercy, "sometimes more / of a contradiction than I can sweat out, /

yet finally the intersection that is both / collision and fusion, stone and seed"
(*The Art of Blessing the Day*, 174).

Endnote

The research for this essay was sponsored by Israel Science Foundation Grant 622/06, and the writing was completed at the Frankel Institute for Advanced Judaic Studies at the University of Michigan. My thanks to Ellen Coin, Deborah Dash Moore, Anita Norich, and David Roskies for good advice.

Works cited

Antin, Mary. *The Promised Land*. Boston: Houghton Mifflin, 1912.

Antler, Joyce, ed. *America and I: Short Stories by American Jewish Women Writers*. Boston: Beacon Press, 1990.

Arendt, Hannah. "Reflections on Little Rock." *Dissent* 6.1 (Winter 1959): 45–56.

Avery, Evelyn. *Modern Jewish Women Writers in America*. New York: Palgrave Macmillan, 2007.

Broner, E. M. *Mornings and Mourning: A Kaddish Journal*. San Francisco: Harper, 1994.

Budick, Emily. "Rebecca Goldstein: Jewish Visionary in Skirts." *The Hollins Critic* 34.2 (1997): 1–13.

Chametzky, Jules, ed. *Jewish American Literature: A Norton Anthology*. New York: W. W. Norton, 2001.

Dropkin, Celia. "A Dancer." 1959. In *Found Treasures: Stories by Yiddish Women Writers*. Ed. Frieda Forman *et al.* Toronto: Second Story Press, 1994.

Falk, Marcia. *The Book of Blessing: New Jewish Prayers for Daily Life, the Sabbath, and the New Moon Festival*. San Francisco: Harper, 1996.

Goldstein, Rebecca. *The Mind/Body Problem*. New York: Penguin, 1983.

    Mazel. New York: Viking, 1995.

Goodman, Allegra. *Paradise Park*. New York: Dial, 2001.

    Kaaterskill Falls. New York: Dial, 1998.

    The Family Markowitz. New York: Farrar, Straus Giroux, 1996.

Gubar, Susan. "Jewish American Women Writers and the Race Question." In *The Cambridge Companion to Jewish American Literature*. Ed. Hana Wirth-Nesher and Michael Kramer. Cambridge: Cambridge University Press, 2003.

Horn, Dara. *The World to Come*. New York: W. W. Norton, 2006.

Hurst, Fannie. *Imitation of Life*. New York: Harper, 1933.

Kaufman, Shirley. "Reasons." In *Roots in the Air*. Port Townsend, WA: Copper Canyon Press, 1996.

    "Sanctum." In *Threshold*. Port Townsend, WA: Copper Canyon Press, 2003.

Klein, Gerda Weissman. *All But My Life*. New York: Hill and Wang, 1957.

Krauss, Nicole. *The History of Love*. New York: W. W. Norton, 2005.

Lagnado, Lucette. *The Man in the White Sharkskin Suit*. New York: Harper Collins, 2007.

Lazarus, Emma. *Selected Poems*. Ed. John Hollander. New York: The Library of America, 2005.

Leitner, Isabella. *Fragments of Isabella: A Memoir of Auschwitz*. New York: Dell, 1978.

Margolin, Anna. *Poems*. Introduction by Avraham Novershtern. Jerusalem: Magnes Press, 1991.

Marom, Daniel. "Who is the 'Mother of Exiles'? Jewish Aspects of Emma Lazarus's 'The New Colossus'." *Prooftexts* 20 (2000): 231–61.

Matza, Diane, ed. *Sephardic-American Voices: Two Hundred Years of a Literary Legacy*. Hanover: University Press of New England, 1997.

Molodowsky, Kadya. "God of Mercy." Trans. Irving Howe. In *The Penguin Book of Modern Yiddish Verse*. Ed. Irving Howe, Ruth R. Wisse, and Khone Shmeruk. New York: Viking, 1987.

    Paper Bridges: Selected Poems of Kadya Molodowsky. Trans. and ed. Kathryn Hellerstein. Detroit: Wayne State University Press, 1999.

Newman, Leslea. "A Letter to Harvey Milk," in Antler, *America and I*.

Norich, Anita. "Yiddish Literature." In *Jewish Women in America: An Historical Encyclopedia*. Ed. Paula Hyman and Deborah Dash Moore. New York: Routledge, 1998.

Obejas, Achy. *Days of Awe*. New York: Ballantine, 2001.

Olsen, Tillie. *Tell Me a Riddle*. New York: Random House, 1990.

Osherow, Jacqueline. *Conversations with Survivors*. Athens, GA, and London: University of Georgia Press, 1994.

    Dead Men's Praise. New York: Grove, 1999.

Ozick, Cynthia. "America: Toward Yavneh." In *What is Jewish Literature?* Ed. Hana Wirth-Nesher. Philadelphia: Jewish Publication Society, 1994.

    The Puttermesser Papers: A Novel. New York: Knopf, 1997.

    The Shawl. New York: Random House, 1990.

Paley, Grace. *The Collected Stories*. New York: Farrar, Straus Giroux, 1994.

Piercy, Marge. *The Art of Blessing the Day*. New York: Knopf, 1999.

    "The Ram's Horn Sounding." In Chametzky, *Jewish American Literature*.

Rukeyer, Muriel. "To be a Jew in the Twentieth Century." In Chametzky, *Jewish American Literature*.

Schor, Esther. *Emma Lazarus*. New York: Schocken, 2006.

Segal, Lore. *Her First American*. New York: The New Press, 1985.

Shapiro, Ann, ed. *Jewish American Women: A Bio-Bibliographical and Critical Sourcebook*. Westport, CT: Greenwood Press, 1994.

Shreiber, Maeera. *Singing in a Strange Land: A Jewish American Poetics*. Stanford: Stanford University Press, 2007.

Sontag, Susan. *On Photography*. New York: Farrar, Straus Giroux, 1973.

Vapnyar, Lara. *There are Jews in My House*. New York: Pantheon, 2003.

Wasserstein, Wendy. *The Heidi Chronicles and Other Plays*. New York: Harcourt Brace Jovanovich, 1990.

Wolosky, Shira, "An American-Jewish Typology: Emma Lazarus and the Figure of Christ." *Prooftexts* 16 (1996): 113–25.

Yezierska, Anzia. *Bread Givers*. New York: Persea, 1925.

    Salome of the Tenements. 1923. Urbana: University of Illinois Press, 1995.

24

Women on the breadlines

JOHN MARSH

The proletarian and radical literature written during the Great Depression has had a famously doomed afterlife. For decades, when it was not being attacked, it was being ignored. The New Critics defined themselves – and the canon of American literature – against it, and Cold War-era English Departments did their best to pretend that it never happened. From the late 1940s to the late 1970s, you can count on two hands the number of scholarly books devoted to radical and proletarian writers of the 1930s. Moreover, when scholars did brave the critical climate, their writing focused almost exclusively on men. True, some women writers from the period – Josephine Herbst, Genevieve Taggard – simply played too big a role in radical literary culture to drop out of the story completely. But in the early literary histories of the movement – Walter Rideout's *The Radical Novel in the United States 1900–1954* (1956), Daniel Aaron's *Writers on the Left* (1961), or Richard Pell's *Radical Visions and American Dreams* (1977) – and the first attempts at constructing a canon of radical and proletarian literature of the 1930s, women remained decidedly in the background.

This essay, following the work of a number of scholars in the last two or three decades, tries to bring those women writers of the 1930s into the foreground. In defense of these early critics, though, one should note that they may not have actively – or even perhaps consciously – written women out of literary history, but, rather, simply responded to the fact that something about the decade itself seemed peculiarly masculine. From certain if not most perspectives, that is, the victims of the Great Depression, as well as their chroniclers, seemed to be mostly men. Unsurprisingly, then, men dominated the histories they told.

Consider photographs of breadlines from the Great Depression. As in Figure 24.1, taken in New York City in February of 1932, most photographs take the long view, framing the snaking, seemingly interminable lines of

Fig. 24.1 "The Great Depression" (1932)

hungry, desperate men. The photograph casts the figures in the breadline as merely one of many, a mass and all but faceless problem. Only rarely, as in Dorothea Lange's famous 1932 photograph, "White Angel Breadline," did photographers focus in on an individual face in one of those interminable breadlines. Whether they took the far or close view, though, what united these photographs of Depression-era breadlines – and the breadlines that went undocumented – was the gender of those standing in lines. Hardly ever does a woman appear. Why? Did women, unlike men, have all the bread they could eat? If not, and it seems unlikely, how did they survive?

This mystery inspired one of the most famous pieces of Depression-era reportage, Meridel Le Sueur's "Women on the Breadlines." Written and published in the same year as the photograph above was taken, Le Sueur's title deliberately misleads. Her point is how few women actually appear in breadlines.

> It's one of the great mysteries of the city where women go when they are out of work and hungry. There are not many women in the bread line. There are no flop houses for women as there are for men, where a bed can be had for a quarter or less. You don't see women lying on the floor at the mission in the free flops. They obviously don't sleep in the jungle or under newspapers in the park. There is no law I suppose against their being in such places but the fact is they rarely are.
>
> Yet there must be as many women out of jobs in cities and suffering extreme poverty as there are men. What happens to them? Where do they go? . . .
>
> I've lived in cities for many months broke, without help, too timid to get in bread lines. I've known many women to live like this until they simply faint on the street from privations, without saying a word to anyone. A woman will shut herself up in a room until it is taken away from her, and eat a cracker a day and be quiet as a mouse so there are no social statistics concerning her. (140–1)

As the final paragraph of this excerpt suggests, part of the mystery of what happens to women in extreme poverty is owed to their isolation, to their being "quiet as a mouse." That is, unlike the very public spectacle of men in breadlines, the unemployment, hunger, and suffering of women remain private, concealed behind doors and left unspoken.

Having registered the mystery of where women go if they do not go to breadlines, the remainder of Le Sueur's "Women on the Breadlines" tries to solve it. Le Sueur does so not through "social statistics" but something equally if not more valuable: stories and narratives. Indeed, the setting of "Women on the Breadline" is not a breadline but the "woman's section" of "the city free employment bureau," where women "sit every day, waiting for a job" even though "there are no jobs" (137). Gradually, out of boredom and loneliness, after hours and days spent waiting, the women begin to share their stories, their own and others, and the mystery is to some extent solved. Some women, contrary to Le Sueur's initial skepticism, do manage to get help from the charities. Other women, confirming her intuition, starve silently. Some women "can get jobs in the stores where there are any, or waiting on table," Le Sueur writes, "but these jobs are only for the attractive and the adroit" (138). One woman waiting for a job, Bernice, "lives alone in little rooms"; she walks "the streets looking for men to take her to a picture show" (138). Another woman, out of work for eight months, goes crazy. Still another woman, Ellen, after experimenting with flashing her legs for spare change behind a restaurant, will now, the consensus holds, take to walking the streets in earnest – though, as Le Sueur puts it, "like every commodity now the body is difficult to sell and the girls say you're lucky if you get fifty cents" (140). Whether they sell their bodies or not, all "refuse to marry, refuse to rear children." "They are like certain savage tribes," Le Sueur observes, "who, when they have been conquered, refuse to breed." So they "get what fun they can" (141).

Which is not much, to judge from the women at the employment bureau. Most women simply survive, "beaten, entrapped" (141). "We sit in this room like cattle," Le Sueur concludes, "waiting for a nonexistent job, willing to work to the farthest atom of energy, unable to work, unable to get food and lodging, unable to bear children; here we must sit in this shame of looking at the floor, worse than beasts at a slaughter" (142). In short, Le Sueur's moving report suggests that while women may not have appeared on breadlines, they suffered the effects of the Great Depression just as much as – if not more than – their male counterparts.

In addition to whatever insight Le Sueur provides about how women weathered the Great Depression, her article suggests that it would take a more persistent art than photography to capture women's experience during that decade. For many writers, including many women writers, literature – stories, poems, novels, and first-person journalism – was that art.

In this essay, I explore how women deployed that art, what stories they told, and how they rendered the experience of the Great Depression. In order to tell this history, I bypass the historical question of what happened to women during the Great Depression – though that inevitably arises in passing – and ask instead the literary-historical question, what happened to women writers during the Great Depression? Where did they go? What did they make? And how was what they made received, either in the moment of its making or among later critics and readers?

In what follows, I describe the major figures of the period and the critical tradition that has built up around these figures. I also offer a word about the direction future scholarship might take. Thus far, most scholarship on women writers during the 1930s has focused on the literary left, on writers who had close – albeit occasionally ambivalent – relationships with the Communist Party. For the most part, I follow that trend here. Nevertheless, one of the directions for future scholarship I will propose is that for the field to remain – and to some extent regain – its urgency, it must start asking new questions, and perhaps asking them of different writers than it heretofore has.

What – and when – were the 1930s?

The field of American women's writing on the left is dominated by two writers, Meridel Le Sueur and Tillie Olsen, and, even more specifically, by two books, Le Sueur's *The Girl* and Olsen's *Yonnondio*. Meridel Le Sueur's *The Girl* is a coming-of-age novel set among the lumpenproletariat of Depression-era St. Paul, Minnesota. Among other incidents – a strike, a love story, a pregnancy, an aborted abortion, a botched bank robbery, and the daily struggle to survive the Great Depression – the book culminates in a feminist revisioning of radical politics. Women, Le Sueur implies, mothers to their children, offer the only hope for the birth of a new, more humane world. Less openly revolutionary, Olsen's *Yonnondio* follows the dissolution of the Holbrook family from coal mine to tenant farm to urban squalor, although that brief description does not do justice to its lyrical force or Olsen's delicate rendering of besieged but defiant hope for a better world.

Rightly so, the books have received an immense amount of critical attention and, if the field of American women's writing during the Great Depression has produced any canonical works, these novels are them.

The only problem is that neither Le Sueur nor Olsen published their major works during the 1930s. Each published stories, journalism, and, in Olsen's case, poetry during the decade, and each participated in the occasionally rarefied subculture of the literary left. (Both Le Sueur and Olsen, for example, were one of a handful of women delegates to the Communist Party-sponsored First American Writers Congress in 1935.) Nevertheless, in Le Sueur's case because she could not find a publisher, and in Olsen's case because she did not try to find one – she would not complete the book until the early 1970s – *The Girl* would not appear until 1978 and *Yonnondio* until 1974 (Rabinowitz, *Labor and Desire*, 99).

Besides what it reveals about the challenges women writers faced getting their work published during this period – challenges Olsen describes and theorizes in her 1978 book *Silences* – the unusual publishing history of these works raises two problems for any effort to survey the field of American women writers during the Great Depression. First, there is the books in print problem. Second, there is the period problem.

As Cary Nelson noted two decades ago in *Repression and Recovery*, literary critics play a major, perhaps decisive role in deciding which texts to recover and the "new discursive life" those texts will have "in the present" (11). As I mention later, for example, in 1981 Deborah Rosenfelt published an essay on "Tillie Olsen and the Radical Tradition" that would inspire renewed attention to Olsen's work. In subsequent years, more and more critics would write about Olsen, and *Yonnondio* would appear on more and more syllabi. But Rosenfelt could only write her essay – and *Yonnondio* appear on syllabi – because Delacorte, now a division of Random House, published the reconstructed manuscript in 1974. The same pattern follows for any number of writers. A work reappears in print, followed by more or less thoughtful reviews, and only then – and not in all cases – does a critical and pedagogical tradition cohere around the work.

It seems like a trivial point, perhaps even a truism, but it is nevertheless worth stating that publishers – and, of course, authors, readers, and critics – shape the canon of American literature. Teachers can only teach, and critics can only debate, works that teachers, critics, and students can easily access. This is especially the case for previously marginalized subfields like American women's writing of the 1930s, when so many works almost immediately fell out of print or, as in the case of *Yonnondio* and *The Girl*, never appeared at all. Over the years, various presses have done yeoman's work in this domain, none more so than the Feminist Press, which has reissued many Depression-era novels by women. Similarly, John Crawford's West End Press has cared for Meridel Le Sueur's work, and many university presses have resuscitated a book or two, perhaps because it had some regional significance. And while it met an untimely demise, the radical novel reconsidered series, published by the University of Illinois Press in the 1990s and overseen by Alan Wald, published many lost novels of the 1930s, several by women. Despite these efforts, more works than not remain out of print and all but inaccessible.

When it comes to journalism, short stories, and poems, the problem is magnified still further. While a handful of women writers working in these genres published discrete books, some of which I discuss below, much writing by women appeared in the newspapers and journals of the era and never appeared again. Charlotte Nekola and Paula Rabinowitz's *Writing Red: An Anthology of American Women's Writing, 1930–1940* (thanks again to the Feminist Press) collects some of the best of this work, but only a fraction.

The result is that some texts have found admirers and publishers, while others, seemingly equally worthy, have not. And that is just the work that we know about. Even after the recovery efforts of the past forty years, no one quite knows what remains or where critics have thus far failed to look. It is enough to inspire a Library of Alexandria-like awe regarding the lost or forgotten works of literary history. What texts have escaped critics' attention, which remain unpublished, even undiscovered? "The more we have dug," Alan Wald writes, "the less we know for certain" (*Writing*, 102), a statement that remains as true today as when Wald published it in 1994.

As a result, one can speak of the major figures in the field, but speaking of these major figures should come with the understanding that many institutions and actors – critics, readers, acquiring editors, estates – had to pull together to establish those figures as the major ones. Conversely, when those institutions and actors did not or could not pull together, often equally strong works – and potentially major figures – languish in library stacks, unread and uncelebrated.

The second problem that Olsen and Le Sueur's slightly unorthodox publishing histories suggest is when the historical clock on the 1930s should start and stop. Begun in the 1930s, both *Yonnondio* and *The Girl* were reconstructed, revised, and published in the 1970s. Both works are "from the thirties," as the subtitle to *Yonnondio* puts it, but neither is, strictly speaking, of the thirties. Should they count as 1930s works? Perhaps because each novel was officially undertaken during the 1930s, one can more easily make the case that they belong to the 1930s. But what about Olsen's 1961 collection of short stories, *Tell Me a Riddle*? Many of those stories deal with themes or legacies of the 1930s, but none of them was written or published until the late 1950s and early 1960s. On the other end of the timeline, where does Agnes Smedley's autobiographical novel *Daughter of the Earth* belong, written in the late 1920s and published in 1929, before the 1930s could even get started? Indeed, it is astonishing how many writers, particularly women writers, moved left before the stock market crashed in late 1929 or before the unemployment rate skyrocketed in the early 1930s – before, that is, what we think of when we think of the 1930s could begin. Some writers, like Le Sueur, grew up in families connected to the old left of socialists and the Industrial Workers of the World. For others, the execution of Sacco and Vanzetti in 1927 seems to have driven them toward radical politics.

Given these ambiguities, critics have revised what counts as 1930s in ways that matter for how we understand the period. In short, scholars no longer feel quite as much confidence in starting the period in 1929 or 1930 and ending it in 1940 or 1941, as various anthologies and monographs did and occasionally still do. In particular, scholars like John Lowney have argued for a generational approach to the 1930s. That is, Lowney has suggested that scholars should focus on a "Depression cohort" of writers, those born between 1904 and 1923. Thus, as I have written elsewhere:

the work of a literary generation would not be limited to what was written and published during any given decade (the 1930s, for example) but, rather, would include work by that generation of writers regardless of the date of publication. In the case of the Depression cohort, then, the literature of the 1930s . . . is not that published between 1930 and 1941 but, rather, from 1930 to, effectively, the last decades of the twentieth century, when this Depression generation gradually began to die off. ("The Depression Cohort," 471–2)

Following Lowney, then, works like Mary McCarthy's *The Company She Keeps* (1942), Ann Petry's *The Street* (1946), or still later works like Olsen's *Tell Me a Riddle* (1961) or, more controversially, Muriel Rukeyser's book of poems *Breaking Open* (1973) would count as Depression-era works. According to this way of thinking, the 1930s were not a period but a generation, a sensibility, and the works of this generation and sensibility remain relevant to a discussion of the 1930s regardless of their publication date.

Lowney helps us solve the riddle of what to do with texts published after the decade of the 1930s, but that leaves works from a slightly earlier generation. Even more expansive than Lowney, Alan Wald has argued for critics to take as their subject what he calls "the Mid-Twentieth-Century Literary Left," which operated from roughly 1911 (the founding of *The Masses*) to the mid-1960s (the birth of the New Left) (*Exiles from a Future Time*). In which case, works like Anna Louise Strong's 1935 pro-Soviet autobiography *I Change Worlds* would belong to the field, but so too would her earlier collection of poems inspired by the Seattle General Strike, *Ragged Verse* (1918). Similarly, Anzia Yezierska's novels of immigrant life and radical politics, *Salome of the Tenements* (1923) and *Bread Givers* (1925), would also "count" in our reckoning of the field, as would Edith Summers Kelly's moving novel of poverty, pregnancy, and motherhood among rural Kentucky tobacco farmers, *Weeds* (1923).

Thus, in the following outline of the field of American women writers of the 1930s, I try to keep in mind that just because some works have fallen out of print, or do not currently preoccupy critics and readers, that is not a judgment – and certainly not a final judgment – on their value or their interest to the field. Moreover, while I focus on works published during the decade of the 1930s, I do not let that decision exclude works that we might still want to consider as part of the field of American women's writing of, about, from – choose your preposition – the Great Depression.

Before I start slotting works of literature into categories, though, it is worth mentioning another undisputed major figure in the field, Josephine Herbst, whose work, to some extent, transcends categories – or belongs in several at once. While Le Sueur and Olsen would have been known to their contemporaries mostly through their uncollected journalism, stories, and poems – though Le Sueur did publish a book of short stories, *Salute to Spring*, in 1940 – Herbst not only published stand-alone novels with a major publisher (Harcourt Brace) but also an ambitious trilogy of novels in the 1930s: *Pity Is Not Enough* (1933), *The Executioner Waits* (1934), and *Rope of Gold* (1939). The novels follow two families, the Trexlers and the Wendels, from Reconstruction through the first three decades of the twentieth century and across several regions of the United States. The final and most highly regarded of the books, *Rope of Gold*, covers the Depression years and offers the (supposedly autobiographical) portrait of Victoria and Jonathan Chance, a couple struggling to make a life together while the old world collapses around them and a new one waits to be built. Also of note is Herbst's journalism, which appeared in various left-wing newspapers and magazines throughout the decade. Remarkably, Herbst seems to have been in all the right places at just the right time: Nazi Germany after Hitler took power; Flint, Michigan for the sit-down strike; and Spain after the start of the Spanish Civil War, among other hot spots. (The journalism, alas, remains uncollected.)

Finally, and for whatever reason, many humanists distrust categories. I have fewer qualms about them. To be sure, categories are not perfect, and some overlap, but that just means we have to accept categories, especially literary categories, for what they are, convenient ways to structure an amorphous field, rather than what they are not, definitive statements about a work's content or value.

Before offering more specific categories, I should add that all of the works that follow belong to the category of American women's writing and most – but not all – belong to the category of women writers addressing the experience of women as wives, mothers, workers, and organizers in what I have come to think of as the long 1930s. Not surprisingly, those are the works that critics – or publishers like the Feminist Press – have chosen to take up and, thus, these are the works that have come to constitute the field.

Fiction

In terms of fiction, the field divides most broadly between strike novels and non-strike novels. Within the category of strike novels, there seem to be two kinds: novels about the Gastonia strike and novels about other strikes. The Gastonia strike illustrates why the conventional dates of the Great Depression will not capture the phenomenon we seek to name when we invoke the 1930s. Beginning in early 1929, workers – many of the women – at the Loray

Mill in Gastonia, North Carolina, began to organize under the banner of the Communist-led National Textile Workers Union. The strike arose in response to the grievances that usually inspire strikes: low wages, inhuman working conditions, and the basic right of workers to organize collectively. What made Gastonia different was the violent response to the strike. A demonstration in June, broken up by the local sheriff, led to the sheriff's death, the arrest of scores of strikers, and charges of murder for more than a dozen strikers and organizers. (If you are wondering how more than a dozen people could be charged with the murder of one sheriff, welcome to the 1930s.) After a mistrial, the region exploded in violence. Strikers were attacked by vigilantes and, in at least one case, that of Ella Mae Wilkins, a local worker turned striker turned organizer turned labor balladeer, murdered. Not least because of the prominent role women played in the strike, Gastonia inspired a number of novels by women. These include Mary Heaton Vorse's *Strike!* (1930), Fielding Burke's *Call Home the Heart* (1932), Grace Lumpkin's *To Make My Bread* (1932), Myra Page's *Gathering Storm: A Story of the Black Belt* (1932), and two sequels of sorts, Grace Lumpkin's *A Sign for Cain* (1935) and Fielding Burke's *A Stone Came Rolling* (1935).

Novelists had no shortage of other strikes to inspire their fiction. Non-Gastonia strike novels include Clara Weatherwax's dramatization of a lumber strike in Aberdeen, Washington, *Marching! Marching!* (1935). The book won a *New Masses* contest for a novel on an American proletarian theme, but that prize seems only to have arrayed critics against it, then and since. It has now come to epitomize the best and the worst – mostly the worst – of proletarian literature of the 1930s. Slightly more successful is Ruth McKinney's modernist-influenced take on the Akron rubber strike, *Industrial Valley* (1939). (McKinney would achieve fifteen minutes of fame when her light-hearted stories describing her and her sister's move from the provinces of Ohio to a Greenwich Village basement apartment, published in *The New Yorker* and later collected in a book, *My Sister Eileen*, were made into a popular Broadway play and later film. Her next book, the chest-beating proletarian novel, *Jake Home* [1943], did not fare nearly so well.) Leanne Zugsmith's intriguing novel, *A Time to Remember* (1936), also dramatizes a strike, but it remains an oddity in that, unusual for the time, it imagines a strike not of industrial workers but among an eclectic group of department store workers in New York City.

Lauren Gilfallan's new woman meets Pennsylvania coal strike novel *I Went to Pit College* (1932) – yes it is as good as it sounds – overlaps the category of strike novel and the next category, lightly fictionalized autobiographies about women on the left. Gilfallan's semi-autobiographical novel depicts a charming if slightly reckless Smith College graduate who travels to a Pennsylvania coal town to see how the other half lives.[1] More conventionally, the category of *roman à clefs* would include Agnes Smedley's frequently taught *Daughter of the Earth* (1929) and, more openly autobiographical still, Mary Heaton Vorse's *A Footnote to Folly* (1935), which covers the years 1912 to 1922. I have mentioned Vorse's Gastonia novel (*Strike!*), and she published an earlier novel on another famous textile strike, *Passaic* (1926), but her autobiography is in many ways her best work. Vorse led a remarkable life, much of it captured in the compelling autobiography: one of the first Greenwich Village bohemians, original member of the Provincetown Players, writer, educational reformer, and, as I discuss below, prominent labor reporter. Another veteran of the political left, Anna Louise Strong, also known for her reportage, published a fascinating autobiography, *I Change Worlds* (1935), which concludes with a now regrettable embrace of the greatness that was the Soviet Union under Stalin.

Tess Slesinger's merciless dissection of New York intellectuals and their enablers, *The Unpossessed* (1934), epitomizes a closely related category, barely fictional fiction that sends up the pretensions, occasionally the absurdities, of radical intellectual life. Slesinger would later publish a splendid collection of short stories with similar themes, *Time: The Present* (1939). A case could be made that Mary McCarthy's risqué and slightly later collection of short stories, *The Company She Keeps* (1942), especially the stories "The Man in the Brooks Brothers Shirt" and "Portrait of the Intellectual as a Yale Man," also belongs to this category.

Finally, there are novels that I think of as devoted to certain places. At this point, perhaps, categories become less useful, since every novel has a setting, but these novels undertake a sustained inquiry into how the Depression played out in certain cities or regions. Somewhere between the novel of place and *roman à clefs* lies Myra Page's *Daughter of the Hills*, about coal-mining in the Cumberland Mountains in Tennessee. Written in the 1930s but published in 1950 with the title *With Sun in Our Blood*, the book is something of an as-told-to, based on the life of Dolly Hawkins Cooper, a daughter, wife, worker, and organizer of the region whom Page had met while teaching at Commonwealth College, one of several labor colleges established during the period. Page also wrote *Moscow Yankee* (1935), a novel about a displaced Detroit autoworker in the adolescent, industrializing years of the Soviet Union.

Catharine Brody's sensationalist but oddly compelling novel *Nobody Starves* (1932) starts in New Jersey but quickly moves to its real subject, automobile factories – and the troubled lives and marriages of automobile factory workers – in 1930s Detroit. (*Nobody Starves* is also a strike novel of sorts.) The next year, Brody published a study of a small, midwestern city, *Cash Item* (1933), which is also, perhaps unexpectedly, one of the few novels about money, credit, and banking during the 1930s. I have mentioned Leanne Zugsmith's *A Time to Remember*, her novel of striking department store workers. Prior to that, Zugsmith published *The Reckoning* (1934), a wide-angled novel of New York City that captures everything from the Italian slums to the city courts and schoolhouses.

Perhaps the best known of these novels, and not just novels of a certain place but all novels produced by the literary left, was Josephine Johnson's *Now in November* (1934), a lyrical, at times claustrophobic novel about a family suffering through the Great Depression, a drought, and other natural and familial disasters on a small Missouri farm. The novel won the Pulitzer Prize in 1935. Johnson later published a study of a small Missouri town coming apart along class lines, *Jordanstown* (1937), which was not as well received. Between *Now in November* and *Jordanstown*, Johnson would publish a book of short stories, *Winter Orchard* (1935) and, in the late 1960s, a classic of environmental writing, *The Inland Island* (1969). (Johnson, better known for her fiction, also published a collection of radical verse in 1937, *Year's End*.)

And while it probably does not count as a category if only one writer occupies it, no survey of Depression-era fiction is complete without mentioning Caroline Slade, who perfected what is sometimes called the social problem novel. Slade, a former social worker, published a trilogy of novels about prostitution, including *Sterile Sun* (1936), *Margaret* (1946), and *Mrs. Party's House* (1948). Her best-known work, *The Triumph of Willie Pond* (1940), in which prostitution figures as an important sub-plot, is an unforgiving attack on the irrationalities and injustices of existing social welfare policies.

Reportage

As could be gathered from the survey above, many 1930s novelists also wrote non-fiction. Indeed, one of the characteristic genres of the 1930s was reportage, a kind of descriptive, at times essayistic, participatory journalism. ("In brief," the editors of the authoritative *Proletarian Literature in the United States* wrote in 1935, "reportage is the presentation of a particular fact, a specific event, in a setting that aids the reader to experience the fact, the event. This is the best reporting" [212]. John Reed's account of the Bolshevik Revolution, *Ten Days That Shook the World* [1919], was often held up as a model.) I referred to Josephine Herbst's journalism above, but Le Sueur's "Women on the Breadlines" is another example of the genre, as is her occasionally anthologized piece, "I Was Marching," about the Minneapolis Teamsters strike of 1934.

As these examples suggest, women excelled at the genre. To my mind, the field divides into two categories: domestic and international reportage. Much of the domestic reportage remains uncollected. (Charlotte Nekola and Paula Rabinowitz's anthology, *Writing Red*, collects some of this work, especially reportage published by African American women [Vivian Dahl, Elaine Ellis, Mollie Lewis, Thyra J. Edwards in journals like *Opportunity* and *Crisis*], but they could only include so much.) Although I have praised Mary Heaton Vorse's autobiography (and remained deliberately silent about her Gastonia novel), her best work may have been as a journalist. Many of her articles would never appear again outside of the newspapers that published them, but she did publish several books based on her journalism, including *Men and Steel* (1920), her account of the 1919 steel strike, and from the 1930s, *Labor's New Millions* (1938), an incisive account of the rise of the most important labor institution in the period, the Congress of Industrial Organizations.

Anna Louise Strong also published a book on her travels in the United States, *My Native Land* (1940), but she is better known for her international reporting. Although other women writers published works explaining and defending the Soviet experiment and the revolutionary struggle of Communists in China, Strong made a career of it. In addition to *I Change Worlds*, her 1935 autobiography, she published a truly astonishing number of pamphlets, books, and travelogues. In a similar vein, Myra Page published *Soviet Main Street* (1933), the basis of her novel *Moscow Yankee* (1935). Although not as committed a Leftist as Strong or Page, Ella Gruber's *I Went to the Soviet Arctic* (1939) also offered to explain the new Soviet Union, including its revolutionary gender relations, to an American audience. Ella Winter's 1933 book, *Red Virtues: Human Relations in the New Russia*, takes up a similar theme, although Winter writes much more from the position of convert than does Gruber. Following her autobiography, Agnes Smedley relocated to China and published a number of books about pre- and post-revolutionary China. The best of these, because the most comprehensive, is probably *Battle Hymn of China* (1943).

As I suggest below, the tradition of radical journalism by American women writers has unfortunately received relatively little attention.

Poetry

Poets obviously pose a bit more of a classificatory problem than do novelists or other narrative writers since poets do not restrict themselves to one form, theme, or setting. Still, one line seems to divide poets on the left from each other during this period: those who managed to publish a collection of verse and those who did not. Unsurprisingly, those who published books have been considered the major figures in the field while those who did not have mostly, although in some cases unjustly, disappeared.[2]

From a slightly earlier generation, Lola Ridge made her name with an ambitious and widely praised first book of poems, *The Ghetto* (1918), whose long title poem affectionately depicts Jewish immigrant life on New York's Lower East Side. In each of the books of poems that followed, Ridge explored one of several left-wing themes: the exploitation of the working class in *Sun-Up* (1920), the Russian Revolution in *Red Flag* (1927), and, in *Firehead* (1929), an imaginative retelling of the execution of Sacco and Vanzetti through Christ's crucifixion. Each collection, it must be said, grew increasingly oblique in image and tone. *Dance of Fire*, from 1935, included poems about various *causes célèbres* of the radical left (Tom Mooney, Sacco and Vanzetti), but by then Ridge had taken to writing an increasingly private and at times obscure, even inscrutable, verse.

More of a precursor to the radical poetry of the 1930s, Lucia Trent's *Children of Fire and Shadow* (1929) satirized bourgeois pretensions and included the still powerful poem, "Breed, Woman, Breed." Trent and her husband, Ralph Cheyney, also a poet, collaborated on a fascinating manifesto-cum-book of criticism, *More Power to Poets* (1934), and a 1937 collection of poems, *Thank You, America!*

Genevieve Taggard, like Trent and Ridge, had a foot in the Bohemian left of the 1920s but, unlike Trent or Ridge, played a major role in the Communist-oriented left of the 1930s. Perhaps no American woman poet had greater influence in the field of the mid-twentieth-century literary left than Taggard. Her reputation, for reasons that remain understandable if undeserved, has since declined. In 1938, Taggard recalled that her earlier volumes of poetry – including *For Eager Lovers* (1922) and *Words for the Chisel* (1926) – "were mostly about love and marriage and having children" (quoted in Berke, *Women Poets on the Left*, 111). While these themes seem to have led Taggard to dismiss these poems, they have proven to be of more rather than less interest to later critics.[3] In the mid-1920s, Taggard turned toward editing and biography. In 1925, she assembled *May Days*, an anthology of revolutionary verse compiled from

The Masses and *The Liberator*, two of the most prominent early cultural organs on the left. In 1929, she published an unusual anthology of metaphysical verse, *Circumference: Varieties of Metaphysical Verse, 1456–1928*. (The subtitle suggests what made it unusual. Taggard traced the metaphysical impulse from Donne and the other usual suspects through Emily Dickinson to T. S. Eliot, Robert Frost, Wallace Stevens, and other modernist poets.) In 1930, Taggard published one of the first – and one of the best – biographies of Emily Dickinson, *The Life and Mind of Emily Dickinson*. The book did much to establish Dickinson as a major American poet. Nevertheless, it is as a poet that Taggard made her mark in the 1930s. In 1934, she published one of the iconic collections of Depression-era poetry, *Calling Western Union*. Later collections, including *Long Music* (1942), continued Taggard's engagement with public themes, including the US response to European fascism, the Spanish Civil War, and racism and segregation.

While not as prominent as Taggard, three poets – Ruch Lechlitner, Joy Davidman, and Marie de L. Welch – published significant volumes of verse in the 1930s. Lechlitner's *Tomorrow's Phoenix* (1937) diagnosed the ills of Depression-era United States – including the oppression of women – and, unusual for the period, championed a return to nature as a possible cure. (Lechlitner would publish another relevant collection of poems in 1944, *Only the Years: Selected Poems, 1938–1944*.) Joy Davidman's first volume of poems, *Letter to a Comrade* (1938), is a quintessential collection of 1930s verse, with poems addressing a range of contemporaneous issues (labor, poverty, fascism) and not-so-contemporaneous issues, like women's oppression. The collection won the prestigious Yale Younger Poet's prize and received a number of (mostly positive) reviews. Davidman later converted to Christianity, married the writer and theologian C. S. Lewis, and drifted away from radical politics. Welch's first volume of poems, *Poems* (1933), caused a minor stir on the left when reviewers attacked it for not being sufficiently revolutionary.[4] Whatever the merits of the attack, Welch's next book of poems, *This Is Our Own* (1940), contains some provocative work. Like Lechlitner, Welch had an abiding interest in the natural world, and it can be exciting to watch that interest merge with the occasionally anti-capitalist poems in the book.

In a testament to how ordinary radical verse would seem in the 1930s, Muriel Rukeyser's first collection of verse, *Theory of Flight* (1937), also won the Yale Younger Poet's prize. (Margaret Walker's *For My People*, which I discuss below, would win the prize in 1942.) Almost alone among women poets on the left, Rukeyser has attracted a good deal of scholarly attention, as much for her later feminist poetry as her earlier feminist-tinged radical poetry, although the balance has recently shifted back to her 1930s poetry. Rukeyser's second volume of poems, *US 1* (1938), contains "The Book of the Dead," her powerful poem about silicosis poisoning in West Virginia and its legislative aftermath.

Finally, and like Rukeyser a poet better known for what she went on to write than what she began by writing, Margaret Walker published *For My People* (1942) at the tail end of the Depression years. Taken as a whole, the poems in the book merge radical politics with a celebration of African American folk culture, as in the often anthologized title poem.

However, to limit a survey of Depression-era poetry to books of poetry ignores much of the everyday life of poetry during the 1930s, which, at least in terms of audience, had as much or more influence than books of poetry. In particular, *The Daily Worker, Partisan Review, New Masses,* and other radical newspapers and journals published many poems written by women, including Tillie Olsen and, heretofore unmentioned, the poet Martha Millet, who would go on to publish a few volumes of poetry in the 1950s but whose 1930s work appeared mostly in newspapers and journals.[5] Of interest here too are several African American poets, many of whom had ties to the Communist Party, who published in the pages of *Opportunity* and *Crisis*.[6]

The labor movement, too, gave room to many women poets in the pages of their newspapers. Perhaps the most accomplished of these was Miriam Tane, the poet laureate of the International Ladies Garment Workers Union, who published dozens of poems in *Justice*, the union's lively newspaper.[7] The poems range in theme and tone from sympathetic depictions of women sweatshop workers to surrealist fantasias on the consumer and march-to-war culture of the late 1930s and early 1940s.

Theory

As Paula Rabinowitz has argued, women writers on the left challenged conventional thinking about not just women and capitalism but also women and communism. Locked out of the closed circle of theoretical analysis, though, which was the domain of (mostly male) party leaders, women did their thinking (and rethinking) about women, capitalism, and communism in the genres – fiction, poetry, reportage – they could command.

That said, some writers on the left did offer sustained theoretical inquiries into the relationship between gender and capitalism, and what this relationship might look like post-capitalism. In 1934, the labor economist Grace Hutchins published *Women Who Work*, which, in addition to describing the place of women in the contemporary labor market, also offered theoretical insights into *why* women occupied that place and its special burdens, including what feminists would later call the double shift. Rebecca Pitts's long essay, "Women and Communism," appeared in *New Masses* in 1935. It located the origins of women's oppression under capitalism in the birth of property rights and, in an argument that hearkens back to Charlotte Perkins Gilman's *Women and Economics* (1898), the distorting influence of sex – and the need to attract men – on women's lives and minds. Finally, in the late 1930s Mary Inman published a series of essays in the left-wing journal *People's World* on the manufacture of femininity and masculinity, on the centrality of women's housework and child-rearing to capitalism, and on other crucial questions of gender and economics. These essays were later gathered into a pamphlet, *In Woman's Defense* (1940). Together, these essays and books anticipated debates about a socialist feminism that would not emerge for another half-decade or so. They remain remarkable – and remarkably understudied – documents.

The critical tradition and future directions
for criticism

If you do an MLA international bibliography search of any of the indisputably major figures discussed so far – Tillie Olsen, Meridel Le Sueur, Muriel Rukeyser – a certain pattern emerges. In the mid to late 1970s, the publication or republication of a major literary work – a novel, a volume of collected poems – leads to a number of reviews in the liberal weeklies and literary monthlies or quarterlies. These are followed by a scholarly article or two, usually straightforward recovery projects. (Deborah Rosenfelt's 1981 article on Tillie Olsen, "From the Thirties: Tillie Olsen and the Radical Tradition," published shortly after the appearance of Olsen's *Yonnondio*, illustrates the pattern rather well.) In the 1980s, scholarly articles begin to appear in literary journals, and more and more dissertations address one or several of these major figures.

Beginning in the early 1990s, however, scholars begin to publish the first book-length treatments of these writers; and these books, more than any others, have shaped the critical tradition about American women's writing in the long 1930s. Three critical works, in particular, were important at the time and appear again and again in the later scholarship: Paula Rabinowitz's *Labor and Desire: Women's Revolutionary Fiction in Depression America* (1991), Laura Hapke's *Daughters of the Great Depression: Women, Work, and Fiction in the American 1930s* (1995), and Constance Coiner's *Better Red: The Writing and Resistance of Tillie Olsen and Meridel Le Sueur* (1995).

An addendum to a text we have already seen, Meridel Le Sueur's "Women on the Breadlines," illustrates – very broadly speaking – the problem that each of these works sought to address. Following Le Sueur's article, the editors of *The New Masses* printed an editorial note in which they scolded her "presentation of the plight of the unemployed woman" for being "defeatist in attitude." "We feel it our duty to add," the editors wrote, getting in the last word, "that there is a place for the unemployed woman, as well as man, in the ranks of the unemployed councils and in all branches of the organized revolutionary movement" (quoted in Coiner, *Better Red*, 96). For many scholars, the note suggests the half-empty glass faced by women writers on the left. While *The New Masses* specifically and the Communist Party more generally provided women writers with a place to publish and with a political movement that valued writing about women, especially exploited and marginalized women, the cautionary note also, perhaps more so, indicates how editors and Party leaders would steer women's writing into directions it otherwise might not have gone and ignored writing that did not meet their political or gendered expectations.

In theory, that is, the Party committed itself to gender equality. In practice, however, it rarely kept these ideals. The rhetoric of revolution, verbal and visual, remained overwhelmingly masculine. Conversely, the feminine, through an association with the bourgeoisie, was ridiculed. Moreover, women's experience, either at home or in the workplace, to say nothing of reigning gender inequalities, struck many radicals as irrelevant to the revolutionary cause or of secondary interest at best. (Recall that when the title character of Ralph Ellison's *Invisible Man* displeases the Party hierarchy, he is assigned to lecture on the Woman Question. "The what!" he responds, dismayed [406].) In sum, the scholarly debate has circled around whether the Communist Party and its various literary institutions and arbiters opened up or foreclosed more opportunities for women writers to answer the sorts of questions that inspired Meridel Le Sueur's "Woman on the Breadlines" and other women writers of the period. For the most part, the Party – and, it perhaps goes without saying, the culture of the period more generally – has been found wanting. The challenge to critics, then, has been to show how women writers on the left struggled under these constraints yet nevertheless managed to articulate a nascent but nevertheless real socialist feminist alternative.

Obviously, this overview does not do justice to the range of criticism about American women writers on the left nor even to the three books themselves. (Despite mostly writing about the work of American women writers with ties to the left, for example, Hapke's larger argument concerns the representation of women's work in the fiction and culture – and not just the revolutionary fiction and culture – of the era.) Nor does it do justice to the close, usually insightful readings of the novels that underlie the larger argument about gender and radical politics that shapes these books. Nor, finally, does it do justice to those who have broken with the critical consensus that has emerged. In *Radical Representations: Politics and Form in US Proletarian Fiction* (1993), for example, Barbara Foley argues that critics have overstated the differences between women writers and the Communist Party and minimized "the conscious commitment of women leftists to the Communist-led movement" (241). "There is no reason to suppose," Foley writes, that the "intelligent and bold women" who comprised the literary left during the 1930s "were suppressing or redirecting feminist leanings that they felt incompatible with their commitment to Marxism" (242). Indeed, for all their differences and challenges to Party orthodoxy, many women writers remained committed to the Party even after its heyday in the 1930s.

Despite these qualifications, the question – the woman question, as it were – continues to inform a good deal of the scholarship written about women writers on the left. And while that question remains crucial and, to some extent, unanswered, it has also, partly because of the number of arguments it has inspired, grown slightly less compelling. Perhaps as a result, after its own heyday in the 1990s, new scholarship on women writers during the long 1930s has fallen off dramatically. For the field to regain its earlier sense of urgency, it must, as I see it, do two things: first, it must ask its motivating questions of genres other than novels; and second, it must ask questions, some old, some new, of a more diverse range of texts within these other genres.

As useful as Le Sueur and Olsen have been to the aspirations and agendas of the field, it needs to range beyond its canonical texts and, even more so, beyond its attachment to a single genre. Indeed, like other fields in the discipline of American literature, it can sometimes seem that critics only have eyes for novels. When they are feeling adventurous or unconventional, they may write about short stories. (In their decisive works, for example, Rabinowitz, Hapke, and, for the most part, Coiner, write exclusively of fiction, usually novels. This seems to have established a precedent.) Part of the reason for this focus, of course, is that the two figures who most dominate the field, Le Sueur and Olsen, worked in fiction. Nevertheless, the result is that other genres – poetry and the considerable body of non-fiction writing – have received far less attention. Beyond Muriel Rukeyser and a few, occasionally anthologized poems, few poets have received any sustained scholarly attention. (Here, even more than with other genres, one runs into the books in print problem. Good luck getting your hands on a book of poems by Genevieve Taggard. All have fallen out of print and no collected or selected edition of the poems exists.) Moreover, and given the recent internationalizing of American Studies, one would expect that the many books of travel writing and reportage written by women in the 1930s, about places as various as Russia, China, Mexico, Cuba, and Spain, would attract more attention than they have thus far received. To some extent, too, the very figure of the roving, radical woman journalist remains understudied as well. Even if scholars remain committed to the question of gender and politics, literary and otherwise, works in these genres may offer different answers to those questions. More ambitiously, they may suggest – perhaps even demand – new historical and theoretical approaches.

In addition to taking up new genres, though, the field may need to start examining new texts, and not just other, less canonical texts of the literary left but texts from across the political spectrum. Laura Hapke's reading of Margaret Mitchell's *Gone with the Wind* (1936) should have, but seems not to have, inspired more of this work. We know relatively little, for example, about the gender and politics of the Great Depression as these played out in middlebrow fiction of the 1930s and even less about how these played out on the rightward end of the political spectrum.[8]

The problem, of course, remains how to embark on these new inquiries while honoring the field's reason for being: the recovery of American women writing from an occasionally androcentric Party apparatus and, at least in its early stages, literary critical tradition. The field, that is, can (and should) stray only so far from the question of how women survived – and how women writers documented their survival – on, or more accurately, off the breadlines.

Notes

1. See Wald's discussion of Gilfallan in *Trinity of Passion*.
2. The discussion that follows is indebted to Wald's chapter, "Sappho in Red," from *Exiles from a Future Time*, and Berke's *Women Poets on the Left*. Later, when I write that poetry has been neglected, Berke is a welcome exception to this rule.
3. See Miller's chapter on Taggard's early poetry, "Love in Greenwich Village: Genevieve Taggard and the Bohemian Ideal," in Miller, *Making Love Modern*.
4. See Berke's discussion of Welch in her essay (and miniature anthology), "Radical Moderns." Alan Filreis also briefly discusses the reviews of Welch in *Modernism from Left to Right*.
5. See Filreis's discussion of Millet's post-Second World War poetry in *Counter-Revolution of the Word*.
6. Again, Nekola and Rabinowitz's *Writing Red* reprints some of this work.

7. For labor poetry of the period in general, see Marsh, *You Work Tomorrow*. On Tane specifically, see Marsh, "The Justice Poetry of Miriam Tane."
8. See Harker, *America the Middlebrow*, and Hutner, *What America Read*.

Works cited

Berke, Nancy. "Radical Moderns: American Women Poets on the Left." In *Gender in Modernism: New Geographies, Complex Intersections*. Ed. Bonnie Kime Scott. Urbana: University of Illinois Press, 2007.

Women Poets on the Left: Lola Ridge, Genevieve Taggard, Margaret Walker. Gainesville: University Press of Florida, 2001.

Brody, Catherine. *Cash Item*. London: Longmans, Green, 1933.

Nobody Starves. London: Longmans, Green, 1932.

Burke, Fielding (Olive Tilford Dargan). *Call Home the Heart*. 1932. New York: Feminist Press, 2002.

A Stone Came Rolling. New York: International, 1935.

Coiner, Constance. *Better Red: The Writing and Resistance of Tillie Olsen and Meridel Le Sueur*. New York: Oxford University Press, 1995.

Davidman, Joy. *Letter to a Comrade*. New Haven: Yale University Press, 1938.

Ellison, Ralph. *Invisible Man*. 1952. New York: Vintage, 1995.

Filreis, Alan. *Counter-Revolution of the Word: The Conservative Attack on Modern Poetry, 1945–1960*. Chapel Hill: University of North Carolina Press, 2008.

Modernism from Left to Right: Wallace Stevens, the Thirties, and Literary Radicalism. Cambridge: Cambridge University Press, 1994.

Foley, Barbara. *Radical Representations: Politics and Form in US Proletarian Fiction, 1929–1941*. Durham, NC: Duke University Press, 1993.

Gilfallan, Harriet Woodbridge (Lauren Gilfallan). *I Went to Pit College*. New York: Literary Guild, 1934.

Gilman, Charlotte Perkins (Charlotte Perkins Stetson). *Women and Economics*. Boston: Small, Maynard, 1898.

Gordon, Linda. *Dorothea Lange: A Life beyond Limits*. New York: W. W. Norton, 2009.

Gruber, Ruth. *I Went to the Soviet Arctic*. New York: Simon and Schuster, 1939.

Hapke, Laura. *Daughters of the Great Depression*. Athens, GA: University of Georgia Press, 1995.

Harker, Jamie. *America the Middlebrow: Women's Novels, Progressivism, and Middlebrow Authorship between the Wars*. Amherst: University of Massachusetts Press, 2007.

Herbst, Josephine. *The Executioner Waits*. New York: Harcourt Brace, 1934.

Pity is Not Enough. 1933. Urbana: University of Illinois Press, 1998.

Rope of Gold. 1939. New York: Harcourt Brace, 1939.

Hicks, Granville, Michael Gold, Isidor Schneider, Joseph North, Paul Peters, and Alan Calmer, eds. *Proletarian Literature in the United States*. New York: International, 1935.

Hutchins, Grace. *Women Who Work*. New York: International, 1934.

Hutner, Gordon. *What America Read: Taste, Class, and the Novel, 1920–1960*. Chapel Hill: University of North Carolina Press, 2009.

Inman, Mary. *In Women's Defense*. Los Angeles: Committee to Organize the Advancement of Women, 1940.

Johnson, Josephine. *Jordanstown*. New York: Simon and Schuster, 1937.

    Now in November. New York: Simon and Schuster, 1934.

    Winter Orchard: And Other Stories. New York: Simon and Schuster, 1935.

    Year's End. New York: Simon and Schuster, 1937.

Kelley, Edith Summers. *Weeds*. 1923. New York: Feminist Press, 1996.

Lechlitner, Ruth. *Only the Years: Selected Poems, 1938–1944*. Prairie City, IL: James A. Decker, 1944.

    Tomorrow's Phoenix. New York: Alcestis Press, 1937.

Le Sueur, Meridel. *The Girl*. 1978. Albuquerque: West End Press, 2006.

    "I Was Marching." 1934. In *Ripening: Selected Work*. Ed. Elaine Hedges. New York: Feminist Press, 1990.

    Salute to Spring. New York: International, 1940.

    "Women on the Breadlines." 1932. In *Ripening: Selected Work*. Ed. Elaine Hedges. New York: Feminist Press, 1990.

Lowney, John. *History, Memory, and the Literary Left: Modern American Poetry, 1935–1968*. Ames, IA: University of Iowa Press, 2006.

Lumpkin, Grace. *A Sign for Cain*. New York: Lee Furman, 1935.

    To Make My Bread. 1932. Urbana: University of Illinois Press, 1996.

Marsh, John. "The Depression Cohort." Rev. of *History, Memory, and the Literary Left: Modern American Poetry, 1935–1968* by John Lowney. *Contemporary Literature* 49.3 (Fall 2008): 470–5.

    "The Justice Poetry of Miriam Tane." *Legacy: A Journal of American Women Writers* 23.1 (2006): 44–59.

Marsh, John, ed. *You Work Tomorrow: An Anthology of American Labor Poetry, 1929–1941*. Ann Arbor: University of Michigan Press, 2007.

McCarthy, Mary. *The Company She Keeps*. 1942. New York: Houghlin Mifflin, 2003.

McKinney, Ruth. *Industrial Valley*. 1939. Ithaca: ILR Press, 1992.

    Jake Home. New York: Harcourt Brace, 1943.

    My Sister Eileen. New York: Harcourt Brace, 1938.

Miller, Nina. *Making Love Modern: The Intimate Public Worlds of New York's Literary Women*. New York: Oxford University Press, 1999.

Mitchell, Margaret. *Gone with the Wind*. New York: Macmillan, 1936.

Nekola, Charlotte and Paula Rabinowitz, eds. *Writing Red: An Anthology of American Women Writers, 1930–1940*. New York: Feminist Press, 1987.

Nelson, Cary. *Repression and Recovery: Modern American Poetry and the Politics of Cultural Memory, 1910–1945*. Madison: University of Wisconsin Press, 1992.

Olsen, Tillie. *Silences*. 1978. New York: Feminist Press, 2003.

    Tell Me a Riddle. 1961. New York: Dell, 1979.

    Yonnondio: From the Thirties. 1974. New York: Delta, 1979.

Page, Myra (Dorothy). *Daughter of the Hills: A Woman's Part in the Coal Miners' Struggle*. 1950. New York: Feminist Press, 1986.

    Gathering Storm: A Story of the Black Belt. New York: International, 1932.

Moscow Yankee. 1935. Urbana: University of Illinois Press, 1996.

Soviet Main Street. Moscow: Co-operative publishing society of foreign workers in the USSR, 1933.

Petry, Ann. *The Street*. 1946. Boston: Mariner Books, 1998.

Pitts, Rebecca. "Women and Communism." *New Masses* (February 19, 1935): 14–18.

Rabinowitz, Paula. *Labor and Desire: Women's Revolutionary Fiction in Depression America*. Chapel Hill: University of North Carolina Press, 1991.

Reed, John. *Ten Days That Shook the World*. New York: Boni and Liveright, 1922.

Ridge, Lola. *Dance of Fire*. New York: Smith, 1935.

Firehead. New York: Payson, 1929.

The Ghetto and Other Poems. New York: B. W. Heubsch, 1918.

Red Flag. New York: Viking, 1927.

Sun-Up and Other Poems. New York: B. W. Heubsch, 1920.

Rosenfelt, Deborah S. "From the Thirties: Tillie Olsen and the Radical Tradition." *Feminist Studies* 7 (Fall 1981): 370–406.

Rukeyser, Muriel. *Breaking Open*. New York: Random House, 1973.

Theory of Flight. New Haven: Yale University Press, 1935.

US 1. New York: Covici-Friede, 1938.

Slade, Caroline. *Margaret*. New York: Vanguard Press, 1946.

Mrs. Party's House. New York: Vanguard Press, 1948.

Sterile Sun. New York: Vanguard Press, 1937.

The Triumph of Willie Pond. New York: Vanguard Press, 1940.

Slesinger, Tess. *Time: The Present*. New York: Simon and Schuster, 1935.

The Unpossessed. New York: Simon and Schuster, 1934.

Smedley, Agnes. *Battle Hymn of China*. New York: Knopf, 1943.

Daughter of the Earth: A Novel. 1929. New York: Feminist Press, 1987.

Strong, Anna Louise. *I Change Worlds: The Remaking of an American*. New York: Henry Holt, 1935.

My Native Land. New York: Viking, 1940.

Ragged Verse by Anise. Seattle: Seattle Union Record, 1918.

Taggard, Genevieve. *Calling Western Union*. New York: Harper, 1936.

For Eager Lovers. New York: Thomas Seltzer, 1922.

The Life and Mind of Emily Dickinson. New York: Knopf, 1930.

Words for the Chisel. New York: Knopf, 1926.

Taggard, Genevieve, ed. *Circumferences: Varieties of Metaphysical Verse*. New York: Covici-Friede, 1930.

May Days: An Anthology of Verse from Masses-Liberator. New York: Boni and Liveright, 1929.

Trent, Lucia. *Children of Fire and Shadow*. New York: Packard, 1929.

Trent, Lucia and Ralph Cheyney. *More Power to Poets! A Plea for More Poetry in Life, More Life in Poetry*. New York: H. Harrison, 1934.

Thank You, America! New York: Suttonhouse, 1937.

Vorse, Mary Heaton. *A Footnote to Folly*. New York: Farrar and Rineheart, 1935.

Labor's New Millions. New York: Modern Age Books, 1938.

Men and Steel. New York: Boni and Liveright, 1920.

Passaic. New York: International Labor Defense, 1931.

Strike! 1930. Urbana: University of Illinois Press, 1991.

Wald, Alan. *Exiles from a Future Time: The Forging of the Mid-Twentieth-Century US Left.* Chapel Hill: University of North Carolina Press, 2001.

Trinity of Passion: The Literary Left and the Antifascist Crusade. Chapel Hill: University of North Carolina Press, 2007.

Writing from the Left: New Essays on Radical Culture and Politics. New York: Verso, 1994.

Walker, Margaret. *For My People*. New Haven: Yale University Press, 1942.

Weatherwax, Clara. *Marching! Marching!* New York: Liveright, 1930.

Welch, Marie de L. *Poems*. New York: Macmillan, 1933.

This is Our Own. New York: Macmillan, 1940.

Winter, Ella. *Red Virtue: Human Relationships in the New Russia.* New York: Harcourt Brace, 1933.

Yezierska, Anzia. *Bread Givers*. 1925. New York: Persea, 2003.

Salome of the Tenements. 1923. Urbana: University of Illinois Press, 1995.

Zugsmith, Leanne. *The Reckoning*. New York: H. Smith and R. Haas, 1934.

A Time to Remember. New York: Random House, 1936.

25

Modern domestic realism in America,
1950–1970

GORDON HUTNER

The history of American women's domestic fiction in the second half of the twentieth century describes a movement from a handful of exemplary careers to a panoply of practitioners. The 1950s are typified by a few stellar careers – Flannery O'Connor, Elizabeth Spencer, and Shirley Jackson – a trend that continues into the 1960s with Joyce Carol Oates among others – but as the decade evolves we find the number of realist writers growing at a pace unprecedented since the beginning of the century. In fact, a closer examination of the history of the period suggests that the conventional analogies concerning gender between nineteenth- and twentieth-century literary production in the USA are not really as neat as we often assume. For the rise of new modern domestic novelists (as opposed to sentimental writers and romancers) is one of the least-appreciated stories comprising twentieth-century American literary history. These writers were rendered invisible in the critical accounts, except for some passing nod to one or another of them, often as niche authors – southern gothicists, like Flannery O'Connor; nasty or charming satirists, like Mary McCarthy; or regionalists, like Eudora Welty. Such attribution may have suited the needs of literary historians intent on promoting war novelists, existentialists, or master comedians and tragedians of manners. Untold, however, is the story of how these women writers more and more often turn their attention to contemporary mores, history, and politics as the scene of their fiction. As a matter of course, that address still turns on women's relationships – with each other, men, their parents, their children – but these relationships are tested, time and again, both for the private power of sustaining identity as well as their implications for the public. More typically, decade by decade, in the second half of the twentieth century, their appeal comes out of a commitment to evolving versions of modern realism and the intensified investigation of social and cultural circumstances as well as gendered ones.

While the careers of several important women writers have gone missing in the archive of American fiction, the sheer number of novels by women that were reviewed favorably for the way they measured the domestic sphere during this half-century is perhaps one of the least appreciated developments in modern American literary historiography. We witness this change specifically in the differing landscapes of the 1950s and '60s and those of 1970s, '80s, and '90s, insofar as the story of 1950s domestic fiction remains a tale of key figures. While it may be that the 1950s brought an unprecedented number of women to colleges and universities, and it is tempting to assume that this rise can be ascribed to the new presence of Creative Writing classes on campus, that phenomenon does not yet achieve the widespread influence it will exert, say, in the last quarter of the century. In their early years, such programs produce one writer or another, even some as august as Flannery O'Connor, but it is not yet clear that, in the 1950s and '60s, so many of the new fiction writers had been Creative Writing students. Instead, the female authors of books reviewed admiringly in major venues turned to writing about the vast change in the American social landscape that resulted from the Depression and World War II. Later, through the 1960s and certainly by the '70s, the increasing number of American domestic realists can seem capable of bringing virtually any political and social question into their ken. What, in the nineteenth century, had been a tradition of exceptional cases, like Lydia Maria Child, or marginalizing conditions that necessitated a literary style intended to subvert social norms, like Elizabeth Stoddard, now achieved general currency.

Consider that American domestic writers were already of such significance that several won Pulitzer Prizes through the 1920s and '30s. Indeed, in the 1920s the several female winners of that prize included such celebrated writers as Wharton and Cather, the popular Edna Ferber, and now largely forgotten figures like Margaret Wilson and Julia Peterkin. Women writers were no less esteemed in the 1930s; inaugurating the decade where women dominated the competition was Margaret Barnes's *Years of Grace*, a tale of American modernity told as the observations of a banker's wife in Chicago where she witnessed the closing decades of the nineteenth century and the first two of the twentieth. Barnes's career might not have proved notable after this book, though she did produce several more novels through the 1930s (again about Chicago's mores and history), but her achievement signaled even more distinction to come for American women regionalists and historical fiction writers during the decade, including Pulitzer Prize-winners such as Pearl Buck (*The Good Earth*, 1931), Carolyn Miller (*Lamb in His Bosom*, 1933), Josephine

Johnson (*Now in November*, 1934), Marjorie Rawlings (*The Yearling*, 1938), and Margaret Mitchell (*Gone With the Wind*, 1936).

While so many of these acclaimed novels of the 1930s addressed regional history and concerns, we also know that there was a significant countermovement to these largely bourgeois books, especially in the number of women novelists writing about partisan affairs, the struggle between labor and capital, in figures like Josephine Herbst, Fielding Burke, and Meridel Le Sueur. There were also novelists who flourished in this decade and into the next, like Jessie Fauset and Zora Neale Hurston, but who slipped from critical memory and were replaced in readers' imagination, though the 1940s saw the emergence of Ann Petry (*The Street*, 1946; *Country Place*, 1947) whose presence for later critics was to prove significant, while Dorothy West's *The Living is Easy* (1948) was admired when it first appeared but vanished for more than three decades before it was republished by the Feminist Press in 1982.

In the 1930s and '40s, there emerged writers like Mildred Walker, who wrote mainly about the west; Caroline Gordon, a regional writer of such well-regarded historical Kentucky tales as *Penhally* (1931) and the more contemporary *Women on the Porch* (1944); as well as Mary Jane Ward, the author of the well-known portrait of a young woman inside a mental institution, *The Snake Pit* (1946), who also wrote a novel about anti-Semitism at a university, *The Professor's Umbrella* (1948). The 1940s saw the first novels by Mary McCarthy (*The Company She Keeps*, 1942; *The Oasis*, 1949), Carson McCullers (*The Heart is a Lonely Hunter*, 1940; *Reflections in a Golden Eye*, 1941), Elizabeth Spencer (*Fire in the Morning*, 1948), and Eudora Welty (*The Robber Bridegroom*, 1942; *Delta Wedding*, 1946). As well known as these writers became, they were scarcely recognized as participating in the new era of American fiction which supposedly came of age in time of war, nor were writers like Martha Gellhorn and Maritta Wolff appreciated as part of a generational change. Indeed, after World War II there was a pronounced effort to liken new male writers to the 1920s novelists who became famous as post-war novelists: Fitzgerald, Hemingway, Dos Passos, and Faulkner. Unsurprisingly, many new authors were found wanting by comparison. By contrast, few women writers were celebrated in the 1920s for their expatriate adventures or their romanticizing of the golden years of youth. Perhaps part of the lingering appeal of Djuna Barnes is that, however late her contribution, *Nightwood* (1936) was the one imaginative work by a woman to be considered to belong to the literature of this lost generation. Nor was it widely maintained that such comparisons were erroneous: American domestic life was in one place in the 1920s and quite another in the 1950s, and writers had very different jobs to do, beyond transforming their war experiences and their return home into novels.

Consider the careers of writers from the late 1930s and '40s whose novels dramatized women's changing social conditions or who saw those circumstances subordinated to larger political and cultural forces. For Catherine Whitcomb, these issues are generally situated in the arena of marriage: *I'll Mourn You Later* (1936) examines family dynamics; *The Grown-Ups* (1937) considers the effects of a divorce on a child; *In the Fine Summer Weather* (1938) investigates the state of three marriages in a writers' colony; *The Malfreys* (1944) is the story of a loveless marriage and its isolating effects; *The Door to the Garden* (1949) recounts a young woman's turbulent coming of age. Perhaps the author whose career exemplifies how women writers of the middle decades would be forgotten and their contributions nullified is Edith (Kniepple) Roberts, who began publishing fiction in 1937 with *Candle in the Sun*, a tale of a young American college student who comes to realize her burden and responsibility when the child of her marriage to a West Indian of local stature is decidedly black. She followed this tale with one about a young American woman who joins the communist movement to fight in Spain, *Reap the Whirlwind* (1938); *Tamarack* (1940) brings the novelist's focus to domestic politics, recounting the stories of two new mothers at a midwest resort, one the mother of an illegitimate child, the other of a legitimate one. *This Marriage* (1941) explores the consequences of a prenuptial agreement that frees husband and wife; *Little Hell, Big Heaven* (1942) takes up the question of altruism in Chicago; *That Hagen Girl* (1946) describes a young woman's struggle to overcome prejudice in a small town, having been born out of wedlock (this was later made into a notoriously bad Hollywood movie starring Shirley Temple and Ronald Reagan). The year 1948 brought *The Divorce of Marcia Moore*, dramatizing the challenges facing a single mother. In *That Loring Woman* (1950), Roberts returns to her *bête-noire*, small-town gossip, in the tale of a virtuous woman of standing and the local physician.

We might also consider briefly the novels by unrecollected writers like Ellen Marsh, who wrote two novels in the post-war 1940s: *Drink to the Hunted* (1945), about how one German family's experience of the preceding two decades provides a historical background for a child's development; and *Dull the Sharp Edge* (1947), a *bildungsroman* of a young American woman during World War II. Then there are the novels by Cornelia Jessy, like *The Growing Roots* (1947), about the ways several people try to establish identity beyond race as a generational tale of Jews; or *Teach the Angry Spirit* (1949), a similar tale about Mexicans. What place would such subjects have among the critics busily trying to determine who was the new Hemingway, or who the new Dos Passos, of these years?

Women writers of the 1940s have usually been shunted aside in the histories of the decade, since so much was understandably made of the war, and so little remains of the fiction from the home-front, especially in the first half of the decade. The general failure to include American women writers when considering post-war fiction has thus led to a vexed misunderstanding, and ignorance, of the achievement of that fiction. Once we appreciate the kind of writing women did contribute, in the form of domestic inquiry, we will have an enlarged, more nuanced vision of US literary history, one that might include Clare Jaynes – the *nom de plume* of two writers, Jane Mayer and Clara Spiegel – who collaborated on such novels of marriage and manners as *Instruct My Sorrows* (1942), about a woman becoming a widow at the age of thirty-three; *These are the Times* (1945), about a wife who tries to obstruct her husband from lending his skills as a doctor to the war effort; and *This Eager Heart* (1947), about marital tensions erupting on a Montana ranch.

The immediate post-war literary scene was, for women writers, strikingly more like the mid-1940s. Notable are books like Elizabeth Janeway's *The Walsh Girls* (1943) or *Daisy Kenyon* (1945), which look at the moral compromises women may have felt compelled to make during or after the war. Maritta Wolff directed her imagination away from the solid bourgeoisie or the respectable "working girl" milieu and toward the impoverished, concentrating instead on how these years affected women in midwestern cities in *Whistle Stop* (1941) and *Night Shift* (1942). Furthermore, she contributed *About Lyddy Thomas* (1947) to the growing shelf of returning-veteran stories, though it was not unheard of for writers, like Kay Boyle, who in the 1920s and '30s enjoyed a career as an expatriate writer (usually focusing on psychological themes) to develop a war novel. In the 1940s, Boyle wrote several novels treating the war, including a story of the French Occupation, *A Primer for Combat* (1941); a spy tale, *Avalanche* (1943); *A Frenchman Must Die* (1946), about the Resistance; and *His Human Majesty* (1949), a quite improbable tale, based on a historical incident of an international cohort of skiers whose mission is to attack the Nazis.

By 1950, it is possible to observe the contours of several developments in women's domestic novels. In the first years of the decade, we encounter important works by familiar novelists like Carson McCullers (*The Ballad of the Sad Café*, 1951), Flannery O'Connor (*Wise Blood*, 1952), Mary McCarthy (*The Groves of Academe*, 1952), Elizabeth Spencer (*This Crooked Way*, 1952), and Shirley Jackson (*Hangsaman*, 1951); but we might also remember several novels by writers once highly regarded, such as Nancy Wilson Ross (*I, My Ancestor*, 1950), Caroline Gordon (*The Strange Children*, 1951), Jessamyn West (*The Witch Diggers*, 1951), Maritta Wolff (*Back of Town*, 1952), May Sarton (*Shadow of a Man*, 1950; *A Shower of a Summer Day*, 1952), and Jean Stafford (*The Catherine Wheel*, 1952). Stalwart authors, like Pearl Buck (*God's Men*, 1951; *The Hidden Flower*, 1952) and Edna Ferber (*Giant*, 1952), continued to publish apace.

Writers about whom even less is known include Alice T. Hobart, who began writing travel books in 1917 and who published *Serpent-Wheeled Staff* (1951), a home-coming novel about a doctor's new social conscience after the war, while Helen MacInnis's *Neither 5 Nor 3* (1951) is devoted to Cold War anxieties of a Red takeover. Such public themes are also articulated in (former Hollywood actress) Ruth Chatterton's *Homeward Borne* (1950), where the southern wife of a New England college president adopts a Jewish refugee. Domestic fiction, however, is more typically driven by private matters, as in novels such as Isabel Bolton's *Many Mansions* (1951), for some a forgotten masterpiece concerning an elderly woman's meditation on her life as it draws to an end, from the author's trilogy, *New York Mosaic*; Nancy Hale's *Sign of Jonah* (1950); Christine Weston's *The World is a Bridge* (1950); Laura Z. Hobson's *The Other Father* (1950), a novel in which a father is in love with another man's daughter, while his daughter is in love with another woman's father. Historical fiction, too, gave domestic writers a vehicle, as in Gwen Bristow's story of female friendship on the way west, *Jubilee Trail* (1950); Eleanor Palffy's tale of the relationship between Mrs. John Lowell Gardner and John Singer Sargent (a countess by marriage, Palffy might be the only American novelist to hold a title), *The Lady and the Painter* (1951); and Mary Anne Amsbary's tale of midwestern corruption, *Caesar's Angel* (1951). One historical novel situated much farther afield is Gladys Schmitt's psychological and historical romance of pagans and Christians in the third century, *Confessors of the Name* (1952).

The mid-1950s witnessed the ascendancy of new domestic novelists as well as the reappearance of those who had previously made their mark. On the one hand, Shirley Jackson published a second novel (*The Bird's Nest*, 1954), a story of multiple personality disorder; so too did Jessamyn West with *Cress Delahanty* (1953), a coming-of-age tale in southern California, and Elizabeth Spencer with *Voice at the Back Door* (1956), a tale of race relations in post-war Mississippi (this was recommended for the year's Pulitzer Prize by the judges but was rejected by the board of overseers!). Novelists from the 1920s (Viña Delmar, *Beloved*, the story of the love affairs of Judah Benjamin, the famous Confederate Jew, 1955), '30s, and '40s continued to publish well-received novels. The year 1953 saw Jackson's *Life Among the Savages*; Marjorie Rawlings's *The Sojourner*, her foray out of Florida in a New England father-and-son tale from the nineteenth century; as well as Ann Petry's *The Narrows*, a story of interracial love in New England, while 1954 provided novels as diverse as Mildred Walker's story of the twentieth-century's rise of the American west, *The Curlew's Cry*; Eudora Welty's *The Ponder Heart*, about a niece's recollection of her beloved, addled uncle; Marcia Davenport's *My Brother's Keeper*, a predecessor to E. L. Doctorow's *Homer and Langley* (2009) in its fictionalizing of the astounding story of the famous recluses, the Collyer brothers of New York City; *Rainbow in the Road*, Esther Forbes's travelogue of a portrait painter in 1830s New England; Harriette Arnow's unforgettable *The Dollmaker*, the experiences of a young Kentucky woman in the industrial north; and Jean Stafford's fascinating novella of a love affair between a former Nazi and Jew in post-war Germany, *A Winter's Tale*.

Other important works from the 1930s and '40s include Mary McCarthy's *A Charmed Life* (1955), which recounts the events at an artist colony; Caroline Gordon's *The Malefactors* (1956), which tells of a man who leaves his wife and returns to Catholicism; Elizabeth Hardwick's portrait of a murder trial, *The Simple Truth*; and May Sarton's Harvard novel, *Faithful are the Wounds* (1955) inspired by F. O. Matthiessen's tragic suicide. Lesser-known authors include several writing about the public sphere: Ilona Karmel's *Stephania* (1954) is about young people working in a hospital ward; Virginia Rowans's *The Loving Couple, Her Story* (1955) is one of the very first novels devoted to suburbia; Hobart returned to her first preoccupation, China, by dramatizing a young man's encounter with the communist regime there in *Venture into Darkness* (1956); and Elizabeth Vining's *The Virginia Exiles* (1956) recounts the story of young Quaker men banished during World War II.

These years also feature such notable historical novels as the first of Mary Lee Settle's West Virginia tetralogy, *O Beulah Land!* (1956), and Inglis Fletcher's *The Scotswoman* (1956), a historical romance about a forgotten episode in the American Revolution. In the 1930s, novelists often turned to history, especially the Revolutionary War but also the Civil War, for analogs to the contemporary sense of challenge; in the 1940s as well, historical novels were per force often political insofar as the reading of history became something like the determining of political choices that revealed moral values. In the 1950s, however, history asserts its interest for its remoteness, for its distance from the contemporary moment. Best-selling author Pearl Buck published two novels during these years: *Come, My Beloved* (1954), about the love of an expatriate American woman for an Indian doctor amid the tumult of independence;

and *Imperial Woman* (1956), about China's last empress. In striking contrast is Eileen Chang's novel of the food shortage in China, *The Rice Sprout Sky* (1955), and Diana Chang's tale of the last days of the Japanese occupation of Shanghai, especially the Eurasians' experience there, *The Frontiers of Love* (1956).

No domestic novel of these years, however, could eclipse Grace Metalious's *Peyton Place* (1956), though 1957 saw the first appearance of Ayn Rand's *Atlas Shrugged*, a kind of antidomestic domestic novel. The phenomenon of Metalious's book has been well studied for its stupendously popular exposé of small-town abuse, cross-class sex, and murder. Rand's book, on the other hand, explains the outrages of individual appetite as much the opposite: a commitment to a fantasy about the triumph of the will in the name of Objectivism.

The year 1957 was not distinguished by novels by writers of particular note, though Buck gave readers *Letters from Peking*, about the correspondence between a Eurasian man and the American wife he left in Vermont, where she is safe from the communist state. Frances Parkinson Keyes's *Blue Camellia* rounded out the fourth decade of her fifty-year career with a historical novel of late nineteenth-century Cajun country. Also to be remembered is Ann Bannon's *Odd Girl Out*, a novel inspired by her experiences at the University of Illinois, chronicling a student's lesbian affair, and the first of the author's series of books over the next several years resisting the postal authorities' constraints.

The final years of the decade, however, give notice of the range and power of domestic novelists' production for the final third of the century. Although there were some novels from earlier writers – including Edna Ferber (*Ice Palace*, 1958), Ruth Suckow (*The John Wood Case*, 1959), Betty Smith (*Maggie Now*, 1958), Elizabeth Janeway (*The Third Choice*, 1959), Lillian Smith's return to fiction in a novel about child rape, *One Hour* (1959), and Sophie Treadwell of *Machinal* (1928) fame now exploring suburban women's anxieties in *One Fierce Hour and Sweet* (1958) – we also see important books by authors specific to the post-war era: Shirley Jackson's eschatological study, *The Sundial* (1958), and a ghost tale *The Haunting of Hill House* (1959); Shirley Ann Grau's novel of bayou life, *The Hard Blue Sky* (1958); Rona Jaffe's group portrait of young New York City career women in *The Best of Everything* (1958); Paule Marshall's tale of a young New York City woman's very different experience, *Brown Girl, Brownstones* (1959); Helga Sandburg's novel about a pregnant Kentucky teenager, *The Wheel of Earth* (1958); as well as Sigrid de Lima's *Praise a Fine Day* (1959), the subtle account of an American artist paid to marry the pregnant Polish mistress of an Egyptian Jew so that their child could enjoy US citizenship.

While it seems portentous to assert that the year 1960 brought with it a new consciousness of the American domestic novel, it is perhaps the first year since the end of World War II that domestic fiction is dominated by women whose careers flourished in the aftermath of the war, rather than prior to, or during, it. Writers from an earlier period do make a special effort to address the present, as in Mildred Walker's tale of a teacher's grief for his student, *Body of a Young Man*, and Kay Boyle's *Generation Without Farewell*, the story of a German journalist who looks upon the ruins of his country and struggles to ascertain a healthy relation to it. More pressing, perhaps, is the effort to reconcile the past, most famously in Harper Lee's *To Kill a Mockingbird*, and Jessamyn West's coming-of-age novel, *South of the Angels*, about the conversion of Californian farm lands into housing developments in the early part of the century. More contemporary novels included Elizabeth Spencer's *Light in the Piazza*, about an unlikely romance between a backward American girl and a handsome Florentine; Jo Sinclair's account of a refugee from the 1956 uprising in Hungary, *Anna Teller*; Barbara Probst Solomon's *avant la lettre* novel of New York yuppies, *The Best of Life*; Vivian Koch's tale of the consequences of a Fulbright fellowship, *Change of Love*; and Ariadne Thompson's tale of suburban adultery, *Copper Beech*.

Either in the sustained development of established writers or in the emergence of new ones, the early 1960s saw a remarkable ascent of American domestic novelists. Not all of these writers would welcome the company in which I place them, but, taken as a group, they show how American novelists have striking resemblances when placed in historical contiguity: Hortense Calisher's mother–daughter study, *Textures of Life* (1963), and a science-fiction comedy, *Journal from Ellipsia* (1965); Mary McCarthy's *succès de scandale*, *The Group* (1963); Susan Sontag's *The Benefactor* (1963); Shirley Ann Grau's *House on Coliseum Street* (1961), about a young woman's neurotic love in contemporary New Orleans, and her celebrated *Keeper of the House* (1964), the year's Pulitzer Prize-winner about a white man, his black domestic servant, and miscegenation; May Sarton's meditation on the creative imagination, *Mrs. Stevens Hears the Mermaids Singing* (1965); Jessamyn West's account of a terminally ill woman contemplating suicide, *A Matter of Time* (1966); Elizabeth Spencer's tale of an American woman in Rome, *Knights and Dragons* (1965); and Shirley Hazzard's first novel, also on a transatlantic theme, *The Evening of the Holiday* (1966).

Several writers published their first novels in these years: Joan Didion's *Run River* (1963); Joyce Carol Oates's *With a Shuddering Fall* (1964); Alison Lurie's novel about an easterner transplanted to Los Angeles, *The Nowhere City* (1965); Diane Johnson's *Fair Game* (1965), about the ways four men love the same woman; Sylvia Plath's *The Bell Jar* (1963); the poet Maxine Kumin's *Through Dooms of Love* (1965), about a father–daughter relationship; Anne Tyler's *If Morning Ever Comes* (1965) and *The Tin-Can Tree* (1966), both about family dysfunction; Alice Adams's divorce novel, *Careless Love* (1966); and Cynthia Ozick's Jamesian account of a young American woman and a European intellectual, *Trust* (1966).

Intriguing, too, are the novels that have all but vanished from historical awareness but whose plots, taken together, reveal the new terrain novelists were exploring. On the one hand, novelists were becoming ever more conscious of their social responsibility, as we see in Lillian Ross's satire of psychoanalysis, *Vertical and Horizontal* (1963); Nancy W. Faber's *Strange Way Home* (1963), about a Jewish boy, kidnapped and taken to Canada, who becomes a priest, written by a novelist who later turned to writing about cognitively challenged children; Mildred Savage's *In Viro* (1964), about the search for an antibiotic. On the other hand, novelists were as committed as ever to adumbrating the challenge of establishing happy intimate relations, as in Jane Rule's *Desert of the Heart* (1964), a lesbian novel set in Reno but published in Canada after she was unable to secure an American publisher; Maude Hutchins's more conventional tale of young love, *Honey on the Moon* (1964); Iowa Workshop graduate Arona McHugh's story of a romance across class lines in post-war Boston, *A Banner with a Strange Device* (1964), and a sequel, *Seacoast of Bohemia* (1966); along with such new perspectives on young women's coming of age as Heather Ross Miller's North Carolina tale, *The Edge of the Woods* (1964); Sylvia Rothschild's treatment of a young Brooklyn girl, *Sunshine and Salt* (1964); Kristin Hunter's story of the hectic life of a young African American woman and the numbers racket, *God Bless the Child* (1964); Shirley Schoonover's *Mountain of Winter* (1965), about the struggles of a young Finnish woman in the Iron Range of North Dakota; Pauline Waugh's *Nanny Goat* (1965), where three young Boston Jews rebel against their parents during the Depression; Rachel Maddux's *A Walk in the Spring Rain* (1966), a novel of adultery left unconsummated. Juxtaposed with these novels of how young women fall in love and achieve identity is the novel that is probably the most ambitious bid for immortality: Marguerite Young's *sui generis* modernist epic *Miss McIntosh, My Darling* (1965), a 1,000-page book some twenty years in the writing that has been celebrated as a masterpiece.

Two directions can be observed in the fiction of the late 1960s. On the one hand, we see the sustained promise of several major talents – Calisher, Oates, Hazzard, Lurie, and Tyler – while, on the other, we can witness an upsurge in domestic fiction that produces an array of new novelists. The year 1967 might be understood as transitional, with the publication of Paula Fox's novel of the new sterility, *Poor George*; Hazzard's treatment of a materialist society in *People in Glass Houses*; Oates's study of migratory workers and a woman who marries above her station, *The Garden of Earthly Delights*; and Lurie's academic satire, *Imaginary Friends*. Writers who were becoming better known include Sylvia Wilkinson, for her study of the intense relationship between a girl and her grandmother in North Carolina, *A Killing Frost*, and Gwen Davis, whose *Sweet William* took on much of the change in manners, such as the turn toward drugs we associate with the 1960s, which she previously surveyed in *The War Babies* (1966), about four female UN guides.

By 1968 and 1969, writers emerged who would have significant careers, and there were a dozen more from whom little would be heard again. Making a first appearance is Lee Smith, with her coming-of-age story, *The Day the Dogbushes Bloomed* (1968), and Marge Piercy, with *Going Down Fast* (1969), a tale of university corruption and the young people whose lives seem bound to the gender, race, and class prejudices of that world. We also encounter novels by Alison Lurie, *Real People* (1968), about a writer's self-discovery in an artists' colony; and Joyce Carol Oates's *Expensive People* (1968), a precursor of sorts to Lionel Shriver's *We Need to Talk about Kevin* (2003), and *them* (1968), a topical account of modern Detroit.

Yet to grasp the new presence of women realists in the USA is to behold the sheer plenitude of novels one might call minor fiction but that, taken together, suggests a dramatic shift. Even as John Updike's *Couples* (1968) and Philip Roth's *Portnoy's Complaint* (1969) were helping, notoriously, to imagine the country's changing sexual attitudes, as was Caroline Bird's and Sarah Welles Briller's *Born Female* (1968), domestic novelists were also reinscribing the American social scene. In 1968, for example, Ruth Wolff's *A Trace of Footprints* recounts how one man learns from his homely neighbors how to make his marriage last, even as his wife is in Europe having an affair; Alice Denham's *My Darling from the Lions* is the story of unhappy newlyweds, with a wife who resists becoming a homemaker while the husband is recalled to the army; Eunice L. Coleman's *The Roaring Shock Test* traces a schizophrenic college drop-out and her efforts to come to terms with reality, especially through a community of Quakers' social actions, a theme similarly treated later in the year by Marjorie Kellogg's *Tell Me That You Love Me, Junie Moon*; Violet Weingarten's *Mrs. Beneker* is the story of a suburban Jewish matron who encounters a variety of 1960s social problems; a milder version of adjusting to the new modernity is Katinka Loeser's empty-nest tale, *The Archers At Home*; Kathrin Perutz, in *Mother is a Country* (1968) portrays the mastery of a successful female academic over her male colleagues (a kind of comic response to the more tragic handling of this theme in Canadian Marian Engel's novel, published a month before, *No Clouds of Glory*); Pearl Buck updates her *modus operandi* in *The New Year*, where a political candidate must deal with the existence of an Amerasian child he fathered during the Korean War; Jane Berry concentrates on the intrigues of a political campaign in *Grass Roots*; *In the Balance*, by M. E. White, dramatizes the plight of a young female drifter who endures multiple rapes and abuses as she travels the Pacific Coast; Alabama writer Babs Deal's *The Walls Came Tumbling Down* describes the consequences for seven women when the remains of an infant are discovered during the demolition of a sorority house. Published just weeks after Updike's famous paean to adultery is Maxine Kumin's *The Passions of Uxport*, which describes the challenges that two women face in a very similar setting, one mourning the loss of a child to leukemia, the other trying to relieve her pain through adultery; Audrey Lee, on the other hand, examines the lives of Philadelphians who pass before the window of a young African American woman newly arrived in the city in *The Clarion People*; as if in response to these witness-to-modernity novels, Frances Rickett, in *A Certain Slant of Light*, returns to 1930s Indiana, where a county auditor faces slander as a single woman, and, along with her niece, encounters bigotry for being a Catholic.

In 1969, we see further evidence of women addressing the cultural moment in novels like *The Open Doors* by Tereska Torres (whose fascinating career has yet to be told), about a young American man's work in transporting European refugees after he falls in love with an older Zionist woman. More historical is veteran writer Martha Gellhorn's novel of 1960s expatriates in Mexico, *The Lowest Trees Have Tops*. Sarah E. Wright's *This Child's Gonna Live* describes one black woman's struggle to complete the migration north. We also find three novels that return us to the post-war era: Sarah Gainham scored a bestseller in *A Place in the Country*, the second part of her trilogy about life in Vienna during and after the war in this story of an actress who tries to assuage the loss of her Jewish husband by turning her attention to an American businessman; Norma Rosen's *Touching Evil*, in turn, imagines the lives of two New York City women whose understanding of Nazi atrocities color their interpretations of their much more contemporary experiences; Ilona Karmel's *An Estate of Memory* is a much-lauded account of how four Polish women collaborate to save the child one of them is carrying despite their internment in a Nazi labor camp. The year 1969 ends with a pair of novels striving very self-consciously to achieve a grand scale of even anthropological proportions: Paule Marshall's *The Chosen Place, The Timeless People* offers a parable of the clash between civilization and the ways of Native peoples when a team of American anthropologists observes the culture of a Caribbean island; similarly, in *Bahadur Means Hero*, Sheila Solomon Klass focuses on the intolerance of another American anthropologist and his wife as they experience Indian mores in Bengal.

However, it is the private sphere that garners the most attention. Serena Sue Hilsinger's *Foxes on the Hill* describes how a suicide victim's friends and family react to her death; Bibi Wein's *Yes* recounts the experiences of a sexually liberated young woman as she makes her way through college and a career in New York; Shirley Schoonover offers a portrait of a lady as a young mother of three in the midst of falling apart after a divorce in *Sam's Song*; Constance Urdang's pastiche, *Natural History*, centers on a young St. Louis woman's collected notes, letters, and literary scraps to forward the story of her developing consciousness and especially her observation of her four friends, a novel not as accomplished as Canadian Margaret Laurence's similar *The Fire-Dwellers*. We also see *bildungsromane* novels, like Bonnie Barrett's *Live in Atlantis*, about a young woman's initiation in a 1930s southern California seaside town; in striking contrast, in *Nine Months in the Life of an Old Maid*, Judith Rossner imagines the subsequent messy lives of daughters left behind during the 1930s, in the care of a grandmother and nanny, when their parents decamp to Hollywood. The latter novel has more in common with Elaine Kraf's *I Am Clarence*, the story of an insane woman and her cognitively impaired son, though it also bears comparison with Helen Tucker's *The Sound of Summer Voices*, which considers the fate of a young boy living with his great uncle, who is a boiling cauldron of assorted bigotries, and the child's struggle to learn about his mother.

As a group, these writers emerged as more numerous, more ambitious, more varied, and a more accomplished generation of women novelists than perhaps any other in American literary history. By 1970, the roll of important publishing novelists included not only Oates, Tyler, Welty, Fox, and Hazzard, but also Didion and newcomers like Toni Morrison, Gail Godwin, and Alice Walker. Indeed, the next thirty years witnessed a further efflorescence of domestic realism.

So much so that historians of modern and contemporary women's writing might consider that a great deal more criticism and research is still to be done. While scholars have already focused on several authors whose careers have been especially luminous, a plethora of modern novelists remain whose achievements should be reassessed. Similarly, there are writers whose names are familiar to contemporary scholars – Sarton, Calisher, Grau, Lurie, and others – but who still have not been subjected to a comprehensive assessment of their oeuvre, either in isolation or in relation to other writers. In short, these novelists and many others might provide the basis for a revisionist enterprise every bit as resourceful and energetic as the one that specialists in women's writing have developed for previous centuries. That endeavor may take the form of studying the work of those women writers who have already come to prominence, or it may involve studying the post-war domestic realists *en bloc*, as a succession of generations whose innovations and variations reveal a more fully nuanced understanding of the era than we have at present. Alternatively, scholars may wish to see these authors as part of a more fully integrated history of American women's writing, tracing in greater detail the history of the genre and its changes. New scholarship might also be directed towards the host of authors about whom little is known, whose accounts of American life are left unread and undervalued in large part simply because they are women.

Works consulted

Davidson, Cathy N. and Linda Wagner-Martin, eds. *Oxford Companion to Women's Writing in the US*. New York: Oxford University Press, 1994.

Hilfer, Anthony. *American Fiction since 1940*. New York: Longman's, 1992.

Hutner, Gordon. *What America Read: Taste, Class, and the Novel, 1920–1960*. Chapel Hill: University of North Carolina Press, 2009.

Kunitz, Stanley, ed. *Twentieth-Century Authors*. 1942. New York: Wilson, 1942; 2nd edn 1955.

Ludwig, Richard M. and Clifford A. Nault, Jr., eds. *Annals of American Literature, 1602–1983*. New York: Oxford University Press, 1986.

Millett, Fred, ed. *Contemporary American Authors*. New York: Harcourt Brace, 1940, 1944.

McGurl, Mark. *The Program Era: Postwar Fiction and the Rise of Creative Writing*. Cambridge, MA: Harvard University Press, 2009.

Warfel, Harry R. *American Novelists of Today*. New York: American Book Co., 1951.

26

Lyric, gender, and subjectivity in modern and contemporary women's poetry

JENNIFER ASHTON

This chapter is intended as a contribution to the history of American women's literature, which is to say, it is intended as a history. But readers will quickly see in it a polemical purpose as well. For the history that I am offering here – one that insists on the coterminous centrality of lyric as a genre and subjective expression as a value (both in their celebration and their critique) – should require us to reconsider, if not abandon, our justifications for studying (or producing) women's poetry as such, that is, as women's poetry.

In the first two sections of this chapter, I attempt to show how, even in the face of the most acute critiques of lyric and its conjunction with subjective expression, particularly in the latter half of the twentieth century, the commitment to poetry as a vehicle for individual expression persists – indeed, it could hardly become any stronger. As I show in the second section, the effort by poets, critics, and scholars to think about the difference women make to poetic production, precisely because it raises the specter of an apparently irreducible and dispositive difference at the level of the body, yields an occasion to think about the relationship between subject position and literary form, with the inevitable effect, I argue, of making form appear to be the indexical trace of particular subject positions. The further effect is that the specificity of any given form, or, we might say, the very drive to innovate forms, becomes an analog of the specificity of any given subject, or the drive to give each subject her proper expression. Finally, given that the ongoing project of studying women's poetry as women's poetry has been part of a feminist project ostensibly devoted to equality – of rights, of recognition, of respect – the third and final section of this chapter asks us to think about the politics of the commitment to subjective expression in the context of the pursuit of social equality. That is, given our ongoing refinements of the imperative to respect (ever more) particularized subject positions, and, through poetry, to give them a voice, the final section asks us how, in the face of such a sustained effort toward acknowledgment, we are to understand the precipitous increase in material inequalities among those we have acknowledged.

That increase in material inequality has coincided with the extent of this chapter's scope, covering modern and contemporary poetry. The "modern and contemporary" designation is not meant to overlook the division that literary historians and theorists have more frequently used to articulate the period from roughly the outbreak of World War I to the present: the division between "modernism" and "postmodernism." It certainly matters for our purposes that without modernism's commitment to the autonomy of the work of art, we would never have had postmodernism's critique of that autonomy; that is, we would never have had the proliferation of interest in subjects and subject positions that exploded it, and that is at the heart of this chapter's history. But postmodernism's critique of modernism's autonomous work of art simply put the foot to the gas pedal of a vehicle that had been idling all along, in the English language, at least, since *Lyrical Ballads*. The periodizing work of this chapter is to chart the progress of that vehicle, which I will be referring to as "lyric," in its relation to the emergence of "women's poetry" as an aesthetic and political project and as a subject of study.

Elizabeth Renker's contribution to this volume suggests very persuasively that rethinking the history of nineteenth-century women's poetry has had the salutary effect of releasing us from various myopias in our periodizing and our theorizing of both gender and genre, including the "genre-effects" that Yopie Prins and Virginia Jackson have argued result from focusing our scholarly attention to poetry too narrowly on "lyric." This chapter in turn proposes that rethinking the history of modern and contemporary women's poetry can have equally salutary effects only if (to shift metaphors) we keep front and center the very same hypostasized "lyric" that is supposed to have been blocking our view. That is, if a much-needed history of nineteenth-century women's poetry "has not yet been written," as Jackson and Prins have claimed, "because of a tendency to read the 'lyric' as a genre defined in terms of subjective expression," the argument here will be that the history of modern and contemporary women's poetry we may need most can only be written with deliberate focus on lyric as a genre of subjective expression ("Lyric Studies," 523). And while this is actually a claim that I would make for modern and contemporary poetry more generally, the subject of "women's poetry" offers us a privileged vantage if only because we inevitably direct our interest to women *as* subjects. More precisely, as I suggested above, the difference their subject position makes seems to derive from something impossible to set aside, the difference their bodies make to their situation in the world.

Of course, lyric could never have emerged as the kind of problem it seems to be if it did not already count for many as a solution. From the myth of Philomela's song of suffering to the marketing messages of writing programs claiming to help students find an "individual voice" (more on this later), lyric has been celebrated as the poetry that gives expression to what has been (in some cases, violently) silenced or even what simply has not yet found its proper voice.

For critics like Jackson and Prins, the problem with focusing on lyric, and more specifically on lyric as subjective expression, is that we see anachronistically. When lyric appears (falsely) as a transhistorical genre, it imposes on poets of the past models of poetic production that actually belong to the present, obscuring the real social and material conditions of poetic production in the past. Emily Dickinson becomes a vivid example in this case, in Jackson's *Dickinson's Misery: A Theory of Lyric Reading*, where critics' treatment of Dickinson's poems as lyrics demanding New Critical-style close readings or as transparent windows on her isolated and eccentric life as a spinster, ignored their more important and more ubiquitous social function as tokens of quotidian exchange and means of facilitating friendship, collaboration, and communication among women. But well before Jackson and Prins, lyric had a different and powerful opposition in the experimental writing of the poets who in the 1970s and '80s came to be identified as part of the so-called "Language" school. For these poets the problem with the lyric and its emphasis on the singular voice was that it entailed a commitment to the priority of the individual over the collective, and one that was symptomatic of contemporary capitalism. For women's poetry, meanwhile, and especially for feminism – without which the category of women's poetry as it has been defined in the modern and contemporary period would be incomprehensible – lyric's connection to the individual speaker, indeed to subjectivity as such, has a further problem, namely that the very idea of *women's* subjectivity has been constituted by structures of patriarchal oppression.

In this chapter, I want to challenge these formulations in two ways. First, by suggesting the degree to which even the most radically anti-lyric arguments in poetry, criticism, and theory have in fact functioned not only to preserve, but to refine and extend the domain of lyric self-expression. And second, by suggesting that the role women's poetry has played in this expansion – even though (and in a way because) it has been motivated by a liberatory social program – has in fact and unfortunately ended up contributing to the least liberatory, i.e. most successfully anti-egalitarian, developments of the period: the neoliberal restructuring of the capitalist economies of the West.

In this respect lyric *is* an artifact of the present. It is also an artifact of the past that produced the present. What that means is that everyone has been doing and is continuing to do lyric, and, more specifically, lyric self-expression – including the Language poets, including Jackson and Prins, including those most recent poetic experiments that would seem to reside in very different precincts from the lyric. The critique of lyric, and even the attempt to ignore it, becomes, I will argue, a way of embracing rather than refusing or avoiding the idea of self-expression. In the case of Jackson and Prins, the critique of lyric has served as a technology for producing more accurate accounts of material and social conditions that women experienced when they wrote their poetry (i.e. more accurate accounts of the subject positions they *really* inhabited instead of the ones they did not inhabit). And although the idea of women's poetry seems like a refusal at least of any individuated ideal of self-expression – certainly the influential idea of the social construction of gender is predicated upon the notion that there is no preexisting self to express – as I will show, women's poetry (like the critique of the lyric) has been especially effective in extending and refining the technologies of self-expression.

But for these effects to materialize fully for our purposes, we need to prepare the ground with some attention to the concept of lyric as such, and the consistent features of its formulation. The concept of lyric has been, after all, central to the discourse about women's poetry, most vividly in its efflorescence in the wake of second-wave feminism and the latter's project of giving every woman a voice.

The difference lyric makes

The emphasis on subjective expression in definitions of lyric is sometimes identified as a reaction against modernism's formal and theoretical imperatives to the "impersonality" of the poem, one that results in minimizing what would otherwise be a much stronger emphasis on voice and musicality, the *melopoeia* that is supposed to have preoccupied lyric's practitioners going back to Sappho. Or, identified with a more specific critical deformation, the manufacture of the so-called "Confessional" school, lyric can also appear as the conflation of voice with authorial self-expression, obscuring what we could otherwise recognize as persona, or the fictiveness of poetic utterance.[1] But in fact if we take as our modern and contemporary purview the twentieth and twenty-first centuries, the interest in lyric subjectivity is not a mid-century anomaly that only later became routine; it has been routine from the start.

A 1911 rhetoric textbook distinguishes lyric from epic and romance, arguing that each of the latter two "hides its author. He does not wish to utter his own loves or griefs. But poetry that does utter the author's love and grief, the poetry of personal feeling, arose in all literatures early. It is called lyric or song" (Baldwin, *Writing and Speaking*, 408). The same year's edition of *The Encyclopedia Britannica* divides "the varieties of poetic art" into those driven by "dramatic imagination" and those driven by "lyric or egoistic imagination" (Vol. 21). In the same year's edition, according to a separate entry on "Lyrical Poetry," "when poetry is objective it is epical, and when it is subjective it is lyrical" (Vol. 17). A consensus on the subjective element of lyric is apparent throughout literature and writing textbooks from the 1910s and '20s:

- "With the lyric subjective poetry begins" (Schelling, *The English Lyric*, 1).
- "There is now a tendency among professional critics to combine both the outer and inner bases of definition by insisting on the dual character of lyric, – its song-like or tuneful quality or form on the one hand, and its subjective or personal content on the other" (Gayley and Kurtz, *Methods and Materials of Literary Criticism*, 6).
- "A lyric poem is a poem of which the main purpose is the expression of the feelings of the author or some imagined person" (Reynolds and Greever, *The Facts and Backgrounds of Literature*, 323).
- "It usually expresses the author's own experience, moods, reflections, and emotions in musical language" (Rich, *A Study of the Types of Literature*, 66).
- "The work of a narrative poet may be nearly if not wholly impersonal. The lyric poet may, on the other hand, be considered to hold the views he expresses in a subjective work" (Hubbell and Beaty, *An Introduction to Poetry*, 147).

These claims persist well beyond the first decades of the twentieth century. Surviving more or less intact from the 1936 *Handbook to Literature* by William Flint Thrall and Addison Hibbard, the definition of lyric that students can still find in the book's 2009 edition begins: "A brief subjective poem strongly marked by imagination, melody, and emotion, and creating for the reader a single, unified impression" (324). Likewise, this definition from the first edition of M. H. Abrams's 1957 *Glossary of Literary Terms* is retained in the current edition: "a lyric is any short poem, consisting of the utterance by a single speaker, who expresses a state of mind or a process of perception, thought, and feeling" (2963).

Obviously, as I have already pointed out, there is an important difference between the persona of a poem's speaker and the actual person of the poet, and an even starker one between either of these and what we might mean by "voice." But we might ask why literary critics, poets, and theorists alike, particularly through the second half of the last century up to the present, consistently feel the pressure to point these differences out, lest we succumb to the impulse to conflate them. At the same time, we must take into account the sustained and highly influential efforts, particularly, as I began to suggest in the previous section, the theoretical work produced by poets associated with the Language movement during the 1970s and '80s, to defeat the lyric project on the basis of a more probing critique of the precise terms of that conflation, rejecting the very idea of the speaker, to which I will return below.

The history I am proposing asks us to treat all of these strains of discomfort with lyric as contributions to the lyric project, and to consider seriously the history that emerges if we regard the lyric / anti-lyric opposition as two sides of the same coin. Suppose we were to accept as accurate – even taking into account the many critiques of lyric that have erupted up to now – the often repeated (and disputed) claim that the lyric genre does in fact dominate Western poetic production more or less since the advent of European Romanticism in the eighteenth century? And what if we also were to accept as definitive, the often repeated (and disputed) conflation of that genre with a range of commitments to self-expression?

Taking (or mistaking) this sweeping generalization at its face value, I am arguing, produces a useful distortion. For instead of allowing us to ignore these claims as false, it demands that we explore the force of them as well as their effects, that we ask why the persistent emphasis on lyric as subjective expression has been sufficiently powerful to invite so many efforts to reject it, indeed, to reject it precisely on its own terms. It demands that we ask why the stereotype takes hold when it does. For this mode of lyric, said to emerge from the liberal revolutions in Europe and America in the eighteenth century, has undergone its modern and contemporary permutations and achieved its proclaimed "dominance" against an equally dominant backdrop, namely the march toward the "End of History" (to recall Francis Fukuyama's 1989 essay announcing the victory of liberal democracy over all other forms of political government), and accompanying that march, the global expansion of markets.

It is clear from the textbook definitions of lyric cited above, even those most cognizant of the fictive possibilities of persona and the formal possibilities of voice, that the representation of subjectivity is central. What else would we need to call "perception, thought, and feeling"? And while none of these necessarily requires the attribution of the term "self" much less "expression," our definitions of lyric persistently succeed in evoking the concept of self-expression.

From the late 1960s onward, however, the imperative to avoid naïvely conflating poet with persona or either with voice gives way, as I began to suggest earlier, to an imperative to reject our interest in all of these. Viewed through the poststructuralist lenses of Saussurean linguistics, Althusserian ideological critique, Lacanian psychoanalysis, and Derridean deconstruction, the identifiable "speaker" of the poem (whatever we might think it represents) becomes a fantasm of intentional agency. On the one hand, the subject lyrically rendered belies the social and linguistic structures of signification within and through which the subject as such is always already "split." On the other – the major contribution of Language poetry to this critique – the intentional authority represented in the lyric speaker places the writer and reader in a false hierarchy. Dispensing with an identifiable speaker and conventional patterns of speech, emphasizing instead ways of dismembering, distorting, and even refusing altogether common grammatical, semantic, and syntactical structures, the solution is a democratizing "open" poetry that "invites participation, rejects the authority of the writer over the reader, and thus, by analogy, the authority implicit in other (social, economic, cultural) hierarchies," as Lyn Hejinian suggests in her influential essay, "The Rejection of Closure" (43). The reader thus activated is imagined to engage with material foundations of language and social traces of linguistic production that otherwise remain transparent, naturalized, or altogether invisible.[2] But what is most important for our purposes is that the reader thus activated is also engaged above all *subjectively* – that is in ways that we might say literally generate the "perception, thought, and feeling" that otherwise are identified with the poet, persona, or voice of the traditional lyric poem. In this respect, the Language poets' claim to produce "the obverse of the autonomous, New Critical lyric" reproduces rather than overturns governing terms of subjectivity that we find in standard definitions of lyric (Silliman *et al.*, "Aesthetic Tendency and the Politics of Poetry," 274).

Moreover, when the lyric subject also appears to its avant-garde, postmodern critics as a hallmark of the "workshop poem," a commodified artifact of Creative Writing programs (which, it is worth pointing out, have expanded exponentially over the second half of the last century and continue to grow in number), we find in the counter to lyric an unwitting idealization of individual expression that is supposedly symptomatic of lyric. As Bob Perelman puts it in *The Marginalization of Poetry*, the creative writing program's

> insistence on individuality, often translated into the aesthetic necessity of "finding your voice," masks the institutional circuits, the network of presses, reviews, jobs, readings, and awards that are the actual sounding board of voice. (114)

The problem with writing programs that encourage students to "find [their] voice" (a commonplace even now in the promotional material on many writing-program websites) is apparently that the voices their students find are insufficiently their own.

Given the recurrent emphasis on subjective expression that we have been tracking, two very recent poetic developments that have followed in the wake of Language poetry might as well have been scripted in advance: the advent of the category of so-called "innovative" writing, where "innovation" is consistently identified with formal techniques that are virtually indistinguishable from those commonly associated with Language-school poetry and, at the same time, is linked predominantly to writing by women, African Americans, Asian Americans, and other identity-based groupings of writers; and second, the backlash against those very same formal techniques and the theory behind them by practitioners of a so-called "New Sincerity" or "New Childishness," whose poetic claim to newness *is* sincerity or innocence of expression.[3] Both movements gesture at reinstating lyric (not that it has ever been removed from office), the former perhaps most vividly in the appearance of Claudia Rankine and Juliana Spahr's 2002 anthology, *American Woman Poets in the 21st Century: Where Lyric Meets Language*. "Mak[ing] room within lyric for language writing's more politicized claims," the collection, according to Spahr's introduction, presents poets of whom the majority "use the word 'lyric' to refer to interiority and/or intimate speech that avoids confession, clear speech, or common sense" (2).

Seeing this persistent identification of lyric with subjective expression, whether it be "confession" or "sincerity" or "interiority" or "intimate speech," even in the refusal of the same, presents us equally persistently with the question of who, in any given poem, is speaking. More precisely, from the standpoint of a literary practice driven by formal invention, it asks us to consider the relationship between who is speaking (or not) and the shape that speaking (or non-speaking) takes.

The difference a woman makes

What do we mean when we organize poetry by women as women's poetry? Why and how does it matter that a poem was produced by a woman?

Consider two statements. First, in the form of a question, from Gertrude Stein: "Why should a woman do the important literary thinking of this epoch" (*The Geographical History of America*, 216–17). The second, from Susan Howe, in the form of an answer to an interviewer's question in 1989: "[t]he difference between say Melville and Dickinson would be (apart from gender) that Melville is from one side of the Connecticut River, and she is from the other side. Trust place to form the voice" (Howe, *The Birth-mark*, 156). We can frame some of the major developments in modern and contemporary women's poetry in terms of the distance between these two statements; that is, how we get from Stein's question (or some version of it) – why should a woman do the important literary thinking – to Howe's statement (or some version of it) to the effect that the subject position (including the gender) of the poet shapes the form of her poetic voice.

For Stein, there is no required connection between the "literary thinking" and the fact that the thinker is a woman. Moreover, the question Stein asks is clearly a permutation of the more obvious negative formulation (why *shouldn't* a woman do the important literary thinking?); indeed, that negative counterpart could perfectly well serve as the answer to the actual question. And the rhetorical force of Stein's question becomes even clearer when we consider that Stein herself, even as she declares "I do it. Oh yes I do it," insists at the same time, "I think nothing about men and women because that has nothing to do with anything" (Stein, *The Geographical History of America*, 214, 206). This may seem to be a remarkable claim coming from the author who composed her earliest writings under the influence of Otto Weininger's *Sex and Character* (published in English translation in 1906), which notoriously argued for essential masculine and feminine traits. But as I have argued elsewhere, Stein abandoned her early "identity"-based model of composition for one based on what she called "entity," effectively renouncing any claim on subjectivity for art.[4] For Stein, in other words, part of the point of the question, "why should a woman do the important literary thinking," is to render the answer irrelevant, and to insist on an idea of art that makes the gender of the artist (and for that matter the reader or beholder) irrelevant.

But if Stein seems to bring gender to the foreground to emphasize its irrelevance, we might say that Howe sets it aside ("apart from gender") in order to keep it in the foreground. For Howe, the poet's voice is shaped by her gender *as well as* the side of the river she comes from, not to mention a host of other conditions, both material and ideological. The difference between Stein's idea of writing as a woman and Howe's, in other words, is that for Stein, the relationship between the poet's subject position and the literary thinking she does is purely contingent; whereas for Howe, it appears necessary, indeed, we might even say, essential.

If we treat these two ways of thinking about why "woman" matters to woman-authored poetry as beginning and endpoints of a trajectory, we obviously get a slightly strange periodization: a modernism committed to diminishing and even disregarding the differences between men and women for the purposes of just social, political, and (as in Stein's comment) literary, recognition; followed by a postmodernism invested in recognizing and valuing difference – not only between men and women, on the basis of sex and gender, but between any given individual and any other, on the basis of any number of ascriptive characteristics, including race, ethnicity, religion, sexual preference, economic class, regional (which "side of the Connecticut river" one is from), or national origin. But in fact, for the history of modern and contemporary women's poetry, and of feminism more generally during this period, it is quite accurate to think of the universalism of the first having given over to the particularism of the second.

The universalist commitment that drove feminism's first wave, that is, the commitment to equality in the form of fair representation, has continued through the course of second- and third-wave feminism to find unfairnesses left untouched by new regimes of fairness – silenced voices and abjected bodies in need of valuing and recognition. Each "wave" has necessitated finer instruments of differentiation to bring acknowledgment and justice to individuals as yet unserved by more universalist programs. Since the 1970s, the ensuing pluralization of feminism into feminisms has been matched by parallel development in poetry toward the commitment to individual difference as such.

We can turn to the earliest years of what we call "modern" poetry, to the years just prior to the passage of the Nineteenth Amendment to the United States Constitution, to witness a proleptic instance of this friction between universality and plurality. In 1914 Margaret Sanger introduced *The Woman Rebel* to raise awareness of women's rights that were not being addressed by the suffrage movement – the rights of working women specifically, but also the rights of all women to birth control and the power to make decisions about their own bodies (a campaign for which the magazine was censored and for which Sanger was charged with violating obscenity laws). The mission of the newsletter was to "fight," as Sanger put it, "for the personal liberty of the women who work. A woman's body belongs to herself alone" (Sanger, "Suppression"). The same year the poet Mina Loy published her "Feminist Manifesto," denouncing, like Sanger, the mainstream feminist movement as "inadequate." But unlike Sanger's radical politics of free choice, which aimed at more complete equality between women and men, Loy's radical poetics consisted in "denying at the outset – that pathetic clap-trap war cry Woman is the equal of man – for she is NOT!" (Loy / Conover, *The Lost Lunar Baedeker: Poems of Mina Loy*, 153).

Published the same year as the "Feminist Manifesto," one of Loy's earliest poems, "Parturition," begins with an obvious figuration of the eponymous physiological process that constitutes the difference she most cares about between male and female bodies – the capacity to give birth – and the literal differentiation ("parturition") that separates one body from another in the birth-giving process. The poem opens by equating the first-person speaker with the experience of her own body, more precisely with the cervical and vaginal openings that stretch painfully to make way for the child: "I am the centre / of a circle of pain / Exceeding its boundaries in every direction" (Loy / Conover, *Poems of Mina Loy*, 4).

We are informed about a third of the way into the poem that this unbounded pain is caused by a "conception   Brute" (the space is in the original line) that is "the irresponsibility of the male" (5). This figure of the "male" appears only once. Otherwise the poem, dominated by imagery of searing bodily pain, focuses exclusively on the "struggle" of the woman speaker as she "climb[s] a distorted mountain of agony" toward a "summit" of "Repose / Which never comes" (5). By the end of the poem, this "pain surpassing itself" has transcended both the body and the consciousness of the speaker, transforming her into a "Mother . . . / Identical / With infinite maternity / . . . absorbed into / The was – is – ever – shall – be / Of cosmic reproductivity" (7). Echoing the claims of her "Feminist Manifesto," Loy's poem ends with compact encomium to sexual difference: "Man and woman God made them – / Thank God" (8). Sanger, in the interest of equality, would give Loy's speaker the choice of avoiding both the "conception Brute" and its consequences. For Loy, however, the speaker's absorption into the "infinite maternity" of "cosmic reproductivity" represents at once a difference from men that she does not choose, as well as a difference that a politics of equality might choose to diminish. The feminist power of choice in Loy's case comes with the decision to celebrate rather than circumvent the difference.

With feminism's second wave came the realization that the equal rights initiatives of the first wave, including successfully mandating universal suffrage, did not remotely succeed in making men and women equal; more-over, even where they did succeed the effects among women were not so universal, as even first-wave feminists like Sanger had long before recognized. That is, many of the mainstream initiatives of feminism tended to be driven by and benefit white women of privilege and to reinforce patriarchal order through what Adrienne Rich famously criticized in 1980 as its tacit acceptance of "compulsory heterosexuality."[5] The often-cited lines of Rich's early poem, "The Roofwalker" (1961) – "A life I didn't choose / chose me" – are echoed in the introduction to her autobiographical treatise, *Of Woman Born: Motherhood as Experience and Institution*, written two and a half decades later, long after Rich married, raised three children, divorced, and came out as a lesbian: "I told myself that I wanted to write a book on motherhood because it was a crucial, still relatively unexplored, area for feminist theory. But I did not choose this subject; it had long ago chosen me" (Rich, *Of Woman Born*, 15).

"The Roofwalker" is not ostensibly about motherhood at all; if anything it is primarily legible as a metapoetic allegory where the lines themselves build a kind of "roof" over the figure at the end of the poem "sitting in the lamplight / against the cream wallpaper / reading" (Rich, *Fact of a Doorframe*, 23). But the building of the roof is enacted through a complex series of gendered identifications, subtly evocative of the language of childbearing and childbirth. The roof's "builders" are also "Giants," with whom the speaker identifies: "I feel like them up there: / exposed, larger than life, / and due to break my neck." We might not make much of the word "due" but in the next line the speaker asks herself, in a striking enjambment, "Was it worthwhile to lay– / with infinite exertion– / a roof I can't live under?"

The labor (pun intended) of the roofwalkers, the "infinite exertion" that allows the speaker to "feel like them," then gives way – an inversion of the logic of Loy's "Parturition" – to a striking conflation of intention with lack of choice. In the lines immediately preceding the moment when "a life I didn't choose / chose me," the speaker lays claim to her own agency and planning: "– All those blueprints, / closings of gaps, / measurings, calculations." But when the speaker then tells us "I'm naked, ignorant / a naked man fleeing across the roofs" the agency of making – both the planning and the lack of choice – are explicitly rendered male. But it is only a "shade of difference" that disables the identification, turning the naked man back into a mere figure, one that leaves the speaker confined to reading about him in a lamplit, wallpapered room. On the one hand, it is the fleeing naked man that makes the conception possible, the identification with whom generates the metapoetic "blueprints, closings of gaps, measurings, calculations" that go into the laying of the lines that form "The Roofwalker." On the other hand, it is the fact that the speaker is not that naked man, the "shade of difference" between them, that returns the speaker to her "cream wallpaper" and a "life I didn't choose."

A decade later, "Diving into the Wreck" would expose the collapse of the identification as itself a myth, its speaker diving into a wreck of patriarchal order to discover beneath it all an abiding androgyny: " . . . I am here, the mermaid whose dark hair / streams black, the merman in his armored body / . . . I am she: I am he" (Rich, *Fact of a Doorframe*, 103). Refusing to limit the gendered inhabitants of the body, this discovery of androgynous origins is a prelude in Rich's writing to the poetic articulation of lesbian desire in her sequence, "Twenty-One Love Poems," which are clearly addressed to "you" who is also a "she." The speaker of these lyrics comes full circle, as it were, from the roofwalker's "life I did not choose," culminating in a declaration of choice, and a narrowing of domain: "I choose to walk here. And to draw this circle" (Rich, *Fact of a Doorframe*, 154).

But lesbian voices were not the only ones that emerged from silence in the second-wave critiques of feminism's universalizing tendencies. The work of theorists like Barbara Christian and bell hooks, and of poets like Audre Lorde, Gloria Anzaldúa, and Cherríe Moraga, exposed the degree to which feminism had not developed adequate space or terms for women writers of color and sought to give voice to subjectivities that were occluded or simply drowned out by more dominant (largely straight, largely white) feminist voices. Anzaldúa's poem "To live in the Borderlands means you" simultaneously articulates and refuses the multiple identities of Rich's early androgynism, shuttling between Spanish and English, "and"'s, "ni"'s, and "neither"'s. "To live in the borderlands," according to Anzaldúa, you are inhabited not by one, not by two identities, but by many: you "carry all five races on your back" and are "half and half – both woman and man, neither– / a new gender" (Anzaldúa, *Borderlands*, 216).

The representational project of feminism that evolved out of first-wave feminism, the desire to ensure all voices are heard, that all women are included, produces out of its universalism an increasing commitment to particularity. But if second-wave feminists like Rich and Anzaldúa offered an individualized universalism in the form of identity – a celebration of diverse and marginalized subjects – third-wave feminism would, in effect, universalize individualism in the form of a critique of the very same identities that second-wave feminism celebrated. The result, paradoxically, has been a whole new set of technologies for generating an ever more finely distinguished array of sub-jectivities, creating, as we shall see, not a better approach to equality but a perfect storm of inequality.

The women's poetry anthology industry, a growth industry since the early 1970s, began, not surprisingly, as a corrective endeavor, and its history mirrors the transition from universalism to particularity that we have been tracing. The editors of the 1978 *Penguin Book of Women Poets*, for example, describe the volume as "redressing the imbalance" in representing women's poetry and "correct[ing] a long neglect" (Cosman *et al.*, *Penguin Book of Women Poets*, 30, 32). But even as the project of bringing visibility to women's writing presented itself in largely egalitarian terms – compatible, for example, with the aims of the Equal Pay Act passed a decade and a half earlier or the Equal Rights Amendment whose ratification deadline was being extended the same year that the *Penguin* anthology appeared – these anthologies also, in effect, demanded that we read their poems not despite the fact that they were written by women, but because of it. In other words, if the egalitarian impulse driving these anthologies was to diminish or erase altogether the differences between men and women, their aesthetic impulse was to delineate and celebrate the differences.

Rising Tides: 20th-Century American Women Poets, for example, opens with a claim to "speak with a woman's voice, through a woman's perceptions, about a woman's experiences; they reflect what may be called a feminine consciousness." Florence Howe and Ellen Bass's anthology, *No More Masks! An Anthology of Poems by Women*, takes its epigraph from Muriel Rukeyser's "The Poem as Mask": "it was myself, split open, unable to speak, in exile from myself" (Howe and Bass, *No More Masks!*, 1). The announcement of the (non-speaking) speaker of the poem that she is a subject in "exile" from her own "self" suggests both that such exile is a shared condition of the women's voices represented in the volume, and that to repair that condition would mean something like a restoration of the female speaker to her proper "self." Within the next decade, the "exile" of Rukeyser's speaker would demand finer tuning to serve poets of color and marginalized sexualities who contended with the pressures not just of male hegemony, but of racism, homophobia, and a myriad other forms of oppression.

This "split" self of Rukeyser or the "border" subject of Anzaldúa, in other words, is hardly the "split subject" of poststructuralist critique, but with the importation and increasing influence of that theory within English depart-ments from the mid 1970s through the early '80s, the kind of double or multiple consciousness implied in their poetic vision acquired the status of a permanent, universal condition of subjective experience. Any fantasy of unmediated self-expression then started to appear naïve at best or in a kind of bad faith at worst. On the heels of anthologies that celebrated identity, such as *No More Masks!* or Anzaldúa and Cherríe Moraga's *This Bridge Called My Back: Writings by Radical Women of Color*, came a sustained critique of the supposedly "accessible" modes of self-expression found in the previous generation's women's poetry.

Viewed through the lenses of feminist poststructuralist critiques, particularly in the form of *écriture féminine* (an adaptation of the more general critique of representation launched by the *Tel Quel* collective that included Roland Barthes, Hélène Cixous, Jacques Derrida, Julia Kristeva, and Jacques Lacan), the unified subject began to appear in the USA in the 1970s and '80s as the fantasmatic product of asymmetrical power relations in which all aspects of discourse, including even the most elemental structures of language, reveal themselves to be shaped by male (especially white male) privilege. Imported into the discourse of women's poetry, such critiques served to render the very idea of the female lyric speaker suspect, on grounds that her speaking could never successfully represent her own subject position, because any representation by linguistic means must inevitably bear the traces of the male-dominated society in which the language evolved. As Rachel Blau DuPlessis puts it in her seminal essay, "Otherhow," it's not just that women are largely the objects rather than the subjects of poetic meditation by the lyric "I":

> The whole *"History of Poetry"* concerns my facing and being haunted by the Western lyric tradition, speaking as a woman poet... "Woman" has been constructed by that tradition as the permanent object of scrutiny, rather than as the speaking subject, even when, as we all know, there have always been a few women poets... Women have been the signifieds with very little or no literary control of signifiers. (149–50)

At the same time, the signifiers over which women have "little or no literary control" are, according to DuPlessis, "overpopulated with the intentions of others,... teeming with, inter alia, gender ideas... Each word *tastes* of the context and contexts in which it has lived its socially charged life" (143–4).

The claim that language bears with it such traces of a gendered and gendering social order is one way of pointing out the extent to which gender is socially constructed, and as such the claim is partly a response to the perceived risks of essentializing socially defined roles or attributes that might accrue to gender and otherwise appear natural, even bodily, and determined in advance. The effort to situate gender discursively was also a way of removing it from the implied claims to authenticity that could be perceived in the effort to cultivate the distinctively feminine poetic voice and consciousness that 1970s anthologies such as *Rising Tides* ("they reflect what may be called a feminine consciousness") or *Psyche: The Feminine Poetic Consciousness* claimed to put on display.

But as I have argued in more detail elsewhere, the effort to organize poetry by women under the auspices of "innovative" and "experimental" forms produces an essentialism of its own.[6] Suppose we organize poets on the basis of some set of shared ideological commitments – to equal rights, say, or the celebration of motherhood, or womynist separatism, or whatever we might care to mean by feminism – in which case, while it might seem from some perspective advantageous to have a disproportionate number of women in the mix, nothing (except maybe in the case of a commitment to separatism) actually requires that the poets we bring into our representative collection be women. And what is even more important for our purposes, nothing requires that the poems they make fall into any particular formal categories. Now suppose we organize our poets on the basis of some set of shared formal commitments – the desire to write sonnets, or write in syllabics, or write in shattered syntax and jarring semantic substitutions, or collage together Google search results – nothing in principle requires that the practitioners of such formal exercises be women. But the moment we insist on both the shared commitments *and* the fact that their adherents are women, we cannot help but produce an essentialized relation between the women and their commitments and, in turn, between the women and the poems that articulate those commitments. And what exactly is it that we care about in the women – whatever we say it is, it has to be what we think makes them women. The identity between poem and producer becomes, in effect, though I doubt any of the practitioners of the "innovative" schools would want to embrace this effect, indexical. To point to something called "innovative poetry by women" – or what Fraser calls the "innovative necessity" is, like it or not, to imply that we could read off the identity of the producer from the poems she has produced, as if the poems were a kind of secretion (one cannot help but think of Marianne Moore's "Paper Nautilus"). And once the relation between form and identity is indexical, we have as many forms, however similar they might be, as there are subjects, however similar they might be. We have, in short, an extremely effective machine whose selling point is its ability to generate multiple and, above all, infinitely differentiable identities.

But whether we think those identities are essential or socially constructed (I am suggesting that the one is always some version of the other), we have arrived simultaneously at an insistence on their *value*, the value both of our identities as such, and of the myriad differences among them. And with this particularizing logic we have achieved a remarkable technology for redressing imbalance in the representation of the marginalized: every subject position is now at once marginal and impossible to marginalize. As DuPlessis writes nearly two decades after "Otherhow," obviously tongue in cheek, but nevertheless in full embrace of subjectivity – indeed, of subjective expression – as such:

> Who doesn't now want female masculinity, males' girlishness, feminine and effeminate texts and acts by males as well as females, androgyny (hey there – lookin' *good*, again); poets embodying "malehood"; queer performativity; butch straight girls; male lesbians; matrisexual people; cross-gender folks; persons-gender-unimportant? Who doesn't want an array of subjectivities in their studios, all engaging in what they imagine as *"self*-fashioning"? How, under these plural conditions of social subjectivity, could we not want "women-as-just-persons" among them? Are these possibilities not, generally, a result of feminism? (DuPlessis, *Blue Studios*, 57)

Even with the requisite scare-quotes, "self-fashioning" is the operative term here.

Contemporary poetry's decentered self, undergoing its constant refashionings, has never been on more vivid display than in the recent anthology *Gurlesque: the new grrly, grotesque, burlesque, poetics.* "In Gurlesque poetry," according to one of the anthology's editors, Laura Glenum,

> human bodies and human language (and thus identity) are not closed, discrete systems. They are grotesque bodies / systems – never finished, ever-morphing, and porous. The body, as the nexus of language and identity, is a strange borderland, the site of erratic and highly specific (and language-mediated) desires. (Glenum and Greenberg, *Gurlesque*, 17)

Third-wave feminism's technology of decentering or splitting the unified subjects of second-wave feminism has proven to be, in short, not an abandonment of identities but a new and improved instrument for individuating them. The difference a woman has made for modern and contemporary poetry is the difference of difference as such.

The difference feminism has not made

As we have seen, the critical discourse that has given us women's poetry, both in its artistic and its academic forms, has shared feminism's broader social justice aims in combating inequalities between men and women, going forward and bringing adequate recognition to women's achievements, both past and present. And as we have also seen, despite the strides made by first- and second-wave feminists, the struggle is ongoing. Contrary to the spirit of the Virginia Slims cigarette ad campaigns launched in the late 1960s, whose message to its target market of female consumers was, "you've come a long way, baby," we have never yet come far enough in dispatching those inequities. Feminism's work is apparently never done.

We do not have to look very far to find ample statistical evidence of the economic inequities that persist for women. In the USA, employed women are still earning less than their male counterparts. Since the enactment of the Equal Pay Act in 1963, the wage gap between men and women has narrowed from 41 percent to 23 percent, but the 77 cents women earn on each dollar that men make is hardly equal pay for equal work. Women are still overrepresented in jobs with poverty-level wages, and underrepresented in corporate boardrooms, top management, and executive offices. And for our purposes here, that is, when we narrow our focus to some of the more prominent institutions of poetic production – Creative Writing programs, presses that publish poetry, journals, and magazines that publish and review poetry, boards and panels for literary grants and prizes, just to name the most obvious – we find women underrepresented once again.

According to the two different reports by the Modern Language Association Committee on the Status of Women in the Profession, women in English Departments are underrepresented among full-time faculty, overrepresented among part-time faculty, and within the tenure-track and tenured ranks, their underrepresentation increases in proportion to rank.[7] Information on poetry publishing tends to be more sporadic and anecdotal, but two recent informal surveys of a limited number of larger publishing houses and smaller university and independent presses suggest that the ratio of volumes by women to those by men is well below parity.[8] A recent survey by VIDA Women in Literary Arts found even more dramatic disproportion in the book-reviewing activities of large-audience magazines such as *The New Yorker* and *The New York Review of Books*, with the number of women book reviewers and the number of women's books reviewed rarely making up more than a third of the pie ("The Count" is presented in a series of pie charts). Other reports found the pattern repeating itself in the distribution of literary grants and prizes, with more than half the total monetary value going to men (Spahr and Young, "Numbers Trouble," 96–7).

What is as important about the disparities themselves, however, is the surprise and disbelief with which they are delivered. "What we found upset and confused us," write Spahr and Young about their "troubling" numbers; "things haven't been that great since the mid-80s" (98). And in response to the more recent survey by VIDA, Meghan Rourke writes, "Even if you might have expected the gender ratios to be skewed, the results are a little surprising." Ruth Franklin's response to the same numbers is more succinct: "The numbers are startling." The headline for the VIDA survey is likewise indicative of this tendency – "'Numbers don't lie.' 'What counts is the bottom line.'" In other words, we *need* to be shown the numbers precisely because we are inclined to believe something different: "We know women write. We know women read," the VIDA survey begins, "It's time to begin asking why the numbers don't reflect those facts with any equity" (VIDA). Or as Robin Romm puts it on *Slate*'s *XXfactor* blog: "VIDA's new count of magazine contributors by gender is distressing. Or maybe it's simply depressing. I suppose it depends on how optimistic you were before you glimpsed the numbers."[9]

But Ruth Franklin's conclusions about the numbers may offer the most telling insight into the false optimism that they are said to expose:

> As a member of third-wave feminism, growing up in the 1970s and '80s, I was brought up to believe we lived in a meritocracy, where the battles had been fought and won, with the spoils left for us to gather. It is sobering to realize that we may live and work in a world still held in the grip of unconscious biases, no less damaging for their invisibility. (Franklin, "A Literary Glass Ceiling?")

The implied lesson of the gender disparities revealed by these accounts is that we need to be all the more vigilant in bringing "unconscious biases" into relief in order to defeat them once and for all. For Franklin, and surely for the others, winning the battles clearly means abandoning a false meritocracy, in which those same biases allow men an unfair advantage, for a true one in which everyone has the same opportunity to succeed. It is the same lesson, in other words, that has played out in the poetry anthology industry and the literary canon reforms that helped to produce their academic market – and, for that matter, in the critical and theoretical enterprise as well, as Renker's contribution to this volume vividly demonstrates.

In one respect, the battles Franklin refers to have been fought and won, and there have been enormous spoils left to gather. But while women may still be disproportionately underrepresented among the gatherers, the disparities that emerge around those spoils suggest that ever-greater vigilance in rooting out and combating invisible biases not only has not solved the problem; it may never solve the problem. For while one important gap – the gender gap in wages – has in fact been closing steadily if slowly in the wake of both feminism's second and third waves, another gap, between the rich and the poor, has reached its widest extreme in US history and continues to widen. In 1967, according to US Census Bureau statistics, the highest quintile of American wealth had 49.4 percent of all income, while the bottom quintile had 3.4 percent. The same figures in 1967 showed the bottom quintile at 5.2 percent and the top at 42.5 percent. Meanwhile the Gini index of income inequality has risen from .37 in 1967 to .46 in 2009 (DeNavas-Walt *et al.*, *Income, Poverty, and Health Insurance Coverage*, 45–8).

In "Feminism, Capitalism, and the Cunning of History," Nancy Fraser points to these stark developments, asking us to look again at the "emancipatory promise" of second-wave feminism, and to see the "cultural attitudes" it effected

> as part and parcel of another social transformation, unanticipated and unintended by feminist activists – a transformation in the social organization of post-war capitalism. This possibility can be formulated more sharply: the cultural changes jump-started by the second wave, salutary in themselves, have served to legitimate a structural transformation of capitalist society that runs directly counter to feminist visions of a just society. (99)

More precisely, "second-wave feminism thrived," Fraser points out, in the context of economic and political forces that "promoted privatization and deregulation; in place of public provision and social citizenship, 'trickle-down' and 'personal responsibility'; in place of the welfare and developmental states, the lean, mean 'competition state'" (107). The "major alteration in the political culture," she goes on to claim, was a shift "from redistribution to recognition," in which "claims for justice were increasingly couched in claims for the recognition of identity and difference" (108). In short, the recognition of identity and difference, rather than combating the most glaring form of social injustice, has aided and abetted it.

How that aiding and abetting has succeeded is not hard to see when we consider the work of the Chicago School economist Gary Becker, whose *Economics of Discrimination* (1971) claimed that discrimination actually reduced the profitability of markets, and whose *Human Capital* (1975) urged us to think of every individual as an investment opportunity. Echoing Becker,

Michel Foucault, in his 1979 lectures at the Collège de France, remarked that neoliberalism announces itself at the precise moment when "the worker himself [now herself] appears as an enterprise for himself" (rather than, say, as a worker whose labor may be exploited by enterprise) (Foucault, *The Birth of Biopolitics*, 226). Becker and Foucault appear to have been proven right if a spate of recent corporate reports is any indication. An in-house report by Goldman Sachs, for instance, offers the following encouragement: "Narrowing the gender gap in employment – which is one potential consequence of expanded female education – could push income per capita as much as 14% higher than our baseline projections by 2020, and as much as 20% higher by 2030" (Lawson, "Women Hold Up Half the Sky," 1). Given the aggregation of wealth at the top that we have already seen, however, most will fail to experience these happy results of the shrinking gender gap.

I hope to have shown in the preceding sections that focusing on the evolutions of lyric as subjective expression, on the one hand, and poetry by women as women's poetry, on the other, allows us to see a distinctively poetic commitment to what is arguably a kindred project of recognizing identity and difference. What the modern and contemporary history of women's poetry framed from this perspective shows us, however, is that the project of recognizing identity and difference may not just be an inadvertent contribution to neoliberalism on the part of second-wave or even third-wave feminism. In both its lyric and its feminist forms, the poetic project of recognizing difference predates the more recent and dramatic liberalizations and expansions of markets, and coincides with a much longer history of "shifts in the social organization of capitalism."

Obviously recognition as such need not in principle have the political content that it does for us – in some other time and place, it might well serve different ends, or even succeed as a project of achieving social justice. Moreover, the fact that the project of recognition and the project of neoliberalism have, as Fraser puts it, "prospered in tandem" suggests a correlative, not necessarily causal, relation between them ("Feminism, Capitalism and the Cunning of History," 108).[10] But in our present moment, the increasingly unregulated expansion of capital, and, with it, an increasing consolidation of wealth to a smaller and smaller elite, does seem to be inevitable without significant structural change (redistribution and social provision). And as long as it is inevitable, recognizing and valuing difference seems to function inevitably in its service. Modern and contemporary women's poetry, in both its lyric and (purportedly) anti-lyric strains, would seem to be one of the Age of Inequality's privileged forms of art.

Notes

1. The term "confessional poetry" was coined by M. L. Rosenthal in 1956 to describe the intimate disclosures figuring in the work of poets like Sylvia Plath, Anne Sexton, and Robert Lowell. It took hold eventually as a description of any poetry in which the speaker of the poem appears to divulge personal information, especially while appearing to be one and the same as the poet.
2. See, for example, Silliman, "Disappearance of the World, Appearance of the Word" in *The New Sentence*, and Bernstein, "Artifice of Absorption" in *A Poetics*.
3. In the interest of space, I will not address this movement here. A preliminary exploration of the movement's implications for lyric can be found in Ashton, "Sincerity and the Second Person."
4. In Ashton, *From Modernism to Postmodernism*.
5. Rich, "Compulsory Heterosexuality," in *Blood, Bread, and Poetry: Selected Prose 1979–1985*.
6. In "Our Bodies, Our Poems."
7. See "Women in the Profession: 2000," "Standing Still," and West and Curtis, "AAUP Faculty Gender Equity Indicators 2006."
8. See Spahr and Young, "Numbers Trouble," 96. See also Franklin, "A Literary Glass Ceiling?".
9. Katha Pollitt's response to the survey is a rare exception to the general tendency to surprise ("The Lack of Female Bylines Is Old News").
10. Eisenstein, *Feminism Seduced*, makes similar claims.

Works cited

"1911 Encyclopædia Britannica." *Wikisource, The Free Library*. <http://en.wikisource.org/w/index.php?title=1911_Encyclop%C3%A6dia_Britannica&oldid=2484343>.

Abrams, M. H. and Geoffrey Galt Harpham. *A Glossary of Literary Terms*, 9th edn. Boston: Wadsworth Cengage Learning, 2009, 2005.

Anzaldúa, Gloria. *Borderlands/La Frontera: The New Mestiza*. San Francisco: Aunt Lute Books, 1999.

Anzaldúa, Gloria and Cherríe Moraga, eds. *This Bridge Called My Back: Writings by Radical Women of Color*. New York: Kitchen Table, Women of Color Press, 1983.

Ashton, Jennifer. *From Modernism to Postmodernism: American Poetry and Theory in the Twentieth Century*. Cambridge: Cambridge University Press, 2005.

    "Our Bodies, Our Poems." *American Literary History* 19.1 (Spring 2007): 211–31.

    "Sincerity and the Second Person: Lyric after Language Poetry." *Interval(le)s* 2.2–3.1 (Fall 2008/Winter 2009): 94–108.

Baldwin, Charles Sears. *Writing and Speaking: A Text-Book of Rhetoric*. New York: Longmans, Green, & Co., 1911.

Becker, Gary. *The Economics of Discrimination*. Chicago: University of Chicago Press, 1971.

    Human Capital: A Theoretical and Empirical Analysis, with Special Reference to Education, 3rd edn. Chicago: University of Chicago Press, 1994.

Bernstein, Charles. *A Poetics*. Cambridge, MA: Harvard University Press, 1992.

Conover, Roger L., ed. *The Lost Lunar Baedeker: Poems of Mina Loy*. New York: Farrar Strauss Giroux, 1996.

Cosman, Carol, Joan Keefe, and Kathleen Weaver, eds. *The Penguin Book of Women Poets*. New York: Viking, 1978.

DeNavas-Walt, Carmen, Bernadette D. Proctor, and Jessica C. Smith. US Census Bureau, Current Population Reports, p.60–238. *Income, Poverty, and Health Insurance Coverage in the United States: 2009*. Washington, DC: US Government Printing Office, 2010.

DuPlessis, Rachel Blau. *Blue Studios: Poetry and its Cultural Work*. Tuscaloosa: University of Alabama Press, 2006.

The Pink Guitar: Writing as Feminist Practice. New York: Routledge, 1990.

Eisenstein, Hester. *Feminism Seduced: How Global Elites Use Women's Labor and Ideas to Exploit the World*. Boulder, CO, and London: Paradigm Publishers, 2009.

Evans, Steve. "Field Notes, October 2003–June 2004." *The Poker* 4 (2004): 66–87.

Foucault, Michel. *The Birth of Biopolitics: Lectures at the Collège de France, 1978–1979*. Ed. Michel Senellart. Trans. Graham Burchell. New York: Palgrave Macmillan, 2008.

Franklin, Ruth. "A Literary Glass Ceiling? Why Magazines aren't Reviewing More Female Writers." *The New Republic*. Online article. February 7, 2011 http://www.tnr.com/article/books-and-arts/82930/VIDA-women-writers-magazines-book-reviews.

Fraser, Nancy. "Feminism, Capitalism and the Cunning of History." *New Left Review* 56 (March/April 2009): 97–117.

Gayley, Charles Mills and Benjamin Putnam Kurtz. *Methods and Materials of Literary Criticism: Lyric, Epic, and Allied Forms of Poetry*. Boston: Ginn and Company, 1920.

Glenum, Laura and Arielle Greenberg, eds. *Gurlesque: The New Grrly, Grotesque, Burlesque, Poetics*. Ardmore, PA: Saturnalia Books, 2010.

Harmon, William and Hugh Holman. *A Handbook to Literature*, 11th edn. Upper Sadler River, NJ: Pearson Prentice Hall, 2009.

Hejinian, Lyn. "The Rejection of Closure." 1983. Reprinted in *The Language of Inquiry*. Berkeley, Los Angeles, and London: University of California Press, 2000.

Howe, Florence and Ellen Bass. *No More Masks! An Anthology of Poems by Women*. Garden City, NY: Anchor Press, 1973.

Howe, Susan. *The Birth-mark: Unsettling the Wilderness in American Literary History*. Hanover: Wesleyan University Press, 1993.

Hubbell, Jay B. and John O. Beaty. *An Introduction to Poetry*. New York: The Macmillan Company, 1922.

Jackson, Virginia. *Dickinson's Misery: A Theory of Lyric Reading*. Princeton: Princeton University Press, 2005.

Jackson, Virginia and Yopie Prins. "Lyric Studies." *Victorian Literature and Culture* 27 (1999): 521–30.

Lawson, Sandra. "Women Hold Up Half the Sky." Goldman Sachs Global Economics Paper No. 164. Online document. March 4, 2008. http://www2.goldmansachs.com/ideas/demographic-change/women-hold-up-half-the-sky.html.

O'Rourke, Meghan. "Women at Work: A New Tally Shows How Female Writers Appear in Magazines." *Slate*. Online article. February 2, 2011. www.slate.com/id/2283605/.

Perelman, Bob. *The Marginalization of Poetry: Language Writing and Literary History*. Princeton: Princeton University Press, 1996.

Pollitt, Katha. "The Lack of Female Bylines is Old News." *Slate*. Online article. February 11, 2011. www.slate.com/id/2284680/.

Rankine, Claudia and Juliana Spahr, eds. *American Women Poets in the 21st Century: Where Lyric Meets Language*. Middletown, CT: Wesleyan University Press, 2002.

Reynolds, George F. and Garland Greever. *The Facts and Backgrounds of Literature: English and American*. New York: The Century Company, 1920.

Rich, Adrienne. *Blood, Bread, and Poetry: Selected Prose 1979–1985*. New York: W. W. Norton, 1986.

　The Fact of a Doorframe: Selected Poems, 1950–2001. New York: W. W. Norton, 2002.

　Of Woman Born: Motherhood as Experience and Institution. New York: W. W. Norton, 1986.

Rich, Mabel Irene. *A Study of the Types of Literature*. New York: The Century Company, 1921.

Romm, Robin. "Why it Matters That Fewer Women are Published in Literary Magazines." *Slate*. Online article. February 2, 2011. www.doublex.com/blog/xxfactor/why-it-matters-fewer-women-are-published-literary-magazines.

Sanger, Margaret. "Suppression." *The Woman Rebel* 1.4 (June 1914): 25. www.nyu.edu/projects/sanger/webedition/app/documents/show.php?sangerDoc=420004.xml.

Schelling, Felix E. *The English Lyric*. Boston and New York: Houghton Mifflin Company, 1913.

Segnitz, Barbara and Carol Rainey, eds. *Psyche: The Feminine Poetic Consciousness, an Anthology of Modern American Women Poets*. New York: Dial Press, 1973.

Silliman, Ron. *The New Sentence*. New York: Roof Books, 1987.

Silliman, Ron, Carla Harryman, Lyn Hejinian, Steve Benson, Bob Perelman, and Barrett Watten. "Aesthetic Tendency and the Politics of Poetry: A Manifesto." *Social Text* 19/20 (Autumn 1988): 261–75.

Spahr, Juliana and Stephanie Young. "Numbers Trouble." *Chicago Review* 53.2/3 (Autumn 2007): 88–111.

Spahr, Juliana and Stephanie Young. "Standing Still: The Associate Professor Survey: Report of the Committee on the Status of Women in the Profession." April 27, 2009. www.mla.org/pdf/cswp_final042909.pdf.

Stein, Gertrude. *The Geographical History of America or the Relation of Human Nature to the Human Mind*. 1936. Baltimore: The Johns Hopkins University Press, 1995.

VIDA. "The Count 2010." Online article. http://vidaweb.org/the-count-2010.

West, Martha S. and John W. Curtis. "AAUP Faculty Gender Equity Indicators 2006." www.aaup.org/AAUP/pubsres/research/geneq2006.htm.

West, Martha S. and John W. Curtis. "Women in the Profession, 2000: MLA Report on the Status of Women in the Profession." www.mla.org/pdf/wip00.pdf.

27

Contemporary American women's writing
Women and violence

HEIDI SLETTEDAHL MACPHERSON

> . . . what feminist thought can and has put into question is the capacity for any
> map to represent more than a fiction of the world's contours. The line traced
> along the eastern edge of North America, for example, the line following the
> extreme border of an American context, for all its inlets and protrusions, its islands
> and peninsulas, still can only demarcate with the fiction of an arbitrarily traced line
> the point at which land moves out to sea and the ground slips from beneath us.
> Peggy Kamuf, "Replacing Feminist Criticism," 46

Peggy Kamuf offers an important caution in relation to mapping a nation's
literature, and her caution also holds for mapping a generation's literature,
or a gender's literary enterprise. Despite her warnings, it is, of course, also
necessary to try to limn the linkages between texts and writers, to establish
a literary history and a way of approaching disparate (though in many ways
connected) texts. Such a mapping cannot hope to include all the terrain, nor
show in details its "inlets and protrusions." However, if the mapping exercise
is not undertaken, women's literature may become invisible in critical terms.
Elaine Showalter argues that women writers need "a critical jury of their
peers to discuss their work, to explicate its symbols and meanings, and to
demonstrate its continuing relevance to all readers" (*Jury*, xi). In this call, she
is not alone. Joanna Russ contends that "[i]f women's experience is defined
as inferior to, less important than, or 'narrower' than men's experience,
women's writing is automatically denigrated. If women's experience is simply
not seen, the effect will be the same" (*How to Suppress Women's Writing*, 47–
8). *Hear me* could well be the cry of many of the women characters who
populate contemporary American women's fiction, whether they reside in
classic (though now perhaps unfairly derided) consciousness-raising novels
from the 1970s such as Erica Jong's *Fear of Flying* (1973) or Marilyn French's

The Women's Room (1977) or novels from the early part of the twenty-first century which reiterate the request to be heard and taken seriously (even when adopting a comic tone).

Contemporary American women's writing offers a forum for contesting dominant representations of women's social and conventional spaces. It therefore demonstrates both a continuation of earlier women's writing, and an extension of it. For example, if, at the end of the nineteenth century, Kate Chopin was unsettling audiences by her depiction of an overtly sexual woman who chose suicide above a loveless marriage in *The Awakening* (1899), so too did Anne Tyler grapple with such issues in her virtual reworking of *The Awakening* almost one hundred years later. Yet Tyler's novel, *Ladder of Years* (1995), is a comic one, in which the central female character accidentally rather than deliberately leaves her family, and the conclusion is one of potential reconciliation to her role, rather than dramatic release. This comic reworking of tragedy is just one example of how women writers have recycled the stories of women's lives (and loves), their "necessary fictions," and their role in the maintenance or subversion of cultural mores.

By the end of the twentieth century and into the early part of the twenty-first century, women writers were also tackling such subjects as women's culpability in the violence and rage of their children, the consequences of their roles as professionals (abortion doctors, coroners, lawyers, and professors, amongst others), their political spaces and whether or not their gender continued to require them to sacrifice their lives for the people within it (in, for example, Ann Packer's *The Dive From Clausen's Pier* [2002], which follows a young woman's "selfish" choice to leave her paralyzed boyfriend). As Rita Felski notes, "a recurring theme of feminist literature is the difficulty many women still experience in defining an independent identity beyond that shaped by the needs and desires of those around them" (*Beyond Feminist Aesthetics*, 78). Yet some themes remain constant – among them the ways in which mothers are judged to fail in their duties to their children and families, though the results of such failure might appear more acute. Consider Jane Hamilton's *The Map of the World* (1994), in which an inattentive mother causes the death of a child in her care through momentary negligence, and consequently suffers guilt in relation to charges of deliberate abuse, or Lionel Shriver's *We Need to Talk about Kevin* (2003), in which a mother confronts the results of her son's actions as a high-school marksman and killer. Contemporary fears and realities come into play in such fiction, against a backdrop of media hysteria over violence, alcohol consumption, bad behavior, sexual license, and the dissolution of the family.

The rise of second-wave feminism and feminist literary theory has brought about substantial and sustained appreciation of women's literature in all its myriad forms. Maria Lauret has proposed that women's literature and the Women's Movement have become inextricably linked, arguing that the "Women's Movement created nothing less than a new, gendered discursive space in which all women's writing would henceforth be written and read, whether it had allegiances to feminism or not" (*Liberating Literature*, 74). Contemporary women's writing is thus marked by feminism, either in its clear adherence to the tenets of equality or in reaction to it (as in some, though not all, forms of postfeminism, which some critics see as an extension of feminism, particularly into third-wave feminism and movements such as grrl power, and others see as a retrogressive movement).[1] Women's romance fiction, for example, has been subject to sustained feminist analysis, by critics such as Tania Modleski, Kay Mussell, and Janice Radway. Contemporary women's literature ranges from, at one end, blockbusters by novelists such as Judith Krantz and Danielle Steele, Harlequin Romances and other formulaic fiction, to experimental fiction such as Kathy Acker's *Blood and Guts in High School* (1984) and *Great Expectations* (1983). The list of genres covered by women's literature is immense: lesbian coming-out novels such as Rita Mae Brown's *Rubyfruit Jungle* (1973), feminist "bonkbusters," a slang term coined in the late 1980s (and now enshrined in the *Oxford English Dictionary*) for popular novels that include numerous and explicit sexual liaisons (an early example being Erica Jong's *Fear of Flying*, which includes the memorable phrase "the zipless fuck");[2] chick-lit such as Candace Bushnell's book based on her *New York Observer* columns, *Sex and the City* (1996), which was made into a successful television series and then two feature films; and both serious and comic "realist" prose, of which there are numerous examples.

Some of these texts are more straightforwardly feminist than others. Marilyn French's *The Women's Room*, for example, a feminist bestseller, overtly outlines a young woman's coming to feminism, and her search through literature for a way to be. French plays a linguistic literary game with the reader by naming her central character Mira, and by letting the narrator separate herself from Mira, even while the reader suspects they are one and the same. The name also evokes the image of a mirror, a trope that is used overtly in the text (though primarily in relation to other women characters). Finally, the name Mira partially inverts the first four letters of French's first name. The fact that French writes a confessional, semi-autobiographical account (or at least pens a book that reads as one) and names her central character after herself is suggestive of a desire for the reader to read such an account as that of a real woman. The turn to literature is thus a sort of double bluff:

> She turned to literature . . . But nothing helped. Like the person who gets fat because they eat unnourishing foods and so is always hungry and so is always eating, she drowned in words that could not teach her to swim. She had a perpetual headache; sometimes she felt she was reading to escape from life, for the escape, at least, occurred. (French, *The Women's Room*, 29)

The narrator notes that Mira is well aware that "to choose a husband is to choose a life. She had not needed Jane Austen to teach her that" (41). Moreover, she recognizes the false division between traditional narrative closures and her own unraveling story:

> In the great literature of the past you either get married and live happily ever after, or you die. But the fact is, neither is what actually happens. Oh, you do die, but never at the right time, never with great language floating all around you, and a whole theater full of witnesses to your agony. What actually happens is that you do get married or you don't, and you don't live happily ever after, but you do live. And that's the problem. (211)

Closely related to the "problem with no name" identified by Betty Friedan in *The Feminine Mystique*, consciousness-raising fiction was popular but in many ways critically maligned. Nicci Gerrard, for example, argues that "the reliance of the realist novel upon the small and self-contained worlds of usually middle-class individuals can seem trivial and self-indulgent. Perhaps it should no longer serve as the most dominant and well-used model for feminist writers" (*Into the Mainstream*, 108). Whether realist fiction is indeed the "dominant" model is perhaps up for debate, and I would argue that even so-called realist texts demonstrate a commitment to experimentation in narrative form and subject matter. Certainly Jong's *Fear of Flying*, while clearly focusing on an individual psyche, attempts to extend the range of the plot beyond self-containment. In alternating between graphic sexual flashbacks and didactic statements of feminism, however, the novel sometimes seems to lose its plot. At the same time, though, the novel's ambivalence towards feminism is a measure of its genesis at a time of social disruption of gender and sexual mores. The ambivalence potentially makes it a more interesting text for feminist literary critics to unpack than a text that might take a more straightforward "party line." In offering a literary overlay (as does French's novel above), *Fear of Flying* also signals its metafictional edge, particularly in its conclusion: "It was not clear how it would end. In nineteenth-century novels, they get married. In twentieth-century novels, they get divorced. Can you have an ending in which they do neither? I laughed at myself for being so literary" (*Fear of Flying*, 277). Whilst metafiction has frequently been linked to male literary endeavors, as a counter to the "realist" nature of women's writing, we can see from this example alone how early metafiction offered an opportunity to explore women's space and women's psyches in the second-wave feminist movement.

Critics once sought to uncover a matrilineage of women's writing, linking contemporary literature to literary foremothers, but such projects of recovery and linkage are perhaps less urgent in the twenty-first century. (That said, the advent of chick-lit, a genre that also seems to follow the "self-contained" worlds of young women, may offer evidence that a link between women's literature across generations, if not centuries, remains a worthy avenue of exploration.) What is clear is that contemporary women's writing has benefited from engaged feminist scholarship that has taken seriously women's issues as they are expressed in fiction, both realist and non-realist, both serious and comic.

In *Feminism and American Literary History*, Nina Baym suggested that critics previously misrepresented women's writing, assuming that "women writers invariably represented the consensus, rather than the criticism of it; [assuming] that their gender made them part of the consensus in a way that prevented them from partaking in the criticism" (9). Clearly such critical shortcuts are no longer appropriate (nor were they ever), and literary scholars have explored women's fiction from a number of critical angles, including Anglo-American feminist criticism, psychoanalytic criticism, French Feminism, structuralist and poststructuralist criticism, and the permutations (and indeed combinations) of each, to which the many readers of editions of feminist literary criticism can attest.[3]

Perhaps one of the best-known scholars of women's writing to establish herself during the rise of second-wave feminism is Elaine Showalter. She stands as a representative of Anglo-American literary criticism. Her groundbreaking edited collection, *New Feminist Criticism* (1985), gathered together a range of essays previously published in other fora and was meant in some respects to be a comprehensive assessment of the field so far. Eighteen essays by Carolyn Heilbrun, Susan Gubar, Sandra Gilbert, Annette Kolodny, and others range across topics as diverse as lesbian and black feminism, pluralism, feminist poetics, and the definition of a "feminist novel." Rosalind Coward, for example, explores whether novels such as Marilyn French's *The Women's Room* should be placed within this category or whether its very popularity – despite its overt use of consciousness-raising as "framing device" ("Are Women's Novels Feminist Novels?," 225) – works against this. In exploring the issue, Coward raises important questions: "Is it that these novels are carrying out subversive politicization, drawing women into structures of consciousness-raising without their knowing it? Or is it that the accounts of women's experiences they offer in fact correspond more closely to popular sentiment than they do to feminist aspirations?" (226). Coward's reply includes a rigorous reading of such novels to ascertain "by what representations of sexuality, of maleness and femaleness, they achieve their version of reality" (228).

One of Showalter's own essays sought to define a new gynocriticism, a form of literary criticism which "begins at the point when we free ourselves from the linear absolutes of male literary history, stop trying to fit women between the lines of the male tradition, and focus instead on the newly visible world of female culture" (Showalter, "Toward," 131). Nancy K. Miller's essay considers the separation of male and female literatures, arguing that such a division is useful because "it locates the problem of identity and difference not on the level of the sentence – not as a question of another language – but on the level of text in all its complexities: a culturally bound and, I would even say, culturally overdetermined production" ("Emphasis Added," 342).

The collection paved the way for future scholars (to be sure, not always in agreement). Later collections of essays build on or depart from the work collected there, and of course, its focus was not entirely on women's writing nor on the contemporary field. In addition, there is not one feminism, any more than there is one version of contemporary women's writing, and there is also critical disagreement over the extent of close reading necessary within the feminist critical apparatus. Showalter argued that "[n]o theory, however, suggestive, can be substituted for the close and extensive knowledge of women's texts which constitutes our essential subject" (Showalter, "Feminist," 266). Although this seems fairly tame with the hindsight of twenty-five years, the reality is that one of the major successes of the (various) feminist projects is that it takes seriously women's writing and offers avenues into critical explorations of diverse women's texts. Showalter uses "essential" to mean "necessary," but she has been criticized for an essentialist view of women's literature, particularly by Toril Moi, whose 1985 book *Sexual/Textual Politics* assesses both Anglo-American feminism and French Feminism, and finds a humanist feminism (which she equates with Showalter) wanting. Moi notes in her preface to the work, "One of the central principles of feminist criticism is that no account can ever be neutral" (xiii). On this issue alone, feminists might agree, and the lack of neutrality is, ironically, a rich platform from which to explore contemporary women's writing.

Showalter herself proves as much with her latest offering, the impressive 586-page *A Jury of her Peers: American Women Writers from Anne Bradstreet to Annie Proulx*, which explicitly sets out to make critical judgments on 350 years of American women's writing, and to forge what Showalter says is the first literary history of its kind. This massive undertaking extends Showalter's earlier critical frameworks from a discussion of the three stages of women's writing which she defines as feminine, feminist, and female in her 1977 book on British women's literature, *A Literature of their Own*, to a new stage she articulates in this book: free. Free is defined as the point where women are not "constrained by their femininity" but are "free to think of themselves primarily as writers, and subject to the same market forces and social changes, the same shifts of popular taste and critical fashion, the same vagaries of talent, timeliness, and luck, as men" (Showalter, *Jury*, 494). Showalter takes the title of a famous early twentieth-century short story by Susan Glaspell as the title of her book. Glaspell's story (called "Trifles" in its one-act play form) offers evidence that a woman's crime is only readable by other women, and not by the men who are given the task of discovering a motive. Showalter argues that particularly in this new "free" stage, women "no longer need specially constituted juries, softened judgment, unspoken agreements, or suppression of evidence in order to stand alongside the greatest artists in our literary history" (*Jury*, xii). What the title also does, however, is indicate in quite clear ways how American women's writing is subject to judgment; moreover, I find it intriguing that in this new "free" stage, many more women are writing about engagement with the law.

The intersection of law and literature has become a fruitful location for literary scholars over the last decade in particular. Although the majority of critics involved in this interdisciplinary field hail from law schools, a significant minority of literary scholars is now actively changing the field and offering a necessary corrective to a too-narrow focus on the law side of the law–literature debate.[4] Contemporary American women's fiction frequently explores how women's narratives (and lives) engage with and pull against the law, whether moral or judicial. Because it is impossible to survey the myriad subjects on which contemporary women write (much less their identity politics, political persuasions, sexuality, ethnic or racial identities, amongst other markers), I have chosen instead to explore, in this second half of the chapter, how contemporary women's writing engages with violence and its aftermath; with law and moral codes; with "goodness" as a default position that is tried (sometimes quite literally) by circumstance.

Toni Morrison's *Beloved* is an obvious example and one of the few texts by African American women that has been given sustained treatment by law and literature experts. The mother of the text, Sethe, kills her child rather than allow her to be captured and transported into slavery; this event quite literally begins to "haunt" Sethe who (like other guilty fictional mothers) seeks not forgiveness or even understanding so much as the opportunity to extend her punishment beyond jail: "It was as though Sethe did not really want forgiveness given; she wanted it refused. And Beloved helped her out" (*Beloved*, 252). The historical slave mother upon whom this story is based, Margaret Garner, was accused of property theft, not murder, and Morrison's book explores how what is lawful or unlawful is subject to cultural pressure rather than any kind of "natural" justice. Instances of what the twenty-first century would see as gross bodily harm (assault, sexual assault, rape, scarring, hangings, and other forms of public and private humiliation and violence – not to mention the purchase of one human being by another) are normal, lawful activities in the nineteenth-century historical landscape, and Morrison skillfully explores how the law alters in the face of human intervention.

Though set in the twentieth century, Alice Walker's *The Color Purple* similarly explores how major crimes against women go unpunished by law (incest, rape, domestic violence), whereas that which is not a crime becomes one: when Sofia, an African American character, "talks back" to the white mayor's wife, she is assaulted. Her retaliation lands her with an initial jail sentence of twelve years. Crime affects almost all of the women characters, none more so than Celie, who is repeatedly violated sexually, emotionally, and physically and whose opportunities to mother her own children are denied her, while she is forced to care for children who are not her own and who continue the cycle of abuse.

The late twentieth century saw novels that referred back to other mass tragedies such as the Holocaust, which saw other perversions of law to align with cultural panics, such as incarceration not only of the Jews but also anyone in Germany deemed unfit by Aryan cultural standards. Emily Prager's 1991 novel *Eve's Tattoo* revisits the moral and judicial containment of women under Nazi Germany. It is a self-consciously postfeminist and postmodern novel that plays with narrative structure as well as the performance of femininity. The protagonist Eve almost impulsively gets the concentration camp number 500123 tattooed on her wrist, with the express aim of educating people through individual (but composite) stories of female victims. She deliberately *tells tales*: always with a specific audience in mind. Inventing a doppelgänger named Eva, the American Eve (and this name is surely no mistake) replicates stories she finds in historical accounts, partially erasing herself in embodying a variety of "others." Yet this erasure can never fully succeed, in that this act of turning attention away from herself ultimately ensures that her own performance is central to the storytelling.

Eve is a forty-year-old never-married woman living in New York in the late 1980s, and as such she embodies the figure of the woman more likely to be gunned down by terrorists than married – or so real American women were frightened by an inaccurate *Newsweek* cover article in 1986, "The Marriage Crunch." Eve's anxiety over this (as well as a second "Holocaust," the AIDS epidemic) causes her to seek a sort of solace in display and performance. She is certainly no stranger to playing roles before she marks her body in what is meant to be a permanent fashion. She performs the role of sardonic author, writing articles for men's magazines with titles such as, "How to Tell if Your Girlfriend is Dying During Rough Sex" (Prager, *Eve's Tattoo*, 36); she pretends to be a geisha but simultaneously describes herself as a "female supremacist" who "never showed it" (37). Thus, she makes a perfect canvas on which to inscribe the stories of various women named Eva, since she self-consciously performs her own womanhood in shifting ways.

Judith Butler argues that gender should be considered as *"a corporeal style, an 'act,'* as it were, which is both intentional and performative, where *'performative'* suggests a dramatic and contingent construction of meaning" (*Gender Trouble*, 177, italics in original). Eve enacts her gender not only in her "real" life but in her narrated one, where she offers stories of various Evas: Eva Klein, Eva Hofler, Eva Berg, Eva Marks, Eva Beck, Eva Hartz, and Eva Flick, not knowing for some time that the "real" Eva is a loyal Nazi woman named Leni, whose marking was at some level a mistake. Eve's tattoo is, she claims, "an emblem of a different perspective, the perspective of women, all kinds of women" (Prager, *Eve's Tattoo*, 13), but even she did not expect the Nazi voice to be the one she ended up, ironically, commemorating on her own body. At the same time, however, while Eve comes across as sometimes naïve in her performances, she is also politically astute, noting, for example, that "Hitler couldn't have made it without the women" (40). The innocence of women (their supposedly innate *goodness*) is hereby undercut, and their complicity and indeed both tacit and overt approval of Hitler become Eve's larger story.

The Vintage paperback edition of the novel contains an edited review from the *Sunday Times* that suggests that the novel "raises queasy questions about entitlement; whether smart, clever, youngish novelists are overstepping some moral boundary in taking the Holocaust as a 'theme' and giving it a bit of a topspin." Yet despite its (deliberately) superficial narrator, the novel offers a complex retelling of history's legal and moral codes, translating the stories of women in Nazi Germany into language that the (fictional) audience in the United States can understand – if only partially, and if only (often) to their own ends: publishing success, sexual conquest, or a sense of community. If Prager ultimately steps back from providing any sense of a lasting shift in judicial (and moral) opinion as a result of the performative experiment, she does at least get her audience(s) to ask questions about gender and legal identity.

Although Eve is a childless woman (ironically, perhaps, given her name), it is more often around motherhood that fictional women come into conflict with the law, where their behavior is deemed inappropriate (as in Sue Miller's *The Good Mother* [1986], where a woman's sexuality is used against her by her ex-husband in a custody fight); negligent (as in Jane Hamilton's *A Map of the World* [1994], where a woman's lapse in attention results in a child's death and further allegations of harm); or when earlier events recode later events as improper (as in Lorrie Moore's *A Gate at the Stairs* [2009], where an adoptive mother's silence on the death of her natural son – and her allegiance to her husband, which is read as inexplicable at one level – renders her apparently unfit to become a mother again).

Perhaps the most challenging recent text on the judicial consequences of the failure of motherhood is Lionel Shriver's *We Need to Talk about Kevin*. Shriver calls the novel a "thought experiment" (Shute, "Lionel Shriver," 64) that traces the absence of mother love and the unnaturalness of expecting "to be drowned by the hormonal imperative" of "maternal heat" (Shriver, *We Need to Talk about Kevin*, 27). It is a novel that pits a larger narrative – the contested US presidential election – against the private grief of one woman, and though it is set in 2000 and 2001, it deliberately ends in April of that latter year, thereby avoiding any reference to that other colossal American story: 9/11. In fact, the novel primarily refers to the events leading up to a day in 1999 when Eva Khatchadourian's son Kevin chooses to become a national figure of hate and, bizarrely, admiration by joining the ranks of high-school marksmen (though he does so with a difference). The novel therefore sets a very public yet ultimately private event (what Eva refers to as *Thursday* throughout, because she cannot find the language to express the true horror of her son's murderous campaign) against a larger political canvas. In doing so, the novel argues, it seems, that the event that affects the American family is in some respects of greater importance and has more lasting consequences than national political wrangles.

Emily Jeremiah suggests that the timeframe "implies the impossibility of change, the absurdity of the political process" ("We Need to Talk about

Gender," 178), but I would argue that Shriver's deliberate juxtapositioning of political landscapes has a larger meaning. Eva herself is a keen observer of America as a nation and a concept. She is by profession a travel writer and entrepreneur, owner of the travel company A Wing and a Prayer, and spends much of her young adult life outside the USA. Moreover, she also resolutely considers her Armenian heritage as somehow more relevant than her US citizenship, so much so that she insists her son takes her surname rather than her husband's to keep their ethnicity visible (here, too, naming remains important, as Kevin becomes a mediated and abbreviated killer, *KK*, in media representations of his violence, and as Eva becomes seen as the originator of his "sins"). Given Eva's position on nationality and her own ironic view of the USA, it is fitting to use her words to describe the political position of the early present tense of the novel: "Only a country that feels invulnerable can afford political turmoil as entertainment" (*We Need to Talk about Kevin*, 25).

The novel is as much about ideas of America – Eva's cynical attitude against her husband Franklin Plaskett's gung-ho patriotism, or Eva's desire to find locations outside of the USA pitted against her husband's insistence as a photographer that he can find reasonable facsimiles of foreign locales within the borders of the vast country – as it is about that iconic symbol of America, mass violence. It is also as much about Eva's judicial encounters as it is her son's; indeed, his trial is skated over,[5] whereas the reader hears "evidence" from her trial – and the novel itself is one long sifting of evidence, and blame – as well as justification, bias, partial stories, and that which is inadmissible – in every sense. Late in her pregnancy, concerned that she is at best ambivalent about becoming a mother, Eva turns to Franklin, who hands down an unexpected judgment: Eva is forbidden from admission of ambivalence; what follows is a bifurcation of experience, where Eva's experience is distrusted. Uncorroborated evidence is disallowed, and Eva's stories are pitted against Kevin's in Franklin's mind, with the benefit of the doubt always offered to the child: "Apparently my testimony was tainted. I would have to bring in other witnesses" (92). Various witnesses (and potential indicators of Kevin's nature) are paraded in front of the reader, including day-care professionals, teachers, and other mothers, in a selection of stories Eva offers almost as if she is preparing a Victim Impact Statement. Certainly she does feel victimized in her relationship with her son, whose odd behavior (including failing to master potty training until Eva is physically violent with him, and a penchant as a teenager for wearing child-sized clothes) makes him unreadable to her. However, her audience is not the court so much as her absent husband, who is not there to support her through this new stage of motherhood.

For Eva, motherhood is figured as a foreign country, which she longs to leave after visiting it. Reflecting on her life post-*Thursday*, Eva sardonically notes, "Well, Kevin has introduced me to a real foreign country. I can be sure of that, since the definition of the truly foreign locale is one that fosters a piercing and perpetual yearning to go home" (392). Yet this feeling of the foreignness of motherhood pre-dates Kevin's public outing of himself as an unhappy, deeply scarred child. Motherhood was a dare for Eva, a way of scaring herself into a challenge for which she was unprepared, and, in this, it was also a repetition of her reaction to travel itself, which she has made her life's work:

> I can't recall a single trip abroad that, up against it, I truly wanted to take, that I haven't in some way dreaded and wanted desperately to get out of. I was repeatedly forced out the door by a conspiracy of previous commitments: the ticket was purchased, the taxi ordered, a host of reservations confirmed, and just to box myself in a little further I would always have talked up the journey to friends, before florid farewells. (31)

The daughter of a reclusive, agoraphobic mother, Eva is forced to engage with the wider world because her mother would not, and the effects of this upbringing persist into her adulthood: "In pushing me to be her emissary while I was still so small, my mother managed to reproduce in me the same disproportionate anguish about minor interactions with the outside world that she herself felt at thirty-two" (31). This is familiar territory – the mother is to blame for the child's fears and behavior – and Shriver sets this backdrop deliberately, for Eva herself will be subject to similar social criticism and deemed to be responsible for her son's murderous activity, both by those who know her, and those who do not.[6]

The novel is composed of a series of letters that Eva pens to her absent husband, trying to explain or understand why their son would murder eleven people with a cross bow, including seven hand-picked classmates, a teacher who expresses interest in him, and a cafeteria worker who was in the vicinity – the high-school gym, another iconic representation of America – by mistake. The epistolary form and one-way correspondence ensure that we have only Eva's viewpoint expressed directly; she tells stories of their past and imagines Franklin's responses, or retells his previous ones, and she allows Kevin only to speak in concert with her. His own story is therefore in a sense at one remove, and the reader never discovers his motivation, nor whether he is a "bad seed" or a child damaged by an unloving mother. This lack of clarity is a fundamental aspect of the novel, the puzzle that is never revealed or explained. To explain away Kevin would be to offer a false haven, an order on chaos, as Eva rightly infers from her own desire to accept blame: "Blame conveys clear lessons in which others may take comfort: *if only she hadn't – ,* and by implication makes tragedy avoidable" (65–6, italics in original).

Eva is a self-confessed "terrible mother," who in fact undergoes her own trial after her son's, a civil case brought against her by Mary Woodford, the mother of one of the murdered teenagers. Eva is accused of parental negligence, and even her lawyer, Harvey Landsdown, thinks she might well be one. His own view of the law, however, makes this an irrelevancy: "Harvey didn't care. He's one of those attorneys who think of the law as a game, not as a morality play. I'm told that's the kind you want" (68). He felt that Eva should settle, that the court case was likely to cost more in money than reputation, but Eva persists, feeling that a public reputation as a Bad Mother is more than she can handle, despite her own private reservations about her role and her own inexorable self-flagellation. Mary's lawyer suggests that Eva has simply *acted* like a good mother, performing a public role, in her weekly visits to her son at Claverack Juvenile Correctional Facility, and Eva herself does not quite deny this: "the trouble with jurisprudence is that it cannot accommodate subtleties" (39). She does, however, note that "trying to be a good mother may be as distant from being a good mother as trying to have a good time is from truly having one" (195). Mary's own goodness as a mother is enshrined in her victimhood, and she argues that parents should take responsibility for their children's destructive behavior (though not, apparently, self-destructive behavior, since her own daughter suffered from anorexia).

Eva's "success" and Mary's "failure" in the courtroom offer neither of them relief. If Mary does not succeed in tempering her grief through litigation, Eva does not achieve the "public exoneration" she thought she wanted: punitively (and potentially unlawfully), she is made to pay the court costs of the case despite being found not guilty. Yet her desire for exoneration is only partial; like Sethe in *Beloved*, Eva wants not forgiveness so much as understanding – primarily from Franklin, the one from whom she will never receive it. As Eva realizes, after agonizing over her own culpability, "The truth is, if I decided I was innocent, or I decided I was guilty, what difference would it make? If I arrived at the right answer, would you come home?" (400).

Her own *decision*, her own judgment, has no legal backing, nor any other remedy, because Franklin will never come home. As the reader learns in the penultimate chapter of the book, he, too, is a casualty of Kevin's rage, along with their daughter Celia. About this tragedy, the novel misdirects the reader from the beginning. Eva writes to Franklin as if they are "separated" (1), "estranged" (7), or "parted" (20). Much later, she tells Franklin about her first visit to his parents after *Thursday*, noting that "it would have been colossally difficult even if you'd been able to come with me, but of course *irretrievable breakdown* prevented that" (138, italics in original), and even later, she talks about "our separation" (224). The novel therefore refrains from revealing the fate of Eva's remaining family until near the book's ending, and refrains from discussing Celia in any detail for the first half.

Celia, who is not mentioned until page 115 of the book, is Eva's second chance, the child whom she loves as fiercely as she rejects her son. Yet even in her amazement and delight over Celia, Eva remains a suspect mother, a fact that she herself may not even quite realize. Eva compares her children thus: "Whereas Kevin [as a baby] had screeched with every conceivable need met, Celia would submit to all manner of material deprivations with barely a mewl or stir, and she could pickle for hours in a wet diaper unless I remembered to check" (225). Eva's mothering is here as patchy as it is for Kevin, but with significantly different results. Celia and Eva cling to each other in mutual adoration. Celia is a fearful child, though unwilling in most instances to tattle on her brother when she comes off the worse for their connection (as it seems she does; she is facially scarred and partially blinded in an "accident" at home under Kevin's care).

No wonder Eva admits to hating her son, an admission that unsettles some critics more than Kevin's atrocities do. Indeed, Jennie Bristow, in an online review from *Spiked*, a forum dedicated to "raising the horizons of humanity by waging a culture war of words against misanthropy, priggishness, prejudice, luddism, illiberalism and irrationalism in all their ancient and modern forms," argues that "Kevin's mass murdering is less shocking than his mother's abject dislike and distrust of her son from pregnancy and infancy onwards." It is perhaps not a surprise that the title of the review is "We don't need to talk about hating our kids." Bristow misses the point of the novel when she argues, "Most children are not Kevin, and we don't need to talk about them as if they were." Similarly, Sarah Smith, in a review from the *Guardian* newspaper, considers the novel "dishonest" and misguided because it is not about a "normal" boy and a "normal" mother, as if the point of literature was to limn the ordinary and not the extraordinary. More academically focused critics, such as Monica Latham, are drawn to the novel precisely because of its exploration of taboo territory (is it really that abnormal to feel emotions other than love for one's offspring?) and its almost excessive discussion of the pitfalls of motherhood, its disgorging of fear and disgust. Emily Jeremiah identifies the novel's indebtedness to American postmodernism and queer and gender theory, noting how it explores "the (relatively recent, Western) idea of maternity as a 'choice,' one that here appears perverse" ("We Need to Talk about Gender," 173). Jeremiah is perhaps too ready to accept Eva's stories of Kevin's base nature as truth, forgetting the selectivity that she employs in offering damning stories of her son, though her exploration of the novel's gendering of motherhood and its deliberations on what constitutes its Americanness are acute. Shriver herself suggests that the novel is one "where everyone is tainted" (Lawless, *Three Monkeys Online Magazine*), not just the individual mother and child. It is in focusing on this aspect of the American family – and its run-ins with the American legal system – that Shriver offers the reader the most scope for considering how literature deals with difficult material, with what is unspeakable and inadmissible.

Although Eva admits that, at some level, she does not want to understand Kevin, "to find a well within myself so inky that from its depths what he did makes sense" (*We Need to Talk about Kevin*, 168), she forces herself to interrogate him at the end, to ask why he has done this inexplicable thing. In receiving no real answer, but only a symbol of rapprochement[7] and an acknowledgment that as he moves from juvenile prison to an adult facility, he still wants her to visit, Eva is ironically at peace. She can let go of her overarching guilt because responsibility cannot be fully traced back to her. She even admits, in the end, to love – an outcome of the trials (in every sense of the word) that is perhaps the most unexpected one. *We Need to Talk about Kevin* is a fitting book with which to close a discussion of contemporary American women's writing, because it *talks about* those things that remain so frequently unsaid: the fact that mother love is not guaranteed; that violence is endemic in the USA; that judicial proceedings do not necessarily lead to resolution; that women's literature can – and does – tackle taboo subjects, and explores the "inky" depths of American life.

Another critic might have taken a different approach to this topic, considering, for example, the overt sexuality expressed in contemporary women's literature, citing amongst others the African American author Zane, a publishing sensation whose erotica (including lesbian erotica and non-fiction) has a strong following, or the author Mary Gaitskill, whose short stories also border on (and cross over into) the pornographic, particularly into S&M activities. Gaitskill came to attention most notably perhaps when her short story "Secretary," from the 1988 collection *Bad Girls*, was made into a film of the same name, starring James Spader and Maggie Gyllenhaal. Still other avenues for exploring contemporary women's literature include their dominance of the short-story market, with authors such as Amy Bloom, Tama Janowitz,

Susan Minot, and Lorrie Moore, or experimental fiction by authors such as Siri Hustvedt. Another approach might be to focus on prize-winning authors who cover a range of literature, including Toni Morrison, who won the Nobel Prize for *Beloved*, and Marilynne Robinson, who made her name in the early 1980s with *Housekeeping*, a lyrical novel about hoboes, and who over thirty years later re-established herself with *Gilead* (which won the Pulitzer Prize). The companion novel to *Gilead*, *Home*, won the Orange Prize, a prize that is potentially controversial given its restriction to women writers – something that Lionel Shriver at least balks at, despite being a winner herself.

There is no one way to approach contemporary women's literature given the diversity of the excellence on offer and the opportunities "free" women, to use Showalter's words, have to explore their necessary fictions. Critical engagement with contemporary literature allows us to identify and benefit from the goodness of American women's writing. Moreover, feminist engagement with questions of goodness (and badness) provides opportunities to explore anew how women's writing moves away from supposedly seeking cultural consensus, to exploring difference, including different modes of behavior – and different measures of goodness overall.

Notes

1. I have elsewhere explored how the term "postfeminism" seems to capture almost as great a range as the term "feminism" does, with a potential consequence that the term itself becomes hollowed out. See Chapter 6 of *Women's Movement: Escape as Transgression in North American Feminist Fiction*. Postfeminism can be both an incorporation of feminism (potentially and in my view problematically apolitically) and an extension of it; perhaps most relevantly, it is a media-hyped construction that can be manipulated to suggest that feminism is over, resolved, and no longer necessary. Given that critics as diverse as Camille Paglia, Katie Roiphe, and Naomi Wolf have either accepted the label postfeminist or had it foisted upon them, one can ascertain the elasticity of the term if it is able to fit such disparate women and their ideologies. What can be said is that postfeminist fiction is often daring and experimental, willing certainly to explore sexuality to its limits as well as performativity and gender.
2. Isadora Wing defines the zipless fuck thus: "The zipless fuck is absolutely pure. It is free of ulterior motives. There is no power game. The man is not 'taking' and the woman is not 'giving.' No one is attempting to cuckold a husband or humiliate a wife. No one is trying to prove anything or get anything out of anyone. The zipless fuck is the purest thing there is. And it is rarer than the unicorn. And I have never had one" (Jong, *Fear of Flying*, 22). It remains, however, a goal of hers.
3. See, for example, Humm's *Feminisms: A Reader*, and Eagleton's *Contemporary Feminist Literature*, amongst others.

4. For a review of the contemporary law and literature debate, see Macpherson, *Courting Failure*.

5. The reader learns that Kevin gets a mere seven years for his crimes, due to his age at the time of the killings, days short of his sixteenth birthday, but also due to the defense claim that he was affected by Prozac – a defense his lawyer admits Kevin himself supplied.

6. It is therefore significant that it is only another "guilty" mother, Loretta Greenleaf, in hearing Eva pour out her guilt in the waiting room of the juvenile detention facility, who calls on Eva not to take the blame: "'It hard to be a momma. Nobody ever pass a law say 'fore you get pregnant you gotta be perfect. I'm sure you try the best you could'" (*We Need to Talk about Kevin*, 166).

7. Earlier in the novel, Eva is horrified to find that Kevin has kept Celia's glass eye as a grisly souvenir. She threatens never to return to visit him in the Claverack Juvenile Correctional Facility if he takes it out again. When he does present it to her at the end of the novel, in a carved box, it symbolizes something else: "Today it was his warning – *don't open it* – that may have constituted the greatest measure of my gift" (*We Need to Talk about Kevin*, 398, italics in original). The warning extends beyond the symbolic, coffin-shaped box, to questions about Kevin's psyche as a whole.

Works cited

Acker, Kathy. *Great Expectations: A Novel*. New York: Grove Press, 1983.

    Blood and Guts in High School. New York: Grove Press, 1984.

Baym, Nina. *Feminism and American Literary History*. New Brunswick: Rutgers University Press, 1992.

Bradshaw, Candace. *Sex and the City*. New York: Atlantic Monthly Press, 1996.

Bristow, Jennie. "We don't need to talk about hating our kids." *Spiked Online* 14 June 2005, www.spiked-online.com/index.php/site/printable/829/ (accessed October 18, 2010).

Brown, Rita Mae. *Rubyfruit Jungle*. 1973. London: Penguin, 1994.

Butler, Judith. *Gender Trouble: Feminism and the Subversion of Identity*. 1990. New York: Routledge, 1999.

Chopin, Kate. *The Awakening and Selected Stories*. 1899. London: Penguin, 2003.

Coward, Rosalind. "Are Women's Novels Feminist Novels?" In Showalter, *New Feminist*.

Eagleton, Mary. *Contemporary Feminist Literature*, 2nd edn. Oxford: Wiley-Blackwell, 1995.

Felski, Rita. *Beyond Feminist Aesthetics: Feminist Literature and Social Change*. N.p.: Hutchinson Radius, 1989.

French, Marilyn. *The Women's Room*. 1977. New York: Jove Books, 1978.

Friedan, Betty. *The Feminine Mystique*. London: Penguin, 1963.

Gaitskill, Mary. *Bad Girls*. 1988. New York: Simon and Shuster, 2009.

Gerrard, Nicci. *Into the Mainstream*. London: Pandora, 1989.

Hamilton, Jane. *A Map of the World*. 1994. London: Black Swan, 1996.

Humm, Maggie. *Feminisms: A Reader*. London: Longman, 1992.

Jeremiah, Emily. "We Need to Talk about Gender: Mothering and Masculinity in Lionel Shriver's *We Need to Talk about Kevin*." In *Textual Mothers/Maternal Texts: Motherhood* in *Contemporary Women's Literatures*. Ed. Andrea O'Reilly and Elizabeth Podnieks. Waterloo, ON: Wilfred Laurier University Press, 2010.

Jong, Erica. *Fear of Flying*. 1973. St. Albans: Panther, 1976.

Kamuf, Peggy, "Replacing Feminist Criticism." *Diacritics* 12.2 (1982): 42–7.

Latham, Monica. "Breaking the Silence and Camouflaging Voices in Lionel Shriver's *We Need to Talk about Kevin*." In *Voices and Silence in the Contemporary Novel in English*. Ed. Vanessa Guignery. Newcastle-upon-Tyne: Cambridge Scholars Publishing, 2009.

Lauret, Maria. *Liberating Literature: Feminist Fiction in America*. London: Routledge, 1994.

Lawless, Andrew. *Three Monkeys Online Magazine*. May 2005, www.threemonkeysonline.com/als_page4/_we_need_to_talk_about_kevin_lionel_shriver_interview.html (accessed October 10, 2010).

Macpherson, Heidi Slettedahl. *Courting Failure: Women and the Law in Twentieth-Century Literature*. Akron: University of Akron Press, 2007.

Women's Movement: Escape as Transgression in North American Feminist Fiction. Amsterdam: Rodopi, 2000.

Miller, Nancy K. "Emphasis Added: Plots and Plausibilities in Women's Fiction." In Showalter, *New Feminist*.

Miller, Sue. *The Good Mother*. 1986. New York: HarperCollins, 2002.

Modleski, Tania. *Loving with a Vengeance: Mass-Produced Fantasies for Women*. Hamden, CT: Archon Books, 1982.

Moi, Toril. *Sexual/Textual Politics*. London: Methuen, 1985.

Moore, Lorrie. *The Gate at the Stairs*. London: Faber and Faber, 2009.

Morrison, Toni. *Beloved*. 1987. London: Picador, 1988.

Mussell, Kay. *Fantasy and Reconciliation: Contemporary Formulas of Women's Romance Fiction*. Westport, CT: Greenwood Press, 1984.

Packer, Ann. *The Dive from Clausen's Pier*. New York: Knopf, 2002.

Prager, Emily. *Eve's Tattoo*. 1991. London: Vintage, 1993.

Radway, Janice A. *Reading the Romance: Women, Patriarchy, and Popular Literature*. Chapel Hill: University of North Carolina Press, 1984.

Robinson, Marilynne. *Gilead*. London: Virago, 2005.

Home. London: Virago, 2008.

Housekeeping. 1980. London: Faber and Faber, 1991.

Russ, Joanna. *How to Suppress Women's Writing*. 1983. London: The Women's Press, 1984.

Showalter, Elaine. *A Jury of her Peers: American Women Writers from Anne Bradstreet to Annie Proulx*. London: Virago, 2009.

"Feminist Criticism in the Wilderness." In Showalter, *New Feminist*.

New Feminist Criticism: Essays on Women, Literature, and Theory. London: Virago, 1986.

"Toward a Feminist Poetics." In Showalter, *New Feminist*.

Shriver, Lionel. *We Need to Talk about Kevin*. 2003. London: Serpent's Tail, 2005.

Shute, Jenefer. "Lionel Shriver." *Bomb* 93 (2005): 60–5.

Smith, Sarah. "Not Mad About the Boy." *The Guardian*, November 15, 2003, www.guardian.co.uk/books/2003/nov/15/featuresreviews.guardianreview27 (accessed October 18, 2010).

Tyler, Anne. *Ladder of Years*. London: Chatto and Windus, 1995.

Walker, Alice. *The Color Purple*. New York: Harcourt, Brace, Jovanovich, 1982.

28

Asian American women's literature and the promise of committed art

LESLIE BOW

Prior to deciding on Asian American women's literature as a research field, I announced my intention to write on Jade Snow Wong's 1945 autobiography, *Fifth Chinese Daughter*, for a 1987 graduate seminar. My professor responded with a less than innocent question, "But, is it *good?*"

I mustered an earnest, but slightly evasive reply, something along the lines that my interest was not based on what a text "is" as much as what it does. His implied aesthetic judgment was nonetheless more subtle than that offered by an Asian American novelist who, upon hearing the gender focus of my work, dramatically rolled his eyes. A decade later, I continued to encounter issues of reception surrounding my object of study. A physics professor and recent immigrant from mainland China could not parse the descriptor, "Asian American women's literature." Casting about for an illustration, I resorted to, "If your daughter were to write a novel here, I would read it."

The irony is that were the hypothetical daughter to publish a novel, she herself might very well reject the rubric, "Asian American women writer," insisting that she writes about the human condition. Or, like novelist Bharati Mukherjee, that she is, in the manner of Bernard Malamud, an "American author in the tradition of other American authors whose ancestors arrived at Ellis Island" (cited in Carb, "An Interview with Bharati Mukherjee," 650). I begin with these examples of axiology and anxiety in order to recognize at the outset the risks of taxonomy, particularly those that cohere around identities and owe their emergence to the legacies of the Civil Rights and Women's movements. Identity-defined literary genres are for some transparently commonsensical, needing no justification, while others find them inherently suspicious, founded on simple-minded equations between experience and art. "Asian American women's writing" is indebted to what Charles Taylor calls the "politics of recognition" and to changes in the literary marketplace. At the same time, both canon expansion arising from liberal notions of representation and ever-subdivided niche readerships continue to circumscribe perceptions about what this body of work does and the range and force of its cultural and aesthetic interventions.

At first it would seem that establishing the value of Asian American women's literature was destined to follow in the footsteps of criticism on nineteenth-century women's writing: feminist recuperation initiates archival recovery leading to expanded notions of both women's empowerment and sentimental advocacy; historical representations of domestic life and gender relations different from our own would produce a putatively more accurate account of women's experience, highlighting the interplay between agency and gendered social structures in new ways. Non-fiction by Asian American women bore testimony to the specificities of intersecting gender, race, and class oppressions: for example, the aforementioned *Fifth Chinese Daughter*; turn-of-the-century journalism by Edith Maud Eaton (Sui Sin Far); Su-ling Wong's *Daughter of Confucius: A Personal History* (1952); Monica Sone's *Nisei Daughter* (1953); Jeanne Houston and James D. Houston's *Farewell to Manzanar* (1973); Akemi Kikumura's *Through Harsh Winters: The Life of an Immigrant Japanese Woman* (1981); Le Ly Hayslip's *When Heaven and Earth Changed Places: A Vietnamese Woman's Journey from War to Peace* (1989); Mary Paik Lee's *Quiet Odyssey: A Pioneer Korean Woman in America* (1990); and the oral histories compiled in Sucheng Chan's *Hmong Means Free: Life in Laos and America* (1994) and Elaine H. Kim and Eui-Young Yu's *East to America: Korean American Life Stories* (1996).

Interest in memoir-as-ethnography ran the risk of limiting Asian American women's writing to a single frame: a body of work bounded by the experiential, it was not universal but particularist, not transcendent but embodied. Its worth lay in its verisimilitude, its contribution to pluralizing the category "woman," its difference from the unmarked, white, middle-class, heteronormative, First World gender norm. As I have argued elsewhere, Asian American women's testimony might serve the purpose of conveying difference while simultaneously offering reassurance of gender commonality, a reassurance opened within the space of – in particular – white women's identification (Bow, *Betrayal and Other Acts of Subversion*). Regarding the uses of postcolonial feminist autobiography, Sara Suleri cautions that lived experience often serves "as fodder for the continuation of another's epistemology, even when it is recorded in a 'contestatory' position to its relation to realism" – a caution that perhaps extends to her own coming-of-age memoir, *Meatless Days* (1989) ("Woman Skin Deep," 766). As with any canon emerging from the rise of liberal multiculturalism and valued primarily for documenting varieties of social injury or grievance, the risk is that visibility and recognition in the public sphere appear to be both the beginning and the end of the story.

In highlighting the irony of contemporary political representation within liberal democracies like the USA, Wendy Brown notes that "just as the mantle of abstract personhood is formally tendered to a whole panoply of those historically excluded from it . . . the marginalized reject the rubric of humanist inclusion . . . Just when polite liberal (not to mention correct leftist) discourse ceased speaking of us as dykes, faggots, colored girls, or natives, we began speaking of ourselves this way" (*States of Injury*, 53). Representation in the eyes of the state in terms of coalitional identities seemingly resistant to absorption paradoxically ends up, she argues, affirming humanist notions of the subject and a limited concept of individual rights. The emergence of ever-specific literary canons – for Suleri, "any one of the pigeonholes constructed for multiculturalism" ("Woman Skin Deep," 766) – risks similar co-optation: including writing by Asian women in the USA might satisfy the dictates of representation by expanding knowledge about women as a class. Too readily attributed to exposure to British or American democracy, Asian women's critical portrayals of, say, *sati*, foot-binding, double-eyelid operations, infanticide, or arranged marriage might fit that bill, one that elsewhere includes depictions of female genital mutilation or the *hijab*. Privileging literature on these terms can promote, in the words of Aiwah Ong, "a view of non-Western women as out of time with the West, and therefore a vehicle for misplaced Western nostalgia" ("Colonialism and Modernity," 85). In this sense, the anti-patriarchical and anti-Orientalist projects of this First World literature can hardly be distinguished from its Orientalist reception.[1]

Of course, the perhaps cynical trajectory I have outlined above is not the complete story; Asian American women's literature grew to prominence with the canonization of Maxine Hong Kingston's *The Woman Warrior: Memoir of a Girlhood among Ghosts* (1976). And while the title and her publisher's deliberately vague and changing classifications ("memoir," "non-fiction," "non-fiction/literature") speak to its selling points as ethnic *bildungsroman* culminating in feminist defiance, it shot to scholarly attention because it was resolutely postmodern at a time in which critics were attempting to define exactly what postmodernism was. When the unnamed narrator queries, "What is Chinese tradition and what is the movies?" (6), she might as well have announced that subjectivity is created, mediated, and disciplined by multiple social discourses. Or questioned along with Nietzsche, "how about those conventions of language? Are they perhaps products of knowledge, of the sense of truth: are designations and things congruent? Is language the adequate expression of all realities?" (*Writing from the Early Notebooks*, 255). Kingston's text was both ethnographic and slyly anti-ethnographic; it spoke to more than one readership, more than one means of critical framing. Given its insistence on the interrelation between subjectivity and fantasy, it is perhaps a further irony that controversy surrounding the book among Asian American literary communities centered around notions of authenticity. Aspiring writers were rumored to have received "Kingston rejection letters" from publishers refusing publication on the basis that their manuscripts were not like *The Woman Warrior*.[2] As critics including myself have shown, debates among writers about creative license arose from anxieties about how to represent the "community," notions of ethnographic empiricism surrounding Chinese culture, and the oppositional valence of liberal feminism.[3]

I highlight the disparities within the text's multiple receptions not to argue for *The Woman Warrior*'s exceptionalism, but to point out competing criteria of value surrounding Asian American artistic production as a whole. Cultural work by Asians in the USA was and continues to be noteworthy not only for its recuperation of racialized history, but also for its destablization of the social identities upon which such history depends. Independent films such as Wayne Wang's *Chan is Missing* (1982), Helen Lee's *Sally's Beauty Spot* (1990), and Rea Tajiri's *History and Memory* (1991) that explore ethnicity as trace; plays such as Velina Hasu Houston's *Tea* (1985) and David Henry Hwang's *M. Butterfly* (1988) that engage transgender or transracial performance; and modern and postmodern literature such as Chuang Hua's *Crossings* (1968), Yoko Ono's *Grapefruit* (1970), and Theresa Hak Kyung Cha's *Dictée* (1982) challenge the art-as-sociology lens that came to be associated with Ethnic Studies at its inception. Thus, the Asian American canon simultaneously came to be recognized and celebrated for one thing while demonstrating something else altogether. In locating "Asian American women's literature," the question is and has always been one of critical framing: there is no single genealogy to affirm, no teleology beginning with realism, testimony, and "coming to voice" and ending with something like, well, *The Woman Warrior*. Defining the underlying coherence within any body of literature is a matter of who looks and why, particularly as political value oscillates between muscular claims of existence and acknowledging "contributions" and recognizing the contingent foundations of identity. The two seemingly divergent pathways converge in the exploration of gendered and racial rhetoric.

Asian American critics have always been suspicious of the "identitarian" nature of literary taxonomy (not to mention culturalist explanations for Asian women's gender oppression), recognizing the irony of casting doubt on the very rubric that makes visible our expertise. In 1987, Amy Ling may have affirmed that, "only as all the diverse peoples that are Americans find their own voices and sing their individual and communal songs, can we enjoy the full richness and depth in this chorus that is America" ("I'm Here," 159). Nevertheless, she also recognized that perspectival multiplicity challenges universalist notions of objectivity that serve as beards for the worldview of white, middle-class men. Moreover, the pathway for Asian American literary criticism opened by Elaine Kim's *Asian American Literature: An Introduction to the Writings and their Social Context* (1982) centered on a critique of nationalism. Focusing on narratives of acculturation and their politicized messages about minority inclusion and segregation, Kim's intersectional analysis was a critical first in Asian American Studies; it was also unabashedly feminist. Lisa Lowe's landmark study, *Immigrant Acts: On Asian American Cultural Politics* (1996), situated literature as one arena through which to explore the contradictions between the democratic promise of equal citizenship and hierarchies of racialized labor required by capitalist exploitation. Asian American cultural forms, she argued, reveal the ways in which the "demand that immigrant subjects 'develop' into an identification with the dominant forms of the nation gives rise to contradictory articulations that interrupt the demands for identity and identification, that voice antagonisms to the universalizing narratives of both pluralism and development, and that open Asian American culture as an alternative site to the American economic, political, and national cultural spheres" (*Immigrant Acts*, 29). As Lowe's work exemplifies, Asian American criticism was quick to develop and embrace theories of racial formation, gender constructivism, and economic globalization in order to interrogate the relationship between discourse and power – now, across national boundaries.

Asian American women's literature serves as the most tangible evidence that American women's writing is diasporic, transnational, and invested in world affairs. It has emerged as a forum for the critique of multinational capital, situating publishing in the USA as a medium for exposing state violence, labor exploitation, and the abrogation of civil rights across the globe. The list goes on: sustainability, sex tourism, transnational adoption, the symbolic use of women by the state. As a practice, literary criticism thus takes on continuing political urgency: in what ways can the project of Asian American feminist criticism illuminate literature's investment in advocacy and social change? This is not to imply that the literature is tendentious, but to emphasize its commitment to challenging the veneer of social reality utilizing, in Adorno's terms, the aesthetic "advantage" of inherent ambiguity.[4] While there are any number of new directions that critics might explore – the tension between commercial and literary prose, emerging genres incorporating the visual, and the unexamined arena of "unraced" texts by women writers – what I highlight here is not simply the proliferation of genres of artistic production, but a continuing critical awareness of literature's activist intervention and the promise of committed art.

*

The popularity of Amy Tan's *The Joy Luck Club* (1989) and her subsequent novels, *The Kitchen God's Wife* (1991), *The Hundred Secret Senses* (1995), and *The Bonesetter's Daughter* (2001), spawned any number of memoirs focused on the daughter's return to the (in particular, East Asian) sites of traumatic matrilineal history: Denise Chong's *The Concubine's Daughter* (1994); Kyoko Mori's *The Dream of Water* (1995); Helie Lee's *Still Life with Rice: A Young American Woman Discovers the Life and Legacy of her Korean Grandmother* (1996); and Adeline Yen Mah's *Falling Leaves: The Memoir of an Unwanted Chinese Daughter* (1997), not to mention novels (for example, Deanna Fei's *Thread of Sky* [2010]). The title of Mah's Young Adult version of her memoir, *Chinese Cinderella: The True Story of an Unwanted Daughter* (1999), perhaps says it all: evil stepmothers, the generation gap, repressed families, migration upheaval, and maternal suicide represent the ongoing inheritance of gender oppression now left to following generations of women to unpack and reconcile. Through harsh winters, indeed. Historical fiction of the foot-binding ilk – work by Gail Tsukiyama, Anchee Min, and now Lisa See – became its own genre, amply demonstrating that Asian women were more than willing to fill the swath of the American marketplace popularized by Tan, but arguably traced to the legacy of Pearl S. Buck. Drawing hard and fast criteria between this genre – perhaps the late twentieth-century incarnation of "scribbling women" – and literary fiction by Asian American women is certainly a task left to future critics who might find it difficult to make categorical distinctions between high art and mass culture when it comes to books published in the USA. Gita Mehta's novel, *Raj* (1989), and Jung Chang's memoir, *Wild Swans: Three Daughters of China* (1991), for example, trade on exotica and veer towards the epic, but deliver a sharp political edge; to find it, one has to look beyond the oftentimes excessively floral packaging. In their overview of gender and sexuality in Asian American literature, Sau-ling Wong and Jeffrey Santa Ana deliberately exclude such texts from consideration, focusing on "print literature of a belletristic character" ("Gender and Sexuality in Asian American Literature," 172). What this exclusion implies is that, by 1999, the theme "gender and sexuality" had become so unwieldy as to necessitate not merely a limited scope that privileged prose over drama and poetry, and highbrow over middlebrow texts, but frameworks so broad as to be relatively incoherent (first, second, and third wave; men's and women's writing).

Thus, if one were willing to undertake a catalogue of writing by Asian American women – which King-kok Cheung and Stan Yogi did and more in 1988 with their *Asian American Literature: An Annotated Bibliography* – much less an academic assessment of what such texts share beyond the race, language, and the (fluid) nationalities of their authors, one would have to confront a now dizzying array of genres that reside within or overlap with Asian American women's literature. There is the subgenre of politically grim, slightly gothic tales of the Cultural Revolution (for example, *Red Scarf Girl*, *Red China Blues*, *Red Azalea*, *The Last Communist Virgin*); Asian American chick-lit (*The Dim Sum of All Things*, *The Hindi-Bindi Club*); and Asian-inflected self-help (*Warrior Lessons: An Asian American Woman's Journey into Power*). The success and infamy of Amy Chua's *Battle Hymn of the Tiger Mother* (2010) may well reignite a genre that (blessedly) never quite took off with *Top of the Class: How Asian Parents Raise High Achievers – and How You Can Too* (2005). Stories of sexual oppression and eventual heteronormative empowerment, publishers discovered, could also be sexually titillating: hence, *Runaway: Diary of a Street Kid*, *Confessions of a Mail Order Bride*, and *Diary of a Manhattan Call Girl*. It remains to be seen whether or not Asian American women will come to dominate an emerging genre, the adoptee memoir (*Lucky Girl*, *The Language of Blood*, *Trail of Crumbs: Hunger, Love, and the Search for Home*). Capitalizing on the association between Asians and food in the USA, Asian American women have begun to establish platforms for their writing with the rise of the culinary memoir, a seemingly commercial category that can belie the literariness of the texts that fall under its purview; I would note, in particular, creative non-fiction by Bich Minh Nguyen (*Stealing Buddha's Dinner*), Leslie Li (*Daughter of Heaven: A Memoir with Earthly Recipes*), Linda Furiya (*Bento Box in the Heartland*, *How to Cook A Dragon*), and Jennifer 8 Lee (*The Fortune Cookie Chronicles*). Following trends in the publishing industry, I think it is important to recognize the strength of "YA" or Young Adult books by authors such as Anjali Banerjee, Linda Sue Park, and Marie Lee. Drawing on the *faux-naïf* voice and coming-of-age structure of her acclaimed adult novel, *The Floating World*, Cynthia Kadohata has added to their ranks, decisively crossing over following her 2005 Newbery award-winning, *kira-kira*.

If it was once possible to have read everything published by Asian women in the USA, it is thus perhaps a sign of progress that such a project is now, if not impossible, at least inordinately time-consuming. More troubling is trying to decipher what the publishing industry thinks it is getting out of commercial fiction and non-fiction. To some extent, it is certainly that trauma, particularly women's trauma, has become a commodity. If there is a common narrative to be wary of within commercial fiction in particular, it is the one that I associate with *The Joy Luck Club* in which stories of gender inequality serve to bolster an exaggeratedly American ideology of self-reliance. That is, inscribing racial subjects in accord with uncritical notions of ethnic pluralism means in part comfortably affirming a teleology of women's progressive advancement bounded by the liberal horizon of self-help; popular texts by Asian American women can tend to represent various Asian countries as sites of repressive contrast, a selling point necessary to distinguishing them from the First World feminist brand. To what extent do these texts inscribe an alternative Asian fetish? Not the stereotypical (and contradictory) turn-on of Asian female hyper-sexuality and modesty, but the feminist's fetish: a specifically American investment in Asia's failure to democratize, an image best conveyed by women's suffering, a female protagonist's struggle to overcome semi-feudal gender codes. Adorno's wariness about politically minded art applies likewise to "multicultural" women's literature in the USA: "The so-called artistic representation of the sheer physical pain of people beaten to the ground by rifle butts contains, however remotely, the power to elicit enjoyment out of it" ("Commitment," 312–13). What underlies the pleasure of watching?

The explosion of work published under the rubric, "Asian American women's literature" since the 1980s produces another problematic: its ephemeral quality. Any number of worthy books that barely registered either with academics or the reading public continue to haunt my bookshelves: *Moon Cakes*, *Eating Chinese Food Naked*, *Face*, *The Interpreter*, *A Bridge Between Us*, *Oriental Girls Desire Romance*, and so on. One author of literary fiction lamented to me that her novels, which had gone out of print, seem to have "disappeared into a black void." It is not an overstatement to suggest that what spells the difference between literary ephemera and longevity is not only commercial impact, but academic interest, canonicity. In the contemporary moment, the question "Is it good?" has heightened stakes. Relatively few works by Asian American women grace the pages of major American or women's literary anthologies but all include them; the five-volume *Norton Anthology of American Literature* anoints six authors: Edith Maud Eaton (Sui Sin Far), Maxine Hong Kingston, Amy Tan, Cathy Song, Kimiko Hahn, and Jhumpa Lahiri. The more ethnically and topically inclusive *Heath Anthology of American Literature* includes more than twelve.[5] Gilbert and Gubar's *Norton Anthology of Literature by Women* focusing on Anglophone writing includes Hisaye Yamamoto, Anita Desai, Bharati Mukherjee, Marilyn Chin, and Gish Jen along with Eaton, Kingston, and Lahiri.[6] Among Asian American literary critics and editors, interest is obviously more expansive; critics routinely engage work by Winnifred Eaton, Theresa Hak Kyung Cha, Fae Myenne Ng, Susan Choi, Meena Alexander, Lois Ann Yamanaka, Monique Truong, Nora Okja Keller, Lan Samantha Chang, Jessica Hagedorn, Ruth Ozeki, Karen Tei Yamashita, Wendy Law-Yone, and Myung Mi Kim.[7] Perhaps the most obvious sign of arrival for Asian American women's literature? *CliffsNotes*.[8]

In 1994, Ann duCille identified a "traffic jam" in black feminist studies due to the rush of white feminist critical interest in African American women's literature, suggesting that it arose from the perception that black women occupy the "quintessential site of difference" ("The Occult of True Black Womanhood," 592). Elizabeth Abel speculated that white feminist critics sought in black women's literature "the text that promises resistance and integrity," given perception of "an increasingly compromised white feminist social position drained by success of oppositionality" ("Black Writing, White Reading," 494). While no such parallel traffic jam has emerged in Asian American feminist studies, I would argue that the "added value" of Asian American women's writing to American women's literature figures somewhat differently; the works do not necessarily extend the promise of oppositionality as much as the promise of diaspora. For Asian American critics there has been a shift from explorations of national identity and inclusion towards transnationalism and multinational capitalism, from minority coalition towards theories of exile, migration, home, and, in Ong's terms, "flexible citizenship" (*Flexible Citizenship: The Cultural Logics of Transnationality*). Thus, the blur between first- and third-world texts, themes, authorship, and circulation signals a keen reversal of Ling's lament regarding the perception that Asian American women writers "were not only third rate but third world and therefore extraneous to the discipline [of English]" ("I'm Here," 153).

Ten years later, David Eng wrote that it was time for Asian American Studies to shift away from a "politics of cultural nationalism to a politics of transnational culturalism":

[I]f earlier Asian American cultural nationalist projects were built on the political strategy of claiming home and nation-state through the domestic and the heterosexual, a new political project of thinking about these concepts in Asian American studies today would seem to center around queerness and diaspora – its rethinkings of home and nation-state across multiple identity formations and numerous locations "out here" and "over there." ("Out Here and Over There," 34)

Lowe's emphasis on Asian American "hetereogeneity, hybridity, multiplicity" ("Heterogeneity, Hybridity, Multiplicity") extended to, for one, deterritorializing the nation-based objects of Asian American Studies. This shift certainly contributed to the canonization of Theresa Hak Kyung Cha's *Dictée*. A highly fragmented prose poem that refuses the conventions of narrative and formally enacts the impossibility of memory and linguistic transparency, it nonetheless enmeshes women's gender submission within the legacies of colonialism and postcolonialism on the Korean peninsula. Mark Chiang argues that Asian American critical interest in the 1982 text might be attributed to the need to "extract legitimacy from cultural works produced by artists who can be 'reclaimed' as Asian Americans" (*The Cultural Capital of Asian American Studies*, 129), thereby transforming the political legitimacy of Asian American Studies based on representation into "aesthetic/academic legitimacy" of the sort offered by avant-garde literature (133). Such an assessment would validate a developmental narrative ascribed to Asian American literature – from socially interventionist, realist writing to literary postmodernism – were it not for the fact that, as Timothy Yu suggests, early Asian American poetry expressive of movement politics challenged the dichotomy between committed and avant-garde art at the outset (*Race and the Avant-Garde*). Like *The Woman Warrior*, *Dictée* performs as interventionist identity politics while simultaneously exposing the subject's coherence and autonomy as an illusion and interrupting "the oppressive rule of the established language and images over the mind and body of man" (Marcuse, *Counterrevolution and Revolt*, 79); more to my point here, it also marks a continuity between theories of American subject-formation and colonial memory, offering critics a means of reconciling (or the impossibility of reconciling) migration to the USA with the international upheavals that precipitated it.

The author likely to benefit from critical interest in the convergence between domestic racialization and American imperialism is Susan Choi, author of critically heralded novels, *The Foreign Student* (1998), *American Woman* (2003), and *A Person of Interest* (2008). Her work is marked by its powerful depiction of the quiet traumas of individuals who suffer misrecognition and thereby also the abuses of state power. The ongoing critical project that attempts to understand the mutual imbrication of domestic and international politics underscores the urgency of transnational literature of the sort exemplified by Choi – in particular, her depictions of segregation and Cold War-era politics, contemporary racial profiling, and the line between radical protest and terrorism. In this sense, her work contributes to what is now a tradition in Asian American women's writing of situating publishing in the USA as a forum for highlighting postcolonial excesses, from Jessica Hagedorn's devastating portrait of the Philippines under a fictionalized Marcos regime (*Dogeaters*, 1990); to Fiona Cheong's veiled commentary on the loss of civil liberties that solidified the rise of Lee Kuan Yew in Singapore (*The Scent of the Gods*, 1991); to Wendy Law-Yone's commentary on the treatment of ethnic minorities by the long-ruling military junta in Myanmar (*The Coffin Tree* [1983], *Irrawaddy Tango* [1993], and the British-published, *The Road to Wanting* [2010]).[9] It will be particularly interesting to see how critics engage Kao Kalia Yang's *The Latehomecomer: A Hmong Family Memoir* (2008), a recounting of history, culture, and migration in keeping with Asian American memoirs represented as being the "first" portrayals of an ethnic group experience. Lauded for its documenting the story of Hmong recruited to fight the CIA's covert war, their forcible expulsion and flight from Laos, and refugee resettlement in Thailand and the USA, in what ways will Yang bear the burdens of representation? As much as *Latehomecomer* offers a sympathetic if overly sentimental account of collective trauma, it will eventually encounter community and/or critical push-back, particularly in its skirting around commentary on General Vang Pao's legacy. For critics, the issue will not involve taking a stand on the accuracy of his portrayal as either (then) liberationist freedom-fighter or (now) suspected arms-dealer and subversive, but establishing the ways in which the duality follows changes in American foreign policy after the Cold War.

My point is that "transnational" literature does not simply celebrate border-crossing or thematize cultural fluidity and exchange. Rather, Asian American women's literature continues to intervene in ongoing political struggles that have heightened consequences for women, whether or not that intervention critiques or endorses multinational capitalism, socialism, or representative democracy, or the nationalist projects of specific regimes. In reading essays such as Gita Mehta's "Banish Charity" celebrating micro-financing and Indian textile workers' economic self-sufficiency under multinational capitalism ("[Your] money bought about one hundred and sixty women and their families out of bondage" [*Snakes and Ladders*, 62]), I am reminded of the varieties of advocacy. Asian American women's literature represents the space between American women's writing and world literature, Asian women's writing in translation, and the objects of postcolonial, feminist, trauma, and critical race studies. While one might be hard-pressed to reconcile the crime novels of Japanese feminist Natsuo Kirino (*Out*, *Grotesque*) with the posthumously published *Last Night I Dreamed of Peace: The Diary of Dang Thuy Tram*, a "found" manuscript by a Vietnamese doctor penned during the "American War," or the magical realism of Arundhati Roy's *The God of Small Things*, such a reconciliation might not reside in expanding literary genres or even recognizing feminism in the plural, but in theorizing an outward-looking politics grounded in feminism and highlighting an unabashed belief in the power of writing as a form of global advocacy. For critics, the payoff lies in exploring the inherent ambiguity of these messages, refusing to assume transparency between the text and the world.

This is not to say that criticism should only concern itself with realist literature and its use as persuasive rhetoric that encourages us to act ethically in the "real"; politics resides in the abstract as well – in understanding the limits of language and signification and theories of the radical contingency of the subject, for example. One of the exciting and yet to be explored arenas of Asian American scholarship concerns what I see as the latency of race, the ways in which narrative circulates racial signifiers without racialized bodies. This might represent the more literal realization of what Kandice Chuh deemed "subjectless" Asian American Studies and one response to Chiang's sense that the discipline must reconcile its legacy of scholarly "cultural capital" derived from social movements based on community representation.[10] That is, rather than privileging realist art and referential language, critics are also engaged with a sense of the political both reconcilable and incommensurate with the liberal multiculturalist imperative of visibility that validates "minority" literature as a conduit of traumatic realism. The movement away from representational literature may reinvigorate the study of poetry, particularly the work of, for example, Victoria Chang or Mei-mei Berssenbrugge who do not, at first glance, appear to engage race in their work. It seems less important to establish these writers as Asian American than to understand the ways in which they enable critics to theorize the link between critical race studies and the aesthetic. For one, this would mean reconciling the quiet, intellectual, early poetry of Carolyn Lau with the work of her later incarnation, right-on woman of color Carolyn Lei-Lanilau ("He did proudly own that he was *marginal*. Me too, me too!" [*Ono Ono Girl's Hula*, 54]). Yoko Ono's Fluxus *Grapefruit*, for example, plays with ideas of differentiation that, I would argue, end up allegorizing social relations and challenging our adherence to visual perception that privileges surface over interior, immanence over impermanence. In its emphasis on the arbitrariness of classification as well as its attempt to "resist by its form alone the course of the world" (Adorno, "Commitment," 304), her poetry has relevance for the ways we think about race as embodied difference.

Moreover, if emerging Asian American literature moves to complicate, veil, or even dispense with the "Asian American subject," it does so not merely by eschewing conventions of the lyric or invoking race via orientalist tropes, but by engaging futuristic fantasies of bodilessness. A 2008 special issue of *Melus* explores the ways in which, according to editor Stephen Hong Sohn, the "Alien/Asian is inextricably tied to science, the future, and technology" ("Editor's Introduction," 6). The volume engages "techno-Orientalist" art exploiting the American association between Asians and dystopia; how might this association enmesh with gender studies' interest in fluid notions of subjectivity and embodiment both within and beyond the genres of science fiction, fantasy, children's literature, and popular culture? How does the "raceless" text impact "Asian American" as a literary category?

Given work by Cha, Ono, and Miné Okubo, tracing a genealogy of Asian American women's literature also necessarily involves understanding visual intertextuality. Elena Tajima Creef and Greg Robinson's *Miné Okubo: Following her Own Road* (2008) reads Okubo's art, including *Citizen 13660*, from a variety of angles, not only for its historical depiction of Japanese American internment, but also for the tension between text and image, for a personal understanding of Okubo's relationship with the art establishment, and for the influences of European art, Japanese woodblock prints or *ukiyio-e*, and *manga*. They recast *Citizen 13660* as an early graphic novel. Work such as Jillian Tamaki and Mariko Tamaki's *Skim* (2008) – undisputedly the best story ever written about a lesbian, multi-racial, Wiccan, Canadian goth girl – represents a merging of genres, the graphic novel as woman's *bildungsroman*. The collage, comic book, family photo-album style of Ann Marie Fleming's *The Magical Life of Long Tack Sam: An Illustrated Memoir* (2007) defies generic classification at the same time that its fragmented, partial re-creation of her magician great-grandfather's life on the vaudeville circuit inherits Kingston's nonlinear, playful, and speculative style.[11] Many of us who claim to do interdisciplinary work recognize the inevitable and uncontroversial direction of literary studies in the twenty-first century as we cultivate visual literacy and expand definitions of literature to encompass text-dependent installation art and performance, illustrated blogs or digital essays, narratives in gaming, and film, in this case, particularly as it engages the tropes of techno-Orientalism and conventions of Bollywood or Hong Kong cinema.

*

In their foreword to *Farewell to Manzanar*, Jeanne Wakatsuki Houston and James D. Houston recount a fellow writer's 1972 advice: don't bother with a book about Japanese American internment because the public is really "issued out." Yet in the early 1970s, memoirs engaging race, gender, and politics represented the tip of an iceberg. Since that time, literature by Asian American women continues to serve as a forum for activism, from Tracy Quan's columns on the rights of sex workers, to Karen Tei Yamashita's eco-literature, to Yiyun Li's essay exposing the practice of selling the organs of condemned Chinese prisoners, to Le Ly Hayslip's use of memoir to fund her non-profit organizations, the East Meets West and Global Village Foundations in Vietnam. What these writers have in common is not necessarily a shared gender politics or even necessarily the conviction that women's rights are human rights. They do not proselytize as much as they pose necessary questions – to wit, Anita Jain's provocative query about feminist relativism, "Is Arranged Marriage Really Any Worse Than Craig'slist?" (2005). Such queries establish an arena of intervention beyond the need to testify to "difference" in the USA, a need most often served by the symbolic figure of the abject Asian woman enlisted to raise the flag about the limitations of her culture. Attending the 1995 United Nations Fourth World Conference on Women in Beijing, activist Mallika Dutt noted the relative weakness of the US Women of Color delegation in comparison to the leadership displayed by third world women. The disparity prompted her to conclude, "If women of color [in the USA] continue only to define themselves in the context of their communities, they perpetuate the problem of white women being perceived as national leaders while women of color are seen only as speaking for their own particular ethnicity or concern" ("Some Reflections," 528). Her caution about the power and limitations of ethnic particularism – the trap of culture – applies to ways of receiving and affirming literature as well.

It remains to be seen how a rubric like "Asian American women's literature" can continue to be useful given texts as disparate as, for example, *Living for Change: An Autobiography* by labor activist Grace Lee Boggs ("a book of revelation") and *I'm the One that I Want* by comedienne Margaret Cho ("an anthem to self-reliance"). Yet the diversity of texts and the multiple arenas of their engagement do not portend the collapse of Asian American feminism as much as the reinvigoration of literature as a forum for activism. Whether exploring the ways in which the body becomes an instrument of state discipline or gender's intersection with other legal identities, ethnic categories, or sexualities, Asian American women's literature is a body of work that does not simply challenge the national borders we place around literature, but holds the USA accountable for its foreign policies in the twentieth century. At the same time, "raceless," visual, and experimental work by Asian American women continues to invite critics to expand notions of the political beyond those of representation and visibility, beyond the liberal projection of the injured subject whose rights have been impugned to differently conceived forms of justice. These directions need not represent contradictions if, to paraphrase Kingston's narrator, we make our minds as large as the universe is large so that there is room for paradoxes.

*

I have no issues with teaching under the course title, "Asian American women's writing" even as some of my colleagues see bio-categorization as a constraint. The rubric works for me not because I retain an unproblematic belief in the relationship between authorship, text, and experience or the shifting foundations upon which these categories become tethered, but because I want to mark the ways in which gendered and racialized rhetoric holds heightened stakes for specific communities and subjects. The title of Ling's 1987 essay, "I'm Here: An Asian American Woman's Response," seems to insist, first and foremost, upon the importance of recognition. And yet, neither the literature nor the body of criticism it inspired seems limited by it. In a speech honoring Asian American members of Congress, legal theorist Mari Matsuda said, "The ability to make the connection between the injustice we have faced as Asian Americans and the injustice that others face is the ultimate test . . . and I believe our Asian-American coalition will live or die by our choice in that regard" ("Why Are We Here?," 160). Asian American women writers and critics continue to affirm that choice.

What is more, this affirmation is not distinct from the question of aesthetic worth. For reasons not wholly different from his own, I would give a more decisive answer to my professor's query about Asian American women's writing: Yes, it's good.

Notes

1. Maxine Hong Kingston herself once noted about reception of *The Woman Warrior*, "The critics who said how the book was good because it was, or was not, like the

oriental fantasy in their heads might as well have said how weak it was, since it in fact did not break through that fantasy" ("Cultural Mis-readings," 55).

2. See Blauvelt, "Talking with the Woman Warrior," 1, 8.

3. See Bow, "'For Every Gesture of Loyalty, There Doesn't Have to Be a Betrayal'"; Cheung, "The Woman Warrior versus the Chinaman Pacific"; Wong, "Autobiography as Guided Chinatown Tour."

4. Adorno's concession to ambiguity as a formal quality is what distinguishes "committed" and nonetheless referential art from propaganda: "Committed art in the proper sense is not intended to generate ameliorative measures, legislative acts or practical institutions – like earlier propagandist (tendency) plays against syphilis, duels, abortion laws or borstals – but work at the level of fundamental attitudes . . . But what gives commitment its esthetic advantage over tendentiousness also renders the content to which the artist commits himself inherently ambiguous" ("Commitment," 304).

5. I say "more than" twelve if one includes writers subheaded under topics such as American imperialism in the Philippines and Vietnam. Moreover, "counting" Asian American women writers is a fraught exercise. For example, the *Heath* anthologizes Lynda Barry who is part Filipina, but rarely if ever engaged as an "Asian American" author.

6. In Showalter's *A Jury of her Peers*, only Min Jin Lee, Amy Tan, and the poet, Reetika Vazirani, get a nod in addition to Lahiri, Kingston, and Mukherjee (Gilbert and Gubar, *Norton Anthology of Literature by Women*).

7. This list is by no means exhaustive, nor have I attempted to quantify it. It does not speak to the range of literary prose or poetry worthy of academic interest or continued print runs. A list of texts included in syllabi might include work by Merle Woo, Nellie Wong, Janice Mirikitani, Shani Mootoo, Le Ly Hayslip, and Miné Okubo. *A Resource Guide for Asian American Literature*, edited by Stephen Sumida and Sau-ling Wong, includes entries on women writers Ronyoung Kim, Wakako Yamauchi, Joy Kogawa, and playwrights Velina Hasu Houston and Momoko Iko. See also early anthologies of Asian American women's literature such as *The Forbidden Stitch*, ed. Shirley Geok-lin Lim, Mayumi Tsutakawa, and Margarita Donnelly, and *Making Waves: An Anthology of Writing by and about Asian American Women*.

8. *CliffsNotes* offers online study guides for *Farewell to Manzanar*, *The Joy Luck Club*, and *The Woman Warrior*. Amy Tan took one validation of her status as "author" with a keen sense of irony: her essay, "Mother Tongue" appeared on the language portion of the SAT (Tan, *The Opposite of Fate*).

9. Anglophone writers publishing in the United States have also produced scathing critiques of Japanese colonial administrations in the Philippines (Cecilia Manguerra Brainard's *When the Rain Goddess Wept*, 1999); Korea (Nora Cobb Keller's *Comfort Woman*, 1997); Singapore (Vyvyane Loh's *Breaking the Tongue*, 2004); and Hong Kong (Janice K. Min's *The Piano Teacher*, 2009).

10. Chuh's call for "subjectless" Asian American Studies does not refer to the absence of "Asian Americans" *per se*. Rather, her call arose from her sense that, even by 2003, Asian American critics did not adequately recognize the discursivity of the subject. Given that its radical historicity is no longer particularly controversial (see, for example, Scott, "The Evidence of Experience"), it is nonetheless interesting to interpret the call more literally: not so much Asian American Studies without Asian Americans, but the very

ways that Asian racialization surfaces via the disembodied tropes of orientalism, Asian objects, metaphor, fantasy, and technology.

11. Women's representation in the Asian/American graphic novel will be particularly welcome given the largely male audience of traditional American comics – subcategories of *manga* intended for female readers notwithstanding – as well as the prominence of Asian American author/illustrators Gene Luen Yang, Adrian Tomine, and Derek Kirk Kim, and Asian Australian Shaun Tan. It is impossible not to notice the masculine overtones of the volume *Secret Identities: The Asian American Superhero Anthology* (2009), for example. Kim's *Good as Lily* (2007), co-authored with Jesse Hamm, and Mariko Tamaki and Steve Rolston's *Emiko Superstar* (2008), both produced for Minx, the short-lived division of DC Comics aimed at girls, are the exceptions here.

Works cited

Abel, Elizabeth. "Black Writing, White Reading: Race and the Politics of Feminist Interpretation." *Critical Inquiry* 19.3 (Spring 1993): 470–98.

Adorno, Theodor W. "Commitment." 1962. In *The Essential Frankfurt School Reader*. Ed. Andrew Arato and Eike Gebhardt. New York: Continuum, 1993.

Baym, Nina, ed. *Norton Anthology of American Literature*. 7th edn. New York: W. W. Norton, 2007.

Blauvelt, William Satake. "Talking with the Woman Warrior." *Pacific Reader: A Review of Books on Asian Pacific Americans* (July 19, 1989): 1, 8.

Bow, Leslie. *Betrayal and Other Acts of Subversion: Feminism, Sexual Politics, Asian American Women's Literature*. Princeton: Princeton University Press, 2001.

"'For Every Gesture of Loyalty, There Doesn't Have to Be a Betrayal': Asian American Criticism and the Politics of Locality." In *Who Can Speak? Authority and Critical Identity*. Ed. Judith Roof and Robyn Wiegman. Urbana: University of Illinois Press, 1995.

Brown, Wendy. *States of Injury: Power and Freedom in Late Modernity*. Princeton: Princeton University Press, 1995.

Carb, Alison B. "An Interview with Bharati Mukherjee." *Massachusetts Review* 29.4 (Winter 1988): 645–9.

Cheung, King-kok. "The Woman Warrior versus the Chinaman Pacific: Must a Chinese American Critic Choose between Feminism and Heroism?" In *Conflicts in Feminism*. Ed. Marianne Hirsch and Evelyn Fox Keller. New York: Routledge, 1990.

Cheung, King-kok and Stan Yogi, eds. *Asian American Literature: An Annotated Bibliography*. New York: MLA, 1988.

Chiang, Mark. *The Cultural Capital of Asian American Studies: Autonomy and Representation in the University*. New York: New York University Press, 2009.

Chuh, Kandice. *Imagine Otherwise: On Asian Americanist Critique*. Durham, NC: Duke University Press, 2003.

duCille, Ann. "The Occult of True Black Womanhood: Critical Demeanor and Black Feminist Studies." *Signs* 19.3 (Spring 1994): 591–629.

Dutt, Mallika. "Some Reflections on US Women of Color and the United Nations Fourth World Conference on Women and NGO Forum in Beijing, China." *Feminist Studies* 22.3 (Autumn 1996): 519–28.

Eng, David. "Out Here and Over There: Queerness and Diaspora in Asian American Studies." *Social Text* 52/53 (Autumn–Winter 1997): 31–52.

Gilbert, Sandra M. and Susan Gubar, eds. *Norton Anthology of Literature by Women: The Traditions in English*. 3rd edn. Vol. 2. New York: W. W. Norton, 2007.

Kim, Elaine. *Asian American Literature: An Introduction to the Writings and their Social Context*. Philadelphia: Temple University Press, 1984.

Kingston, Maxine Hong. *The Woman Warrior*. 1976. New York: Vintage, 1989.

  "Cultural Mis-readings by American Reviewers." In *Asian and Western Writers in Dialogue: New Cultural Identities*. Ed. Guy Amirthanayagam. London: Macmillan, 1982.

Lauter, Paul, ed. *Heath Anthology of American Literature*. 6th edn. Boston: Wadsworth, 2010.

Lei-Lanilau, Carolyn. *Ono Ono Girl's Hula*. Madison: University of Wisconsin Press, 1997.

Lim, Shirley Geok-lin, Mayumi Tsutakawa, and Margarita Donnelly, eds. *The Forbidden Stitch: An Asian American Women's Anthology*. Corvallis, OR: Calyx Books, 1989.

Ling, Amy. "I'm Here: An Asian American Woman's Response." *New Literary History* 19.1 (Autumn 1987): 151–60.

Lowe, Lisa. "Heterogeneity, Hybridity, Multiplicity: Marking Asian American Difference." *Diaspora* 1.1 (1991): 24–44.

  Immigrant Acts: On Asian American Cultural Politics. Durham, NC: Duke University Press, 1996.

Making Waves: An Anthology of Writing by and about Asian American Women. Ed. Asian Women United. Boston: Beacon, 1989.

Marcuse, Herbert. *Counterrevolution and Revolt*. Boston: Beacon, 1972.

Matsuda, Mari. "Why Are We Here? Thoughts on Asian-American Identity and Honoring Asian-Americans in Congress." 1996. In *Screaming Monkeys: Critiques of Asian American Images*. Ed. M. Evelina Galang. Minneapolis: Coffee House Press, 2003.

Mehta, Gita. *Snakes and Ladders: Glimpses of India*. New York: Doubleday, 2009.

Nietzsche, Friedrich. *Writings from the Early Notebooks*. Ed. Raymond Geuss and Alexander Nehamas. Trans. Ladislaus Löb. Cambridge: Cambridge University Press, 2009.

Ong, Aiwah. "Colonialism and Modernity: Feminist Re-presentations of Women in Non-Western Societies." *Inscriptions* 3.4 (988): 79–93.

  Flexible Citizenship: The Cultural Logics of Transnationality. Durham, NC: Duke University Press, 1999.

Robinson, Greg and Elena Tajima Creef, eds. *Miné Okubo: Following her Own Road*. Seattle: University of Washington Press, 2008.

Scott, Joan. "The Evidence of Experience." *Critical Inquiry* 17 (Summer 1991): 773–97.

Showalter, Elaine. *A Jury of her Peers: American Women Writers from Anne Bradstreet to Annie Proulx*. New York: Knopf, 2009.

Sohn, Stephen Hong. "Editor's Introduction: Alien/Asian: Imagining the Racialized Future." *Melus* 33.4 (Winter 2008): 5–22.

Suleri, Sara. "Woman Skin Deep: Feminism and the Postcolonial Condition." *Critical Inquiry* 18 (Summer 1992): 756–69.

Sumida, Stephen and Sau-ling Wong, eds. *A Resource Guide for Asian American Literature*. New York: Modern Language Association Book Publications, 2001.

Tan, Amy. *The Opposite of Fate: A Book of Musings*. New York: G. P. Putnam's Sons, 2003.

Taylor, Charles. *Multiculturalism: Examining the Politics of Recognition*. Ed. Amy Gutmann. Princeton: Princeton University Press, 1994.

Wong, Sau-ling C. "Autobiography as Guided Chinatown Tour? Maxine Hong Kingston's *The Woman Warrior* and the Chinese-American Autobiographical Controversy." In *Multicultural Autobiography: American Lives*. Ed. James Robert Payne. Knoxville: University of Tennessee Press, 1992.

Wong, Sau-ling C. and Jeffrey J. Santa Ana. "Gender and Sexuality in Asian American Literature." *Signs* 25.1 (1999): 171–226.

Yu, Timothy. *Race and the Avant-Garde: Experimental and Asian American Poetry since 1965*. Stanford: Stanford University Press, 2009.

29

Straight sex, queer text

American women novelists

LYNDA ZWINGER

In the Introduction to the landmark collection, *The New Feminist Criticism: Essays on Women, Literature, and Theory* (1985), Elaine Showalter traces the evolution of feminist academic study of women writers from its birth in 1970 with Kate Millet's *Sexual Politics*. She notes that "the second phase of feminist criticism was the discovery that women writers had a literature of their own, whose historical and thematic coherence, as well as artistic importance, had been obscured by the patriarchal values that dominate our culture" (6). The subsequent focus on women's writing

> led to a massive recovery and rereading of literature by women from all nations and historical periods. As hundreds of lost women writers were rediscovered, as letters and journals were brought to light, as new literary biographies explored the relationship between the individual female talent and the literary tradition, the continuities in women's writing became clear for the first time. (6)

In addition to her own *A Literature of their Own* (1977), Showalter points to Patricia Meyer Spacks's *The Female Imagination*, Ellen Moers's *Literary Women* (published in 1975 and 1976, respectively), and Sandra Gilbert and Susan Gubar's *The Madwoman in the Attic* (1979) as beginning to define women's writing in feminist terms, which declared that starting from the time of these landmarks of feminist work, we

> now have a coherent, if still incomplete, narrative of female literary history, which describes the evolutionary stages of women's writing during the last 250 years from imitation through protest to self-definition, and defines and traces the connections throughout history and across national boundaries of the recurring images, themes, and plots that emerge from women's social, psychological, and aesthetic experience in male-dominated cultures. (6)

Others in the field might not have seen it quite so rosily, but it is certainly the case that the scholarship in the many fields dealing with women writers is voluminous and illuminating. To take a modest subset of such work as a kind of measure of substantial accomplishment: typing in the keywords "lesbian writers American" into the Worldcat search engine yields 330 items. Taking a more academic approach, entering the keywords "lesbian American writing" yields the slightly less boggling, but every bit as intimidating (for the woman writer attempting a twenty-page essay) number of 118 entries. And good stuff too: from the now-venerable "Compulsory Heterosexuality and Lesbian Existence" to an entire issue of *Journal of Women's History* devoted to that epoch-making essay; from "Serious Play: Drag, Transgender, and the Relationship between Performance and Identity in the Life Writing of RuPaul and Kate Bornstein" and "Queering Euro-American Jews"; to special journal issues devoted to Queer Race and Carolyn Dinshaw's *Getting Medieval*.

So maybe it is time to return to the place we perforce started from, back when we had to take the stance that writing by women could not be the same as writing by men because women have different social, psychological, and aesthetic experiences, should not be judged by the same standards as writing by men because women writers were not aiming at the same effects, and that these assertions have value in discourses about literature. Now that there is ample evidence that there were indeed women writers in, say, the American nineteenth century, that there were many, many women writers there in fact, maybe it is time to ride the critical pendulum back to our crucially strategic beginnings and ask another set of questions: what do we lose when we taxonomize literary texts?

We might lose sex, as women write it.[1]

Take, for instance, the classification "sentimental novels" (which morphs into "domestic novels" and is often lost within that category as an assumed synonym). The taxonomic maneuver that produced this label rescued, redis-covered, and rehabilitated a significant body of American women writers and their texts, once abandoned to the oblivion of non-serious literature. Occurring after Showalter's essay was published, the establishment of the sentimental and/or domestic novel as a worthy category of scholarly and pedagogical attention reproduces all of the accomplishments she therein celebrates, and it creates a not-so-minor academic industry that continues to flourish. The impulse to taxonomize is, of course, a foundational and necessary one, as is the impulse I am about to give way to: that of interrogating and dismantling the results, in order to begin again. Now that we have rediscovered and rescued from oblivion a vast pantheon of women writers, we need to (re)decide – we need to continually decide – what we are going to do with them.

Charlotte Temple, by Susanna Rowson, was published in the United States in 1794, and is arguably, therefore, the first American novel written by an American woman novelist (both labels, notably, the product of Rowson's own active construction).[2] The story, and the author of it, are transatlantic: Charlotte Temple and her author traveled from England to America at the dawn of America's existence; each to give birth – one to a child; one to a career. We all know the story: "seduced and betrayed" (in mid-Atlantic, no less), Charlotte Temple pines away all alone in her rural cottage, waiting for her seducer and betrayer to come to her. Too noble to allow her pollution to contaminate by sentimental osmosis the purity of the more fortunate members of her sex, she wiles her time away with sighings and plaintive ballad singing ("For what are nature's charms combin'd, / To one whose weary breast / Can neither peace nor comfort find, / Nor friend whereon to rest?" [*Charlotte Temple*, 78]).[3]

Her neighbor, Mrs. Beauchamp, hears the "soft melodious voice" whilst walking, leaning on her husband's arm, in her garden early one morning, and with a "pellucid drop of humanity stealing down her cheek," resolves to "offer her friendship" – to become, that is, the friend whereon the unhappy Charlotte can rest her weary breast (78). Captain Beauchamp heartily approving his wife's plan to follow "the impulse of [her] generous heart," Mrs. Beauchamp prepares to visit Charlotte (79). The attentive reader will hardly miss the tropes of sentimentality, in all their glorious perversity, pervading the account of the subsequent meeting, despite its ostensibly (or actually) platonic nature.

Mrs. Beauchamp reflects that she needs to avoid the possible imputation of "impertinent curiosity." Upon giving the problem some thought, "she stepped into the garden, and gathering a few fine cucumbers, took them in her hand by way of apology for her visit" (80). Welcome bouquet in hand, she arrives at Charlotte's abode, whereupon:

> A glow of conscious shame vermilioned Charlotte's face as Mrs. Beauchamp entered.
>
> "You will pardon me, Madam," said she, "for not having before paid my respects to so amiable a neighbour; but we English people always keep up that reserve which is the characteristic of our nation wherever we go. I have

taken the liberty to bring you a few cucumbers, for I had observed you had none in your garden."

Charlotte, though naturally polite and well bred, was so confused she could hardly speak. (80)

The reader gets to the garden smoothly enough, but when the introductory handful is named, she pulls up. She probably rereads the sentence. Yes, says she to herself, it is "cucumbers." A few fine ones, to be exact. Because the pregnant and abandoned, vermilion-faced Charlotte has none in her garden.[4]

It is an odd textual moment, bracketed by quiveringly sentimental passages that intend to lay their figurative hands on the reader's heart in the best tradition of the inculcation of female virtue by negative example. The cucumbers at first glance add nothing much to the heterosexual parable but a coarse and not very funny joke, an elbow dug into the side of the palpitating reader (whether her palpitations are those of virtuous sympathy for Charlotte's plight or delicious savoring of her woes). But they are, in fact, an odd stumble in the narrative. It is impossible to read the passage without at least a kind of temporal hiccup, a "what?" response, however momentary.

In fact, it could be called a rather queer hesitation in the narrative flow. For now, let us call it a temporal anomaly: the otherwise unoffending gourds pull the reader up, obscurely signal a kind of place-holder for something else, function as a kind of readerly speedbump. The readerly eye pauses, the readerly mind registers a resistance to an oddity in the text, and then moves on. But that "speedbump" is located at a carefully chosen moment in the novel's action and in the reader's reading: the tender albeit intrusive affiliation and initiation of intimacy, with all due sentimental-masochistic trappings, between two women (one of whom intends to rescue the other from her heterosexually caused plight).[5]

Take another writer with a rhetorical interest in cucumbers, Louisa May Alcott, whose 1863 *Hospital Sketches* bears the epigraph "Which, namin' no names, no offense could be took," a remark made by one of Alcott's favorite Dickens characters, the "cowcumber"-devouring Sairy Gamp. Sairy, a home nurse and premier opportunist, voraciously consumes food and drink at her patients' expense and is the polar opposite of the sentimental angel figure so often found at the bedsides of the sick and dying in nineteenth-century texts. We can find sly references to Sairy in most of Alcott's writings (letters, journal entries, stories, novels – including *Little Women*).

Alcott, whose academic rescue began in the 1960s and who has ridden the succeeding waves of academic taxonomies quite comfortably, has moved from a forgotten, though once-popular, woman writer, to a writer expressing a uniquely female experience in a male-defined culture, to a novelist of the domestic/sentimental which has lately become so significant in the literary and cultural history of US writers. If we consider her novels to be written in the sentimental modality, rather than expressing sentimental content, we can rescue them once again, this time from ourselves. Long considered a woman's (sub)genre (a taxonomizing gesture that belies the sentimental's roots in writing by men), the sentimental, becoming synonymous with the domestic, was transformed to a legitimate literary category which in turn became a way to liberate women writers from the limbo of insignificant scribbling women to which they had been too long consigned. This critical movement came, of course, with a price. While the work of re-evaluating the function and value of the sentimental novel has resulted in the removal of the stigma formerly associated with reading it, this recuperation has exacted a price. It has become much harder to account for the perversity of the sentimental and, therefore, much harder to read the complexities of the texts' deployment of sex and sexuality. The tear-jerking propensity of sentimental stories has been sanitized, perhaps, but other propensities have been lost in the wash. Domesticating the content of sentimental novels means that the homely garden fruit proffered to the seduced, betrayed, and pregnant Charlotte becomes less readable than it can be when we read sentimentality queerly.

I am using – perhaps abusing – the term "queer" to point to a destabilization of binaries, narrative expectations, and heteronormalizing character identities. The term has a vexed and useful history in many arenas of discourse, and this essay cannot begin to engage with all of them. My modest ambition is to apply its torque to generic assumptions and taxonomies typically assumed by readers of the kinds of novels and novel issues I am grappling with in this essay.

Sentimental narratives invite us to revel in pleasures we prefer not to acknowledge. The "seduced and betrayed" novel allows us to seduce and betray the heroine, for instance. It also allows us to seduce and *not* betray her, simultaneously, along with Mrs. Beauchamp and her cucumbers – to eat our cukes and have them too. In the instance of *Little Women*, we can cheer for the sentimental (and sadistic) pedagogy which transforms Jo into a more or less proper heterosexual woman (wife, mother) while simultaneously engaging, empathetically and viscerally, both her masochistic, tearful submission as well as her peculiar and peculiarly pleasurable resistances to it. "'Does genius burn Jo?'"[6] her sisters mischievously inquire, every few weeks, when "she would shut herself up in her room, put on her scribbling suit, and 'fall into a vortex,' as she expressed it . . . " (*Little Women*, 328), sometimes "writing away at her novel with all her heart and soul," sometimes "little romances" / "rubbish" for "The Spread Eagle" (295).[7]

A passionate young woman, secluded in her garret, burning with bliss as she falls into a vortex might well remind us of Eve Sedgwick's watershed analysis in "Jane Austen and the Masturbating Girl" (1991), an essay which contends that

> in our reimaginings of the history of sexuality "as" (we vainly imagine) "we know it," through readings of classic texts, the dropping out of sight of the autoerotic term is also part of what falsely naturalizes the heterosexist imposition of these books, disguising both the rich, conflictual erotic complication of a homoerotic matrix not yet crystallized in terms of "sexual identity," and the violence of heterosexist definition finally carved out of these plots.[8] (826)

There is indeed sex in the uncategorized novel entitled *Little Women*, in short, but perhaps there is none in the *domestic* novel of the same title.[9] The sex that is there inheres in the *modality* of the sentimental – by which term I mean to focus on the non-content elements of the sentimental – and intrudes queerly. Sex, auto-erotic, protolesbian, non-heterosex, is there in textual eruption, in language rather than content.

One more example of the kind of sex-intrusion I am pointing to in *Little Women*: "The Spread Eagle" is the outlet in which Jo publishes the romances and tales that (sentimentally enough) become "comforts for them all" (*Little Women*, 333). One tale pays the butcher's bill; another buys a new carpet; a third funds "groceries and gowns" (333). Thus, the generic content of these gothics and romances ("The Duke's Daughter," "A Phantom Hand," "The Curse of the Coventrys") is transformed "by the magic of a pen" into domestic content. As we absorb, and, possibly, palpitate with, the charming twist that sentimentalizes the lurid fiction Jo so enjoys writing, we experience a miniscule but noticeable pause – another speedbump – in the title of the paper. The *Oxford English Dictionary* provides as the first definition of "spread eagle" a description of the eagle with spread wings we know from the tops of flag poles everywhere.[10] It is the second definition that justifies the slight pause the reader experiences as she passes her eyes over the name of the story paper. This definition, "A person secured with the arms and legs stretched out, esp. in order to be flogged," was contemporaneous with Alcott's novel, and the perverse torque of the title she chooses for Jo's outlet was as available to Alcott as it is to us.

The telling detail that does not tell is another kind of manifestation of queer moments in novels otherwise classified as straight.[11] We might turn to Edith Wharton's *The House of Mirth* (1905) for one such detail: before she succumbs to an apparent overdose of chloral, Lily Bart wanders through the streets and is taken in momentarily by a protégé of her friend Gerty Farish. Nettie Struther is a young working-class woman who has worked her way out of despair, fallen-woman-ness, and poverty into sentimental working-class respectability largely due to Gerty and Lily's assistance. Lily warms herself in the Struther flat and holds Nettie's baby. Later, in her dying delirium, Lily finds that

> Nettie Struther's child was lying on her arm: she felt the pressure of its little head against her shoulder. She did not know how it had come there, but she felt no great surprise at the fact, only a gentle penetrating thrill of warmth and pleasure. She settled herself into an easier position, hollowing her arm to pillow the round downy head, and holding her breath lest a sound should disturb the sleeping child. (*The House of Mirth*, 263)

Lily's lack of surprise is not duplicated in the reader: Lily has not until now been presented as even faintly interested in children, much less interested enough to hold her breath for one. Yes, the words "thrill," "warmth," and "pleasure" are unsurprising as applied to Lily's history of desire; pillowing downy heads, however, is new. The baby is a conspicuous and odd presence in the climax of Lily's narrative.

Lily has just written a cheque that will restore her (financial) respectability and leave her utterly impoverished; she also has dangerously increased her nightly dose of chloral in order to induce the sleep she desperately needs. She is destitute due to a chain of events precipitated by her flight from Gus Trenor's adulterous heterosexual proposition: she has fled to Gerty Farish's apartment. Gerty is in love with Lawrence Selden; so is Lily. When Lily takes refuge with her, Gerty realizes that Lawrence loves Lily, and that she, Gerty, will never take Lily's place with him. Despite the torture that this realization is for her, Gerty soothes the hysterical Lily into bed and joins her in it. At first the heart-broken Gerty shrinks from Lily's conquering beauty, but relents when Lily "moan[s]": "'Hold me, Gerty, hold me, or I shall think of things'..." (136). And Gerty "silently slipped an arm under her, pillowing her head in its hollow as a mother makes a nest for a tossing child" (136).

When Lily adjusts her arm to pillow the head of the imaginary baby, she repeats the scene in which her head was similarly pillowed. The duplication merges, momentarily, these two women shut out of heterosexuality – one by virtue of an absence of heterosexual desirability; the other by virtue of a plenitude of heterosexual desirability.

The House of Mirth queries and interrogates heterosexuality and its complicit social institutions. Does the novel advocate for a different sexuality? No. Does it present us with suggestive moments of refusal and resistance complicated by verbal and visual deviations from both the happy and the star-crossed hetero-romance? Yes. Gerty and Lily, Lily and Nettie are conjoined, and in their comings together produce the phantom baby who comforts Lily in her last hours.

The House of Mirth was a bestseller in its time, as were *Charlotte Temple* and *Little Women*. They each tell a tale of a female character entangled in the more or less standard plots of heteronormativity. They each find ways to present their readers with odd moments in their protagonists' journeys into, through, and out of their predestined roles in heterosex. The novelists I have discussed chose to write in traditions that precluded the representation of literal sex, but certainly found ways to imply its presence. The sex-intrusions are presented deviously and include deviations, evasions, and outright refusals of heterosex.

Finally, I would like to say a parting word about Charlaine Harris's best-selling series, the first of which, *Dead Until Dark*, published in 2001, is a twenty-first-century woman's revisioning of the perennially popular vampire story. This is a genre marketed to an audience for which explicit sex is very much *de rigueur*.

Sookie Stackhouse is a barmaid living in a small town in northern Louisiana, and she has what she describes as a disability: she is telepathic. All day, every day, her mind is invaded by the thoughts of those around her. She experiences this telepathy, unsurprisingly, as intrusive and unpleasant – she is aware not only of how mundane and uninteresting much of the mental life of her friends and neighbors is, but also of the true results of the constant physical assessment of every man around her. This results, naturally enough, in behavior that earns her the label "Crazy Sookie" and a limited social life. As she puts it, explaining why she has never looked at her boss Sam as a "beddable man":

> I never looked at anyone that way, not because I don't have hormones – boy, do I have hormones – but they are constantly tamped down because sex, for me, is a disaster. Can you imagine knowing everything your sex partner is thinking? Right. Along the order of "Gosh, look at that mole . . . her butt is a little big . . . wish she'd move to the right a little . . . why doesn't she take the hint and . . . ?" You get the idea. It's chilling to the emotions, believe me. (*Dead until Dark*, 25)

Then, one day, "HE" walks into her bar.

"HE" is a vampire. *And* she cannot hear his thoughts.

Long story short, they become lovers and in this and every succeeding novel in the series, Sookie has wonderful sex, finds and loses romantic love, gets lusted after by both appropriate and inappropriate objects, remains monogamous (albeit serially), gets beaten up, is targeted for death, beats people (and other beings) up, escapes death, helps others escape death, kills the occasional sentient being, and learns what to wear to fangbanger bars and royal summit meetings. Through it all she remains a down-to-earth, albeit telepathic, blue-collar working gal – who just happens to solve crimes while sleeping with and fending off sleeping with vampires and were-people. In both her working lives – the human and the supernatural – her body is an asset: being attractive to humans results in more income at the bar; being attractive to vampires initiates her more lucrative but more sporadic second shift job.

Nina Auerbach in *Our Vampires, Ourselves* asserts that in both British and American stories, vampires "turn to women to perform the extreme implications of their monstrosity" (7). There are vampires in Sookie's world – right *next to her* usually. And shapeshifters and werewolves and goblins and witches and fairies. But mostly, the Sookieverse revels in the essentially scary, more or less than human, definitely not entirely straight nature of female sexuality.

Not for nothing does Vampire Bill ask her three different times in the first novel: "What are you?" Sookie, despite her occasional doubts (which make us identify with her all the more), is really good at being a Woman: a working girl with good strong blue-collar values, but one whose sentimental desire to be Good is not in conflict with her nonheterosex activities and desires, which are directed toward and performed with (mostly) dead guys.

> I raised my head from his neck, and a wave of dark delight carried me out to sea.
>
> This was pretty exotic stuff for a telepathic barmaid from northern Louisiana. (197)

Exotic, yes. And not precisely heterosexual despite the presence of two morphologically different bodies.

Leslie Fiedler taught us to read certain components of American literature as composing and participating in an American myth of homoerotic, cross-ethnic camaraderie between boy-men running away from Aunt Sally's "sivilization," and toward the frontier. Annette Kolodny has taught us ways to read the sources of that myth and the materials from which it is constructed as inflected by gender and sexuality. The American landscape is feminized in our literature; the story of civilizing the frontier is homologous to that of masculine heterosexuality. "The metaphorical experience of 'the land-as-woman'" (*The Lay of the Land*, 158), Kolodny argues, underscores our canonical literature and, therefore, our canonized experience. "At its core," says Kolodny, "lay a yearning to know and to respond to the landscape as feminine, a yearning that I have labeled as the uniquely American 'pastoral impulse'" (8). Gendering the land was nothing new; what is new in America is "the revival of that linguistic habit on the level of personal experience" (8). For both Fiedler and Kolodny, then, the American hero in American literature generally runs away from heterosexuality.

Louisa May Alcott's novel *Little Women* has usually been read as a story of reaching heterosexual maturity and *refraining* from lighting out for the Territory. But, as we have seen, there are other territories lurking within novels written by women. Fiedler was writing well before the beginning of the tidal wave of feminist re-readings and revisionings that we now call the Second Wave. It is not news to anyone now, one hopes, that there are female characters in American novels who are in search of equivalents to Huck's raft – who seek to evade if not confound the cultural narrative of heterosexuality. And they do it within genres that are not typically classified as the rebellion stories so dear to the hearts of American critics and scholars.[12] In popular American novels written by women, the female protagonist's alternative to "sivilization" (i.e. heteronormative lives) often turns out to be death (for example, Little Eva, Edna Pontellier, Clare Kendry . . .). Some, however, survive their inscription into heterosexuality. In both plot lines, heterosexuality is hard on heroines, but even when they survive it, not absolutely triumphant. If we can see around and through our taxonomic pieties to return to the messy peculiarities of texts by women novelists, if we can retreat from our once-strategic political and rhetorical classification systems and instead charge forward (or backward) into sheer textuality, we may (re)discover the hidden pleasures of cucumbers, spread eagles, invisible babies, nonhuman sex.

Am I suggesting that when women novelists write sex, there is always something queer going on? And how would this suggestion work with "the lesbian novel"? On the one hand, Terry Castle's insistence that Queer Theory's tendencies contribute to the "ghosting" of the lesbian is persuasive (*The Apparitional Lesbian*, 13). On the other hand, Martha Vicinus, pondering the limiting nature of labels of sexual identity, argues that "lesbian history is best understood as part of a larger history of women" (*Intimate Friends*, xxiii). Insofar as the "speedbumps" I isolate above are reactions to the constraints of a sexual identity label, and given that "the lesbian novel" is inevitably a presexualized taxonomic label, one would expect to find literary lesbian versions of cucumbers and spread eagles, if not invisible babies and nonhuman sex. It remains to be seen if looking for what I am calling "queer intrusions"[13] in lesbian novels by American women (or American novels by lesbian women) might produce oscillations and resistances similar to those in *Charlotte Temple*, *Little Women*, *The House of Mirth*, and *Dead until Dark*. To answer this question, it seems to me, one must perform slow, close reading in spite of or at least adjacent to whatever taxonomic labels have been affixed to a given text or texts. In other words, I want to argue that the question to carry from my readings above to, say, *Nightwood* or *O Pioneers!* is not so much "Does it work on lesbian novels/novelists?" but "What are this particular novel's 'speedbumps?'"; not "Are lesbian novels Queer?" but "What is queer in this novel?"

In short, do lesbian novels by women resist lesbian sex the way heterosexual novels by women resist heterosex? Can we, should we assume that lesbian novels (if we know what those are) by American women writers are hegemonic as to sex while nonlesbian novels (if we know what *those* are) by American women writers are not?

Reader, I query you.

Notes

1. And this includes, of course, writing *against* it.
2. See Homestead and Hansen, "Susanna Rowson's Transatlantic Career," for a review of differing claims made for the status of both the novel and the novelist, and for an extensive and illuminating analysis of the process by which Rowson constructed her career.
3. This is a stanza from a ballad almost certainly of Rowson's own composing, as she was a prolific poet and lyric writer. Elias Nason describes it thus: "The plaintive song of the heroine in the twentieth chapter is in Mrs. Rowson's happiest vein" (*Memoir of Mrs. Susanna Rowson*, 51). Susanna Rowson is generally considered the first professional writer in America. She wrote novels, poetry, plays, and textbooks; she also acted on the stage and wrote lyrics for the stage music of the companies she worked with, and was a pioneer in the movement for the serious education of women, founding and teaching in her own vastly successful "Young Ladies Academy" of Boston. She supported her husband, his illegitimate son, a sister-in-law, three nieces, and an adopted daughter through her literary, theatrical, and pedagogical careers. Her own experience of heterosexual institutions may well be summed up in her advice on marriage: "Do not

marry a fool," reported by Ann Douglas in her wide-ranging and valuable introduction to *Charlotte Temple and Lucy Temple*. *Charlotte Temple* was first published in the USA in 1794 (1791 in England); *Lucy Temple* was first published in 1828 in the USA as *Charlotte's Daughter: The Three Orphans*.

4. "Gerard's *Herball* (1597) contains the first detailed instructions for hotbeds used for growing cucumbers . . . All of the ancient Roman writers on agriculture mention the cucumber. Marcus Terentius Varro (116–27 BCE) gives the Latin name of *Curvimur* for the cucumber, referring to the curvature of the fruit. The Greek name for cucumber is *sikys*, meaning the plant has no aphrodisiac qualities, hence the Greek proverb, *Let a woman weaving a cloak eat a cucumber; because female weavers, if we believe Aristotle, are unchaste, and eager for love making*. It was introduced to England during the reign of Edward III but was lost during the mayhem of the Hundred Year War and reintroduced during the reign of Henry VIII in the 16th century" (Greene, "Gardening Under Cover").

5. In *Daughters, Fathers, and the Novel*, I argue that sentimentality *is* heterosexuality. For other examples of arguably perverse readings of the sentimental, see Burgett, *Sentimental Bodies*; Brissenden, *Virtue in Distress*; Hagstrum, *Sex and Sensibility*; and Noble, *The Masochistic Pleasures of Sentimental Literature*.

6. For an excellent discussion of the queer valences of this word in *Little Women*, see Stadler, "Louisa May Alcott's Queer Geniuses."

7. She stores her manuscripts in an "old tin kitchen in the garret" – suggestive of a wonderful mélange of the privileged feminine spaces of domestic and sentimental women's novels.

8. In this essay, Sedgwick also praises Paula Bennett's work on Emily Dickinson as offering "a model for understanding the bedrock, quotidian, sometimes very sexually fraught, female homosocial networks in relation to the more visible and spectacular-ized, more narratable, but less intimate, heterosexual plots of pre-twentieth-century Anglo-American culture" ("Jane Austen and the Masturbating Girl," 824). Eve Sedgwick was one of the founders of queer theory, an ardent and passionate close reader, and a rebel against pieties and easy binaries wherever she found them. Her contribution to literary, cultural, and sexuality studies is revolutionary and unparalleled.

9. See also Doyle, "Jo March's Love Poems," Kent, *Making Girls into Women*, and Quimby, "The Story of Jo," for readings locating *Little Women* as a lesbian novel.

10. This definition includes a reference to a figure in ice skating, which reminds us of the ice-skating accident Jo's anger rather magically causes the manuscript-burning Amy to experience.

11. Cf. "'The story *won't* tell' said Douglas; 'not in any literal, vulgar way'" (James, *The Turn of the Screw*, 3).

12. See Nina Baym's celebrated, "Melodramas of Beset Manhood" for the germinal reading of this predilection.

13. My choice of the lower case is deliberate and tendentious.

Works cited

Alcott, Louisa M. *Little Women*. 1868–9. New York: Modern Library, 1983.
Auerbach, Nina. *Our Vampires, Ourselves*. Chicago: University of Chicago Press, 1997.

Barnard, Ian. "Queer Race." *Social Semiotics* 9.2 (1999): 199–212.

Baym, Nina. "Melodramas of Beset Manhood: How Theories of American Fiction Exclude Women Authors." *American Quarterly* 33.2 (1981): 123–39.

Brissenden, F. *Virtue in Distress: Studies in the Novel of Sentiment from Richardson to Sade.* New York: Harper & Row, 1974.

Burgett, Bruce. *Sentimental Bodies: Sex, Gender, and Citizenship in the Early Republic.* Princeton: Princeton University Press, 1998.

Castelli, Elizabeth A. "History's Queer Touch: A Forum on Carolyn Dinshaw's *Getting Medieval: Sexualities and Communities, Pre- and Postmodern.*" *Journal of the History of Sexuality* 10.2 (2001): 165–212.

Castle, Terry. *The Apparitional Lesbian: Female Homosexuality and Modern Culture.* New York: Columbia University Press, 1993.

Douglas, Ann. "Introduction." In *Charlotte Temple and Lucy Temple.* New York: Penguin Books, 1991.

Doyle, Jennifer. "Jo March's Love Poems." *Nineteenth-Century Literature* 60.3 (2005): 375–402.

Fiedler, Leslie. *Love and Death in the American Novel.* New York: Stein and Day, 1960.

Greene, Wesley. "Gardening Under Cover." *Garden Smart.* <www.gardensmart.tv/?p=articles&title=Under_Cover_Colonial Williamsburg> (accessed December 15, 2010).

Hagstrum, Jean H. *Sex and Sensibility: Ideal and Erotic Love from Milton to Mozart.* Chicago: University of Chicago Press, 1980.

Harris, Charlaine. *Dead until Dark.* London: Little, Brown, 2004.

Homestead, Melissa J. and Camryn Hansen. "Susanna Rowson's Transatlantic Career." *Early American Literature.* 45.3 (2010): 619–54.

James, Henry. *The Turn of the Screw.* 1898. New York: W. W. Norton, 1999.

Kent, Kathryn R. *Making Girls into Women: American Women's Writing and the Rise of Lesbian Identity.* Durham, NC: Duke University Press, 2003.

Kolodny, Annette. *The Lay of the Land: Metaphor as Experience and History in American Life and Letters.* Durham, NC: University of North Carolina Press, 1984.

Nason, Elias. *Memoir of Mrs. Susanna Rowson, with Elegant and Illustrative Extracts from her Writing in Prose and Poetry.* Albany, NY: Joel Munsell, 1870.

Noble, Marianne. *The Masochistic Pleasures of Sentimental Literature.* Princeton: Princeton University Press, 2000.

Quimby, Karin. "The Story of Jo: Literary Tomboys, Little Women, and the Sexual-Textual Politics of Narrative Desire." *GLQ: A Journal of Lesbian and Gay Studies* 10.1 (2003): 1–22.

Rich, Adrienne. "Compulsory Heterosexuality and Lesbian Existence (1980)." *Journal of Women's History* 15.3 (2003): 11–48.

Rofel, Lisa. "Queering Euro-American Jews." *GLQ: A Journal of Lesbian and Gay Studies* 11.3 (2005): 476–8.

Rowson, Susanna. *Charlotte Temple and Lucy Temple.* 1794; 1828. Ed. Intro. Ann Douglas. New York: Penguin Books, 1991.

Rupp, Leila J., ed. "Women's History in the New Millennium: Adrienne Rich's 'Compulsory Heterosexuality and Lesbian Existence': A Retrospective." *Journal of Women's History* 15.3 (2003): 7–89.

Schewe, Elizabeth. "Serious Play: Drag, Transgender, and the Relationship between Performance and Identity in the Life Writing of RuPaul and Kate Bornstein." *Biography: An Interdisciplinary Quarterly* 32.4 (2009): 670–95.

Sedgwick, Eve Kosofsky. "Jane Austen and the Masturbating Girl." *Critical Inquiry* 17.4 (1991): 818–37.

Showalter, Elaine, ed. *The New Feminist Criticism: Essays on Women, Literature, and Theory.* New York: Pantheon Books, 1985.

Stadler, Gustavus. "Louisa May Alcott's Queer Geniuses." *American Literature* 71.4 (1999): 657–77.

Vicinus, Martha. *Intimate Friends: Women Who Loved Women, 1778–1928.* Chicago: University of Chicago Press, 2004.

Wharton, Edith. *The House of Mirth.* 1905. Mineola, NY: Dover Publications, 2002.

Zwinger, Lynda. *Daughters, Fathers, and the Novel: The Sentimental Romance of Heterosexuality.* Madison: University of Wisconsin Press, 1991.

30

Latina writers and the usable past

KIMBERLY O'NEILL

During her confirmation hearings in June of 2009, Supreme Court Justice Sonia Sotomayor became infamous for arguing that the experiences of a "wise Latina woman" could make her a more effective judge and an important voice in the US judiciary (Sotomayor, "A Latina Judge's Voice," 92). Sotomayor's remarks suggest how histories of migration, marginalization, and misogyny prepare Latinas to intervene in the political future of the USA. Her assertion that Latina identity has intellectual and ethical utility mirrors that of generations of Latina and Chicana artists, writers, and thinkers who have traced the historical dimensions of *Latinidad*. They have mined pre-Columbian mythologies, the competing imperialisms of Spain, Britain, and the USA, and centuries of turbulent hemispheric politics to understand their implications for the Latin American diaspora and especially for women.[1]

This essay focuses on the political movements and crises that provoked dialogue among women writers of multiple national and cultural identifications, among them Mexican and Chicana, Cuban American, Puerto Rican, Salvadoran, and Dominican. Particularly in the past thirty years, these authors and poets have developed rhetorical and political practices in response to shared conflicts and in conversation with one another. That conversation comprises the literary history of Latinas and Chicanas and the usable past they have constructed.[2]

Origins

A distinctive Chicana and Latina corpus first emerged in response to the civil rights discourses of the 1960s Chicano and Feminist Movements. Latina activists were inspired by these coalitions – along with allied movements such as the Black Panthers and Young Lords – but argued that the masculinist, heteronormative rhetoric of *El Movimiento* and the white bias of 1960s feminism undermined their objectives. Chicana writers such as Gloria Anzaldúa and Cherríe Moraga recuperated the strengths of *Chicanismo* – especially its struggle for workers' rights, social justice, and its defense of Chicana/o culture, identity, and community – but criticized its sublimation of women and queers.[3] Blending the genres of poetry, narrative, and essay, Moraga's *Loving in the War Years: lo que nunca pasó por sus labios* (1983) theorizes Chicana lesbianism as an act of cultural resistance. Searching for community in memories of her mother, exploring spirituality through Aztec mythological heritage, and analyzing race as a *güera/mestiza*, Moraga recounts her individual history as a piece of the intersecting histories of women of color and oppressed peoples in and beyond the USA.

Perhaps the most quoted and anthologized Chicana feminist writer, Gloria Anzaldúa grounds her central text, *Borderlands/La frontera: The New Mestiza* (1987), in her memories of growing up in Texas and in her collaboration with third-world women and lesbian communities, especially in the landmark anthology *This Bridge Called My Back: Writings by Radical Women of Color* (1981). Inspired by Moraga, *Borderlands* is a collage of poetry, memoir, essay, and theory in multiple dialects of English and Spanish. Anzaldúa's imagined history migrates from 1950s Texas to the clash between indigenous peoples and conquistadors during Spanish colonization in the sixteenth century. The racial and cultural *mestizaje* that characterizes Latin America and its diasporas begins with this violent contact between "old" and "new" worlds.

Along with many other Chicana writers, Gloria Anzaldúa explores this point of origin through the legend of la Malinche (1505–51).[4] (Fig. 30.1.) La Malinche was born into a prominent Nahua family and stolen or sold into slavery by the Mayans, who in turn gave her to Hernán Cortés. Because she spoke both Nahua and Maya, la Malinche translated for Cortés as he conquered the Aztecs. La Malinche has since become a symbol of the rape of indigenous America. Anzaldúa writes, "Not me sold out my people but they me. *Malinali Tenepat*, or *Malintzin*, has become known as *la Chingada* – the fucked one. She has become the bad word that passes a dozen times a day from the lips of Chicanos. Whore, prostitute, the woman who sold out her people to the Spaniards are epithets Chicanos spit out with contempt" (*Borderlands*, 22). La Malinche is mythologized as the mother of all *mestizos*. As Anzaldúa argues, her story reflects a gendered history of conquest in which the indigenous woman is cast as a betrayer. Along with Anzaldúa, Chicana writers such as Cherríe Moraga and Pat Mora and artists such as

Fig. 30.1 "La Malinche" by Santa Barraza (1991)

Santa Contreras Barraza have recuperated la Malinche, and her allegorical sister La Llorona, as feminine subjects who defy the power of colonizers and patriarchs alike.

Just as la Malinche embodies the contradictory position of women in Latin America, other iconic women have served as forebears and symbols for contemporary Latina writers. Sor Juana Inés de la Cruz (1648–95), a Spanish nun, author, poet, and champion of education in colonial Mexico, is often cited as the first woman writer in the New World and a literary ancestress of modern Latin American and Latina writers. Alicia Gaspar de Alba and Estela Portillo Trambley have examined her life and its resonance for Chicanas.[5] The mythical Virgin of Guadalupe, said to appear before an indigenous Mexican campesino named Juan Diego in 1531, blends the Virgin Mary with sacred feminine images from Mexican indigenous cultures. Like la Malinche, the Virgin of Guadalupe is a fraught figure for Chicanas.[6] As a Catholic symbol of sexual purity and submission, the Catholic virgin seems to enact male fantasies of female passivity, but the indigenous goddesses who inspire the Virgin of Guadalupe signify female power beyond the grasp of Spanish colonialism or heteropatriarchy.[7]

Historical and mythological icons such as la Malinche, Sor Juana, and the Virgin of Guadalupe have been central to the dialogue between Chicana writers and theorists of Latina/o ethnicity and culture. Writers such as Emma Pérez have followed Anzaldúa's example by publishing both fiction and critical scholarship. Pérez, for example, published her first novel *Gulf Dreams* in 1996 and her scholarly monograph, *The Decolonial Imaginary*, in 1999. Chicana feminism has inspired key literary scholars such as Rosaura Sánchez and Norma Alarcón, even as Chicana writers have collaborated with Nuyoricans like Sandra María Esteves, whose "My Name is Maria Christina" (1980) is among the most widely read poems of the Nuyorican Poets Café. For all of these writers, the concept of *mestizaje* – the race mixture of African, indigenous, and European races – is a vital analogy for the cultural hybridity of contemporary Latinas. As Rafael Pérez-Torres explains, "The transnationality of [Latina/o] identity manifests the idea of mixture. The linguistic interplay between Spanish, English, and [indigenous languages] illustrates the synthesis of this identity in expression. The uniquely hybrid nature of [Latina/o] culture is discussed as a correlative to the racial condition of mestizaje" (*Mestizaje*, xi). Latina writers have described their bodies as traces of Spanish colonization and indigenous oppression; *mestiza* subjectivity reconciles the multiple, often-conflicting allegiances that diasporic peoples experience. Furthermore, writers such as Moraga and Anzaldúa have connected the fluid and "transgressive" identity of *mestizas* to that of queer women of color (Pérez-Torres, *Mestizaje*, 155).

Puerto Rican mother and daughter Rosario and Aurora Levins Morales have long been celebrated for their groundbreaking collaborative work *Getting Home Alive* (1986), which explores the relationship between Puerto Rican and US subjectivity and its impact on their lives as Boricua women, Jewish Americans, mother and daughter. The text, like Anzaldúa's *Borderlands* or Cherríe Moraga's *Loving in the War Years*, intermixes poetry and prose to represent the multiplicity of *mestiza* identity. In their widely read and anthologized "Ending Poem" from *Getting Home Alive*, Morales and Levins Morales list the array of identifications that describe children "of the Americas." The poem collapses the imperial legacies of Spain and the USA in the Caribbean with the racial legacy of empire in contemporary New York:

I am what I am.
A child of the Americas.
A light-skinned mestiza of the Caribbean.
A child of many diaspora, born into this continent at a crossroads.
I am Puerto Rican. I am US American.
I am New York Manhattan and the Bronx.   (212)

The polyvocal narrator locates herself in multiple geographies, using the metaphor of the crossroads to signal the intersection between the east to west migration of Jewish diasporas and enslaved Africans with the south to north (and back again) travel of Puerto Rican migrants. The poem goes on to recount the authors' diverse connections with these ancestral travelers – indigenous Taínos, Africans, Europeans: "I am the child of many mothers. / *They have kept it all going* / All the civilizations erected on their backs." The poem ends with the assertion that *"History made us. . . . And we are whole"* (212). In this way the authors position themselves – not as global citizens or even Latinas – but as children of history, complete even in their transnational ancestries. Their insistence on the present tense suggests the current importance of these repressed and distorted histories.

Histories

In his preface to the brand new *Norton Anthology of Latino Literature* (2010), Ilan Stavans identifies the 1980s as the decade in which Latina / o literature becomes "mainstream" (lvi). The 1980s saw a torrent of celebrated Latina novels, stories, poetry, memoirs, and fictional memoirs, including prominent books by Judith Ortiz Cofer, Ana Castillo, and Helena María Viramontes.[8] These writers laid the groundwork for the historical novels that have dominated Latina literary production in the 1990s and 2000s, many of which deal explicitly with racial, cultural, and individual memory during the state-sponsored imperialism and xenophobia of the "American century."

Historical novels by US Dominican author Julia Alvarez, Cuban Americans Cristina García and Achy Obejas, Chicana Sandra Cisneros, and Salvadoran American Sandra Benítez (among many others) trace the connections between US power in the hemisphere and the lives of the contemporary Latin American diaspora. These writers have located the US national climate of hostility toward Latin American peoples in the narratives of violence by which Americans have come to understand their southern neighbors.[9] They have returned again and again to this genealogy to upset its entrenched assumptions and to explore the ramifications of that racial narrative for Latina/o identities and communities.

Occupied by the empires of Spain, France, and later the USA, the Dominican Republic's colonial history has played a key role in the race, class, and gender structures of its citizens. Perhaps the most dramatic exemplar of that historical clash has been Rafael Trujillo, whose dictatorship enjoyed US support from his coup in 1930 until his assassination in 1961. Trujillo's racism, military authoritarianism, and exploitation of women have scarred the people who lived under his regime.

To recover these silenced voices from the censorship of the Trujillo regime and to represent the cultural relationship of the DR and the USA, Dominican American writers such as Nellie Rosario, Loida Maritza Pérez, Angie Cruz, and Julia Alvarez have turned to fiction. Rosario's *Song of the Water Saints* (2002) reconstructs the lives of Dominican women during the US occupation of the DR in the 1920s and the consequent Trujillo Regime, while Cruz's *Soledad* (2002) and Pérez's *Geographies of Home* (1999) imagine the contemporary DR as a site of both fracture and healing for Dominican migrant families in New York.

Among the most widely read and commercially successful Dominican writers, Julia Alvarez focuses on the political agency of Dominican women. As Alvarez explains the impetus for her historical writing, "You wouldn't know it from reading the official stories, but Latin America has had its share of amazing women" (juliaalvarez.com). Her historical novels, *In the Time of the Butterflies* (1994) and *In the Name of Salomé* (2000), tell the fictional tales of real Dominican women who participated in nationalist revolutions: Salomé Ureña's poetry inspired the future of the Dominican nation and her advocacy fostered its education system. In 1960, the Mirabal sisters were assassinated by the Trujillato as vengeance for their participation in insurrectionary activities. The regime fell less than a year later. Alvarez's immigrant narratives, *How the García Girls Lost their Accents* (1991) and its sequel *¡Yo!* (1997), build on Dominican history and US culture to expose the harmful unequal power relations between the USA and the DR, as well as those between upper and lower classes, whites and nonwhites, and men and women in both countries.

The four García girls suffer visibly from the trauma of exile.[10] Alvarez describes this strain through the girls' nightmarish memories of the Trujillo regime. The USA offers refuge from the regime, but the Garcías' poverty as recent immigrants and their isolation from culture and family offer little solace. The García girls soon lose themselves in the paralyzing clash between the prescriptive gender roles and sexual scruples of Dominican culture and the US liberal feminist "freedom" that celebrates heteronormative pleasure and demonizes religiosity and sexual conservatism. The novel proceeds in reverse chronological order, uncovering details from the Garcías's past to illustrate the ongoing consequences of US imperialism and xenophobia in their lives as immigrants. Alvarez alludes to US military and economic control of the hemisphere through the trauma caused by Trujillo. She also registers the sexualized racism that has enabled US imperialism and continues to taint attitudes toward immigrants like the Garcías. Their yearning for individualism and their rampant consumerism signal their contradictory positions as women, racialized and classed differently in the DR and the USA. The four girls try to maneuver within race, gender, and class prescriptions, but their unhappiness – and nervous breakdowns – serve as symptoms for the inescapability of these identifications.

In one scene from the four girls' childhood, Carla García encounters an American pedophile when she walks home from school. As a Latina child in the foreign United States, Carla has been bullied by white boys at her Catholic school, is far from fluent in English, and finds herself alone on the streets of New York: "Carla dreaded being asked directions since she had just moved into this area right before school started, and all she knew for sure was the route home from the bus stop. Besides, her English was still just classroom English, a foreign language" (*How the García Girls Lost their Accents*, 156). Here the child Carla fails to perceive the sexual threat embodied by the American man. She feels apologetic for her inadequacy as an American; Carla only sees the danger when confronted directly by the man's nakedness.

The trauma of this moment is prolonged when her mother calls the police. These men comprise a visible and known threat to Carla. Alvarez writes that "Carla and her sisters feared the American police almost as much as the SIM [Trujillo's secret police] back home" (158). The officers probe her uncertain English for the sexual language she does not understand. They reinforce Carla's powerlessness by representing the knowledge and power of the institutional state. This power echoes that of the Trujillato, and Carla feels the crosscurrents between old country and new in the masculine authority that subjects her to its scrutiny.

Carla's sexualized fear remains long after the police withdraw. "The cop snapped his pad closed, and each officer gave Carla and her mother a salute of farewell. They drove off in their squad car, and all down the block, drapes fell back to rest, half-opened shades closed like eyes that saw no evil" (164). Alvarez portrays Carla, Yolanda, and the other sisters as vulnerable subjects that operate under the constant threat of attack. In this scene, they feel both watched and unprotected. Neither the police nor their neighbors are allies. The isolation the Garcías feel in the Trujillo DR migrates with them to the USA, illustrating the power of past trauma in the present.

Alvarez's novels dramatize the consequences of hemispheric politics for migrant peoples. Similarly, Cuban American writers have focused on the cultural aftermath of the animosity between the USA and Cuban dictator Fidel Castro. Few scholars have explored the place of the Cold War in Latina literary expression. The Cold War has structured US political and cultural relations with Latin America since the CIA overthrew left-leaning Guatemalan president Jacobo Arbenz in 1954. Following the 1959 Cuban Revolution, the USA responded to the rise of Castro by welcoming refugees from his "Red" regime.

In the coming decades, Cuban exiles have congregated in US cities, especially Miami, where they have spoken out against Castro in periodicals and propaganda. These exiles have registered their relationship to Cuba as one of loss – families and communities torn apart by the revolution. The children of exiles, however, experience a very different relationship with Cuba: one of kinship, desire, and curiosity in addition to loss. Cristina García's *Dreaming in Cuban* (1992) inaugurated a new era in Cuban American literature. Women writers like García, Achy Obejas, and Ana Menéndez explore daughters of exile who long for reconciliation but criticize the disappointments of the Castro regime: its delusions and especially its hostility toward transgender subjects. Furthermore, they represent the revolutionary present as coeval with the post-Cold War triumph of capitalism in the USA.[11]

García's *Dreaming in Cuban* and *The Agüero Sisters* (1997) follow the lives of families split by the revolution. In Havana, Miami, or New York, mothers and daughters, sisters, fathers, and sons feel the ongoing effects of the historic clash between left and right, north and south. Like García, Achy Obejas explores the lives of Cuban exiles and their descendants in the USA, illustrating the displacement, nostalgia, despair, and hope fueled by Castro's triumph. Obejas's novels, *Memory Mambo* (1996) and *Days of Awe* (2003), refuse to relegate revolutionary Cuba to foreign space or past tense. Instead, she exposes the temporal disconnection between the curiosity of Cuban American daughters and the nostalgia of their parents. *Days of Awe* also portrays post-revolutionary Cuba and its mutually antagonistic and dependent relationship with the USA. In much of her work, Obejas describes the sense of alienation her protagonists feel as Cuban Americans, lesbians, and women, never feeling completely Cuban or American.

"Is life destiny or determination?" (*We Came All the Way From Cuba So You Could Dress Like This?*, 115). In the title story from her first collection, "We came all the way from Cuba so you could dress like this?," Achy Obejas rethinks the history of the Cuban Revolution through the unanswered questions of one child refugee. As a Cuban American lesbian, the daughter of exiled parents, a social justice activist, and a traveler, Obejas's nameless narrator explores the big and small events that have shaped her life, the moments that have determined "who I am" (125). She connects these scenes with a few stark images: the green sweater she wears during her voyage from Cuba to the USA and a blond doll she receives from an immigration officer. Her rhetorical questions signal Obejas's resistance to the teleology imposed on her story by US officials, even by her parents. She rejects solutions and conclusions and protects the problems, contradictions, and questions at the heart of her Cuban counter-history.

The tale defies the logic of chronology; the narrator mixes the story of her first day in the USA with reflections on lovers, lingering over revealing scenes with her parents. Obejas narrates the past in present tense:

> As I speak, my parents are being interrogated by an official from the office of Immigration and Naturalization Services. It's all a formality because this is 1963, and no Cuban claiming political asylum actually gets turned away. We're evidence that the revolution has failed the middle class and that communism is bad. My parents – my father's an accountant and my mother's a social worker – are living, breathing examples of the suffering Cubans have endured under the tyranny of Fidel Castro. (113)

This passage evokes the contrast between undesirable immigrants – Mexican "wetbacks" and Central American refugees from civil war and genocide – and Cubans, whose "suffering" under the "tyranny" of Castro makes them powerful symbols worthy of material consideration. The narrator notes that even as her parents have symbolic value for the US government, she has symbolic value for her parents: "We came for her, so she could have a future" (114). Her parents dream of the money she will make and the family she will have, but both their daughter and their new country disappoint. The narrator remembers (in future tense) how she has defied her parents with her hippy clothing, lesbianism, and leftist politics. When her father asks the central question of the story, "We came all the way from Cuba so you could dress like this?," she rejects their dreams by replying: "Look, you didn't come for me, you came for you; you came because all your rich clients were leaving, and you were going to wind up a cashier in your father's hardware store if you didn't leave, okay? . . . It's a free country, I can do anything I want, remember?" (121). To stave off their disappointment, her parents grasp for resolutions, nostalgic fantasies of return, but all the narrator finds are more unanswered questions. She does not know what would happen if her parents never left Cuba or if Castro never came to power, but she does know that these events have shaped her future.

The historical project of writers like Obejas and García is multifarious: their historical novels restore the Cuban present from its relegation to the days of yore, a relic of the bygone Cold War. They also reconstruct the Cuban American past. Scholars such as Emma Pérez and Kirsten Silva Gruesz have argued that conventional US history denies an American past to Latina/os, especially women.[12] By insisting on the entwined histories of Cuba and the USA and connecting them with the lives of Cuban American women in the contemporary era, these authors reveal the covert power of the USA in the hemisphere and recuperate the place of Cuba in the USA.

Perhaps the most deliberately historiographical Latina writer is Sandra Cisneros, whose epic *Caramelo* (2003) builds on the historical methods of the novelists who precede her. Cisneros revises official narratives of the Mexican Revolution – a hemispheric event long ignored in orthodox US history – through historical fiction, tracing its legacies for Mexican Americans and women in particular. *Caramelo* interweaves the family history of Celaya (named after the 1915 battle) with the tangled history of Mexico and the USA. Celaya's grandfather Narciso, like Juan Rubio in Villarreal's *Pocho* (1959), alters the course of generations when he leaves war-torn Mexico during the revolution. Cisneros's *Caramelo* returns to revolutionary Mexico to revise the racialized narratives by which the USA made that conflict legible. Gone are the voiceless peons and the militant *indios*, the bullet-festooned rebels, the stodgy generals, the corrupt dictators, the opulent *hacendados*. Instead, Cisneros views the Mexican middle and working classes as the progenitors of contemporary Mexican American culture. Her novel explores subjects who are poor but not abject, soldiers who feared to fight, and women who defied relegation to swooning aristocracy or mercenary prostitution. Further, Cisneros recalls the role that US interventionism played in and after the revolution. Woodrow Wilson serves as the US counterpart to Mexican dictator Porfirio Díaz. For Cisneros, Mexican history is neither insular nor dependent, but transcendent and entangled.

Caramelo's genealogy ties the racial discourses of revolution to the cultural specificity of Chicana/os. The novel's protagonist and narrator, Celaya, employs the history of her family to understand her childhood and adult identity. She writes: "I don't know how it is with anyone else, but for me these things, that song, that time, that place, are all bound together in a country I am homesick for, that doesn't exist anymore. That never existed. A country I invented. Like all emigrants caught between here and there" (*Caramelo*, 434). In this section Cisneros blends her voice with that of her narrator. Both are writers. Both have intermingled fact and fiction to collect the tangled plots and characters that make up *Caramelo*. Furthermore, Cisneros argues here that all migrants invent a homeland, something to be "homesick for." For both Cisneros and Celaya, the Mexican Revolution serves as the moment of rupture, the paradigm shift that galvanizes migration and the trauma that erases old histories, making room for new ones.

Caramelo is also a story of women – campesinas who marry into wealthy families, mothers who survive the revolution by any means necessary, illegitimate and legitimate daughters, and finally a young woman whose history is both Mexican and American. She builds the story from the partial facts and pure *cuento* she has gathered from her elders, and so also finds herself an actor in the national, cultural, and gendered drama she creates.

Celaya is to be the success story built on so many struggles, or so she believes. Standing at a balcony on a hotel in the Zócalo, Celaya feels grateful for a freedom that she does not really possess:

> But I'm thinking of the women, the ones who had no choice but to jump from these bell towers not so long ago, so many they had to stop letting visitors go up there. Maybe they'd run off or been run off. Who knows? Women whose lives were so lousy, jumping from a tower sounded good. And here I am leaning on an iron balustrade at the holy center of the universe, a boy with his hands under my skirt, and me with no intention of leaping for nothing or nobody. (383)

She compares herself to women who would throw themselves from the bell towers, unable to imagine their alternatives as Mexican women. In the Zócalo, a monumental square and the heart of the nation built on the site of violent cultural memories, Celaya believes herself free from their legacy. Yet Celaya, like millions of men and women before her, is caught in the systemic strictures that enfold Mexico and the USA. Her migration between countries has not secured her equity as a woman. In Mexico, her family is respectable but penniless. In the USA, the family makes money enough, but is marked by their dependence on the upholstery trade (leftover furnishings even fill their house). Their home itself is a motley structure, built in pieces for a family that is forever spilling out.

Caramelo insists on the mutually constitutive relationship among literature, history, and identity. The novel is replete with references to race and color. Cisneros builds on US accounts of the Mexican Indian, using Spanish-inflected English to underscore the mingling of US and Mexican racial traditions.[13] Cisneros plays with such rhetorical slippage through Celaya's translation of Candelaria. Candelaria is the dark sister, beautiful but inscrutable in the racial hierarchy that Celaya has inherited: "Her mother, the washerwoman Amparo, comes every week on Monday, a woman like a knot of twisted laundry, hard and dry and squeezed of all water. At first I think Amparo is her grandmother, not her mama. – But how could a girl with skin like a *caramelo* have such a dusty old mother?" (34). To Celaya, Candelaria *is* beauty. The American in Celaya longs to consume such beauty – she continually compares her half-sister to food – but Celaya cannot forget that she and her family have abandoned Candelaria. Her father does not recognize her. The Awful Grandmother sends her back to the capital on a bus, her address pinned to her dress. Cisneros implicates both the USA and Mexico in the gulf that separates two girls connected by blood. Both nation-states have co-opted the heritage of indigeneity, only to ignore Native peoples. The Reyes's disavowal of Candelaria harms both the legitimate and the illegitimate daughters.

Thus, Cisneros uses historical fiction to write a usable past that connects third-world subjects, even as she points out how both men and women have exceeded the constraints of their past. In recent years, women writers of Central and South American descent have added their literary histories to more numerous accounts by Mexican, Cuban, Puerto Rican, and Dominican Americans. Chilean writer Isabel Allende lives permanently in the USA but continues to write in Spanish, usually about Latin American contexts. Sandra Benítez focuses on the lives of working-class families during decades of political conflict in El Salvador in novels such as *Bitter Grounds* (1998) and *The Weight of All Things* (2002). Another underexplored avenue of Latina/o scholarship has been Latina participation in the human rights struggles of indigenous and laboring Latin Americans, women, children, and queer and transgender peoples under the military regimes long supported or ignored by the US government. Writers such as Demetria Martínez, Cherríe Moraga, Sandra Cisneros, Cristina García, and Gloria Anzaldúa have all argued for coalition between citizens of the third world and women of color. The rhetoric they employ and the narratives they craft have also been key to the articulation of *Latinidad* in the twenty-first century.

Futures

Latina critical scholars and literary writers reconstruct and reimagine hemispheric history to advocate Latina/o culture in the USA, Latina/o Studies in the academy, and Latina identity. One pivotal facet of these projects has been the recovery of earlier writers whose alternative historical narratives presage those of contemporary authors. The Recovering the US Hispanic Literary Heritage Project, housed at the University of Houston and managed by Arte Público Press, has combed the archives to publish now-essential writers such as María Amparo Ruiz de Burton, María Cristina Mena, and Luisa Capetillo, finding in the process that women writers of Spanish and Latin American heritage have participated in public debates about the political and cultural future of the hemisphere since the nineteenth century.

The earliest woman novelist recovered by the project is California novelist María Amparo Ruiz de Burton, who wrote in the 1870s and '80s on behalf of Mexican Americans disenfranchised by the Treaty of Guadalupe Hidalgo (1848). The treaty ceded much of Mexico's northern territory to the USA. Stripped of their Mexican citizenship, these conquered people became citizens of the USA, only to find their lands and customs under siege by industrialists and squatters. Ruiz de Burton challenges the marginalization of Latin American peoples (particularly *Californios* of Spanish descent) by Anglo-American society. Her historical romances, *Who Would Have Thought It?* (1872) and *The Squatter and the Don* (1885), depict Spanish American characters as bastions of European civilization and morality. Her Anglo characters thrive only when they learn from and establish (financial and marital) connections with Californio and Mexican protagonists.

In the early twentieth century, once-obscure Mexican American authors such as María Cristina Mena and post-revolutionary author and playwright Josefina Niggli borrowed from Mexican history to understand the lives of women in Mexico and the USA. A recent migrant to the USA who saw herself as a "refugee" from the increasingly volatile economic and social climate of pre-revolutionary Mexico, Mena wrote entirely in English, acting as translator and interpreter of a Mexican life that she distinguished from the stories of violent strife that filled the newspapers. Her 1913–16 portraits of Mexican subjectivity and culture, like Ruiz de Burton's, argue that Americans should learn from the traditions and values of their southern neighbors.

Although she is most famous for her novel *Mexican Village*, Josefina Niggli's plays feature Mexican women as agents in Mexican revolutionary history. Furthermore, Niggli's Mexico is immune to US incursion. If masculine revolutionaries and brave *soldaderas* have won the day with no help from the north, then the myriad Hollywood Westerns that featured American heroes "saving" Mexico have been mistaken in their keenness for "Good Neighbor" aggression. The gun-slinging women and hot-blooded men that Niggli's plays favor suggest that post-revolutionary Mexico, toughened by its decades of conflict, is no place for the theater-going American.[14]

In addition to Latina and Chicana fiction writers, extensive collections such as the Benson Collection at the University of Texas in Austin and the Cuban Heritage Collection at the University of Miami offer access to thousands of periodicals, books, propaganda, and ephemera in Spanish and English that circulated among Hispanic communities in the nineteenth and early twentieth centuries. This recovery work has been important to Latina scholarship because it offers an alternative literary genealogy that better represents the intercultural and transnational dimensions of the USA. Diverse accounts by recovered Tejana and southwestern women writers like Jovita Gonzalez and autobiographies by Leonor Villegas de Magnón, Nina Otero-Warren, and Cleofas Jaramillo demonstrate the political and literary agency of Hispanas in the formation and reformation of the nation.

The twenty-first century has also seen the proliferation of Latina/o anthologies, critical collections, bibliographies, and encyclopedias. As Kirsten Silva Gruesz notes, these have been essential to our current understanding of Latina/o cultural expression and our formulation of a Latina/o canon, but recent scholars have also begun to develop interdisciplinary projects to explore the dialogue, community, and coalition between Latinas and other historically underrepresented groups, as well as between these groups and mass culture.

Scholars of Latina feminism and queerness such as Juana María Rodríguez, Ricardo Ortiz, and Richard T. Rodríguez have examined the narratives and subjectivities of queer Latina/os in the context of heteronormative Latina/o and US cultures. Immigration and racialization scholars such as Eithne Luibhéid and Mai Ngai have studied the relationship between US immigration policy and discriminatory practices toward racial Others like Asian and Latina/o migrants, especially border-crossing women. Border theorists and critical regionalists like Mary Pat Brady and Rachel Adams have borrowed from disciplines like geography to understand the racial and gendered parameters of space. Scholars of US empire such as Shelley Streeby, Gretchen Murphy, and Amy Kaplan have studied how popular cultural expressions endorse or contest US imperial power in Latin America. Furthermore, Hemispheric American scholars such as Kirsten Silva Gruesz, Anna Brickhouse, and David Luis-Brown bridge political and linguistic borders between North and South America to account for transnational subjects whose identities shift with travel or migration and those who position themselves between borders.

My own work focuses on the international alliances that Latin American, Latina / o, and mass cultural US writers forge in response to hemispheric political crises. By engaging public debates over US intervention in Latin America or by challenging military dictatorships or human rights abuses, journalists, literary writers, filmmakers, and activists create ties to multiple nations and redefine community across linguistic, political, and cultural borders. During the torrent of coups, civil wars, and revolutions that characterized the Cold War in Latin America, for example, refugees from Guatemala and El Salvador formed strategic alliances with human rights and Latina / o activist groups and used film and propaganda to urge US support for indigenous and working-class peoples in Central America. Artists like Susan Meiselas and Mark Vallen and films such as *Salvador*, *Under Fire*, and *El Norte* dramatize human rights abuses in Central America and imagine how journalists, activists, and donors can intercede. They also worked to obtain official refugee status for Central American immigrants, a difficult goal in a Cold War climate of xenophobia. By examining the possibilities and problems of international coalition among Latin American diasporas, I hope to redefine the relationships among citizens, undocumented peoples, and the governments that often fail to contain them.

In this essay I have argued that Latina writers anticipate our own scholarly efforts to expand and amend hemispheric history. Latina literature coalesces around political struggle. Searching for literary origins and political futures, Latina writers reveal the histories that define third-world women and imagine new possibilities for subjectivity and community. Exposing imperialism, patriarchy, racism, and heteronormativity, women writers of Mexican and Latin American descent have shaped a literary tradition to empower dispossessed, exploited, and silenced peoples in and beyond the Americas.

Notes

1. Although women's experiences and stories have been vital to this project, Latina writers have also expressed solidarity with gay and transgender, working-class, and indigenous peoples oppressed by imperial racial hierarchies and by heteropatriarchy.
2. Literary scholar Lois Parkinson Zamora's *The Usable Past* explores writers in both the USA and Latin America who employ historical events and historiographic rhetorical strategies in order to rethink the making of history itself. She argues that the "anxiety of origins" "impels American writers to search for precursors (in the name of community) rather than escape from them (in the name of individuation), to connect to traditions

and histories (in the name of a usable past) rather than dissociate from them (in the name of originality)" (5). Also inspired by Zamora, Kirsten Silva Gruesz has argued that "no one has yet ventured to build a comprehensive narrative around the tens of thousands of texts produced over time by Latinos living in what is now the United States... It seems to me that if 'Latino' is to have any long-term conceptual staying power, it must grapple with the construction of a usable past that would be, if not *common* to all Latinos (what historical stories are?), intelligible and meaningful to that constituency" ("The Once and Future Latino," 116–17).

3. The Chicano Movement borrowed pre-Columbian mythology as well as early Mexican nationalist icons like the Virgin of Guadalupe to represent the ancient cultural history of Mexican America. Perhaps the most famous of these was their recuperation of Aztlán, the mythical homeland of Nahua peoples like the Toltecs and Aztecs.

4. In her essay for *This Bridge Called My Back*, "Chicana's Feminist Literature," Norma Alarcón identifies several early Chicana literary representations of la Malinche, including poems by Alma Villanueva and Lorna Dee Cervantes. Likewise, Sonia Saldívar-Hull's *Feminism on the Border* reads Chicana theory and fiction for its resistance to the essentialisms of feminism and nationalist agendas. Saldívar-Hull encourages "women of color" politics as they further solidarity and non-essentialist resistance. Reading Anzaldúa, Sandra Cisneros, and Helena María Viramontes, Saldívar-Hull argues that these Chicana writers search for an indigenous past as a space for Chicana subjectivity. She writes that they, as well as Cherríe Moraga and others, write *mestiza* texts that blend genres and problematize ideologies, fighting against traditional representations of women such as those found in *telenovelas*. Saldívar-Hull also examines Cisneros's and other Chicanas' use of la Malinche and la Llorona as *feminismo popular*, or praxis instead of abstract theory.

5. See Estela Portillo Trambley's play, *Sor Juana* (1983) and Gaspar de Alba's novel, *Sor Juana's Second Dream* (1999).

6. In *Women Singing in the Snow*, Rebolledo analyzes the "literary myths and archetypes" that pervade Chicana narrative. In the case of the Virgin, she discusses how writers such as Sandra Cisneros and Demetria Martínez have recuperated the "strengths and power" of the Virgin through the Nahuatl goddesses who precede her (57).

7. It is also important to note that the Virgin of Guadalupe plays a key role in other Latin American cultures as well, especially Guatemala's.

8. For an exhaustive list, see *Latinas in the United States: A Historical Encyclopedia* by Vicki Ruíz and Virginia Sánchez Korrol.

9. These writers are by no means alone in tracing this connection. Dominican American writers Julia Alvarez and Junot Díaz, the Haitian American writer Edwidge Danticat, and countless others have imagined Latin American and Caribbean revolutions as the genesis of contemporary race relations in the USA.

10. Many scholars have posited Yolanda as an exemplar of the hybrid, marginalized, and fractured alien subject. Perhaps the first to make this argument explicitly is Ricardo Castells, who contends that "the novel does not demonstrate the four sisters' successful assimilation into American life, and that even this incomplete transition occurs to a great extent because of the displacement of their Hispanic language and culture. Rather than forging an assimilated dual identity as Hoffman believes, the sisters repeatedly find themselves at odds with their bicultural surroundings, experiencing a form of alienation

that is often symbolized by either silence or by an absolute failure to communicate with the other characters" ("The Silence of Exile," 34).

11. Johannes Fabian suggests in *Time and the Other: How Anthropology Makes its Object* that Western anthropology denies coevalness to the peoples it studies. Kirsten Silva Gruesz picks up this idea in "The Once and Future Latino" arguing that Latina/o Studies needs to consider "the overall conception of *temporality* that shapes our work" (117).

12. See Pérez, *The Decolonial Imaginary*, and Gruesz, "The Once and Future Latino."

13. Bill Johnson González argues that *Caramelo* employs translation to interrogate Mexican traditions and American hegemony in the lives of Chicana/os. He argues that "By representing elements of her family's speech to herself (and to the reader) in a language that is foreign to the original, and by moving back and forth between languages in different contexts, Celaya is able to notice subtle differences and slippages of meaning between Spanish and English that give her a heightened awareness of the contingency of meaning in both tongues, as well as their different modes of signifying" ("The Politics of Translation," 4).

14. Niggli allows Bob Webster, the protagonist of *Mexican Village*, to return to Mexico to fulfill his own masculine promise precisely because Webster is as Mexican as he is American. Like Niggli herself, Webster deploys his cultural hybridity. His familiarity with the customs of the village makes him a more sensitive ambassador for the USA, a body that can transfer the best in US individualism and industry to the rich traditions of the Mexican community.

Works cited

Alarcón, Norma. "Chicana's Feminist Literature." In *This Bridge Called My Back: Writings by Radical Women of Color*. Ed. Cherríe Moraga and Gloria Anzaldúa. New York: Kitchen Table, Women of Color Press, 1981.

Alvarez, Julia. *How the García Girls Lost their Accents*. Chapel Hill: Algonquin Books, 1991.

In the Name of Salomé: A Novel. Chapel Hill: Algonquin Books, 2000.

In the Time of the Butterflies. Chapel Hill: Algonquin Books, 1994.

¡Yo! New York: Plume, 1997.

Anzaldúa, Gloria. *Borderlands/La frontera: The New Mestiza*. San Francisco: Spinsters/Aunt Lute Books, 1987.

Benítez, Sandra. *Bitter Grounds*. New York: Hyperion, 1997.

The Weight of all Things. New York: Hyperion, 2001.

Castells, Ricardo. "The Silence of Exile in *How the García Girls Lost their Accents*." *Bilingual Review/La Revista Bilingüe* 26.1 (January–April 2001): 34–42.

Cisneros, Sandra. *Caramelo*. New York: Knopf, 2002.

Cruz, Angie. *Soledad*. New York: Simon and Schuster, 2001.

Fabian, Johannes. *Time and the Other: How Anthropology Makes its Object*. New York: Columbia University Press, 1983.

Gaspar de Alba, Alicia. *Sor Juana's Second Dream: A Novel*. Albuquerque: University of New Mexico Press, 1999.

García, Cristina. *The Agüero Sisters*. New York: Knopf, 1997.

Dreaming in Cuban. New York: Knopf, 1992.

González, Bill Johnson. "The Politics of Translation in Sandra Cisneros's *Caramelo*." *Differences: A Journal of Feminist Cultural Studies* 17.3 (2006): 3–19.

Gruesz, Kirsten Silva. "The Once and Future Latino: Notes Toward a Literary History *Todavía Para Llegar*." In *Contemporary US Latino/a Literary Criticism*. Ed. Lyn Di Iorio Sandín and Richard Perez. New York: Palgrave Macmillan, 2007.

Mena, María Cristina. *The Collected Stories of Maria Cristina Mena*. Ed. Amy Doherty. Houston: Arte Público Press, University of Houston, 1997.

Moraga, Cherríe. *Loving in the War Years: Lo Que Nunca Pasó Por Sus Labios*. Boston: South End Press, 1983.

Morales, Aurora Levins and Rosario Morales. *Getting Home Alive*. New York: Firebrand Books, 1986.

Niggli, Josefina. *Mexican Village*. Chapel Hill: University of North Carolina Press, 1945.

    The Plays of Josefina Niggli. Ed. William Orchard and Yolanda Padilla. Madison: University of Wisconsin Press, 2007.

Obejas, Achy. *Days of Awe*. New York: Ballantine Books, 2001.

    Memory Mambo: A Novel. Pittsburgh: Cleis Press, 1996.

    We Came All The Way From Cuba So You Could Dress Like This? Pittsburgh: Cleis Press, 1994.

Pérez, Emma. *The Decolonial Imaginary: Writing Chicanas into History*. Bloomington: Indiana University Press, 1999.

    Gulf Dreams. Berkeley: Third Woman Press, 1996.

Pérez, Loida Maritza. *Geographies of Home: A Novel*. New York: Viking, 1999.

Pérez-Torres, Rafael. *Mestizaje: Critical Uses of Race in Chicano Culture*. Minneapolis: University of Minnesota Press, 2006.

Rebolledo, Tey Diana. *Women Singing in the Snow: A Cultural Analysis of Chicana Literature*. Tucson: University of Arizona Press, 1995.

Rosario, Nelly. *Song of the Water Saints*. New York: Pantheon Books, 2002.

Ruíz, Vicki and Virginia Sánchez Korrol, eds. *Latinas in the United States: A Historical Encyclopedia*. Bloomington: Indiana University Press, 2006.

Ruiz de Burton, María Amparo. *The Squatter and the Don*. Ed. R. Sánchez and B. Pita. 1885. Houston: Arte Público Press, 1992.

    Who Would Have Thought It? Ed. R. Sánchez and B. Pita. 1872. Houston: Arte Público Press, 1995.

Saldívar-Hull, Sonia. *Feminism on the Border: Chicana Gender Politics and Literature*. Berkeley: University of California Press, 2000.

Sotomayor, Sonia. "A Latina Judge's Voice." *La Raza Law Journal* 13 (Spring 2002): 87–94.

Stavans, Ilan. "Preface." In *Norton Anthology of Latino Literature*. Ed. I. Stavans. New York: W. W. Norton, 2010.

Trambley, Estela Portillo. *Sor Juana and Other Plays*. Ypsilanti: Bilingual Press/Editorial Bilingüe, 1983.

Villarreal, José Antonio. *Pocho*. 1959. Garden City, NY: Anchor Books, 1970.

Zamora, Lois Parkinson. *The Usable Past: The Imagination of History in Recent Fiction of the Americas*. Cambridge: Cambridge University Press, 1997.

31

Where is she? Women / access / rhetoric

PATRICIA BIZZELL

Location has been as important to rhetoric as discovering the available means of persuasion, to paraphrase Aristotle. Classifying orations as forensic, deliberative, and ceremonial has had as much to do with where they are uttered (courtroom, legislature, and celebratory platform or pulpit) as with their content. That these are all public locations provides the main reason why women have been excluded from such rhetorical occasions since classical times, though as litteraturazione (the application of oral rhetoric principles to written language) and rhetorical arts of conversation developed, private venues in which women could be persuasive were legitimated. The problem has always been that a woman in public seems to be a public woman, in the same sense that a lodging serving all comers is a "public" house: in other words, she seems to be a whore; or else, no woman at all.

Accusations of sexual impropriety were leveled against American women activists from early in the nineteenth century. For example, in 1837 the Congregationalist clergy of Massachusetts, provoked by the public speeches of abolitionists Sarah and Angelina Grimké, issued a Pastoral Letter against female activists, which suggests that such women take a prurient interest in the sexual exploitation of female slaves (Bizzell and Herzberg, *The Rhetorical Tradition*, 1046–7). One minister sermonized that abolition women venture out of their proper domestic sphere only in search of illicit sexual adventure, while another predicted that the Grimké sisters' audacity would soon lead them to appear on the speakers' platform nude (Folsom, "Abolition Women"; Lerner, *Grimké Sisters*, 148–9). This in spite of the fact that the sisters were always attired in public in the exceptionally modest Quaker dress (Mattingly, *Appropriate[ing]*, 24ff.). Or if she is not a whore, then she is no woman at all: with great dignity, African American activist Sojourner Truth actually did uncover her bosom to prove to hecklers that she was not a man (Buchanan, *Regendering Delivery*, 111).

American women seeking access to rhetoric, then, had either to restrict their activities to acceptably enclosed locations, or make arguments for their right to speak in public spaces along with the arguments they wanted to make about the social issues their public speaking addressed. Such arguments were often explicit in the nineteenth century and became more implicit since 1900, but some sort of defense always had, and has, to be there. Critical to successful defense was, and is, how a woman could answer the question, "Where is she, when she is speaking?" Gender trouble did not evaporate for American women once they achieved the national franchise in 1920, as the trajectories of women politicians have recently shown. Nevertheless, women have continued to develop rhetorical competence in a variety of places.

In the parlor

An acceptable location for women's rhetorical activities in the nineteenth century was the parlor, the room where middle- and upper-class families gathered to share various sociable rhetorical activities that required some education (and a home large enough to have a parlor). Thus access to rhetoric, at least in this location, related to social class and race as well as gender. Women's Studies scholar Catherine Hobbs presents evidence that, by 1800, about 50 percent of white Protestant women in the northern United States were literate to some degree ("Introduction," 2). For enslaved women, this attainment was illegal, although secret, self-sponsored study or the convenience of slave-owners sometimes resulted in its acquisition; by 1860, estimates suggest from 5 to 10 percent of enslaved persons were literate (this number includes more men than women) (12). Both white and black women steadily increased their literacy rates over the nineteenth century, and, by its end, about 50 percent of African American women were literate, while the rate was well over 90 percent among northern Protestant white women (2).

Hobbs explains, however, that assessing literacy levels is difficult (7). Early in the century, it was not uncommon for women to be taught to read but not to write (5). Reading they might learn from the women who managed the informal child-care arrangements in private homes where boys and girls often learned their letters. But writing was considered a higher-order skill, the province of male teachers and available mostly in formal schools (8). By the time American children were eight or ten years old, even if they had acquired some minimal literacy, their educational experiences started to diverge, with most receiving only training in manual arts that were often gender-specific, and only a tiny minority, mostly white and mostly male, attaining any further organized instruction. Looking for women of any race who could practice parlor rhetorics, then, requires ascending an ever-narrowing socio-economic pyramid.

Few historians of rhetoric today contest Hobbs's support for the view that the nineteenth century was dominated successively by gender ideologies termed "Republican Motherhood" and "True Womanhood" (terms launched in contemporary scholarship by historians, the first by Linda K. Kerber, and the second by Nancy F. Cott and Barbara Welter). Nor do they dispute Hobbs's contention that these ideologies, while insisting that women were best suited by nature and divine intent to center their lives within their homes, devoted especially to raising children, also provided an opening for arguments in favor of better formal education for women, to equip them for the more intellectual domestic tasks of beginning their children's education and inculcating proper Christian and republican virtues (5). More recently, scholar of English education Sarah Robbins has confirmed this contention and shown how the maternal role of first reading teacher, particularly for her sons, came to be deemed essential to the health of the Republic, necessitating maternal education and even dramatized repeatedly in nineteenth-century fictions she terms "domestic literacy narratives" (*Managing Literacy, Mothering America*, 3, 9).

In response to this felt need for better education for women, academies or "seminaries" for teen-aged girls began to arise. Scholars sometimes cite as early models Emma Willard's Troy Female Seminary (founded 1827), Catharine Beecher's Hartford Female Seminary (1828), and Mary Lyon's Mount Holyoke Seminary (1837) (see Hobbs, "Introduction," 14). Be it noted that these were all located in the northeast and admitted only white Protestant girls, but historian of rhetoric Carol Mattingly documents the foundation of Catholic schools for girls as early as 1727 in New Orleans ("Uncovering," 161), and in much of the south and west, they provided the only education for girls at this level (including non-Catholics) until well into the nineteenth century. Historian of rhetoric Shirley Wilson Logan notes that the Reverend William Watkins opened his Academy for Negro Youth, which educated both boys and girls, in 1820, before Willard's school; his niece, the important activist Frances Ellen Watkins Harper, was educated there (*"We Are Coming"*, 48). Historian Devon A. Mihesuah (Choctaw) has described a seminary founded in 1857 for Cherokee girls by Mount Holyoke graduates, which produced some tribal leaders. Historian Mary Kelley has shown that seminary-type schools for young women spread rapidly, and by 1850 about 250 could be found throughout the United States, about the same number as colleges for men (*Learning to Stand and Speak*, 41).

But what sort of rhetorical training did young women receive in these seminaries? Herein lies scholarly controversy. Seminaries never taught all the subjects found in comparable schools for young men. Typically, natural sciences and classical languages were avoided, although this changed gradually; Emma Willard was an early pioneer (Kelley, *Learning to Stand and Speak*, 89). But even when the young women's curriculum became almost identical to the men's, the one topic that remained off limits was rhetoric. Mary Kelley argues that seminaries empowered women who later became public activists; she cites a letter in which abolitionist and women's rights advocate Lucy Stone states that it was at Mount Holyoke where she "'learned to stand and speak'" (quoted in *Learning to Stand and Speak*, 275). Kelley claims that seminary education equipped women to enter what she terms "civil society" and to contend about current issues; but the definition she establishes for this activity early in her study explicitly rules out the pursuit of "organized politics" and public office (6). In the antebellum USA, only Oberlin College (founded 1833) admitted both white and black women, a fact that is generally cited as evidence of a progressive view there; but at least at first, women could not take all the same courses as were available to men, particularly excluding rhetoric (Hobbs, "Introduction," 14; Buchanan, *Regendering Delivery*, 57ff.). Historian of rhetoric Nan Johnson reports Lucy Stone as saying about her time at Oberlin: "'I was never [before] in a place where women were so rigidly taught that they must not speak in public'" (*Gender and Rhetorical Space*, 22). Communications scholar Lindal Buchanan reports that when a woman student tried to give a classroom address about women's rights at Oberlin, she was hooted down by not only her male classmates but also the male professor too (*Regendering Delivery*, 59).

Buchanan's study and other evidence suggest a rising tide of female rhetorical competence in the nineteenth century, which pushed against barriers erected by the dominant gender ideologies but did not succeed in breaching them for most women. Buchanan notes that girls might first learn to raise their voices when they learned to read, since reading was commonly done out loud until the very end of the nineteenth century (12). From reading aloud, one could easily progress to delivering memorized readings expressively, an activity cherished in nineteenth-century culture as "elocution" and taught to both sexes (12). Young women might even mount a speaker's platform at school – Buchanan calls such venues the "academic platform," a somewhat protected space since not open to the general public. Nevertheless, this venue was not uncensored for females (44–5). Buchanan surveys school textbooks to show that those for girls did not include the examples of public oratory on patriotic and political topics or the instruction on how to speak dynamically on a public platform that could be found in textbooks for boys (32–3, 38), differences that are perhaps the more striking in that other categories of readings, such as poems and dramatic soliloquies, were represented in relatively equal numbers. Moreover, while young women might be allowed to compose essays on relevant social themes, they were not allowed to deliver these essays as orations until much later: at first, a male professor would read a young woman's piece while she sat on the stage, eyes lowered. By the late 1850s, she might read it herself, if she remained seated. Not until 1874 do the records Buchanan examined show a young woman standing in front of a school audience and delivering her own words as an oration, and this she did without permission (61–2, 79)!

Certainly, women found other ways to develop their rhetorical abilities. Experiences with formal schooling could be frustrating, and many did not have access to them anyway. There were many informal organizations in which women could practice writing and speaking about all sorts of intellectual topics and contemporary issues, such as all-female "literary societies" like the Gleaning Circle, founded in Boston in 1805 (Kelley, *Learning to Stand and Speak*, 133), or the Semi-Colon Club, open to both women and men, where Harriet Beecher Stowe honed her ways with words (Tonkovich, "Writing in Circles"). An unusually well-educated woman might hold organized "Conversations" with other women to discuss intellectual issues in private homes, as Margaret Fuller did in Boston in the 1840s (Kelley, *Learning to Stand and Speak*, 146ff.). While African American women were often excluded from such white organizations, they formed their own, as Shirley Wilson Logan has documented, and their literary societies featured "elocutionary activities, debates, [and] dramatic performances" as well as the reading and critique of original essays, poetry, and fiction (*Liberating*, 8). Aspiring to use their rhetorical abilities in the public sphere motivated women such as Judith Sargent Murray and Lydia Maria Child to seek role models in history and to recover the stories of women leaders from the past who were noted for their eloquence (Kelley, *Learning to Stand and Speak*, 191ff.).

Nevertheless, the number of women who became public speakers remained vanishingly small throughout the nineteenth century. As Nan Johnson suggests, most women were "stranded in the parlor" and relegated only to those types of rhetorical activities that could be pursued in private (*Gender and*

Rhetorical Space, 14). To be sure, they used the pen to gain a public voice through fiction; Catherine Hobbs reports that by 1874, about 75 percent of all novels being published were written by women ("Introduction," 18), and, arguably, such works reached what Sarah Robbins calls their "apex of political influence" in Stowe's *Uncle Tom's Cabin*, an internationally known antislavery novel widely deemed to be politically effective (*Managing Literacy, Mothering America*, 9). But as Johnson shows, the writing of private letters was presented by most conduct books as a more appropriate use for a woman's pen (*Gender and Rhetorical Space*, 79–80). Very few women could actually speak from the public platform about slavery or any other political issue, and the exclusion of rhetoric from girls' and women's curricula was justified in order to avoid "'too great a strain'" on their feminine modesty (quoted in Johnson, *Gender and Rhetorical Space*, 24). Conduct literature emphasized that woman's place was in the home (49).

Fiction, poetry, essays, and private letters, genres that might comprise parlor rhetoric because they could be written, and shared or consumed, in private, were of course composed by men as well as by women. But, as Johnson points out, only women were explicitly restricted to these genres and warned away from the public platform (26). Johnson also shows that oral forms of parlor rhetoric, while practiced by both sexes, were gendered. One anthology of selections suitable for elocutionary performance shows a man giving a formal recitation in evening dress to a crowded parlor, while depicting a woman performing a comic poem (one that is explicitly anti-feminist!) in an exaggerated costume. Another similar text shows the male speaker poised for serious speech while the female is garbed as a gypsy to entertain (36–40). The implication is that women's oral parlor rhetorics aimed only to ornament domestic life while men's might prepare for action in the public sphere. Moreover, Johnson shows that many conduct books actually demonized talkative women and praised silence as the domestic woman's most attractive adornment (64). Indeed, some conduct books actually linked oratory and sexual misconduct; historians of rhetoric Janet Carey Eldred and Peter Mortensen provide an example (*Imagining Rhetoric*, 29). It appears that a woman may have access to rhetoric if she is in the parlor, but only certain kinds of rhetoric.

On the speaker's platform

If a woman did decide to try to mount the public platform with rhetorical abilities developed in seminary, literary society, or parlor, she had to contend with popular characterizations of such speakers as "freedom shriekers who forget their position and their womanhood, who leave their families neglected and their homes forsaken to rant on platforms" (quoted in Johnson, *Gender and Rhetorical Space*, 64). Johnson analyzes how women public speakers tried to ward off charges of unwomanly behavior by performing what the era deemed to be appropriately feminine personae in public, the "noble maid" (if unmarried) or "wise mother" (if married; see 113). These personae dramatize the activist's public agenda as an extension of her domestic concerns, and, moreover, work hard to shield her from the familiar charge of sexual impurity. The concern for purity lurks just under the surface when Johnson describes how writers framed the biographical sketches of well-known women public speakers:

> [such women were] always *modest* and gentle in their speaking roles . . . co-opting the public lectern as a domestic site from which to exert their feminine *moral* force . . . eloquent not because they were skilled, but because they were *moral* and loving women . . . [who] spoke from their *moral* authority as wives and mothers . . . (112, 113, 114, emphasis added)

The words "modest" and "moral" recur again and again, seemingly intended to link these women's social activism to acceptably feminine, domestic values, while evoking a subtext pointing to physical modesty and sexual morality. These would be the types of modesty and morality most crucial for a woman public speaker to demonstrate if she were to avoid the kind of criticism leveled against the Grimkés and other women activists. Johnson provides further evidence for the cultural context of such concerns, quoting from nineteenth-century writings on rhetoric instruction that allow women some parlor eloquence but evince anxiety that "'the *purity* and delicacy of the young Female mind cannot be too assiduously guarded'" against the risks of more public rhetoric (quoted in Johnson, *Gender and Rhetorical Space*, 24, emphasis added).

In the face of such opposition, particularly as it called their chastity into question, I find nineteenth-century women who did ascend the speaker's platform presenting three types of argument for why they should be heard: because I am essentially different from you men and so my insight is needed; because I am divinely inspired; or because I am essentially the same as you men and so have the same right as you to speak.

It may seem paradoxical that women would trade on repressive definitions of woman's sphere in order to enlarge their sphere of action, but such an approach might gain approval as relatively unthreatening to accepted values.

Indeed, it would build upon what women probably learned in the secluded spaces, discussed above, in which they first began to speak: what Lindal Buchanan calls a "feminine delivery style," which, even when a woman spoke her own words standing before a mixed audience, displayed a tone more suited to conversation than oratory, conspicuously cited her support by male family members and other authorities, and "[avowed] a commitment to conventional gender roles while behaving contrary to them" (*Regendering Delivery*, 79). Frances Willard exemplifies the strategy of turning the feminine style to account for public address on a wide range of issues, as can be seen in these contemporary accounts (by men) of her delivery:

> When Miss Willard rose and began to speak I felt instantly that she had something to say; something that she felt it was important that we should hear, and how beautifully, how impressively, how simply it was said! not a thought of self . . . no affectation, nor pedantry, nor mannishness to mar the effect. (quoted in Johnson, *Gender and Rhetorical Space*, 109–10)

> If a great heart, fed by fiery streams from on high, glowing and molten with burning love for humanity . . . lifting millions of human beings from out the noise and dullness of unreason into the serene radiance of reason, so that they are willing to obey the highest ideals and to serve at any cost the noblest demands of humanity and God – if these be of the characteristics or results of eloquence, then without doubt, Frances Willard must be considered one of the most eloquent orators of our time. (quoted in Bizzell, "Frances Willard," 389–90)

While she headed the Woman's Christian Temperance Union (1879–98), Willard enlarged the organization's agenda to include many social causes, including woman suffrage, and created "the largest and most effective organization for teaching women rhetorical skills in the nineteenth century" (Mattingly, *Well-Tempered*, 58). Her principal authorization for doing so arose out of the special characteristics of purity and piety she was supposed to possess as a woman, and on which she drew in her most important work on women's right to speak, *Woman in the Pulpit* (1888).

Willard, be it noted, was not a preacher, but she chose to frame her argument for women's public speaking as a defense of their preaching at least in part because, as Roxanne Mountford has shown, the pulpit as a location for speaking was strongly gendered as masculine (*The Gendered Pulpit*, 16 *et passim*). A woman in a pulpit, in other words, is a sort of worst-case scenario. Wrapping her argument in a shawl of feminine style, Willard begins the book with an introduction comprising three letters from male ministers praising it, and ends with four chapters citing other male authorities on her behalf (see Bizzell and Herzberg, *The Rhetorical Tradition*, 1120–1, cited because no modern, readily available edition of this work exists). In her first chapter, she begins by contending with biblical exegetes who cite texts from Paul's letters to forbid all public speaking by women (I Timothy 2:11, I Corinthians 14: 34–5). Initially presenting her position as that of "any reasonable human being" (and not necessarily a woman's view), Willard concludes this analysis by noting that "there are thirty or forty passages in favor of women's public work for Christ, and only two against it, and these not really so when rightly understood" (quoted in Bizzell and Herzberg, *The Rhetorical Tradition*, 1127, 1131). Her argument quickly moves, however, to the contention that erroneous exegesis, and, indeed, incomplete if not downright erroneous teaching of the Christian gospel has resulted from the male monopoly of the pulpit:

> "We want the earth," is the world-old motto of men. They have had their desire, and we behold the white male dynasty reigning undisputed until our own day; lording it over every heritage, and constituting the only "apostolic succession" ... Men preach a creed; women will declare a life. Men deal in formulas, women in facts. Men have always tithed mint and rue and cumin in their exegesis and their ecclesiasticism, while the world's heart has cried out for compassion, forgiveness, and sympathy ... It is men who have given us the dead letter rather than the living Gospel. The mother-heart of God will never be known to the world until translated into terms of speech by mother-hearted women. (quoted in Bizzell and Herzberg, *The Rhetorical Tradition*, 1132–3)

In arguing that women bring something unique and essential to promulgating Christianity, Willard employs language that evokes conventional nineteenth-century gender ideologies: women bring their insights as mothers and empha-size tender emotions over sterile intellectualism. Moreover, although her ostensible topic is only preaching the gospel, many of her phrases carry a subtext defending women's involvement in broader social issues, as when she stringently condemns "the white male dynasty" for "lording it over every heritage" in the world. Listen to me and to other women, says Willard, or else you will never understand Christianity rightly nor will you know how to approach all our social ills most productively.

It is, perhaps, a short step from this argument to claiming the right to speak on grounds of divine inspiration. Willard does not take this step here, but Maria W. Stewart does. Active in Boston abolition circles, she was one of the first African American women to speak in public on social and political issues – indeed, one of the first women of any race to do so. Her vocation as a speaker emerged after she suffered several personal disasters, including the death of her husband, which led to her religious conversion and the conviction that God was calling her to address her community, and anyone else who cared to listen, on the topics of African American and women's rights (see Richardson, "Introduction"). Stewart typically began her speeches by asserting her divine call:

> Soon after I made this profession [of her faith in Christ], The Spirit of God came before me, and I spake before many. When going home, reflecting on what I had said, I felt ashamed, and knew not where I should hide myself. A something said within my breast, "Press forward, I will be with thee." And my heart made this reply, Lord, if thou wilt be with me, then I will speak for thee as long as I live. ("Farewell Address to her Friends in the City of Boston," 67)

Stewart's audiences would have been familiar with such accounts of divine call from women who preached (without ordination) in Methodism (see Bizzell and Herzberg, *The Rhetorical Tradition*, 1085–8), but Stewart's topics are political rather than religious. She chastises the white community for keeping African Americans in servile positions and exhorts her own people to accelerate their efforts to better themselves and claim their rights, urging them to emulate such American icons as the pilgrims and George Washington (see, for example, "Lecture Delivered at the Franklin Hall," 45–9). Challenged as to the propriety of her speaking, Stewart avers:

> What if I am a woman; is not the God of ancient times the God of these modern days? Did he not raise up Deborah, to be a mother, and a judge in Israel [Judges 4:4]? . . . St. Paul declared that it was a shame for a woman to speak in public, yet our great High Priest and Advocate did not condemn the woman for a more notorious offense than this; neither will he condemn this worthless worm . . . Did St. Paul but know of our wrongs and deprivations, I presume he would make no objections to our pleading in public for our rights. Again; holy women ministered unto Christ and the apostles; and women of refinement in all ages, more or less, have had a voice in moral, religious and political subjects. ("Farewell Address," 68)

On the one hand, Stewart displays the submission and humility demanded of women by nineteenth-century gender ideologies – she is a mere "worthless worm." She even compares herself implicitly to the adulterous woman whom Jesus pardoned, evoking this "more notorious [sexual] offense" to confront those who would impute unchastity to the woman public speaker. Yet God has chosen her, like Deborah and other biblical precedents. Therefore she can face down Paul (whom we saw Willard also debating), and Stewart goes so far as to suggest that the Apostle would approve the public speaking of Stewart and her contemporaries not only on religious subjects but also concerning their secular "wrongs and deprivations." "For God makes use of feeble means, sometimes, to bring about his most exalted purposes" ("Farewell Address," 69).

Defending women's rhetoric on grounds of divine inspiration did not entirely disarm the disapproval Stewart experienced, however, and her 1833 "Farewell" address may have been her last. In it, she mentions "prejudice" and "opposition" coming her way from the Boston African American community, and "some of you have said, 'do not talk so much about religion'" (70, 71). A third kind of argument for women's right to speak is more egalitarian, though springing from religious roots in the Society of Friends. Founder of the denomination, Margaret Fell Fox began the Quaker tradition of outspoken women in Renaissance England, and it carried over into nineteenth-century America (see Bizzell and Herzberg, *The Rhetorical Tradition*, 748–53). Early abolitionist Sarah Grimké theorized this egalitarian strategy in ways that are still persuasive today.

As I noted earlier, Sarah and her sister Angelina, who had grown up in a slave-holding family in South Carolina, excited intense opposition to their abolitionist activism in antebellum New England. Condemned by a Congregationalist Pastoral Letter, Sarah undertook to defend the sisters' rhetorical practices in a series of formal letters "on the Equality of the Sexes and the Condition of Women" addressed to fellow abolitionist Mary S. Parker with the understanding that they would be published. The bedrock of her argument is equality before God:

> [When] The Lord Jesus defines the duties of his followers . . . I follow him through all his precepts, and find him giving the same directions to women as to men, never even referring to the distinction now so strenuously insisted upon between masculine and feminine virtues . . . Men and women were CREATED EQUAL; they are both moral and accountable beings, and whatever is right for man to do, is right for woman. (*Letters*, 38, emphasis in original)

Even more stringently than Willard, Grimké condemns male attempts to dominate women, saying that talk of female "influence" "has ever been the flattering language of man since he laid aside the whip as a means to keep women in subjection" (39). It may be that "Our powers of mind have been crushed, as far as man could do it, our sense of morality has been impaired by his interpretation of our duties; but no where [*sic*] does God say that he made any distinction between us, as moral and intelligent beings" (39). Thus, says Grimké:

> The woman who goes forth, clad in the panoply of God, to stem the tide of iniquity and misery, which she beholds rolling through our land, goes not forth to her labor of love as a female. She goes as the dignified messenger of Jehovah, and all she does and says must be done and said irrespective of sex. (43)

It will be seen that like Stewart, Grimké believes she is doing divinely sanctioned work, but Grimké does not make divine sanction the basis of her authorization to speak. She has not been specially chosen or called; she is simply trying to follow Christ's commands like any other Christian. And unlike Willard, Grimké does not suggest that, as a woman, she brings something unique and essential to the task based in her feminine experience; on the contrary. She analyzes the Apostle Paul's strictures at length, and she points out (like Willard) that they appear to contradict other important biblical texts, and resolves the contradiction by asserting that "the directions given to women not to speak, or to teach in the congregations, had reference to some local and peculiar customs, which were then common in religious assemblies," but which no longer hold today (95). In spite of her learned arguments, Sarah Grimké was unable to defend her and her sister's public speaking from mob violence, which drove them from the speaker's platform in the same year, 1838, that Sarah's letters were published in book form. Nevertheless, women's historian Gerda Lerner avers: "I see Sarah Grimké not only as the first woman to write a coherent feminist argument in the United States, but also as a major feminist thinker" (Lerner, *Feminist*, 5). Her egalitarian arguments seemed eventually to prevail, in the gains women made as her life was drawing to a close (she died in 1873). But how well they work for today's women in public life remains to be seen.

In the voting booth

The turn of the twentieth century presented paradoxes for the development of women's rhetoric. In many ways, positive changes were happening. Educational opportunities for women, indeed, had been improving since the mid-nineteenth century. Land-grant universities, mostly in the midwest and west, were co-ed from their inception (for example, Iowa, 1856; Michigan, 1870; Hobbs, "Introduction," 16). Women's colleges with curricula equal to men's also began to appear; perhaps the earliest was Mary Sharp College in Winchester, Tennessee (1851), but what Catherine Hobbs calls "true degree-granting colleges" emerged after the Civil War (for example, Vassar, 1865; Wellesley and Smith, 1875; Bryn Mawr, 1885; Barnard, 1889; Hobbs, "Introduction," 16). The number of female college graduates in proportion to the rest of the population was still very small, but women were becoming equipped to follow learned professions such as medicine and law, and eventually a woman, Jeannette Rankin, was elected to the House of Representatives in 1916 (Eldred and Mortensen, *Imagining Rhetoric*, 2). Women's right to vote in national elections was secured by the Nineteenth Amendment to the Constitution passed in 1920. Alice Paul, another woman activist emerging from the Quaker tradition, had fought for final passage of this amendment by making especially effective use of visual rhetoric, using parades, banners, cartoons, and, sadly, after she and fellow members of her National Women's Party had been arrested for picketing, the marks of police abuse on their bodies, as explained by historians of rhetoric Katherine H. Adams and Michael Keene and dramatized in the film *Iron-Jawed Angels* (*Alice Paul and the American Suffrage Campaign*, 200).

Women were becoming university professors in a variety of fields, and some of them taught rhetoric to female students. Indeed, Frances Willard herself had done so at a women's college affiliated with Northwestern University where she was the college president (Bizzell and Herzberg, *The Rhetorical Tradition*, 1114–15). Hobbs has argued that "for much of the nineteenth century," rhetoric was defined as "the theory and practice of male public discourse" ("Introduction," 3) – that is, male only – and she reviews the scholarly controversy over whether coeducation caused a decline in the importance of rhetoric in college curricula (13). The fact remains that women found increasing opportunities to study rhetoric at the college level, and these studies were clearly aimed at civic participation, not parlor entertainments. For example, Gertrude Buck's students at Vassar debated political and economic topics (see Campbell, *Toward a Feminist Rhetoric*), and Mary Augusta Jordan's at Smith were encouraged to speak their minds on suffrage and to plan how to use their rhetorical talents for social reform (Kates, *Activist Rhetorics*, 47ff.). At Wilberforce University, Hallie Quinn Brown made sure that African American students' lessons in elocution included material that critiqued white-supremacist racism and emphasized the important roles African Americans of both sexes had played and would play in American civic life (Kates, *Activist Rhetorics*, 61ff.). Scholar of African American rhetoric Jacqueline Jones Royster has traced the ways nineteenth- and early twentieth-century black women used literacy and rhetoric "to better themselves, to change their worlds . . . [and to insert] themselves directly and indirectly into arenas for action" (*Traces of a Stream*, 110).

Moreover, new institutions such as Brookwood Labor College and the Bryn Mawr Summer School for Women Workers were moving higher education out of elite social spheres and training working-class women and men in writing and speaking "for social responsibility" (Kates, *Activist Rhetorics*, 90). Brookwood educated both men and women, but the school at Bryn Mawr (from 1922 to 1939) served women workers only, preparing them for "transforming their oppressive work environment into a more humane, equitable experience for themselves and other workers" and also encouraging them to "grow in purely aesthetic and intellectual realms" (Hollis, *Liberating Voices*, 1). Working-class liberation rather than feminism was the primary goal of these women's rhetorical training; they tended to "put the 'woman question' inside a critique of capitalism" (3). Some students at the Summer School were supported by their labor unions (school rules required that at least half the students be union members), while others received scholarships provided by donors solicited by the school's leaders, M. Carey Thomas and Hilda Worthington Smith. Writing instruction aimed to teach correct English to a diverse student body, some of whom were barely literate and others of whom spoke little English. Course materials, however, were drawn from students' own lives, and "classist" textbooks were avoided (39). The women wrote reflective autobiographies (61ff.). They collected testimony on working conditions and compiled this anecdotal evidence in "scrapbooks" (42ff.). They undertook statistical study of working conditions and wrote reports that were published by the US Department of Labor (45). They performed in various types of "labor drama," for example acting out a trial in which a company is indicted by its women workers for unfair labor practices (103ff.). They studied canonical literature and wrote poems themselves (117ff.). Many examples of their writing in all these genres are included in Women's Studies scholar Karyn Hollis's book on the Summer School (see also *The Women of Summer* in which students at the School speak about their experiences). The students also participated actively in the School's governance and took the initiative not only to request curricular innovations but also to insist that both African American workers and housekeepers and waitresses of all races be admitted to the School on an equal footing. Many Summer School students went on to become leaders in trade unionism, government labor departments, and workers' education (168).

Even as women's opportunities to study and teach rhetoric expanded, however, the accomplishments of nineteenth-century women activist-orators were gradually erased from public consciousness, as Nan Johnson has shown. A very few were noticed, but only if they employed, or could be depicted as employing, feminine rhetorical styles. In one influential account, Frances "Willard does not emerge as a skilled public speaker and politician who successfully claimed the male preserve of the podium as her own for twenty-five years; she is described instead as a loving woman who found in public life a wider home to oversee" (*Gender and Rhetorical Space*, 146). Similarly, while literary histories included women writers, women largely disappeared from turn-of-the-century anthologies of American oratory: one included only two speeches by women among seventy-five selections (and no African Americans of either sex), another printed three among "over 3,335 speeches" (163, 164). Lest this neglect appear to be a thing of the past, William Safire includes no more than fifteen women among over 200 "great speeches in history" selected mostly from the American twentieth century in his well-regarded, "revised and expanded" 1997 anthology. Karlyn Kohrs Campbell was among the first to recover nineteenth-century women's oratory in her groundbreaking collection, *Man Cannot Speak for Her* (vol. 2), and as the preceding discussion has shown, contemporary scholarship has extensively explored and analyzed nineteenth-century women's rhetoric. Much more work is needed, however, on women and rhetoric from 1900 to the present; and no historical narrative has emerged to establish leading figures of the stature of earlier activists such as Stewart, Grimké, or Willard. Indeed, as women's historian and activist Sheila Tobias notes, most high-school and college history texts published between 1940 and 1975 mention only four "historically significant" women: Betsy Ross, Amelia Bloomer, Carrie Nation, and Eleanor Roosevelt (*Faces of Feminism*, 38).

Nevertheless, women's rhetoric has never been practiced only by "great women." Indeed, almost everyone represented in Campbell's collection inspired activism by legions of women whose names never appear in dominant historical narratives, and women's rhetorical competence continued to spread in the twentieth century. A unified women's movement concentrating on one primary goal dispersed after national suffrage was achieved; but the kind of transition women's activism made is both enacted and symbolized by the decision of Carrie Chapman Catt, last president of the National American Women's Suffrage Association, to transform that organization in 1920 into the League of Women Voters (LWV) (Tobias, *Faces of Feminism*, 31). As Tobias explains, LWV chapters around the country worked to pass legislation at the state level that was socially progressive and often focused on both traditionally feminine and domestic issues, such as child welfare, and on feminist issues, such as women's access to work (31).

Women's historian Wendy Sharer's account shows that the LWV and the Women's International League for Peace and Freedom (one of whose founders was American settlement house innovator Jane Addams) made it part of their particular mission to provide instruction and experience at the grassroots level for women to develop their written and oral rhetorical skills, similar to what the Woman's Christian Temperance Union had done in the previous century. The LWV's goal was "to train women as political rhetors" (Sharer, *Vote and Voice*, 127), linked to earlier activists' efforts both by invoking them and by employing some of their pietistic language: as Sharer explains, the LWV presented "Voting [as] a sacred duty, one owed to God and to the leaders of the suffrage movement" (131). The LWV ran "citizenship schools" that offered adult education courses, sometimes in conjunction with major universities and colleges such as Yale and Radcliffe (133–4), and sometimes in venues that might be more accessible to some women, such as The Outlet Department Store in Providence, Rhode Island (140). LWV programs trained women in written rhetoric, through handbooks on political participation (142–4) and through writing courses such as one offered at Wheelock College, which aimed to teach women "to express [their ideas] clearly, convincingly, and graciously," to deal with hostile audiences, and to debunk propaganda (137–9). Women also received training in public speaking, for example, by enacting the roles of real-life Senators in a model Senate (133); and by taking parts in dramatic productions designed to convey information about political processes and to inspire activism (149ff.). It seems clear that to this day, the League of Women Voters has provided what Sharer, following Lorraine Code, calls a "rhetorical space" in which women could flourish (162–3). A 1983 study found that "57.5 percent of state senators and 49.7 percent of state representatives had belonged to the League at one time" (cited in Sharer, *Vote and Voice*, 160).

Unfortunately, the LWV also expressed openly anti-Irish bias in some of its literature. Anti-black racism was more subtle, and some African American women did join the League, but their concerns were not given prominence (156). The League's political agenda was essentially reformist rather than radical, for which it was criticized by Alice Paul, who in 1923 rallied the National Woman's Party to push for an Equal Rights Amendment to the US Constitution, to finish the work the Nineteenth Amendment began and erase discrimination against women in all areas of social and political life (Tobias, *Faces of Feminism*, 34–5). The LWV opposed the ERA for fear it would eliminate protections the League believed were needed by working women (Sharer, *Vote and Voice*, 158). Nevertheless, it can be seen that in various ways, enfranchised women sought to use the voting booth as a location in and around which to exercise rhetorical power.

In the mid-twentieth century, women's progress was uneven. The Great Depression of the 1930s was hard on almost everyone, but impacted women in specific ways, for example, by employers' practice of firing married women first when job cuts had to be made (see Tobias, *Faces of Feminism*, 38–9). Both the gains in employment World War II brought to women, especially in access to well-paying blue-collar jobs, and the concerted effort to push them out of these jobs when the war ended, are graphically documented in *The Life and Times of Rosie the Riveter* (1980); women's rhetoric is displayed both by the working women who eloquently describe their experiences in this film and by the film itself as a rhetorical artifact. In the 1950s, women's college graduation rates dropped back below what they had been in the 1920s (Tobias, *Faces of Feminism*, 60), and women got married at a younger age (twenty), on average, than they had at any time since the turn of the century (88). Prevailing gender ideologies, as domestic as the nineteenth-century ones but without their high moral tone, promoted the idea that "The ideal American woman was white and middle-class and frivolous and spoiled and fun loving and materialistic and beautiful and boy-crazy and – if not already living it – dreaming of wifehood and motherhood in the middle-class heaven, the envy of her sisters all over the world" (61).

Into this atmosphere of retrenchment burst Betty Friedan's *The Feminine Mystique*, published in 1963 and arguably a powerfully effective instance of women's rhetoric. Sheila Tobias relives the days after it appeared and explains how it changed the self-perception of so many white, middle-class women of her generation, each of whom, like Tobias, "can remember where she was the day she first came across" it (58). Reactions to Friedan's opus comprise one strand in the complex story Tobias tells of how women's specifically feminist activism resurged in mid-century, creating what some historians (Tobias included) have termed "second" and "third" waves, which aimed to move beyond the nineteenth century's "first wave" to seek not merely inclusion in, but radical change of, American social and political institutions.

The Civil Rights Movement by white and black women generated another source of feminist activism in the mid-twentieth century, similar to the way the abolition movement gave rise to women's rights activism in the nineteenth century. As historians Davis W. Houck and David E. Dixon explain, "the movement was not [only] a series of great speeches by Martin Luther King, Jr." ("Introduction," xviii). More women than men were active in the movement, and, as Houck and Dixon show, their contributions were essential "to serve as local leaders who could recruit, raise money, and mobilize protest activities," all of which "need rhetorical leadership – public and persuasive messages strategically calibrated to movement aims" (xvii). Sadly, history repeated itself in documenting the Civil Rights Movement, in that once again, women's contributions were slighted and many speeches by women either were not recorded at the time or were preserved in media that have proved evanescent (see xviii ff.). Houck and Dixon begin the recovery effort with an anthology of thirty-nine full-text speeches in which women present "a critique of movement sexism, a narrative of personal involvement, or the challenges of local white and black intransigence" (xx). While some women included here, such as Fannie Lou Hamer and Mary McLeod Bethune, are well-known leaders, many more are now obscure, once again exemplifying that effective rhetorical activity was not, and is not, the exclusive province of "great women."

Tobias's history of women's activism in the 1960s, '70s, and '80s attempts to acknowledge how social class, race, and sexual orientation played into women's experiences and agendas in those decades, while admitting that her own view is tinted by whiteness, heterosexuality, and relative class privilege. Nevertheless, her perspective principally treats "woman" as a unitary category of analysis and will strike contemporary readers as limited and dated for that reason. For present purposes, however, her catalog of mid-century milestones is illustrative of the climate in which women's rhetoric continued to use the voting booth as a location of power.

Discrimination in employment on the basis of sex or race was not explicitly prohibited until passage of Title VII of the 1964 Civil Rights Act (Tobias, *Faces of Feminism*, 80–1). Enforcement of its regulations, however, could not be taken for granted and formed a major impetus for the National Organization for Women's founding in 1966 (84–5). In 1969, a police assault on the "Stonewall" gay bar provoked vigorous resistance that put activism for the rights of lesbians and gay men on the national map as never before (163). Literary scholars began to rediscover hundreds of works of women's fiction, aided by the founding of the Feminist Press in 1970, the same year that saw the first college-level Women's Studies course taught, at Cornell (196, 265). Discrimination in education on the basis of sex was not explicitly prohibited (for schools receiving federal funds) until Title IX of the 1972 educational reform act (122). In that same year, the first widely supported national campaign to pass an Equal Rights Amendment to the Constitution launched, and made great gains, only to be eventually defeated amid conservative backlash ten years later (see 137ff.). In 1973, the US military formally integrated men and women by eliminating its female-only service branches (267). Also in 1973, the US Supreme Court declared state laws banning abortion to be unconstitutional. The first woman on the court, Sandra Day O'Connor, took her seat in 1981 (228). Meanwhile, women began to be elected to high public office: Ella Grasso, for example, became Governor of Connecticut in 1974, and Nancy Landon Kassebaum became a US Senator in 1978 (248). In 1977, a key document stating the black feminist agenda coalesced ongoing activism: the Combahee River Collective's much-reprinted "A Black Feminist Statement" (for an analysis of its rhetoric, see Norman, *The American Protest Essay*). One year later, Shirley Chisholm became the first black woman elected to Congress.

Further milestones can be gleaned from the detailed chronology Tobias prints at the end of her book (*Faces of Feminism*, 260–72). These gains of the recent past (Tobias's list ends in 1996), still fresh in the minds of many older women, including myself, are distant indeed for women born in 1990 and after. They find almost every institution of higher learning in the country open to them; they find women practicing almost every occupation. For many of these women, "feminism" is an outmoded concept that they explicitly disavow (see Bauer, "The Other 'F' Word"). They take for granted the presence of women-focused material in their college courses, women students on debate teams and in student government, and women faculty in every academic department. On the national scene, women have risen to levels of prominence undreamed of even a few decades ago. A black woman has been Secretary of State, an office now filled by a white woman who campaigned, almost successfully, for nomination to be President. A Latina and two Jewish women sit on the Supreme Court. Nevertheless, one may be able to detect ongoing challenges to the public exercise of rhetorical skills by women; and to define these challenges in specifically gendered terms.

On the campaign trail

The campaign trail would be the most challenging rhetorical venue for a woman if any nineteenth-century-style sanctions against her public activism persisted. After all, to campaign, she must not only speak in public but do so repeatedly, over an extended period of time, in a wide variety of public locations. From the picture of women's burgeoning civic participation that I have just been painting, one might assume that such sanctions do not indeed persist. And yet, there are some disquieting signs.

Throughout Hillary Clinton's campaign for the Democratic Presidential nomination (2007–8), her clothing was a constant topic of press scrutiny, attention that was given to no male candidate. For the most part, she was not criticized for immodest dress, though an episode when she showed a bit of cleavage aroused, if not stern disapproval, similarly punitive mocking scorn: one news report was headlined, "Now, Wait Chest a Minute!" (Bazinet). Mostly, she was mocked for lacking fashion sense in relying on modestly tailored pantsuits as her "signature," hoping that the masculine style would convey her competence for leadership and even joking on the David Letterman show: "'In my White House, I'll wear the pantsuits'" (see Gerstel, "Campaign Calls for Pantsuits"). As journalist Hadley Freeman observed when reporting on Clinton's declining to be photographed for the cover of *Vogue*:

> Hillary avoids looking too stylish because she doesn't want to ruin her credibility with voters (which is the reason she turned down the *Vogue* shoot). If she looks as if she cares too much about her appearance people will start crying that she's too vain or too focused on lipstick to be caring about the world's toughest issues. If she looks as if she doesn't care about her appearance, people immediately pick her image apart. It's a no win situation no matter what she wears, sadly to say.

This particular no-win situation besets the woman public speaker with a problem in visual rhetoric that male public figures are usually spared.

Shortly before Martha Coakley began her campaign for the US Senate seat left vacant by the death of Edward Kennedy, I saw her speak at a fund-raising breakfast for a battered women's shelter in Worcester, Massachusetts. I would say that her appearance could be described as business-like yet feminine. She wore a skirted suit with light make-up and a short, softly curly hair style. Her address replicated the combination of traits suggested by her dress, living up to her reputation as a "charismatic" public speaker, not only "funny and smart" but also "hard-charging," especially when it comes to the legal protections for women and children that she has made her signature issues as Massachusetts Attorney General (see Rucker, "Martha Coakley"). However, as is now well known, she spectacularly lost her Senate race to an under-dog Republican, Scott Brown. Journalist Philip Rucker suggests that a contributing factor in this defeat was her decision to "[make] her case to the voters the way she made her closing arguments to countless juries: she was measured and dispassionate . . . she avoided talking about her personal life while campaigning." As a result, according to commentator James Carroll, she evoked this reaction from voters: "She was sort of cold, don't you think?" Coakley has subsequently begun to rehabilitate her image with self-mockery, for example by using the pop song "She's Cold as Ice" as her background music at public appearances (see Vennochi, "For Coakley"). I find it rather sad that women public figures need to make fun of themselves to gain credibility, a rhetorical tactic rarely used by men.

When Elena Kagan was proposed for a seat on the US Supreme Court, African American law professor and public intellectual Patricia J. Williams noticed some of the same disquieting signs in the media scrutiny of her candidacy, what Williams describes as "another season of vulgar sexism":

> Sonia Sotomayor had to refute allegations that she was too strident and bossy; Kagan is already facing speculation that she's a lesbian – in that unfortunate schoolyard universe where, as with Hillary Clinton before her, "lesbian" is defined only as "unwomanly" . . . Forty years after the birth of modern feminism, we are still not able to think about women who attain certain kinds of professional success as normatively gendered.

As a result, in order to take Kagan seriously as a candidate, according to Williams, the press had to gender her as masculine:

> This chatter isn't really about Kagan's sexual preference as much as it is about whether she exhibits masculine traits . . . She likes poker! She swings a softball bat! Not only does anything she touches suddenly get characterized as a male pursuit; she is amply endowed with a Midas touch of testosterone. Success itself is masculinized.

Williams cites this chatter as alarming evidence of how "the languages we speak shape the way we think," a formidable rhetorical problem for the woman in public. Of course, Kagan was spared the experience of Sarah and Angelina Grimké, who were driven from the podium by a mob that burned down the hall where they were speaking. She was confirmed to the Supreme Court. But she still had to account for her gender in ways that public men do not.

Where is rhetoric?

The primary focus of this essay has been rhetoric in the public sphere, as forecast by my opening allusion to classical rhetoric, which concentrates there. The paradigmatic practice of rhetoric, in this approach, can be found in the speaker or writer addressing an audience on an issue of civic importance. If this is the model, then a search for women practicing rhetoric must begin with questions about how women could acquire the language-using skills that would enable them to hold an audience. Hence a recurring theme in this essay concerns women's educational opportunities and rehearsals of rhetorical skills in a variety of more private venues. From these backgrounds, another theme builds up a picture of women's increasing participation in public deliberations in the more than two centuries since the United States came into being. This picture may have certain figures in the foreground, women whose individual accomplishments have now been restored to the historical record, and I have named a few of them and described their rhetorical strategies here. But the picture must also include a densely populated background of anonymous women who worked tirelessly for various activist campaigns, and I have also named some of their organizations and noted their rhetorical efforts and the gains they have made. Inclusion in, and reform of, American civic institutions has been a recurring goal of women's activism since the nation's founding, a goal nicely illustrated by activist women's proclivity for appropriating the Declaration of Independence and turning it to account for the social agenda they favor. Women's Studies scholar Brian Norman describes the rhetorical force of three such significant appropriations: the 1848 Seneca Falls "Declaration of Sentiments and Resolutions," of which Elizabeth Cady Stanton was a principal author; "A New Declaration of Independence," published in 1909 by Emma Goldman in her anarchist magazine *Mother Earth*; and the 1970 "Declaration of Women's Independence" promulgated by the "Boston-based socialist feminist organization Bread and Roses" (*The American Protest Essay*, 63).

I am aware, of course, that defining rhetoric in these ways arguably narrows its potential scope. Defining rhetoric and its scope has always been an issue for historians and theorists, never more so than now, when the "rhetorical turn" in Western intellectual life has declared virtually every effort at human communication to be rhetorical, when, as literary theorist Stanley Fish puts it, "the givens of any field of activity – including the facts it commands, the procedures it trusts in, and the values it expresses and extends – are socially and politically constructed, are fashioned by man [*sic!*] rather than delivered by God or nature" ("Rhetoric," 485). Thus virtually every chapter in the present volume could be considered to provide more information on women's persuasive discourses. Moreover, my focus has been primarily on rhetorics that employ language, although I have alluded to non-verbal rhetorics from time to time. Furthermore, while I have attempted to at least acknowledge the interplay of race, social class, and sexual orientation with gender in American rhetorical developments, I have essentially treated "woman" as a biologically unproblematic category, treating as "woman" those figures who have been construed as such by their contemporaries, although Queer rhetorics scholar K. J. Rawson reminds us that this is risky business if we seek scholarly rigor. The best I can do in conclusion is to plant a marker over the space where everything that has been left out should be included. You readers will fill that space in.

Works cited

Adams, Katherine H. and Michael L. Keene. *Alice Paul and the American Suffrage Campaign.* Urbana: University of Illinois Press, 2008.

Bauer, Dale. "The Other 'F' Word: The Feminist in the Classroom." *College English* 52 (April 1990): 385–96.

Bazinet, Kenneth R. "Now, Wait Chest a Minute! Hil Irate over Report on her Cleavage." *New York Daily News* (July 28, 2007): News 3.

Bizzell, Patricia. "Frances Willard, Phoebe Palmer, and the Ethos of the Methodist Woman Preacher." *Rhetoric Society Quarterly* 36 (2006): 377–98.

Bizzell, Patricia and Bruce Herzberg. *The Rhetorical Tradition: Readings from Classical Times to the Present.* 2nd edn. Boston: Bedford Books of St. Martin's Press, 2001.

Buchanan, Lindal. *Regendering Delivery: The Fifth Canon and Antebellum Women Rhetors.* Carbondale: Southern Illinois University Press, 2005.

Campbell, Joann, ed. *Toward a Feminist Rhetoric: The Writing of Gertrude Buck.* Pittsburgh: University of Pittsburgh Press, 1996.

Campbell, Karlyn Kohrs. *Man Cannot Speak for Her.* 2 vols. New York: Praeger, 1989.

Carroll, James. "Misogynist Massachusetts." *The Daily Beast*: www.thedailybeast.com/blogs-and-stories/2010–01–19/misogynist-massachusetts/full.

Cott, Nancy F. *The Bonds of Womanhood: "Woman's Sphere" in New England, 1780–1835.* New Haven: Yale University Press, 1977.

Eldred, Janet Carey and Peter Mortensen. *Imagining Rhetoric: Composing Women of the Early United States.* Pittsburgh: University of Pittsburgh Press, 2002.

Fish, Stanley. "Rhetoric." In *Doing What Comes Naturally.* Durham, NC: Duke University Press, 1989.

Folsom, Reverend Albert A. "Abolition Women." *The Liberator* (September 22, 1837): 1.

Freeman, Hadley. "Race for the White House: Clinton Faces a Harsh Wintour." *The Guardian* (January 19, 2008): International 30.

Gerstel, Judy. "Campaign Calls for Pantsuits: Hillary Clinton's Uniform Ensures Talk Won't Focus on her Wardrobe." *The Toronto Star* (February 8, 2008): L04.

Grimké, Sarah. *Letters on the Equality of the Sexes, and Other Essays.* Ed. Elizabeth Ann Bartlett. 1838. New Haven: Yale University Press, 1988.

Hobbs, Catherine. "Introduction." In *Nineteenth-Century Women Learn to Write.* Ed. Catherine Hobbs. Charlottesville: University of Virginia Press, 1995.

Hobbs, Catherine, ed. *Nineteenth-Century Women Learn to Write.* Charlottesville: University of Virginia Press, 1995.

Hollis, Karyn L. *Liberating Voices: Writing at the Bryn Mawr Summer School for Women Workers.* Carbondale: Southern Illinois University Press, 2004.

Houck, Davis W. and David E. Dixon. "Introduction: Recovering Women's Voices from the Civil Rights Movement." In *Women and the Civil Rights Movement, 1954–1965.* Ed. Davis W. Houck and David E. Dixon. Jackson: University Press of Mississippi, 2009.

Iron-Jawed Angels. Dir. Katja von Garnier, with Hilary Swank, Anjelica Huston, HBO Home Videos, 2004. Film.

Johnson, Nan. *Gender and Rhetorical Space in American Life, 1866–1910*. Carbondale: Southern Illinois University Press, 2002.

Kates, Susan. *Activist Rhetorics and American Higher Education: 1885–1937*. Carbondale: Southern Illinois University Press, 2001.

Kelley, Mary. *Learning to Stand and Speak: Women, Education, and Public Life in America's Republic*. Chapel Hill: University of North Carolina Press, 2006.

Kerber, Linda K. *Women of the Republic: Intellect and Ideology in Revolutionary America*. Chapel Hill: University of North Carolina Press, 1980.

Lerner, Gerda, ed. *The Feminist Thought of Sarah Grimké*. New York: Oxford University Press, 1998.

   The Grimké Sisters from South Carolina. Boston: Houghton Mifflin, 1967.

The Life and Times of Rosie the Riveter. Dir. Connie Field, Clarity Educational Productions, 1980. Film.

Logan, Shirley Wilson. *Liberating Language: Sites of Rhetorical Education in Nineteenth-Century Black America*. Carbondale: Southern Illinois University Press, 2008.

   "We Are Coming": The Persuasive Discourse of Nineteenth-Century Black Women. Carbondale: Southern Illinois University Press, 1999.

Mattingly, Carol. *Appropriate[ing] Dress: Women's Rhetorical Style in Nineteenth-Century America*. Carbondale: Southern Illinois University Press, 2002.

   "Uncovering Forgotten Habits: Anti-Catholic Rhetoric and Nineteenth-Century American Women's Literacy." *College Composition and Communication* 58 (December 2006): 160–81.

   Well-Tempered Women: Nineteenth-Century Temperance Rhetoric. Carbondale: Southern Illinois University Press, 1998.

Mihesuah, Devon A. "'Let Us Strive Earnestly to Value Education Aright': Cherokee Female Seminarians as Leaders of a Changing Culture." In Hobbs, *Nineteenth-Century Women Learn to Write*.

Mountford, Roxanne. *The Gendered Pulpit: Preaching in American Protestant Spaces*. Carbondale: Southern Illinois University Press, 2003.

Norman, Brian. *The American Protest Essay and National Belonging*. Albany: State University of New York Press, 2007.

Rawson, K. J. "Queering Feminist Rhetorical Canonization." In *Rhetorica in Motion: Feminist Rhetorical Methods and Methodologies*. Ed. Eileen E. Schell and K. J. Rawson. Pittsburgh: University of Pittsburgh Press, 2010.

Richardson, Marilyn. "Introduction." In Stewart, *Maria W. Stewart*.

Robbins, Sarah. *Managing Literacy, Mothering America: Women's Narratives on Reading and Writing in the Nineteenth Century*. Pittsburgh: University of Pittsburgh Press, 2004.

Royster, Jacqueline Jones. *Traces of a Stream: Literacy and Social Change among African American Women*. Pittsburgh: University of Pittsburgh Press, 2000.

Rucker, Philip. "Martha Coakley Argued her Case and Lost in Massachusetts Senate Race." *The Washington Post* (January 19, 2010): www.washingtonpost.com/wp-dyn/content/article/2010/01/19/AR2010011904684.html.

Safire, William, ed. *Lend Me Your Ears: Great Speeches in History*. 2nd edn. New York: W. W. Norton, 1997.

Sharer, Wendy B. *Vote and Voice: Women's Organizations and Political Literacy, 1915–1930*. Carbondale: Southern Illinois University Press, 2004.

Stewart, Maria W. *Maria W. Stewart, America's First Black Woman Political Writer: Essays and Speeches*. Ed. Marilyn Richardson. Bloomington: Indiana University Press, 1987.

Tobias, Sheila. *Faces of Feminism: An Activist's Reflections on the Women's Movement*. Boulder, CO: Westview Press, 1997.

Tonkovich, Nicole. "Writing in Circles: Harriet Beecher Stowe, the Semi-Colon Club, and the Construction of Women's Authorship." In Hobbs, *Nineteenth-Century Women Learn to Write*.

Vennochi, Joan. "For Coakley, a Lonely Reinvention." *The Boston Globe* (May 13, 2010): www.bostonglobe.com/editorial_opinion/oped/articles/2010/05/13/for_coakley/.

Welter, Barbara. "The Cult of True Womanhood, 1820–1860." *American Quarterly* 18 (1966): 151–74.

Williams, Patricia J. "She-Lawyers and Other Improbable Creatures." *The Nation* (June 7, 2010): 9.

The Women of Summer. Dir. Suzanne Bauman, Filmakers Library, 1985. Film.

32

Reading women in America

SUSAN M. GRIFFIN

The history of how American women readers have been studied is tied closely to the history of Women's Studies in America. This is true in several senses: one is that Women's Studies from the start concerned itself with identifying and describing the woman reader (and, later, women *readers* – an important distinction). The second is that the history of Women's Studies is, quite literally, largely a history of women – in this case, feminists – reading. After all, as Judith Fetterley declared in 1978, "At its best feminist criticism is a political act whose aim is not simply to interpret the world but to change it by changing the consciousness of those who read and their relation to what they read." This essay has, then, a dual focus: describing some of the many ways in which women readers have been and are being studied and suggesting why certain kinds of studies appeared at different historical moments.[1]

Twentieth-century feminists were not, of course, the first to address the *topic* of the woman reader, a controversial matter dating back to Classical Greece. Indeed, every advance in the technologies of literacy brought with it protests against, and sometimes arguments for, women reading. The history of the novel in particular is deeply imbricated with advice for, fears about, warnings to educators, parents, girls themselves. Fiction was considered especially dangerous for women who were thought to be, by their very natures, more sensitive, emotional, and empathetic – and thus more susceptible to sensational influences. As late as 1886, Frances Willard, the highly influential educator, was warning girls against novel reading in *How to Win: A Book for Girls*: "Much as I disliked the restriction then, I am now sincerely thankful that my Puritan father not only commanded me not to read novels, but successfully prohibited the temptation from coming in his children's way" (117). In *The Woman Reader, 1837–1914*, Kate Flint points out the "range of contexts in which 'the woman reader' was constructed as a discrete topic" in the nineteenth century: "These included articles in newspapers and periodicals;

medical and psychological texts; advice manuals for young girls, wives, servants, governesses; educational and religious works; autobiographies; letters; journals; fiction; and verse, as well as paintings, photographs, and graphic art" (4).

But women's reading does not become a *field* of critical study as such until the last quarter of the twentieth century (Flint's book, for example, was published in 1993). This field was constituted by multiple approaches to the topic, including feminist literary theory, work on female authors, the feminist turn to personal experience, critiques of the literary canon, and sociological studies focused on gender and genre. Several early and influential works of feminist scholarship are illustrative. Judith Fetterley's *The Resisting Reader: A Feminist Approach to American Fiction* (1978) introduced the consideration of gender to then-current reader-response theory. The starting point for Fetterley's study was personal: her own reading journal. Finding that "powerlessness characterize[s] woman's experience of reading" (xiii), Fetterley argues that American literature poses a particular challenge – even threat – to the female reader: "I see my book as a self-defense survival manual for the woman reader lost in 'the masculine wilderness of the American novel'" (viii) and constrained by a nationalist critical tradition: "The woman reader's relation to American literature is made even more problematic by the fact that our literature is frequently dedicated to defining what is peculiarly American about experience and identity." Rehearsing and analyzing the experience of reading specific American canonical texts by Irving, Anderson, Hawthorne, Faulkner, Hemingway, Fitzgerald, James, and Mailer, Fetterley's book goes on to explore how the traditional equation of "male" with "universal" leaves the woman reader in an uneasy position. In order to read masculinist American literature, the female reader must identify with male characters and define herself against the female. Fetterley's example illustrates how feminist critics began to introduce questions of gender into current literary theories. Significant too is her interest in the topic of "identification," a concept that studies of women's reading will return to again and again.

As feminist scholars devoted themselves to the recovery of "lost" women writers and their works, the female readerships of those rediscovered texts came in for critical attention. Perhaps the most influential work of recovery was Nina Baym's *Woman's Fiction: A Guide to Novels by and about Women in America, 1820–1870* (1978), which reports on "a body of once popular but now neglected American fiction" (11). These novels were, Baym argues, not only written by, but also written for, women. They were successful because the story that they told – that of a young girl who, losing her natural support and protection, makes her own way in the world – succeeded in "engaging and channeling the emotions of readers through identification with the heroine" (17). Baym expanded on this work in *Novels, Readers, and Reviewers* (1984) which, while it focuses on (often male) reviewers more than on readers, demonstrates that "the novel was recognized to be a woman's form – crucially to involve women readers, authors, and characters" (24). With the 1986 inauguration of the American Women Writers series, published by Rutgers University Press and edited by Joanne Dobson, Judith Fetterley, and Elaine Showalter, contemporary readers began to gain access to some examples of "woman's fiction," like Maria S. Cummins's *The Lamplighter* (1854), Fanny Fern's *Ruth Hall* (1854), and E. D. E. N. Southworth's *The Hidden Hand; or, Capitola the Madcap* (1859). In 1987 the Feminist Press issued what was to be the novel that was most intensively and widely read by late twentieth-century scholars of American women's writing: Susan Warner's *The Wide, Wide World* (1851).

With the rise of Women's History, the autobiographies and letters of significant American women were located, read, and, in many cases, republished. A central aspect of many of these life stories was the young woman's reading history, and reading habits are often a matter of discussion in letters and diaries. While such women were not representative of the general female population, their examples give concrete instances of how parental influence, friendships, formal schooling, personal tastes, and economic status all shape a reader. Elizabeth Cady Stanton's *Eighty Years and More: Reminiscences, 1815–1897* was reissued by Schocken in 1971. Stanton, whose education began with *Murray's Spelling Book*, studied Latin, Greek, and mathematics in a class with boys in the (always defeated) hope of showing her father that a daughter could be as good as a son. Turned away from Union College, where her male companions continued their education, she was enrolled at Miss Willard's. She tells of the shared delight in listening, with her sisters, to Dickens read aloud, as well as their disgust as they encounter Blackwell, Kent, and Story on the status of women under the law. Charlotte Perkins Gilman's autobiography, *The Living of Charlotte Perkins Gilman*, first published posthumously in 1935, was reprinted by Harper and Row in 1975. Gilman, whose father was a librarian, described her mother's program of early education (which excluded novels): furtive reading of the scandalous and forbidden *The Wandering Jew*, a subscription to *Our Young Folks*, in which she particularly enjoyed the natural science papers, and the gift of some *Popular Science Monthlies*, which she described as the beginning of her "real education" (*The Living of Charlotte Perkins Gilman*, 37). Many twentieth-century feminists had been educated to dismiss nineteenth-century females as faintly ridiculous Victorians or had come to think of these earlier women as simple victims of patriarchy. Reading their foremothers' life stories altered and expanded these scholars' understanding. And doing so, in turn, aided the continuing development of Women's Studies.

Some female writers did not, of course, need rediscovering. But increased awareness of masculinist critical and cultural hegemonies made feminist critics newly interested in how women authors had struggled with male literary traditions. Sandra Gilbert and Susan Gubar's much-debated study, *The Madwoman in the Attic: The Woman Writer and the Nineteenth-Century Literary Imagination* (1979), which aimed to delineate a feminist poetics, did so in large part by analyzing how female authors had read – and been constrained by their reading of – canonical male texts. Gilbert and Gubar explicitly relate their study of female authors reading to their own critical reading of female writing and lives, including their own: "Reading metaphors in this experiential way, we have inevitably ended up reading our own lives as well as the texts we study" (*The Madwoman in the Attic*, xiii). A central section of their study, "Milton's Daughters," proposes that the work of writers like Mary Shelley and Emily Brontë can best be understood as responses to the experience of reading *Paradise Lost* as a woman. The one major American women writer whom Gilbert and Gubar discuss, Emily Dickinson, is, interestingly, described as rewriting both her male and her female predecessors by creating her own life as a gothic narrative.

While Gilbert and Gubar addressed how the female writer's identity was complicated by her reading, Rachel Brownstein, in *Becoming a Heroine: Reading about Women in Novels* (1982), argued that women readers in general form their identities, in part, around female fictional characters. Using herself as an example, Brownstein calls her first chapter "My Life in Fiction." Her point is that she, like many women, identified and developed a self through reading: "Young women like to read about heroines in fiction so as to rehearse possible lives and to imagine a woman's life as important" (*Becoming a Heroine*, xxiv). Admiring Jane Eyre or Emma Woodhouse, the female reader is, in effect, creating and loving "an idealized image of oneself" (xiv).

Brownstein's study, which uses works by Austen, Brontë, Meredith, Eliot, James, and Woolf as examples, is genre-specific. She points to the historical and cultural identification of novels as books that women read: "The history of both women and fiction has been influenced by the fact that the self has been identified, in novels, with the feminine" (xvi). Barbara Welters's widely influential "The Cult of True Womanhood: 1820–1860" (1966), an historical investigation of nineteenth-century feminine ideals, was genre-based as well, but focused on a range of non-fictional materials read by women.

The women's magazines, conduct manuals, and gift books that she examined became primary reading material for many subsequent works of feminist history and criticism.[2] Studying what and how earlier women read became a larger and more varied endeavor. And the later readership of those "non-literary" women's texts continued to grow. By 2000, *Mrs. Beeton's Book of Household Management* of 1861 had been reissued as an Oxford World Classic, edited by Nicola Humble. Catharine Beecher and Harriet Beecher Stowe's *American Woman's Home* (1869), was reprinted in 2002 by Rutgers University Press, edited and introduced by Nicole Tonkovich. Such sources continue to be uncovered and analyzed, as in Nan Johnson's *Gender and Rhetorical Space in American Life, 1866–1910* (2002), which looks at, among other materials, elocution manuals and letter-writing handbooks, as well as conduct books and parlor rhetoric texts, studying how they affected postbellum women's rhetoric.

The best-known, and perhaps most revolutionary, instance of a feminist critic working with neglected "female" forms is Janice Radway's *Reading the Romance: Women, Patriarchy, and Popular Fiction* (1984). Radway used sociological methodology to look at a commercially successful but critically disdained literary form whose reading audience is comprised almost entirely of women: the Romance novel. Working against critical assumptions about the cheap thrills that the Romance novel afforded shallow-minded female audiences, Radway investigated how and why individual women said that they read these books using, among other methods, a "Romance Reader Survey" questionnaire (included as an appendix in *Reading the Romance*). What she delineates are the complex and varied cultural, economic, and personal factors involved in this often sophisticated form of women's reading. The work of ethnography that Radway introduced has continued to expand and reconfigure our understanding of women's reading with, for example, the now-extensive work that has been done on women's reading groups and book clubs. Women's Studies scholars, some of whom had themselves participated in consciousness-raising and reading groups, would later turn their attention to the kinds of reading that took place (and continue to take place) at these communal sites: African American literary societies, Oprah's Book Club, etc. In *Book Clubs: Women and the Uses of Reading in Everyday Life* (2003), Elizabeth Long recounts how, when she began her research on women's book clubs in the late 1980s, her proposed topic was met with skepticism and indifference by male colleagues. In contrast, "women could often understand that a gathering of women to discuss books and their lives might hold some intrinsic value" (x). It is just this sort of "women's culture" that Lauren Berlant comes to describe and critique in her 2008 *The Female Complaint*: an American "mass cultural intimate public . . . distinguished by the view that the people marked by femininity have already something in common and are in need of a conversation that feels intimate, revelatory, and a relief even when it is mediated by commodities, even when it is written by strangers who might not be women, and even when its particular stories are about women who seem, on the face of it, vastly different from each other and any particular reader" (viii–ix).

"Around 1981," as Jane Gallop put it,[3] the critiques of postcolonialist critic Gayatri Spivak and African American writers like Alice Walker and critics like Barbara Christian and Hazel Carby made mainstream feminists aware of how much work in Women's Studies had been based solely on the experiences of white, middle-class females.[4] This population had also been the source of generalized statements about women and reading. Such a situation is neither surprising nor particularly invidious, given that materials regarding such women (diaries, letters, etc.) were in greater supply. Now, however, work began to move beyond (implicit) assumptions about "the woman reader": the heterogeneity of women's reading experiences began to be descried and described; scholars foregrounded place, race, ethnicity, and class. Feminist scholars were able to uncover archival material that diversified their work. New texts became available through the Schomburg Library of Nineteenth-Century Black Women Writers publications, begun in 1988. Recognizing the need to celebrate black women writers, white feminists had championed the work of Toni Morrison and others. Elizabeth Abel's "Black Writing, White Reading" (1993) explored the unrecognized difficulties of just such reading by discussing Morrison's "Recitatif," a short story that deliberately sets out to trouble black and white readers' racial assumptions.

Other minority (usually immigrant) women's autobiographies wherein authors recounted their own reading experiences were discovered and reprinted (for example, those of Mary Antin, including *The Promised Land* [1912]). Scholars investigated the records of African American Literary Societies and the educational experiences of Native American girls in boarding schools (Cobb-Greetham, *Listening to Our Grandmother's Stories*). The title of Elizabeth McHenry's *Forgotten Readers: Recovering the Lost History of African American Literary Societies* (2002) names directly the gap in knowledge that her study seeks to fill. In an introduction called "In Search of Black Readers," McHenry explains that the postbellum history of free black readers has remained invisible because of assumptions about African American illiteracy, an almost exclusive focus on slave narratives (which were often also literacy narratives), scarce records, and the difficulty of tracing reading (as opposed to writing) practices. McHenry calls for scholars to look beyond records of formal schooling to expand their definitions of "literature," and, indeed, of literacy.

For information on working-class women, feminist scholars turned to *The Long Day: The Story of a New York Working Girl* (1905) (republished in 1990 by the University of Virginia Press)[5] in which Dorothy Richardson described the reading preferences and habits of the factory girls she met. But periodical literature offered a much wider field of information. Ellen Gruber Garvey's "Less Work for 'Mother': Rural Readers, Farm Papers, and the Makeover of "The Revolt of 'Mother'"" (2009) looks at non-urban women readers, a relatively neglected area of study, finding that Mary Wilkins Freeman's story of farm life, "The Revolt of 'Mother,'" "was read in city and rural homes, high school and college classrooms, and was performed in public readings and amateur theatricals. It furnished a starting point for early twentieth-century discussions of the lives of farm women and inspired other stories about farm women's control of finances and improving the lives of rural families" (119). Garvey's work here is representative of how research in periodical literature continues to uncover new information about women and reading, a trend that has been greatly accelerated by the increasing number of digitized databases.[6] Garvey herself created and maintains the online "Research Resource Site" of the RSAP, the Research Society for American Periodicals.[7] This frequently updated site, which contains a section on "Women Periodical Readers, Writers, and Editors," is a rich resource for archival scholarship and pedagogy.

The presence of lesbian writers and readers was foregrounded by works of criticism, autobiography, and theory, but also by effective efforts to discover, recover, and uncover lesbian literature. Scholars like Lillian Faderman and Susan Koppelman edited literary anthologies that not only republished forgotten texts but also insisted on the re-reading of works whose "lesbian" nature had been previously ignored. Perhaps the best example is Koppelman's 1994 collection *Two Friends and Other Nineteenth-Century American Lesbian Stories by American Women Writers*. The language of Koppelman's title – "Lesbian," "19th-Century," "American" – was deliberately polemical. Presenting stories by Mary Wilkins Freeman, Sarah Orne Jewett, and Elizabeth Stuart Phelps as depictions of female–female love and eroticism, Koppelman demanded their re-reading. At the same time, work in Gender and Queer Studies, led by theorists like Judith Butler, called into question the category of "woman," and with it, of course, the woman reader.

If such studies redefined "woman," they also broadened the meanings of "reading." Janet Cornelius's pathbreaking essay, "'We Slipped and Learned to

Read': Slave Accounts of the Literacy Process, 1830–65," gave documentary evidence of the multiple, often communal ways in which African American slaves had learned to read and write. Cornelius showed that slave literacy was frequently limited, hidden, stolen, and shared. Later scholars who were more specifically focused on women's experiences built on this new paradigm. For example, Elizabeth McHenry's study of nineteenth-century African American literary societies led her to question the universality of standard notions of literacy as a "solitary or individual activity with an explicit directive to write as its ultimate goal" – the very American notion that individuality is, in fact, a *function* of reading and especially writing ("An Association of Kindred Spirits," 12–13). The women that McHenry studied attended meetings where texts were read aloud, reported on, and debated. Comparing the literacy narrative of Frederick Douglass's autobiographies with the experiences of his wife, Anna Murray Douglass, proved instructive, especially given that Frederick Douglass's iconic story of self-making is so centrally a literacy narrative. Anna Douglass, who never learned to read or write, was an active member of the East Baltimore Mental Improvement Society. McHenry writes, "many early nineteenth-century literary societies endorsed a broader notion of oral literacy that did not valorize the power of formal or individualized literacy over communal knowledge" (13). Amanda J. Cobb, in describing the educational experiences of her grandmother and others at the Bloomfield Academy for Chickasaw Females, proposes a model of literacy that includes, not only the intertwined skills of reading and writing, but also "related skills": "the appropriate social skills and cultural conventions, traditions, and ideologies" associated, in these cases, with citizenship.[8] Jewish women immigrants' literacy was different still. Many came to the United States with minimal reading skills: competent enough in Yiddish to conduct business, able to follow along in Hebrew prayerbooks, but, relatively speaking, unlearned and unlettered. Coming from a culture that highly valued (male) learning, many Jewish women eagerly embraced the opportunities that American public schooling and public libraries offered.

Indeed, the rise of History of the Book as a field made libraries objects of increasing scholarly attention. Studying libraries, Thomas Augst and Kenneth Carpenter argue, "we can situate reading more fully within its many physical and historical contexts, and better understand its place at the crossroads of collective behavior and individual experience" (*Institutions of Reading,* 4). Their collection *Institutions of Reading: The Social Life of Libraries in the United States* (2007) shows women reading in a variety of contexts. Essays by Barbara A. Mitchell and Karin Roffman focus on the female who, in the popular imagination, both stands for and controls access to reading: the librarian. Mitchell looks at how a technological change in antebellum libraries – the introduction of the card catalogue – created demand for a new workforce of educated women. Roffman reorients our thinking about two women writers, Marianne Moore and Nella Larsen, arguing that "for modern women writers, authorship and librarianship were related critical experiences" ("Women Writers and their Libraries in the 1920s," 203).

As this example illustrates, work on middle-class white women itself became more nuanced and specific. E. Jennifer Monaghan shows that, given the gendered distinctions made between reading and writing instruction in Colonial America, we cannot rely upon women's inability to sign their names as proof of their illiteracy. Reading, which was considered easier to teach and to learn, was required of all students; writing, which was considered more difficult as well as "job-related," was taught by men and often only to boys. Women's reading, Monaghan's study suggests, may have been more common than formerly thought.[9]

Monaghan's essay appeared first in Cathy N. Davidson's *Reading in America*, an influential collection that included Sharon O'Brien's tracing of the publication, reading, and critical histories of Willa Cather's writing,[10] and Davidson's own "Biography" of Susanna Rowson's *Charlotte Temple*. Davidson had been instrumental in advancing American History of the Book scholarship with *Revolution and the Word: The Rise of the Novel in America* (1986), which had demonstrated how, for many average and even unprivileged Americans, and especially for women, what she calls "the reading revolution" of the late eighteenth and early nineteenth centuries, "conferred an independence as profound as that negotiated in Independence Hall" (vii). The democratization of reading that Davidson describes is crucially tied to the novel and, not incidentally, the sentimental novel, directed at and read by women.

Also included in *Reading in America* was Barbara Sicherman's "Sense and Sensibility," a study of the Hamilton sisters of Fort Wayne, Indiana, important not only for the new archival material it introduced but also because it demonstrated "how reading functioned as a cultural style and how it affected women's sense of self" (202). Working out from the example of the highly literate Hamilton sisters, two of whom went on to widely recognized successful careers – Alice, who worked in industrial medicine and became the first woman professor at Harvard, and Edith, author of bestselling popularizations of the Classics – Sicherman theorized the psychological, cultural, and historical inflections and experience of these women's reading. "Reading," she argued, "provided space – physical, temporal, and psychological – that

permitted women to exempt themselves from traditional gender expectations, whether imposed by formal society or by family obligation" ("Sense
and Sensibility," 202). Sicherman's study is also important in that, by drawing
on the work of Norman Holland and Cora Kaplan, she complicates the idea of
female readerly "identification." The Hamilton girls, Sicherman found, often
identified with multiple characters within a novel, rather than seeing themselves solely in terms of the heroine. Indeed, she suggests that the settings
and plots provided space for free mental play that allowed these Gilded Age
young women to imagine alternative realities for themselves.

Sicherman went on to write a biography of Alice Hamilton, in which
her subject's reading played an important part. In 2010, *Well-Read Lives: How
Books Inspired a Generation of American Women* built out from the Hamilton
family to a thorough study of the rich, varied, and powerful forms taken by
American women's reading from 1855 to 1875. Included in this larger study are
not only white and African American women, but also investigations of how
specific books (for example, *Little Women*) and particular places (for example,
Jane Addams's Hull-House) functioned as sites of female self-making through
reading. In Gilded Age America, Sicherman demonstrates, "many women's
most significant literary experiences were collaborative" (*Well-Read Lives*,
68). "[B]ooks and reading," she argues, "were central to the web of female
friendship" (68). Sicherman's language invokes Carroll Smith-Rosenberg's
cornerstone essay of 1975, "The Female World of Love and Ritual," here
with the emphasis on reading's central role in creating and sustaining that
world.

And what constituted women's reading turned out to be more varied than
the strictures of conduct books and manuals had led historians to believe.[11]
There were (and are) gender differences to be sure: American women have
always read more fiction than their male peers; writers and publishers created and marketed texts specifically aimed at, and largely read by, girls and
women; women's journals and magazines have been, since the nineteenth
century, steady commercial successes. Nonetheless, males also read much of
this "female" reading material. And the reading histories described in female
autobiographies as well as the investigative work by later scholars revealed
that, while women were less likely to have formal higher education, many
educated themselves in science, history, classics. Elizabeth Cady Stanton studied Latin, Greek, and mathematics, and read law; Margaret Fuller too received
a classical education from her father. In *American Women Writers and the Work
of History, 1790–1860*, Nina Baym demonstrated that, for American females, the
study of history was presented as the positive alternative to novel reading. "By

the 1830s," Baym argues, "advice that women should learn history was thoroughly conventional, the subject itself had long since been installed in female academies, and American history was also becoming a required subject in the common schools of the northeast" (13). Nor was female reading of "male" genres and materials confined to scholarly works: for example, dime novels and story papers had been thought of by scholars of popular culture as exclusively male genres. However, archival work, including that of Felicia Carr, uncovered the fact that, especially between 1870 and 1929, women not only wrote dime novels,[12] but often wrote them with a specifically female audience in mind. Carr's invaluable website on American Women's Dime Novels explains that these texts had been ignored by historians because later collectors had sought out stories focused on male adventure. For example, Charles Bragin's 1938 bibliography of dime novels for collectors was comprised of what he considered "real" dime novels, excluding books and series aimed at women readers. Carr lists and describes these in fact very popular series, including: *Belles & Beaux: A Home Weekly for Winter Nights and Summer Days* (1874), *Girls of Today: A Mirror of Romance / New York Mirror of Romance* (1875–6), *Waverly Library*: "The Only Young Ladies Library of First-Class Copyright Novels Published" (1879–86), and *New York Monthly Fashion Bazaar* (1879–85). A female audience was extremely eager for dime novels like *All for Love of a Fair Face or, A Broken Betrothal* (1885) and *Only a Mechanic's Daughter: A Charming Story of Love and Passion* (1892) by Laura Jean Libbey; *The Unseen Bridegroom, or, Wedded for a Week* (1881) and *The Midnight Queen* (1876) by May Agnes Fleming.[13] While the readers of these romantic, sensational, and adventure fictions were largely young working-class women, dime novels also circulated among middle-class women and girls. The fact of circulation is itself significant: such texts were shared, borrowed, passed along, often literally read to shreds.

Kate Flint's work is symptomatic of an additional change in the studies of women's reading that came about as the insularity of American Studies began to break down at the turn of the twentieth century. Based primarily on British sources, Flint's *The Woman Reader, 1837–1914* (1993) nonetheless describes in detail nineteenth-century gendered reading theories and female reading practices that existed in the United States as well. International Copyright law, the Anglo-American nature of nineteenth- and early twentieth-century feminism, and individual relationships between American and British women of letters (for example, Harriet Beecher Stowe's friendship, correspondence, and shared reading with George Eliot), the burgeoning of Transatlantic Studies[14] and Hemispheric Studies: all worked to redefine what might count as both an American book and an American reader. As with

African American, immigrant Jewish, and other minority female populations, the publication of autobiographies provides windows on the reading practices of Chicana women. Books like *Migrant Daughter*, the life story of Frances Esquibel Tywoniak, who became a Berkeley student and, later, teacher and school administrator, helped to give a broadened and more diverse history of women's literacy.[15] Tywoniak's earliest reading memory is of her mother pondering purchases from a Sears Roebuck or Montgomery Ward catalogue: "These moments with my mother linger as memories of an auditory, visual, and emotional experience – moments of joyful anticipation shared through the medium of a catalog, the wish book" (*Migrant Daughter*, 7). Critical work on Chicana, Mexican, and Cuban women writers is still typically focused on introducing this work to the Anglo-American academy and therefore tends to concentrate on analyzing the writing itself, as well as its historical, political, and cultural circumstances. Nonetheless, there is often attention to the implied readership. For example, Joanna O'Connell, in *Prospero's Daughter*, takes the writings of Rosario Castellanos as a reading lesson: "I read Castellanos' fiction and essays as lessons in how to read with integrity" (viii). Especially in her discussion of Castellanos's essays, O'Connell describes the audiences that Castellanos addresses and constructs in her work. More work remains to be done here, including studies of multilingual American female readers.

An instructive way to see how the history of Women's Studies is the history of women's reading is to look at the changing readings received by a particular text. Charlotte Perkins Gilman's "The Yellow Wall-Paper" is exemplary in this regard. Part of its history is familiar: published first in *New England Magazine* in January 1892 and reprinted by William Dean Howells in *Great Modern American Short Stories* (1920), Gilman's story was famously "recovered" with the Feminist Press's 1973 reissue of the story in book form. Taken up as the exemplum of a lost feminist literature by a neglected-because-female writer, "The Yellow Wall-Paper" was widely reprinted initially in collections of women's writing and textbooks for courses in Women's Studies but eventually in standard surveys of American Literatures, entering, for example, the *Norton Anthology of American Literature* in its third, 1989, edition. This story, not incidentally a narrative of a woman forbidden to read, was read as an allegory for the infantilization and restriction of women in marriage and of how patriarchy constructs female madness. The knowledge that Gilman herself had undergone the rest cure fortified the story's status as evidence in the feminist investigation of women's medical history. And especially in light of the assumptions that followed with *The Madwoman in the Attic*, Gilman's loosely autobiographical story was read as allegory for the female writer: forbidden, frustrated, and finally driven mad.

During the 1980s, debates about what we used to call the canon of American Literature included references to Gilman's story, but the most powerful challenge to women readers who championed the status of "The Yellow Wall-Paper" as a representative American women's text came from within Women's Studies itself. In 1989, Susan Lanser read both the story's canonization and its interpretation as symptomatic of American feminism's exclusive focus on white middle-class women. Foregrounding turn-of-the-century cultural meanings of "yellow," Lanser argued that the reading history of "The Yellow Wall-Paper" in the 1970s and '80s illustrates how feminist criticism had "embraced contradictory theories of literature, proceeding as if men's writings were ideological sign systems and women's writings were representations of truth, reading men's or masculinist texts with resistance and women's or feminist texts with empathy" ("Feminist Criticism," 422). Critiquing, rather than simply celebrating, "The Yellow Wall-Paper" both complicated what had become its standard interpretation as a narrative of the victimized female artist voice and undercut the image of Gilman as a democratic feminist champion.

By the publication of Dale M. Bauer's 1998 Bedford Cultural edition of "The Yellow Wall-Paper," readers were invited to approach the story in the context of contemporary writings on "Conduct Literature and Motherhood Manuals," "Invalid Women," "Sexuality, Race, and Social Control," "Movements for Social Change," "Literary Responses and Literary Culture." Of these, it is the inclusion of materials on "Sexuality, Race, and Social Control" that makes clearest the changes in how "The Yellow Wall-Paper" has come to be read. Recognition of Gilman's support of racist eugenics has made later critics ambivalent about championing her as a feminist forerunner.

The upsurge in scholarship on nineteenth-century reading practices brought about by the resurgence and revitalization of the History of the Book has brought attempts to resituate Gilman's story within contemporary debates about reading. Historian Barbara Hochman's "The Reading Habit and 'The Yellow Wallpaper'" (2002) argues that "The Yellow Wall-Paper" was primarily and precisely a narrative concerned with nineteenth-century reading practices. Sari Edelstein focuses on reading and "The Yellow Wall-Paper" as well, but sees the story as part of Gilman's paradoxically sensational crusade against yellow journalism.

The re-examination of feminist readings of "The Yellow Wall-Paper" also continued. In 1996, an essay in *PMLA* by Julie Bates Dock, Daphne Ryan Allen, Jennifer Palais, and Kristen Tracy argued that "The Yellow Wall-Paper" offers a narrative of feminist mis-reading. They claim that twentieth-century feminists actually to some extent created a narrative in which a male literary establishment rejected the work of a brave woman writer. This "reception myth," as Dock and her co-authors label it, asserted that the benighted Victorian readers of the story saw only a Poe horror story, thus missing Gilman's subversive feminist intent. According to this narrative, the text had to await later feminist readers who could discern its true, revolutionary meaning. A sharp line is thus drawn between male (bad) and female (good) readers. The deliberately controversial counter-claim – the *PMLA* article is titled "'But One Expects That'" – is that these feminist critics found what they wanted to find. Disrupting and complicating the standard twentieth- (and to some extent twenty-first-)century reading, Dock and her co-authors go on to show that many turn-of-the-century readers, male and female, recognized the sexual politics of Gilman's story, some endorsing, some objecting to, its critique of gender roles. The "horror" that earlier readers found in "The Yellow Wall-Paper" was not some gothic misreading but perhaps something more frightening still: an agreement with Gilman that life for many women was, precisely, horrific.

Jane Thrailkill, too, is interested in analyzing the history of feminist critics' readings of "The Yellow Wall-Paper." Thrailkill argues that previous critics have "doctored" the story less through (intentional or unintentional) ignoring of counter-evidence and more by "recasting . . . its 'un-narration' into a recognizable Ur-feminist tale and then by conceiving of their readings as a form of therapy as well as a form of criticism" ("Doctoring 'The Yellow Wallpaper'," 553). Thrailkill sees interpretation itself as "therapeutic," especially when, as in this case, it is "collaborative." Indeed, she claims "The Yellow Wall-Paper" as it exists in the history of its reading by feminists effected "the founding of a vibrant, contentious field of study and myriad institutional venues that have helped propel women into the academy in startling numbers since the 1970s."

The historical narrative of an "unread" text, rescued by women readers, thus becomes an historical narrative of (mostly) women readers. Stopping with Thrailkill's essay is, of course, arbitrary: every indication is that "The Yellow Wall-Paper" will continue to be read by feminist critics (as well, of course, as others). Indeed institutional and professional attitudes towards scholarly publication virtually guarantee that this will be so.

The direction of current reading studies vividly illustrates the ways that technological change alters the patterns and perhaps the nature of reading. Janice Radway, for example, has, with "Girls, Zines, and the Miscellaneous Production of Subjectivity in an Age of Unceasing Circulation," begun a major investigation of girl culture, e-zines, and female subjectivity. Studies of fan sites and gender multiply daily. Psychologists and narratologists speculate on the nature of electronic reading. And authors now interact with their readerships via online interviews and chats. This last is part of a shift in contemporary marketing techniques that has made one aspect of women's reading highly visible: its economics. Women's reading groups or book clubs which were, in the nineteenth century, sites for self-improvement and, in the twentieth, spaces for feminist consciousness-raising are now a targeted niche market. Books that are marketed as book-group appropriate provide guides, interviews, and suggested questions for discussion. Then there are the coffee-table books and post-card packages that gather depictions of women readers; tee-shirts declaring "Book Lady" or "Book Woman," or even "Book Slut"; coffee mugs, magnets, and jewelry aimed at "women who read."

Scholars have focused on the psychologies, socialization, histories, and experiences of women readers. Perhaps the most consistently used term in these discussions is "identification": women "identify" with characters who are comfortingly like or thrillingly unlike them. Important, too, has been the metaphor of "space": reading creates an imaginary realm or a shared sphere or a protected enclave, gives women room and latitude. Both of these concepts have proved rich and flexible means of understanding women readers and are likely to continue to do so. But both have limits as well. Studying female identification tends to mean focusing on characters and, to a lesser extent, on genres rather than on how factors like narrative structure or style affect women's reading. And "space," except when it is used literally to refer to physical place, often remains an unexamined, even unacknowledged trope. The temporal aspects of reading are given lesser, if any, consideration. Critical self-awareness of these normalized terms of analysis might well open the field up to new methodologies and insights. What would we learn, for example, by studying the role of the senses in reading? In "The Reader as Artist," Toni Morrison, for one, traces her own history and habits as a reader to listening:

> my pleasure in, my passion for the art of reading came . . . in childhood and it began with listening. Not only was I a radio child who grew up in the decades when radio was paramount, when being mesmerized by the dramas and reenactments from a speaker box was commonplace, I was also surrounded by adults who told stories, reshaped and solicited them from each other as well as their children . . . Listening required me to surrender to the narrator's world while remaining alert inside it. That Alice-in-Wonderland combination of willing acceptance coupled with intense inquiry is still the way I read literature: slowly, digging for the hidden, questioning or relishing

the choices the author made, eager to envision what is there, noticing what is not. In listening and in reading, it is when I surrender to the language, enter it, that I see clearly. Yet only if I remain attentive to its choices can I understand deeply. Sometimes the experience is profound, harrowing, beautiful; other times enraging, contemptible, unrewarding. Whatever the consequence, the practice itself is riveting. I don't need to "like" the work; I want instead to "think" it.

Reading as creation, reading as listening, reading as thinking. From a family gathered to hear a book read aloud to the child crouched by a radio to the power walker with her downloadable audio book, changing technologies perpetually shift definitions of reading. And the new semiotic systems that come with innovation in reading technologies insure that our notions of "reading" will continue to evolve. What, precisely, is happening when tween girls spend the day reading (and writing) in the evolving language of text messaging? Perhaps the new field of literature and cognition,[16] for which gender has not yet been a significant area of study, may help us toward answers.

Given not only the preponderance of female readers of nineteenth-century serial literature, but also the emergence in the twentieth and twenty-first centuries of comics and graphic novels written by and directed toward a female audience, recent critical attempts to understand and theorize the reading of illustrated texts[17] offer promising possibilities for research. And, as immigration patterns for the United States shift, there will be new groups of readers who bring different literacy backgrounds to their reading in America. The complex positions and experiences of multi-lingual and creole women readers deserve careful attention.[18]

Women's Studies in the United States began by recognizing, perhaps we might even say admitting, what it is to read as a woman. The terms of that recognition have since been complicated, historicized, diversified, and contested, as has the field of Women's Studies itself.[19] Today, an Amazon search for 2010 texts on "women reading" brings up much that is commercial – predictably, The Reading Women 2011 Calendar; unpredictably, Jackie Kennedy's "Autobiography in Books," written by a male author. But there is also Megan Sweeney's 2010 study *Reading is My Window: Books and the Art of Reading in Women's Prisons*, which analyzes "the material dimensions of women's reading practices, as well as the modes of reading that women adopt when engaging with three highly popular categories of books: (1) narratives of victimization, (2) African American urban fiction, and (3) self-help and inspirational texts" (2). Oprah's Book Group is over, but Women and Children First, a feminist bookstore, first opened in 1979, still sponsors four women's reading groups: Feminist Book Group, The Family of Women, Women's Book Group, and Women's Classics. Hillary Chute's *Graphic Women* focuses on female graphic artists, but her analyses demonstrate how graphic novels at once interpellate and accommodate gendered readings: "That it cedes the pace of consumption to the reader, and begs rereadings through its spatial form makes comics a categorically different visual-verbal experience for its audience" (8–9). Looked at together, these examples position contemporary reading women as variously commodified and empowered. Reading is represented as comfort, redemption, titillation, creativity. More for women to read. More kinds of women reading and being read.

The following is a partial list of websites/databases that are useful resources for the study of women and reading

American Women's Dime Novel Project. http://chnm.gmu.edu/dimenovels/

International Reading Association: searchable database. www.reading.org/General/Default.aspx

Nineteenth-Century American Children and What They Read. www.merrycoz.org/kids.htm

Nineteenth-Century Girls' Series. http://readseries.com/index.html

A Place of Reading: locations where individuals performed the act of reading in America. www.americanantiquarian.org/Exhibitions/Reading/index.htm

Reading Experience Database: searchable by gender, age, etc. Reading histories of "British subjects and overseas visitors to Britain from 1450–1945." www.open.ac.uk/Arts/RED/

Reading: Harvard Views of Readers, Readership, and Reading History. http://ocp.hul.harvard.edu/reading/

Research Society for American Periodicals: includes a section on "Women Periodical Readers, Writers, and Editors." http://home.earthlink.net/~ellengarvey/index1.html

RSVP (Research Society for Victorian Periodicals): contains a bibliography of current work in the field. www.rs4vp.org/index.html

SHARP (Society for the History of Authors, Reading, and Publishing): extensive links to resources in all aspects of History of the Book. www.sharpweb.org/

Women's Genre Fiction Project: contains some information on readers.
http://womenwriters.library.emory.edu/genrefiction/about.php

Notes

1. The scholarship on the history of reading and readers is vast. And there is a solid body of scholarship on British women readers. My essay is informed by and intersects with some of this work but is in no way a complete survey of the field.
2. See also Welter's *Dimity Convictions*.
3. Or 1985, according to Elizabeth Abel, whose 1993 article "Black Writing, White Reading" analyzes the reading stances and practices of white feminist critics dealing with texts written by black women.
4. Spivak's article foregrounds reading from its first sentence: "It should not be possible to read nineteenth-century British literature without remembering that imperialism, understood as England's social mission, was a crucial part of the representation of England to the English" ("Three Women's Texts," 243). Spivak reads the opening scene of *Jane Eyre* as setting up the reader's identification with the heroine through reading: "Here, in Jane's self-marginalized uniqueness, the reader becomes her accomplice: the reader and Jane are united – both are reading" (246).
5. It was also republished in 1972 as part of a collection titled *Women at Work*.
6. Digitization of periodical literature has not been without its controversies, especially when materials like advertisements and illustrations are omitted.
7. Also useful are the SHARP (Society for the History of Authorship, Reading, and Publication) and RSVP (Research Society for Victorian Periodicals) websites.
8. Cobb-Greetham, in *Listening to Our Grandmother's Stories*, gives a good overview of previous work on Native American education.
9. This work was extended in *Learning to Read and Write in Colonial America*.
10. "Becoming Noncanonical" became part of *Willa Cather: The Emerging Voice*.
11. Indeed, as Nina Baym has pointed out, the American Puritan heritage of hostility to fiction notwithstanding, novels were, from the start, avidly and widely read in the United States.
12. The first dime novel *Malaeska* (1860) was, in fact, written by a woman, Ann Stephens. See Brown, *Reading the West*, which reprints *Malaeska*.
13. See The American Women's Dime Novel Project (http://chnm.gmu.edu/dimenovels/intro.html) as well as the Women's Genre Fiction website (http://womenwriters.library.emory.edu/genrefiction/).
14. For example, Hackel and Kelly, *Literacy, Authorship, and Culture*.
15. *Automitografías* is an important genre in Chicana/o literature. Gloria Anzaldúa's *Borderlands/La Frontera: The New Mestiza* was a pioneering example for feminist critics and writers.
16. See, for example, the work of Lisa Zunshine.
17. See, for example, Leighton and Surridge, "The Plot Thickens."
18. In suggesting these possibilities for future research and scholarship, I inevitably follow my predecessors in Women's Studies, reflecting the intellectual concerns and trends of the moment, my own background in nineteenth-century studies, an addiction to

audiobooks, an interest in the material history of books, and a curiosity about what Eva Hoffman calls the triangulated (in time, in space) identities that come with geographic, class, and cultural mobility.

19. For example, at many colleges and universities, Gender Studies has replaced Women's Studies.

Works cited

Abel, Elizabeth. "Black Writing, White Reading: Race and the Politics of Feminist Interpretation." *Critical Inquiry* 19 (1993): 470–98.

Antin, Mary. *The Promised Land.* Ed. Werner Sollors. New York: Penguin, 1997.

Anzaldua, Gloria. *Borderlands/La Frontera: The New Mestiza.* San Francisco: Aunt Lute Books, 1987.

Augst, Thomas and Kenneth Carpenter, eds. *Institutions of Reading: The Social Life of Libraries in the United States.* Boston: University of Massachusetts Press, 2007.

Baym, Nina. *American Women Writers and the Work of History, 1790–1860.* New Brunswick: Rutgers University Press, 1995.

   Novels, Readers, and Reviewers: Responses to Fiction in Antebellum America. Ithaca: Cornell University Press, 1984.

   Women's Fiction: A Guide to Novels by and about Women in America, 1820–1870. Champaign: University of Illinois Press, 1993.

Beecher, Catharine and Harriet Beecher Stowe. *American Woman's Home, or, Principles of Domestic Management.* Ed. Nicole Tonkovich. New Brunswick: Rutgers University Press, 2002.

Beeton, Isabella. *Mrs. Beeton's Book of Household Management.* Ed. Nicola Humble. New York: Oxford University Press, 2000.

Berlant, Lauren. *The Female Complaint: The Unfinished Business of Sentimentality in American Culture.* Durham, NC: Duke University Press, 2008.

Bragin, Charles. *Dime Novels Bibliography, 1860–1928.* Brooklyn: Charles Bragin, 1938.

Brown, Bill, ed. *Reading the West: An Anthology of Dime Westerns.* New York: Bedford Books, 1997.

Brownstein, Rachel. *Becoming a Heroine: Reading about Women in Novels.* New York: Viking, 1982.

Butler, Judith. *Gender Trouble: Feminism and the Subversion of Identity.* New York: Routledge, 1990.

Carby, Hazel. *Reconstructing Womanhood: The Emergence of the Afro-American Woman Novelist.* New York: Oxford University Press, 1987.

Christian, Barbara. *Black Women Novelists: The Development of a Tradition, 1892–1976.* Westport, CT: Greenwood Press, 1980.

Chute, Hillary. *Graphic Women: Life Narrative and Contemporary Comics.* New York: Columbia University Press, 2010.

Cobb-Greetham, Amanda J. *Listening to Our Grandmother's Stories: The Bloomfield Academy for Chickasaw Females.* Lincoln, NB: University of Nebraska Press, 2000.

Cornelius, Janet, "'We Slipped and Learned to Read': Slave Accounts of the Literary Process, 1830–1865." *Phylon* 44 (1983): 171–98.

Cummins, Maria S. *The Lamplighter*. 1854. Ed. Nina Baym. New Brunswick: Rutgers University Press, 1988.

Davidson, Cathy N. "The Life and Times of *Charlotte Temple*: The Biography of a Book." In Davidson, *Reading in America: Literature and Social History*.

Revolution and the Word: The Rise of the Novel in America. New York: Oxford University Press, 1986.

Davidson, Cathy, ed. *Reading in America: Literature and Social History*. Baltimore: The Johns Hopkins University Press, 1989.

Dock, Julie Bates, Daphne Ryan Allen, Jennifer Palais, and Kristen Tracy. "'But one expects that': Charlotte Perkins Gilman's 'The Yellow Wallpaper' and the Shifting Light of Scholarship." *PMLA* 111 (1996): 52.

Edelstein, Sari. "Charlotte Perkins Gilman and the Yellow Newspaper." *Legacy* 24.1 (2007): 72–92.

Faderman, Lillian. *Chloe Plus Olivia: An Anthology of Lesbian Literature from the 17th Century to the Present*. New York: Penguin, 1995.

Fern, Fanny. *Ruth Hall and Other Writings*. Ed. Joyce W. Warren. New Brunswick: Rutgers University Press, 1986.

Fetterley, Judith. *The Resisting Reader: A Feminist Approach to American Fiction*. Bloomington: University of Indiana Press, 1978.

Fleming, May Agnes. *The Midnight Queen*. New York: Beadle and Adams, 1876.

The Unseen Bridegroom, or, Wedded for a Week. New York: George Munro, 1892.

Flint, Kate. *The Woman Reader, 1837–1914*. New York: Oxford University Press, 1993.

Gallop, Jane. *Around 1981: Academic Feminist Literary Theory*. London: Routledge, 1992.

Garvey, Ellen Gruber. "Less Work for 'Mother': Rural Readers, Farm Papers, and the Makeover of 'The Revolt of "Mother."'" *Legacy* 26.1 (2009): 119–35.

Gilbert, Sandra and Susan Gubar. *The Madwoman in the Attic: The Woman Writer and the Nineteenth-Century Literary Imagination*. New Haven: Yale University Press, 1979.

Gilman, Charlotte Perkins. *The Living of Charlotte Perkins Gilman*. New York: Harper and Row, 1975.

The Yellow Wallpaper. Ed. Dale M. Bauer. New York: Bedford Books, 1998.

The Yellow Wallpaper. New York: Feminist Press, 1973.

"The Yellow Wall Paper." In *A Book of the Short Story*. Ed. E. A. Cross. New York: American Book Co., 1934.

"The Yellow Wallpaper." In *The Great Modern American Stories*. Ed. William Dean Howells. New York: Boni & Liveright, 1920.

"The Yellow Wallpaper." *New England Magazine*. January 1892: 647–56.

Hackel, Heidi Brayman and Catherine E. Kelly, eds. *Literacy, Authorship, and Culture in the Atlantic World, 1500–1800*. Philadelphia: University of Pennsylvania Press, 2008.

Hochman, Barbara, "The Reading Habit and 'The Yellow Wallpaper'." *American Literature* 74.1 (March 2002): 89–110.

"Uncle Tom's Cabin in the National Era: An Essay in Generic Norms and the Contexts of Reading." *Book History* 7 (2004): 143–69.

Hoffman, Eva. *Lost in Translation: A Life in a New Language*. New York: Penguin, 1989.

Johnson, Nan. *Gender and Rhetorical Space in American Life, 1866–1910*. Carbondale: Southern Illinois University Press, 2002.

Koppelman, Susan, ed. *Two Friends and Other Nineteenth-Century American Lesbian Stories by American Women Writers*. New York: Plume, 1994.

Kuhn, William. *Reading Jackie: Her Autobiography in Books*. New York: Nan Talese, 2010.

Lanser, Susan S. "Feminist Criticism, 'The Yellow Wallpaper,' and the Politics of Color in America." *Feminist Studies* 15.3 (1989): 415–41.

Leighton, Mary Elizabeth and Lisa Surridge. "'The Plot Thickens: Toward a Narratological Analysis of Illustrated Serial Fiction in the 1860s." *Victorian Studies* 51.1 (Autumn 2008): 65–101.

Libbey, Laura Jean. *All for Love of a Fair Face or, A Broken Betrothal*. New York: George Munro, 1885.

    Only a Mechanic's Daughter: A Charming Story of Love and Passion. New York: George Munro, 1892.

Long, Elizabeth. *Book Clubs: Women and the Uses of Reading in Everyday Life*. Chicago: University of Chicago Press, 2003.

McHenry, Elizabeth. "An Association of Kindred Spirits." In *Institutions of Reading*. Ed. Thomas Augst and Kenneth Carpenter. Amherst: University of Massachusetts Press, 2007.

    Forgotten Readers: Recovering the Lost History of African-American Literary Societies. Durham, NC: Duke University Press, 2002.

Mitchell, Barbara A. "Boston Library Catalogues, 1850–1875: Female Labor and Technological Change." In *Institutions of Reading: The Social Life of Libraries in the United States*. Boston: University of Massachusetts Press, 2007.

Monaghan, E. Jennifer. *Learning to Read and Write in Colonial America*. Boston: University of Massachusetts Press, 2007.

    "Literacy Instruction and Gender in Colonial New England." In Davidson, *Reading in America: Literature and Social History*.

Morrison, Toni. "The Reader as Artist." *O, The Oprah Magazine*. July 1, 2006.

O'Brien, Sharon. "Becoming Noncanonical: The Case against Willa Cather." In Davidson, *Reading in America: Literature and Social History*.

O'Connell, Joanna. *Prospero's Daughter: The Prose of Rosario Castellanos*. Austin: University of Texas Press, 1995.

Radway, Janice. "Girls, Zines, and the Miscellaneous Production of Subjectivity in an Age of Unceasing Circulation." *Center for Interdisciplinary Studies of Writing Lecture Series*. 18 (2001): 1–24.

    Reading the Romance: Women, Patriarchy, and Popular Fiction. Durham, NC: University of North Carolina Press, 1984.

Richardson, Dorothy. *The Long Day: The Story of a New York Working Girl*. Charlottesville: University of Virginia Press, 1990.

Roffman, Karin. "Women Writers and their Libraries in the 1920s." In *Institutions of Reading: The Social Life of Libraries in the United States*. Boston: University of Massachusetts Press, 2007.

Sicherman, Barbara. "Sense and Sensibility: A Case Study of Women's Reading in Late Victorian America." In Davidson, *Reading in America: Literature and Social History*.

    Well-Read Lives: How Books Inspired a Generation of American Women. Durham, NC: University of North Carolina Press, 2010.

Smith-Rosenberg, Carroll. "The Female World of Love and Ritual." *Signs* 1.1 (Autumn 1975): 1–29.

Southworth, E. D. E. N. *The Hidden Hand; or, Capitola the Madcap.* Ed. Joanne Dobson. New Brunswick: Rutgers University Press, 1988.

Spivak, Gayatri Chakravorty. "Three Women's Texts and a Critique of Imperialism." *Critical Inquiry* 12 (1985): 243–61.

Stanton, Elizabeth Cady. *Eighty Years and More: Reminiscences, 1815–1897.* New York: Schocken, 1971.

Sweeney, Megan. *Reading is my Window: Books and the Art of Reading in Women's Prisons.* Chapel Hill: University of North Carolina Press, 2010.

Thrailkill, Jane F. "Doctoring 'The Yellow Wallpaper'." *English Literary History* 69.2 (2002): 525–66.

Tywoniak, Frances Esquibel and Maria T. Garcia. *Migrant Daughter: Coming of Age as a Mexican American Woman.* Berkeley: University of California Press, 2002.

Walker, Alice. *In Search of Our Mothers' Gardens: Womanist Prose.* New York: Harcourt, 1983.

Warner, Susan. *The Wide, Wide World.* New York: Feminist Press, 1987.

Welter, Barbara. "The Cult of True Womanhood: 1820–1860." *American Quarterly* 18.2 (Summer 1966): 151–74.

    Dimity Convictions: The American Woman in the Nineteenth Century. Athens, OH: Ohio University Press, 1977.

Willard, Frances. *How to Win: A Book for Girls.* New York: Funk & Wagnall's, 1886.

Zunshine, Lisa. *Strange Concepts and the Stories They Make Possible: Cognition, Culture, Narrative.* Baltimore: The Johns Hopkins University Press, 2008.

    Why We Read Fiction: Theory of Mind and the Novel. Columbus: Ohio State University Press, 2006.

Index

Notes: Titles of works which receive frequent mention or detailed analysis are indexed under their titles; works receiving only passing reference appear as subheadings under the author's name. Anonymous works are grouped under 'Anon' unless receiving detailed treatment.